HIDDEN® Washington

HIDDEN®

Washington

Including Seattle, Puget Sound, San Juan Islands, Olympic Peninsula, Cascades and Columbia River Gorge

Eric Lucas

SIXTH EDITION

Ulysses Press®

BERKELEY, CALIFORNIA

Published by:
ULYSSES PRESS
P.O. Box 3440
Berkeley, CA 94703
www.ulyssespress.com

ISSN 1521-4397
ISBN10 1-56975-617-1
ISBN13 978-1-56975-617-1

Printed in Canada by Transcontinental Printing

10 9 8 7

UPDATE AUTHOR: Nicky Leach
MANAGING EDITOR: Claire Chun
PROJECT DIRECTOR: Elyce Petker
COPY EDITOR: Lee Micheaux
EDITORIAL ASSOCIATES: Ruth Marcus, Laurel Shane, Lauren Harrison
TYPESETTERS: Lisa Kester, Tamara Kowalski, Judy Metzener
CARTOGRAPHY: Pease Press
INDEXER: Sayre Van Young
FRONT COVER PHOTOGRAPHY: Mt. Rainier courtesy of Lewis County Convention & Visitors Bureau/Loren Lane; white-water rafting courtesy of Washington State Tourism
ILLUSTRATOR: Glenn Kim

Distributed by Publishers Group West

Write to us!

If in your travels you discover a spot that captures the spirit of Washington, or if you live in the region and have a favorite place to share, or if you just feel like expressing your views, write to us and we'll pass your note along to the author.

We can't guarantee that the author will add your personal find to the next edition, but if the writer does use the suggestion, we'll acknowledge you in the credits and send you a free copy of the new edition.

ULYSSES PRESS
P.O. Box 3440
Berkeley, CA 94703
E-mail: readermail@ulyssespress.com

*

*

Ulysses Press would like to thank the following readers who took the time to write in with suggestions that were incorporated into this new edition of *Hidden Washington*:

Vicci Rudin from Port Angeles, WA; Dean and Kathe Miller from Kilgore, TX.

What's Hidden?

At different points throughout this book, you'll find special listings marked with this symbol:

◄ HIDDEN

This means that you have come upon a place off the beaten tourist track, a spot that will carry you a step closer to the local people and natural environment of Washington.

The goal of this guide is to lead you beyond the realm of everyday tourist facilities. While we include traditional sightseeing listings and popular attractions, we also offer alternative sights and adventure activities. Instead of filling this guide with reviews of standard hotels and chain restaurants, we concentrate on one-of-a-kind places and locally owned establishments.

Our authors seek out locales that are popular with residents but usually overlooked by visitors. Some are more hidden than others (and are marked accordingly), but all the listings in this book are intended to help you discover the true nature of Washington and put you on the path of adventure.

Contents

Maps

OUTDOOR ADVENTURE SYMBOLS

The following symbols accompany national, state and regional park listings, as well as beach descriptions throughout the text.

Camping

Hiking

Biking

Horseback Riding

Downhill Skiing

Cross-country Skiing

Swimming

Snorkeling or Scuba Diving

Surfing

Waterskiing

Windsurfing

Canoeing or Kayaking

Boating

Boat Ramps

Fishing

ONE

The Evergreen State

A place of emerald beauty and scenic grandeur, Washington is the heart of a region that has long fascinated explorers and entrepreneurs, environmentalists and dreamers. This northwesternmost corner of the contiguous United States is nicknamed "The Evergreen State"—an appropriate label for a land that boasts eight national forests. Sharing a border with Canada to the north and Idaho on the east, Washington is divided from Oregon on the south by the course of the Columbia River.

Water is a major force, as the Pacific Ocean batters the state's rugged western edge and numerous rivers carve the landscape. Come to Washington and you'll discover wondrous waterfalls, glistening waterways and verdant rainforest. You'll also find mysterious bays, sounds and tributaries, wind-sculpted trees on wave-battered capes and inlets, gossamer mists on towering evergreens, icy summits that cast shadows on pastoral valleys, bustling cityscapes with a cosmopolitan flair, warm breezes through juniper boughs, even a powerful volcano or two.

The heavy rainfall for which Washington is famous helps keep its vegetation lush. The drizzle and clouds that blanket the coastal region during much of the winter and spring nourish the incredibly green landscape that grows thick and fast and softens the sharp edges of alpine peaks and jagged sea cliffs. But there's a flip side: Over half the state (meaning points east of the Cascade Range) is actually warm and dry throughout much of the year.

Much of Washington remains undeveloped and there are vast expanses of wilderness close to all metropolitan centers. In fact, nearly half of the state is covered by forest. Almost without exception, each of its cities is surrounded by countless outdoor recreational opportunities, with mountains, lakes, streams and an ocean within easy reach. It's no surprise that residents and visitors tend to have a hardy, outdoorsy glow. After all, it is the proximity to nature that draws people here.

Hidden Washington will help you explore this diverse area, introduce you to its flora and fauna, tell you of its history. Besides taking you to countless popular spots, it will lead to unusual and unique locales. Each chapter will suggest places to eat, stay, sightsee and shop and to enjoy the outdoors and nightlife. We think you'll find Washington is a place where you can explore for a day, a week or much longer.

Where to Go

The number of tourists visiting Washington continues to grow as the secrets of its beauty and sunny summer and fall weather get out. Because the landscape is so widely varied, each area with its own appeal, here are brief descriptions of the regions presented in this book to help you decide where you want to go. We begin in the Seattle area, move through southern Puget Sound, the Olympic Peninsula and the Coast, northern Puget Sound and the San Juan Islands, and then to the Cascades and central Washington, finishing with the vast stretch east of the Cascades.

Seattle offers a comfortable mix of cultural sophistication and natural ruggedness. The clustered spires of its expanding skyline hint at the growth in this busy seaport, the shipping and transportation hub of the Northwest. In addition to the downtown/Seattle Center district, this metropolitan community has a number of attractive neighborhoods ideal for strolling, shopping and nightlife. Pastoral Vashon Island is just a quick ferry ride away, while east of the city center is the fashionable Lake Washington district and bedroom/corporate communities such as Bellevue, Renton, Kirkland and Redmond.

Within easy reach of Seattle, **Southern Puget Sound** is a popular day trip and a great way to get acquainted with the Washington State Ferry System. The state capital of Olympia, Tacoma and the charming little community of Gig Harbor all offer easy access to wildlife refuges. Tacoma, Washington's third-largest city, is home to Point Defiance Park, considered the best saltwater park in the state. Bainbridge Island offers art galleries and plenty of scenic beauty. On the Kitsap Peninsula is the Navy town of Bremerton, gateway to the picturesque hamlet of Poulsbo. To the north is the company town of Port Gamble, while south of Bremerton you can discover the rural charms of the Longbranch Peninsula and Harstine Island.

American Indians were probably the first to discover the beauty and bounty of the **Olympic Peninsula and Washington Coast**, with its lush rainforests, stretches of driftwood-cluttered beach, tumbling rivers and snow-capped mountains. Several tribes still live in the area on the outskirts of the massive Olympic National Park alongside fishing villages such as Sequim and Port Angeles and the Victorian-styled logging town of Port Townsend. On the coast, Grays Harbor is a popular maritime area, while the pristine Long Beach–Willapa Bay estuary is famed for oyster farming. This region is ideal for beachcombers, kite flyers and seafood lovers.

Northern Puget Sound and the San Juan Islands, regarded in this book as the coastal area stretched between Seattle and Blaine

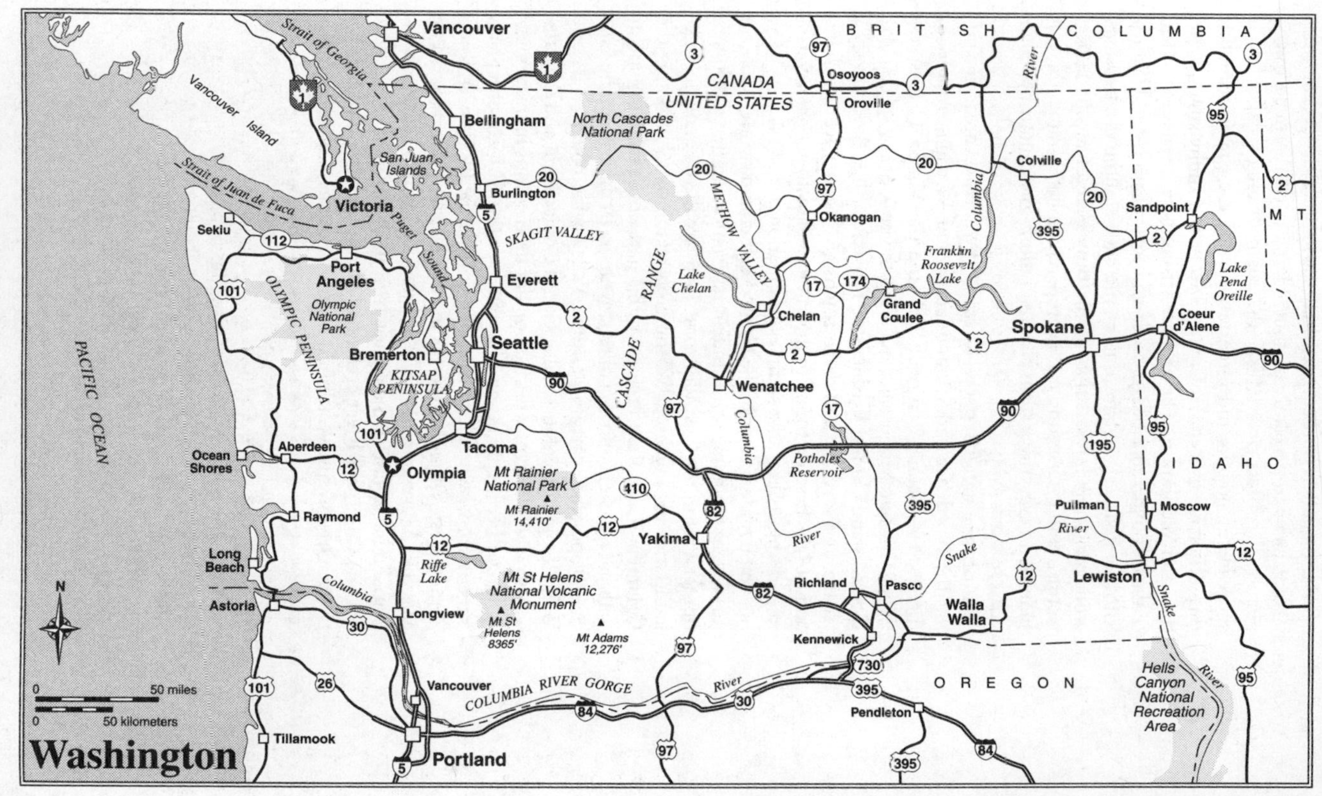
Washington
PACIFIC OCEAN
0 50 miles
0 50 kilometers
N
BRITISH COLUMBIA
CANADA
UNITED STATES
IDAHO
MT
OREGON
Vancouver Island
Strait of Georgia
Strait of Juan de Fuca
San Juan Islands
Puget Sound
Vancouver
Victoria
Sekiu
Bellingham
Burlington
Everett
Seattle
Tacoma
Olympia
Bremerton
KITSAP PENINSULA
Port Angeles
Olympic National Park
OLYMPIC PENINSULA
Ocean Shores
Aberdeen
Raymond
Long Beach
Astoria
Tillamook
Longview
Vancouver
Portland
Riffe Lake
Mt St Helens National Volcanic Monument
Mt St Helens 8365'
Mt Rainier National Park
Mt Rainier 14,410'
Mt Adams 12,276'
COLUMBIA RIVER GORGE
Columbia
River
Yakima
SKAGIT VALLEY
North Cascades National Park
CASCADE RANGE
Lake Chelan
METHOW VALLEY
Wenatchee
Chelan
Okanogan
Osoyoos
Oroville
Grand Coulee
Franklin Roosevelt Lake
Potholes Reservoir
Columbia River
Richland
Kennewick
Pasco
Pendleton
Walla Walla
Snake River
Colville
Spokane
Sandpoint
Coeur d'Alene
Lake Pend Oreille
Pullman
Moscow
Lewiston
Hells Canyon National Recreation Area
Snake River
Columbia River
1 1 3 3 3 97 20 20 20 20 2 2 2 2 5 5 5 90 90 90 101 101 101 12 12 12 12 12 112 26 30 30 410 82 82 97 97 97 97 97 17 17 174 395 395 395 395 195 95 95 95 84 84 730

on the Canadian border, is entirely enchanting, from sea-swept island chains to pastoral coastline. Here are rich farming tracts, picturesque forest-covered islands, quaint fishing villages and a shoreline of sloughs and estuaries. Among the cities covered in this section are Everett, La Conner, Mt. Vernon, Bellingham, Ferndale and Snohomish. The arts are strong here, perhaps because of the preponderance of artists drawn by the area's natural beauty. The San Juan Islands are one of the state's authentic treasures and a very popular vacation destination. Island-hopping is perfect for both cyclists and campers. A region lost in time, the San Juans offer everything from plush mansions to romantic bed-and-breakfast hideaways.

A strip of national parks, forests and wilderness areas, including the North Cascades, Snoqualmie and Wenatchee national forests, Mt. Rainier National Park and the Mt. St. Helens National Volcanic Monument, make up the bulk of the spectacular **Cascades and Central Washington.** Leavenworth, a Bavarian-style village, and several small resort towns are also key features here. Some of the best are found in the Lake Chelan area, one of Washington's most desirable summer destinations.

You'll find sagebrush-filled high desert country with shoot-'em up western towns and quiet Indian reservations scattered throughout the **East of the Cascades** zone. Here are the Okanogan Highlands, a scenic northeast Washington region that runs along the Columbia River. Rich in history, this part of the state is popular with backpackers and day hikers, who find it dryer than the Cascades. Spokane, pastoral Yakima Valley wine country, historic Walla Walla, the Palouse Hills, Grand Coulee Dam and the gateway to Hell's Canyon are also popular destinations in this region. Among other highlights are the state's original British settlement, Vancouver, which helped open the door to the Oregon Trail migration west. Other landmarks include Beacon Rock, the remote Maryhill Museum and the Klickitat River, where American Indian dip net fishing remains a way of life.

The Columbia River creates a spectacular natural border between Oregon and Washington known as the **Columbia River**

OBSERVATIONS

Native son William O. Douglas once wrote that visiting his favorite Washington spot, Bird Creek Meadows on the southeast shoulder of Mt. Adams, always made him feel as though he were "standing on the threshold of another world." He also observed "how badly we need high alpine meadows which can only be reached on foot, how badly we need peaks which can only be conquered by daring."

Gorge, a region characterized by towering cliffs, waterfalls and forested bluffs. Here you'll find tremendous opportunities for hiking, salmon fishing, and some of the best windsurfing in the country. The region can be explored by a scenic loop drive over Routes 14 and 84, or by crisscrossing the Gorge and taking time out to explore the spectacular beauty of the Cascade Locks. Watch tugboats ply the waters of the river or marvel at the natural beauty and power of the more than 70 waterfalls in the area.

Seasons

Washington isn't just rain-soaked, snow-covered tundra. In fact, summer and fall days (June–September) are generally warm, dry and sunny. Overall temperatures range from the mid-30s in winter to the upper 80s in summer. There are distinct seasons in each of the primary zones, and the climate varies greatly with local topography.

The enormous mountain ranges play a major role in the weather, protecting most areas from the heavy rains generated over the Pacific and dumped on the coastline. Mountaintops are often covered in snow year-round at higher elevations, while the valleys, home to most of the cities, remain snow-free but wet during the winter months. East of the mountain ranges are temperature extremes and a distinct lack of rain. Travelers can enjoy the rivers, lakes and streams during the hot, dry summers and frolic in the snow during the winter.

The mountainous zones are a bit rainy in spring, but warm and dry during the summer when crowds file in for camping, hiking and other outdoor delights. Fall brings auto traffic and visitors attracted by the changing seasonal colors, while winter means snow at higher elevations that provides the perfect playground for coldweather sports.

The coastal region is generally soggy and overcast during the mild winter and early spring, making this the low season for tourism. However, winter is high season among Washingtonians drawn to the coast to watch the fantastic storms that blow in across the Pacific. Be forewarned, however: These coastal mountain roads can be treacherous, especially in winter. When driving in snow-packed conditions, let someone know your itinerary and stick to it. Travel early in the day and keep simple signaling devices such as mirrors and whistles in the car. Summers are typically warm and dry in the coastal valleys and along the crisp, windy coast, making it the prime season for travelers, who show up in droves, clogging smaller highways with recreational vehicles.

Keep in mind that no matter when you visit Washington, the weather is subject to abrupt change. It is not unusual for surprise snowstorms to hit the Cascades in late spring or early fall. Always bring along warm clothing when traveling in the high country.

CALENDAR OF EVENTS

Festivals and events are a big part of life in Washington, especially when the rains disappear and everyone is ready to spend time outdoors enjoying the sun. Washington's larger cities average at least one major event per weekend during the summer and early fall. Below is a sampling of some of the biggest attractions. Check with local chambers of commerce to see what will be going on when you are in the area.

JANUARY

Seattle Honor **Martin Luther King, Jr.**, at Seattle Center's birthday celebration, featuring step shows, hip-hop dances and African drumming.

The Cascades and Central Washington In addition to catching a dog-sled ride, you'll hear carillon bells and perhaps munch wienerschnitzel at the **Icefest** in Leavenworth. Winthrop is home of the **Methow Valley Pursuit Ski Race**, one of the few two-day cross-country ski marathons in the United States.

Columbia River Gorge High school bands and vocalists compete for prizes at the **Clark College Jazz Festival** in Vancouver.

FEBRUARY

Seattle The **Lunar New Year Celebration** is a day-long community event, with crafts, music, food and live entertainment. Seattle blooms with demonstration gardens and floral displays during the **Northwest Flower and Garden Show. Wintergrass** in Tacoma features bluegrass music and a street dance.

Northern Puget Sound and the San Juan Islands Amateur detectives have a field day during Whidbey Island's **Langley Mystery Weekend**, when local merchants offer clues and prizes to solve a whodunit.

The Cascades and Central Washington Join spring training at the **Winthrop Snowshoe Softball Tournament**, where participants play ball with a winter twist—in snowshoes. Also popular is Winthrop's **Rendezvous Mountain Ski Tour**, featuring a 30K cross-country ski race up and over Rendezvous Pass.

East of the Cascades In Spokane, the **Northwest Bach Festival** highlights works by the German composer. The **Ag Expo/Farm Forum** in Spokane features farm-machinery demonstrations and horseshoe-throwing contests.

MARCH

Southern Puget Sound South of Olympia, you can enjoy the sounds of fiddles, accordions and ragtime piano music at the **Tenino Old Time Music Festival.**

Northern Puget Sound and San Juan Islands Watch a cooking demonstration, enter a mussel-eating contest or compare your favorite shellfish recipes at the **Penn Cove Mussel Festival** in Coupeville on Whidbey Island. The luck of the Irish will surely be with you at the **Oak Harbor St. Patrick's Day Parade.**

Olympic Peninsula and Washington Coast Step back in time at Port Townsend's **Victorian Festival**, a celebration of this historic port's heritage, with events portraying Victorian lifestyles.

The Cascades and Central Washington Snow-castle and sculpture competitions are the highlight of the **White Pass Winter Carnival.**

APRIL

Seattle Enjoy some of the first blossoms of spring at the **Daffodil Festival Grand Floral Parade**, which also passes through Tacoma, Puyallup and nearby communities.

Northern Puget Sound and San Juan Islands If you'd rather catch those early-spring colors in all their natural glory, queue up for the drive through the rich farmlands of La Conner and Mt. Vernon during the **Skagit Valley Tulip Festival.**

The Cascades and Central Washington Enjoy more than 40 different apple-oriented events during the **Washington State Apple Blossom Festival** in Wenatchee, which continues into May.

East of the Cascades One of the most colorful events in the area, Clarkston's **Dogwood Festival** celebrates the coming of spring with garden tours, crafts booths, music and road races.

Columbia River Gorge In Woodland, the Hulda Klager Lilac Gardens are open for tours during the **Annual Lilac Festival**, which ends on Mother's Day.

MAY

Seattle Bring your umbrellas to watch contestants lure gulls in Port Orchard's **Seagull Calling Festival.** The **Northwest Folklife Festival** features food and over 6000 musicians, dancers and artists from around the world. Considered one of the five best in the nation, the **Seattle International Film Festival** views more than 300 feature films.

Olympic Peninsula and Washington Coast **Sequim Irrigation Festival**, the state's oldest continuous event, features park picnics, an old-fashioned pancake breakfast, dance, parade and a show where loggers demonstrate their skills.

Northern Puget Sound and San Juan Islands A parade, carnival rides, and arts-and-crafts show are held in conjunction with the 85-mile **Ski To Sea Race** between Mt. Baker and Bellingham. The festivities continue at **It All Ends in Fairhaven** with live bands, food, crafts and a beer garden.

The Cascades and Central Washington Cyclists from all over the evergreen state compete at the **Lake Chelan Mountain Bike Festival**, a major event in this region.

East of the Cascades The ten-day **Spokane Lilac Festival** features a carnival, bed race, torchlight parade, food booths and more. There's also a **Hot Air Balloon Stampede** with nearly 50 balloons in Walla Walla. The **Maifest** in Leavenworth celebrates spring with Bavarian maypole dancing, a grand march and oompah bands. The Grand Coulee Dam sparkles with a **Laser Light Show** extravaganza every night from Memorial Day through Labor Day.

JUNE

Seattle The three-day **Pagdiriwang Philippine Festival** at Seattle Center celebrates the island chain's Independence Day and cultural heritage with music, dance, food and exhibits. Live music plus a *biergarten* and a "coffee garden" are featured at the **Pike Place Market Festival.**

Southern Puget Sound The **Tacoma Highland Games** celebrate all things Scottish—food, games, dancing and music (kilts and bagpipes not required for admission). Puyallup's **Meeker Days Festival**, named after one of the town's earliest citizens, celebrates the region's history and its namesake with food stands, crafts booths and music. You'll enjoy hearty servings of strawberry shortcake and performances by Norwegian dancers at the **Strawberry Festival** in Marysville.

Olympic Peninsula and Washington Coast Booths sell sausage, doughnuts, ice cream, baskets and dolls made of garlic at the **Northwest Garlic Festival** in Ocean Park on the Long Beach Peninsula.

Northern Puget Sound and San Juan Islands Traditional war-canoe races and ceremonial songs and dances are among the highlights of the **Lummi Stommish Water Festival**, held on the Lummi Indian Reservation northwest of Bellingham.

East of the Cascades Spokane takes basketball to the streets during the **Spokane Hoopfest 3-on-3**, when over 2500 teams participate in courts set up all over downtown. Festivities also include a mini food fair, contests and special activities in Riverside Park.

JULY

Seattle Get ready for alder-smoked salmon and live music at the **Ballard Seafoodfest. Bite of Seattle**, the city's annual food festival, offers the chance to sample food and wine from dozens of restaurants and wineries. Northwest talent is showcased at the **Bellevue Arts and Crafts Fair**, host to over 300 artists, craftspeople and performers.

Southern Puget Sound Behold bagpipe, drum and dance competitions at Enumclaw's **Scottish Highland Games.**

Olympic Peninsula and Washington Coast **Splash Festival!**, on July 4 in Aberdeen, features Indian canoe races, a grand parade and a street dance.

Northern Puget Sound and San Juan Islands Festivities at the three-day **Kla Ha Ya Days** in Snohomish include a hot-air balloon show, road race, soccer game and car show. Another winner is the music- and clown-filled **Mount Vernon Children's Art Festival** in Mount Vernon, with hands-on opportunities to make pottery and magic wands. An ideal place to celebrate Independence Day is in La Conner at the **Fireworks Over the Swinomish.**

The Cascades and Central Washington The historic river town of Cathlamet hosts the popular **Cathlamet Wooden Boat Festival.**

East of the Cascades In Lynden is the **Threshing Bee and Antique Equipment Show,** which displays old steam engines and antique farm machinery. The **Sweet Onion Fest** is a celebration of Walla Walla's famous produce, with food booths, arts and crafts, onion contests—and, of course, live music.

Columbia River Gorge Downtown Vancouver's **International Festival** celebrates Washington's varied heritage with food, music and dance. **Sternwheeler Days** marks the return of the Sternwheeler Columbia Gorge to its summer port in Cascade Locks with entertainment and an arts and crafts fair.

AUGUST

Olympic Peninsula and Washington Coast World champions descend on Long Beach to compete in the **Washington State International Kite Festival.**

Northern Puget Sound and San Juan Islands Many of the Northwest's finest artists display their work at top local shows like the **Historic Coupeville Arts & Crafts Festival** on Whidbey Island. Friday Harbor hosts the **San Juan County Fair,** with arts and crafts, agricultural and animal exhibits, a carnival and food booths featuring the bounty of the islands. Also recommended for a selection of Washingtonian art is the **Anacortes Arts Festival.**

The Cascades and Central Washington Located in the shadow of Mt. Adams, the **Trout Lake Community Fair** is a good place to find local color.

East of the Cascades Classic hot rods, complete with flame-painted hoods, take center stage during Yakima's **Vintiques Northwest Nationals Rod Run.**

Columbia River Gorge The **Clark County Fair** has big-name entertainment, horse and art shows, great food and a carnival.

SEPTEMBER

Seattle **Bumbershoot** brings music, plays, art exhibits and crafts to Seattle Center. Learning to live in harmony with the environment is the emphasis of the **Salmon Homecoming Celebration** next to the Seattle Aquarium. American Indian dancing, ceremonies, storytelling and crafts are featured. "Do the Puyallup" is the catch phrase of the **Puyallup Fair,** one of the country's largest agricultural fairs.

Southern Puget Sound The state's capital is the port of call for **Olympia Harbor Days,** which celebrates the Sound's maritime heritage with arts and crafts booths, tugboat races and music.

Olympic Peninsula and Washington Coast Many of Port Townsend's grand Victorian homes are open to the public during the town's **Historic Homes Tour. Logger's Play Day** celebrates the life and times of the lumberjack in the coastal town of Hoquiam.

East of the Cascades Broncobusting awaits at the **Ellensburg Rodeo,** held on Labor Day weekend is ranked among the top 25 rodeos in the nation. Enjoy the *biergarten* and German food circus at the **Odessa Deutchesfest.** Wine aficionados can tour the region's wineries and sip estate-bottled vintages at **Catch the Crush** in the tri-cities of Richland, Pasco and Kennewick.

The Cascades and Central Washington See prize-winning livestock, sample produce and local crafts, nibble cotton candy and enjoy a ride or two at the **Central Washington State Fair** in Yakima, from late September through early October. Leavenworth is ablaze during the **Washington State Autumn Leaf Festival** complete with oompah bands and Bavarian costumes.

Columbia River Gorge Candles provide the only light as you step back into 1845 during the **Fort Vancouver Candlelight Tours.**

OCTOBER

Seattle The **Issaquah Salmon Days Festival** in Issaquah features a salmon bake, races, live entertainment, arts and crafts and a parade.

Olympic Peninsula and Washington Coast There's plenty of seafood and entertainment along with a shucking contest at the **OysterFest** in Shelton. **Dungeness Crab & Seafood Festival,** held each year in Port Angeles the second week in October, is the ideal place to try fresh salmon, Willapa oysters and dozens of other specialties.

Northern Puget Sound and San Juan Islands A great way to get into the Halloween spirit is to visit the ghosts and ghoulies in Mt. Vernon's **Hillcrest Haunted Forest.**

NOVEMBER

Seattle Eat a sugar skull and dance with a skeleton at the Seattle Center's **Día de los Muertos** celebration.

Southern Puget Sound Get into the Christmas spirit at Centralia's **Festival of Trees,** complete with games, storytelling, carolling and, of course, Santa Claus.

Northern Puget Sound La Conner hosts **Arts Alive,** a three-day celebration of art including demonstrations, live music and displays.

The Cascades and Central Washington The **Christkindlmarket** in Leavenworth is a colorful Bavarian-style celebration that attracts visitors from all over the state.

East of the Cascades Spokane's **Winter Knights Snowmobile Show** draws big crowds.

DECEMBER

Seattle To get in the holiday mood, join the hordes of people who gather on Seattle's shoreline to watch the festively decorated

Seattle Christmas Ship. Seattle Center is all decked out with an ice-skating rink, Christmas train display and arts-and-crafts booths during **Winterfest**, which runs through New Year's Eve.

Southern Puget Sound The Point Defiance Zoo hosts **Zoolights**, with half a million lights depicting zoo animals on December evenings. Tacoma's **Fantasy Lights** is one of the region's leading Christmas events. Also popular is the **TideFest Arts Fair** in Gig Harbor, which features fine arts and crafts for show and sale.

Washington's nickname, "The Evergreen State," stems from its abundance of evergreen forests. Curiously, the moniker has never been officially adopted despite being commonly used.

The Cascades and Central Washington The Bavarian village of Leavenworth looks like a scenic Christmas card during the **Christmas Lighting Festival.**

East of the Cascades It's holiday time down at the farm during the **Sunnyside Lighted Farm Implement Parade.**

Columbia River Gorge Stevenson's **Christmas in the Gorge** offers a tree lighting, crafts bazaar and a parade. Boats decorated with Christmas lights sail the Columbia and Willamette Rivers during the **Christmas Ship Parade.**

Before You Go

VISITORS CENTERS

For a free copy of the *Washington State Visitor's Guide*, contact **Washington State Tourism.** ~ www.experiencewashington.com, e-mail tourism@cted.wa.gov.

Large cities and small towns throughout the state have chambers of commerce or visitor information centers; a number of them are listed in *Hidden Washington* under the appropriate chapter.

For visitors arriving by automobile, Washington provides numerous **Welcome Centers** at key points along the major highways. Visitors can pull off for a stretch, a cup of coffee or juice and plenty of advice on what to see and do in the area. The centers are clearly marked and are usually open during daylight hours throughout the spring, summer and fall.

PACKING

Comfortable and casual are the norm for dress in Washington. You'll want something dressier if you plan to catch a show, indulge in high tea or spend your evenings in posh restaurants and clubs, but for the most part, your topsiders and slacks are acceptable garb everywhere else.

Layers of clothing are your best bet, since the weather changes so drastically depending on which part of the state you are visiting; shorts will be perfectly comfortable during the day in the hot, arid interior, but once you pass over the mountains and head for the coastline, you'll appreciate having packed a jacket to protect you from the nippy ocean breezes, even on the warmest of days.

Wherever you're headed, during the summer bring some long-sleeve shirts, pants and lightweight sweaters and jackets along with your shorts, T-shirts and bathing suit; the evenings can be quite crisp. Bring along those warmer clothes—pants, sweaters, jackets, hats and gloves—in spring and fall, too, since days may be warm but it's rather chilly after sundown. Winter calls for thick sweaters, knitted hats, down jackets and snug ski clothes. It's not a bad idea to call ahead to check on weather conditions.

The mosquito thrives in Washington's moist climate, with over 45 species buzzing around the state. Don't forget the bug spray, whether you embark on a fishing trip or a hike through the woodlands or bogs.

Sturdy, comfortable walking shoes are a must for sightseeing. If you plan to explore tidal pools or go for long walks on the beach, bring a pair of lightweight canvas shoes that you don't mind getting wet.

Scuba divers will probably want to bring their own gear, although rentals are generally available in all popular dive areas. Many places also rent tubes for river floats and sailboards for windsurfing. Fishing gear is often available for rent, as well. Campers will need to bring their own basic equipment.

Don't forget your camera for capturing Washington's glorious scenery and a pair of binoculars for watching the abundant wildlife that live here. Also pack an umbrella, just in case. And by all means, don't forget your copy of *Hidden Washington*!

LODGING

Lodging in Washington runs the gamut, from rustic cabins in the woods to sprawling resorts on the coastline. Chain motels line most major thoroughfares and mom-and-pop enterprises still vie successfully for lodgers in every region. Large hotels with exceptional service, lavish Sunday buffets and complete business facilities, comfortable pensiones on the European model and waterfront establishments accommodate visitors in all price ranges.

Bed and breakfasts, small inns and cozy lodges where you can have breakfast with the handful of other guests are appearing throughout the region as these more personable forms of lodging continue to grow in popularity. In fact, in areas like the San Juan Islands, they are the norm.

Whatever your preference and budget, you can probably find something to suit your taste with the help of the regional chapters in this book. Remember, rooms are scarce and prices rise in the high season, which is generally summer along the coastline and winter in the mountain ranges. It's a good idea to book ahead in the prime tourists season when conventions can overwhelm the lodging market in cities like Seattle. Off-season rates are often drastically reduced in many places. In general, you can get your best rates in rural areas during the week and in big cities on weekends and holidays.

Lodging in this book is organized by region and classified according to price. Rates referred to are for two people during high season, so if you are looking for low-season bargains, it's good to inquire. *Budget* facilities are generally less than $60 per night and are satisfactory and clean but modest. *Moderate*-priced lodgings run from $60 to $110; what they have to offer in the way of luxury will depend on where they are located, but they often offer larger rooms and more attractive surroundings. At a *deluxe* hotel or resort, you can expect to spend between $110 and $150 for a double; you'll usually find spacious rooms, a fashionable lobby, a restaurant and a few shops. *Ultra-deluxe* properties, priced above $150, are a region's finest, offering all the amenities of a deluxe hotel plus plenty of extras.

Whether you crave a room facing the surf or one looking out on the ski slopes, be sure to specify when making reservations. If you are trying to save money, keep in mind that places a block or so from the waterfront or a mile or so from the ski lift are going to offer lower rates than those right on top of the area's major attractions.

DINING

Seafood is a staple in Washington, especially along the coast where salmon is king. Whether it's poached in herbs or grilled on a stake Indian-style, plan to treat yourself to this regional specialty often. While each area has its own favorite dishes, ethnic influences and gourmet spots, Seattle cuisine as a whole tends to be hearty and is often crafted around organically grown local produce. The city's restaurant community is particularly strong on Asian cuisine, including Chinese, Vietnamese and Thai dishes. With numerous open-air eateries and waterfront restaurants, Seattle is also blessed with a generous supply of coffee bars serving first-rate espresso and cappuccino. For an offbeat experience, you might want to try one of Seattle's wheatgrass bars, which serve the ultimate health food drink, clipped fresh and ground into a chlorophyll-laden treat.

Within a particular chapter, restaurants are categorized geographically, with each entry describing the type of cuisine, general decor and price range. Restaurants listed offer lunch and dinner unless otherwise noted. Dinner entrées at *budget* restaurants usually cost under $8. The ambience is informal, service usually speedy and the crowd a local one. *Moderate*-priced restaurants range between $8 and $16 at dinner; surroundings are casual but pleasant, the menu offers more variety and the pace is usually slower. *Deluxe* establishments tab their entrées from $16 to $25; the cuisine may be simple or sophisticated, depending on the location, but the decor is plusher and the service more personalized. *Ultra-deluxe* dining rooms, where entrées begin at $25, are often gourmet places where the cooking and service have become an art form.

Some restaurants change hands often, while others are closed in low seasons. Efforts have been made to include in this book places with established reputations for good eating. Breakfast and lunch menus vary less in price from restaurant to restaurant than do the evening offerings. If you are dining on a budget and still hope to experience the best of the bunch, visit at lunch when portions and prices are reduced.

TRAVELING WITH CHILDREN

By all means, bring the kids to Washington. Besides the many museums, boutiques and festivals set aside for them, the state also has hundreds of beaches and parks, and many nature sanctuaries sponsor children's activities, especially during the summer months. Here are a few guidelines that can help make travel with children a pleasure.

Many Washington bed and breakfasts do not accept children, so be sure of the policy when you make reservations. If you need a crib or cot, arrange for it ahead of time. A travel agent can be of help here, as well as with most other travel plans.

If you're traveling by air, try to reserve bulkhead seats where there is plenty of room (unless you want to view a movie). Take along extras you may need, such as diapers, a change of clothing for both yourself and your child, snacks and toys or books. When traveling by car, be sure to carry the extras, along with plenty of juice and water. And always allow plenty of time for getting places.

A first-aid kit is a must for any trip. Along with adhesive bandages, antiseptic cream and something to stop itching, include any medicines your pediatrician might recommend to treat allergies, colds, diarrhea or any chronic problems your child may have.

When spending time at the beach or on the snow, take extra care the first few days. Children's skin is especially sensitive to sun, and severe sunburn can happen before you realize it, even on overcast days. Hats for the kids are a good idea, along with liberal applications of sunblock. Be sure to keep a constant eye on children who are near the water or on the slopes.

Even the smallest towns usually have stores that carry diapers, baby food, snacks and other essentials, but these may close early in the evening. Larger urban areas usually have all-night grocery or convenience stores that stock these necessities.

Many towns, parks and attractions offer special activities designed just for children. Consult the calendar listings in this chapter, check local newspapers and/or phone the numbers in this guide to see what's happening where you're going.

WOMEN TRAVELING ALONE

Traveling solo grants an independence and freedom different from that of traveling with a partner, but single travelers are more vulnerable to crime and must take additional precautions.

It's unwise to hitchhike and probably best to avoid inexpensive accommodations on the outskirts of town; the money saved does not outweigh the risk. Bed and breakfasts, youth hostels and YWCAs are generally your safest bet for lodging, and they also foster an environment ideal for bonding with fellow travelers.

Keep all valuables well-hidden and clutch cameras and purses tightly. Avoid late-night treks or strolls through undesirable parts of town, but if you find yourself in this situation, continue walking with a confident air until you reach a safe haven. A fierce scowl never hurts.

These hints should by no means deter you from seeking out adventure. Wherever you go, stay alert, use your common sense and trust your instincts. If you are hassled or threatened in some way, never be afraid to yell for assistance. It's also a good idea to carry change for a phone call and to know a number to call in case of emergency, such as the **King County Sexual Assault Resource Center.** ~ P.O. Box 300, Renton, WA 98057; 24-hour crisis line: 888-998-6423 (call for advice and referrals); www.kcsarc.org.

For more helpful hints, get a copy of *Safety and Security for Women Who Travel* (Travelers' Tales).

GAY & LESBIAN TRAVELERS

Seattle's Capitol Hill is the hub of urban gay life in Washington, but information hotlines and social and support groups for gay and lesbians also exist in several of the state's other larger cities and towns. Information on gay services and events in the Seattle area can be obtained from the **Gay City Health Project Wellness Center.** ~ 511 East Pike Street, Seattle, WA 98122; 206-860-6969; www.gaycity.org, e-mail info@gaycity.org. **PFLAG Information and Referral Line** offers support and information in Spokane. ~ 509-489-2266. Also in Spokane is the **Inland Northwest LGBT Center**, with gay and lesbian contacts and activities. ~ 509-489-1914; www.spokanerainbowcenter.org, e-mail info@spokanerain

EVERGREEN ALL-STARS

Among the famous folks who hail from Washington are Bing Cosby (Tacoma); Jimi Hendrix, Bill Gates and Fred Couples (Seattle); Hilary Swank (Bellingham); Adam West (Walla Walla); Bob Barker (Darrington); Kurt Cobain (Hoquiam); and Kenny "Footloose" Loggins (Everett).

bowcenter.org. The Seattle–King County Department of Public Health runs an AIDS referral hotline, 206-205-7837, AIDS Care Access Project, 206-284-9277 and CDC National AIDS hotline, 800-458-5231.

SENIOR TRAVELERS

Senior citizens will find Washington a hospitable place to visit, especially during the cool, sunny summer months that offer respite from hotter climes elsewhere in the country. Countless museums, historic sights and even restaurants and hotels offer senior discounts that can cut a substantial chunk off vacation costs. The national park system's **Golden Age Passport**, which must be applied for in person, allows free admission for anyone 62 and older to the numerous national parks and monuments in the region. The Passport can be obtained at any national park ranger's office or park office, or in Seattle at the **Pacific Northwest Outdoor Recreation Information Center.** ~ REI Building, 222 Yale Avenue North, Seattle; 286-470-4060.

Washington is the only state to be named after a U.S. president: George Washington, the nation's first.

The **AARP** offers membership to anyone age 50 or over. AARP's benefits include travel discounts with a number of firms and escorted tours with Gray Line buses. ~ 601 E Street Northwest, Washington, DC 20049; 888-687-2277; www.aarp.org.

Elderhostel offers reasonably priced, all-inclusive educational programs in a variety of Pacific Northwest locations throughout the year. ~ 11 Avenue de Lafayette, Boston, MA 02111; 800-454-5768; www.elderhostel.org.

Be extra careful about health matters. In addition to the medications you ordinarily use, it's a good idea to bring along prescriptions for obtaining more. Consider carrying a medical record with you—including your medical history and current medical status, as well as your doctor's name, phone number and address. Make sure your insurance covers you while you're away from home.

DISABLED TRAVELERS

Washington is striving to make more destinations accessible for the disabled traveler.

For more specific advice on traveling in the state, turn to Access Seattle from the **Easter Seal Society**. The Accessible Traveler's Database can be found on their website. ~ 157 Roy Street, Seattle, WA 98109; 206-281-5700, 800-678-5708; www.easterseals.com.

There are several places to find more information, including the **Travel Information Center.** ~ 215-456-9603. The **Society for Accessible Travel & Hospitality** is another organization that can provide information. ~ 347 5th Avenue #605, New York, NY 10016; 212-447-7284, fax 212-447-1928; www.sath.org. **Mobility International USA** is another helpful organization for international exchange travel programs. ~ 132 East Broadway, Suite 343, Eugene, OR 97401; 541-343-1284; www.miusa.org. Or try **Flying Wheels Travel.** ~ 143 West Bridge Street, Owatonna, MN 55060; 507-451-5005; www.flyingwheelstravel.com; e-mail bjacobson@ll.net. **Travelin' Talk**, a networking organization, also provides information. ~ P.O. Box 1796, Wheat Ridge, CO 80034; 303-232-2979; www.travelintalk.net, e-mail travelin@travelin talk.net. **Access-Able Travel Source** has worldwide information online. ~ 303-232-2979; www.access-able.com.

FOREIGN TRAVELERS

Passports and Visas Entry into Canada and the U.S. calls for a valid passport, visa or visitor permit for all foreign visitors. U.S. visitors are not technically required to show a U.S. passport to gain entry to Canada—proof of citizenship (voter's registration, birth certificate, driver's license), including two pieces of photo identification, are all that's required—and may visit without a visa for up to 180 days. However, in 2007, tighter U.S. Department of Homeland Security regulations now mandate that all those traveling to the U.S. by air, including U.S. citizens, must show a valid passport to enter or reenter the U.S. This requirement will expand to include those entering by land and sea (including ferries) by January 2008. So, in a nutshell, everyone, including U.S. citizens, should now carry a valid passport at all times if they plan on visiting British Columbia and returning to the U.S.

Customs Requirements Foreign travelers are allowed to bring in the following: 200 cigarettes (1 carton), 50 cigars or 2 kilograms (4.4 pounds) of smoking tobacco; one liter of alcohol for personal use only (you must be at least 21 years of age to bring in alcohol); and US$100 worth of duty-free gifts that can include an additional quantity of 100 cigars. You may bring in any amount of currency (amounts over US$10,000 require a form). Americans who have been in Canada over 48 hours may take out $400 worth of duty-free items ($25 worth of duty-free for visits under 48 hours). Carry any prescription drugs in clearly marked containers; you may have to provide a written prescription or doctor's statement to clear customs. Meat or meat products, seeds, plants, fruits and narcotics are not allowed to be brought into the United States. The same applies to Canada, with the addition of firearms. ~ www.cbp.gov.

Driving If you plan to rent a car, an international driver's license should be obtained prior to arrival. United States driver's licenses are valid in Canada and vice versa. Some rental car companies require both a foreign license and an international driver's license along with a major credit card and require that the lessee be at least 25 years of age. Seat belts are mandatory for the driver and all passengers. Children under the age of 5 or 40 pounds should be in the back seat in approved child safety restraints.

Currency American money is based on the dollar. Bills in the United States come in six denominations: $1, $5, $10, $20, $50 and $100. Every dollar is divided into 100 cents. Coins are the penny (1 cent), nickel (5 cents), dime (10 cents) and quarter (25 cents); half-dollar and dollar coins are used infrequently. You may not use foreign currency to purchase goods and services in the United States. Consider buying traveler's checks in dollar amounts. You may also use credit cards affiliated with an American company such as Interbank, Barclay Card, VISA and American Express.

Electricity and Electronics Electric outlets use currents of 110 volts, 60 cycles. To operate appliances made for other electrical systems, you need a transformer or other adapter. Travelers who use laptop computers for telecommunication should be aware that modem configurations for U.S. telephone systems may be different from their European counterparts. Similarly, the U.S. format for videotapes is different from that in Europe; National Park Service visitors centers and other stores that sell souvenir videos often have them available in European format on request.

Weights and Measurements The United States uses the English system of weights and measures. American units and their metric equivalents are as follows: 1 inch = 2.5 centimeters; 1 foot = 0.3 meter; 1 yard = 0.9 meter; 1 mile = 1.6 kilometers; 1 ounce = 28 grams; 1 pound = 0.45 kilogram; 1 quart (liquid) = 0.9 liter.

Outdoor Adventures

CAMPING

Parks in Washington rank among the top in North America as far as attendance goes, so plan ahead if you hope to do any camping during the busy summer months. Late spring and early fall present fewer crowds to deal with and the weather is still fine.

Though much of Washington's scenic coastline is privately owned, there are a few scattered parks along the shore and even more situated inland in the mountains. It is possible to reserve campsites at several state parks from May 15 through September 16 by calling **Oregon State Reservations Northwest.** ~ 800-452-5687. You can also contact the **Washington State Parks and Recreation Commission** for more details. ~ P.O. Box 42650, Olympia, WA 98504; 360-902-8844 (general information), 888-226-7688 (reservations); www.parks.wa.gov.

PERMITS

Wilderness camping is not permitted in the state parks of Washington, but there are primitive sites available in most parks. Permits (available at trailheads) are required for wilderness camping in parts of the Alpine Lakes wilderness area of the Mt. Baker–Snoqualmie and Wenatchee national forests in Washington. For more information call 800-627-0062. For permits in the Lake Enchantment Area, make reservations (509-548-6977). Campers should check with all other individual parks to see if permits are required. Keep in mind that the popular Mt. Rainier region fills up first in the busy summer months. Consider the Mt. Baker area, the North Cascades or the Okanogan as less-crowded alternatives.

Follow low-impact camping practices in wilderness areas: "Leave only footprints, take only pictures." When backpacking and hiking, stick to marked trails or tread lightly in areas where no trail exists. Be prepared with map and compass since signs are limited to directional information and don't include mileage.

BOATING

With miles of coastline and island-dotted straits to explore, it's no wonder that boating is one of the most popular activities in Washington. Many of the best attractions in the state, including numerous pristine marine parks, are accessible only by water and have facilities set aside for boaters. Write, call or visit the **Washington State Parks and Recreation Commission** for a boater's guide to Washington. ~ P.O. Box 42650, Olympia, WA 98504; 360-902-8844; www.parks.wa.gov.

There are several waterways suitable for extended canoeing and kayaking trips. The **American Canoe Association** can provide more information. ~ 7432 Alban Station Boulevard, Suite B232, Springfield, VA 22150; 703-451-0141; www.acanet.org.

Whitewater rafting is particularly popular, especially on the White Salmon where you will find outfitters renting equipment and running tours throughout the summer months.

For general information on wilderness camping contact Outdoor Recreation Information Center. ~ REI Building, 222 Yale Avenue North, Seattle; 206-470-4060.

WATER SAFETY

The watery region of Washington offers an incredible array of watersports to choose from, be it on the ocean, a quiet lake or stream or tumbling rapids. Swimming, scuba diving, walking the shoreline in search of clams or just basking in the sun are options when you get to the shore, lake or river.

Shallow lakes, rivers and bays tend to be the most popular spots since they warm up during the height of summer; otherwise, the waters of Washington are generally chilly. Whenever you swim, never do so alone, and never take your eyes off of children in or near the water.

FISHING

With its multitude of rivers, streams and lakes, and miles of protected coastline, Washington affords some of the best fishing in the world. Salmon is the main draw, but each area features special treats for the fishing enthusiast that are described in the individual chapters of *Hidden Washington*.

Fees and regulations vary, but licenses are required for both salt- and freshwater fishing throughout the state and can be purchased at sporting-goods stores, bait-and-tackle shops and fishing lodges. You can also find leads on guides and charter services in these locations if you are interested in trying a kind of fishing that's new to you. Charter fishing is the most expensive way to go; party boats take a crowd, but are less expensive and usually great fun. On rivers, lakes and streams, guides can show you the best place to throw a hook or skim a fly. Whatever your pleasure, in saltwater or fresh, a good guide will save you time and grief and will increase the likelihood of a full string or a handsome trophy.

For more information on fishing in Washington, contact the **Washington Department of Fish and Wildlife** concerning shellfish, bottomfish, salmon, saltwater sportfish and freshwater game fish. Ask for the Department of Fish Management. ~ 600 Capitol Way North, Olympia, WA 98501; 360-902-2200; www.wdfw.wa.gov, e-mail fishpgm@dfw.wa.gov.

SKIING

As winter blankets the major mountain ranges of Washington, ski season heats up at numerous resorts. Ski enthusiasts head for Mt. Adams, Mt. Rainier and Mt. Baker. For additional information on skiing in Washington, contact the **Pacific Northwest Ski Areas Association.** ~ P.O. Box 1720, Hood River, OR 97031; 541-386-9600; www.pnsaa.org.

TWO

The Washington Landscape

Washington, the northwest placeholder of the contiguous United States, has enough different ecological zones to turn even the most jaded visitor into an amateur geographer. There's a wealth of dramatic scenery found here: rugged coastline, dense forests and two large mountain ranges—one young and aspiring and the other part of a dominant and established volcanic chain.

The young, low-lying Olympic Mountains, home to the only rainforest in the United States outside of Hawaii, reign over the Olympic Peninsula, but are overshadowed by the Cascades to the east, a volcanic chain that starts in western Canada, runs down the middle of Washington and spills out over the state's southern border into Oregon. The Cascades' lower peaks reach over 8000 feet, while Mt. Rainier, the tallest, stretches to a dizzying 14,411 feet and, like some of its neighbors, hosts a family of glaciers. These and other geological wonders fill the state and divide it into its various climate zones. The monumental crests of the mountains trip the clouds, casting a vast "rain shadow" over the eastern part of the state. This rain shadow gives eastern Washington about 12–20 inches of annual rainfall, while the coastal plain to the west of the mountains receives some of the heaviest precipitation in the United States—over 150 inches douses parts of the Olympic Peninsula and sustains the moss-draped rainforest.

The only natural link east to west across the Cascades is the Columbia River, which acts as the Oregon/Washington border. One of the longest rivers in the United States, the Columbia meanders for some 700 miles through Washington alone. The dry, warm flatland climate sucks the cool ocean breezes through the Columbia River Gorge, following the snaking river into the patchwork of rolling plains, irrigated fields and vineyards of eastern Washington.

The greatest concentration of people live in a relatively narrow depression along Washington's western edge that's known as the Puget Trough. Here, you'll find Puget Sound, speckled with the San Juan Islands—more than 170 of them in total.

Wherever you go in the state, there's an abundance of wildlife, from bears to birds, and more types of vegetation than we can do justice to in a few short pages. What follows is a brief overview of some of the highlights of the Washington landscape.

GEOLOGY

The eruption of Mt. St. Helens in 1980 was only the most recent reminder of the dramatic geological forces that have shaped this state. The Cascade Range began to rise just 20 million years ago, about the time the massive Columbia lava flow, second-largest in the world, formed the Columbia Plateau, which includes Washington and neighboring Oregon. Volcanic eruptions reached a peak about two million years ago with the formation of the Northwest's long chain of "fire mountains," part of the Pacific Rim Ring of Fire.

Volcanoes may have built the mountains, but glaciers carved them into their present form. For the last million years or so they have crept through the valleys and around the mountains, naturally sculpting the land. Within the past 10,000 years, a warmer climate has caused much of the ice mass to melt, adding to the power of already formidable rivers like the Columbia, which has cut its way into the plateau and continental shelf. The withered remains of some glaciers can still be seen on Cascade mountain slopes, still slowly chipping away at their summits. Mt. Baker is dressed with 20 square miles of them.

Some of the state's most intriguing geology is found along the Columbia River basin. A series of volcanic eruptions, giant floods and landslides have combined to create one of Washington's most dramatic landscapes. Traveling through this region, you'll find evidence of numerous lava flows. A geological wonder, the Columbia River basin is littered with pleistocene cinder cones, submerged pinnacles, high benches and eroded scablands.

FLORA

Washington's forests contain some of the world's biggest trees, holding records in height and circumference, with fir, pine, hemlock and cedar topping 300 feet. While everyone equates coniferous trees with Washington, there is much more to the flora of the region than its abundance of Douglas fir, white pine, red cedar and other evergreens. In fact, the pine-like Western hemlock with its irregular needles is the official state tree, populating the Olympic rainforest, as well as the low slopes of the Cascade mountains, and commonly growing to a height of 200 feet (some reach 300 feet). Each of the distinct geological zones hosts its own particular ecosystem. No matter where you go in Washington, expect to find yourself dazzled by such surprises as the Palouse Hills grasses in spring, the wildflowers of the San Juan Islands or the avalanche fawnlily that grows among patches of snow in Gifford Pinchot National Forest. Throughout western Washington, you will find bright displays of rhododendron, the state flower. Hundreds of varieties, with their mass of colorful blooms in shades of pink, red and purple, are found growing wild in meadows and parks, making this species a popular icon for photographers. They also have become a cornerstone of Washington backyard gardens.

Thanks to heavy precipitation, this state is one of the greenest in America. Visit the unique rainforests of the Olympic Peninsula, where some 12 feet of rainfall annually support over 1000 species of plant life—trees, flowers and thick carpets of moss and fern. This is the place to look for swordfern, red paintbrush, glacier lily and wood sorrel. Moss-blanketed fir, cedar, maple and spruce create a majestic canopy overhead.

Washington State is the number-one producer of raspberries, cherries, hops, pears, and, of course, apples. In fact, more than half of the apples grown in the U.S. come from Washington.

The rainforest is heaven for the spidery, low-lying ferns that enjoy the dank climate. Among the ferns you are likely to find here and elsewhere around Washington are bracken, oak and maidenhair. The maidenhair spleenwort, a short wiry plant with matted roots, grows in the rocky ravines. The high country houses the beautiful mountain holly fern. Up to two feet in length, this scythe-shaped plant is commonly found in cooler shaded areas. The bracken fern thrives in Washington's shaded woodlands and open fields. This triangular plant, ranging up to three feet or more in height, grows fronds all summer long.

In the moist woodlands of the coast, glossy madrones and immense Douglas firs tower over Pacific trilliums and delicate lady's slippers. Bogs full of skunkcabbage thrive alongside fields of fragrant yellow Scotch broom in a riot of color. Look for dune goldenrod, American dunegrass, coastal strawberry and rushes along the shore. Arrowgrass abounds in the salt marshes and you can also expect to find huckleberry, salmonberry and California wax myrtle.

Many different forms of seaweed commonly wash onto the seashore. The hollow tubular plants frequently found along the shoreline at low tide, in tide pools or attached to rocks are known as *enteromorpha intestinalis* (they're the ones used by beachgoing bullies to bludgeon their little brothers). Green hairlike urospora plants are frequently discovered on rocks or driftwood. *Bryopsis corticulans* is a bright green plant with featherlike branches growing from a central tube. You'll find it attached to rocks, shells and driftwood.

In the lowland valleys, alder, oak, maple and other deciduous trees provide brilliant displays of color against an evergreen backdrop each spring and fall. Daffodils and tulips light up the fields, as do azaleas, red clover and other grasses grown by the many nurseries and seed companies prospering in the region. Wild berry bushes run rampant in this clime, offering blackberries, huckleberries, currants and strawberries for the picking. Indian paintbrush, columbine, foxglove, butter cups and numerous other wildflowers line the paths and brush the fields with color.

In the wetlands along the Columbia River and Puget Sound, tall tufts of Douglas fir and hemlock pocketed with maple and alder sprout at the river's edge and creep up the banks. In the spring, scores of violets poke out through the underbrush.

Thick groves of fir and cedar filter the sunlight, providing the perfect environment for mushrooms, lichens, ferns and mosses. As a result, mushrooming has become a favorite pastime of fungus-loving locals, as well as a tourist attraction for fine food lovers. Each spring, after a good rainfall, you can spy mushroomers sneaking off alone to their favorite gathering spot, always scanning the ground for the ultimate find: a crop of truffles, part of the mushroom family and an expensive delicacy in French restaurants. **Warning:** New gatherers should bring along an expert to decipher the poisonous mushrooms from the edible. While they will not show you their secret spots, they will steer you away from some serious health problems.

As the snow recedes, alpine wildflowers struggle to live on the rain-soaked meadows, yet a breathtaking array survive. The elegant tiger lily, beargrass, aster, fawnlily and sandwort with its small pin-wheel flowers above a mat of tough leaves, form a rainbow of colors that compliment the gray-green hillsides and decorate the rocky crevasses. Other hardy wildflowers peak through the short wiry grass and dwarf shrubs. Crowberry, red and white mountain heathers and tasty alpine huckleberries blossom and ripen in the early fall.

With the dramatic decrease in rainfall in the plateaus and desert zone comes a paralleling drop in the amount of plant life in eastern Washington, though it is still rich in pine, juniper, cottonwood and sagebrush. Flowers found here include wild iris, foxglove, camas, balsam root and pearly everlasting.

BE BEARFUL

Washington ranks within the top five of the lower 48 states in total black bear population. Combine this statistic with the fact that natural habitats are shrinking, chance encounters between humans and bears have invariably risen. An inherently shy animal that tends to avoid humans, a black bear can become aggressive if it feels threatened, so avoid hiking alone and make enough noise to avoid any that might be around. Don't let the name fool you—black bears' coats may range from black to cinnamon to reddish-blond in color.

FAUNA

It was the abundance of wildlife that first brought white settlers to Washington, beginning with the trappers who came in droves searching for fur. Beaver and otter pelts, highly valued in China during the 19th century, were heavily hunted. Nearly decimated colonies, now protected by law, are coming back strong. Playful otters are often seen floating tummy up in coastal waters, while the bald eagle can be seen frequently on the Skagit River.

Fish, especially salmon, were also a major factor in the economic development of the region, and remain so to this day, though numbers of spawning salmon are dropping drastically. Nonetheless, fishing fanatics are still drawn here in search of the five varieties of Pacific salmon along with flounder, lingcod, rockfish, trout, bass and many other varieties of sportfish. Angler or not, check out the fish ladders of the Columbia River in the spring where salmon launch themselves out of the water to make it up the huge dams.

The banana slug thrives in Washington's moist climate. Not quite large enough to be mistaken for a speed bump, they leave telltale viscous trails. While it's the bane of gardeners, the slug is still regarded as a sort of mascot for the state. In many souvenir shops, you'll even find plush toy replicas and gag cans of slug soup.

Among the more readily recognized creatures that reside in the Pacific Northwest's waters are the orca (killer whales), porpoises and dolphins often spotted cavorting just offshore. When the orca show up, the playful seals and sea lions (the orca's prey) disappear. Constantly one-upping the resident shorelife is the colony of California gray whales that migrate between the Bering and Chukchi seas near Alaska and their warm breeding waters around Baja California. Each year, you can see herds of whales passing the Washington coastline from April through June on their trip north, and again from November through December heading south. Fleets of excursion boats take whalewatchers out to witness these behemoth water mammals that can grow to 42 feet long, weigh over 30 tons and awe spectators with an occasional breach—where 30 tons of whale launches itself completely out of the water. Minke whales are more numerous, as are Dall's porpoises, often mistaken for baby orca because of their similar coloration and markings. Special museums and exhibits throughout the coastal zone attest to the importance of these marine animals to the region. The San Juan archipelago is an excellent place to whalewatch, thanks to three resident pods of killer whales. On whale watching trips, you're also likely to see Dall's porpoises, splotchy brown harbor seals, bald eagles, great blue herons, cormorants and tufted puffins.

Coastal tidepools offer a closeup look at many fascinating species such as starfish, sea cucumbers, clams, oysters, sea urchins, hermit crabs, anemone, mussels and barnacles. When beachcombing along the coast, you'll find a wide variety of attractive shells. In the Puget Sound area, look for the yellow-gray Japanese littleneck clam. In shallow water you're likely to discover hairy triton, a large yellow white shell. In the same vicinity, keep an eye out for channeled dogwinkle, an inch-long yellow-brown dye shell, or the bluish-white barrel bubble. Mudflat areas are a good place to find a shiny tan mollusk called the *cooperella subdiaphana* or a tiny white pear-shaped shell called carp. The brown or black *acmaea limatula* is a limpet found in rocks between tides.

Watch for the Pacific giant salamander in fallen, rotting logs; it is the largest of its kind in the world—growing up to a foot in length and capable of eating small mice.

Among Washington's larger creatures, of the varieties of bear living in the Northwest's remote forests, black bear are most common in southern Washington. Weighing upwards of 300 pounds and reaching six feet tall, they usually feed on berries, nuts and fish and avoid humans unless provoked by offers of food or danger to a cub. Grizzly bears, officially called *horribilis*, are much more aggressive. While extinct in California, these bears, top dog of the bear kingdom, still survive in northern Washington. Even in small numbers, this furry carnivore is a legend. Reportedly, the Lewis and Clark party shot one of these fearsome creatures six times at short range, which apparently only made the animal mad enough to get its half-ton body in motion for a half-hearted chase around the woods. Color does not differentiate a black bear from a grizzly. Some black bears can be light brown, while grizzlies can be almost black. Grizzlies, however, are bigger, have humped shoulders and wield longer claws. They are also known to be meaner and tougher.

Big-game herds of deer, elk, antelope along with moose, cougar and mountain goats range the more remote mountainous areas. Scavengers such as chipmunks, squirrels, raccoons, opossums and skunks are abundant, as well.

The coastal Johns River Habitat Management Area is a good place to look for Roosevelt elk, muskrat, weasel and river otter. An unusual animal, unique to the Olympic Mountains, is the Olympic marmot. These gregarious creatures look like a cross between a ferret and a squirrel, are slightly more curious than lazy and when they are not basking in the sun on top of the pile of rocks they call home, they are exploring and testing, whether its neighboring animals, a sibling, humans or your picnic basket. Visit Olympic National Park and you may run into one of the colonies of marmots who reside there and are said to be the animal world's best people-watchers.

One of the best places in the state to see deer, as well as beaver and mink, is the Columbian White-Tailed Deer National Wildlife

A Salmon's Odyssey

The life of a salmon is a long round-trip journey from birth to ocean and back to birthplace. A salmon first enters the world in a small inland stream, where it grows for about a year before departing on its great journey.

Unlike most other fish, salmon live part of their life in saltwater and another part in fresh. Salmon swim downstream to the open sea, changing their camouflage from dots for the river to smooth white for the ocean where they will flow with the currents for about two years. Then they head "home," finding the route back to their original streams by the smell of their home waters and by using the sun as a navigational reference.

These fish are driven to battle ferocious river rapids, swimming upstream against the current to spawn in the same placid pools where they were born. The journey can be as long as 900 miles (to Idaho's Salmon River) and the fish often have to jump up small waterfalls to get to their mates. Ironically, after this long trip and their ritual spawning, the salmon die.

Now with many of the rivers dammed, salmon use manmade fish ladders (that look more like steps) to get back to their streams. Many salmon don't make it upstream past the huge dams, a fact that has prompted government authorities to actually truck some back to their spawning grounds to procreate and then perish.

Refuge. It's located on the Columbia River near Cathlamet. At Birch Bay State Park on the coast near the Canadian border, beavers, opossums and muskrats can often be seen running along the muddy shoreline. In North Cascades National Park, you're likely to find snowshoe hare, red squirrels, bats, wolverines, mountain goats and, with luck, the elusive bobcat. Eastern Washington's Okanogan National Forest is full of porcupine, black bear and snowshoe hare. The flying squirrel also makes its rounds in the trees of this park, and is actually known more for its gutsy leaping abilities than its aerodynamics. In fact, the flying squirrel cannot "fly," but rather uses the flaps of skin that stretch from its legs to its front paws as a small set of glider wings to extend the range of its leap.

Washington State has more glaciers than the other 47 contiguous states combined.

With a proliferation of protected refuges and preserves providing homes for great flocks of snow geese, trumpeter swans, great blue herons, kingfishers, cranes and other species, birdwatchers will be in seventh heaven in Washington, one of the fastest-growing birder destinations on the continent. In fact, when juvenile Pacific Salmon are readily available, nearly 500 species of birds live in the Pacific Northwest for at least a portion of the year. Easily accessible mudflats and estuaries throughout Washington provide refuge for egrets, cormorants, loons and migratory waterfowl making their way along the Pacific Flyway. Hundreds of pairs of bald eagles nest and hunt among the islands of Washington along with great blue herons and cormorants. You might see goshawks and spotted owls if you venture quietly into the state's old-growth forest zones.

The spotted owl has been the center of controversy in recent years, the focus of the recurring nature-versus-commerce debate. As logging companies cut deeper into the old-growth forests, which have taken 150 years or more to grow, the habitat for this endangered owl grows smaller. (These nocturnal birds need thousands of acres per pair to support their indulgent eating habits.) The old-growth forests of the Pacific Northwest provide adequate nesting spots in the protected snags and broken branches of tall trees that shelter their flightless young. Recently, old-growth forest has become increasingly hard to come by and the owl's numbers are diminishing—at last count a few years ago, there were only about 500 pairs in Washington and that number is believed to be rapidly declining. Some scientists predict their extinction early in the 21st century if logging continues at its present rate. Environmental activists are fighting to keep Washington's forests free and clear of commercial logging roads to preserve their fragile ecosystems.

If you hear a rapid pounding noise, it's probably coming from the pileated woodpecker. Identified by its erect head feathers, it is the largest woodpecker in North America and the model for the cartoon character "Woody Woodpecker." Unlike its cartoon cousin, this bird lives primarily in old-growth forests, drilling for insects under tree bark.

The Olympic Peninsula area has become a refuge for birders as well as birds. You can see both these groups in full force at Dungeness National Wildlife Refuge near Sequim. Here, you're likely to find a number of binoculars following a wide array of ducks, including greater scaup, bufflehead and green-winged teal. The Nisqually National Wildlife Refuge near Tacoma houses thousands of wintering waterfowl, as well as gulls, sandpipers and passerines. On the Columbia near Vancouver, Ridgefield National Wildlife Refuge has a wide range of birds big and small: widgeons, mallards, red-tailed hawks, goldfinches and red-winged blackbirds are commonly seen darting through the air. At Mt. Baker, far less crowded than popular Mt. Rainier, you'll see red-tailed hawks, bald eagles circling overhead preying on a plentiful supply of grouse, sapsuckers and warblers. In the Spokane area, Turnbull National Wildlife Refuge has a large congregation of forest birds. Bring your binoculars to spot western meadowlark, song sparrows, ducks, killdeer, great horned owls and mountain chickadees.

THREE

History

There's an intrepid outdoor spirit at the heart of the Washington population. Pacific Northwesterners feel as comfortable lying against a tree as they do sitting behind a desk. This should come as no surprise—anyone raised in a land dotted with lakes, carpeted with forests and cleaved by mountains would grow up familiar with the outdoors. But Washingtonians' love of the outdoors goes well beyond the familiar. They're unfazed by heavy rainfall—true natives leave the umbrellas in the closet—and they revel when the warm sun pokes its head through the usually gray skies. They have an immunity to the harshness of nature, but they also have a strong appreciation for it, which comes from a tradition of explorers and fast growth, retold by living grandparents, remembered by great-grandparents and still present today—it comes from their history. Many have learned of Washington's charms thanks to poets and writers like Theodore Roethke, Gary Snyder , Annie Dillard, Timothy Egan and David Gutterson.

The story of Washington and the Pacific Northwest is a young one. Romanticized tales of frontier life, from fixing wagon wheels and weathering devastating storms to hunting for food and water in the yet-unsettled territory, dominate our Eurocentric textbooks. But, like other states, Washington's history can be traced back long before the arrival of the Europeans.

THE FIRST TO ARRIVE A popular theory today suggests that 25,000 years ago, at the end of the last ice age, the seas were 300 feet lower and a stretch of land traversed the Bering Strait. The first humans to arrive on the west coast of North America are thought to have used this "land bridge" to walk from Asia to what is now Alaska. From there, they wandered through Canada and down into Washington in search of a warmer climate. Archaeologists have discovered solid evidence of human existence dating back 10,000 years with the find of the "Marmes Man," which are some of the oldest documented skeletal remains in the Western Hemisphere. Along with the partial remains of several individuals, Washington archaeologists, working the dig in the Marmes Rock Shelter (located in eastern Washington), uncovered many of the tools left by this ancient hunter-and-gatherer tribe.

Other, more recent evidence of human culture was found at Ozette on the Olympic Coast, the site of one of five major Makah villages. Archaeologists have unearthed well-preserved baskets, harpoons and clothing of the people who lived here an estimated 500 years ago until a mud slide, probably triggered by an earthquake, engulfed and buried the settlement. Because the slide caught the American Indians by surprise, it buried utensils in all stages of use and development. While wooden and textile artifacts have often been destroyed by the region's damp climate, Ozette was beautifully preserved by the great slide. Eleven years of excavation turned up more than 55,000 artifacts, making it possible to paint a complete picture of the early Makah. This find has dwarfed all other projects of its kind and today, 97 percent of all Northwest Coast Indian artifacts excavated on the outer coast of Washington State are from Ozette.

These ancient people were the ancestors of the numerous tribes that later populated the North American continent. Among them are the Kwakiutl, Haida, Bella Coola, Tlingit, Salish, Yakima, Nez Percé, Paiute, Shoshone, Umpqua and Rogue tribes.

The varying climate of the Pacific Northwest both provided for and dictated the lifestyles of these tribes. Those living inland, east of the mountain ranges, were forced into a nomadic existence, depending primarily on fishing, foraging and hunting game for survival, moving as the climate and animal migrations demanded. They lived in caves during warmer times and constructed large pit houses for winter camp. Many Northwest Coast Indians lived in "longhouses," wooden buildings as much as 100 feet long and 40 feet wide, which could house several families.

The mild climate and abundant resources of the Puget Trough and Pacific coastline led to a fairly sedentary life for the tribes west of the mountain ranges. Here, they constructed permanent villages from the readily available wood, fished the rich waters, foraged in lush forests and had enough free time to develop ritualized arts and ceremonies, as well as an elaborate social structure.

American Indian tribes living on the coast had a wealth of food. Their diets depended on seafood (mostly shellfish, salmon and whale) supplemented by a surplus of potatoes, a common crop for settled tribes. Materialistic and organized, these people had time to create beautiful basketry, hats and wooden whale-fin sculptures inlaid with hundreds of sea otter teeth.

They were also very resourceful people, taking advantage of the malleable consistency of the western red cedar, using its wood for everything from medicinal teas and ointments to houses and canoes. The Makah, one of Washington's most developed coastal Indian cultures, used cedar so proficiently that their woven baskets could be made to hold water and their boxes were used to boil food. Cedar bark was pounded to make soft clothing and woven cedar rain hats helped to keep the people dry in the wet weather of the Olympic Peninsula.

Much of the Makah people's resourcefulness came from their religious beliefs. They took pride in efficiency, using the inedible portions of animals for household utensils so as to please the spirits of the animals who, as they believed, had given themselves up for human benefit. According to their legends, the mountains and the rivers contained great spirits and the salmon were residents of the sea who fed themselves to mankind. For these reasons, the Makah tossed fish bones back into the streams so the salmon people could regenerate to serve the hungry human race once again.

To the east, the Yakima and other mid-Columbia Indians developed an elaborate trading culture built around the region's rich fisheries. These tribes were seminomadic, depending on spear-hunted deer, elk, bear, rabbit and squirrel. The tribes that settled by the Columbia River depended on salmon as their main food source.

EXPLORATION AND SETTLEMENT In the 1700s, the heads of several European nations interested in expanding their borders sent explorers to claim chunks of the Northwest coast. The explorers also searched continually for the fabled Northwest Passage, which supposedly connected the Pacific and Atlantic oceans by water. The search for the passage actually had begun much sooner. In the late 1500s, Juan de Fuca, the first recorded explorer to sail along the Washington coastline, thought he had discovered it. However, this Greek traveler, who had adopted his Spanish name as well as flag, was mistaken. What he really found was the mouth of Puget Sound, now called the Strait of Juan de Fuca in his honor.

The Spanish sent out two more parties in 1774 and 1775. Juan Perez, leader of the former, was the first to describe in-depth the region's natural beauty. The other Spanish expedition, led by Bruno de Heceta and Juan Francisco de la Bodega, was much greater in number, as well as purpose. Heceta went ashore along the Washington coastline and claimed the whole Northwest in the name of Spain.

The Russians, not ones to be left out, had sent an expedition in the mid-1700s. They liked what they saw here and sent another group to follow up. Both missions were led by Vitus Bering, who quickly realized the capital potential of the land with its abundance of sea otters and beavers. The Russians moved quickly and erected a number of trading and hunting posts all along the coast, from Alaska as far south as what today is northern California. Bolstered by the prospects of a lucrative fur trade, the Russians were making their first bold move to annex the territory, either ignoring or just ignorant of Spain's outrageous claim.

Arrival of the white explorers brought many changes to the generally peaceful tribes of this relatively well-off region. There is no documentation of the Americans Indians' early interactions with white men, but it is thought that Spanish explorers introduced the horse to the native tribes in the early 18th century, revolutionizing their nomadic lifestyle. The horse allowed hunters to cover much more territory, so tribes were able to remain settled for longer periods of time. By the century's end, traders were beginning to swap guns and ammunition for furs. These weapons helped make the mid-Columbia American Indians proficient bison hunters and fierce warriors. Unfortunately, along with the horses and guns came smallpox. As early as 1775, ships arriving on the Washington coast introduced western diseases that decimated indigenous peoples who had no immunity.

Before becoming the 42nd state to enter the union in 1889, Washington was known as Columbia, named after the Columbia River. The name was changed to avoid confusion with the District of Columbia.

Ironically, the Spanish and Russians were the first foreigners in the region, but they had started a diplomatic territorial battle that they were never to enter. Their sailing expeditions were nothing compared to England's imperialistic machine. The dominating force at the time, England flexed its financial muscle and sent Captain James Cook in 1778 to investigate the maritime fur trade. In 1792, the British commissioned George Vancouver to find the Northwest Passage and map the region, giving him extra leeway with supplies and money. He traveled the inland water routes and named every prominent geological feature after members of his crew.

About the same time, the young and independent United States started looking west. Robert Gray, an American fur trader sent by the Boston Company, explored the Washington coast in 1792 to verify its treasure trove of furry animals. The explorations took him to the mouth of the Columbia River, a discovery that later became the basis for America's claim to the territory. Many American trade companies followed the Boston Company's example and sent hunting parties west. By 1812, the United States dominated the fur trade. The Russians slowly packed up many of their outposts, distracted by the Napoleonic Wars, while the Spanish also lost interest, deterred perhaps by the English presence.

The most famous overland expedition to the west coast was started in 1804 at St. Louis by Meriwether Lewis and William Clark. Their journey, made mostly by canoe and on foot, took the 40-man party two years round-trip. Their goal was a lofty one: to study the geology, plant and animal life of the Louisiana

Purchase. And even with that huge task in hand, they did more. They crossed the Rocky Mountains and headed into Washington, paddling down and charting nearly 400 miles of the Columbia River, from the foothills of the Rockies to the Pacific Ocean. In their travels, they encountered many obstacles, from rattlesnakes and grizzly bears to exposure and near starvation, yet only one man died en route. Their success was secured by good relations with the regional American Indians. Lewis and Clark employed French Canadian interpreter Toussaint Charbonneau and, more importantly, his American Indian wife, Sacajawea, who promoted friendship with the Shoshoni and kept the party on good footing with other tribes. The detailed journals and studies kept by Lewis and Clark helped finally dispel the notion of a Northwest Passage.

After Lewis and Clark returned east, a new generation of explorers headed west, convinced they could make a quick fortune in the fur trade. Perhaps the most ambitious of these enterprises was organized by John Jacob Astor, at the time the richest man in America. Eager to monopolize the lucrative fur trade in the uncharted Northwest, he dispatched the ill-fated ship *Tonquin* from New York in the fall of 1810.

In the spring of 1811, just about the time the *Tonquin* was sailing across the Columbia River Bar, a second, overland group sponsored by Astor left St. Louis. They began by following the river route pioneered by Lewis and Clark, but then forged a new trail across the Rockies that would ultimately become part of the Oregon Trail. Among the leaders was Wilson Price Hunt, who was plagued by practically every conceivable misfortune on the journey west. Members of Hunt's party drowned, nearly starved to death, were ambushed by Indians and victimized by strange diseases.

By 1812, when this party limped into the coastal outpost at Astoria, virtually the entire *Tonquin* crew had perished in an Indian raid. A surviving crew member, in a final insane act of revenge, lured the American Indians back on the ship, went below and lit the ship's magazine, killing everyone aboard.

The War of 1812 (in which the United States allied with France against the English) hardly affected the Northwest except

FLOWER POWER

Before women in Washington State were granted the right to vote, they chose the coast rhododendron as the state flower in 1892. In an effort to select an official flower to enter in a floral exhibit at the 1893 World's Fair in Chicago, voting booths were set up for ladies throughout the state. In the end, the "rhodie" triumphed over the clover.

for some skullduggery on the part of a British trade company. In September 1812, the remaining Astorians residing on the banks of the Columbia were visited by a party from the English-owned North West Fur Company, a business rival. These newcomers announced that a British warship was en route to seize the new American base Fort Astoria. To make matters worse, they announced that the British had just won the War of 1812. Cut off from the news that would have exposed this lie, the Astorians decided to sell off their pelts for pennies on the dollar and control of the region shifted to the British.

Once the trading companies established permanent outposts in Washington and laid some of the foundation for settlement, the missionaries came to "civilize" the American Indians with their western religion and medicine. However, the intentions of the missionaries often resulted in tension between the American Indians and the new settlers. Eventually, skirmishes escalated into the various Indian Wars of the region, which started in the mid1800s and ended by the turn of the century.

Over time, the territorial struggle came down to the United States and England. After the dust had settled on the War of 1812 (which actually stalemated in 1815), the American and British governments signed a Treaty of Joint Occupation giving both nations the right to trade and settle in the northwest region known as Oregon Country. In 1821, the two reigning British enterprises, Hudson's Bay Company and North West Company, merged and went on to set up a base at Fort Vancouver. This new regional headquarters on the banks of the Columbia exemplified the ability of the British to blend economic and political goals. Unlike Astor's ill-fated pioneers, the region's new landlords showed a deft ability to master this untamed land. Under the aegis of the Hudson's Bay Company, the British turned their Columbia River base into a prosperous trading hub, attracting American Indian tribes from throughout the region.

At the same time, Dr. John McLoughlin, the chief Hudson's Bay factor who befriended American missionaries and settlers, was a superb diplomat. Recognizing the inevitability of American westward expansion, he helped smooth the way for the creation of the new Oregon Territory and the lowering of the British flag in 1848.

Homesteading, fishing, logging, ranching and other opportunities kept the flow of settlers coming. Gold was another early attraction to Washington. A small strike was hit at Walla Walla in the 1850s; however, it was not gold found in Washington that helped this state to prosper. It was the Alaska and Yukon strikes of the late 1890s that attracted droves of prospectors, most of whom passed through Washington buying supplies for their trip up north. Stage routes were established, and river traffic increased steadily. Over the next 40 years, the population expanded from

4000 to over 100,000. As the logging, fishing and shipping industries grew, railroads began pushing into the region, reaching Puget Sound in 1883. Six years later, Washington became our 42nd state and Olympia was named its capital.

THE 20TH CENTURY Rapid industrial development came with the world wars, and Washington emerged as a major player in the shipbuilding and shipping industries. Expansion in lumber, agriculture and fishing continued apace. During World War II, the shipbuilding, aircraft and atomic energy industries all boomed. Modern Washington first found itself in the international spotlight when it hosted two World's Fairs in 12 years: in Seattle in 1962 and Spokane in 1974.

Seattle became the western head of the American airplane industry with the emergence of Boeing as one of the world's largest commercial aircraft companies. Microsoft set up base here in 1975 and within a decade rose to dominate the software industry. Other companies settling in Washington included Sega Corporation, Nike and the Nordstrom corporate headquarters.

The rush of young successful companies combined with the backbone of Boeing attracted a huge influx of people. Until very recently, Seattle was expanding at a phenomenal rate. They could hardly build roads fast enough to handle the traffic. As a result, Seattle is young—from the hoards of yuppie coffee drinkers to the development-speckled suburbs and ultramodern road system.

The early 1990s were tough for Washington, particularly Seattle. Boeing took some blows, losing big contracts to McDonnell Douglas and Air Bus—and when Boeing hurts, so does Seattle. The regional economy, however, is still very much on its feet, driven by the strong computer and technology companies.

A MOUNTAIN BY ANY OTHER NAME ...

Long before European explorers set foot on North American soil, Northwest American Indians knew the mountain as Takhoma, Tahoma and even Ta-co-bet, among other names. Many of these names mean "snowy peak," "big mountain," or even "place where the waters begin." The peak was rechristened by Captain George Vancouver, who encountered the awesome sight when he sailed into Puget Sound on May 8, 1792. He named it after his friend Rear Admiral Peter Rainier, who had fought in His Majesty's Navy against the colonists during the Revolutionary War, but had never even visited America, let alone beheld this majestic landmark. Although the names Tacoma or Tachoma were used interchangeably with Mt. Rainier over the years, in 1880, the U.S. Geographic Board declared Mt. Rainier the official name to be used on all government maps.

On a cultural level, many American Indian tribes have proudly reclaimed their heritage. A new generation of American Indians has gained prominence in business, education, the environmental movement and the arts. Tribal organizations are also reclaiming lands and fishing rights.

In the early '90s Seattle had its 15 minutes of cultural fame when unlikely members of its lively music scene gained national attention. The "grunge" phenomenon, associated with flannel shirts and a rough rock sound, was shunned by hardcore music fans as pure media hype. Seattle's thriving arts and music scene, however, is anything but hype—it is, after all, Jimi Hendrix's hometown. The large number of students who live there ensure the town's status as a mecca for the young and talented. For alternative sounds, local and otherwise, tune in to KEXP 90.3.

Washington's current challenge is to reconcile its business opportunities with its natural resources, to strike a balance between expansion and preservation that will maintain its rich environmental and economic resources.

FOUR

Seattle and Vicinity

Rain city? Not today. Last night's storm has washed the air clean, swept away yesterday's curtain of clouds to reveal Mt. Rainier in all its astonishing glory. From your hotel room window, you can see the Olympics rising like snow-tipped daggers beyond the blue gulf of Puget Sound. Below, downtown Seattle awakens to sunshine, espresso and the promise of a day brimming with discovery for the fortunate traveler.

The lesson here is twofold: Don't be daunted by Seattle's reputation for nasty weather, and don't limit yourself to anticipating its natural setting and magnificent greenery, awesome as they may be. For this jewel surrounded by water, earning it the nickname "The Emerald City," sparkles in ways too numerous to count after a decade or more of extraordinary growth.

Greater Seattle has changed dramatically. The city, squeezed into a lean, hour-glass shape between Elliott Bay and Lake Washington, covers only 84 square miles, and its population is still under 600,000. But the greater metropolitan area, reaching from Everett to Tacoma and east to the Cascade foothills, now boasts some 4 million.

While most newcomers have settled in the suburbs, Seattle's soaring skyline downtown is the visual focus of a region on the move. No longer the sleepy sovereign of Puget Sound, Seattle today is clearly the most muscular of the Northwest's three largest cities. Its urban energy is admired even by those who bemoan Seattle's freeway congestion, suburban sprawl, crime and worrisome air and water pollution. Growth has been the engine of change, and although the pace has slowed in the '90s, the challenges posed by too rapid an expansion remain persistent topics of discussion.

Seattle offered no hint of its future prominence when pioneers began arriving on Elliott Bay some 150 years ago. Like other settlements around Puget Sound, Seattle survived by farming, fishing, shipbuilding, logging and coal mining. For decades the community hardly grew at all. One whimsical theory has it that because the frontier sawmill town offered a better array of brothels to the region's loggers, miners and fishermen, capital tended to flow into Seattle to fund later investment and expansion.

Whatever the reason, the city quickly rebuilt after the disastrous "Great Fire" of 1889. But it would be another eight years before the discovery of gold in Alaska put Seattle on the map. On July 17, 1897, the ship *Portland* steamed into Elliott Bay from Alaska, bearing its legendary "ton of gold" (actually, nearly two tons), triggering the Klondike Gold Rush. Seattle immediately emerged as chief outfitter to thousands of would-be miners heading north to the gold fields.

Today, Seattle remains tied to its traditions. It's so close to the sea that 20-pound salmon are still hooked in Elliott Bay, at the feet of those gleaming, new skyscrapers. It's so near its waterfront that the boom of ferry horns resonates among its buildings and the cries of gulls still pierce the rumble of traffic. But the city's (and the state's) economy has grown beyond the old resource-based industries. International trade, tourism, agriculture and software giants like Microsoft now lead the way. The spotlight has passed from building ships to building airplanes, from wood chips to microchips, from mining coal to cultivating the fertile fields of tourism.

Seattle has also achieved national—even global—cultural status. Grunge rock swept the music industry in the early '90s, led by local groups such as Pearl Jam, Nirvana, Soundgarden (named after a Seattle park), Alice in Chains and legendary record label Sub Pop. All these bands still live and work here (except Nirvana, disassembled by the death of grunge king Kurt Cobain), and music fans can hear the next generation of stars in the city's innumerable clubs and small concert halls.

Starbucks, a home-grown company founded by three University of Washington graduates, fueled the international specialty coffee boom; now Seattle considers itself the coffee capital of the world, and visitors can sample an astonishing array of roasts and blends. With more than two dozen specialty coffee retailers, there's literally a coffee shop on every corner. Nordstrom brought true customer service to the retail industry; Eddie Bauer and REI, two other home-grown institutions, melded flannel and fashion; the city was the test market that proved America would embrace Altoids. In other words, like San Francisco and Los Angeles, Seattle is a good place to see what's coming down the cultural pike.

In the process, one of the nation's most vibrant economies has emerged. You can see that energy in Seattle's highrises, feel it in the buoyant street scene fueled in part by locals' infatuation with espresso. And there is fresh energy beneath your very feet. An "underground" of retail shops (as distinguished from the historic Pioneer Square Underground) has taken shape around the downtown Westlake stations in the Metro Transit Tunnel.

Civic energy has produced a glorious art museum downtown, a small but lively "people place" in Westlake Park, a spacious convention center and additions to Freeway Park. Private enterprise has added hotels, office towers with grand lobbies brimming with public art, shopping arcades, restaurants, nightclubs and bistros.

During the late '80s, as locals struggled with construction chaos, Seattle's downtown briefly suffered the nickname "little Beirut." Now, in the early years of the new millennium, downtown Seattle is once more under construction. But this time the atmosphere is one of urban revitalization, as the city has gained a new symphony hall, a plethora of condominiums and several upscale shopping and entertainment complexes. As vibrant as it is, downtown also exhibits the famed Seattle social courtesy and informality. Drivers on many downtown streets still stop to let waiting pedestrians cross, and it's not considered polite to honk your horn. Ask directions of anyone who looks like they know their way around; they'll almost always do their best to help. Only bankers and corporate executives wear suits to work, and not even all of those do. Casual wear is acceptable in almost every social situation; even the symphony and opera draw fans dressed in jeans. Historically, weather bureau statistics show that mid-July to mid-August brings the driest, sunniest, warmest weather—a sure bet for tourists, or so you'd suppose. But in the last decade or two, that midsummer guarantee all too often has been washed away by clouds or rain. What's the sun-seeking tourist to do?

Consider September. In recent years it has brought modestly reliable weather. Or, simply come prepared—spiritually and practically—for whatever mix of dreary and sublime days that fate delivers. An accepting attitude may be the best defense of all in a region once described in this way: "The mildest winter I ever spent was a summer on Puget Sound."

Have goofy weather, growth, gentrification of downtown neighborhoods and a tide of new immigrants eradicated the old Seattle? Not by a long shot. Pike Place Market's colorful maze is still there to beguile you. Ferry boats still glide like wedding cakes across a night-darkened Elliott Bay. The central waterfront is as clamorous, gritty and irresistible as ever. Pioneer Square and its catacomb-like underground still beckons. The soul of the city somehow endures even as the changes wrought by regional growth accumulate.

But despair not. The legendary Northwest may take a bit more effort to discover, but by almost any standard Seattle and its environs still offer an extraordinary blend of urban and outdoor pleasures close at hand. And growth seems only to have spurred a much richer cultural scene in Seattle—better restaurants serving original cuisines, more swank hotels, superb opera and a vital theater community, more art galleries and livelier shopping in a retail core sprinkled with public plazas that reach out to passersby with summer noon-hour concerts. In this chapter we will point you to familiar landmarks, help you discover some "hidden" treasures and find the best of what's new downtown.

Downtown Seattle

When you fly into Seattle, the central part of this lush region looks irresistible. From the air you'll be captivated by deep bays, harbors, gleaming skyscrapers, parks stretching for miles and hillside neighborhoods where waterskiing begins from the backyard. Central Seattle's neighborhoods offer a seemingly inexhaustible array of possibilities from the International District to Lake Union and the waterfront to Capitol Hill. Eminently walkable, this area can also be explored by monorail, boat and bike. From the lofty heights of the Space Needle to the city's underground tour, this is one of the Northwest's best bets.

SIGHTS

Downtown Seattle (Pioneer Square to Seattle Center, the waterfront to Route 5) is compact enough for walkers to tour on foot.

Energetic folks can see the highlights on one grand loop tour, or you can sample smaller chunks on successive days. Since downtown is spread along a relatively narrow north–south axis, you can walk from one end to the other, then return by public transit via buses in the Metro Transit Tunnel or aboard the Waterfront Streetcar trolleys, each of which have stations in both Pioneer Square and the International District. The Monorail also runs north–south between Westlake Center and Seattle Center.

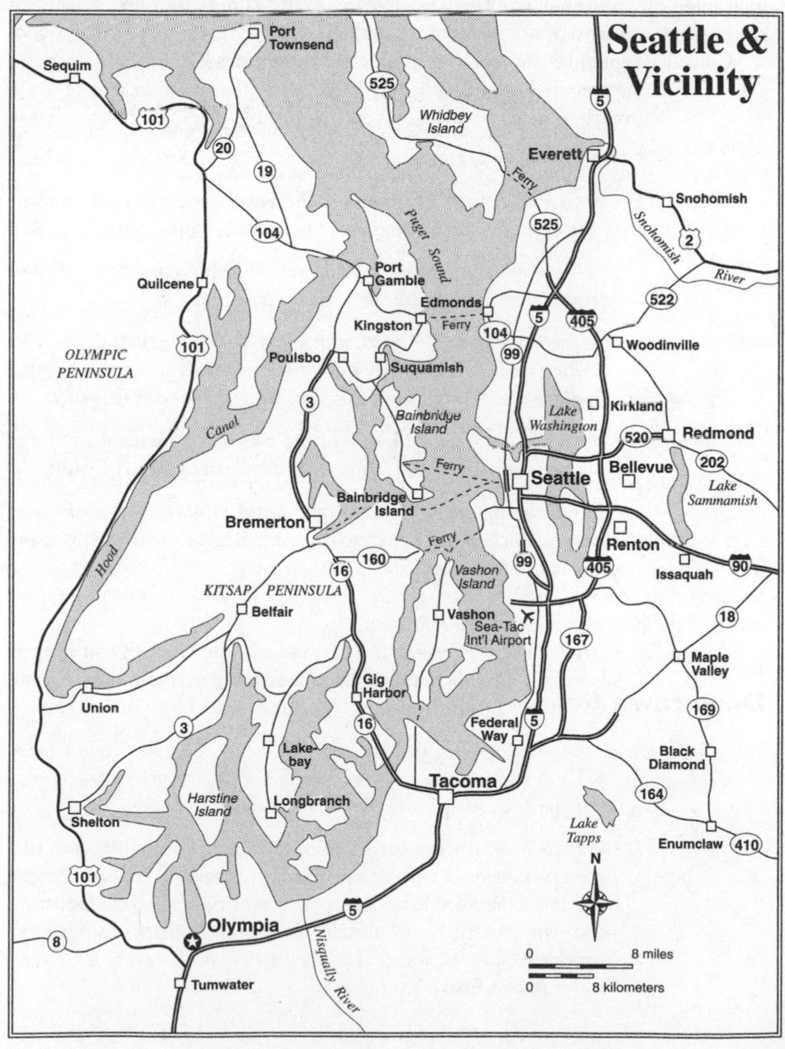

Text continued on page 44.

Three-day Weekend

Seattle

Day 1

- Check in. It makes sense to stay downtown, where most of the key sights are located. Driving from other parts of this long, narrow city can be time consuming. If you *do* stay outside the downtown area, your best bet is to park at Seattle Center and ride the monorail instead of looking for downtown parking.
- If you haven't done so before starting your trip, make reservations for dinner and the theater tonight and the Underground Tour tomorrow. Seattle runs on reservations, and most locals plan far ahead.
- Stroll **Pike Place Market** and the **waterfront** (see the walking tour on pages 50–51) and visit the **Seattle Aquarium** (page 47).
- Rest your feet on a low-cost, scenic **Washington State Ferry** cruise from the Pier 52 terminal to Bremerton and back.
- On terra firma once more, climb the steep hill to the Westlake Center monorail terminal. Ride the **monorail** to Seattle Center. Take the elevator to the top of the **Space Needle** (page 69).
- Dine atop the Space Needle at the **Sky City Restaurant** (page 71) or, more affordably, at the **Seattle Center Food Court**.
- In the evening, enjoy your choice of Seattle Center performing-arts events, which may range from operas and ballets to stage plays and folk-dancing lessons.

Day 2

- Stroll down to **Pioneer Square** and take the **Underground Tour** (page 44) for a look at the abandoned city that lies hidden beneath downtown Seattle's streets.
- Above ground, ride the elevator to the top of **Smith Tower** (page 45) and imagine the long-ago time when this mini-skyscraper was the tallest building west of the Mississippi.
- Wander through the **International District** (page 46) and take your pick from the many small Asian restaurants along Main and Jackson streets for lunch. Feast your eyes on the exotic foodstuffs and fine Asian home furnishings at **Uwajimaya** (page 46). Complete your exploration of the district with a visit to the **Wing Luke Asian Museum** (page 46).

- For dinner this evening, why not enjoy Seattle's favorite food, alder-grilled salmon, at **Ivar's Salmon House** (page 88) on the Lake Union shoreline? Start driving up there early or take a cab; for a popular tourist restaurant, it's a little tricky to find.
- This could be the evening to check out the city's exceptionally lively nightclub scene. (If you don't feel like dyeing your hair green, simply wear your most authentically grungy camping clothes . . . .)

Day 3

- Is it raining? If not, this could be an ideal morning for sightseeing on attractive **Bainbridge Island** (page 138).
- If it *is* raining, check out the nearby **Museum of History and Industry** (page 76)—the name may sound boring, but the museum is fascinating. The same is true for the new **Seattle Central Public Library** (page 46).
- For lunch, try one of the interesting, affordable meals at the popular **Sound Food Café** (page 99).
- Sun still shining? How about a bike ride along **Alki Beach** (page 94) in West Seattle, with its old-time California atmosphere and its great views of the Seattle skyline across the bay?
- Still raining? The city has plenty of other good museums to stay dry in. One good bet is the Boeing's **Museum of Flight** (page 94), tracing the century-long history of the Seattle area's largest employer.
- Consider finishing up your Seattle spree with a big-splurge dinner at **Campagne** (page 62), one of the city's finest restaurants.

A good place to orient yourself is the Seattle Convention and Visitors Bureau's **Citywide Concierge & Visitors Center.** Folks staffing the desk will supply you with sightseeing advice and reservations for ground transportation and area restaurants. Closed Saturday and Sunday except in summer. ~ Within the Washington State Convention & Trade Center, 800 Convention Place; 206-461-5840; www.seeseattle.org.

Pioneer Square and its "old underground" remain one of Seattle's major fascinations. It was at this location that Seattle's first business district began. In 1889, a fire burned the woodframe city to the ground. The story of how the city rebuilt out of the ashes of the Great Fire remains intriguing to visitors and locals alike.

To learn exactly how the underground was created after the new city arose, then was forgotten, then rediscovered, you really need to take the one-and-a-half-hour **Underground Tour.** Several of these subterranean pilgrimages are offered daily to the dark and cobwebby bowels of the underground—actually the street-level floors of buildings that were sealed off and fell into disuse when streets and sidewalks were elevated shortly after Pioneer Square was rebuilt (in fire-resistant brick instead of wood). Admission. ~ 608 1st Avenue; 206-682-4646, fax 206-682-1511; www.undergroundtour.com.

Above ground, in sunshine and fresh air, you can stroll through 91 acres of mostly century-old architecture in the historic district (maps and directories to district businesses are available in most shops). Notable architecture includes gems like the **Grand Central Building,** 1st Avenue South and South Main Street, **Merrill Place,** 1st Avenue South and South Jackson Street, the **Maynard Building,** 1st Avenue South and South Washington Street, the cast-iron **Pergola** in Pioneer Square Park and facing buildings such as the **Mutual Life and Pioneer buildings,** 1st Avenue and Yesler Way. More than 30 art galleries are located in the Pioneer Square area. Here you can shop for American Indian art, handicrafts, paintings and pottery. (Incidentally, the Pioneer Building houses Seattle's first electric elevator.)

Yesler Way, located in the heart of the Pioneer Square area, itself originated as the steep "Skid Road" for logs cut on the hillsides above the harbor and bound for Henry Yesler's waterfront mill, and thence to growing cities like San Francisco. Later, as the district declined, Yesler Way attracted a variety of derelicts and became the prototype for every big city's bowery, alias "skid row."

The new city boomed during the Alaska Gold Rush in 1897–98. For a look back at extraordinary times, stop by the Seattle Unit of the **Klondike Gold Rush National Historical Park,** one of the tiniest National Park Service sites in the lower 48. In this historic red-brick building in downtown Seattle, you can see gold-panning demonstrations (only in summer), a collection of artifacts, films and other memorabilia. Other units of the park are in Southeast Alaska. ~ 319 2nd Avenue South; 206-220-4240; www.nps.gov/klse.

The main pedestrian artery is **Occidental Mall and Park**, a tree-lined, cobbled promenade running south from Yesler Way to South Jackson Street allowing pleasant ambling between rows of shops and galleries (don't miss the oasis of **Waterfall Park** off Occidental on South Main Street).

For an overview of the whole district, ride the rattling old manually operated elevator to the observation level of the 42-story **Smith Tower**, built in 1914. Closed weekdays from November through March. Admission. ~ 506 2nd Avenue and Yesler Way;

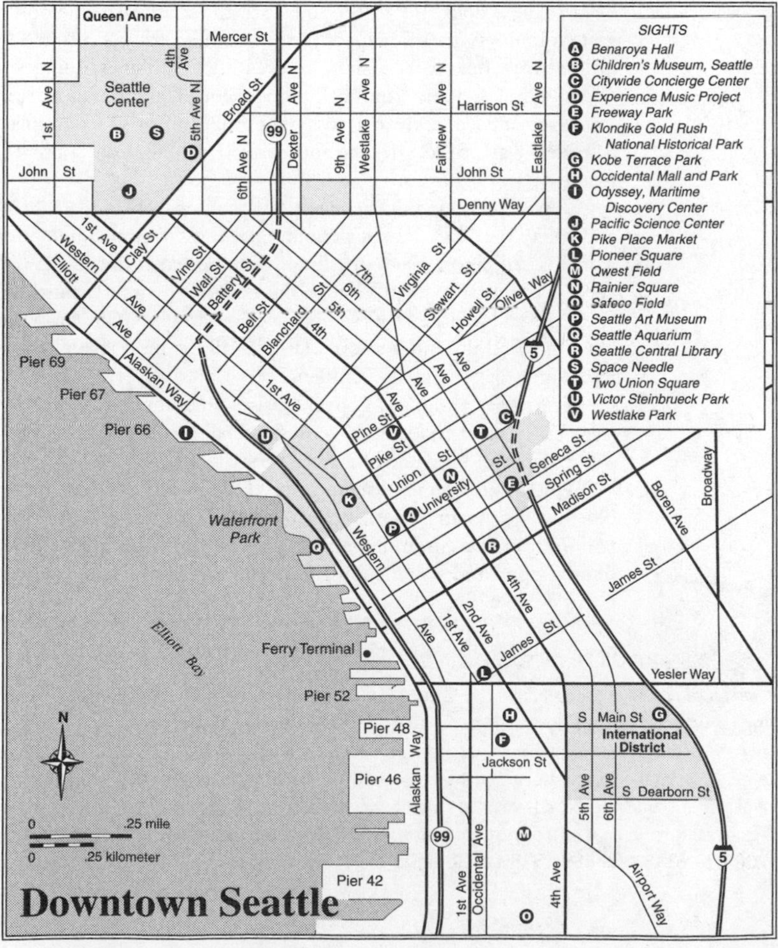

206-622-4004, fax 206-622-9357; www.smithtower.com, e-mail info@smithtower.com.

Designed to take full advantage of views of downtown and glimpses of Elliott Bay, each floor of the new cantilevered, 11-story **Seattle Central Public Library** is linked by a spiral of shocking-yellow escalators leading from the parking area up through public spaces to the research, collections and administrations floors. Much of the furniture is bright and funky. In true Seattle tradition, one floor has a coffee stand, and computers with wi-fi access are available. This is definitely not your grandma's library. A must for every book and architecture lover. ~ 1000 4th Avenue; 206-386-4636; www.spl.org.

Sharp ethnic diversity has always marked the **International District**, next door to Pioneer Square to the southeast. The polyglot community that emerged on the southern fringes of old Seattle always mixed its Asian cultures and continues doing so today, setting it apart from the homogeneous Chinatowns of San Francisco and Vancouver, across the border in British Columbia. ~ Yesler Way to South Dearborn Street, 4th Avenue South to Route 5.

Chinese began settling here in the 1860s, Japanese in the 1890s, and today the "I.D.," as it's commonly known, is also home to Koreans, Filipinos, Vietnamese and Cambodians. For all its diversity, the district clearly lacks the economic vitality, bustling street life and polished tourist appeal of other major Chinatowns. Yet some find the International District all the more genuine for its unhurried, even seedy, ambience.

A variety of mom-and-pop enterprises predominates in the I.D. —specialty-food and grocery stores, herbal-medicine shops, dim sum palaces and fortune-cookie factories.

Wing Luke Asian Museum offers a well-rounded look at the Northwest's Asian American history and culture, representing ten groups of Asian immigrants. Presentations include historical photography and social commentary on the Asian-American ex-

sights

AUTHOR FAVORITE

Pike Place Market is lots of fun, but I find it even more fascinating to wander up and down the food aisles of **Uwajimaya**, trying to identify the strange and exotic ingredients sold there—many of them bright pink. This retail store is not only the largest family-owned Asian grocery and gift store in the Northwest but also a worthwhile experience of Asian culture even if you're not shopping. ~ 600 5th Avenue South; 206-624-6248, 800-889-1928, fax 206-405-2996; www.uwajimaya.com.

perience. You may also see paintings, ceramics, prints, sculpture and other art. Closed Monday. Admission. ~ 407 7th Avenue South; 206-623-5124, fax 206-623-4559; www.wingluke.org, e-mail folks@wingluke.org.

Named after Seattle's sister city in Japan, **Kobe Terrace Park** offers pleasant strolling among Japanese pine and cherry blossom trees. An adjacent community garden is tended by local residents. ~ 221 6th Avenue South; 206-684-4075.

Hing Hay Park is the scene of frequent festivals—exhibitions of Japanese martial arts, Chinese folk dances, Vietnamese food fairs, Korean music and the like. It's colorful pavilion comes from Taipei, Taiwan. ~ South King Street and Maynard Avenue South.

The old **waterfront** beginning at the western edge of Pioneer Square remains one of the most colorful quarters of the city and what many consider Seattle's liveliest "people place." On sunny summer days, it is the most popular tourist draw in the city. The waterfront grows more interesting by the year, a beguiling jumble of fish bars and excursion-boat docks, ferries and fireboats, import emporiums and nautical shops, sway-backed old piers and barnacle-encrusted pilings that creak in the wash of wakes.

The action's concentrated between Piers 48 and 60, and again around Pier 70. Poking around by foot remains the favorite way to explore, but some folks prefer to hopscotch to specific sites aboard the **Waterfront Streetcar**, which runs from the International District to Pier 70. You also can climb into a horse-drawn carriage near Pier 60 for a narrated tour. Still another way to do it is via boat (see "Hey! The Water's Fine" at the end of this chapter). Here's a sampler of attractions: As you stroll south to north, you'll encounter a harbor-watch facility, a dozen historical plaques that trace major events, a public boat landing, the state-ferry terminal at Colman Dock and the waterfront fire station whose fireboats occasionally put on impressive, fountainlike displays on summer weekends. Ye Olde Curiosity Shop houses a collection of odd goods from around the world, Ivar's is the city's most famous fish bar, and cavernous shopping arcades include pier-end restaurants, outdoor picnic areas and public fishing. **Waterfront Park** is a crescent-shaped retreat from commercialism presenting sweeping views over the harbor.

Dating back to 1899, **Ye Olde Curiosity Shop** is a combination souvenir shop and museum that draws crowds with odd displays such as a Siamese twin calf, rare Eskimo walrus-tusk carvings and one of the world's largest collections of shrunken heads. The antique, coin-operated games are an easy way to get rid of pocket change. ~ 1001 Alaskan Way, Pier 54; 206-682-5844; www.yeolde curiosityshop.com.

After a $41 million fund-raising campaign, the **Seattle Aquarium** is now greatly expanded. The centerpiece is the new

Puget Sound Great Hall, a three-story, light-filled building with interactive educational kiosks, sea life art, and thought-provoking conservation exhibits focused on Puget Sound's ecosystems. Through a 40-foot-long window, visitors can view rock blades filled with salmon, colorful rockfish, vibrant sea anemones and other marine life swimming amid a kelp-filled sea. Other new amenities include a full-service café and gift store, and viewing platforms that offer a three-dimensional look into Window on Washington Waters, a 120,000-gallon showcase exhibit of the offshore environment at Neah Bay. ~ Pier 59, 1483 Alaskan Way; 206-386-4300, fax 206-386-4328; www.seattleaquarium.org, e-mail aquariumprograms@seattle.gov.

The Pike Hillclimb across Alaskan Way leads up—almost straight up, 155 steps' worth—past several decent restaurants and shops to the famed **Pike Place Market**. (There's an elevator for the walk-weary. You can also reach the north end of the Market from a stairway/elevator complex opposite the Pier 62/63 public wharf.) You'll also pass some piers whose sheds have been leveled to provide public access, the last vestiges of working waterfront on the central harbor—fish-company docks and such—as well as the Port of Seattle headquarters.

The venerable market, born in 1907, has proved itself one of the city's renewable treasures. Saved from the wrecking ball by citizen action in the early '70s, the market was later revitalized through long-term renovation. In August 2007, nine-acre Pike Place Market celebrated the centennial of its founding. **Pike Place Market National Historic District** and the surrounding neighborhood are, in many respects, better than ever. The main historic market, with its famous neon-lit clock, brass pig and fish-throwing vendors, now offers hundreds of different products in hundreds of categories, from clothing to different types of zucchini, even fresh crumpets. It currently has about 100 regular farmers, 200 craftspeople, 240 shops and restaurants, and 200 musicians and performers, and is visited by nearly 10 million visitors a year. In all, a market experience unparalleled in the nation! To learn more, visit the market's website or stop at the Info Booth at 1st Avenue and Pike Street. ~ Virginia Street to just south of Pike Street, 1st to Western avenues; 206-682-7453, fax 206-625-0646; www.pikeplacemarket.org, e-mail info@pikeplacemarket.org.

There are so many ways to enjoy the market that we can scarcely begin to list them. Come early for breakfast and wake up with the market (at least a dozen cafés open early). Come at noon for the ultimate experience of marketplace clamor amid legions of jostling shoppers, vendors hawking salmon and truck-farm produce, and street musicians vying for your contributions. Come to explore the market's lower level, often missed by tourists, a warrenlike collection of secondhand treasures, old books, magazines, posters and vintage clothing. Come to shop for the largest collection of handmade merchandise in the Northwest on handcraft tables at the market's north end. Come to browse all the "nonproduce" merchandise surrounding the main market—wines, exotic imported foods, French kitchenware, jewelry and avant-garde fashions.

Seattle's buses run free within the Central Business District. The Monorail ($2.50 roundtrip) zips between Seattle Center and Westlake Center in 90 seconds. For a leisurely ride along the waterfront, hop aboard the 1927 vintage streetcar ($1.25 each way).

Among the market's many virtues, perhaps the best is that it is a real-life urban amenity popular with Seattleites every bit as much as visitors. What downtown workers do lends itself to travel itineraries equally well: Walk to the market late morning and enjoy the atmosphere for a few minutes. You could buy a coffee drink at Starbucks and listen to the street musicians invariably set up out front—perhaps the King Jesus Disciples, four excellent gospel singers who once prowled downtown streets as transients. Yes, this is the original **Starbucks** store, the very first of some 3600 around the world; it opened in 1971. ~ 1912 Pike Place; 206-448-8762.

After you've loaded up on coffee and tasty treats from the food vendors, wander down to **Victor Steinbrueck Park**, a small plaza at the north end of Pike Place, overlooking Elliott Bay and the Olympics. On sunny days the crowd here ranges from backpacking European youths to bankers to religious proselytizers to Japanese schoolgirls on tour, holding hands. There's no better place to gain an appreciation of Seattle's cultural diversity. On your way back to your hotel, pick up some gifts to take home, or maybe just a loaf of bread for dinner. ~ Pike Place and Western Avenue.

The next pier north, **Pier 62/63**, is a public park ten months of the year where you can often see anglers for squid at high tide. During July and August, the pier becomes a world-class outdoor theater, with evening concerts by pop, rock and blues music acts such as Chris Isaak and Robert Cray. The setting is unparalleled, with the Olympic Mountains across the sound lit pink by the summer sunset. Admission. ~ Summer Nights at the Pier, 206-281-7788; www.onereel.org.

Just a bit north is the Port of Seattle's **Pier 66**, the Bell Street Pier. With a small-craft marina, three restaurants, a museum, a conference center and a skybridge leading up to the booming Belltown shopping/restaurant district along 1st Avenue, this recent development has become a popular stop for travelers.

At Pier 66 on the waterfront, **Odyssey Maritime Discovery Center** contains four galleries of high-tech interactive exhibits for kids and adults that reveal how the industrial waterfront works, focusing on fishing, trade and boating. Children can steer a con-

WALKING TOUR

Seattle's Waterfront

Nowhere is the distinctive character of Seattle more visible than along the waterfront between Piers 52 and 70 and the adjacent Pike Place Market. (Of course, the waterfront contains many more piers south of this area, but they are used for industrial shipping and are inaccessible on foot. The best way to get a look is from a harbor tour boat.) This walking tour covers about two and a half miles. Although it can be completed in less than two hours, along the way you'll find enough points of interest to fill a whole day.

PIKE PLACE MARKET Start at Pike Place Market, near the intersection of Pike Street and 1st Avenue on a steep hillside above the waterfront. (If you must park in this area, you're most likely to find a space beneath the Alaskan Way Viaduct downhill from the market. A better plan for drivers, though, is to park at one of the big lots around the Seattle Center and ride the monorail downtown. It lets you off just four blocks from the market.) On the street level are more than 100 food vendors' stalls where you'll find plenty of fresh fruits and veggies to snack on while you wander, free samples of tasty edible souvenirs, and fishmongers hawking fresh local seafood such as giant geoduck (pronounced "gooey duck") clams, along with arts-and-crafts stands. The lower level has small eateries and shops that sell exotica imported from such far-off lands as Egypt and India.

HARBOR STEPS PARK From the south end of Pike Place Market, head south a short distance to Harbor Steps Park. (Here you're practically in front of the **Seattle Art Museum** (page 50); if time permits, it's well worth a visit either now or on the way back.) Walk down the broad 16,000-square-foot steps to Western Avenue. The waterfront promenade is just across the avenue. The steps take you down to Pier 59, site of the **Seattle Aquarium** (page 47). The aquarium is a must-see stop, where undersea attractions include jellyfish, migratory salmon and the

tainer ship into port, load a 20-ton cargo container onto a ship, and explore a scaled-down fishing boat. Other displays explain fishery management, the global economy, marine safety and environmental preservation. Closed Monday from May through September and Monday and Tuesday from October through April. Admission. ~ Pier 66, 2205 Alaskan Way; 206-374-4000, fax 206-374-4002; www.ody.org, e-mail info@ody.org.

South of Pike Place Market is the **Seattle Art Museum,** designed by the husband/wife architectural team of Robert Venturi

largest octopus in captivity. The aquarium is in the middle of the public waterfront area.

PIERS 62–70 If you walk north, you'll pass **Pier 62/63**, a bare-wood park serving as a 4000-seat municipal concert venue that has hosted such performers as Lyle Lovett, Jonny Lang, Judy Collins and Los Lobos. Between Anthony's Pier 66 Restaurant and the Edgewater Inn on Pier 67 is **Odyssey, Maritime Discovery Center** (page 49). Beyond the Edgewater Inn is the departure pier for the **Victoria Clipper** (high-speed ferry service to Victoria, B.C.; Pier 69). At the northern end of the waterfront is **Pier 70**, now home to offices and two restaurants but better known as the filming site for MTV's *The Real World: Seattle*.

PIERS 55–57 If you walk south from the aquarium, you'll pass a large dining and shopping complex at **Pier 57**, where the central attraction for kids is a vintage carousel. **Pier 55** is the departure point for tour boats to **Tillicum Village** (206-933-8600, 800-426-1205), a replica Salish Indian village on a small island where trips include a traditional grilled salmon buffet. The pier is also home to **Argosy Cruises** (206-623-1445), offering daily boat tours of Seattle Harbor.

PIER 54 Pier 54 is the site of two venerable Seattle landmarks. **Ivar's Fish Bar** (206-467-8063), the original home of the clams and fish-and-chips restaurant that now has locations all over the Northwest, was started in 1938 by the late Ivar Haglund while he was director of Seattle's first aquarium next door. **Ye Olde Curiosity Shop** (page 47) is a combination souvenir shop and free museum.

PIER 52 Pier 52 is the terminal for the **Washington State Ferries** that run frequently to Bremerton, Bainbridge Island and Vashon Island. Taking any of these ferries as a foot passenger makes for a relaxing, low-cost scenic cruise and an introduction to the ferry system that will serve you well as you travel to other parts of the Puget Sound area.

PIONEER SQUARE From the ferry terminal, you can either return the way you came, climbing back up the Harbor Steps, or go a few more blocks south to Pioneer Square, returning to central downtown along 2nd Avenue with its towering skyscrapers.

and Denise Scott. The five-story, limestone-faced building highlighted with terra-cotta and marble has quickly become a regional, postmodern landmark. Known for its Northwest Coast American Indian, Asian and African art, the museum also features Meso-American, modern and contemporary art, photography and European masters. In 2007, the museum expanded next door into the first four floors of the 42-story Washington Mutual Bank building. The seamlessly integrated spaces afford SAM a new museum café and store, as well as the $1 *billion* of new art given by collectors. Also new is the Olympic Sculpture Park, created on a reclaimed nine-acre industrial site on Elliott Bay. Closed Monday. Admission. ~ 1300 1st Avenue; 206-654-3100, fax 206-654-3135; www.seattleartmuseum.org.

Located across the street from the Seattle Art Museum, the Seattle Symphony's massive **Benaroya Hall** gives the symphony its own dedicated concert facility after years of sharing space at Seattle Center with the opera and ballet. The grounds include a memorial garden dedicated to Washington residents who died in military conflicts from World War II to the present. ~ 200 University Street; 206-215-4700, 866-833-4747, fax 206-215-4701; www.seattlesymphony.org, e-mail info@seattlesymphony.org.

City center, or **Downtown**, has undergone a remarkable rejuvenation. It's a delightful place to stroll whether you're intent on shopping or not. Major downtown hotels are clustered in the retail core, allowing easy walks in any direction. Here's one way to sightsee:

Start at the south end of **Freeway Park**, which offers five-plus acres of lawns, gardens and fountains, and is the nation's first major park to be built over a freeway. The park's many waterfalls and pools create a splashy, burbling sound barrier to city noise. Beds of summer-blooming flowers, tall evergreens and leafy deciduous trees create a genuine park feeling, inspiring picnics by office workers on their noon-hour break. Amble north through the park, and take a short detour beneath a street overpass toward University Street (steps next to more waterfalls zigzag up to Capitol Hill and dramatic views of city architecture). ~ 6th Avenue and Seneca Street.

Continue north as the park merges with similarly landscaped grounds of the **Washington State Convention & Trade Center**, which features impressive architecture and a large collection of public art. Maps and information are on hand at the Citywide Concierge & Visitor Center (206-461-5888), located on the first level of the Convention Center. ~ 800 Convention Place; 206-694-5000; www.wsctc.com, e-mail info@wsctc.com.

Head west through linking landscaping that leads you past yet more waterfalls and flowers in the main plaza of **Two Union Square**. Cross 6th Avenue and enter the **US Bank Centre**, located on the corner of Union Street. This handsome building's lower levels contain the City Centre mall, featuring upscale shops and a theater complex, bold sculptures and stunning exhibits of colorful art glass. Wander and admire for a bit, stop for a meal or an espresso, then continue by leaving the building at the 5th Avenue and Pike Street exit. Cross 5th Avenue past what used to be the striking Coliseum Theater, now renovated and occupied by Banana Republic. Head west on Pike Street to 4th Avenue and turn right to enter triangular **Westlake Park** at 4th Avenue and Pine Street, which offers a leafy copse of trees and an intriguing pattern of bricks that replicate a Salish Indian basket-weave design best observed from the terraces on the adjoining Westlake Center.

Westlake Center is an enormously popular, multilevel shopping arcade, a people place offering espresso bars, flower vendors, handicrafts and access to what's been heralded as downtown's "new underground." The marbled, well-lighted, below-street-level arcades were created as part of the city's new downtown transit tunnel. Metro buses (propelled electrically while underground) rumble by on the lowest level. Just above it are mezzanines full of public art, with vendors and shops, and underground access to a string of department stores.

Walk south on 4th Avenue a few blocks to **Rainier Square**, between 4th and 5th avenues and University and Union streets, and discover another burgeoning underground of upscale enterprises. Follow its passageways eastward past a bakery, restaurants and access to the venerable **Fifth Avenue Theatre**. Continue east, up an escalator back to Two Union Square and Freeway Park.

LODGING

Lodgings vary widely in style and price throughout the Seattle area. Downtown, there's a thick cluster of expensive luxury hotels interspersed with a few at moderate and even budget rates.

◄ HIDDEN

The **Pioneer Square Hotel**, a Best Western property, combines a prime location with Four-Diamond historic charm. The essence of comfort is captured here by turn-of-the-20th-century decor and remarkably quiet rooms. Rates are quite reasonable by downtown standards. The Pioneer Square Historic District surrounding the hotel is a haven for fascinating restaurants, taverns,

AUTHOR FAVORITE

For grandeur and luxury check in to the **W Seattle.** This Italian Renaissance–style hotel was built in 1924 on land that was the site of the original University of Washington. Conveniently located in the heart of downtown close to Pike Place Market and the Seattle Art Museum, this grande dame is the ultimate statement of refined elegance. The 450 guest rooms are tastefully appointed, and modern conveniences combine gracefully with the classic furnishings. The public rooms, adorned with impressive floral arrangements and crystal chandeliers take you back to another era while the fantasy blown-glass arrangements in the main dining room bring you back to the 21st century. Add a health club with pool and huge jacuzzi and you need look no further. ~ 1112 4th Avenue; 206-264-6000, 877-946-8357, fax 206-264-6100; www.whotels.com, e-mail wseattle.whatwhen@whotels.com. ULTRA-DELUXE.

art galleries, shops and more. The ferry terminal and Seattle Art Museum are also within a few blocks. ~ 77 Yesler Way; 206-340-1234, 800-800-5514, fax 206-467-0707; www.pioneersquare.com, e-mail info@pioneersquare.com. ULTRA-DELUXE.

The Edgewater has changed completely since the days when the Beatles used to fish for sand sharks from the windows, but the location—directly on the waterfront—is still hard to beat. The property began as a top-flight hotel on Pier 67, built in the 1960s for the World's Fair. It later slid into decay and was renovated in "mountain lodge" style—meaning stone fireplaces and natural-log furniture in the rooms. Half of the 223 rooms and suites have stunning views of Elliott Bay, West Seattle and the Olympic Peninsula. Rooms are comfortable, and the staff is accommodating. The restaurant has a fine water view. ~ 2411 Alaskan Way; 206-728-7000, 800-624-0670, fax 206-441-4119; www.edgewaterhotel.com, e-mail contactus@edgewaterhotel.com. ULTRA-DELUXE.

Writer Thomas Egan likened Seattle to "living in a leaky basement." But despite its legendary propensity for relentless rain, Seattle averages only about 36 inches of rain yearly—less than Atlanta and New York.

The **Alexis Hotel** is an elegant little haven two blocks from the waterfront and close to downtown stores and business centers. The 109 rooms have soft colors and contemporary furnishings mixed with a few antiques, all done in good taste. Some of the roomy suites have fireplaces, and others have two-person jetted tubs. The service is unmatched in this renovated historic hotel. Pet-friendly. ~ 1007 1st Avenue; 206-624-4844, 866-356-8894, fax 206-621-9009; www.alexishotel.com, e-mail reservations@alexishotel.com. ULTRA-DELUXE.

Another luxury hotel, **The Inn at Harbor Steps** has perhaps the best possible location for exploring downtown Seattle on foot. Across the street from the Seattle Art Museum and two blocks from Pike Place Market, the 28-room inn occupies the lower floors of a condominium highrise overlooking the heart of the waterfront. Each spacious guest room features a king- or queen-size bed, a sitting area, a gas fireplace and an oversize jetted bathtub. The rooms have high ceilings and floral print decor. ~ 1221 1st Avenue; 206-748-0973, 888-728-8910, fax 206-748-0533; www.innatharborsteps.com, e-mail inn@harborsteps.com. ULTRA-DELUXE.

HIDDEN ► The downtown location for the **Green Tortoise Hostel** is convenient to most central-Seattle attractions. With functional private and dorm rooms, 24-hour check-in, a common room and a fully equipped kitchen, it's much like a traditional hostel, with one extra advantage: a free full-service breakfast including unlimited eggs, fresh fruit, make-your-own waffles and fresh-baked brownies. There are also 11 computers with free internet access.

Many guest services, such as tours and discounts at local clubs, pubs and restaurants, add value as well. ~ 105 Pike Street; 206-340-1222, 888-424-6783, fax 206-623-3207; www.greentortoise.net, e-mail info@greentortoise.net. BUDGET.

Feel like a local by renting the fully furnished, nonsmoking **Convention Center Guest Quarters** apartment. The charmingly furnished suite, located in a 1950s building within walking distance of Pike Place, sleeps two. It has a comfy queen-size bed (with a memory foam mattress and 100 percent cotton linens), wi-fi access and a CD/DVD player in an armoire. Amenities include a kitchenette with a microwave, coffeemaker and mini fridge stocked with continental breakfast items. Three-night minimum. ~ The Electra, 1400 Hubbell Place, 206-697-6585, 800-684-2932; www.seattlebedandbreakfast.com, e-mail information@seattlebedandbreakfast.com. MODERATE.

Pensione Nichols offers European-style lodging within a block of Pike Place Market. Ten rooms on the third floor of a historic building share three baths and a large common space with a view of the bay, while two rooms share one bath on the second floor. The rooms are painted a cheerful yellow and have antique furnishings; some have windows, while others only have skylights. There are also two ultra-deluxe suites that sleep four and have views of the sound, fully equipped kitchens and private baths. A continental breakfast is served. ~ 1923 1st Avenue; phone/fax 206-441-7125, 800-440-7125; www.pensionenichols.com, e-mail info@pensionenichols.com. DELUXE TO ULTRA-DELUXE. ◄ HIDDEN

A retreat from the throngs in Pike Place Market is **Inn at the Market.** The hotel, several shops and a restaurant are centered by a brick courtyard with an old cherry tree. Light and airy and furnished in contemporary European style, the 70-room inn is one of Seattle's best. Guest rooms have views of the city, courtyard or water. ~ 86 Pine Street; 206-443-3600, 800-446-4484, fax 206-448-0631; www.innatthemarket.com, e-mail info@innatthemarket.com. ULTRA-DELUXE.

Hotel Monaco offers stylish, upscale accommodations in 189 funky, plush rooms and suites. The grand high-ceilinged lobby has columns and pilasters and a white stucco fireplace. Make sure to take advantage of their in-room pet goldfish adoption program. ~ 1101 4th Avenue; 206-621-1770, 800-715-6513, fax 206-261-7779; www.monaco-seattle.com. ULTRA-DELUXE.

Considered a luxury hotel in the 1930s, the **Executive Hotel Pacific** is now a dignified, quiet downtown classic with 150 rooms. Though updated and decorated with modern furniture, it hasn't lost its old-fashioned flavor, with windows that open, ceiling fans and rather small rooms. The concierge is very helpful. Wi-fi access available. ~ 400 Spring Street; 206-623-3900, 888-388-3932, fax 206-623-2059; www.pacificplazahotel.com, e-mail resehp@executivehotels.net. MODERATE TO DELUXE.

The **Renaissance Madison Hotel** offers luxury accommodations with views of Puget Sound, Lake Union and downtown. The 553 rooms are furnished in casual and contemporary earth-toned decor and guests enjoy access to the workout room, pool and whirlpool spa on the top floor. ~ 515 Madison Street; 206-583-0300, 800-546-9184, fax 206-447-0992; www.themadison.com, e-mail res@themadison.com. ULTRA-DELUXE.

The **Sheraton Seattle Hotel & Towers** manages to deftly combine the facilities of a large urban hotel with a personal touch. It has 840 rooms and suites, a cozy lobby with stunning displays of art, mostly glass. The pool and exercise room on the 35th floor have a grand view of the city with the Olympic Mountains as a backdrop. Stay in the Club Level (floors 31–33) and you'll have private breakfast, tea and evening hors d'oeuvres in the Club Lounge. The Towers (top floor) offer the same perks as the Club Level, but with even more luxuries and amenities including butler service. ~ 1400 6th Avenue; 206-621-9000, 800-325-3535, fax 206-621-8441; www.sheraton.com/seattle. ULTRA-DELUXE.

Two smaller boutique hotels offer elegant lodging in more intimate settings in the heart of the shopping district. The **Mayflower Park Hotel** is right next to Westlake Center and Nordstrom; in fact, it's connected to Westlake and offers covered access to Nordstrom and Macy's. A handsome, renovated 1927 stone building whose thick walls ensure quiet, the Mayflower's 171 rooms are furnished with Queen Anne–style furnishings and mahogany armoires. As was common in the '20s, the rooms are somewhat small, but its location is hard to beat. Closed until September 2007. ~ 405 Olive Way; 206-623-8700, 800-426-5100, fax 206-382-6997; www.mayflowerpark.com, e-mail mayflowerpark@mayflowerpark.com. ULTRA-DELUXE.

Just three blocks away, the **Hotel Vintage Park** is a refurbished classic, with 126 upscale rooms and an excellent Italian restaurant. It offers luxury hotel amenities such as terry-cloth robes, fully stocked honor bars and soundproofed double-pane windows. The hotel provides a nightly hosted wine hour by the wood-burning fireplace in its lobby. ~ 1100 5th Avenue; 206-624-8000, 800-624-4433, fax 206-623-0568; www.hotelvintagepark.com. DELUXE TO ULTRA-DELUXE.

The Warwick, on 4th Avenue a few blocks north of Westlake, has 230 rooms; those on the upper floors have great views of Queen Anne Hill and downtown. Most rooms are in the Sheraton class, with king-size beds, balconies and Italian marble bathrooms. It has a swimming pool and exercise facilities, and an in-house dining room. The Seattle Center is within easy walking distance. Wi-fi access available. ~ 401 Lenora Street; 206-443-4300, 800-426-9280, fax 206-448-1662; www.warwickwa.com, e-mail res.seattle@warwickhotels.com. MODERATE TO DELUXE.

Freshest in Seattle

Nothing beats strolling through a local farmer's market to take in the colorful sights and tempting smells of Washington's bounty. In recent years, a number of street-side markets have cropped up around Seattle neighborhoods. All feature local goodies—meats, cheeses, eggs, honey and other foodstuffs straight from small farms. Depending on the season, you'll have your pick of juicy pears, peaches, cherries, a variety of berries, mushrooms, potatoes or other root vegetables. Each market reflects the neighborhoods it's in, and many offer cooking demos, live music, produce tasting and activities for the kids.

The **Broadway Farmers Market** is open on Sunday from mid-May to late November. ~ Entrances are on Broadway, Thomas Street and 10th Avenue.

The **Columbia City Farmers Market** operates on Wednesday from mid-May to late October. ~ 4801 Rainier Avenue.

The **Lake City Farmers Market** is open on Thursday from mid-May to late October. ~ Northeast 127th and Northeast 30th streets.

Magnolia Farmers Market runs on Saturday from early June to late September. ~ 2550 34th Avenue West.

University District Farmers Market is open on Saturday from early May to mid-December. ~ Northeast 50th Avenue.

The **West Seattle Farmers Market** is open on Sunday from early May to mid-December. ~ Located in the Alaska Junction, on the 4500 block of California Avenue Southwest and Southwest Alaska streets.

For more information, contact the **Neighborhood Farmers Market Alliance**. ~ 206-547-2278; www.seattlefarmersmarkets.org.

Located in a former 1920s apartment building, the **Hotel Andra** provides spacious guest rooms converted from studio apartments. Decorated in earth tones, the 119 rooms include sitting areas with love seats. There's also a fitness room. ~ 2000 4th Avenue; 206-448-8600, 877-448-8600, fax 206-441-7140; www.hotelandra.com, e-mail hotelandra@hotelandra.com. DELUXE TO ULTRA-DELUXE.

Between downtown and Seattle Center is **Sixth Avenue Inn**, a five-story motor inn with 167 rooms. The rooms are a cut above those in most motels. They contain brass beds, desks and large windows. Those on the north and in back are the quietest. There's a restaurant overlooking a small garden, a fitness facility and wireless internet. ~ 2000 6th Avenue; 206-441-8300, 888-627-8290, fax 206-441-9903; www.sixthavenueinn.com, e-mail sixth.avenue@starwoodhotels.com. MODERATE TO DELUXE.

The **Sorrento Hotel** is known for its personal service and attention to detail. A historic building that has been remodeled, Sorrento is at the top of what is locally known as "Pill Hill" (for its proximity to the hospital), a few blocks from the downtown area to the north and the International District immediately south. Beyond the quiet, plush lobby are a notable restaurant and an inviting lounge with a piano bar that is a popular spot for a nightcap. The Sorrento has been called one of the most romantic hotels in Seattle. All 76 rooms and suites have a warm, traditional, European atmosphere. ~ 900 Madison Street; 206-622-6400, 800-426-1265, fax 206-343-6155; www.hotelsorrento.com, e-mail mail@hotelsorrento.com. ULTRA-DELUXE.

The **Inn at Virginia Mason** is an attractive, nine-story brick building owned by the medical center next door. On the eastern edge of downtown, it caters to hospital visitors and others looking for a convenient location and pleasant accommodations at reasonable prices. The 79 rooms have dark-wood furnishings and teal and maroon decor. Two suites have a fireplace and whirlpool tub. There's a small restaurant by a brick terrace. ~ 1006 Spring Street; 206-583-6453, 800-283-6453, fax 206-223-7545; www.innatvirginiamason.com. DELUXE TO ULTRA-DELUXE.

Villa Heidelberg is a bed and breakfast in a Craftsman-style home on a corner hillside. The inn has a wide wraparound porch that overlooks gardens of roses and rhododendrons. Inside, the atmosphere is comfortable and relaxed. The house features leaded glass windows, beamed ceilings and the original 1909 gaslight fixtures and embossed wall coverings. The six guest rooms feature brass or oak beds and oak dressers. Some have views of the Puget Sound and the Olympic Mountains. A full breakfast is served. ~ 4845 45th Avenue Southwest, West Seattle; 206-938-3658, 800-671-2942, fax 206-935-7077; www.villaheidelberg.com, e-mail info@villaheidelberg.com. MODERATE TO DELUXE.

DINING

The fine **al Boccalino** serves some of the city's best Italian dinners. Located in a brick building in Pioneer Square, the restaurant's atmosphere is unpretentious and intimate, the antipasti imaginative, and the entrées cooked and sauced to perfection. Saddle of lamb with brandy, tarragon and mustard is a favorite choice. There are daily specials for every course. No lunch on Saturday or Sunday. ~ 1 Yesler Way; 206-622-7688, fax 206-622-1798; e-mail alboccalino@aol.com. MODERATE TO DELUXE.

For a romantic dinner, try **Il Terrazzo Carmine** in the Merrill Place Building. For patio diners, a cascading reflecting pool drowns out some of the freeway noise. Entrées include roast duck with cherries or veal piccata with capers and lemon. The restaurant also features an extensive Italian wine list. No lunch on Saturday. Closed Sunday. ~ Pioneer Square, 411 1st Avenue South; 206-467-7797, fax 206-447-5716; www.ilterrazzocarmine.com. DELUXE.

Locals rave about **Harried and Hungry**, a great little sandwich café just north of Benaroya Hall. The café excels in fast and fresh takeout soups, sandwiches and salads. At breakfast, pick up a smoothie or a breakfast bagel with peanut butter and banana drizzled with honey. For lunch, sandwiches include homemade falafel (on wheat bread, not pita), as well as chicken pesto and turkey club. Large salads make an entire meal. Free wi-fi. No dinner. Closed weekends. ~ 1415 3rd Avenue; 206-264-7900. BUDGET.

◄ HIDDEN

It's impossible not to get thoroughly filled at **Zaina**, a friendly, low-key Greek eatery in the midst of the lower downtown business district. The place is packed with office workers at lunch, but the crowd thins out after 1 p.m. The food is filling and flavorful. Closed Sunday. ~ 108 Cherry Street; 206-624-5687. BUDGET.

A favorite among downtowners is the **Botticelli Café**. The small café is known for its *panini*—little sandwiches made of toasted

AUTHOR FAVORITE

Fresh, homemade crumpets–flat, toasted English teatime bread with the soft consistency of an English muffin–are almost impossible to find in the United States. What joy, then, to come upon them starring in their very own show in a tiny shop in Pike Place Market. **The Crumpet Shop** is a friendly place serving homemade crumpets the classic way, piping hot and crunchy with lots of butter, jam or honey, and a cup of imported black tea. For a more substantial meal, do like the Brits do and make a "high tea" out of a crumpet by ordering it toasted with English cheese, smoked salmon or pesto-colored eggs with ham. Soups, sandwiches and scones are also served. ~ 1503 1st Avenue; 206-682-1598. BUDGET.

focaccia bread and topped with olive oil, herbs, cheeses, meats and vegetables. The espresso and ices are good, too. Breakfast and lunch only. Closed Saturday (except in summer) and Sunday. ~ 101 Stewart Street; 206-441-9235. BUDGET.

Inside the Alexis Hotel, the **Library Bistro** is a sleek 1940s-style eatery, featuring faux lizard-skin high-backed booths, copper and bronze checkerboard tiles and gleaming oak floors. The cuisine is American contemporary, with entrées such as house-made creamy macaroni and cheese and a slow-cooked pulled pork sandwich with Dr. Pepper barbecue sauce. Wines hail from the Pacific Northwest. Breakfast and lunch only. ~ 92 Madison Street; 206-624-3646, 888-850-1155, fax 206-340-8861; www.librarybistro.com. DELUXE.

White-linen tablecloths, black-rattan furnishings and loads of plants await you at **Jade Garden**, an upscale Cantonese restaurant in the International District. In the foyer, the specials—such as hot and smoky crab in a spicy sauce, fresh fish with vegetables or clams in black-bean sauce—are posted on the blackboard. ~ 424 7th Avenue South; 206-622-8181. MODERATE TO DELUXE.

Shoppers and theatergoers love **Palomino** and its large, airy dining room, which lends itself to prime people watching. The food's good, too—this bustling downtown spot is best known for thin-crust pizzas that barely support the heap of toppings. Also on the menu is a variety of regional American and southern European–inspired salads, pasta and roasted meat and poultry dishes. Though crowded, you can still count on fast and efficient service. ~ 1420 5th Avenue, Suite 350; 206-623-1300; www.palomino.com. MODERATE TO DELUXE.

Hidden away in the Pike Place Market is **Place Pigalle.** Wind your way past a seafood vendor and Rachel, the bronze pig (a popular market mascot), to this restaurant with spectacular views of Elliott Bay. The dark-wood trim, handsome bar and other touches make for a European-bistro atmosphere. The restaurant makes the most of fresh ingredients from the market's produce tables. Dine on fresh Penn Cove mussels with bacon, celery and shallots in balsamic vinaigrette, calamari in a dijon-ginger cream sauce, or one of the daily fresh salmon specials. The dishes are artfully presented. Patio dining available in summer. Closed Sunday. ~ 81 Pike Street; 206-624-1756. DELUXE TO ULTRA-DELUXE.

Tucked into a hillside in Pike Place Market, **Il Bistro** is a cozy cellar spot with wide archways and oriental rugs on wooden floors. Light jazz, candlelight and well-prepared Italian food make it an inviting spot on a rainy evening. Several pastas are served; the entrées include rack of lamb, veal scallopine, fresh salmon and roasted free-range chicken. Dinner only. ~ 93-A Pike Street; 206-682-3049, fax 206-223-0234; www.ilbistro.net. DELUXE TO ULTRA-DELUXE.

Seattle's Coffee Wars

It doesn't take long for visitors to notice that Seattle's primary energy source is coffee. Coffee bars, the preferred business and social meeting spots, do a booming business, and it seems as if there's a drive-up espresso kiosk on every block. Conventional wisdom blames the weather for making the steamy, mood-lifting beverage more popular than Prozac, but on sunny summer days, you'll still see people waiting in line for iced lattes and granitas.

In 1971, "fresh coffee" still meant a new five-pound can of Folger's from the supermarket. Then Jim Stewart, with backing from his brother Dave, started Stewart Brothers Coffee, a small stand selling coffee beans in Pike Place Market. Jim first used a peanut roaster he'd bought from a vendor on a southern California beach but soon traveled to Italy to learn the art from master espresso roasters and purchased a real coffee-bean roaster. The unfamiliar smell of fresh roasted coffee wafted through the market and made his stand an instant hit. Later that same year, a second coffee-bean stand opened in Pike Place Market under the name Starbucks.

Soon the two rivals began buying coffee beans from different parts of the world, developing assorted distinctive blends and adding flavorings. In 1984 Starbucks started its first coffee bar at 4th and Spring streets in downtown Seattle. Meanwhile, Stewart Brothers began selling whole-bean coffee in bulk through supermarkets. Learning that there was another coffee wholesaler named Stewart, the brothers abbreviated the company's name to SBC Inc., which in turn inspired its trade name, Seattle's Best Coffee.

SBC grew to become the world's leading seller of specialty coffee beans, while Starbucks has expanded to nearly 4000 coffee bars, including locations in Tokyo, Beijing, Manila and Kuwait. Starbucks finally bought its in-city rival in 2003 but SBC retains an independent identity. The city now boasts 26 other retail and wholesale coffee-roasting companies as well as five green brokers (importers of unroasted coffee beans).

Across the cobbled street, you can observe the eclectic mix of shoppers and artists in the Pike Place Market at **Three Girls Bakery**, a popular hangout. This tiny lunch counter and bakery with just a few seats serves good sandwiches—the meatloaf sandwich is popular—and hearty soups, including chili and clam chowder. You have more than 50 kinds of bread to choose from. The sourdough and rye breads are recommended. If you don't have room for pastries, buy some to take home. You won't regret it. ~ 1514 Pike Place, Suite 1; 206-622-1045, fax 206-622-0245. BUDGET.

HIDDEN ► The food at **Oriental Mart** is a combination of Filipino and Asian—and it's very good and very inexpensive. Try the pork *adobo* if they have it that day; otherwise, any of the chicken preparations are excellent. There's no better place for lunch at the Market. The lunch counter is in back of the food-and-novelties store. ~ 1506 Pike Place Market; 206-622-8488. BUDGET.

In Post Alley, behind some of the market shops, you will find more than just a wee bit of Ireland at **Kells**. This traditional Irish restaurant and pub will lure you to the Emerald Isle with pictures and posters of splendid countryside. A limited menu includes Irish stew and meat pies. From the heavy, dark bar comes a host of domestic and imported beers. Irish musicians play live music seven days a week. ~ 1916 Post Alley; 206-728-1916, fax 206-441-9431; www.kellsirish.com/seattle. MODERATE

HIDDEN ► Talk about hidden—this place doesn't even have a sign. You enter through the pink door off of Post Alley. **The Pink Door**, with its Italian kitsch decor, is lively and robust at lunchtime. Especially good are the *lasagna della porta rosa* and a delicious cioppino. In the evening, the pace slows, the light dims and it's a perfect setting for a romantic dinner. In the summer, rooftop dining offers views of the Sound. Closed Sunday. ~ 1919 Post Alley; 206-443-3241, fax 206-443-3341; www.thepinkdoor.net. DELUXE.

Off a brick courtyard above Pike Place Market, **Campagne** is one of the city's top restaurants. Diners enjoy French country cooking in an atmosphere both warm and elegant. The menu changes six times a year. Entrées may include rack of lamb brushed with puréed anchovy and garlic sauce or roasted sea bass with

THE REAL DEAL

When I'm craving authentic Mexican food, I head to **El Puerco Lloron**. Every meal served here includes wonderfully fresh tortillas made by hand while hungry diners watch from the cafeteria line. The chiles rellenos compares with the best, and the tamales and taquitos are all authentic and recommended. There's a fiesta atmosphere in the warm, steamy room. ~ Pike Place Market Hillclimb, 1501 Western Avenue; 206-624-0541. BUDGET.

tarragon, lemon and tiny herb dumplings. The simply prepared dishes are usually the best: young chicken stuffed with ricotta, spinach and roasted herbs and served with sage-infused *jus* and rosemary roasted potatoes, for example. Dinner only. ~ 86 Pine Street; 206-728-2800, fax 206-448-7562; www.campagnerestaurant.com. DELUXE TO ULTRA-DELUXE.

Right below Campagne, off Pine Street, is **Cafe Campagne**, the larger restaurant's hugely popular, less expensive bistro. The café's food is even heartier than that upstairs, typified by sausages, roast meats, extravagant breakfasts and country-style desserts. The atmosphere is definitely more homey, with long tables and benches. ~ 1600 Post Alley; 206-728-2233; www.campagnerestaurant.com. MODERATE TO DELUXE. ◄ HIDDEN

Overlooking the market itself, **Copacabana Café** is Seattle's only Bolivian restaurant, but that isn't its greatest virtue. Tucked into the second floor of a lengthy, triangular historic brick building, its outdoor balcony tables offer mind-boggling views on sunny days. In the distance, the Olympic Mountains loom above the shimmering waters of Puget Sound. In the foreground below is the market's colorful bustle. Copacabana's food, typified by shrimp soup and *huminta*, a spicy corn pie, is decent; it's the view that causes local office workers to line up at the entrance, a curved wrought-iron stairway at the foot of Post Alley, before it opens at 11:30 for lunch. All the outside tables are gone by noon on clear days, so get there early. No lunch on Friday and Saturday in winter. ~ 1520½ Pike Place; 206-622-6359. MODERATE. ◄ HIDDEN

A stone's throw away is **Chez Shea**, also occupying the upper floor of a historic brick building. This intimate cubbyhole dining room offers great views (all indoors, alas) and superb Northwest regional cuisine with French influences, and enhancements such as excellent seafood. The prix-fixe menus include rich, inventive soups, salads and main dishes based on hearty ingredients such as roast chicken and lamb. Timing your dinner to coincide with sunset will produce an incomparably romantic experience. Closed Monday. ~ 94 Pike Street; phone/fax 206-467-9990; www.chezshea.com. ULTRA-DELUXE.

Inside Hotel Monaco is the upscale **Sazerac**, named for a New Orleans cocktail of bourbon and peychaud bitters. The seasonal Southern-inspired menu may feature spicy gumbo, fried catfish with cole slaw or cider-glazed pork ribs. Mahogany booths and windows, velvet curtains and cushions, whimsical artwork and music playing in the background complete this trendy scene. ~ 1101 4th Avenue; 206-624-7755, fax 206-624-0050; www.sazeracrestaurant.com. DELUXE.

The decor is spare and clean in **Wild Ginger**, and the menu is pan-Asian. Dark-wood booths fill the main dining room. There's also a satay bar where skewered chicken, beef, fish and vegetables are grilled, then served with peanut and other sauces. The wondrous Seven Elements Soup, an exotic blend of flavors, is a meal in itself. No lunch on Sunday. ~ 1401 3rd Avenue; 206-623-4450, fax 206-623-8265; www.wildginger.net. MODERATE TO DELUXE.

Padded white tablecloths, carpeting and an amber glow from the light fixtures give **Tulio** appealing warmth. Usually packed and festive, it's a place for great food and lively conversation rather than a quiet rendezvous. Go for the specials, such as duck breast and crispy confit with fennel, and the desserts, which range from a rich tiramisu to delicate pistachio gelato. Brunch on Saturday and Sunday. ~ 1100 5th Avenue, 206-624-5500, fax 206-623-0568; www.tulio.com. DELUXE.

Contemporary, international cuisine prepared with imagination is served at the **Dahlia Lounge** near the shops of Westlake Center. Bright red walls, a neon sign and paper-fish lampshades create a celebratory atmosphere. The chef draws upon numerous ethnic styles and uses Northwest products to develop such dishes as roasted mussels, smoky lamb sausage and yam souffle with carmelized apples and ginger. No lunch on weekends. ~ 2001 4th Avenue; 206-682-4142, fax 206-467-0568; www.tomdouglas.com, e-mail office@tomdouglas.com. DELUXE TO ULTRA-DELUXE.

Just north of downtown, you'll find the thriving Belltown shopping, dining and nightlife scene.

HIDDEN ►

Dark and intimate, **Marco's Supperclub** is a little-known purveyor of fine, eclectic multiregional dishes; the deep-fried sage leaves, an appetizer, are a true original. The staff is friendly and experienced, the music is '30s and '40s jazz, and the filling meals are reasonable by Belltown standards. Dinner only. Closed Sunday. ~ 2510 1st Avenue; 206-441-7801; www.marcossupperclub.com. MODERATE TO DELUXE.

Scarlet walls, high-backed booths and dim lighting help **Belltown Pizza** stand apart from your average pizza joint. It helps, too, that the pies here are damn tasty. Also on the menu is a small selection of pasta, salads and focaccia sandwiches. But after 10 p.m. on weekends, expect a hip, lively crowd that's more interested in the bar than the food. Dinner only. ~ 2422 1st Avenue; 206-441-2653; www.belltownpizza.net, e-mail jimmyd09@comcast.net. BUDGET TO MODERATE.

Artists and others without a lot of money for eats hang out at **The Two Bells Bar & Grill.** Local artwork on the walls changes every two months. This funky bar with 25 kinds of beer and a host of inexpensive good food is a busy place. You can always find good soups, sandwiches, burgers, salads and cold plates. Some favorites are an Italian-sausage soup and the hot beer-sausage sandwich. ~ 2313 4th Avenue; 206-441-3050, fax 206-448-9626. MODERATE.

Named for the region between the Cascade Mountains and the Pacific Ocean, **Cascadia** specializes in haute cuisine crafted entirely from local ingredients. Carmelized spice-rubbed wild king salmon and fenugreek-crusted spring lamb are just a few of chef Kerry Sear's elegant offerings, served against a backdrop of a nine-foot cascading waterfall. Dinner only. Closed Sunday. ~ 2328 1st Avenue; 206-448-8884, fax 206-448-2242; www.cascadiarestaurant.com. ULTRA-DELUXE.

An elegant 1950s-style supperclub, **El Gaucho** does dramatic versions of American classics. Martinis are a specialty, and table-side performances include caesar salad tossings and aged-steak carvings. In the Pampas Room there's live music and dancing on weekends. Dinner only. ~ 2505 1st Avenue; 206-728-1337, fax 206-728-4477; www.elgaucho.com, e-mail gwright@elgaucho.com. DELUXE TO ULTRA-DELUXE.

A Belltown institution with sleek, modern lines, the **Flying Fish** is devoted to the sea's bounty (except for a couple of meat dishes). The seasonal menu changes daily, but may include crispy monkfish in a spicy peanut sauce, salt-and-pepper Dungeness crab with spicy noodles, or sockeye salmon with a wild mushroom sauté. The award-winning wine list is extensive and varied. Try not to gawk—you may be sharing space with Seattle's pro athletes or glitterati at this hip hangout. Reservations suggested. ~ 2234 1st Avenue; 206-728-8595; www.flyingfishseattle.com, e-mail info@flyingfishseattle.com. DELUXE.

SHOPPING

The oldest and loveliest structure in Pioneer Square is the Pioneer Building. In the basement, the **Pioneer Square Antique Mall** has more than 6000 square feet of space devoted to antiques and collectibles and maintained by some 60 dealers. ~ 602 1st Avenue; 206-624-1164.

Grand Central Building houses 18 shops. Visitors can also enjoy drinks and baked goods at lobby tables adjacent to a brick fireplace. ~ 214 1st Avenue South; 206-903-0603.

Need a Morris Graves painting or a portrait of grunge legend Kurt Cobain? Several Pioneer Square galleries specialize in local artists, including **Linda Hodges Gallery** (Closed Sunday and Monday; 316 1st Avenue South; 206-624-3034; www.lindahodgesgallery.com), **Davidson Galleries** (313 Occidental Avenue South; 206-624-6700; www.davidsongalleries.com) and **Greg Kucera Gallery** (212 3rd Avenue South; 206-624-0770; www.gregkucera.com).

In the heart of the Pioneer Square district is the **Elliott Bay Book Company**, featuring over 150,000 titles, including an outstanding stock of Northwest books. You're bound to enjoy browsing, snacking in the on-premises café or listening in on frequently scheduled readings by renowned authors. ~ 101 South Main Street; 206-624-6600, 800-962-5311; www.elliottbaybook.com.

On the first Thursday of every month, Pioneer Square stores remain open late to premiere art exhibits accompanied by wine-and-cheese soirees and artist lectures.

Seattle's connection with the Pacific Rim is legendary, and **Uwajimaya** demonstrates the tie with shoji screens and lamps, kanji clocks, goldimari ceramic pieces and Japanese, Chinese, Thai, Vietnamese, Filipino and American canned and frozen foods. ~ 600 5th Avenue South; 206-624-6248, fax 206-405-2996; www.uwajimaya.com.

Housed in the old Higo Variety Store building (a neighborhood institution from the 1920s), the **KOBO Gallery** showcases traditional Japanese handicrafts and contemporary Pacific Northwest. Handmade cedar bowls, lacquerware, vintage textiles, modern photography and ceramics are all available. Closed Sunday. ~ 604 South Jackson Street; 206-381-3000.

John W. Nordstrom, founder of his namesake department store, is another of Seattle's native sons. His first store was founded here in 1901.

Along the waterfront, Piers 54 through 70 are shoppers' delights. You'll love **Ye Olde Curiosity Shop**, a Seattle landmark where the mummies "Sylvia," "Sylvester" and "Gloria" preside over souvenirs, American Indian totem poles and masks, Russian stacking dolls, lacquerware and Ukrainian eggs. ~ 1001 Alaskan Way, Pier 54; 206-682-5844; www.yeoldecuriosityshop.com.

Called the "Soul of Seattle," the **Pike Place Market** has been in business since 1907. Saved from the wrecking ball by citizen action in the early '70s, Pike Place is now a bustling bazaar with nearly 300 businesses (about 40 are eateries), 100 farmers (selling produce and flowers at tables and stalls) and 200 local artists and craftspeople. ~ 85 Pike Street; 206-682-7453; www.pikeplacemarket.org.

A notable establishment within the market is the **Pure Food Fish Market**, which ships fresh or smoked salmon anywhere in the U.S. ~ 1511 Pike Place; 206-622-5765; www.freshseafood.com.

Just south is **DeLaurenti Specialty Food and Wine**, a wondrously well-stocked gourmet store and café with hundreds of cheeses, pâtés, canned goods, spices, breads, meats and, in season, fresh truffles that can go for over $1500 a pound. ~ 1435 1st Avenue; 206-622-0141. Near Rachel, the market's famous bronze pig, is **Marketspice**, which offers, among dozens of teas and spices, its own distinctive clove-tinged spiced tea blend; it makes a great Christmas gift. ~ 85-A Pike Place; 206-622-6340.

HIDDEN ►

HIDDEN ►

Across Pike Place from the main arcade is **Jack's Fish Spot**, where the fish is as good as that at the more famous fish stands, the prices are at least 50 cents a pound better—in some cases as much as $3 cheaper per pound—and the Dungeness crab, cooked on the spot, is the freshest in the market. They'll ship fresh salmon anywhere in the country, and Jack's smoked salmon, which comes from the only smokehouse in the market, is also the best. ~ 1514 Pike Place; 206-467-0514; www.jacksfishspot.com, e-mail jack@jacksfishspot.com.

A few feet away, at the foot of Post Alley, **El Mercado Latino** carries Caribbean and Central American delights ranging from plantains to pasilla chiles to habañero sauces. ~ 1514 Pike Place; 206-623-3240.

On 1st Avenue just above the market, two stores across the street from each other offer uniquely Seattle wares. At **Dilettante Chocolates,** the family recipes, rich and dark, derive from the delights ancestor Julius Rudolph Franzen made as chocolatier for the last Romanov czar, Nicholas II. ~ 400 Pine Street; 206-903-8595; www.dilettante.com. Literally across the street, **Simply Seattle** is the best place downtown to get a gift or memento reflecting the city. It could be a Seattle Mariners T-shirt; it could be a carved wooden slug. ~ 1600 1st Avenue; 206-448-2207; www.simplyseattle.com.

Close by is **Opus 204,** a small shop filled with a wondrous display of unusual and fine clothing, handicrafts, imports and gifts. ~ 2004 1st Avenue; 206-728-7707.

◄ HIDDEN

In the downtown area, 5th Avenue, Seattle's fashion street, is lined with shops displaying elegant finery and accessories. **Nancy Meyer** specializes in very fine European lingerie. Closed Sunday. ~ 1318 5th Avenue; 206-625-9200, 800-605-5098; www.nancymeyer.com. **Rainier Square** houses several prestigious retail establishments. ~ 1333 5th Avenue. **Turgeon Raine** is an exceptionally good, locally owned jewelry store. ~ 1407 5th Avenue; 206-447-9488, 800-678-0120; www.turgeonraine.com. Off 5th Avenue on Union is **Totally Michael's,** which has contemporary, upscale clothing. Closed Sunday. ~ 521 Union Street; 206-622-4920; www.totallymichaels.com.

At the **Westlake Center,** located at 4th Avenue and Pine Street, there's the **Fireworks Gallery** (206-682-6462; www.fireworksgallery.net) which takes its name from unusually fired sculptures. Also offered are a variety of intriguing home accessories, gifts and jewelry. **Millstream** (206-233-9719) sells Northwest sculpture, prints, pottery and jewelry by local artisans. ~ 400 Pine Street. Fast foods, available on the third floor, include teriyaki, pizza, enchiladas and yogurt. Nearby, **Alhambra** offers high-end women's clothing, Indonesian furniture and a variety of jewelry. ~ 101 Pine Street; 206-621-9571; www.alhambranet.com.

NIGHTLIFE

Seattle's nightlife, music and club scene is astounding for a city its size. More than 50 clubs, lounges, restaurants and taverns feature live or deejay-spun music, and dozens more have occasional performances. The offerings run the gamut from folk to punk/metal; dance venues range from midnight raves in port district warehouses to salsa nights at Latin bars.

The best guide to the city's entertainment scene is *The Stranger*, an alternative weekly newspaper that carries a complete calendar of shows, dances, plays, cinema, performances, readings, art galleries and other goings-on. It offers the most entertaining classifieds section in town, as well as advice from down-and-dirty love-life columnist Dan Savage, a local Seattle celebrity. It's available free every Thursday at coffee shops, cafés, taverns, bookstores and newsstands throughout the Seattle area.

A competing weekly, the *Seattle Weekly*, also provides comprehensive nightlife coverage; it's free every Wednesday. The *Seattle Times* also publishes a club guide in its Friday entertainment section.

HIDDEN ► Half-price same-day tickets to many Seattle musical events, as well as most theater stagings, are available at **Ticket/Ticket**, which maintains a downtown booth at Pike Place Market as well as locations at Pacific Place and Broadway Market on Capitol Hill and at Meydenbauer Center in Bellevue. Call for directions, but they won't say over the phone what tickets they have that day. Closed Monday. ~ Pike Place Market, 1st Avenue and Pike Place; 206-324-2744; www.ticketwindowonline.com.

Unexpected Productions offers comedy performances and workshops in improvisational theater techniques. ~ The Market Theater, 1428 Post Alley, Pike Place Market; 206-587-2414; www.unexpectedproductions.org. And at **Comedy Underground**, comics entertain nightly. Cover. ~ 222 South Main Street; 206-628-0303; www.comedyunderground.com.

There are many fine nightclubs in Pioneer Square, and on "joint-cover" nights, one charge admits you to nine places within a four-block radius. Among them is **Doc Maynard's**, heavy on rock-and-roll with live music on weekends. Cover. ~ 610 1st Avenue; 206-682-3705; www.docmaynards.com. The **New Orleans Creole Restaurant** offers live jazz and blues nightly along with Cajun Creole food in an eclectic, laidback atmosphere. Cover on weekends. ~ 114 1st Avenue South; 206-622-2563; www.neworleanscreolerestaurant.com. Over at **Trinity Night Club**, a mixed crowd enjoys deejay dance music. Cover. ~ 111 Yesler Way; 206-447-4140; www.trinitynightclub.com.

The Showbox nightclub features local, national and international live bands and all types of music and a full bar. Cover. ~ 1426 1st Avenue; 206-628-3151; www.showboxonline.com.

Belltown, near the Pike Place Market, has lots of activity after dark. **Crocodile Café**, one of Seattle's legendary spawning grounds for grunge, punk, rock and alternative bands, attracts a young crowd for live music. Closed Monday. Cover. ~ 2200 2nd Avenue; 206-441-5611; www.thecrocodile.com.

A venerable jazz outpost, **Tula's** provides scat lovers with live music every night, plus a full menu and bar. Cover. ~ 2214 2nd Avenue; 206-443-4221; www.tulas.com.

Dimitriou's Jazz Alley is a downtown dinner theater and premier jazz club with international acts. Closed Monday. Cover. ~ 2033 6th Avenue; 206-441-9729; www.jazzalley.com.

The **Seattle Symphony**'s large performance space, **Benaroya Hall**, has enabled it to vastly expand its schedule and repertoire. Noted especially for its attention to American composers, the symphony, under the direction of Gerard Schwarz, is one of the top recording orchestras in the United States. ~ 200 University Street; 206-215-4700, tickets 206-215-4747; www.seattlesymphony.org.

For satirical/comical revues on Friday, Saturday and some Wednesday nights, try the **Cabaret de Paris** dinner theater at the Crepe de Paris restaurant. Cover. ~ Rainier Square, 1333 5th Avenue; 206-623-4111.

The **Paramount Theatre**, the elaborate movie palace of the 1920s, now offers diverse events from Broadway musicals to political programs. ~ 911 Pine Street; 206-467-5510; www.theparamount.com.

Video games, beer and pub food—sounds like a classic video arcade. But **Gameworks** is much more than that. With the latest in electronic games, virtual-reality games and adventures, this has become the highly successful (and highly publicized) prototype for what is now an international chain. ~ 1511 7th Avenue; 206-521-0952; www.gameworks.com.

Seattle Center–Queen Anne Area

Northwest of downtown a familiar landmark rises skyward—the Space Needle. This symbol of the city nestles comfortably among museums, cultural centers and a sports arena at the Seattle Center. Just north of the arts and entertainment complex sits the stunning Queen Anne area, a hilly neighborhood of fanciful homes and great views. This is the part of Seattle where the downtown bustle starts to give way to the more peaceful charms of the outlying neighborhoods.

SIGHTS

Seattle Center, once the site of the 1962 World's Fair, is now a 74-acre campus with more than a dozen buildings housing a variety of offices, convention rooms and theaters. Locals and visitors continue to flock to the **Space Needle** (admission; 206-905-2100; www.spaceneedle.com, e-mail info@spaceneedle.com) for the view or a meal, to summer carnival rides at the **Fun Forest**, to the **Center House**'s short-order ethnic eateries, to see nearby opera and live theater and to check out wide-ranging exhibits and demonstrations at the **Pacific Science Center** (admission; 206-443-2001, fax 206-443-3631; www.pacsci.org). The **Seattle Children's Theatre** (206-443-0807, fax 206-443-0442; www.sct.org, e-mail info@sct.org) has jovial performances geared to a young audience. The **Pacific Northwest Ballet** (tickets, 206-441-2424, fax 206-441-2420; information, 206-441-9411; www.pnb.org) has

> The 605-foot tall Space Needle, built to withstand wind velocities of up to 200 miles an hour, sways approximately one inch for every ten miles an hour of wind.

its offices and rehearsal space at the Phelps Center (where the public can watch the corps rehearse through a glass wall). ~ Seattle Center: Two miles north of the downtown core between Denny Way and Mercer Street at 305 Harrison Street; 206-684-7200, fax 206-684-7342; www.seattlecenter.com.

Kids will also enjoy visiting the **Children's Museum, Seattle** on the ground floor of Center House. The collection features a kid's-size neighborhood and multicultural global village, a two-story walk-through re-creation of a mountain forest and mechanically oriented displays. There is also a small lagoon for children and a drop-in art studio. Admission. ~ Seattle Center; 206-441-1768, fax 206-448-0910; www.thechildrensmuseum.org.

For an interactive history lesson on American rock-and-roll, stop by **Experience Music Project (EMP)**, a must for music lovers of all stripes. Among the many highlights at this 140,000-square-foot space-age facility are a vintage guitar collection, a rock fashion exhibit and the Jimi Hendrix Gallery. Those with rock-star fantasies will get a kick out of the Sound Lab, where you can perform on stage. Closed Tuesday from early November to late May. Admission. ~ 325 5th Avenue North; 206-367-5483, 877-367-5483, fax 206-770-2727; www.emplive.org, e-mail experience@emplive.org.

For a rewarding, spur-of-the-moment visit, drop by Seattle Center on a summer evening for a contemplative quarter-hour of gazing at the **International Fountain**. The combination of changing lights and waterworks synchronized to music during the first 15 minutes of every hour against a rose-tinted summer sunset can lull you into a dreamy state.

The Seattle Center grounds are the home of three popular and worthwhile annual events. The **Folklife Festival** (206-684-7300; www.nwfolklife.org) on Memorial Day weekend attracts hundreds of thousands of fans for music of every possible description, especially ethnic. Folklife also features art and crafts, food, dance, mime, improv theater, juggling and acrobatics—all

AMPHIBIOUS FROLIC

For an amusing tour of Seattle, hop aboard **Ride the Ducks of Seattle**'s amphibious World War II vehicles that tread both land and water. The 90-minute excursion covers downtown Seattle, Pioneer Square and Pike Place Market, among other well-known attractions. Popular with families, reservations are recommended. Seasonal hours; call ahead. Fee. ~ 516 Broad Street, across from the Space Needle; 206-441-3825, 800-817-1116; www.ridetheducksofseattle.com, e-mail info@ridetheducksofseattle.com.

free, though a donation is suggested. **Bumbershoot** (206-281-7788; www.bumbershoot.org) occupies the other end of summer, Labor Day weekend, charging a modest admission but offering an equally kaleidoscopic lineup of music, food and arts, including national acts like B. B. King, Pearl Jam, Bonnie Raitt and George Thorogood. The midsummer **Bite of Seattle** (206-684-7200; www.biteofseattle.com) attracts dozens of the city's restaurants to the grounds, where patrons can try modestly priced samples of everything from ostrich to sautéed geoduck.

For a breathtaking view of Seattle's skyline and Elliott Bay, go up Queen Anne Hill to **Kerry Park** at West Highland Drive and 2nd Avenue West.

LODGING

Conveniently located two blocks from Seattle Center, half of the **Best Western Executive Inn**'s rooms offer views of the Space Needle. In the lobby guests enjoy a fitness center with jacuzzi, a full-service restaurant and lounge. ~ 200 Taylor Avenue North; 206-448-9444, 800-351-9444, fax 206-441-7836. DELUXE.

On Lower Queen Anne Hill is the **Hampton Inn & Suites**. Standard rooms have either a king-size or two double beds. One- and two-bedroom suites are also available and include fireplaces and full kitchens. Full breakfast buffet included. ~ 700 5th Avenue North; 206-282-7700, 800-426-7866, fax 206-282-0899; www.hamptoninnseattle.com. DELUXE.

DINING

At the Space Needle's **Sky City Restaurant**, the entertainment—from 500 feet up—in either the restaurant or the observation deck is seeing metropolitan Seattle, its environs, Puget Sound, the Olympic Mountains and Mt. Rainier, the Queen of the Cascade Range, as you rotate in a 360° orbit. The restaurant serves various seafood, beef, pasta and poultry dishes, such as tea-smoked wild salmon and *sake* beef short ribs. Weekend brunch. ~ 400 Broad Street; 206-905-2100, fax 206-905-2211; www.spaceneedle.com/restaurant, e-mail skycitymanagers@spaceneedle.com. ULTRA-DELUXE.

On the plaza at Five Point Square, next to the Chief Seattle statue, the **Five Point Cafe** is a distinctive Seattle landmark. The drinks are stiff, the portions are huge and the ambience is part bar scene, part mom-and-pop diner. The jukebox is usually playing and the lights are dim. Try the meatloaf sandwich or the fish and chips. ~ 415 Cedar Street; 206-448-9993. BUDGET.

◄ HIDDEN

For sublime breakfast pastries and delicious Mediterranean-inspired lunch items, head for **Macrina Bakery**, a cozy European-style bakery and café where the moss green walls are adorned with scrolls, ironwork, paintings and other work by local artists. Breakfast items include house-made coffee cakes, cereals and fruit pastries, while a changing lunch menu may offer such dishes as roasted duck tartines with watercress, aioli, rhubarb jam and shaved radishes. ~ 2408 1st Avenue; 206-448-4032, fax 206-374-1782; www.macrinabakery.com. MODERATE.

Hip to the max, **BOKA** (not a mispelled Spanish word for mouth, but an acronym meaning "bold artistic kitchen artistry") channels old Hollywood for modern Seattle foodies. Here you'll find clever little renditions of chef Kamimura's "urban cuisine": pigs in a blanket, Dungeness crab "cupcakes" and lobster croquettes for starters, alongside gazpacho and roasted tomato bisque. Entrées include Moroccan-spiced lamb and New York steak with a syrupy veal-stock-and-red-wine reduction, while the dessert menu boasts red velvet cake. Dress like Nick and Nora. ~ Hotel 1000, 1010 1st Avenue; 206-357-9000; www.bokaseattle.com, e-mail info@bokaseattle.com. ULTRA-DELUXE.

Seattle is a derivative of "Sealth"—a chief of the Suquamish tribe at the time the first white settlers arrived in 1851.

Near Seattle Center, **Rice N Spice** serves authentic Thai cuisine in a friendly, comfortable setting. There are art objects from Thailand to look at while you wait for your order of Swimming Angel (chicken in a peanut-chili sauce over spinach) or another of the menu's 50-plus items. They vary in hotness and are rich with the flavors of coconut, curry, garlic, peanuts and peppers. No lunch on weekends. ~ 101 John Street; 206-285-9000. BUDGET.

Chutney's occupies a tidy, elegant space just a block from the Seattle Center. Its Indian menu is rich and varied, leaning heavily on hearty lentil and vegetable concoctions. The lunch buffet is unbelievably filling. Ask for the excellent garlic/chile chutney. No lunch on Sunday. ~ 519 1st Avenue North; 206-284-6799, fax 206-284-6801. MODERATE.

Three blocks away, but still within easy walking distance of Seattle Center, **Tup Tim Thai** is the Thai restaurant locals favor over its better-known cousins north of the center. Tup Tim's soups and curries are the best in Seattle; it's advisable to arrive early for lunch, or for dinner on nights there are events at the center. No lunch on Saturday. Closed Sunday. ~ 118 West Mercer Street; 206-281-8833. BUDGET TO MODERATE.

Hearty Northwest fare with a German accent is on the menu at **Szmania's**, a popular spot with an exhibition kitchen in the residential area of Magnolia. The specialties include seared ahi tuna over a black rice-cake with a red curry sauce; rack of lamb with minted mashed potatoes; and stuffed quail with spinach and pine nuts in a black grape glace. No lunch on the weekend. Closed Monday. ~ 3321 West McGraw Street; 206-284-7305, fax 206-283-7303; www.szmanias.com. MODERATE TO ULTRA-DELUXE.

On the south shore of Lake Union is **Chandler's Crabhouse**, where the whiskey crab soup is good for starters before digging into a steamed crab, grilled salmon or other fresh seafood plate.

During happy hour (3 to 6:30 p.m. and 9:30 to closing), grab a table with a view of the water and enjoy. ~ 901 Fairview Avenue North; 206-223-2722, fax 206-223-9380. DELUXE TO ULTRA-DELUXE.

Bicycles hang from the rafters. T-shirts are on sale in the lobby. **Cucina! Cucina!** is an open, spacious, noisy Italian restaurant with a large deck overlooking Lake Union where you can watch float planes land and take off or see kayakers gently paddling by. Diners can see into the open kitchen to watch the staff making pizzas large and small for baking in the woodburning ovens. One of the most interesting toppings is the barbecue chicken. You will find a variety of pasta dishes, such as linguine with roasted chicken and goat cheese, vegetarian or meat-filled calzones and good mixed and caesar salads. ~ 901 Fairview Avenue North; 206-447-2782, fax 206-223-9372. MODERATE.

Also on Lake Union's east shore is a sushi restaurant much loved by north downtown workers. **I Love Sushi** overlooks Lake Union and a small marina; enjoy a plate of expertly prepared sushi while you dream of bidding on the boats for sale in the water next to the deck. ~ 1001 Fairview Avenue North; 206-625-9604; www.ilovesushi.com. MODERATE TO DELUXE.

The **14 Carrot Café** has been serving breakfast and brunch since 1978. In addition to standard breakfast fare, hungry Seattleites come for the huge, home-baked cinnamon rolls and 25 different kinds of omelets. Lunch consists of sandwiches, lasagna, salads and soups. Sit inside and gaze at the work of local artists, or claim a quaint, sidewalk bistro table. No dinner. ~ 2305 Eastlake Avenue East; 206-324-1442. BUDGET.

NIGHTLIFE

Home of the 1962 World's Fair, the **Seattle Center** still offers numerous nighttime diversions. ~ 305 Harrison Street; 206-684-8582; www.seattlecenter.com.

The **Marion Oliver McCaw Hall for the Performing Arts** is the city's opera and ballet companies' glamorous concert hall. Founded in 1964, **Seattle Opera** is dedicated to producing theatrically compelling, musically accomplished opera. The leading Wagner company in America, the company stages five operas a year. ~ 321 Mercer Street; 206-389-7676, 800-426-1619; www.seattleopera.org.

Pacific Northwest Ballet's annual production of Tchaikovsky's *Nutcracker*, with fanciful sets designed by famed children's illustrator Maurice Sendak, is a perennial favorite. ~ 301 Mercer Street; 206-441-2424; fax 206-441-2420; www.pnb.org, e-mail tickets@pnb.org.

Music director Gerard Schwarz has led the **Seattle Symphony** to prominence by focusing on baroque and romantic classics and formerly little-known American composers such as Alan Hovhaness (a longtime Seattle resident), David Diamond and Howard Hanson. Masterpiece symphony concerts are Thursday and Saturday evenings and the occasional Sunday afternoon. The fact that symphony concerts rarely sell out offers visitors the chance to see one of the top orchestral ensembles in the United States. No shows mid-July to early September. ~ 206-215-4747, 866-833-4747; www.seattlesymphony.org, e-mail info@seattlesymphony.org.

The **Seattle Repertory Theatre** plays an eclectic mix from musicals to classic dramas at the **Bagley Wright Theatre** and the **Leo K. Theatre.** ~ 155 Mercer Street between Warren Avenue and 2nd Avenue North; 206-443-2222, 877-900-9285; www.seattlerep.org. The nearby **Intiman Theatre** presents plays by the great dramatists, as well as new works. ~ 201 Mercer Street at 2nd Avenue North; 206-269-1900; www.intiman.org, e-mail intiman@intiman.org.

ACT Theatre in the old Eagles Auditorium next to the Convention Center specializes in works by new playwrights. ~ 7th and Union streets; 206-292-7676; www.acttheatre.org, e-mail service@acttheatre.org.

Capitol Hill and East of Lake Union

Seattle's sizable gay population and diverse array of gay inns, clubs and meeting places is one of the many reasons travelers are increasingly flocking to the city. While gay activities and nightlife are found throughout the city, the highest concentration is in Capitol Hill, one of Seattle's most cosmopolitan neighborhoods. Take a walk down Broadway in Capitol Hill, and you'll see one of the most vibrant gay communities in the country.

SIGHTS

Capitol Hill is a mixed neighborhood that is a fun place to browse. Within a block or two you can toss back an exotic wheatgrass drink at a vegetarian bar, slowly sip a double espresso at a sidewalk café, shop for radical literature at a leftist bookstore or hit a straight or gay nightclub. If you can't find it on Capitol Hill, Seattle probably doesn't have it. Broadway Avenue is the heart of this region known for its boutiques, yuppie appliance stores and bead shops.

Home of some of the city's finest Victorians, this neighborhood also includes **Volunteer Park.** Be sure to head up to the top of the water tower for a great view of the region. ~ 15th Avenue East from East Prospect Street to East Galer Street.

The building that used to house the Seattle Art Museum is now the home of the **Seattle Asian Art Museum.** This Art Moderne building was a gift to the city in the 1930s by Dr. Richard Fuller, who was the museum's director for the next 40 years. The Japanese, Chinese and Korean collections are the largest, but the museum also has south and southeast Asian collections. Japanese folk textiles, Thai ceramics and Korean screen paintings are some of the highlights. One admission fee will get you into here and the Seattle Art Museum if you visit within the same week. Admission. Closed Monday. ~ Volunteer Park, 1400 East Prospect Street; 206-654-3100, fax 206-654-3191; www.seattleartmuseum.org.

Not far away, **St. Mark's Episcopal Cathedral** is an imposing Romanesque edifice from the outside; an austere, cavernous space inside with an unusual shape (more a square than a long rectangle) dictated by its location on a bluff overlooking downtown. The cathedral's superb acoustics and massive Flentrop organ mean it is often the site of recitals. The gift shop offers books, CDs and knickknacks. ~ 1245 10th Avenue East; 206-323-0300, fax 206-323-4018; www.saintmarks.org.

Nostalgia reigns in Capitol Hill's **Harvard Exit Theater**. Once the elegant home of a women's club, it still has the parlor with a fireplace and piano. This is the place to see award-winning foreign and art films. Auditoriums are wheelchair accessible. ~ 807 East Roy Street; 206-781-5755 ext. 4.

On the south side of Union Bay, 230-acre **Washington Park** at Lake Washington Boulevard East and East Madison Street presents enough diversions indoors and out to fill a rich day of exploring in all sorts of weather. Most famous is the **Washington Park Arboretum** (which occupies most of the park with 10,000 plants), at its best in the spring when rhododendrons and azaleas—some 10 to 15 feet tall—and groves of spreading chestnuts, dogwoods, magnolias and other flowering trees leap into bloom. Short footpaths beckon from the Visitors Center. But two in particular deserve mention—Azalea Way and Loderi Valley—which wend their way down avenues of pink, cream, yellow, crimson and white blooms. The arboretum's renowned Japanese Garden (admission) is especially rewarding in the spring months, and both arboretum and garden present splendid fall colors in October and early

STARGAZING

Robert Redford's Sundance Festival may be more famous, but the **Seattle International Film Festival** is actually the largest independent film event in the country. Each spring, SIFF draws hundreds of thousands of cinema lovers for its 25-day run, usually in Capitol Hill, downtown theaters and on the East Side. Each year at least one of the SIFF favorites goes on to national acclaim. Screenings, lectures and receptions abound at this large, well-attended film festival. Admission. ~ 206-324-9996 (box office), 206-464-5830; www.seattlefilm.org, e-mail info@seattlefilm.org.

November. In the Winter Garden, everything is fragrant, and the Woodland Garden highlights the arboretum's acclaimed collection of Japanese maples. ~ Visitors Center: Arboretum Drive East; 206-543-8800, fax 206-325-8893; www.wparboretum.org, e-mail uwbg@u.washington.edu.

Miles of duff-covered footpaths lace the park. For naturalists, the premier experience will be found along the one-and-a-half-mile (each way) **Foster Island Trail** at the north end of the park on Foster Island behind the Museum of History and Industry (see below). This footpath takes you on an intriguing bog-walk over low bridges and along boardwalks through marshy wetlands teeming with ducks and wildfowl, fish and frogs and aquatic flora growing rank at the edge of Lake Washington.

Washington State is the number one producer of lentils, dry peas, raspberries, cherries, hops, pears and of course, apples.

In summer, you can join the canoeists paddling the labyrinth of waterways around **Foster Island,** sunbathers and picnickers sprawling on lawns, anglers casting for catfish and trout and the swimmers cooling off on hot August afternoons. Canoes are for rent through the University of Washington.

On rainy days the **Museum of History and Industry** is a fitting retreat. It's the city's best early-day collection and pays special tribute to Puget Sound's rich maritime history, as befits any museum located next door to this vital waterway. Admission. ~ 2700 24th Avenue East; 206-324-1126, fax 206-324-1346; www.seattlehistory.org, e-mail information@seattlehistory.org.

LODGING

Just one block north of the Harvard Exit Theater sits **Bed & Breakfast on Broadway,** a 1906 home with four bedrooms, all with private baths. Breakfast is continental (pastries, fruit, coffee) but with Broadway literally at your feet, you won't go hungry for food or entertainment. ~ 722 Broadway Avenue East; 206-329-8933, fax 206-726-0918; www.bbonbroadway.com. DELUXE TO ULTRA-DELUXE.

The **Salisbury House Bed & Breakfast** is a quiet, dignified, gracious Capitol Hill home two blocks from Volunteer Park. The five crisp, clean rooms (all have private baths) are furnished with antiques and wicker. Fresh flowers, duvets on the beds, a full (meatless) breakfast and thoughtful innkeeper make this a well-done B&B. There are fireplaces in the living room and library and a refrigerator guests may use. A fully equipped 600-square-foot suite offers the lone television. ~ 750 16th Avenue East; 206-328-8682, fax 206-720-1019; www.salisburyhouse.com, e-mail sleep@salisburyhouse.com. DELUXE TO ULTRA-DELUXE.

Also in the popular, busy Capitol Hill area, **Gaslight Inn** is a bed and breakfast brimming with urban flair. The 1906 house is furnished with oak, maple and glass antiques. Various period styles have been effectively combined with modern amenities in the eight guest rooms. Most have private baths, and one boasts a fireplace. Gaslight has a heated, outdoor swimming pool (closed in winter) and an outdoor deck that overlooks the city. A continental buffet breakfast is served. ~ 1727 15th Avenue East; 206-325-3654, fax 206-328-4803; www.gaslight-inn.com, e-mail innkeepr@gaslight-inn.com. DELUXE.

Bed and Breakfast on Capitol Hill is a 1903 nonsmoking private home abutting the Harvard-Belmont Historical District. It has three guest rooms, each beautifully furnished with antiques. Double beds have 100 percent cotton linens and down comforters. Two rooms share a bath; one has a private bath and sitting area. A healthy continental breakfast is served. The owners' pets are on the premises. Guests over 16 only. Two-night minimum. ~ 739 Broadway East; 206-325-0320, fax 206-568-5886; www.bbcapitolhill.com, e-mail innkeeper@bbcapitolhill.com. BUDGET TO MODERATE.

On Capitol Hill near Volunteer Park in the Harvard-Belmont Historic District is the **Bacon Mansion**, a historic 1909 Tudor stucco home. In addition to the two-story carriage house, which has a living room, dining room and two guest rooms with a private bath in each, there are nine guest rooms in the main house, seven with private bath. The Capitol suite has a sun room with wet bar, fireplace, queen-size bed, big bathtub and view of the Space Needle (in winter). ~ 959 Broadway East; 206-329-1864, 800-240-1864, fax 206-860-9025; www.baconmansion.com, e-mail info@baconmansion.com. DELUXE TO ULTRA-DELUXE.

DINING

West of Broadway, on Pike and Pine streets, is a collection of bars and restaurants catering to the hipster population. **611 Supreme** is a cheery, comfy café specializing in crêpes both sweet and savory. Try the Gruyere and sautéed vegetables crêpe, or the citron version. No lunch on weekdays. Weekend brunch. Closed Monday. ~ 611 East Pine Street; 206-328-0292. BUDGET.

Ayutthaya is a corner restaurant in Capitol Hill renowned for its Thai cookery. Small, clean-lined and pleasant in light wood, Ayutthaya features plenty of chicken and seafood dishes along with soups and noodles. Flavors blend deliciously in the curried shrimp with green beans, coconut milk and basil. Or try the chicken sautéed in peanut-chili sauce. No lunch on Sunday. ~ 727 East Pike Street; 206-324-8833, fax 206-324-3135. BUDGET.

Low prices make **Oasis Cafe** stand out on restaurant-rich Capitol Hill: At lunch, you can get four dishes for under $10. The Buddhist tofu is rich and tasty, and the *pad thai* is good, too. ~ 1024 East Pike Street; 206-323-3293. BUDGET.

At **Osteria La Spiga**, the fare is down-home Italian, the decor rustic tile, and the crowded tables lively. Soups, salads, panini and pastas are done with flair, and the atmosphere is about as charmingly romantic as Broadway dining gets. Dinner only. ~ 1429 12th Avenue; 206-323-8881; www.laspiga.com, e-mail hello@laspiga.com. BUDGET TO MODERATE.

You can feast on thick slices of fresh sashimi that virtually melt on your tongue at **Aoki Japanese Grill & Sushi Bar.** This casual and relaxed eatery also offers bento boxes and combo plates that include *donburi* and *robata* for palates that prefer their meals cooked. No lunch on Sunday. Closed Monday. ~ 621 Broadway Avenue; 206-324-3633. MODERATE.

Café Septième is a re-creation of the small Parisian cafés that cater to the literati and students. This full-service restaurant carries plenty of reading material and turns out cups of good coffee, lattes and light fare. Sandwiches and salads are standard, but the real treat is the mouth-watering display table, loaded with cakes, pies and cookies. Breakfast, lunch and dinner. ~ 214 Broadway East; 206-860-8858, fax 206-860-0760. MODERATE.

The **Broadway Grill** is a famed mainstay of the Capitol Hill scene. Its food is mainstream-grill breakfast and burger fare, moderately priced and dependable if unimaginative. But it's better known as a place to hang out and watch the passing parade on Broadway. ~ 314 Broadway East; 206-328-7000, fax 206-325-4734. BUDGET TO MODERATE.

Since Capitol Hill never truly closes, its two dessert emporia are integral to the area's atmosphere. You can buy a box of chocolate truffles at **Café Dilettante**, but you'd be missing a divine late-evening experience—a midnight table in a crowded, mirrored room. Try the Coupe Dilettante, the restaurant's exceptional ice cream sundae swimming in Dilettante's dark Ephemere sauce, or any of dozens of other desserts. This is among the best chocolate in the country. ~ Dilettante Chocolates, 416 Broadway East; 206-329-6463, 800-482-0281; www.dilettante.com. BUDGET.

HIDDEN ►

AUTHOR FAVORITE

With thematic menus and a decor as eclectic as the neighborhood that surrounds it, **The Coastal Kitchen** has no trouble maintaining a loyal clientele. Chef Jeremy Hardy rotates his menu every three months, transporting diners to faraway coastal regions in Argentina, Italy and Spain. Past themes have included Morocco, graced by a live belly dancer, and the Deep South, serenaded by a gospel choir. Choices are expectedly heavy on seafood, but steak and chicken dishes make a frequent appearance. The ever-changing wall art contributes additional flair. Breakfast, lunch and dinner. ~ 425 East 15th Avenue; 206-322-1145. MODERATE TO DELUXE.

At **B & O Espresso**, the emphasis is less on chocolate, the atmosphere is a bit more cozy than glitzy and the late-night crowds are large. B & O offers breakfast, lunch and dinner with Middle Eastern specialties. But dessert is the main course. Diners can choose from more than two dozen different pies, cakes and European-style tortes. ~ 204 Belmont Avenue East; 206-322-5028, fax 206-322-5707; www.boespresso.com, e-mail b_oespresso@yahoo.com. MODERATE.

◄ HIDDEN

In a small house surrounded by gardens, **Rover's** specializes in Northwest cuisine with a French accent and is just the place for those romantic occasions. Chef Thierry Rautureau creates the ever-changing menu based on locally available, fresh produce. In addition to seafood in imaginative sauces, entrées might include rabbit, venison, pheasant and quail. A good selection of Northwest and French wines is available. Service is friendly and helpful. Lunch on Friday only. Closed Sunday and Monday. ~ 2808 East Madison Street; 206-325-7442, fax 206-325-1092; www.rovers-seattle.com. ULTRA-DELUXE.

A colorful and lively Spanish-eclectic restaurant in the Madison Park area, **Cactus** serves a cuisine representative of many different cultures, but mostly influenced by Southwestern food. Start with one of the most unusual items on the menu—Navajo fry bread—and round out your meal with a butternut squash enchilada or cactus fajitas. No lunch on Sunday. ~ 4220 East Madison Street; 206-324-4140; www.cactusrestaurants.com. MODERATE.

SHOPPING

The trendy boutiques of Capitol Hill draw shoppers looking for the unusual, though there are many standard stores, too. You'll see dozens of shops with new and vintage clothing, pop culture items, and ethnic wear and artifacts, all interspersed with myriad cafés and coffeehouses.

Yes, it's a sex shop. But **Toys in Babeland** isn't what you'd expect. Plate-glass front windows, plenty of lighting and a comfy bench have turned this purveyor of toys, books and body products into a neighborhood hangout. Come here to feel empowered, admire the tasteful-albeit-pornographic glass art and meet more locals than at the corner café. ~ 707 East Pike Street; 206-328-2914; www.babeland.com.

At the **Washington Park Arboretum Visitor Center Gift Shop** are gardening books, cards, china, earrings, necklaces, serving trays and sweatshirts. You can also buy plants from the arboretum greenhouse. ~ 2300 Arboretum Drive East; 206-325-4510.

Seattle-based **Recreational Equipment, Inc.**, better known as **REI**, is the largest consumer cooperative in the United States. Its flagship store offers an astonishing array of outdoor clothing and equipment—as well as a 65-foot climbing wall, the tallest indoor freestanding climbing structure in the country. ~ 222 Yale Avenue North; 206-223-1944, 888-873-1938; www.rei.com/stores/seattle.

Capitol Hill's **Broadway Market** is filled with popular shops like **Urban Outfitters**. Featuring casual urban wares, this shop offers new and vintage clothing, jewelry, housewares and shoes for the hip crowd. ~ 401 Broadway East; 206-322-1800.

Bailey/Coy Books is well-stocked with reading material, including gay and lesbian literature. ~ 414 Broadway East; 206-323-8842.

Chocoholics can get their fix in the Capitol Hill district at **Dilettante Chocolates**, a combination chocolatier and café. ~ 416 Broadway East; 206-329-6463; www.dilettante.com, e-mail info@dilettante.com.

NIGHTLIFE

In the "Pike-Pine corridor," west of Broadway, a string of stylish (and stylized) bars stretches toward downtown. East of Broadway, the clubs along Pike and Pine drop down a notch on the scene scale and gain in loungeability.

With its mohair booths and starry ceiling, the **Baltic Room** is a glamourous retro cocktail lounge. Music (both live and deejayed) ranges from jazz to hip-hop to Bollywood. Cover. ~ 1207 Pine Street; 206-625-4444; www.thebalticroom.net.

Barça is another slinky lounge, but less crowded and lacking in live music. Prime viewing is from the balcony. ~ 1510 11th Avenue; 206-325-8263; www.barcaseattle.com.

GAY SCENE Capitol Hill offers a number of popular gay and lesbian clubs and bars, including the following:

One of the biggest clubs in the area is **R Place Bar & Grill**. Depending on your mood, you can plunk down at the sports bar, throw darts, enjoy a music video, shoot pool, enjoy tunes from the jukebox or deejay, take advantage of the dancefloor or feast on quesadillas and taco salad. ~ 619 East Pine Street; 206-322-8828; www.rplaceseattle.com, e-mail rplace@qwest.net.

Gay clubs and stores are concentrated on Broadway, as well as nearby streets like 15th Avenue East and East Olive Way.

The oversized martinis are the main attraction at **Manray Video Bar**, a temple of cool high-tech decor and beautiful bods. It's also a popular spot for CD and DVD release parties. ~ 514 East Pine Street, 206-568-0750; www.manrayvideo.com.

Also popular is **Neighbours**, offering deejay dance music Friday and Saturday, including retro disco and Latin nights. Cover. ~ 1509 Broadway; 206-324-5358; www.neighboursonline.com.

Founded in 1984, the **Wild Rose** claims to be the oldest women's bar on the West Coast, offering food and drink, pool tables and video games as well as camaraderie. Occasional live music. ~ 1021 East Pike Street; 206-324-9210; www.thewildrosebar.com.

The leather crowd favors **The Cuff** and **Seattle Eagle,** two more Capitol Hill taverns. ~ The Cuff, 1533 13th Avenue, 206-323-1525; Seattle Eagle, 314 East Pike Street; 206-621-7591.

Madison Pub is a laid-back neighborhood local. It's just the place to enjoy a few pints, a game of pool or darts, and watch the game. ~ 1315 E. Madison Street, 206-325-6537.

For a comprehensive list of gay Seattle's arts and entertainment scene, pick up a copy of the weekly *Seattle Gay News.* ~ www.sgn.org.

PARKS

BOREN/INTERLAKEN PARKS A secret greenway close to downtown is preserved by these neighboring parks on Capitol Hill; it's just right for an afternoon or evening stroll. ~ Entry points are on 15th Avenue East across from the Lakeview cemetery and at East Galer Street and East Interlaken Boulevard.

◄ HIDDEN

Northern Neighborhoods

While downtown is the city's magnet, some of Seattle's best parks, sightseeing and nightlife can be found in its nearby neighborhoods. Arboretums and science museums, lakeside dining and shopping worth a special trip are all in this region.

Heading north from Green Lake, you'll cross the county line (into Snohomish County) toward the less urban and more maritime cities and villages lining Northern Puget Sound. Edmonds is of most interest to visitors. You don't have to travel far to catch a glimpse of the region's past, before Seattlemania lured businesses and families to relocate here.

SIGHTS

Few guidebooks look at the **Lake Washington Ship Canal** as a single unit. Yet it ties together a wondrous diversity of working waterfront and recreational shoreline along eight miles of bay, lake and canal between Puget Sound and Lake Washington. Construction of the locks and canal began in 1911 and created a shipping channel from Lake Washington to Lake Union to Puget Sound. Along its banks today you can see perhaps the liveliest continuous boat parade in the West: tugs gingerly inching four-story-tall, Alaska-bound barges through narrow locks; rowboats, kayaks, sailboards and luxury yachts; gill-netters and trawlers in dry dock; government-research vessels; aging houseboats listing at their moorings; and seaplanes roaring overhead.

All in all, the ship canal presents a splendid overview of Seattle's rich maritime traditions. But you'll also discover plenty that's new—rejuvenated neighborhoods like Fremont and south Lake Union's upscale shoreline, a renovated Fisherman's Terminal and a handful of trendy, waterside restaurants. Amid the hubbub of boat traffic and ship chandlers, you'll also encounter quiet, street-end parks for birdwatching, foot and bike paths, the best historical museum in the city and one of the West's renowned arboretums. Here's a summary, west to east. **Ballard** is one of Seattle's most distinctive neighborhoods, exemplified by the wry slogan, "Ya, sure, y'betcha," a nod to its Nordic heritage. Ever tried lutefisk? If you want to (few do), this is the place. Ballard shut down to greet Norway's royal family on one of their state visits to the United States. The royals even checked out the **Nordic Heritage Museum**, the only facility of its kind in the country. Here artifacts such as antique boats demonstrate why timber and fisheries are what drew Scandinavians here more than a century ago; the museum also maintains an extensive research library. Closed Monday. Admission. ~ 3014 67th Street Northwest; 206-789-5707, fax 206-789-3271; www.nordicmuseum.org, e-mail nordic@nordicmuseum.org.

Hiram M. Chittenden Locks in Ballard is where all boats heading east or west in the ship canal must pass and thus presents the quintessential floating boat show; it's one of the most-visited attractions in the city. Visitors crowd railings and jam footbridges to watch as harried lock-keepers scurry to get boats tied up properly before locks are either raised or lowered, depending on the boat's direction of passage. Terraced parks flanking the canal provide splendid picnic overlooks. An underwater fish-viewing window gives you astonishing looks at several species of salmon, steelhead and sea-going cutthroat trout on their spawning migrations (June to November). Lovely botanical gardens in a parklike setting offer yet more diversion. ~ 206-783-7059, fax 206-782-3192.

Fisherman's Terminal is home port to one of the world's biggest fishing fleets, some 700 vessels, most of which chug north into Alaskan waters for summer salmon fishing. But you'll always be able to see boats here—gill-netters, purse-seiners, trollers, factory ships—and working fishermen repairing nets, painting boats and the like. Here, too, are net-drying sheds, shops selling marine hardware and commercial fishing tackle. One café opens at 6:30 a.m. for working fishermen; there's a fish-and-chips window and one good seafood restaurant (Chinook's) overlooking the waterway. ~ On the south side of Salmon Bay about a mile east of the locks. ~ 206-728-3395, 800-426-7817, fax 206-728-3393; www.portseattle.org, e-mail ft@portseattle.org.

The **Fremont District** is locally famous for the sculpture *Waiting for the Interurban*, whose collection of lifelike commuters is frequently seen adorned in funny hats, scarves and other cast-off clothing. Centered around Fremont Avenue North and North 34th Street at the northwest corner of Lake Union, the district is

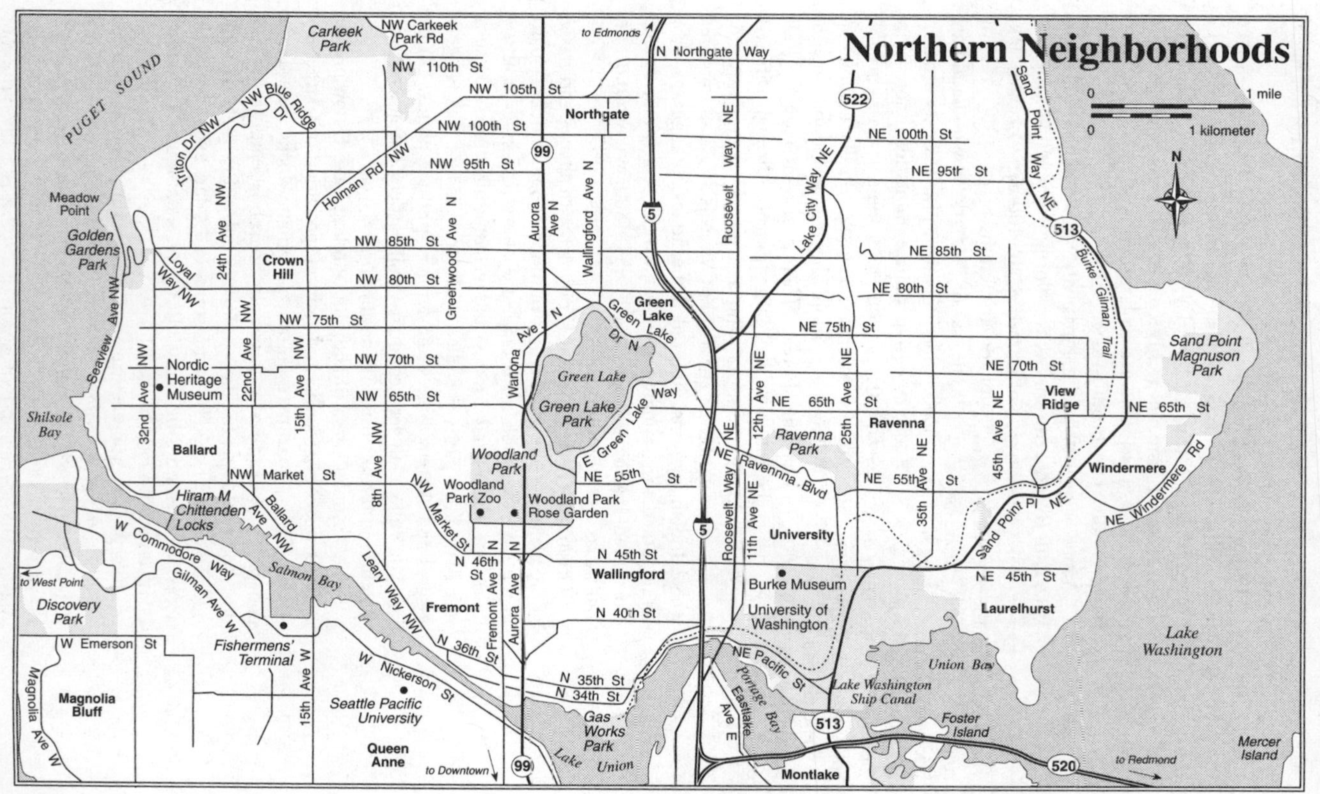
Northern Neighborhoods
0 1 mile
0 1 kilometer
N
Puget Sound
Carkeek Park
NW Carkeek Park Rd
Meadow Point
Golden Gardens Park
Shilsole Bay
Crown Hill
Ballard
Nordic Heritage Museum
Hiram M Chittenden Locks
Salmon Bay
Fishermens' Terminal
Discovery Park
Magnolia Bluff
Queen Anne
Seattle Pacific University
Fremont
Woodland Park
Woodland Park Zoo
Woodland Park Rose Garden
Green Lake
Green Lake Park
Northgate
Wallingford
Gas Works Park
Lake Union
Portage Bay
Union Bay
Lake Washington Ship Canal
Foster Island
Montlake
University
Burke Museum
University of Washington
Ravenna
Ravenna Park
View Ridge
Windermere
Laurelhurst
Sand Point Magnuson Park
Lake Washington
Mercer Island
Burke - Gilman Trail
Sand Point Way NE
Lake City Way NE
N Northgate Way
Roosevelt Way NE
Ravenna Blvd
NE Pacific St
Eastlake Ave E
Wallingford Ave N
Aurora Ave N
Wanona Ave N
Greenwood Ave N
Holman Rd NW
NW Market St
Leary Way NW
W Nickerson St
Ballard Ave NW
W Commodore Way
Gilman Ave W
W Emerson St
Magnolia Ave W
Seaview Ave NW
Loyal Way NW
Triton Dr NW
NW Blue Ridge Dr
Green Lake Dr N
Green Lake Way
E Green Lake Way
N 35th St
N 34th St
N 36th St
N 40th St
N 45th St
N 46th St
Fremont Ave N
NE Windermere Rd
Sand Point Pl NE
to Edmonds
to Downtown
to West Point
to Redmond
5
99
513
520
522

top-heavy with shops proffering the offbeat (handmade dulcimers, antiques and junk).

Perhaps most offbeat of all is the **Fremont Troll**, another famous sculpture found beneath the north footings of the Aurora Bridge. When the nearby Magnolia Bridge was damaged by mudslides, Fremont residents archly averred that their bridge escaped harm because it was under a troll's guardianship. ~ 35th Street North, under the Aurora Bridge.

A mile or so north of the ship canal, Woodland Park and Green Lake Park straddle Aurora Avenue North (Route 99) and together offer more than 400 acres of park, lake and zoo attractions.

The Fremont Outdoor Cinema runs campy, edgy cult classics on Friday and Saturday nights from late June to late August. Outrageous games, contests and themed costume nights are encouraged and expected. ~ www.fremont outdoormovies.com.

The star of the parks is **Woodland Park Zoo**, which has won praise for its program of converting static exhibits into more natural, often outdoor environments. Most notable are the African Savannah, Gorilla Exhibit, the Willawong Station, the Jaguar Exhibit and the Elephant Forest. There's also a Tropical Rain Forest, heralded as a "journey through different levels of forest," and a seasonal contact yard and family farm. The Trail of Vines is an Asian rainforest where Indian pythons, lion-tailed macaques, orangutans, Malayan tapirs and siamangs live. Admission. ~ Fremont Avenue North and North 50th Street; 206-684-4800; www.zoo.org, e-mail webkeeper@zoo.org.

Green Lake Park, enormously popular with all ages and classes of Seattleites, is simply the best outdoor people-watching place in the city. Two loop trails circle the shore (the inner trail is 2 miles long, the outer 3.2 miles) and welcome all comers. On summer days, both paths are filled with strollers and race-walkers, joggers and skaters, bikers and nannies pushing prams. On the lake you will see anglers, canoeists, sailboarders, swimmers, birdwatchers and folks floating in inner tubes.

The six miles or so of shoreline circling **Lake Union** present a varied mix of boat works and nautical specialty shops, street-end pocket parks, boat-in restaurants, seaplane docks, rental-boat concessions, ocean-research vessels, houseboats and flashy condos. You could spend a day exploring funky old warehouses and oddball enterprises. The lake's south end offers extensive public access to the shore behind a cluster of restaurants, a wooden-boat center and new park.

Exceptional architecture, a garden setting and easy access make a campus tour of the **University of Washington** (or U-Dub, as locals call it) a highlight of a Seattle visit. The university began downtown in 1861; in 1895, it was moved to its present site. The Alaska–Yukon–Pacific Exposition of 1909 was held on the campus, and several of its fine buildings date from that event. The campus borders the canal north of Montlake Cut (part of the waterway) and is a haven for anyone who enjoys the simple pleasure of strolling across a college campus. It boggles the mind to think of what awaits you on its 693 acres—handsome old buildings in architectural styles from Romanesque to modern; Frosh Pond; red-brick quads and expanses of lawn and colorful summer gardens; canal-side trails on both sides of the Montlake Cut; access to the Burke-Gilman Trail; and a lakeside **Waterfront Activity Center** (206-543-9433) with canoe and rowboat rentals. ~ Husky Stadium parking lot, off Montlake Boulevard.

The **Burke Museum of Natural History and Culture** is the oldest university museum in the West. Established in 1889, it has a notable collection of American Indian and Pacific Rim artifacts. There's a popular coffeehouse, the **Burke Café** (206-543-9854), in the basement. ~ Northeast 45th Street and 17th Avenue Northeast; 206-543-5590, fax 206-685-3039; www.burkemuseum.org, e-mail theburke@u.washington.edu.

The **Henry Art Gallery** focuses on modern and contemporary art of the Pacific Northwest. Don't miss the excellent photography collection on display here, including James Turrell's *Skyspace*. Closed Monday. Admission. ~ 15th Avenue Northeast and Northeast 41st Street; 206-543-2281, fax 206-685-3123; www.henryart.org, e-mail info@henryart.org.

At the **Visitors Information Center**, you can pick up a useful (and free) walking tour map. The map describes quirky bits of UW history as the hour-plus walk meanders under tall trees and past stately brick buildings. The Henry Suzzallo Library resembles a Gothic cathedral. The Medicinal Herb Garden may be the largest of its kind in the United States. The tree-enclosed Sylvan Grove Theater is the site of numerous trysts, plays and weddings. Fountains, ponds, a rose garden and views of Lake Washington add texture to the lovely campus. The visitors center is closed weekends. ~ 4014 University Way Northeast; 206-543-9198, fax 206-616-6294; www.washington.edu, e-mail uwvic@u.washington.edu.

North of Seattle, the long-time mill town of **Edmonds** has a lively charm and provides a link to the Olympic Peninsula. Ferries leave hourly from the Edmonds ferry landing, on a waterfront that has a recently redeveloped beach park, a long fishing pier and an underwater park that is popular with divers. The park teems with marine life that swims around sunken structures: boats, a dock, a bridge model and others. On shore, the **Edmonds Discovery Program** hosts summer beach walks. Closed Sunday. ~ 425-771-0230, fax 425-771-0253; www.ci.edmonds.wa.us, e-mail lider@ci.edmonds.wa.us.

The **Edmonds Chamber of Commerce** wins the prize for quaintness. Its information center is housed in a pioneer log cabin that looks like a storybook house. Closed weekends. ~ 121 5th Avenue North, Edmonds; 425-670-1496, fax 425-712-1808; www.edmondswa.com, e-mail chamberofcommerce@edmondswa.com.

A visit to the **Edmonds Historical Museum** with its working shingle-mill model, maritime heritage exhibits and collections of logging tools and household furnishings gives a better understanding of the pioneer heritage and industrial history of Edmonds. Rotating exhibits and a gift shop are upstairs on the second floor. Closed Monday and Tuesday. ~ 118 5th Avenue North, Edmonds; 425-774-0900; www.historicedmonds.org.

LODGING

Seattle's neighborhoods offer several hotels and numerous bed-and-breakfast accommodations. A bed and breakfast can be a great value, offering a casual atmosphere, home-cooked food included in the room rate and personal contact with an innkeeper who usually knows the city well. Contact **Pacific Reservation Service.** Closed weekends. ~ 206-439-7677, 800-684-2932, fax 206-282-4354; www.seattlebedandbreakfast.com, e-mail information@seattlebedandbreakfast.com.

A favorite of visitors to the University of Washington, both gay and straight, the **Chambered Nautilus Bed and Breakfast Inn** is only four blocks from the campus. Breezily casual, the spacious home has a family atmosphere. Games and books, soft chairs by the fireplace and all-day tea and cookies add to the homeyness. Ten guest rooms on the second and third floors have antique furnishings. All have private baths and four feature private porches; two have gas fireplaces, and four offer kitchens. A business room with printer, computer and fax machine is always open. A full gourmet breakfast is served, sometimes on the sun porch. ~ 5005

AUTHOR FAVORITE

Located across the street from the University of Washington, **The College Inn** has been a popular recommendation among younger Seattlites lacking couch space for their out-of-town guests. This 1909 Tudor inn offers 27 clean, no-frills guest rooms that, despite the sparse furnishings, boast picture windows with lovely views of Lake Union and downtown. Communal men and women's bathrooms are down the hall. There's a café, restaurant, convenience store and raucous college bar at ground level, so ask for a quieter room on the higher floors if noise bothers you—but be forewarned: this is a four-story walk-up. The staff is friendly and knowledgeable about Seattle's "hidden" treasures. A generous expanded continental breakfast is included. ~ 4000 University Way Northeast; 206-633-4441, fax 206-547-1335; www.collegeinnseattle.com, e-mail mgr@collegeinnseattle.com. BUDGET TO MODERATE.

22nd Avenue Northeast; 206-522-2536, 800-545-8459, fax 206-528-0898; www.chamberednautilus.com, e-mail stay@chambered nautilus.com. DELUXE TO ULTRA-DELUXE.

Also in the University District is the **Hotel Deca**, a 15-story tower with 155 corner rooms and three suites with balconies. All units have views of the mountains or the lake and cityscape. Standard hotel furnishings adorn the spacious rooms, decorated in art deco style. A handsome restaurant and lounge are on the floor below the lobby. ~ 4507 Brooklyn Avenue Northeast; 206-634-2000, 800-899-0251, fax 206-547-6029; www.hoteldeca.com, e-mail hoteldeca@aol.com. MODERATE TO ULTRA-DELUXE.

For a pleasant stay in Edmonds, consider the **Inn on Third & Dayton**, a 1917 Craftsman-style B&B with five comfortably appointed rooms. Guests return year after year to these themed-havens: the Pagota room with Japanese artwork, the Fishing Lodge room with views of the Olympic Mountains and Puget Sound. Although all accommodations have private baths, only two of them are actually in the rooms themselves. No children under nine allowed. ~ 202 3rd Avenue South, Edmonds; 425-775-1600, 800-823-1466; www.innonthird.com, e-mail info@inn onthird.com. MODERATE TO DELUXE.

The **Maple Tree**, a renovated 1923 vintage home, offers charming accommodations for up to three people, complete with private bath and balcony. A light breakfast is included. ~ 18313 Olympic View Drive, Edmonds; 425 774-8420; themapletree b_b.home.comcast.net, e-mail themapletreeb_b@comcast.net. MODERATE.

Hidden away in a little business complex full of shops and restaurants, the **Edmonds Harbor Inn** provides basic motel-style accommodations with updated pastel decor and light wood furnishings, a breakfast area (where a continental breakfast is served) and a meeting space. Sadly, none of the rooms has a view of the harbor. ~ 130 West Dayton, Edmonds; 425-771-5021, 800-441-8033, fax 425-672-2880; www.nwcountryinns.com/edmonds, e-mail harborinn@seanet.com. MODERATE TO ULTRA-DELUXE.

Rooms in the three-story **Travelodge** are comfortably decorated and clean, with dark blue carpets, curtains and bedspreads, cable television and wi-fi access. There are even a few units with microwaves and fridges. Other amenities include hot tubs and continental breakfast. ~ 23825 Route 99, Edmonds; 425-771-8008, 800-578-7878, fax 425-771-0080; www.travelodge.com. BUDGET TO MODERATE.

DINING

On a drab, busy street, the unprepossessing **Le Gourmand** is one of Ballard's best-kept secrets. Since 1985, this intimate family-run restaurant has offered classic French food prepared with fresh local ingredients, including shrimp mousseline and a crackly crème brûlée. They now offer a bar in their beautiful garden. Dinner only. Closed Sunday through Tuesday. ~ 425 Northwest Market Street; 206-784-3463, fax 206-789-4348. ULTRA-DELUXE.

Ponti Seafood Grill is near the Fremont Bridge on the Lake Washington ship canal. The Mediterranean-style restaurant offers spectacular views of the canal from flower filled patios. The menu has mostly seafood, though there are good pasta, steak and chicken dishes as well. Dinner only. ~ 3014 3rd Avenue North; 206-284-3000, fax 206-284-4768; www.pontiseafoodgrill.com, e-mail info@pontiseafoodgrill.com. DELUXE TO ULTRA-DELUXE.

When you're nostalgic for a neighborhood restaurant with an upbeat, casual flavor, head for **35th Street Bistro**. Set in the unpretentious Fremont District, it has high windows, a friendly atmosphere, music, and a seasonal southern European–inspired menu. Try the lemon and ricotta ravioli or the grilled steak with horseradish and hand-cut french fries. Closed for lunch on Monday. ~ 709 North 35th Street; 206-547-9850; www.35bistro.com, e-mail info@35bistro.com. MODERATE TO DELUXE.

Seattle is a poor place to sample Mexican food. One happy exception is the **Chile Pepper**, an unpretentious Wallingford café where they know what pasillas, moles and poblanos are. The chiles rellenos are quite good. Closed Sunday. ~ 1427 North 45th Street; 206-545-1790. BUDGET TO MODERATE.

Located in the bottom of a condo complex overlooking Gas Works Park, **Elemental** is a tiny *bijou* eatery that lives up to its own billing as "an eclectic culinary endeavor." The free-form menu changes every Tuesday and draws inspiration from whatever is organic, fresh and local that week. Entrées range from the delightfully unusual (espresso roast duck with grape flatbread) to the frankly far-out (pickled lamb tongue with onion strudel). For $10 a head, owner Phred Westfall, a wine connoisseur, will select a glass of wine for you to accompany each course. This is adventurous eating at its best. ~ 3309 Wallingford Avenue North; 206-547-2317; www.elementalatgasworks.com. MODERATE.

Touristy though it may be, the great view, alder-grilled fish and historic photos of native Salish people in old-time Seattle combine to make **Ivar's Salmon House** a great Seattle restaurant. The restaurant is a replica Northwest American Indian longhouse complete with an open-pit barbecue, and also features views of the kayak, canoe, tugboat, windsurfer and yacht activity on Lake Union. The menu includes Northwest American Indian–style alder-roasted salmon, pork loin and halibut. ~ 401 Northeast Northlake Way; 206-632-0767; www.ivars.net, e-mail webmail@keepclam.com. MODERATE TO DELUXE.

Union Bay Café serves Northwest regional foods with an Asian and Italian influence. The seasonal entrées might include grilled sturgeon with roasted garlic, tomato and dill and hazelnut chicken on sautéed spinach with lemon butter. More unusual is the filet of ostrich grilled and served with Walla Walla sweet onions and a sauce of port wine, green peppercorn and sage. Lighter entrées are available in the simple, classic café. The appetizer list is almost as long as the regular menu. Dinner only. Closed Monday. ~ 3515 Northeast 45th Street; 206-527-8364, fax 206-527-0436; www.unionbaycafe.com, e-mail info@unioncafe.com. DELUXE.

The **Santa Fe Cafe** is more upscale, offering a fussier version of Southwestern cuisine, more avocados and cilantro than beans and tortillas. Chile-flavored beer, anyone? Wags might call it Northwest/Southwest Contemporary cuisine; it's worth a visit after a trip to the Woodland Park Zoo. No lunch on weekends. ~ 5910 Phinney Avenue North; 206-783-9755. MODERATE.

For waterfront dining on the marina, **Anthony's HomePort Edmonds** fits the bill. This upscale eatery decked out in nautical decor is the place locals come to celebrate and sink their teeth into fresh, local seafood. Specialties include charbroiled yellowfin ahi in a ginger soy sauce and pineapple chutney, fishermen's cioppino, and Puget Sound oysters on the half shell. Come early on Sunday night for your share of the all-you-can-eat Dungeness crab extravaganza. **Anthony's Beach Café** on the ground level provides a more casual dining experience. Dinner and Sunday brunch only. ~ 456 Admiral Way, Edmonds; 425-771-4400, fax 425-771-2331; www.anthonys.com, e-mail edmonds@anthonys.com. MODERATE TO DELUXE.

Every table at **Arnies at Edmonds** has a dandy second-floor view of Puget Sound and the Edmonds harbor. Chicken, steak and pasta are on the regular menu, but your best bet is to order from the fresh daily seafood list. There's a variety of fresh broiled fish, and the clam chowder has won awards. The three-course

AUTHOR FAVORITE

In 1992, a group of star chefs from some of Seattle's best-known restaurants got together to create a unique training program aimed at teaching commercial kitchen skills to the homeless. Since its inception, **FareStart** has trained over 1500 homeless and now prepares meals for local shelters and also serves daily lunch and Thursday-night dinners in their own Lake Union building. Most popular are the Guest Chef Dinners, where 200 lucky diners get to sample what the young trainees have been learning. An assortment of soups, salads and sandwiches are served. The meals are a frequent sellout, so book well in advance. ~ 7th Avenue and Virginia Street; 206-443-1233 ext. 6210; www.farestart.org, e-mail reservations@farestart.org. MODERATE.

early dinner (until 6 p.m.), available Sunday through Friday, is a bargain. Sunday brunch. ~ 300 Admiral Way, Edmonds; 425-771-5688, fax 425-771-7624; www.arniesrestaurant.com. MODERATE TO DELUXE.

Located a block from the ferry landing, **Café de Paris** is known for its French cuisine, served in a small dining room or on the glass-enclosed sunporch. No lunch on weekends. ~ 109 Main Street, Edmonds; 425-771-2350. MODERATE TO DELUXE.

Chanterelle has a rustic atmosphere, with wooden floors and American cuisine. It's bright, cheerful and busy at mealtimes with patrons ordering salads and sandwiches. Open daily for breakfast, lunch and dinner. ~ 316 Main Street, Edmonds; 425-774-0650, fax 425-771-5783; www.chanterellewa.com, e-mail chan terelle.restaurant@gmail.com. MODERATE TO DELUXE.

SHOPPING

If you're in the market for a potato gun, would like to snack on Pez or are searching for a popping Martian, head on over to **Archie McPhee's** in Ballard. This novelty-and-toy store offers more than 10,000 exotic items from all over the world. ~ 2428 Northwest Market Street; 206-297-0240; www.mcphee.com, e-mail mcphee@mcphee.com.

Dominated by the UW campus is the University District, a commercial neighborhood overflowing with a vast array of retail shops. One that attracts many tourists is **La Tienda/Folk Art Gallery**. Here you'll find handpicked craft items, jewelry and textiles from all over the world, including those made by 200 selected American artisans. Closed Sunday. ~ 2050 Northwest Market Street, 206-297-3605; www.latienda-folkart.com.

The largest bookseller in Washington is **University Book Store**, where addicted readers can browse happily for hours. There's a huge selection of literature, technical books and college texts, as well as music and camera sections, some clothing and stationary. ~ 4326 University Way Northeast; 206-634-3400, 800-335-7323, fax 206-634-0810; www.ubookstore.com, e-mail ubsbooks@u.washington.edu.

There are a number of good shops in the renovated **Old Mill Town**. Within it, check out the **Edmonds Antique Mall**, where

NORTHWEST CUISINE, SEATTLE STYLE

In the Northwest, regional cooking at its best emphasizes the bounty of fresh produce and seafood available; in Seattle, innovative chefs have turned it into a distinctive cuisine showcasing the dazzling variety of ingredients that pour in from farms and boats. Combined with fine wines from Washington's 200-plus wineries, it makes for meals that critics rave about.

you can find dolls, glasses and antique furniture. ~ 201 5th Avenue South, Edmonds; 425-670-1496.

More than 150 dealers sell their wares at the **Aurora Antique Pavilion**. ~ 24111 Route 99, Edmonds; 425-744-0566.

NIGHTLIFE

In Ballard, **Conor Byrne's** has live music, specializing in Irish, folk, bluegrass and blues. The Old World building has exposed bricks, high ceilings, original art and low light. Weekend cover. ~ 5140 Ballard Avenue Northwest; 206-784-3640; www.conorbyrnepub.com.

The Tractor tavern offers a mix of live rock, country, Celtic, jazz and alternative music. Cover. ~ 5213 Ballard Avenue Northwest; 206-789-3599; www.tractortavern.citysearch.com.

Sunset Bowl offers night owls 'round-the-clock lanes and a karaoke lounge (Wednesday through Sunday) for wannabe American Idols. ~ 1420 Northwest Market Street; 206-782-7310; www.sunsetbowl.com.

Fremont, while small, is home to several bars and clubs, including **El Camino**, a vibrantly colored venue famous for its delicious margaritas, decent Mexican menu and rubbernecking clientele. ~ 607 North 35th Street; 206-632-7303; www.elcaminorestaurant.com.

For a good game of pool, the **Ballroom** is the place to be. The dancing here is less ballroom than rump-shaking. ~ 456 North 36th Street; 206-634-2575.

Near the University of Washington, you will find an array of clubs and places to park yourself at night.

There are cocktail service, full dinner and comedy shows Thursday through Sunday at **Giggles Comedy Club**. Cover on Friday and Saturday. ~ 5220 Roosevelt Way Northeast; 206-526-5653; www.gigglescomedyclub.com.

Located just barely off campus, the happening student hangout in the University District is the **Big Time Brewery & Alehouse**, which offers beer, pizza and a rowdy young crowd. Seattle's oldest brewpub (c. 1988), it has an antique bar, shuffleboard in the back room and a museum-like collection of beer bottles, cans, signs and memorabilia. ~ 4133 University Way Northeast; 206-545-4509; www.bigtimebrewery.com, e-mail comments@bigtimebrewery.com.

Nearby, **Tommy's Nightclub & Grill** features deejay dance music and live reggae and rock on alternating nights and some of the cheapest beer in town. ~ 4552 University Way Northeast; 206-634-3144; www.tommysnightclub.com.

Seattle's most active small **cinema district** is near the University of Washington in a cultural mecca along and near 45th Street. These theaters are all operated by the same company and show popular, foreign, art and independent films. ~ **The Guild 45th Street Theatre**, 2115 North 45th Street; **Metro Cinemas**, 4500

9th Avenue Northeast; **Neptune Theatre,** 1301 Northeast 45th Street; **Seven Gables Theatre,** 911 Northeast 50th Street; and **Varsity Theatre,** 4329 University Way Northeast; 206-781-5755. This neighborhood is also home to a profusion of small cafés and restaurants catering to the evening before- and after-show crowd.

BEACHES & PARKS

DISCOVERY PARK With two miles of beach trail and nine miles of footpaths winding through mixed forest and across open meadows, this bluff-top preserve (Seattle's largest at more than 534 acres) protects a remarkable "urban wilderness." Here are sweeping vistas, chances to watch birds (including nesting bald eagles) and study nature, the **Daybreak Star Cultural Center** (206-285-4425, fax 206-282-3640) featuring art and cultural exhibits from various tribes, an interpretive center (closed Monday) with environmental displays and educational programs, four miles of road for bicycling and an 1881 lighthouse (oldest in the area). Fort Lawton Historic District includes Officers' Row and military buildings surviving from the park's days as an Army fort. There are areas suitable for picnics; restrooms and a visitor center are at the park's east gate. ~ Located a quarter-hour drive north of downtown in the Magnolia district. The main entrance is at 3801 West Government Way and 36th Avenue West; 206-386-4236, e-mail discover@seattle.gov.

CARKEEK PARK Tucked into a woodsy canyon reaching toward Puget Sound, this 216-acre wildland protects Piper's Creek and its resurrected runs of salmon and sea-going trout. Signs explain how citizens helped clean up the stream and bring the salmon back. Trails lead past spawning waters, to the top of the canyon and through a native-plant garden. You will find picnic areas, restrooms, play areas and beachcombing (as long as you take nothing home with you) and a pioneer orchard. ~ 950 Northwest Carkeek Park Road. Take 3rd Avenue Northwest to 110th Street Northwest, turn and follow the signs; 206-684-0877, fax 206-364-4685.

LIVE MUSIC AND LIVE ANIMALS

One of Seattle's most eagerly anticipated and fun summer events is the evening concert series, **Zoo Tunes,** held on the lawn at Woodland Park Zoo. Bring a lawn chair, a picnic and the whole family and enjoy great music by artists like the Indigo Girls, Little Feat, Leo Kottke, Shawn Colvin, David Wilcox and others (with a little bit of lions, tigers and bears, oh my! chorusing in the background). All proceeds benefit the zoo. ~ Fremont Avenue North and North 50th Street; 206-615-0076; www.zoo.org, e-mail concerts@zoo.org.

GAS WORKS PARK Gas Works Park occupies property that dangles like a giant green tonsil from Lake Union's north shore. Until 1956, the park's namesake "gas works" produced synthetic natural gas from coal and crude oil. Some of the rusting congeries of pipes, airy catwalks, spiraling ladders, tall towers and stubby tanks were torn down during park construction, but enough remains (repainted in snappy colors) to fascinate youngsters and old-timers alike. On windy days, kite enthusiasts come out in full force; the bobbing, colorful displays can be seen from much of the park. ~ 2101 North Northlake Way; 206-684-4075.

GOLDEN GARDENS North of Ballard on Shilshole Bay, this 88-acre park has waterfront, woods, a creek and a sandy beach that swarms with young picnickers and sunbathers in summer. You can watch glorious sunsets from here. There are fire pits, a boat ramp, basketball hoops, wheelchair accessible soccer and football fields and trails, and a public fishing pier. There's a bathhouse on the beach which is usually teeming with activity. On the slope east of the beach, the park has numerous walking paths under the trees. ~ 8498 Seaview Place Northwest; 206-684-4075, fax 206-684-4853; e-mail parksinfo@seattle.gov.

WARREN G. MAGNUSON PARK This 350-acre site carved from the Sand Point Naval Air Station presents generous access to Lake Washington and wide views across the lake. It's a favorite place to launch a boat, swim or toss a frisbee. You'll find picnic areas, restrooms, softball fields, tennis courts, swimming beaches with summer lifeguards, a community center and garden and a wheelchair-accessible wading pool. Adjacent to the park is the National Oceanic Atmospheric Administration's **Sound Garden**, which is full of sculptures that move and chime when the wind blows. The melodic garden gave the Seattle multiplatinum rock band its name. (Visitors who want to tour the garden must show picture ID at a checkpoint entrance at 77th Street and Sand Point Way.) ~ Located on Lake Washington, northeast of downtown Seattle, at 7400 Sand Point Way Northeast and 65th Avenue Northeast; 206-684-4946, fax 206-684-4853; e-mail parksinfo@seattle.gov.

◄ HIDDEN

Southern Neighborhoods

Meander from the heart of the city and you'll find one of the world's great aviation museums. Inviting saltwater beaches provide a convenient retreat from urban living. Seattle South serves as the city's back door to the wilderness.

South and west of downtown West Seattle is one of the city's neighborhood treasures. West Seattle offers the city's finest aggregation of seaside parks and paths, along with stupendous views of the downtown skyline shining across the waters of Elliott Bay. Ferries depart West Seattle's Fauntleroy Dock for pastoral Vashon Island, a 37-square-mile mecca for artists, writers and bed-and-breakfast operators.

Back on the mainland, Renton and Kent are sprawling cities in their own right, Boeing towns still recovering from the severe sting of layoffs that preceded and followed the aerospace giant's corporate move to Chicago.

SIGHTS

About ten miles to the south of downtown Seattle, off Route 5 at Boeing Field, you'll encounter the **Museum of Flight**. Centered in a traffic-stopping piece of architecture called the Great Gallery, the museum is a must. In the glass-and-steel gallery, 22 aircraft hang suspended from the ceiling, almost as if in flight. In all, more than 135 air- and spacecraft (many rare) trace the history of a century of aviation. You'll see the world's first fighter airplane, the first airliner to carry stewardesses, the first presidential jet Air Force One and the only existing M-21 Blackbird spyplane.

The 1909 **Red Barn** houses one wing of the museum. The so-called barn was originally a boat-building factory on the banks of the nearby Duwamish River. Later Bill Boeing bought it and turned it into the original headquarters for the Boeing Corporation. Relocated several times, the Red Barn now houses exhibits on Boeing's early days in the airplane business, a far cry from today's mammoth factories. Visitors can also tour the operating air traffic control tower. Admission. ~ 9404 East Marginal Way South; 206-764-5720, fax 206-764-5707; www.museumofflight.org, e-mail info@museumofflight.org.

> Alki Beach was the site of Seattle's first flight: In 1908, L. G. Mecklem flew an air balloon from what was then known as Luna Park to Meadows Race Track in Georgetown.

Two-mile-long **Alki Beach** is the place to find Seattle's approximation of a beach scene. Though the waters of Puget Sound are chilly, to say the least, the summer sun beckons hordes of bikini-clad teens and twenty-somethings to gather for barbecues and volleyball games. A long, double-wide sidewalk is ideal for joggers, bicyclists and in-line skaters (rentals available); a strand of casual cafés follows the northwest-facing beach for several blocks. Look for a monument to the Denny party, Seattle's first white settlers who established landfall here, and a three-foot-high replica of New York's Statue of Liberty. At the beach's west end, the 1913 **Alki Point Lighthouse** (3201 Alki Avenue Southwest, West Seattle; 206-217-6124), operated by the Coast Guard, invites visitors for half-hour guided tours of the 37-foot-tall facility on summer weekends.

Look offshore from Alki Point and you'll spot forested Blake Island. Here is **Tillicum Village**, built around a huge cedar longhouse (styled after the dwellings of the Northwest Coast American Indians) situated on the edge of a 475-acre marine state park. The village presents traditional salmon bakes and performances by the Tillicum Village Dancers. Tillicum Village charters Argosy vessels from Pier 55 on Seattle's central waterfront year-round. ~ 206-933-8600, 800-426-1205, fax 206-933-9377; www.tillicumvillage.com.

No shopping malls, no fast-food restaurants—just natural beauty and a hometown feel. That's the draw to 14-mile-long **Vashon Island**. In addition to the Fauntleroy crossing, Vashon is accessible by another 15-minute ferry from Tahlequah, near Tacoma's Point Defiance Park, creating a lovely Seattle-to-Tacoma country-road alternative to Route 5.

Since Vashon is also served by a passenger-only ferry that leaves from downtown Seattle's main ferry dock, it's a popular destination for bicyclists and backpackers heading for the island's youth hostel or one of its many B&Bs. The island's little-traveled back roads offer long, leisurely rides through deep second-growth forests and pastoral farmland, with a smattering of U-pick berry and fruit farms. Vashon is home to a thriving community of artists, potters, weavers and other craftspeople—many of whose studios are periodically open to passersby, especially during holiday weekends—as well as writers and musicians. It's also home to a growing gay and lesbian community.

Vashon Highway runs the length of the island, passing through the town of Vashon, with its smattering of small shops and restaurants. **Burton**, a small community halfway down the island, has a few small galleries and stores, a post office, a restaurant and two inns. It's also the turnoff for a secluded, lovely beach park, **Burton Acres Park**, an excellent place to go for a picnic or a beach stroll, to launch canoes or kayaks, or even to swim in the cool salt water of Quartermaster Harbor. On July Fourth, a local anonymous benefactor pays for a fireworks show on a barge in the middle of the harbor; it's one of the best displays on the West Coast. ~ Burton Acres Park, Bayview Drive Southwest, outer loop.

◄ HIDDEN

Side roads beckon from the highway to a handful of poorly marked state beaches and county parks. **Point Robinson County Park** on Maury Island (linked to Vashon via an isthmus at the hamlet of Portage) is easier to find and particularly interesting since it's next door to the Coast Guard's picturesque Point Robinson Lighthouse (not open to the public).

Back on the mainland, historical museums in the adjacent Boeing communities of **Renton** and **Kent** showcase that area's 19th-century roots. The **Renton History Museum**, near the Cedar River, exhibits reminders of an era when this town at the south end of Lake Washington was an important coal-shipping port. Closed Sunday and Monday. Admission. ~ 235 Mill Avenue South, Renton; 425-255-2330; www.rentonhistory.org.

In fall, my favorite place to watch spawning salmon journeying upriver is outside **Renton Public Library**. The library is built right over the Cedar River, and salmon swim through Lake Washington from Puget Sound up into the Cascade foothills via this little-known route on the southeast side of the lake. 100 Mill Avenue South, Renton; 425-436-6610. And the **Greater Kent Historical Society Museum** displays furnishings from the 1930s in the historic Brieter House. Closed Sunday through Tuesday. ~ 855 East Smith Street, Kent; 253-854-4330; www.cyberkent.com.

Seattle's rock legend Jimi Hendrix is buried in Renton. A caretaker can show you the guitarist's grave at **Greenwood Memorial Park**. ~ 350 Monroe Avenue Northeast, Renton; 425-255-1511.

LODGING

A stone's throw from Sea-Tac Airport, the **Seattle Marriott** is a wonderfully luxurious hotel featuring a 20,000-square-foot tropical atrium five stories high. Around it are 459 guest rooms. A restaurant, lounge, whirlpool, health club with massage therapy (by appointment) and gameroom round out the amenities. Airport shuttle is provided. ~ 3201 South 176th Street; 206-241-2000, 800-314-0925, fax 206-248-0789; www.marriott.com. DELUXE.

Vashon Island, befitting its pastoral, low-key nature, has no hotels or motels, and attempts to build anyway would provoke local outcry. It does, however, have more than two dozen fine small inns and B&Bs. Most of Vashon's inns and B&Bs are secluded, idyllic places where quiet prevails and the island's beauty is at the visitor's doorstep.

Vashon Island abounds with bed-and-breakfast inns, some of them in quaint old farmhouses surrounded by meadows and orchards. One is the **Betty MacDonald Farm**, the former home of Betty MacDonald who authored *The Egg and I*, *Onions in the Stew*, and all the Mrs. Piggle Wiggle children's books. The first two books wryly chronicle life on the Olympic Peninsula and Vashon Island. The six-acre farm overlooks Puget Sound and Mt. Rainier and offers two guest accommodations, a cedar-paneled loft and a private cottage, both furnished with oriental carpets, Northwest Indian print fabrics, antiques, full kitchens stocked with breakfast supplies and wood-burning stoves. Guests also enjoy beach access, trail bikes, private decks and gardens. For nighttime reading, there are books by MacDonald. ~ 12000 99th Avenue Southwest, Vashon Island; 206-567-4227, 888-328-6753, fax 206-567-4555; www.bettymacdonaldfarm.com, e-mail info@bettymacdonaldfarm.com. DELUXE TO ULTRA-DELUXE.

A 15-acre retreat within walking distance of town, the **Lavender Duck B&B** operates out of a charming 1896 converted farmhouse. Run by the AYH Ranch/Hostel, the comfortable, no-frills Duck offers four bedrooms all decorated in—you guessed it—various shades of lavender or purple and outfitted with private baths. The shared kitchen sets the scene for the morning pancake breakfast. ~ 16503 Vashon Highway, Vashon Island; 206-463-2592, fax 206-463-6157; www.vashonhostel.com, e-mail jake@vashonhostel.com. MODERATE.

There are eight one- and two-bedroom cottages in four different locations at **Swallow's Nest Guest Cottages**. All are fully equipped with beds, separate baths, armchairs or rocking chairs, light cooking facilities and supplies; two have views of Mount Rainier and Puget Sound. A shared hot tub is on the premises. Full breakfast included. Well-behaved pets and children allowed with advance notice. ~ 6030 Southwest 248th Street, Vashon Island; 206-463-2646, 800-269- 6378, fax 206-463-2646; www. vashonislandcottages.com. MODERATE TO DELUXE.

Actress Dyan Cannon was once the proud title holder of Miss West Seattle.

Also in a pastoral setting, **Artist's Studio Loft** has five acres of gardens and a carriage house cottage with a beamed ceiling, skylights, ceiling fan, kitchenette and outdoor hot tub. Other accommodations include two luxury mission-style cottages with fireplaces and whirlpool tubs, a suite with a private entrance, French doors, cathedral ceilings, and potted palms and a smaller room decorated with Mexican tiles and wicker furnishings. The rate includes breakfast. ~ 16529 91st Avenue Southwest, Vashon Island; 206-463-2583; www.asl-bnb.com, e-mail info@vashon bedandbreakfast.com. DELUXE TO ULTRA-DELUXE.

Situated in the tiny town of Burton, the **Back Bay Inn** is a New England–style lodging with an airy, open dining room downstairs (open in season) and four spare, elegant bedrooms up. A brick entryway is edged with bright flowers six months of the year, and a brick patio is open for dining in warm weather. Sunday brunch is excellent. It's also open for dinner Wednesday through Saturday, serving Northwest cuisine. ~ 24007 Vashon Highway Southwest, Burton; 206-463-5355; www.backbayinn.net. MODERATE TO DELUXE.

The **AYH Ranch/Hostel**, about a mile outside the town of Vashon, caters to bicycle and foot travelers; free pickup is provided from the Thriftway Grocery in town. Hostel lodgings range from campsites and tepees to seven private rooms with bath. Extensive grounds allow room for roaming. Free pancakes for all. No camping available November through April; private rooms available year-round. ~ 12119 Cove Road Southwest, Vashon Island; 206-463-2592; www.vashonhostel.com, e-mail jake@vashonhostel.com. BUDGET TO MODERATE.

DINING

An excellent Thai restaurant in Tukwila is **Bai Tong**. This eatery is known for its steamed curry salmon, grilled beef with Thai sauce and marinated chicken. The carpeted dining room is lush with potted plants, and the walls are adorned with photos of mouthwatering dishes. ~ 16876 Southcenter Parkway, Tukwila; 206-575-3366; www.baitongrestaurant.com. BUDGET.

For an unusual experience in low-priced dining, head west of the airport to the increasingly Latino suburb of Burien, where you'll find **El Trapiche Pupusería & Restaurant**. This homespun, unpretentious little restaurant serves authentic Salvadoran specialties such as *pollo asado* (a skinless, boneless chicken breast chargrilled in annatto-seed marinade), *pescado frito* (whole deep-fried tilapia), *pupusa de chicharrón* (cornmeal rounds stuffed with shredded pork and served with spicy slaw) and beef hoof soup (an acquired taste, to be sure). Practically the only Central American eatery in the greater Seattle area, El Trapiche's novelty draws a growing clientele from all parts of the city. ~ 127 Southwest 153rd Street, Burien; 206-244-5564, fax 206-242-2120. BUDGET TO MODERATE.

Spend a perfect summer day at Alki Beach, then take in dinner at the **Alki Café Beach Bistro**, where a well-rounded menu includes great salads (that change seasonally), seafood, meat, chicken and pasta dishes. Specials of the evening are listed in the dining area. ~ 2726 Alki Avenue Southwest, West Seattle; 206-935-0616; alkicafe.home.comcast.net. BUDGET TO MODERATE.

The **Alki Bakery** just down the street offers up a host of muffins and cinnamon rolls, scones, coffee, espressos and lattes. If you've overindulged, you can always take another stroll on the beach. ~ 2738 Alki Avenue Southwest, West Seattle; 206-935-1352; www.alkibakery.com. BUDGET.

Opened in 2007, **Beato** ("blessed" in Italian) offers *perfecto* Italian food and wine pairings in a light relaxed setting. Seafood, meats and pastas all get the gourmet touch here. Try the antipasto starter of cured meats, cheeses, olives and artichoke paste followed by lamb loin with *cipollini* onions and beets or pan-seared albacore with green garlic puree, olives and tomato oil.

AUTHOR FAVORITE

When I want to roll up my sleeves and dine as the locals do, I claim a picnic table at the **Alki Crab and Fish Company** at West Seattle's Seacrest Marina. This small hole-in-the-wall seafood joint has breathtaking city and water views and is heavily frequented by anglers fishing off the pier and scuba divers returning to dry land. Best known for fried halibut and chips, the kitchen also cranks out fresh shrimp, crab, and shellfish by the pound, as well as standards like cheeseburgers and chicken sandwiches. ~ 1660 Southwest Harbor Avenue, West Seattle; 206-983-0975. BUDGET.

Bittersweet chocolate ravioli stuffed with mascarpone cheese and dates makes an appropriately seductive dessert. A great place to linger with friends after a day at the beach. ~ 3247 California Avenue Southwest, West Seattle; 206-923-1333; www.beatoseattle.com, e-mail info@beatoseattle.com. MODERATE TO DELUXE.

Vashon Island is one of the least likely places to find decent Mexican food, but there it is at **Casa Bonita**, a small family-run enclave in the town of Vashon. Here are such unusual (for the Northwest) delights as chicken *en mole* and *molcajete*, a hearty stew. Meals are filling and economical. ~ 17623 100th Avenue Southwest, Vashon Island; 206-463-6452. MODERATE.

If you want to act like a real islander on Vashon, breakfast consists of a visit to **Bob's Bakery**, a tiny storefront on the main highway in town. Each morning Bob bakes up more than three dozen different delights, ranging from sweets like lemon-rosemary pound cake and cranberry-orange muffins to such savories as pizzas and tofu burgers. Grab a goodie, a cup of coffee and the newspaper, have a seat on the bench out front and watch the world go by for a half hour or so. Closed Sunday and Monday. ~ 17506 Vashon Highway, Vashon Island; 206-463-1441. BUDGET.

The old island hangout is **Sound Food Café**. The restaurant is known for its casual atmosphere—windows overlooking the gardens and lots of wood inside. A variety of soups, salads and sandwiches of baked bread is available for lunch. Dinner entrées include pasta primavera, seafood dishes and a number of large salads. Desserts—sigh—come fresh from the bakery. Take your pick of lime curd French tart, raspberry apple pie, chocolate cream cake or any of the daily goodies. Closed on Sunday and Monday. ~ 20312 Vashon Highway Southwest, Vashon Island; 206-463-0888; www.soundfoodcafe.com. BUDGET.

SHOPPING

For music lovers, a good stop in West Seattle is **Easy Street Records**, where many of the area's bands and deejays shop for their own tunes. The newest indie-rock CDs share shelf space with historic vinyl and rare imports; astute staff will direct you to listening stations before you make your purchase. There's even a bar and budget-priced café here. ~ 4559 California Avenue Southwest, West Seattle; 206-938-3279.

Consignment boutiques have come a long way from the slightly moth-eaten charity shops beloved by poverty-stricken students everywhere. **Funky Jane's** in West Seattle has a great selection of fashionable clothing for all sizes. Designer samples and handbags quickly sell out, so check back often. ~ 4706 California Avenue Southwest, West Seattle; 206-937-2637.

The **Country Store and Gardens** offers an eclectic collection of clothing, garden supplies, food products, gifts and nursery plants. Spring is a great time to stroll the grounds and experience the vast array of flowers. ~ 20211 Vashon Highway Southwest, Vashon Island; 206-463-3655, 888-245-6136; www.vashoncountrystore.com.

Across the street, **Minglement** has handicrafts from around the world, including pottery and jewelry, plus a selection of natural foods, teas and herbs. ~ 19529 Vashon Highway Southwest, Vashon Island; 206-463-9672.

NIGHTLIFE

Salty's on Alki is a marvelous spot for a quiet drink with a sunset view across Elliott Bay toward the downtown Seattle skyline. On Monday and Friday nights and weekend days the bar is packed with contemporary music lovers who come for the weekly show. Seafood dinners here are special-occasion pricey, but there's a great Sunday brunch. ~ 1936 Harbor Avenue Southwest, West Seattle; 206-937-1600, fax 206-937-1430; www.saltys.com.

West Seattle's younger crowd frequents **Rocksport,** a sports bar that books local rock bands for dancing on weekend nights. ~ 4209 Southwest Alaska Street, West Seattle; 206-935-5838, 866-935-5838; www.rocksport.net.

For a flashback to the fabulous '50s, have a martini at **West 5** and take in the memorabilia. There's a daily happy hour and occasional deejay music. Closed Monday. ~ 4539 California Avenue Southwest, West Seattle; 206-935-1966; www.westfive.com.

PARKS

SEWARD PARK On Bailey Peninsula, this 300-acre park jutting into Lake Washington encompasses Seattle's largest virgin forest. Walking through it on one of several footpaths is the prime attraction, but many come to swim and sunbathe, launch a small boat, fish or visit a fish hatchery. Seward Park offers a rare opportunity to see nesting bald eagles in an urban setting. The best introductory walk is the two-and-one-half-mile shoreline loop stroll; to see the large Douglas firs, add another mile along the center of the peninsula. The swimming beaches' gentle surf is ideal for children, and there are lifeguards in summer. You can fish from the pier for crappie and trout. There are tennis courts, picnic areas, restrooms, an art studio and play areas. ~ Located on the west shore of Lake Washington, southeast of downtown, at 5902 Lake Washington Boulevard South and South Orcas Street; 206-684-4075, fax 206-684-4853; e-mail parksinfo@seattle.gov.

LINCOLN PARK This major multipurpose park in southwest Seattle is situated on a nose-shaped bluff just south of the Fauntleroy Ferry Terminal. There are rocky beaches strewn with tidepools and a network of quiet paths winding through groves of madrona, Douglas fir, cedar and redwoods. The park also offers play and picnic areas, an outdoor heated saltwater pool, tennis courts, a horseshoe pit, a football field and several

Where Are They Now?

Nearly 30,000 visitors each year make pilgrimages to Seattle to visit the gravesites of deceased superstars. The headstone of martial arts film hero **Bruce Lee** (1940–1973), engraved in English and Chinese, is found in Lake View Cemetery on Capitol Hill, just north of Volunteer Park. Alongside, another headstone marks the final resting place of his son, **Brandon Lee** (1965–1993), who died in a freak gunshot accident while filming *The Crow*. ~ 1554 15th Avenue East, Seattle; 206-322-1582.

Lake View Cemetery is also the final resting place of several Seattle historical figures—among them founding fathers Henry L. Yesler (1830–1892) and David "Doc" Maynard (1808-1873), and Chief Seattle's daughter Princess Angeline (1820?–1896).

Legendary guitarist **Jimi Hendrix** (1942–1970), who reigned as Seattle's most famous rock musician until his fatal drug overdose a year after his landmark appearance at Woodstock, is interred at Greenwood Memorial Park in suburban Renton. Because of the large number of fans who still visit the grave, a large open-air family mausoleum has been built on the site. ~ 350 Monroe Avenue Northeast, Renton; 425-255-1511.

Incidentally, Jimi Hendrix attended central Seattle's Garfield High School, where Bruce Lee met his future wife Linda Emery (class of '63) while he was giving a guest lecture on Chinese philosophy at Garfield High. Jimi and Bruce also shared the same birthday, November 27.

Don't look for the grave of Seattle's other deceased rock superstar, **Kurt Cobain** (1967–1994), lead singer and guitarist of the grunge group Nirvana. His remains were cremated and the ashes scattered in the Wishkah River near the south boundary of Olympic National Park. The river provides the water supply for the city of Aberdeen, Washington. If you can't make the pilgrimage out to Aberdeen, head for Seattle's Viretta Park instead. This tiny park, due south of Cobain's former home, has become an informal memorial site, complete with flowers, candles and graffiti left by fans. ~ 151 Lake Washington Boulevard East.

miles of bike paths. ~ 8011 Fauntleroy Avenue Southwest, south of West Seattle; 206-684-8021, fax 206-233-7023.

SEAHURST PARK A well-designed, 152-acre site where landscaping divides 4000 feet of saltwater shoreline into individual chunks just right for private picnics and sunbathing. A nature trail and some three miles of primitive footpath explore woodsy uplands and the headwaters of two creeks. Other facilities include picnic areas, restrooms, and a marine laboratory with a small viewable fish ladder. ~ Located at Southwest 140th Street and 16th Avenue Southwest, via Exit 154B from Route 5, Burien; 206-988-3700.

GENE COULON BEACH PARK At the south tip of Lake Washington in Renton, this handsomely landscaped site is most notable for the loads of attractions within its 55 acres: one and a half miles of lakeside path, the wildfowl-rich estuary of John's Creek and a "nature islet," a lagoon enclosed by the thousand-foot water walk and "Picnic Gallery," a seafood restaurant, a fast-food restaurant, and interesting architecture reminiscent of old-time amusement parks. A logboom-protected shoreline includes a fishing pier. There's a boat harbor with an eight-lane boat launch, and good fishing from the pier for trout and salmon. The bathing beach is protected by a concrete walkabout with summer lifeguards. There are two restaurants, picnic grounds and floats, restrooms, play areas, and volleyball and tennis courts. ~ Bordered by Lake Washington Boulevard North in Renton, north of Route 405 via Exit 5 and Park Avenue North; 425-430-6600, fax 425-430-6603.

SALTWATER STATE PARK You'll share this busy park with lots of locals, nearly 800,000 visitors a year, so don't expect solitude. But among the 88 acres, do revel in the fine views, some

A SIDE TRIP TO VICTORIA

The picturesque Canadian town of **Victoria** in British Columbia combines a rich British heritage with a relaxed lifestyle. Winsome, gracious and colorful, Victoria is full of history and natural beauty, offering museums and gardens, grand old hotels and quaint shops. Located west of the San Juan Islands and just across the Strait of Juan de Fuca from Washington's Olympic Peninsula, Victoria is just a pleasant ferry ride away from the Seattle area and makes for a scenic day trip or overnight excursion. Whichever you choose, consider capping off your visit with high tea at the landmark Empress Hotel. (For information on getting to Victoria, see the "Ferry" section at the end of the chapter.)

1500 feet of shoreline and quiet woods with two miles of hiking trails. A sunken barge about 150 yards offshore from a prominent sandspit attracts a variety of perch and seasonal fish and divers. There are picnic areas, restrooms, an outdoor shower, play areas, a café and a concession stand. ~ Located on Marine View Drive (Route 509) about halfway between Seattle and Tacoma, west of Route 5 via Exit 149; 253-661-4956, fax 206-870-4294.

▲ There are 50 campsites ($19 per night), of which 22 can accommodate RVs. No reservations. Closed in winter.

Eastside Neighborhoods

Seattle East, extending from the eastern shore of Lake Washington to the Cascade foothills, blends the urban and rural assets of this metropolitan region. Here you'll find wineries and archaeological sites, prime birdwatching areas and homey bed and breakfasts.

SIGHTS

I highly recommend a visit to the **Château Ste. Michelle** winery, even for teetotalers, because the spacious, parklike grounds surrounding the château are among the most beautiful places in the Seattle area for a relaxing stroll or a picnic. Located just south of Woodinville, Château Ste. Michelle is the state's largest winery with daily tasting and tours. Situated on a turn-of-the-20th-century estate, it also has duck and trout ponds, experimental vineyards and outdoor concerts on summer weekends. ~ 14111 145th Street Northeast, Woodinville; 425-415-3300, fax 425-415-3657; www.ste-michelle.com, e-mail info@ste-michelle.com.

Bellevue is the fifth-largest city in Washington, its suburban sprawl broken by high-rise complexes of office buildings, shops and department stores. Crossing Lake Washington between Seattle and Bellevue is the **Evergreen Point Floating Bridge**, the world's longest floating bridge (1.4 miles).

Bellevue Square, with some 200 stores, is one of the largest malls in the state. ~ Northeast 8th Street and Bellevue Way Northeast, Bellevue; 425-454-8096; www.bellevuesquare.com.

At Bellevue Square is the **Bellevue Arts Museum**, where exhibits and public programs emphasize the work of Northwest contemporary artists, craftspeople and designers. Admission. ~ 510 Bellevue Way Northeast at Northeast 6th Street, Bellevue; 425-519-0770; www.bellevuearts.org, e-mail info@bellevuearts.org.

To see what Bellevue used to be like before freeways, commuters and office towers, stroll the short stretch of shops along Main Street westward from Bellevue Way Northeast in **Old Bellevue.**

Adults and children alike are enchanted with the **Rosalie Whyel Museum of Doll Art.** Hundreds of antique and modern dolls are on display in a building that is patterned after a brick Victorian mansion. Admission. ~ 1116 108th Avenue Northeast, Bellevue; 425-455-1116, fax 425-455-4793; www.dollart.com, e-mail dollart@dollart.com.

Bellevue boasts a surprisingly diverse network of parks embedded within its neighborhoods. Adjacent to Bellevue Square is **Downtown Park**, whose 20 acres include a broad waterfall and a five-acre meadow enclosed by a canal. **Mercer Slough Nature Park** boasts 320 acres of natural wetland habitat and over seven miles of trails, as well as a blueberry farm and an environmental education center. ~ 2102 Bellevue Way Southeast, Bellevue; 425-452-6881.

Wilburton Hill Park is centered around the Bellevue Botanical Garden, filled with native and ornamental Northwest plants. The park covers over 100 acres and has more than three miles of hiking trails as well as softball and soccer fields. ~ 12001 Main Street off 116th Avenue Northeast, Bellevue; 425-452-2750; www.bellevuebotanical.org.

North of Bellevue, hugging the Lake Washington shore, is **Kirkland**, with remnants of small-town charm. Pedestrian traffic is encouraged, with easy access to the lake and a one-and-a-half-mile walking/biking path. At Moss Bay, there's a public boat ramp and marina, shops, cafés and a brewery.

LODGING

Woodinville is famous for its wineries. Bucolic Chateau Ste. Michelle and Columbia Winery are the main draws for oenophiles, along with the smaller boutique wineries such as DeLille Cellars, Facelli and Matthews Cellars that are quickly gaining in popularity. The sumptuous **Willows Lodge** resort on the Sammamish River adjoins the wineries, making it the perfect base for Wine Country touring. The 84 elegant rooms and suites in this rustic retreat have balconies and patios overlooking the gardens. Other amenities include stone fireplaces, DVD/CD players, French press coffee, beds with 300-thread-count sheets and down comforters and large soaking tubs. There is also a pool, a spa and a fitness center. Pet-friendly. ~ 14580 Northeast 145th Street, Woodinville; 877-424-3930; www.willowslodge.com, e-mail mail@willowslodge.com. ULTRA-DELUXE.

Set on three-plus acres, **A Cottage Creek Inn** has its own creek, pond, waterfall and gazebo on the grounds. The English Tudor house features four rooms, one with a brass bed, one with an antique bed, all with their own bathrooms and highspeed internet access. There are full jacuzzis in the two larger rooms and a communal outdoor hut tub. There's a pleasant sitting room with a piano, which guests are encouraged to play. Full breakfast included. ~ 12525 Avondale Road Northeast, Redmond; phone/fax 425-881-5606; www.cottagecreekinn.com, e-mail innkeepers@cottagecreekinn.com. MODERATE TO DELUXE.

Hey! The Water's Fine

Even if you're a diehard landlubber, do not fail to go sightseeing here by boat at least once. Simply put, if you leave Seattle without plying its surrounding waters your trip will be incomplete. So don't hesitate, dear traveler: Head to the downtown central waterfront and make some waves.

On a clear day you can see forever, or so it would seem aboard one of the **Washington State Ferries**. Headquartered at Colman Dock, the ferries make frequent departures to Bremerton and to Bainbridge Island, both across Puget Sound to the west. But getting there is much of the fun because from your watery perch you'll be treated to grand views of Mt. Rainier, Mt. Baker and the Olympics (the Mountains, not the Games, silly). Up closer you'll see pleasure boats and other craft, and you may even catch a glimpse of an orca (killer) whale. To Bremerton, you can ride the car-and-passenger ferry, the passenger-only boat or the high-speed ferry for pedestrians. At Pier 50 next door, you can board a passenger-only ferry to Vashon Island. ~ Pier 52; 206-464-6400; www.wsdot.wa.gov/ferries.

This is your captain speaking. That's just part of the show on **Argosy Cruises**, which offer at least two tours every day year-round. On the harbor spin you'll get grand mountain views and see boat traffic like you won't believe: freighters, tugboats, sailboats, ferries, you name it. The narrator spices up the trip. ~ Pier 55; 206-623-4252, 800-642-7816; www.argosy cruises.com.

Argosy and **Gray Line of Seattle** join forces for their "locks tour." The tour goes north to Shilshole Bay, eastward through the Hiram M. Chittenden Locks into the Lake Washington Ship Canal and then on to the south tip of Lake Union. You return to the waterfront by bus. Going through the locks is an experience in itself, plus you'll get to see zillions of other boats doing the same. And along the way you might even see salmon jumping. ~ Pier 55; 800-426-7505.

S.S. Virginia V is the last authentic operating steamboat of the legendary "Mosquito Fleet," the motley flotilla of steamboats that once carried foot passengers and cargo around Puget Sound before the coming of highways and autos. Recently renovated, the *Virginia V* is available for charter cruises. ~ 206-624-9119; www.virginiav.org.

A quieter, more peaceful way to see Elliott Bay is **Emerald City Charters**' sailboat tours. Pick a daytime or sunset tour and float gracefully past motorboats, ferries and tankers from May to mid-October. ~ Pier 54; 206-624-3931, 800-831-3274; www.sailingseattle.com.

Big and broad-shouldered, the **Hyatt Regency Bellevue** is the classiest place to stay in Bellevue. The mood is corporate, the quality's high and access is convenient. The 382 rooms are painted in earth tones, and have soft lighting, contemporary furnishings and all the amenities, including room service. Guests are welcome to use the adjoining health club. ~ 900 Bellevue Way Northeast, Bellevue; 425-462-1234, 800-233-1234, fax 425-646-7567; www.bellevue.hyatt.com. ULTRA-DELUXE.

The **Woodmark Hotel on Lake Washington** is a handsome, four-story brick structure on Lake Washington's shore. Its small scale, residential-style lobby, and comfortable bar with a fireplace and shelves of books create the ambience of a welcoming, stylish home. The 100 rooms have all the amenities: mini-bars, televisions, robes and hair dryers. Ask for a room on the West side—they have lake views. ~ 1200 Carillon Point, Kirkland; 425-822-3700, 800-822-3700, fax 425-822-3699; www.thewoodmark.com, e-mail mail@thewoodmark.com. ULTRA-DELUXE.

HIDDEN ►

In a quiet wooded area southeast of Seattle is the **Maple Valley Bed and Breakfast.** The two-story stone home has open-beamed ceilings, peeled-pole railings, cedar walls and detailed wood trim. Guests like to relax on the antique furniture in the sitting room. The two guest rooms are individually decorated and color coordinated with French doors that open onto a large deck. Both have log beds. On cool nights, heated, sand-filled pads ("hot babies") are used to warm the beds. A full breakfast is served on country-stencil pottery in a dining area that overlooks trees, wandering birds and ponds with ducks. ~ 20020 Southeast 228th Street, Maple Valley; 425-432-1409, 888-432-1409, fax 425-413-1459; www.seattlebestbandb.com/maplevalley, e-mail wildlifepond@hotmail.com. BUDGET TO MODERATE.

DINING

Reservations are hard to come by, and it's a bit of a challenge getting there, but **The Herbfarm** is the Seattle area's equivalent to the Napa Valley's French Laundry: the ultimate in exquisite meals prepared from locally grown ingredients. Each week, the restaurant picks a theme (e.g., "A Summer Sketchbook") and builds a nine-course tasting menu with paired wines to illustrate it. Never tried miner's lettuce or ice cream flavored with maple blossoms? You will at The Herbfarm. Dinner only. Closed Monday through Wednesday. ~ Willows Lodge, 14590 Northeast 145th Street, Woodinville; 425-485-5300; www.theherbfarm.com, e-mail reservations@theherbfarm.com. ULTRA-DELUXE.

It's not all wineries in Woodinville. Seattle's popular **Redhook Brewery** more than holds its own amid the wine tastings. Tour the brewery, then pull up a leather chair next to the fireplace in the brewery's eatery, the Forecaster's Public House, and order a burger, pita sandwich, ribs or other pub grub, washed down with a pint of Redhook IPA. A popular local hangout. ~ 14300 Northeast 145th, Woodinville; 425-483-3232; www.redhook.com, e-mail redhook@redhook.com. BUDGET.

The open kitchen at **Andre's Eurasian Bistro** is as entertaining as the food. This restaurant offers a menu with Vietnamese specialties like spring rolls or chicken with lemongrass, as well as Continental selections, such as lamb with garlic. Vietnamese chef Vu Nguyen comes with experience from some of Seattle's best restaurants. No lunch on Saturday. Closed Sunday. ~ 14125 Northeast 20th Street, Bellevue; 425-747-6551, fax 425-747-4304; www.andresbistro.com. MODERATE.

You wouldn't expect to find a good restaurant in this little shopping strip, but here it is. At **Pogacha**, a Croatian version of pizza is the mainstay. The pizzas, crisp on the outside but moist inside, are baked in a clay oven. Because the saucing is nonexistent or very light, the flavor of the toppings—pesto and various cheeses, alone or over vegetables or meat—is more apparent. Other entrées include Adriatic-inspired grilled meats and seafood, salads and pastas. ~ 119 106th Avenue Northeast, Bellevue; 425-455-5670; www.pogacha.com. MODERATE.

One of the best Japanese restaurants in all of Puget Sound is hidden in the Totem Lake West shopping center in suburbia. **Izumi** features an excellent sushi bar. Entrées are fairly standard—beef, chicken sukiyaki and teriyaki and tempura—but the ingredients are especially fresh and carefully prepared. Service is friendly. No lunch on weekends. Closed Monday. ~ 12539 116th Avenue Northeast, Kirkland; 425-821-1959. MODERATE TO DELUXE.

◄ HIDDEN

A couple of local residents who grew up in Pakistan and Bangladesh have opened **Shamiana**. The food is cooled to an American palate but can be spiced to a full-blown, multistar *hot*. A buffet

ALL ABOARD FOR DINNER

Dining cars built in the 1930s and 1950s, refurbished in style, offer unusual views of the Seattle area to passengers who book a ride on the **Spirit of Washington**. The train travels from Renton north for 22 miles along the east shore of Lake Washington to Woodinville. Top-quality meals at ultra-deluxe prices are served during the journey—dinners daily, and lunch and brunch on weekends. In Woodinville, passengers disembark for a tour of the beautifully landscaped Columbia winery. On the return journey, they enjoy dessert and coffee and watch the scenery go by. The train crosses Wilburton Trestle, the longest (975 feet) wooden trestle in the Northwest. Closed Monday in winter. ~ 625 South 4th Street, Renton; 800-876-7245; www.spiritofwashingtondinnertrain.com. ULTRA-DELUXE.

of four curries, salad, *nan* and *dal* is offered at lunch. Dinner is à la carte, and includes entrées such as lamb curry with rice *pulao* or chicken *tikka*. ~ 10724 Northeast 68th Street, Kirkland; 425-827-4902, fax 425-828-2765. MODERATE TO DELUXE.

Incongruously located in a strip mall in Redmond, **Neville's at the British Pantry** has been serving authentic British cuisine in its lace-tableclothed dining room since 1978. Traditional items on both lunch and dinner menus include bangers and mash, roast beef and Yorkshire pudding, Lancashire pasty, and steak and kidney pie, followed by custard tart or sherry trifle. Stop in for a pot of tea and a scone or crumpet. No dinner Monday and Tuesday. Breakfast on Sunday only. ~ 8125 161st Avenue Northeast, Redmond; 425-883- 7511, fax 425-895-0464; e-mail alvia@thebritishpantryltd.com.

SHOPPING

In Bellevue, **Bellevue Square** has 200 of the nation's finest shops, department stores and restaurants. ~ Northeast 8th Street and Bellevue Way Northeast, Bellevue; www.bellevuesquare.com.

One of the most elegant shops in Bellevue is **Alvin Goldfarb Jeweler**. Specializing in 18-carat platinum and gold pieces crafted by an in-house goldsmith who also works with precious and semiprecious gems, this is a mecca for discriminating people who desire a one-of-a-kind item. Closed Sunday. ~ 305 Bellevue Way Northeast, Bellevue; 425-454-9393; www.alvingoldfarbjeweler.com.

If you're looking for the unusual, browse through **Ming's Asian Gallery**, two stories full of Asian antiques and art from China, Korea, Japan and Southeast Asia. ~ 10217 Main Street, Bellevue; 425-462-4008; www.mingsgallery.com.

Doll collectors will revel in **Absolute Quality Dolls**, which proffers realistic, handcrafted dolls. Closed Sunday. ~ 119th Avenue Southeast, Bellevue; 425-644-6019.

Owned by potters, **Wilburton Pottery** offers a wide range of home and garden ornaments. Their specialty is artisan garden tiles. A tour of the studio is possible by appointment. Call ahead for directions and hours. ~ 425-455-9203; www.wilburtonpottery.com, e-mail mail@wilburtonpottery.com.

CANDYLAND

Satisfy your sweet tooth at **Boehm's Candies**, where hundreds of chocolates are hand-dipped every day. You can tour the factory (reservations are required; this is a popular spot) and watch the skilled workmanship that goes into making candies of this quality. ~ 255 Northeast Gilman Boulevard, Issaquah; 425-392-6652, fax 425-557-0560; www.boehmscandies.com, e-mail info@boehmscandies.com.

Hunters of antiques appreciate the **Antique Mart at Kirkland.** The mall has nearly 100 dealers selling antiques and collectibles. ~ 151 3rd Street, Kirkland; 425-827-7443.

Excellent Northwest ceramics, jewelry and blown glass make **Lakeshore Gallery** a fine place to stop even if you have no intention of buying. The carved woodwork is especially well done. ~ 107 Park Lane, Kirkland; 425-827-0606.

Refurbished farmhouses, a barn and a feed store are stocked with handicrafts and artful, designer clothing at Issaquah's **Gilman Village.** Among the 40-plus shops clustered in these historic structures is **The Revolutionary Gallery** (425-392-4982, www.revolution-gallery.com), an artists co-op featuring fun and functional artwork fashioned from recycled materials. ~ 317 Northwest Gilman Boulevard, Issaquah; www.gilmanvillage.com.

Hedges Family Estate is a Yakima Valley winery that has opened a full-fledged tasting room on the west side of the Cascades; some aging is done here. Hedges is known for its blends. ~ 195 Northeast Gilman Boulevard, Issaquah; 425-391-6056, 800-859-9463; www.hedgescellars.com.

NIGHTLIFE

Enjoy live blues tunes on Saturday at **Forecasters Public House at the Redhook Ale Brewery.** ~ 14300 Northeast 145th Street, Woodinville; 425-483-3232; www.redhook.com.

Daniel's Broiler has a live pianist playing contemporary hits seven nights a week. ~ Bellevue Place, 10500 Northeast 8th Avenue, 21st Floor, Bellevue; 425-462-4662.

There is live music Wednesday through Sunday nights at the **0/8 Seafood Grill and Twisted Cork Wine Bar,** located in the Hyatt Regency Bellevue. ~ 900 Bellevue Way Northeast, Bellevue; 425-462-1234; www.08seafoodgrill.com.

With a welcoming fireplace and free appetizers Monday through Friday, the **Coast Bellevue Hotel** invites you into their lounge. ~ 625 116th Avenue Northeast, Bellevue; 425-455-9444.

Good things come in small packages, and the **Village Theatre** proves it. The local casts here will tackle anything, be it Broadway musicals, dramas or comedy. ~ 303 Front Street North, Issaquah; 425-392-2202; www.villagetheatre.org.

BEACHES & PARKS

MARYMOOR COUNTY PARK This roomy, 640-acre preserve at the north end of Lake Sammamish in Redmond is a delightful mix of archaeology and history, river and lake, meadows and marshes, plus an assortment of athletic fields. A one-mile footpath leads to a lakeside observation deck, and there's access to the ten-mile Sammamish River Trail. The circa-1904 Clise Mansion, near a pioneer windmill, was built as a hunting lodge. Facilities include picnic areas, restrooms, play areas, baseball and soccer fields, tennis courts, a model-airplane airport, a bicycle velodrome with frequent races, a climbing wall and archaeological site. ~ Located on West Lake Sammamish Parkway Northeast off Route 520, just south of Redmond city center; 206-205-3661, fax 206-296-1437.

KELSEY CREEK PARK This unique park is a 150-acre farm with an old homestead and farm animals in the barnyard. There are hiking trails, jogging paths, wooded glens, a creek and an 1888 log cabin. ~ 410 130th Place Southeast; 425-452-7688.

JUANITA BEACH PARK Juanita Beach Park draws big crowds of area residents from late June through September, with good reason. The roped-off swimming area is vast and the water warms up fairly early in the shallow bay. There's a concession building and adequate changing facilities, a picnic area and plenty of room for anglers to ply their craft without interfering with swimmers. ~ Access from Juanita Drive Northeast, five minutes north of downtown Kirkland. Across the bay, **Juanita Bay Park** is basically undeveloped (aside from restrooms), offering wildlife watchers a huge wetland area that attracts waterfowl, blackbirds and the occasional eagle or osprey. ~ Access is from Market Street North, five minutes north of downtown Kirkland; 425-587-3300.

Volunteer park rangers offer guided tours of wildlife-rich Juanita Bay Park the first Sunday of each month. Don't forget your binoculars!

O.O. DENNY PARK Also located on Lake Washington, just north of Kirkland, O.O. Denny offers miles of heavily wooded hiking trails and a sheltered picnic area on the lake. While there are no lifeguards, people do swim and fish. Restrooms are available. ~ From Route 405 take Northeast 116th Street Exit, head west on Juanita Drive Northeast, and turn left on Holmes Point Drive Northeast; e-mail parkinfo@finnhillparks.net.

SAINT EDWARDS STATE PARK This former Catholic seminary still exudes the peace and quiet of a theological retreat across its 316 heavily wooded acres and 3000 feet of Lake Washington shoreline. Except for a handful of former seminary buildings, the park is mostly natural, laced by miles of informal trails. To reach the beach, take the wide path just west of the main seminary building. It winds a half mile down to the shore, where you can wander left or right. Side trails climb up the bluff for the return loop. There's also a beach (no lifeguard) and year-round indoor pool (fee). You'll also find picnic areas, restrooms, a horseshoe pit, soccer and baseball fields, basketball, volleyball, badminton and a gymnasium (fee). ~ Located on Lake Washington's northern shore, between Kenmore and Kirkland on Juanita Drive Northeast; 425-823-2992.

LUTHER BURBANK PARK At the northeast corner of Mercer Island in Lake Washington, this little jewel presents some 3000 feet of shoreline to explore along with marshes, meadows and woods. The entire 77-acre site is encircled by a loop walk. You can fish from the pier for salmon, steelhead, trout and bass, and in summer swim at the beach. Among the facilities are picnic areas, restrooms, a play area, tennis courts and an amphitheater with summer concerts. ~ Entrance is at 2040 84th Avenue Southeast and Southeast 24th Street, via the Island Crest Way exit from Route 90 on Mercer Island, east of Seattle; 206-236-3545.

LAKE SAMMAMISH STATE PARK A popular, 512-acre park at the southern tip of Lake Sammamish near Issaquah, it offers plenty to do, including swimming (no lifeguard), boating, picnicking, hiking and birdwatching along 6858 feet of lake shore and around the mouth of Issaquah Creek. Look for eagles, hawks, great-blue heron, red-wing blackbirds, northern flickers, grebes, kingfishers, killdeer, buffleheads, widgeon and Canada geese. Picnic areas, restrooms, showers, soccer fields and a jogging trail are the facilities here. ~ Located at East Lake Sammamish Parkway Southeast and Southeast 56th Street, two miles north of Route 90 in Issaquah (15 miles east of Seattle) via Exit 17; 425-649-4275.

Outdoor Adventures

SPORTFISHING

Salmon is the Sound's most famous fish, but scores of other species make sportfishing a signature attraction here. A combination of migratory and "resident" stocks offer angling for Chinook and Coho almost year-round. And when salmon fishing slows, you can try your luck for some 80 types of bottom-fish that also populate these waters—colorful fellows like the Red Irish Lord and copper rock fish, as well as greenling, halibut and many varieties of cod.

SEATTLE AREA Downtown, you can drop your line right into Elliott Bay at **Waterfront Park** (Piers 57-61). But for the real deal, head to Ballard, where the city's commercial fishing fleet is based (at Fisherman's Terminal) and sportfishing tours can be chartered. **Adventure Charters** offers full-day salmon-fishing trips year-round. Afternoon tours are offered in summer, and all gear is provided. ~ 7001 Seaview Avenue Northwest, Shilshole Bay Marina; 206-789-8245, 800-789-0448; www.seattlesalmoncharters.com.

NORTHERN NEIGHBORHOODS **All Seasons Charter Service** operates two boats for salmon or bottomfish. ~ Port of Edmonds; 425-743-9590.

KAYAKING & SMALL BOATING

If your nautical knowhow extends no further than a good row across a lake, then head for Lake Union, on the northern edge of Seattle's downtown center. On a bright summer day, the waters of Lake Union are dotted with kayaks, small wooden rowboats and sailboats.

SEATTLE AREA To rent a single or double kayak, call **Northwest Outdoor Center** to reserve ahead. Kayaking on Lake Union is very popular, and it's not unusual for all the center's 100-plus kayaks to be rented on a nice day. Classes and guided trips from one day to five days are available. ~ 2100 Westlake Avenue North; 206-281-9694, 800-683-0637; www.nwoc.com. At the **Center for Wooden Boats**, not only can you rent one of several different kinds of classic wooden rowboats, you can also learn a bit about their history. There are also several small sailboats for rent, but only experienced boaters can rent one. The center is a non-profit, hands-on museum that also offers sailing instruction and other heritage maritime skills such as knot-tying, navigation and boat building. ~ 1010 Valley Street; 206-382-2628, fax 206-382-2699; www.cwb.org. To rent a "kicker boat" for do-it-yourself sportfishing, you'll have to leave the lake.

A mere two hours of preservation work at the Center for Wooden Boats will earn you a "free" hour of sailing time.

VASHON ISLAND The owners of **Puget Sound Kayak Company** both rent and sell kayaks. They offer instruction as well, and in summer months lead kayak tours around the island's shores, a day-long odyssey that almost always includes heron, eagle, sea lion and seal sightings. The island's inner harbor is safe for novices; tricky tidal currents can make a foray out into the main channels more risky. Reservations are required for off-season rentals. ~ P.O. Box 2957, Vashon, WA 98070; 206-463-9257; www.pugetsoundkayak.com.

WINDSURFING

Serious windsurfers head south to Columbia Gorge—when they have the time for a four-hour drive. When they don't, **Lake Washington, Elliott Bay** and **Quartermaster Harbor** on Vashon Island are prime spots for windsurfing—there's almost always a breeze, often fairly stiff, and the air temperature is usually above 40°.

The water is another story: Puget Sound boarding requires a dry suit, and it's a good idea on Lake Washington as well in spring and fall. Prime put-ins are beach parks on the east side of Lake Washington, especially Houghton Beach Park in Kirkland, Luther Burbank Park on Mercer Island and Gene Coulon Beach Park in Renton. On Lake Sammamish, Lake Sammamish State Park at the south end of the lake, in Issaquah, is popular. On Elliott Bay, Alki Beach in West Seattle is best, although some boarders put in at Myrtle Edwards park in downtown Seattle.

The top rental and general information place in the Seattle area is **Urban Surf**, near the University of Washington on the shores of the Lake Washington Ship Canal. ~ 2100 North Northlake Way; 206-545-9463; www.urbansurf.com.

SWIMMING

Do people swim in Puget Sound? Sure—most of the time on a dare. The area's salt waters don't warm much past 50°, even in August. But a few sheltered bays get considerably warmer than that, and on a sunny summer day a dip can be stimulating. Any other place, any other time, requires caution, not to mention foolhardiness—hypothermia can arrive in less than two minutes if you're unprepared. Puget Sound's many freshwater lakes are another story; by midsummer they've usually warmed near 70° and attract hordes of bathers on sunny days.

Nude beaches? Try Hawaii.

FRESHWATER The best swimming beaches on Lake Washington are at Juanita Beach Park and Houghton Beach Park in Kirkland; Gene Coulon Park in Renton; and Seattle's Seward Park, Colman Park, Madrona Park, Madison Park and Matthews Beach Park. Lake Sammamish State Park is the place to go on Lake Sammamish in Issaquah; many smaller outlying lakes offer public beaches.

SALTWATER There aren't any truly warm bays in the immediate Seattle area; hardy souls hit the saltchuck at Alki Beach in West Seattle when the sun burns bright in August.

Better swimming is found west and south, at Ostrich Bay in Bremerton; Quartermaster Harbor on Vashon; and Penrose Point State Park on the Key Peninsula west of Tacoma. It's not for wimps; even Puget Sound natives are prone to ask if you really did go in that water. But if you truly want to immerse yourself in a visit to Puget Sound, immerse yourself.

SCUBA DIVING

Puget Sound's hundreds of miles of shoreline, scores of public beaches, extraordinary marine life and numerous underwater parks offer considerable opportunities for diving. But the Sound's average temperature of around 55° means wetsuits are de rigueur, and full scuba gear is the frequent choice of divers. Of the many exciting dive spots in the area, one standout is **Brackett's Landing Underwater Park** in Edmonds. Numerous dive shops with equipment rentals and lessons are located around major population centers. With 11 locations between them, **Underwater Sports Inc.** (800-252-7177; www.underwatersports.com) and **Lighthouse Diving Centers** (800-777-3483; www.lighthousediving.com) are convenient to most Seattle-area locations. They offer lessons and trips, and they rent and repair equipment.

NORTHERN NEIGHBORHOODS **Underwater Sports Inc.** has eight shops between Everett and Olympia. ~ Seattle: 10545 Aurora Avenue North; 206-362-3310, 800-252-7177. Edmonds: 264 Railroad Avenue; 425-771-6322. Everett: 205 East Casino Road #4; 425-355-3338; www.underwatersports.com.

Lighthouse Diving Centers offers outposts in Seattle and Lynnwood. ~ Seattle: 8215 Lake City Way Northeast; 206-524-1633. Lynnwood: 5421 196th Street Southwest #6; 425-771-2679.

SOUTHERN NEIGHBORHOODS A full-service scuba shop, **Northwest Sports Divers Inc.** rents any equipment you might need. They also offer scuba certification classes. Closed Sunday. ~ 8030 Northeast Bothell Way, Suite B, Kenmore; 425-487-0624; www.nwsportsdivers.com.

EASTSIDE NEIGHBORHOODS You'll find local branches of **Underwater Sports** in Bellevue and Kirkland. ~ Bellevue: 12003 Northeast 12th Street; 425-454-5168. Kirkland: 11743 124th Avenue Northeast; 425-821-7200; www.underwatersports.com.

In Bellevue, **Silent World** has classes, gear and rentals. There are beach dives on Sunday, as well as some one-day and two-day trips to the San Juans, Canada and tropical destinations. Closed Sunday. ~ 13600 Northeast 20th Street; 425-747-8842, 800-841-3483; www.silent-world.com.

INLINE SKATING

It takes about an hour to skate around Seattle's **Green Lake** on the paved multi-use trail. You can rent inline skates at **Gregg's Greenlake Cycle**. ~ 7007 Woodlawn Avenue Northeast; 206-523-1822; www.greggscycles.com.

JOGGING

In a generally cool climate, with pastoral back roads on the outskirts of much of Seattle and Tacoma, and an extensive network of public trails and greenbelts, runners will find innumerable routes. Some of the better-known trails, such as Seattle's Burke-Gilman and Green Lake, are often quite crowded, especially on weekends and after work in the summer.

Seattle's Washington Park Arboretum is an exceptionally beautiful mid-city forest enclave, landscaped with hundreds of native and exotic shrubs and trees. Trails are numerous; a typical loop would comprise a 5K.

GOLF

Except when the occasional snowstorm closes them down, golf courses in the area are open year-round.

NORTHERN NEIGHBORHOODS **Jackson Park Golf Club** is a public 18-hole course with a par 3. Though the course has a few hills, it isn't very challenging. ~ 1000 Northeast 135th Street, Seattle; 206-363-4747. Golf pro Freddy Couples grew up at the **Jefferson Park Golf Club**, which has 18 holes with an executive par 3. You can rent carts and clubs, and you can see the lake and the city at some points. ~ 4101 Beacon Avenue South, Seattle; 206-762-4513. **Kayak Point Golf Course**, about 30 miles north of Seattle, is hilly and overlooks the Olympic Mountains and Puget Sound. This public championship course with a double fairway is worth the drive. Amenities include an 18-hole putting course; rentals; and a restaurant in the same building. ~ 15711 Marine Drive Northeast, Stanwood; 360-652-9676.

EASTSIDE NEIGHBORHOODS The 18-hole **Bellevue Municipal Golf Course** is one of the most active courses in the state, probably because it's a good walking course with moderate hills. Cart rentals available. ~ 5500 140th Avenue Northeast; 425-452-7250.

TENNIS

Northwest precipitation practically turns tennis into an indoor sport. You'll have to call a few days in advance to reserve an indoor court at one of these public facilities.

SOUTHERN NEIGHBORHOODS It helps to mention that you're an out-of-town visitor when you call—at least six days in advance—to reserve one of the ten hardtop indoor courts at the **Amy Yee Tennis Center.** The center also has four public outdoor courts. Tennis pros are available for lessons by appointment. ~ 2000 Martin Luther King Jr. Way South; 206-684-4764.

EASTSIDE NEIGHBORHOODS The city of Bellevue operates the public courts at **Robinswood Tennis Center.** There are four indoor and four lighted outdoor courts; call six days in advance (start dialing at 8:30 a.m.). Lessons are available. Fee. ~ 2400 151st Place Southeast at Southeast 22nd Street; 425-452-7690.

RIDING STABLES

Take off on a guided ride to the top of a mountain east of Seattle or a slow meander through a wooden tract near Tacoma.

EASTSIDE NEIGHBORHOODS On a clear day, you can see more than 100 miles atop Tiger Mountain. **Tiger Mountain Outfitters** will get you there in a three-hour trail ride that will let you see Mt. Rainier 65 miles away in the distance and possibly black bear, deer and cougar within several yards. Call for reservations. ~ 24508 Southeast 133rd Street, Issaquah; 425-392-5090.

BIKING

Helpful information, including bicycle route maps, is available from several agencies. The Washington Department of Transportation operates the **Bicycle Hotline** to request a route map and informative brochure. ~ P.O. Box 47393, Olympia, WA 98504; 360-705-7277; www.wsdot.wa.gov/bike. **The Seattle Bicycling Guide Map** is available from the Seattle Transportation Department and

TOP TWO-WHEELING TOWN

It's no surprise to learn that Seattle has earned a nod from *Bicycling* magazine as one of the top bicycling cities in the country. Bicycle programs are administered by state, city and county transportation agencies, which has resulted in a network of bicycle lanes and trails throughout the region, many of them convenient for visitor recreational use.

can usually be found in bike stores and public libraries, or ordered online at www.seattle.gov/transportation/bikemaps.htm. ~ 600 4th Avenue, Room 708, Seattle, WA 98104; 206-684-7583. **King County** publishes a bicycling guide map; it's distributed free at bike shops countywide and at Metro Transit centers, or online at www.metrokc.gov/bike.htm. Or call the King County Bike Hotline at 206-263-4700. The **Cascade Bicycle Club** serves as an all-purpose club, for riders of all skill levels. The club operates a hotline, which provides general information about bicycling in the area and club-sponsored weekend rides. ~ 206-522-3222; www.cascade.org.

DOWNTOWN SEATTLE In West Seattle, the **Alki Bike Route** (6 miles) offers miles of shoreline pedaling—half on separated bike paths—from Seacrest Park to Lincoln Park. Besides changing views of the city and Puget Sound, you should have great views of the Olympic Peninsula mountains.

OUTLYING AREAS The three-mile loop around **Green Lake** is the most leisurely and rich in recreational detours. Although the central city is fairly hilly, especially if you're biking in an east–west direction, there are trails within Seattle that run near the water and on lower and flatter terrain that are ideal for recreational bicyclists. The most famous, of course, is the multi-use **Burke-Gilman Trail**, popular with bikers, walkers and joggers. It's flat, paved and, following an old railroad right of way, it extends from Gas Works Park on Lake Union, through the university campus, past lovely neighborhoods next to Lake Washington and on to Kenmore. This well-used corridor offers both urban and wooded stretches, highlighting why the Emerald City is one of the nation's top cycling cities. In Kenmore, it links up with the **Sammamish River Trail**, which winds through Woodinville (and its wineries) and on to suburban Redmond. It's a lovely city-to-farmlands tour.

NORTHERN NEIGHBORHOODS Pedal past Puget Sound parks, beaches and the bustling Edmonds port, home of the largest charter fleet on Puget Sound, on the three-mile **Edmonds Waterfront Trail** running between Edmonds Underwater Park and Deer Park Reserve.

Bike Rentals For bike rentals, repairs, new bikes and accessories in Seattle, try **Gregg's Greenlake Cycle.** ~ 7007 Woodlawn Avenue Northeast; 206-523-1822; www.greggscycles.com. **The Bicycle Center of Seattle**, near the Burke-Gilman Trail, has mountain bikes, hybrids and tandems. ~ 4529 Sand Point Way Northeast; 206-523-8300; www.bicyclecenterseattle.com. The place to buy and repair a bike on Alki Beach is the **Alki Bike & Board.** ~ 2606 California Avenue Southwest, Seattle; 206-938-3322; www.alkibikeandboard.com.

HIKING

Nearly every park mentioned in the "Beaches & Parks" sections of this chapter offers at least a few miles of hiking trail through forest or along a stream or beach. Some are outstanding, such as Nisqually National Wildlife Refuge, Green River Gorge, Point Defiance Park in Tacoma and Discovery Park in Seattle. All distances listed are one way unless otherwise noted.

DOWNTOWN SEATTLE For short strolls in downtown Seattle, try **Freeway Park** and the grounds of the adjoining Washington State Convention Center (.5 mile) and **Myrtle Edwards and Elliott Bay parks** (1.25 miles) at the north end of the downtown waterfront. Just across Elliott Bay, West Seattle offers about four miles of public shoreline to walk around Duwamish Head and Alki Point.

NORTHERN NEIGHBORHOODS For a longer walk, the **Burke-Gilman Trail** (12 miles) extends from Gas Works Park in Seattle to Logboom Park in Kenmore and on to Redmond.

The **Shell Creek Nature Trail** (.5 mile), in Edmonds' Yost Park at 96th Avenue West and Bowdoin Way, is an easy walk along a stream. Contact Edmonds Parks and Recreation for a guide to the area. ~ Edmonds Parks Department: 700 Main Street; 425-771-0227.

SOUTHERN NEIGHBORHOODS The trail along **Big Soos Creek** (4.5 miles), now protected in two parks, is an inviting ramble on a blacktop path next to one of the few wetland streams still in public ownership hereabouts. The trail winds from Kent-Kangley Road to Gary Grant Park. In Kent, south of Seattle, follow signs off Route 516 (Kent-Kangley Road) at 150th Avenue Southeast.

EASTSIDE NEIGHBORHOODS Three foothills peaks nicknamed the "Issaquah Alps" (King County's Cougar Mountain

AUTHOR FAVORITE

Make time to take a detour to **Cougar Mountain Regional Wildland Park.** This little-known and somewhat neglected 4000-acre park offers miles of hiking and horseback riding trails through old-growth fir, spruce and cedar forests. The rest of its charms include a mishmash of offerings such as 19th-century coal mine shafts, waterfalls, caves and even a Nike missile site—a remnant of the Cold War. As its name suggests, this park teems with wildlife, and bobcats, coyote, black-tailed deer, bald eagles and Pileated woodpeckers are frequently spotted in the more remote areas. ~ Off Route 90, about 35 miles east of Seattle; 206-296-4232.

Regional Wildland Park, Squak Mountain State Park and Tiger Mountain State Forest) south of Issaquah (about 15 miles east of Seattle) include miles and miles of trail and road open to hikers year-round. **Cougar Mountain Regional Wildland Park** (206-296-4145) is the best bet for visitors with resident deer, porcupines, bobcats, coyotes, black bears and four square miles of untouched land with trails. Call for trail maps. Another good resource is the **Issaquah Alps Trails Club** (www.issaquahalps.org), which publishes several hiking guidebooks and offers excursions, group hikes and general hiking information. One representative hike is the **West Tiger 3, 2, 1 Trail** (8–10 miles), which meanders to an elevation of 3000 feet at the summit of West Tiger 3 for stunning aerial views. Leave Route 90 at the High Point exit (the first exit east of Issaquah) and you will see the small parking lot where the trailhead is located.

Transportation

CAR

Seattle lies along Puget Sound east of the Olympic Peninsula in the state of Washington. **Route 5** enters Seattle from Olympia and Tacoma to the south and from Everett from the north. **Route 90** from Eastern Washington goes near Snoqualmie and through Bellevue on its way into Seattle. **Route 405** serves the Eastside suburban communities of Bellevue, Kirkland and Redmond. **Route 169** leads from Route 405 southeast of Renton to Maple Valley, Black Diamond and Enumclaw.

AIR

About 20 miles south of downtown Seattle is **Seattle-Tacoma International Airport**, also called Sea-Tac, which is served by Aeromexico, Air Canada, Alaska Airlines, America West Airlines, American Airlines, Asiana Airlines, ATA, British Airways, Continental Airlines, Delta Air Lines, EVA Air, Frontier Airlines, Hawaiian Airlines, Horizon Air, JetBlue Airways, Northwest Airlines, Scandinavian Airlines, Southwest Airlines, Sun Country Airlines, United Airlines, US Airways and several smaller charter airlines. For general information, call 206-431-4444. There's a visitors information center on the baggage level of Sea-Tac International Airport (206-433-5218; www.portseattle.org/seatac).

FERRY

The **Washington State Ferry System** serves Seattle, Port Townsend, Tacoma, Southworth, Vashon Island, Bainbridge Island, Bremerton, Kingston, Edmonds, Mukilteo, Clinton, the San Juan Islands and Sidney, B.C. All are car ferries. ~ 206-464-6400; www.wsdot.wa.gov/ferries.

The **Victoria Clipper** passenger catamaran service operates daily trips (a two-and-a-half-hour trip) between Seattle and Victoria, B.C. ~ 206-448-5000, 800-888-2535; www.clippervacations.com.

BUS

Greyhound Bus Lines serves Seattle. The terminal is at 811 Stewart Street. ~ 800-231-2222; www.greyhound.com. **Gray Line of Seattle** provides inexpensive bus service from the airport to hotels and the downtown area. ~ 206-624-5077, 800-426-7532; www.graylineofseattle.com.

TRAIN

Rail service in and out of Seattle is provided by **Amtrak** on the "Empire Builder," "Coast Starlight" and "Amtrak Cascades." Call for more information on connections from around the country. ~ 800-872-7245; www.amtrak.com.

CAR RENTALS

Most major car-rental businesses have offices at Seattle-Tacoma International Airport. Rental agencies include **Avis Rent A Car** (800-331-1212), **Budget Rent A Car** (800-527-0700), **Dollar Rent A Car** (800-800-4000), **Hertz Rent A Car** (800-654-3131) and **Thrifty Car Rental** (800-367-2277).

PUBLIC TRANSIT

Bus transportation provided by **Metro Transit** is free in downtown Seattle. Metro Transit provides service throughout the Seattle-King County area. ~ 206-553-3000, 800-542-7876; www.transit.metrokc.gov.

Deemed transportation for the future, the **Monorail** was built for the 1962 World's Fair. It runs between downtown and the Seattle Center every ten minutes. ~ 206-905-2600; www.seattlemonorail.com.

The downtown hub for both the monorail and the bus system is at Westlake Center, on Pine Street between 4th and 5th Avenues. The Monorail arrives on an elevated platform above the street-level mall, while buses load in an underground terminal. The buses are uniquely designed so they can switch from diesel to electric power when they enter the subterranean tunnels.

Waterfront Streetcar trolleys run from Seattle's historic Chinatown to Pier 70. ~ 206-553-3000; www.transit.metrokc.gov.

TAXIS

In the greater Seattle area are **Farwest Taxi** (206-622-1717), **North End Taxi** (206-363-3333) and **Yellow and Redtop Cab** (206-622-6500).

FIVE

Southern Puget Sound

First-time visitors to southern Puget Sound may find that it's the constantly changing geography that's the region's most memorable and striking feature. On a map, Southern Puget Sound looks like a fistful of bony fingers clawing at the earth. This maze of inlets, peninsulas and islands presents plentiful saltwater access and invites days of poking around.

What nature created here, partly by the grinding and gouging of massive lowland glaciers, is a complex mosaic. From the air, arriving visitors see a green-blue tapestry of meandering river valleys weaving between forested ridges, the rolling uplands dotted by lakes giving way to Cascade foothills and distant volcanoes, the intricate maze-way of Southern Puget Sound's island-studded inland sea.

From on high it seems almost pristine, but a closer look reveals a sobering overlay of manmade changes. Even as Seattle's downtown becomes "Manhattanized," the region is being "Los Angelesized" with the birth of a freeway commuter culture stretching from Olympia on the south to Everett on the north and beyond Issaquah on the east. Some commuters arrive by ferry from Bainbridge Island to the west. Farmlands and wetlands, forests and meadows, are giving way to often poorly planned, hastily built housing tracts, roads and shopping centers.

For the traveler, such rapid growth means more traffic and longer lines for the ferry; more-crowded campgrounds, parks and public beaches; busier bikeways and foot trails; more folks fishing and boating and clam-digging. Downtown parking can be hard to find and expensive. But don't despair. South of the heart of Seattle you'll still find a wealth of parks and wilderness, waterways and beaches. With an ample array of outdoor activities, southern Puget Sound serves as Seattle's back door to the wilderness.

To the southwest of Seattle, the Tacoma/Olympia region is rich in history, parks, waterfalls and cultural landmarks. Tacoma features numerous architectural gems; nearby villages like Gig Harbor are ideal for daytrippers. One of the nation's prettier capital cities (and here you may have thought Seattle was the capital of Washington!), Olympia is convenient to the wildlife refuges of southern Puget Sound, as well as to American Indian monuments and petroglyphs.

Venture west of Seattle across Puget Sound and you'll find some rare treasures such as a company town operating in the time-honored manner, a fascinating Indian cultural show, a marine-science center and inns that look like they were created for a James Herriott book. From the islands of Puget Sound west to Hood Canal, this is also a region rich in parks and natural areas. You'll also want to tour the Kitsap Peninsula, Bremerton's Naval Heritage and the parks of Southern Puget Sound.

Tacoma and Olympia

Despite a lingering mill-town reputation, Tacoma, the city on Commencement Bay, has experienced a lively rejuvenation in recent years and offers visitors some first-rate attractions. Charles Wright, president of the Great Northern Railroad, chose it as the western terminus of his railroad, and he wanted more than a mill town at the end of his line. Some of the best architects of the day were commissioned to build hotels, theaters, schools and office buildings.

SIGHTS

Today, **Tacoma** is the third largest city in the state with a population of just under 200,000. The city jealously protects its treasure trove of turn-of-the-20th-century architecture in a pair of historic districts overlooking the bay on both sides of Division Avenue. The 1893 **Old City Hall** at South 7th and Commerce streets was modeled after Renaissance Italian hill castles. The 1889 **Bostwick Hotel** at South 9th Street and Broadway is a classic triangular Victorian "flatiron."

The **Pantages Theater**, an exquisitely restored 1918 masterpiece of the vaudeville circuit, is the centerpiece of Tacoma's thriving theater district. A classic of the vaudeville circuit (W. C. Fields, Mae West, Will Rogers and Houdini all performed here), this theater offers dance, music and theater. The Pantages is worth visiting simply to gawk at its glittering grandeur. It's joined in the Broadway Center for the Performing Arts by the **Rialto Theater**, another restored 1918 belle, and the **Theatre on the Square**, devoted to its resident drama company, Tacoma Actors Guild. ~ Broadway Center, 901 Broadway, Tacoma; tickets, 253-591-5894; tours and general information, 253-591-5890, fax 253-591-2013; www.broadwaycenter.org.

The new and improved **Tacoma Art Museum** (now doubled in size) is located in the new Museum District downtown. The building is artfully designed to take advantage of views of nearby Mount Rainier and includes a series of galleries showcasing the museum's premier collection of American, Asian and European art, as well as traveling exhibitions that wrap around an open-air interior stone garden. The work displayed is of the highest caliber and includes recently a photo exhibit about famed Mexican artist Frida Kahlo, works on paper and ceramics by

Picasso, and landscape sculptures by innovative Scottish environmental artist Andy Goldsworthy. The permanent collection focuses on the work of Tacoma's most famous contemporary artist, Dale Chihuly. Closed Monday Labor Day through Memorial Day. Admission. ~ 1701 Pacific Avenue, Tacoma; 253-272-4258, fax 253-627-1898; www.tacomaartmuseum.org, e-mail info@tacomaartmuseum.org.

History adds more depth to Tacoma's appeal at the **Union Station/Washington State History Museum** complex. The side-by-side buildings not only are aesthetically appealing—the restored copper-domed Union Station is now the federal courthouse, the history museum is a sweeping, arched modern counterpart—they also offer cultural wealth inside. **Union Station**'s 70-foot diameter rotunda dome rises 60 feet above ground level; the Beaux Arts neoclassical–style building dates from 1911. The rotunda holds one of the world's finest exhibits of glass art made entirely by Tacoma native Chihuly, the renowned founder of the Pilchuck School of blown-glass art. Closed Saturday and Sunday. ~ 1717 Pacific Avenue, Tacoma; 253-572-9310, www.chihuly.com/installa tions/unionstation.

The **Washington State History Museum** located next door offers a comprehensive view of the state's human cultures, from the original inhabitants dependent on salmon to the logging, fishing and farming that first brought settlers to the Northwest. Interactive exhibits allow visitors to sit in the driver's seat of a covered wagon, take a stab at separating wheat from chaff and experience a coal mine cave-in. Closed Monday from Memorial Day through Labor Day. Admission. ~ 1911 Pacific Avenue, Tacoma; 253-272-9747, 888-238-4373, fax 253-272-9518; www.wshs.org.

The **Chihuly Bridge of Glass**, a tunnel of light and color created by the renowned Tacoma glass artist Dale Chihuly, connects the History Museum to the **Museum of Glass**. The museum's most distinctive architectural feature is its tilted, 90-foot-high, steel-clad, inverted cone, which houses a working glass studio, which has become an identifiable cultural landmark on the Tacoma skyline. Dedicated to showcasing glass art from around the world, the museum also features contemporary painting, sculpture, and mixed media pieces. Visitors can stroll along the waterfront or ascend the steps to the rooftop plaza to enjoy views of downtown Tacoma and Mount Rainier in the distance. Closed Monday and Tuesday from Labor Day to Memorial Day. Admission. ~ 1801 Dock Street, Tacoma; 253-284-4750, 866-468-7386, fax 253-396-1769; www.museumofglass.org, e-mail info@museumofglass.org.

The **Asia Pacific Cultural Center** is a facility designed to promote 47 cultures—from Japan and China to Polynesia, and Tibet to New Zealand. Housed in the historic former home of the

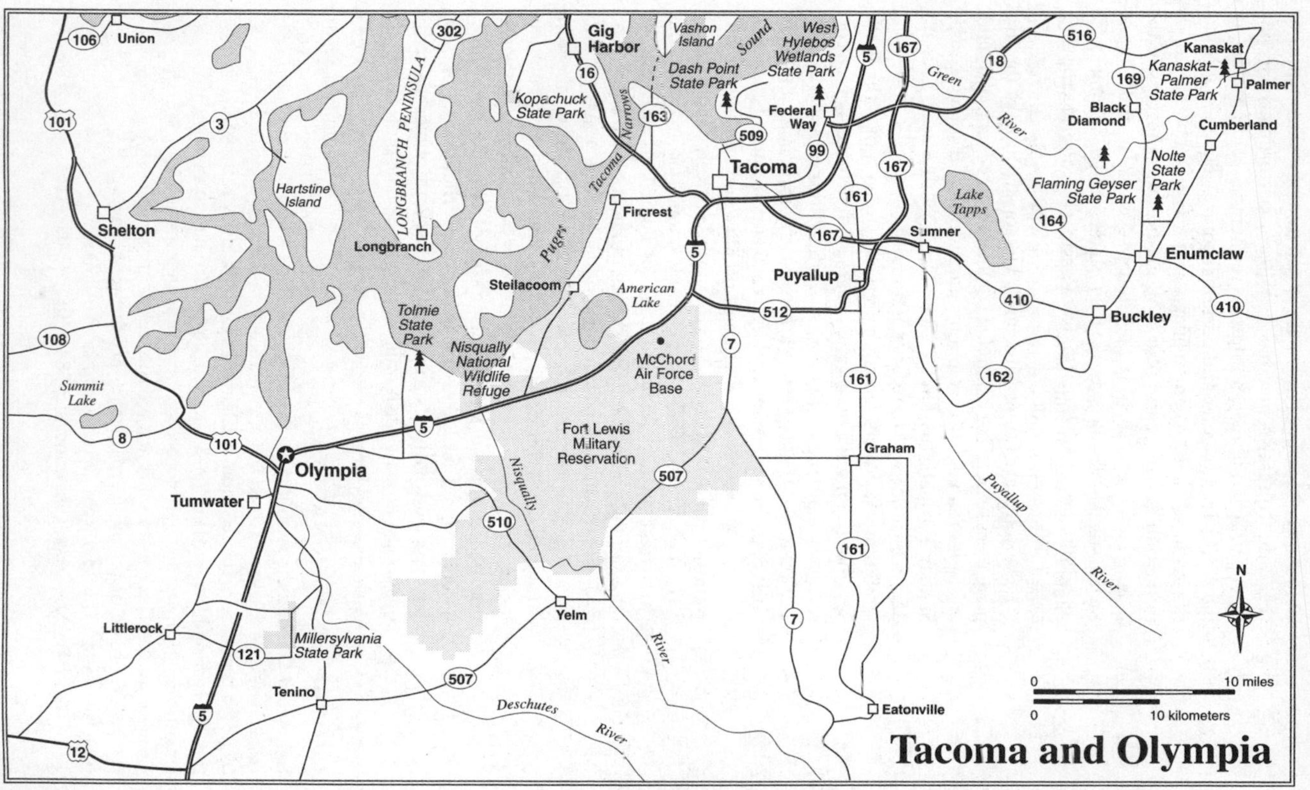
Tacoma and Olympia
0 10 miles
0 10 kilometers
N
Kanaskat
Palmer
Kanaskat–Palmer State Park
Cumberland
Enumclaw
Nolte State Park
Black Diamond
Flaming Geyser State Park
Buckley
Green River
Lake Tapps
Sumner
Puyallup River
Graham
Eatonville
West Hylebos Wetlands State Park
Federal Way
Tacoma
Puyallup
Sound
Vashon Island
Dash Point State Park
Fircrest
American Lake
McChord Air Force Base
Gig Harbor
Tacoma Narrows
Kopachuck State Park
Puget
Steilacoom
Fort Lewis Military Reservation
Nisqually River
Yelm
Deschutes River
Nisqually National Wildlife Refuge
Tolmie State Park
LONGBRANCH PENINSULA
Longbranch
Hartstine Island
Olympia
Tumwater
Millersylvania State Park
Tenino
Littlerock
Union
Shelton
Summit Lake
516
169
164
410
18
162
167
5
161
99
512
509
7
163
507
16
302
510
3
101
121
106
8
108
12

Tacoma Art Museum (which expanded into new digs that same year), the cultural center has a 250-seat performance/meeting space, an Asian library, an upscale restaurant, and an office of the World Trade Center and Port of Tacoma. Classes on *ikebana* (flower arranging), Asian languages and tea ceremonies are open to the public. The center also sponsors traditional events in the Asian community, such as the Chinese New Year and Dragon Boat Festival. ~ 934 Broadway Street, Suites 5 and 6, Tacoma; 253-383-3900, fax 253-722-5700; www.asiapacificculturalcenter.org, e-mail info@apccusa.org.

The **Job Carr Cabin Museum** is a reconstruction of the first permanent settlers' log cabin that commemorates Tacoma's founding with original artifacts, photos and historical displays. Closed Sunday through Tuesday. ~ 2350 North 30th Street, Tacoma; 253-627-5405; www.jobcarrmuseum.org.

Without a doubt, Tacoma's prettiest garden spot is the **W. W. Seymour Botanical Conservatory**, a graceful Victorian domed conservatory constructed at the turn of the 20th century with over 12,000 panes of glass. Inside are exotic tropical plants, including birds of paradise, ornamental figs, cacti and bromeliads; seasonal displays of flowers; a collection of orchids; and a fish pond with waterfall. Closed Monday. ~ 316 South G Street, Tacoma; 253-591-5330, fax 253-627-2192; e-mail seymour@tacomaparks.com.

A treat for both kids and adults is **Point Defiance Park**, set on a sloping peninsula above the south Puget Sound shore. This 700-acre urban park has an outstanding zoo and aquarium with a Pacific Rim theme. You can watch the fish from above or through underwater viewing windows. You'll also see an outdoor logging museum with steam trains; Fort Nisqually, a reconstruction of the original 1850 Hudson's Bay Company post (closed Monday and Tuesday except in summer); rhododendron, rose, Japanese and native Northwest gardens; and numerous scenic overlooks. A good beach walk is at the base of the bluff edging the

COMMUNING WITH NATURE

Lakewold Gardens, located just south of Tacoma, offers a horticultural respite you'd be hard-pressed to find anywhere else in the area. Designed by noted landscape architect Thomas Church, Lakewold's lovely paths wind through rose and fern gardens. You'll also have an opportunity to saunter amidst the Northwest's largest collections of rhododendrons and Japanese maples. Docent-led tours are available during spring and summer. Closed Monday and Tuesday from April to September, and Monday through Thursday from October to March. Admission. ~ 12317 Gravelly Lake Drive, Lakewood; 253-584-4106, 888-858-4106.

park, heading west from Owen Beach. Since the water is swift here, it's best to walk at low tide. The **Boathouse Marina** offers boat rentals and fishing (253-591-5325). ~ 5912 North Waterfront Drive, off Pearl Street, Tacoma; 253-305-1000.

Halfway between Point Defiance and downtown, tucked along Foss Waterway, **Thea's Park** is a little-known oasis in the city. Not only is this idyllic little enclave rarely crowded, it is exceptionally well landscaped, with a walking path, kayaking access, picnic area and breathtaking views of Mt. Rainier and Commencement Bay. ~ On South 4th Street and Dock Street, Tacoma; 253-305-1000, fax 253-305-1098; e-mail lindsayf@tacomaparks.com.

A half hour east of Tacoma, in the **Puyallup Valley**, a series of river-bottom flower farms blaze with daffodil and tulip blooms. One of the largest growers is **Van Lierop Bulb Farm**, a family-operated farm since 1934. Van Lierop welcomes visitors to its shop and gardens during the height of the bloom season in March and April. Closed June through January. ~ 13407 80th Street East, off Pioneer Avenue East, from Route 512, Puyallup; 253-848-7272, fax 253-848-9142.

Gig Harbor, situated across the Tacoma Narrows off Route 16, is a classic Puget Sound small town. The community that arose around the harbor was founded as a fishing village by Croatians and Austrians. Today you're more likely to see every sort of pleasure craft here; it's one of the best boat-watching locales on Puget Sound. The tight harbor entrance funnels boats single-file past dockside taverns and cafés where you can watch the nautical parade. Or, rent a boat from Gig Harbor Rent-A-Boat and join the flotilla. ~ 8829 North Harborview Drive; 253-858-7341; www.gigharborrentaboat.com, e-mail gigharborrentaboat@comcast.net.

Steilacoom about five miles south of Tacoma is a quiet counterpoint to Gig Harbor's bustle. Founded by Yankee sea captains in the 1850s, it exudes a museum-like peacefulness and preserves a New England look among its fine collection of clapboard houses. Get a self-guiding brochure at **Steilacoom Historical Museum**. Open Friday through Sunday in February, November and December; open Friday through Sunday from April through October. Closed Monday and the month of January. ~ 1801 Ranier Street, Steilacoom; 253-584-4133; www.steilacoomhistorical.org. ◄ HIDDEN

Don't miss the **Pioneer Orchard**; it surrounds the **Nathaniel Orr Home.** Closed Monday through Thursday. ~ 1811 Rainier Avenue. At the 1895 **Bair Drug and Hardware Store**, you can order an old-fashioned float from the 1906 soda fountain. ~ 1617 Lafayette Street near Wilkes Street, Steilacoom; 253-588-9668, fax 253-588-0737; www.thebairrestaurant.com.

Fort Lewis, astride Route 5 south of Tacoma, is one of the most important Army posts in the United States, having gained strength during the Pentagon consolidation. Nearby **McChord Air Force Base** has grown in stature as well. Both posts offer museums open to the public. The **McChord Air Museum** has historic aircraft, flight simulators for visitor use, and other artifacts covering the base's history from World War II on. Closed Saturday through Tuesday. ~ On the base near the main entrance, Route 5, Exit 125; 253-982-2485, fax 253-982-9560; www.mcchordairmuseum.org. The **Fort Lewis Military Museum** covers the history of the post from 1917 to the present. Pick up a visitor's pass at the main gate. Open Wednesday through Sunday afternoon. ~ Building 4320, on Post, right off Route 5, Exit 120; 253-967-7206, fax 253-966-3029; www.lewis.army.mil.

At the southern tip of Puget Sound, **Olympia**'s state capitol dome rises boldly as you approach on Route 5, a tempting landmark for travelers and an easy detour from the busy freeway. But this community of some 39,000 offers visitors more to peruse than government buildings and monuments. Nevertheless, the capitol campus may be the best place to begin your explorations.

You can take a daily guided tour seven days a week through the marbled halls of the Romanesque **Legislative Building** and see other buildings on the grounds—**Temple of Justice** and **Executive Mansion.**

The nearby **State Capitol Museum** includes a fine collection of Northwest Coast Indian artifacts. Closed Sunday through Tuesday. Admission. ~ 211 Southwest 21st Avenue, Olympia; 360-753-2580, fax 360-586-8322; www.wshs.org/wscm.

Downtown, the handsomely restored **Old Capitol**, at 7th Avenue and Washington Street across from stately Sylvester Park, will catch your eye with its fanciful architecture. But most of downtown is a potpourri of disparate attractions—the **Washington Center for the Performing Arts** at 512 Washington Street Southeast, galleries, the **Capitol Theater** at 5th Avenue and Washington Street with its old films and local theater, and a bit of Bohemia along 4th Avenue West.

HIDDEN ►

Percival Landing is an inviting, harborside park with observation tower, kiosks with historical displays, picnic tables, cafés and boardwalks next to acres of pleasure craft. ~ At the foot of State Avenue at Water Street, Olympia.

For a longer walk, head south on Water Street, cross 4th and 5th avenues, then turn west and follow the sidewalk next to the Deschutes Parkway (or get in your car and drive) around the park-dotted shores of manmade **Capitol Lake**, which is two and a half miles from the town of Tumwater.

Tumwater marks the true end of Puget Sound. Before Capitol Lake was created, the sound was navigable all the way to the Deschutes River. **Tumwater Historical Park**, at the meeting of river and lake, is rich in both history and recreation. One of two pioneer houses here was built in 1860 by Nathaniel Crosby III (Bing Crosby's grandfather). Down by the river you can fish, have a picnic, explore fitness and hiking trails, watch birds in reedy marshes and see more historical exhibits. Across the river, a handsome, six-story, brick brew house built in 1906 marks an early enterprise that lives on in a 1933 brewery a few hundred yards south. ~ 777 Simmons Avenue, Tumwater; 360-754-4160, fax 360-754-4166.

While in Tumwater, you can also visit the **Washington State Library**, which was moved here from Olympia in 2001, following the Nisqually earthquake. Opened in 1853, the library is a major archive of Washington history. Closed weekends. ~ Point Plaza East, 6880 Capitol Boulevard, near the Olympia Airport in Tumwater; 360-704-5200; www.statelib.wa.gov, e-mail askalibrarian@secstate.wa.gov.

Follow Deschutes Parkway south to **Tumwater Falls Park** (not to be confused with Tumwater Historical Park), a small park that's a nice spot for a picnic lunch and whose main attraction is the namesake "falls," twisting and churning through a rocky defile. Feel the throb of water reverberating through streamside footpaths. Listen to its sound, which the Indians called "Tumtum." You'll find plenty of history in the headquarters exhibit, including an American Indian petroglyph and a monument recounting the travails of the first permanent settlement north of the Columbia River here in 1845. ~ Deschutes Way and C Street, Tumwater; phone/fax 360-943-2550; e-mail otf@olytwnfoundation.org.

Ten miles south of Olympia are **Mima Mounds**, an unusual group of several hundred hillocks spread across 450 acres. Scientists think they could have been created by glacial deposits or, believe it or not, busy gophers. There is a self-guided interpretive trail offering a close look at this geologic oddity, as well as several miles of hiking trails. Wildflowers paint the mounds yellow, pink

BLACK DIAMOND—COAL AND BREAD

Black Diamond (about 35 miles southeast of Seattle on Route 169) is an old coal-mining town with the odds and ends of its mining, logging and railroading history on display at the **Black Diamond Historical Society Museum**. This intriguing museum is housed in an 1880 railroad depot. Open Thursday, Saturday and Sunday afternoons or by appointment. ~ Baker Street and Railroad Avenue; 360-886-2142. But the real reason most folks stop here—on their way to Mt. Rainier, the Green River Gorge or winter ski slopes—is the famous **Black Diamond Bakery**. At last count, the bakery and its wood-fired ovens produced some 30 varieties of bread. ~ 32805 Railroad Avenue; 360-886-2741.

and blue from April through June. ~ Wadell Creek Road, Littlerock; 360-902-1004, fax 360-902-1775; www.dnr.wa.gov/nap.

Howl with the wolves at **Wolf Haven International** southeast of Olympia. The 80-acre refuge shelters about 42 gray wolves. Guides give tours daily from April through October and on weekends in other months. On summer weekends, visitors gather for singing, storytelling and joining in the wolves' howls. Closed Tuesday and the month of February. Admission. ~ 3111 Offut Lake Road, Tenino; 360-264-4695, fax 360-264-4639; www.wolfhaven.org, e-mail info@wolfhaven.org.

LODGING

Many of Tacoma's historic residences have been transformed into small inns and B&Bs. **The Villa** is a 1925 Italianate mansion also on the National Historic Register. Six sizable guest rooms have jacuzzis or soaking tubs, fireplaces and views. The verandas, patio with fountain, and landscaped gardens add to the Mediterranean allure. Guests will also enjoy a hot tub, complimentary wine and other beverages and snacks. ~ 705 North 5th Street, Tacoma; 253-572-1157, 888-572-1157; www.villabb.com, e-mail innkeeper@villabb.com. DELUXE TO ULTRA-DELUXE.

Chocolates left on my pillow is but one of the reasons I have sweet dreams when I stay at **Chinaberry Hill**. This luxurious 1889 Victorian bed and breakfast offers two spacious romance suites with bay windows, double jacuzzis, private baths with showers and harbor views or a fireplace, as well as a guestroom overlooking the side garden. The adjacent two-story carriage house, with its cabin atmosphere, is ideal for families featuring a queen-sized curved iron canopy bed, a queen sofa sleeper and a

AUTHOR FAVORITE

Just 15 minutes from downtown Tacoma brings you to the breathtaking **Thornewood Castle Inn and Gardens**. Built in 1908 by a local eccentric for his lady love, the building is actually a 400-year-old Elizabethan manor that was painstakingly disassembled and rebuilt on its present four-acre site. Everything in this Tudor Gothic is original, from the 500-year-old staircase to the crystal windows and stained-glass accents dating from the early 13th–18th centuries to the wooden dowels that hold the castle doors together. All eight rooms and suites are appointed with cherrywood Victorian antiques; most have private decks, fireplaces and gleaming hardwood floors. Amenities include a sunken English garden, a hot tub, and a private dock and beach. A full gourmet breakfast is served. No children under 12 allowed. Reservations required. ~ 8601 North Thorne Lake Southwest, Lakewood; 253-584-4393, fax 253-584-4497; www.thornewoodcastle.com, e-mail info@thornewoodcastle.com. ULTRA-DELUXE.

jacuzzi alcove. Appointed with period antiques and surrounded by gardens, the inn is an inviting retreat. ~ 302 Tacoma Avenue North, Tacoma; 253-272-1282, fax 253-272-1335; www.chinaberryhill.com, e-mail chinaberry@wa.net. DELUXE TO ULTRA-DELUXE.

The **Sheraton Tacoma Hotel** is an elegant hotel next to the Tacoma Convention Center. The 319 rooms have a contemporary decor and most have views of Mt. Rainier or Commencement Bay. The concierge levels (24th and 25th floors) serve complimentary continental breakfast. ~ 1320 Broadway Plaza, Tacoma; 253-572-3200, 800-325-3535, fax 253-591-4105; www.sheratontacoma.com. ULTRA-DELUXE.

No Cabbages Bed and Breakfast is a lovely home with a view of the water and access to the beach. It has three guest rooms with both private and shared bathrooms, and a suite with its own private entrance. The house is laden with eclectic, primitive folk art and interesting conversation. The grounds feature deer, fox, woodpeckers and a prayer labyrinth for introspection and walking meditation. The innkeeper serves an outstanding breakfast. ~ 10319 Sunrise Beach Drive Northwest, Gig Harbor; 253-858-7797; www.nocabbages.com, e-mail info@nocabbages.com. DELUXE.

High above Capitol Lake, on a grassy bluff with a view of the manmade lake and capitol dome, is the **Red Lion Hotel Olympia.** Popular with business and government travelers, it has 190 commodious rooms with practical furnishings, a lounge, a restaurant overlooking the lawns and water, and an outdoor swimming pool and jacuzzi. Waterside rooms have the best views and are the quietest. ~ 2300 Evergreen Park Drive, Olympia; 360-943-4000, fax 360-357-6604; www.redlion.com. DELUXE.

The **Lighthouse Bungalow** is a beautifully restored 1920s-era beachfront property with waterfront access to Budd Inlet on Puget Sound. The four-bedroom, four-bath upstairs unit sleeps eight comfortably and is furnished with antiques, hardwood floors, a full kitchen, two fireplaces, and views of the Sound and Olympic Mountains from its deck. The cozy two-bedroom, lower-level unit includes a sitting room and sleeps up to four. The owners lend bicycles, kayaks and a canoe. ~ 1215 East Bay Drive, Olympia; 360-754-0389, fax 360-754-7499; www.lighthousebungalow.com, e-mail info@lighthousebungalow.com. DELUXE TO ULTRA-DELUXE.

Eight blocks from the Capitol, the **Governor Hotel** is the latest version of a vintage downtown hotel. Its 119 rooms—some with views of the lake, harbor and Capitol building—are spread over eight floors. The hotel has above-standard furnishings, though most rooms are small, and a seasonal pool, indoor jacuzzi, exercise room and sauna. A number of packages and discounts are available. ~ 621 South Capitol Way, Olympia; 360-352-7700, 877-352-7701, fax 360-943-9349; www.olywagov.com, e-mail guestservices@olywagov.com. MODERATE.

The three-story **Tumwater Guest House & Suites** offers a bit more character than one might expect from a chain hotel. It's set amidst evergreens, for one, and guests are greeted by a two-story waterfall in the lobby. The 59 mini-suites are equipped with a fridge and microwave; some have counter space and a small sink. For longer stays or larger groups, the spa suite has a kitchenette, and the two-room children's suites are outfitted with bunk beds. An indoor pool and spa and exercise room round out the amenities. ~ 1600 74th Avenue Southwest, Tumwater; 360-943-5040, 800-214-8378, fax 360-943-5066; www.guesthouseintl.com. MODERATE TO ULTRA-DELUXE.

DINING

Named for the Lakota Sioux word for bison, **Tatanka Takeout** near Tacoma (try saying that fast) showcases ultra-lean, grass-fed bison. Here, it turns up in energy-boosting burgers, wraps, taco and burrito fillings, barbecue, stir fries and nachos. Many veggie options are available as well as free-range chicken. Try the tasty nonfat yogurt shakes. Yum! ~ 4915 North Pearl Street, Ruston (near Vashon Ferry); 253-752-8778. BUDGET.

Sophistication and elegance describe the ambience at **Altezzo** in the Sheraton Tacoma Hotel. There are superb views of Commencement Bay and Mt. Rainier from this gourmet Italian restaurant, located several stories above the city. The menu changes daily; entrées include grilled pork loin chop stuffed with fontina cheese and artichoke hearts and cioppino, a hearty tomato-based stew of Dungeness crab, prawns, calamari, clams and other fresh seafood. Reservations recommended. Dinner only. Closed during summer holidays. ~ 1320 Broadway Plaza, Tacoma; 253-591-4155, fax 253-591-4105. MODERATE TO DELUXE.

One of those time-warp kind of restaurants that has had the same waitresses and clientele for decades, **Harbor Lights** is where locals go for certified Angus beef and chops, huge buckets of steamed clams, Dungeness crab, grilled salmon and other unpretentious seafood dishes. ~ 2761 Ruston Way, Tacoma; 253-752-8600, fax 253-752-4679. MODERATE TO DELUXE.

If you've a hankering for barbecued ribs, fried chicken or catfish, try **Southern Kitchen**. This is no antebellum mansion, just a plain, well-lighted café with good food. Just as good as the entrées are the greens, grits, yams, fried okra, biscuits, homemade strawberry lemonade and melt-in-your-mouth corncakes served up alongside. The cooks are Southern stock themselves, so you can count on this fare being authentic. Breakfast is served all day. ~ 1716 6th Avenue, Tacoma; 253-627-4282. MODERATE.

For pizza and beer, do as the locals do and make a beeline for **Katie Downs Waterfront Restaurant.** The pies at this casual tavern have been deemed "Best Pizza in Western Washington" by its community several years in a row. Also on the menu are staples such as burgers, salads, sandwiches, and fish and chips, as well as charbroiled salmon and halibut. The deck gets busy when the weather's warm. Must be 21 years or older. ~ 3211 Ruston Way, Tacoma; 253-756-0771; www.katiedowns.com. MODERATE.

At **The Spar** in Old Town (Tacoma's original settlement site, two miles north of downtown), pub food reaches unaccustomed heights. The Spar is famous for "chicken & jos," deep-fried chicken and potato pieces not recommended for health enhancement. You can also get a remarkably good caesar salad, along with crab sandwiches in season. Breakfast served on weekends. ~ 2121 30th Street North, Tacoma; 253-627-8215, fax 253-534-9377; www.the-spar.com. BUDGET. ◄HIDDEN

Boasting one of the finest views of any harbor, **The Green Turtle** is hidden away in an unlikely but fantastic waterfront location. Diners are treated to views of Mt. Rainier, Puget Sound and the entrance to Gig Harbor. The food is excellent, served by friendly and competent waitstaff. Pacific Rim inspired, the menu weighs heavily on seafood, but roast duck, chicken and filet mignon are also featured; vegetarian dishes are available upon request. No lunch on Saturday and Sunday, no dinner on Monday. ~ 2905 Harborview Drive, Gig Harbor; 253-851-3167; www.thegreenturtle.com. DELUXE TO ULTRA-DELUXE. ◄HIDDEN

Gardner's Seafood and Pasta is no secret to locals, who flock to this small restaurant. While seafood is the specialty here, there are several pastas that are very good, too. Try the pasta primavera. The Dungeness crab casserole is rich with cream, chablis and several cheeses. Homemade ice cream and other desserts fill out the meal. Dinner only. Closed Sunday and Monday. ~ 111 West Thurston Street, Olympia; 360-786-8466. DELUXE.

AUTHOR FAVORITE

If your cravings for wasabi, buttery slices of fresh raw fish and melt-on-your-tongue tempura become too hard to bear while in Tacoma, **Fujiya** will be a godsend. The chicken sukiyaki is delicious, too. In addition, owner/chef Masahiro Endo is a great entertainer with his knife at the sushi bar. No lunch on Saturday or Sunday. ~ 1125 Court C, Tacoma; phone/fax 253-627-5319. MODERATE.

Patrons don't usually go to a restaurant for the drinking water, but at **McMenamin's Spar Café Bar** it truly is exceptional because it comes from the eatery's own artesian well. Once a blue-collar café, the restaurant features large photographs of loggers felling giant Douglas firs. On the menu are thick milkshakes, giant sandwiches, prime rib and Willapa Bay oysters. ~ 114 East 4th Avenue, Olympia; 360-357-6444, fax 360-786-1716. MODERATE.

Tacoma, Washington's third-largest city, derived its name from *Tacobet*, or "mother of the waters," the Indian name for Mt. Rainier.

Boaters, legislators, lobbyists, tourists and waterfront strollers congregate at the **Budd Bay Cafe** at Percival Landing. You can sit outside on the big deck and watch the boats come and go while you enjoy some of the specialties: fresh pasta and seafood, homemade soups, micro beers, Northwest wines and desserts from the in-house bakery. Breakfast is offered Monday through Saturday and an elaborate champagne brunch is served Sunday. ~ 525 North Columbia Street, Olympia; 360-357-6963, fax 360-786-8474; www.buddbaycafe.com, e-mail contactus@buddbaycafe.com. DELUXE.

The **Dockside Deli & Pizza** is a bright little café on the boardwalk at Olympia's Percival Landing. Fast and friendly service, tasty homemade soups and sandwiches, deep-dish quiche, hand-tossed pizza and a fine view of Budd Bay have made this spot a favorite. Try the muffins, hand-dipped ice creams and espresso. ~ 501 North Columbia Street, Olympia; 360-956-1928, fax 360-956-0110. BUDGET.

In a neighborhood less frequented by tourists, **Portofino Ristorante** is a charming restaurant in a turn-of the-20th-century home. Seven tables fill the former living and dining rooms, with more tables on the enclosed porch. Classical music plays softly in a subdued atmosphere. Fresh Northwest foods are served, often under mild sauces. Dinner only. ~ 101 Division Street, Olympia; 360-352-2803. MODERATE.

In downtown Olympia, the **Urban Onion** serves sizable breakfasts, good sandwiches and hamburgers and a hearty lentil soup. Dinners include chicken, seafood and *gado gado*—a spicy Indonesian dish of sautéed vegetables in tahini and peanut sauce, along with Mexican entrées. They also offer several vegetarian specials. The restaurant is part of a complex of shops in the former Olympian Hotel. ~ 116 Legion Way, Olympia; 360-943-9242, fax 360-754-2378. MODERATE.

The Olympia area isn't the place you'd expect gourmet French-Northwest cuisine, but chef Jean-Pierre Simon exceeds expectations at **Jean-Pierre's**. Located in a historic old home near the Olympia Brewery, Simon serves up luscious three-course or six-course dinners that meld French Provincial influences with local ingredients such as Dungeness crab. Reservations recommended. No lunch Saturday through Monday. ~ 316 Schmidt Place, Tumwater; 360-754-3702, fax 360-754-1352; www.jean-pierres.com. ULTRA-DELUXE.

One of the best views in Olympia is from **Falls Terrace**, through huge windows overlooking Tumwater Falls on the Deschutes River. A good way to start your meal is with some oysters. The menu features pasta dishes, an excellent bouillabaisse and an array of chicken and beef entrées. Reservations recommended. ~ 106 South Deschutes Way, Tumwater; 360-943-7830, fax 360-943-6899; www.fallsterrace.com. MODERATE TO DELUXE.

SHOPPING

In the Proctor District in north Tacoma you can find Northwest foods, gifts and clothing at the **Pacific Northwest Shop.** ~ 2702 North Proctor Street, Tacoma; 253-752-2242, 800-942-3523. Fine Irish imports are in stock at **The Harp & Shamrock.** ~ 2704 North Proctor Street, Tacoma; 253-752-5012. The **Old House Mercantile** offers gifts for the kitchen and garden as well as a selection of teapots and jewelry. ~ 2717-A North Proctor Street, Tacoma; 253-759-8850. Educational toys are found at **Teaching Toys.** ~ 2624 North Proctor Street, Tacoma; 253-759-9853. The **Northwest Museum Store** at the Washington State History Museum features American Indian gifts, jewelry and pottery. ~ 1911 Pacific Avenue, Tacoma; 253-798-5880.

Near the Tacoma Dome downtown, **Freighthouse Square** is a thriving collection of shops and eateries in an old railroad warehouse. Dozens of shops offer local crafts, jewelry, ethnic gifts, flowers and food items. ~ 25th and East D streets, Tacoma; 253-305-0678; www.freighthousesquare.com.

Park Avenue Books carries more than 30,000 used and new titles on its shelves. Closed Sunday. ~ 8304 Park Avenue South, Tacoma; 253-471-2099; www.parkavenuebooks.com.

For sportswear and outdoor gear in Tacoma, try **Sportco.** Shop warehouse-style for hunting, fishing, camping gear and guns. ~ 4602 East 20th Street, Tacoma; 253-922-2222; www.sportco.com. Or visit **Duffle Bag Army Navy Inc.** for camping, hunting and workwear. ~ 8207 South Tacoma Way, Tacoma; 253-588-4433, 800-588-4432; www.thedufflebag.com.

In Gig Harbor, **The Beach Basket** features, of course, baskets and other gifts. ~ 4102 Harborview Drive, Gig Harbor; 253-858-3008. Scandinavian utensils, books and gifts can be found at **Strictly Scandinavian.** ~ 7803 Pioneer Way, Gig Harbor; 253-851-5959. **Mostly Books** stocks books (you're kidding), bookmarks and postcards. ~ 3126 Harborview Drive, Gig Harbor; 253-851-3219.

Downtown Puyallup has several fine antique stores within walking distance of each other on Stuart and Meridian streets.

Check out the **Pioneer Antique Mall** for a hodgepodge of paintings, glass and knickknacks from all eras. ~ 113 Meridian Street, Puyallup; 253-770-0981.

In Olympia, contemporary women's clothing and accessories are found at **Juicy Fruits.** ~ 111 Market Street, Suite 103, Olympia; 360-943-0572. **Olympic Outfitters** is housed in a restored, brick-and-metal building and is stocked with everything from bicycles to backpacking and cross-country ski gear. ~ 407 East 4th Avenue, Olympia; 360-943-1114.

NIGHTLIFE

For drinks and occasional music, a longtime favorite is **The Swiss Pub,** at the top of a flight of stairs connecting the State History Museum with the campus of the University of Washington—Tacoma. It's renowned for its collection of Chihuly glass, not a common thing for a college pub. ~ 1904 South Jefferson Avenue, Tacoma; 253-572-2821. **Katie Downs Tavern** is an adults-only pub overlooking Commencement Bay with a menu featuring local microbrews, seafood and pizza. ~ 3211 Ruston Way, Tacoma; 253-756-0771. Boasting one of the largest selections of draught beer in the state is the **Ale House Pub.** ~ 2122 Mildred Street West, Tacoma; 253-565-9367; www.alehousepub.com.

The **Tacoma Little Theatre** is a community theater producing five plays a year. ~ 210 North I Street, Tacoma; 253-272-2281; www.tacomalittletheatre.com.

South of Tacoma is **Happy Days Casino,** where people try their luck at blackjack, hold 'em, and other poker games. ~ 11521 Bridgeport Way Southwest, Lakewood; 253-582-1531.

The Tides Tavern in Gig Harbor features live bands on Saturday nights playing '50s and '60s rock and some rhythm-and-blues. ~ 2925 Harborview Drive, Gig Harbor; 253-858-3982; www.tidestavern.com.

BEACHES & PARKS

The **Green River Gorge** is less than an hour from downtown Seattle but is worlds away from the big city. The heart of the gorge covers only some six miles on the map but is so twisted

LISTEN AND LEARN

Interested in glass artist Dale Chihuly but can't schedule a guided tour? Opt for the new **Ear for Art Chihuly Glass Cell Phone Walking Tour,** the first of its kind in Washington state. Available through Tacoma Art Museum, and activated through your cell phone by calling 888-411-4220 any time day or night, the innovative audio tour is partly narrated by Chihuly himself. It features 12 audio stops throughout the Museum District.

into oxbows that it takes kayakers 14 river miles to paddle through it. Just 300 feet deep, the steep-walled gorge nevertheless slices through solid rock (shale and sandstone) to reveal coal seams and fossil imprints and inspire a fine sense of remoteness. State and county parks flank the gorge.

The **Green River Gorge Conservation Area** includes three state parks. Here we pick the two developed parks at the entrance and exit of the gorge and one nearby state park on a lake. ~ 360-902-8844.

FLAMING GEYSER STATE PARK Once a resort, this 480-acre park downstream from the exit of Green River Gorge offers four miles of hiking trails and nearly five miles of riverbank. Originally, the flaming geyser area was a test site for coal samples, but miners found natural gas instead, which, when lit, produced a 20-foot flame. The "flaming geyser" is only eight inches high now, and can be seen off one of the trails. Pick up a trail map and brochure at the main office. Fish for rainbow trout and steelhead in season (check the posted regulations). There are picnic areas, restrooms, play areas, volleyball courts, a horseback riding area (but no stables) and horseshoe pits. ~ Green Valley Road, three miles west of Route 169, south of Black Diamond; 253-931-3930, fax 253-931-6379.

KANASKAT-PALMER STATE PARK Lovely walking on riverside paths, especially in summer, is the hallmark of this 320-acre park upstream from the entrance to Green River Gorge. During fishing season, try for steelhead and trout (check posted regulations). Picnic areas, restrooms, showers, volleyball courts and horseshoe pits are the facilities here. ~ On Cumberland-Kanaskat Road off Southeast 308th Street, 11 miles north of Enumclaw and Route 410; 360-886-0148, fax 360-886-1715; e-mail kanaskat-palmer@parks.wa.gov.

▲ There are 31 standard sites ($19 per night) and 19 with partial hookups ($25 per night). Reservations: 888-226-7688.

NOLTE STATE PARK Surrounding Deep Lake, 117-acre Nolte Park is famous for its huge Douglas firs, cedars and cottonwoods. A one-and-a-quarter-mile path circles the lake taking you around nearly 7200 feet of shoreline and past the big trees; a separate nature trail interprets the forest. You can swim at the lake (no lifeguards); motorboats are prohibited. The lake is open for fishing year round, offering trout, bass, crappie, catfish and silvers. There's a minimal picnic area. ~ On Veazie-Cumberland Road just south of Southeast 352nd Street, six miles north of Enumclaw and Route 410; 360-825-4646.

WEST HYLEBOS WETLANDS A rare chunk of urban wetland tucked between industrialization and subdivisions, the 68-acre park offers examples of all sorts of wetland formations along a ◄ HIDDEN one-mile boardwalk trail—springs, streams, marshes, lakes, floating bogs and sinks. You'll also see remnants of ancient forest, plentiful waterfowl, more than a hundred species of birds and many mammals. Facilities are limited to portable toilets. ~ On South 348th Street at 4th Avenue South, just west of Route 99 and Exit 142; 253-835-6901, fax 253-835-6969.

DASH POINT STATE PARK Nearly 400 acres of forested wildland with 3300 feet of saltwater shoreline preserve a bit of solitude just barely outside the Tacoma city limits. Seven and a half miles of trail ramble through mixed forest of second-growth fir, maple and alder. The park's beach is one of the few places on Puget Sound where you'll find enjoyable saltwater swimming—shallow waters in tide flats are warmed by the summer sun. Tides retreat to expose a beachfront nearly a half-mile deep. There's fishing from the pier at Brown's Point Park south of Dash Point State Park, and swimming in tide flat shallows (no lifeguard). Facilities include picnic areas, restrooms and showers. ~ Located just northeast of Tacoma on Southwest Dash Point (Route 509); 253-661-4955, fax 253-661-4995.

▲ There are 114 developed sites ($19 per night) and 27 sites with hookups ($26 per night). Reservations: 888-226-7688.

POINT DEFIANCE PARK Jutting dramatically into Puget Sound, this 700-acre treasure is hailed by some as the finest saltwater park in the state, by others as the best city park in the Northwest. Here are primeval forests, some 50 miles of hiking trails, over three miles of public shoreline and enough other attractions to match almost any visitor's interests. Five Mile Drive loops around the park perimeter with access to trails, forest, beach, views, attractions and grand overlooks of Puget Sound. The park is also known for its zoo and aquarium, particularly the shark tank (fee). Popular with boaters, there's a fully equipped marina with boat rentals, a boathouse (253-591-5325) and a restaurant. You can fish from the pier or in a rented boat. You'll find picnic areas, restrooms, play areas, tennis courts and a snack bar at the boathouse. ~ The entrance is on North 54th and Pearl streets; 253-305-1000, fax 253-305-1098.

LET'S MAKE A DEAL

Midwestern timber baron George Weyerhaeuser arrived in Tacoma in September 1900 ready to do a deal. He wound up buying 900,000 acres of wilderness timberland for $1 million. Not only was that the start of the Northwest's giant timber companies, it was the largest single check ever written to that point.

KOPACHUCK STATE PARK Spectacular views across Carr Inlet toward the Olympic Mountains from a half-mile of shoreline gives Kopachuck much to boast about. Many car-top boaters launch from the beach near the park to fish for bottomfish and salmon or paddle out to Cutts Island Marine State Park a half-mile away. No lifeguard is on duty. There are picnic areas, restrooms and showers. ~ Located on Kopachuck Drive Northwest at Northwest 56th Street, about seven miles west of Gig Harbor and Route 16; 253-265-3606, fax 360-644-8112.

▲ There are 41 sites for tents and RVs ($19 per night); no hookups are available.

NISQUALLY NATIONAL WILDLIFE REFUGE This 3000-acre refuge's ecosystem is a diverse mix of conifer forest, deciduous woodlands, marshlands, grasslands and mud flats and the meandering Nisqually River (born in Mt. Rainier National Park). Here, the river mixes its fresh waters with the salt chuck of Puget Sound. The refuge is home to mink, otter, coyote and some 50 other species of mammals, over 200 kinds of birds and 125 species of fish. Trails thread the refuge; longest is the five-and-a-half-mile dike-top loop that circles a pioneer homestead long since abandoned. Fishing yields salmon, steelhead and cutthroat. Facilities include a visitor's center, a nature shop and restrooms. Day-use fee, $3 per family. ~ Route 5 Exit 114, about 25 miles south of downtown Tacoma; 360-753-9467, fax 360-534-9302; www.fws.gov/nisqually.

TOLMIE STATE PARK A salt marsh with interpretive signs separates 1800 feet of tide flats from forested uplands overlooking Nisqually Reach. The sandy beach is fine for wading or swimming; at low tide you may find clams. A two-and-a-half-mile wheelchair-accessible perimeter hiking trail loops through the park's 106 acres. An artificial reef and three sunken barges 500 yards offshore and almost-nonexistent current make the underwater park here popular for divers. Fishing yields salmon and cod. You'll find picnic areas, restrooms and showers. Closed Monday and Tuesday from October through March. ~ Hill Road Northeast, northeast of Olympia via Exit 111 from Route 5; phone/fax 360-456-6464.

MILLERSYLVANIA STATE PARK Some 842 acres of primeval conifer forest and miles of foot trail are this park's big appeals. But visitors also come to enjoy its 3300 feet of shoreline along Deep Lake, where you can swim, launch a small boat (no wake) or fish for trout, bass, perch and crappie. Facilities include picnic areas and restrooms. ~ Exit 95 just east of Route 5, ten miles south of Olympia; 360-753-1519, fax 360-664-2180.

▲ There are 120 standard sites ($19 per night) and 48 sites with hookups ($26 per night). No reservations necessary October to May. Reservations: 888-226-7688.

Bainbridge Island

To the north, **Bainbridge Island** offers a much more attractive destination for most travelers, and you can see it on foot. The picturesque town is located on an island of the same name, just a 35-minute ferry ride from Coleman Dock (pick up a self-guiding brochure with map, *A Downtown Guide to Bainbridge Island*, before boarding).

SIGHTS

To see more than obvious attractions on **Bainbridge Island**, head for the mile-long waterfront footpath called **Walkabout** to the left of the ferry landing. Follow it along the shoreline, past shipyards and hauled-out sailboats under repair, to **Eagle Harbor Waterfront Park** and its fishing pier and low-tide beach. Carry on to a ship chandler and pair of marinas. Return as you came or make it a loop trip by walking up to **Winslow Way**, where you can stop for espresso or shop.

Bainbridge Island Vineyards and Winery is the only winery in the Seattle area that grows its grapes on-site. There is a tasting room, gardens, a wine museum of antiques and a picnic area on this family farm estate winery. The Ferryboat White label is popular with visitors. Open afternoons Friday through Sunday. ~ 8989 East Day Road, Bainbridge Island; 206-842-9463.

If you enjoy gardens, don't miss a tour of the famous **Bloedel Reserve**. Once a private estate, the reserve has 150 acres of forest, meadows, ponds and a series of beautifully landscaped gardens. Reservations are required for a tour. Closed Monday and Tuesday. Admission. ~ 7571 Northeast Dolphin Drive, Bainbridge Island; 206-842-7631, fax 206-842-8970; www.bloedelreserve.org, e-mail email@bloedelreserve.org.

LODGING

If you've enjoyed traditional country inns in Japan, you'll love **Fuurin-Oka Futon & Breakfast**, a private, detached guesthouse surrounded by a bamboo grove, Zen garden, orchards and the last Japanese-American organic berry farm on Bainbridge Island. With a name meaning "wind-bell hill," this romantic getaway is authentic in every detail, with tatami rice-grass mats on hardwood floors, sliding shoji screens and luxurious futons. You can make a cup of soothing green tea or cook in the kitchenette, which is furnished with a hot plate, microwave, refrigerator and rice cooker. A traditional Japanese soaking bath overlooks the garden and there is a peaceful deck. Other amenities include kimonos, a stereo, a library, high-speed Internet, and CDs and videos. Full organic breakfast (vegetarian-friendly). ~ 12580

Vista Drive Northeast, Bainbridge Island; 206-842-5045; www.futonandbreakfast.com, e-mail afborwick@yahoo.com. DELUXE.

Set on a seven-acre farm overlooking a placid pond, **Blackberry Hill Farm Bicycle Inn** has two large guest accommodations just three miles from Winslow and the ferry dock. The upstairs unit is a three-room suite with a family hostel room, while the downstairs apartment has a private entrance, fireplace and kitchen. Deer and raccoon are frequently seen traversing the property, and guests are invited to pick blackberries, apples and strawberries in season. A full Scandinavian breakfast is served, and may include homemade muesli as well as fresh eggs guests may gather themselves if they're inclined to lend a hand. As the name suggests, bicycles are available. Closed November through February. ~ 8400 Paulanna Lane, Bainbridge Island; 206-842-4870, fax 206-842-1680; e-mail bainbridgebicycleinn@hotmail.com. DELUXE TO ULTRA-DELUXE.

Take time to tour the Bainbridge Island library's award-winning Northwest-Japanese garden "Haiku no Niwa," dedicated to the Issei (the first generation of Japanese Americans).

DINING

Specializing in steaks, seafood and pan-Asian dishes, the **Island Grill** provides casual fine dining amid a dark green and burgundy color scheme with hardwood floors. Dishes include grilled salmon in black bean basil sauce, lobster in ginger and onion sauce and barbeque baby back ribs. Weekend brunch. ~ 321 High School Road Northeast, Bainbridge Island; 206-842-9037. MODERATE.

The white-linen tablecloths and low lighting at the **Bistro Pleasant Beach** bespeak a comfortable island elegance. The chef specializes in Mediterranean seafood but includes a couple of succulent chicken dishes, pastas and aged beef entrées. The leg of lamb, served with roasted garlic, fresh herbs and shallot–rose cabernet sauce, comes recommended. Made-to-order pizzas are baked in the wood-fired oven. When the weather's nice, patio seating is available. Champagne brunch on Sunday. Closed Monday. ~ 241 Winslow Way West, Bainbridge Island; 206-842-4370, fax 206-842-6997; www.bicomnet.com/bistropb, e-mail ramadanbistro@aol.com. MODERATE.

Exotic flavors and innovative sauces are what you'll find at the **Four Swallows**, an upscale Italian restaurant located in a spacious 1880s farmhouse. The kitchen staff, utilizing fresh Northwest ingredients, whips up gourmet, thin-crust pizzas and zesty pastas. The entrées show the chef's creativity, and include grilled veal chops with porcini-mushroom sauce and *brodetto*, a fresh fish-and-shellfish stew in a rustic saffron-tomato-fennel broth. Dinner only. Closed Sunday and Monday. ~ 481 Madison Avenue, Bainbridge Island; 206-842-3397; www.fourswallows.com. MODERATE TO DELUXE.

A pleasant spot to relax with a beer and a sandwich or fish and chips is the deck at **Doc's Marina Grill**. The view from the deck above the water is always a delight, and it's only about five blocks from the ferry dock. The food, which includes bourbon barbeque salmon, Northwest seafood stew and gorgonzola chicken fettuccine, is reasonably priced, but high for what you get—stick with something simple and enjoy the view. Breakfast served daily. ~ 403 Madison Avenue South, Bainbridge Island; 206-842-8339. MODERATE.

The cozy **Pegasus Coffee House and Gallery** is a traditional coffeehouse with lots of reading material, conversation, freshly baked pastries and assorted coffees. ~ 131 Parfitt Way, Bainbridge Island; 206-842-6725; www.pegasuscoffeehouse.com. BUDGET.

Walk into the **Streamliner Diner** and it's like stepping back into a Midwestern diner. There are eight tables, a small bar and an open kitchen that serves up breakfast burritos, fried egg sandwiches, scrumptious omelettes and buttermilk waffles. Lunches include soups, salads and quiches. Breakfast and lunch only. ~ 397 Winslow Way, Bainbridge Island; 206-842-8595. BUDGET.

NIGHTLIFE

For relaxing after-dinner entertainment, drop by **Pegasus Coffee House and Gallery**. There's live music Thursday through Sunday, featuring local folk and blues musicians, as well as the occasional indie-rock band. Listen while you peruse their selection of local art. ~ 397 Winslow Way, Bainbridge Island; 206-842-8595.

BEACHES & PARKS

FAY BAINBRIDGE STATE PARK A small park (17 acres), it nevertheless curls itself around a long sandspit to present some 1400 feet of shoreline. The only campground on Bainbridge Island is here. Facilities include picnic areas, restrooms, showers, a play area, horseshoe pits and volleyball courts. ~ At Sunrise Drive Northeast and Lafayette Road about six miles north

BAINBRIDGE BARGAINS

When shopping on Bainbridge Island, most will breathe a sigh of relief that it doesn't involve towering shopping centers and crowded parking lots that seem to plague urban areas. But while the local boutiques are sweet, the prices aren't easy on the wallet. Not so at the **Bainbridge Bargain Boutique**, a quaint local thrift shop that's been around since 1968. They usually have a good selection of knickknacks such as a scented candle ensconced in a ceramic seashell and many other must-have Bainbridge Island souvenirs. Closed Sunday. ~ 572 Winslow Way East, Bainbridge Island; 206-842-5567.

of the town of Bainbridge Island at the island's northeast tip; 206-842-3931.

There are 10 standard sites ($19 per night) and 26 sites with hookups ($26). Restrooms and showers available. Camping availability during winter depends on snow conditions.

FORT WARD STATE PARK Located at the south end of Bainbridge Island, this park offers 137 acres of paths, forest and picnic sites, as well as a beach stretching nearly a mile long, complete with salmon and lingcod fishing and an underwater park for scuba divers. Locked service road is accessible by walking. ~ 206-842-4041.

Kitsap Peninsula

Only an hour from the heart of Seattle, the Kitsap Peninsula is framed on the east side by Puget Sound and the west by Hood Canal. Historic company towns, naval museums and remote parks make this area a fine retreat from the city. In June and July, Kitsap and Olympic Peninsula visitors should watch the roadsides for the delicate pink blossoms of native rhododendron bushes, which thrive in the understory of the Douglas fir forests.

SIGHTS

Another interesting loop trip west of Seattle begins in the Navy town of **Bremerton.** You can explore some of the region's history, as well as the remote reaches of southern Puget Sound.

If you take the ferry or drive to Bremerton, you'll pass by the **Puget Sound Naval Shipyard.** The best way to get here is the Washington State Ferry (cars and walk-ons; one hour) or state foot-ferry (50 minutes) or the passenger-only fast ferry (35 minutes) from Seattle's Colman Dock (Pier 52) through Rich Passage to Bremerton. Although the shipyard is not open for public tours, it's an amazing sight even from a distance. ~ Burwell Street and Pacific Avenue, near the ferry dock, Bremerton; 360-476-7111, fax 360-476-0937; www.psns.navy.mil.

Bremerton Naval Museum looks back to the days of Jack Tar and square-riggers and includes a wood cannon from 1377. Closed Sunday from October through April. ~ 402 Pacific Avenue, a half-block north of the ferry dock, Bremerton. Closed Sunday.; 360-479-7447.

Award-winning horticulturalist Dan Robinson displays many of his best specimens at **Elandan Gardens,** his family's six-acre landscaped garden near Bremerton. Now reclaimed and beautified, the former landfill features many ancient bonsai (one is 1300 years old), all set against a backdrop of boulders, ponds, waterfalls, stylized plantings and large-scale naturalistic sculptures on the shores of Puget Sound. Learn about bonsai, buy equipment and plants, and visit the gift shop/gallery, which sells unique antiques and handmade clothing. Closed Monday and in January.

~ 3050 West Route 16, Bremerton; 360-373-8260; dianerobin son@prodigy.net; www.elandangardens.com.

In the small town of Keyport, off Route 308 between Poulsbo and Silverdale, you'll find the **Naval Undersea Museum.** Historical exhibits here focus on the Navy's undersea activities from the Revolutionary War to the present. Diving and defense displays explore such subjects as nautical archaeology and the history of the submarine. There's also an interactive installation on the ocean environment. ~ 1 Garnett Way, Keyport; 360-396-4148; http://keyportmuseum.cnrnw.navy.mil, e-mail underseainfo@kpt.nuwc.navy.mil.

Looking like a lane in faraway Scandinavia, the main street of Poulsbo is lined with wonderful galleries and boutiques.

From Bremerton, Route 3 runs up the eastern side of the Kitsap Peninsula. Turn down Route 305 past Liberty Bay and you'll come to the charming town of Poulsbo. "Velkommen til Poulsbo" is an oft-repeated phrase in "Washington's Little Norway." Looking like a lane in faraway Scandinavia, the main street of Poulsbo is lined with wonderful galleries and boutiques. There are some wonderful samples of his-toric architecture on a walking tour of town; the **Greater Poulsbo Chamber of Commerce** can provide more information. ~ 19351 8th Avenue, Poulsbo; 360-779-4848, fax 360-799-3115; www.poulsbochamber.com, e-mail admin@poulsbochamber.com.

HIDDEN ►

A good place to learn about the region's American Indian heritage is the town of **Suquamish**. Chief Seattle and the allied tribes he represented are showcased at the **Suquamish Museum.** There's an outstanding collection of photographs and relics, along with mock-ups of a typical American Indian dwelling and the interior of a longhouse. Two award-winning video presentations are shown in a small theater. Closed Monday through Thursday in winter. Admission. ~ 15838 Sandy Hook Road off Route 305, Suquamish; 360-598-3311 ext. 422; www.suquamish.nsn.us/museum.

Chief Seattle's Grave, set under a canopy of dugout canoes in a hillside graveyard overlooking Seattle (his namesake), is just a few miles down Suquamish Way. Follow the road signs.

HIDDEN ►

One of the West's last company towns, **Port Gamble** is a favored visitor stop. Situated on a bluff at the intersection of Admiralty Inlet and Gamble Bay, this century-old community is owned by the Pope Resources lumber firm.

The oldest running lumber mill in the United States (operating since 1853) was closed in 1995. The town had long been home to about 150 sawmill workers and their families, who rented homes by the company. Picturesque frame houses, towering elms and a church with Gothic windows and a needle spire give the community a New England look. Don't miss the mock-ups of Captain Talbot's cabin and A. J. Pope's office at the **Port**

Gamble Historic Museum. Admission. ~ #3 Ranier Avenue, Port Gamble; 360-297-8074, fax 360-297-7455; www.portgamble.com.

◄HIDDEN

South of Bremerton is the **Longbranch Peninsula**, a showcase of Southern Puget Sound's outdoor treasures. Quiet coves and lonely forests, dairy farms, funky fishing villages with quiet cafés, shellfish beaches and oyster farmers, a salmon hatchery, fishing piers and wharves all await leisurely exploration. Take Route 16 to Route 302, proceeding west until you reach Key Center. The

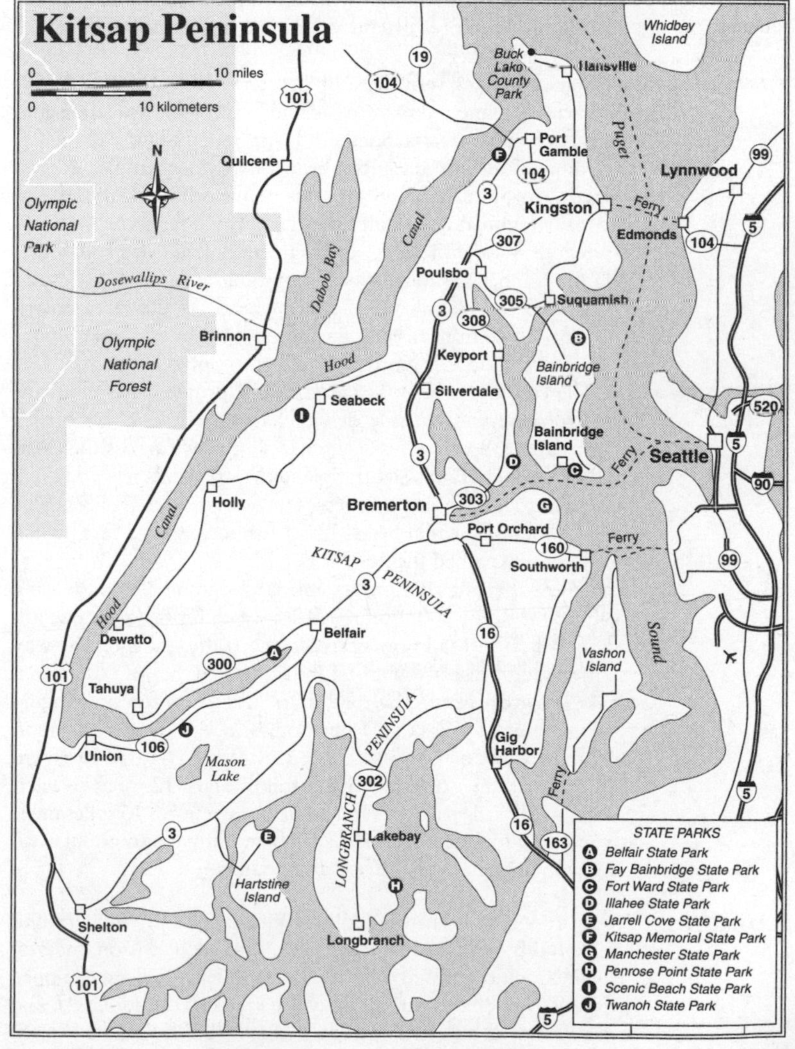

Key Peninsula Highway, running south from this community, is the main road bringing you to most attractions.

To visit the hamlet of **Lakebay** on Mayo Cove, turn east from Peninsula Highway three and a half miles south of Home (the town, not your Home Sweet) onto Cornwall Road and follow it to Delano Road. On the south side of the cove is **Penrose Point State Park** with 152 acres of forest, more than two miles of beaches, hiking trails, fishing, picnicking and camping. ~ 321 158th Avenue K.P.S., Lakebay; 253-884-2514, fax 360-753-1594.

At the end of the highway is another bayside village, **Longbranch**, on the shores of Filucy Bay, one of the prettiest anchorages in these waters.

HIDDEN ► **Harstine Island** (northeast of Shelton via Route 3 and Pickering Road) is connected to the mainland by a bridge, providing auto access to a quintessential Southern Puget Sound island experience.

Many of the island's public beaches are poorly indicated, but **Jarrell Cove State Park** and a marina on the other side of the cove are easily found at the island's north tip. You'll see plenty of boats from both sides of the cove, and at the park you can stroll docks, fish for perch, walk bits of beach or explore forest trails. Main roads loop the island's north end, or head for the far southern tip at Brisco Point near Peale Passage and Squaxin Island. ~ Foot of Wingert Road, off North Island Drive; 360-426-9226.

HIDDEN ► The eastern shore of **Hood Canal** is located a mere mile or two from the western side of the channel, but in character it's worlds apart. Beach access is limited, but views across the canal to the Olympic Mountains are splendid, settlements few and quiet and back roads genuine byways—few tourists ever get here. This is also where the canal bends like a fishhook to the east, which has been nicknamed the "Great Bend."

To see the east shore in its entirety, begin at Belfair, leaving Route 3 for Route 300. At three miles, watch for Belfair State Park on the left. The road now narrows and traffic thins on the way to the modest resort town of Tahuya; shortly beyond, the canal makes its great bend. The road dives into dense forest, bringing you in about 11 miles to a T-junction; bear left, then left again to the ghost town of Dewatto. Take Dewatto Bay Road eastward out of town, then turn north and follow signs 12 miles to a left turn into the little town of **Holly**, or continue north 15 miles more to **Seabeck**, founded in 1856 as a sawmill town and popular today with anglers, scuba divers and boaters.

LODGING

Guest rooms at Poulsbo's **Holiday Inn Express** are modern and comfortably furnished with big beds, satellite television, individual air conditioning and other basic amenities; a few are equipped with kitchenette or jacuzzi. There is a seasonal outdoor pool and continental breakfast is included. ~ 19801 7th Avenue Northeast, Poulsbo; 360-697-4400, 888-465-4329, fax 360-697-2707; www.hiexpress.com/poulsbowa. DELUXE.

DINING

The family-run **Mor Mor Bistro and Bar** offers eclectic Northwest cuisine in a large but intimate dining room. The selection focuses on locally harvested seafood, and uses natural and organic ingredients. Sunday brunch is served. ~ 18820 Front Street, Poulsbo; 360-697-3449, fax 360-697-9904; www.mormorbistro.com, e-mail info@mormorbistro.com. MODERATE TO DELUXE.

Casa De Luna features fast and cheap traditional Mexican or Mexican-American fare. Diners are treated to colorful murals and sweet ballads while munching on tacos and burritos and sipping Negra Modelo. ~18830 Front Street Northeast, Poulsbo; 360-779-7676. BUDGET.

Linger over a memorable meal in a quiet rural valley north of Poulsbo at **Molly Ward Gardens.** The family-run restaurant (Molly was their dog) is atmospherically housed in a big old barn next to organic gardens that provide much of the seasonal produce. The changing menu might include fried Dabob Bay oysters or Thai chicken satay for starters, followed by entrées of rack of New Zealand lamb, Dungeness crab cakes, Copper River salmon with balsamic vinegar or marinated Kurabato pork tenderloin. Sunday brunch features delicious local lamb sausage and eggs, fresh vegetable-and-goat-cheese frittatas, omelettes with Dungeness crab, and rib steak and eggs. Closed Monday; no lunch Sunday through Tuesday. ~ 27462 Big Valley Road, Poulsbo; 360-779-4471; www.mollywardgardens.com, e-mail mollyw@mollywardgardens.com. MODERATE TO ULTRA-DELUXE.

SHOPPING

You'll find paintings, pottery, weavings, cards, rosemaling, baskets and woodturnings created by local artists at the **Verksted Gallery.** ~ 18937 Front Street Northeast, Poulsbo; 360-697-4470; www.verkstedgallery.com. The **Potlatch Gallery** carries a fine selection of prints, glasswork, woodwork and jewelry by Northwest artists. ~ 18830-B Front Street Northeast, Poulsbo; 360-779-3377; www.potlatchgallery.com.

OLD MAN HOUSE STATE PARK

Old Man House State Park was once the home of Chief Sealth (Seattle) before it was turned over to the Suquamish tribe. Check out the interpretive and historical displays. A small, sandy beach overlooks the heavy marine traffic that cruises through Agate Passage. You'll find pit toilets and picnic tables. Closed in winter. ~ On the Kitsap Peninsula north of Agate Pass off Route 305; 206-842-3931, fax 206-385-7248.

Head to **Boehm's Chocolates** for Swiss-European chocolates, truffles and fudge. ~ 18864 Front Street Northeast, Poulsbo; 360-697-3318. Get your fill of Norwegian strudels, bear claws, breads, pastries and cookies at **Sluys Bakery.** ~ 18924 Front Street Northeast, Poulsbo; 360-779-2798.

BEACHES & PARKS

MANCHESTER STATE PARK This one-time fort overlooking Rich Passage includes abandoned torpedo warehouses and some interpretive displays explaining its role in guarding Bremerton Navy Base at the turn of the 20th century. The park is infamous for its poison oak—stay on the two miles of hiking trails, or try the 3400 feet of beach. The rocks off Middle Point attract divers. Fishing yields salmon and bottomfish. There are picnic areas, restrooms and showers. ~ Located at the east foot of East Hilldale Road off Beach Drive, east of Bremerton; 360-871-4065, fax 503-378-6308.

▲ There are 35 standard sites ($19 per night) and 15 RV hookup sites ($26 per night). Reservations: 888-226-7688.

BUCK LAKE COUNTY PARK Near Hansville on the northern tip of the Kitsap Peninsula, picturesque Buck Lake is a good spot for quiet, contemplative fishing or a relaxing summer swim. Trout fishing is excellent on the lake or from the shore. Facilities include restrooms, picnic tables, a baseball diamond, a volleyball court, barbecue pits and a playground. ~ Buck Lake Road; take Route 104 from Kingston to Hansville Road and follow it north; 360-337-5350, fax 360-337-5385.

The Southern Puget Sound is an outdoor-lover's paradise—it boasts more than 40 city, county and state parks. In addition, there are nearly 20 beaches or tidelands areas and over 40 public or commercial boat launches.

SALISBURY POINT This tiny, six-acre park with a small stretch of saltwater beach is next to Hood Canal Floating Bridge and gives views of the Olympic Mountains across the canal. Shrimping is popular here. There are restrooms, picnic shelters and a playground. ~ North of Hood Canal Floating Bridge, turn left on Wheeler Road and follow the signs; 360-337-5350, fax 360-337-5385.

KITSAP MEMORIAL STATE PARK This 58-acre park four miles south of Hood Canal Floating Bridge has a quiet beach well suited for collecting oysters and clams. Between the canal, beach and playground facilities there's plenty to keep the troops entertained, making this a good choice for family camping. Restrooms, showers, a shelter, tables and stoves, boat moorage buoys, a playground and a volleyball court are available; some facilities are wheelchair accessible. Day-use fee, $5. ~ From

Kingston take Route 104 (which turns into Bond Road) to Route 3, then follow it north until you reach the park; 360-779-3205, fax 360-779-3161.

▲ There are 21 standard sites ($17 per night); 18 sites with hookups ($26 per night); and a trailer dump ($5). Four sleeper cabins can accommodate up to five adults and have small kitchenettes, picnic tables and fire pits with grills ($55). A blufftop log cabin with full bedding, bath towels and a kitchenette (no stove) is also available; $147 per night in peak season.

ILLAHEE STATE PARK Wooded uplands and 1800 feet of saltwater shoreline are separated by a 250-foot bluff at this site. A steep hiking trail connects the two park units. On the beach is a wheelchair-accessible fishing pier where anglers can cast for perch, bullhead and salmon; at the south end are tide flats for wading. Facilities include a picnic area, restrooms, showers, a baseball field, a play area and horseshoe pits. ~ Located at the east foot of Sylvan Way (Route 306) two miles east of Route 303 northeast of Bremerton; 360-478-6460, fax 360-792-6067.

▲ There are 24 standard sites (no hookups); $19 per night; two utility spaces ($26 per night).

TWANOH STATE PARK With many amenities of a city park, Twanoh's 182 acres also include the forests, trails and camping of a more remote site. A two-mile hiking trail takes you through a thick forest of second-growth conifers next to Twanoh Creek; nearly a half-mile of saltwater beach attracts divers. Fishing yields cutthroat, salmon and trout. There are picnic areas, restrooms, showers, tennis, horseshoe pits and a concession stand. ~ Route 106, eight miles southwest of Belfair; 360-275-2222.

▲ There are 25 tent sites ($19 per night) and 22 full hookup sites ($26 per night).

BELFAIR STATE PARK Two creeks flow through this 63-acre park en route to Hood Canal, affording both fresh and saltwater shorelines. Along its 3720 feet of beachfront the saltwater warms quickly across shallow tide flats, but pollution makes swimming here risky; many instead swim in a lagoon with a bathhouse nearby. Shellfish are usually posted off-limits. There are picnic areas, restrooms and showers. ~ Route 300, three miles west of Belfair; 360-275-0668.

▲ There are 137 tent sites ($19 per night) and 47 full hookup sites ($26 per night); dump station ($5). Closed September through May. Reservations: 888-226-7688.

SCENIC BEACH STATE PARK Nearly 1500 feet of cobblestone beach invites strolls; scuba divers also push off from here. Every year in May, 88 acres of native rhododendrons burst into bloom. Anglers try for salmon and bottom fish at the nearby artificial reef, and there's a boat launch less than a mile from the park. There are picnic areas, restrooms, showers, a play area, horseshoe pits and volleyball areas. ~ Located just west of Seabeck on Miami Beach Road Northwest, about nine miles northwest of Bremerton; 360-830-5079, fax 360-830-2970.

▲ There are 52 standard sites ($19 per night) and 18 pull-through sites ($25); no hookups. Weather-related closures possible in winter. Reservations: 888-226-7688.

PENROSE POINT STATE PARK With more than two miles of saltwater shoreline, this 152-acre park provides some of the most accessible public beaches on Southern Puget Sound. You can swim at the park's sandy, shallow-water beaches, hike along two miles of trail, launch a canoe or kayak, fish for bottomfish and salmon, picnic and camp. The entire park closes for the winter. Restrooms, showers, restaurant and grocery store are close by. ~ Off Delano Road at the foot of 158th Avenue, near Lakebay on the Longbranch Peninsula; 253-884-2514, fax 253-884-2526.

▲ There are 82 standard sites ($19 per night). Reservations: 888-226-7688.

Outdoor Adventures

FISHING

Salmon, of course, is the big draw for anglers on Puget Sound. State hatchery programs see to it that the anadromous fish are available year-round, but the months from midsummer to mid-fall bring the bulk of salmon—and anglers—to these waters. From mid-July to late August, chinook salmon are king; by Labor Day coho take over until October. Then chum arrive, but since they tend to be plankton eaters they don't bite. Pink salmon return in odd numbered years in August, and are most plentiful in the Sound north of Seattle near Everett. Sockeye can be found in Lake Washington from late June to August.

Several charter companies operate fishing trips on the Sound. The cost, which can range from $35 to $80 and up, usually includes everything except lunch and the fishing license (which you can purchase through the charter company).

KITSAP PENINSULA **Great Bend Charters** serves the whole of Hood Canal. You can charter the C-Dory 22 Cruiser with Captain Paul Schaumburg at the helm for either short scenic cruises or all-day fishing trips. ~ 360-490-2777; www.greatbendcharters.com, e-mail info@greatbendcharters.com.

If you're in Tacoma, you can fish from a dinghy in Puget Sound off Point Defiance Park.

KAYAKING

TACOMA AND OLYMPIA Located near the tip of the peninsula in Point Defiance Park, the **Boathouse Marina** has 20 14-foot dinghies for rent. Most of the time they're rented by anglers, but you can take them out to explore the Sound if you prefer. Also for rent are motors to power the boats. ~ 253-591-5325.

Washington State fishers catch more than 1.3 billion pounds of fish and seafood annually, more than half the nation's total edible catch.

A wide range of rentals including sea kayaks and single kayaks, powerboats, sailboats and sportfishing boats are available from **Gig Harbor Rent-a-Boat.** ~ 8829 North Harborview Drive, Gig Harbor; phone/fax 253-858-7341; www.gigharborrentaboat.com.

KITSAP PENINSULA Kayak rentals and instruction are the specialty of **Olympic Outdoor Center.** Custom group trips for three or more take paddlers throughout the Puget Sound. ~ 18971 Front Street, Poulsbo; 360-697-6095; www.olympicoutdoorcenter.com.

SCUBA DIVING

Although the water temperature in Puget Sound averages a cool 45° to 55°, diving is quite popular, especially from October through April, when there's no plankton bloom because of reduced sunlight during those months. With several dive clubs in the Seattle-Tacoma area, there are usually many dives scheduled each weekend: a wall dive off Fox Island perhaps, or a shore dive at Three Tree Point (near Federal Way) or Sunrise Beach (near Gig Harbor). Southern Puget Sound and the area around Vashon Island are considered the best places to dive—you'll see starfish, crabs, ling cod, scallops and many more species. Be prepared, however: Currents are extremely strong south of Seattle so you'll need to check the tides and currents carefully before diving. The dive shops listed below can provide details about these hazards as well as information on local dive spots. If you're not an experienced diver, you can arrange lessons with these shops, although it takes several days to complete training for certification. The outfits listed all rent and sell gear and accessories as well as offer a variety of instruction.

TACOMA AND OLYMPIA In Tacoma, **Lighthouse Diving** takes divers to Canada, the San Juan Islands and other destinations for trips that range from one to two days. Night dives are available. Lighthouse pros meet divers at designated locations. They use one tank per dive. ~ 2502 Pacific Avenue, Tacoma; 253-627-7617, fax 253-627-1877; www.lighthousediving.com. In Port Orchard, contact **Tagert's Dive Locker** for diving, camping trips and holiday dives, such as an Easter egg hunt underwater. Night dives are available. Trips are no more than a half day and use two to three tanks per dive. ~ 1230 Bay Street; 360-895-7860.

Exotic Aquatics Scuba & Kayaking offers dives of all levels to over 15 sites around the Puget Sound. Nighttime and overnight dive trips are available. ~ 146 Winslow Way West, Bainbridge Island; 206-842-1980; www.exoticaquaticsscuba.com.

Underwater Sports Inc. offers shore and boat dives as well as dives abroad—both tropical and night dives. They repair gear. Dives are a day long and use two or three tanks. ~ Tacoma: 9606 40th Avenue Southwest, 253-588-6634; Olympia: 3330 Pacific Avenue Southeast, 360-493-0322; www.underwatersports.com.

JOGGING

In Tacoma, the main road through Point Defiance Park, Five Mile Loop, is a spectacular hilly passage through deep old-growth forest, with occasional breakouts offering lovely views of Puget Sound. This is the route used by the Sound-to-Narrows, an early summer 12K that's one of the country's most popular road races.

Olympia's Capitol Lake greenbelt trails pass through pretty woods, and offer great views of the State Capitol Building and the lake itself. A loop would encompass five kilometers or more.

GOLF

Just south of Tacoma is the **Lake Spanaway Golf Course** in Pierce County Park. The 18-hole public course was cut out of a forest, so it's treelined but fairly open. It has a putting green and a pro shop and rents power and pull carts. ~ 15602 Pacific Avenue, Tacoma; 253-531-3660; www.lakespanawaygc.com.

TENNIS

Call two or three days in advance to reserve one of the four public hardtop indoor courts (or five racquetball courts) at **Sprinker Recreation Center**. Professionals are available for lessons. Fee. ~ 14824 South C Street at Military Road, Tacoma; 253-531-6300.

RIDING STABLES

Su Dara Riding offers a "tranquil, peaceful" one-hour ride for up to seven people through woodland thick with firs and maples. On a clear day there are views of Mt. Rainier. Su herself says, "We ride rain or shine." ~ 8104 Canyon Road East, Puyallup; 253-531-1569; www.sudara.com.

BIKING

TACOMA AND OLYMPIA When it comes to bicycling in Tacoma and Pierce County, "things are just getting going," according to one of the city's public works planners. The area does not yet have the extensive network of lanes and trails that they have up in Seattle, but continues to develop its bicycle and pedestrian plan. Meanwhile, the **Pierce County Department of Public Works** puts out a bike route map. ~ 2702 South 42nd Street, Suite 201, Tacoma; 253-798-7250; www.co.pierce.wa.us. The **Tacoma**

Wheelmen's Bicycle Club operates a recorded Ride Line. ~ 253-759-2800; www.twbc.org.

Among the more popular and convenient places to ride in the city is a two-mile lane along the **downtown waterfront.** Beginning at Schuster Parkway and McCarver Street, this multi-use lane (it's separated from traffic, however) extends to Waterview Street along Ruston Way and Point Defiance Park. Within **Point Defiance Park,** a shoulder lane of Five Mile Drive loops around the peninsula. Call the Metropolitan Park District for more information. ~ 253-305-1000; www.metroparks tacoma.org.

For a pleasant bike ride sans cars, head to Point Defiance Park's Five Mile Drive, which is closed to vehicular traffic every Saturday morning until 1 p.m.

KITSAP PENINSULA Cyclists find the moderate **Poulsbo–Port Gamble Loop,** with its 20 miles featuring outstanding views of Hood Canal, the Cascade Range and the Olympic Mountains, a worthwhile ride.

HIKING

Nisqually National Wildlife Refuge, Green River orge and Point Defiance Park in Tacoma are a hiker's haven. All distances listed for hiking trails are one way unless otherwise noted.

TACOMA AND OLYMPIA A wonderful river-delta walk, **Brown Farm Dike Trail** (5.5 miles), which starts on the Brown Farm Road, loops through the Nisqually National Wildlife Refuge. You may see bald eagles, coyotes, great blue heron, red-tail hawks and a variety of waterfowl such as wood, canvasback and greater scaup ducks, as well as mallards and pintails. Views stretch from Mt. Rainier to the Olympics. You'll also see many of the islands in the south, Steilacoom and the Tacoma Narrows Bridge.

KITSAP PENINSULA Located southwest of Bremerton, **Gold Mountain Hike** (4 miles) is a moderate-to-strenuous climb with a 1100-foot elevation gain. You will survey the twisting waterways of Southern Puget Sound and Hood Canal from a 1761-foot point that also offers vistas from the Olympics to the Cascades and Edmonds to Olympia. The best access is from Holly Road at the trailhead called Wildcat.

Transportation

CAR

Route 5 is the main north–south highway connecting Seattle, Tacoma and Olympia. **Route 16** leads north from Tacoma, across the Tacoma Narrows Bridge toward Gig Harbor and farther north toward Bremerton. On Bainbridge Island, the main thoroughfare is **Route 305** that runs northwest across the island and onto Kitsap Peninsula to Poulsbo.

AIR

Ten miles north of Tacoma and 20 miles south of downtown Seattle is **Seattle-Tacoma International Airport,** also known as Sea-Tac, which is served by Aeromexico, Air Canada, Alaska Airlines,

America West Airlines, American Airlines, British Airways, Continental Airlines, Delta Air Lines, EVA (Evergreen) Air, Hawaiian Airlines, Horizon Air, JetBlue, KLM, Northwest Airlines, Southwest Airlines, Scandinavian Airlines, United Airlines, US Airways and several smaller charter airlines. For general information, call 206-433-5388; www.portseattle.org/seatac/.

Shuttle service to the northern Kitsap Peninsula is available through the **Bremerton-Kitsap Airporter.** ~ 360-876-1737.

BUS

In the Kitsap Peninsula area, **Kitsap Transit** provides routed service in Poulsbo, Bremerton, Kingston, Port Orchard and Bainbridge Island; otherwise, you will have to depend on car or taxis for transportation around the peninsula. ~ 800-501-7433; www.kitsaptransit.org.

CAR RENTALS

Rental agencies at Seattle-Tacoma International Airport include **Avis Rent A Car** (800-331-1212), **Budget Rent A Car** (800-527-0700), **Dollar Rent A Car** (800-800-4000), **Hertz Rent A Car** (800-654-3131) and **Thrifty Car Rental** (800-367-2277). **Payless Car Rentals** (800-227-5397) offers low rates and shuttle service to the airport.

SIX

Olympic Peninsula and Washington Coast

One of the most spectacular sights for many Pacific Northwest visitors is sitting on the dock of the bay (Seattle's Elliott Bay, that is) watching the sun set behind the stark profile of the Olympic Mountains. The area is even more memorable looking from the inside out.

The Olympic Peninsula is a vast promontory bounded on the east by Puget Sound, the west by the Pacific Ocean and the north by the Strait of Juan de Fuca. With no major city—the largest town is Port Angeles, a community of only 19,000 people—it retains a feeling of country living on the edge of wilderness, which indeed it is. Remote it may be but the Olympic Peninsula is where much of the seattle Metropolitan area comes to play. Be sure to make reservations when possible at lodges, motels and campgrounds or arrive very early to get a spot, especially on weekends.

Olympic National Park, which dominates the peninsula, is a primeval place where eternal glaciers drop suddenly off sheer rock faces into nearly impenetrable rainforest, where America's largest herd of Roosevelt elk roams unseen by all but the most intrepid human eyes, where an impossibly rocky, protected coastline (at 73 miles the longest wilderness beach in the Lower 48) cradles primitive marine life forms as it has done for millions of years. No fewer than five Indian reservations speckle sections of a coast famed as much for its shipwrecks as for its salmon fishing.

South of the national park, the Washington coast extends down the Northwest's finest sand beaches and around two enormous river estuaries, to the mouth of the Columbia River and the state of Oregon. In this region, two towns have become major resort centers: Ocean Shores and Long Beach.

The Washington coast is known for its heavy rainfall, and justifiably so. Although the Olympics are not high by many standards—its tallest peaks are under 8000 feet—they catch huge amounts of precipitation blowing in from the Pacific Ocean. So much snow falls that more than 60 glaciers survive at elevations as low as 4500 feet. Even greater amounts fall on the windward slopes: 120 to 167 inches a year and more in the Forks area. Not only does this foster the rapid growth of mushrooms and slugs, but it has also led to the creation of North America's greatest rainforest in the soggy Hoh River valley. Yet a mere 40 miles away as the raven flies, Sequim—in the Olympic rain shadow—is a comparative desert with only about 15 inches of rain per year.

The first residents of the peninsula and coast were tribes like the Makah, Ozette and Quileute, whose descendants still inhabit the area today. A seafaring people noted for their woodcarving, they lived in a series of longhouses facing the sea and are known to have inhabited this region for as long as 2500 years.

Their first contact with Europeans came in 1775, when they massacred a Spanish landing party. Three years later, the ubiquitous British captain James Cook sailed the coast and traded for sea otter furs with Vancouver Island natives; his report opened the gates to the maritime fur trade.

American entrepreneur John Jacob Astor established a fort at the mouth of the Columbia River in 1803, and two years later Meriwether Lewis and William Clark led a cross-country expedition that arrived at Cape Disappointment, on the Washington side of the Columbia, in the winter of 1805. White settlement was at first slow, but by the mid-19th century Port Townsend had established itself as Puget Sound's premier lumber-shipping port, and other communities sprang up soon after.

Olympic National Park was annexed to the national park system in 1938. But long before that, Washingtonians had discovered its natural wonders. A fledgling tourism industry grew, with lodges constructed at several strategic locations around the park, including lakes Crescent and Quinault, Sol Duc Hot Springs and Kalaloch, overlooking the Pacific. Coastal communities were also building a visitor infrastructure, and quiet beach resorts soon emerged.

Today, typical Olympic Peninsula visitors start their tour in Port Townsend, having traveled by ferry and car from Seattle or Whidbey Island, and use Route 101 as their artery of exploration. Port Townsend is considered the most authentic Victorian seacoast town in the United States north of San Francisco, and its plethora of well-preserved 19th-century buildings, many of them now bed and breakfasts, charms all visitors. Less than an hour's drive west, the seven-mile Dungeness Spit (a national wildlife refuge) is the largest natural sand hook in the United States and is famed for the delectable crabs that share its name. Port Angeles, in the center of the north coast, is home to the headquarters of Olympic National Park and is its primary gateway. The bustling international port town also has a direct ferry link to Victoria, Canada, across the Strait of Juan de Fuca.

Neah Bay, the northwesternmost community in the continental United States, is the home of the Makah Indian Museum and Cultural Center and an important marina for deep-sea fishing charters. Clallam Bay, to its east, and La Push, south down the coast, are other sportfishing centers. The logging town of Forks is the portal for visitors to the national park's Hoh Rainforest.

Route 101 emerges from the damp Olympic forests to slightly less moist Grays Harbor, with its twin lumber port towns of Aberdeen and Hoquiam. Though these towns combined have a population of over 25,000, they have limited appeal to travelers, who typically head over the north shore of Grays Harbor to the hotels

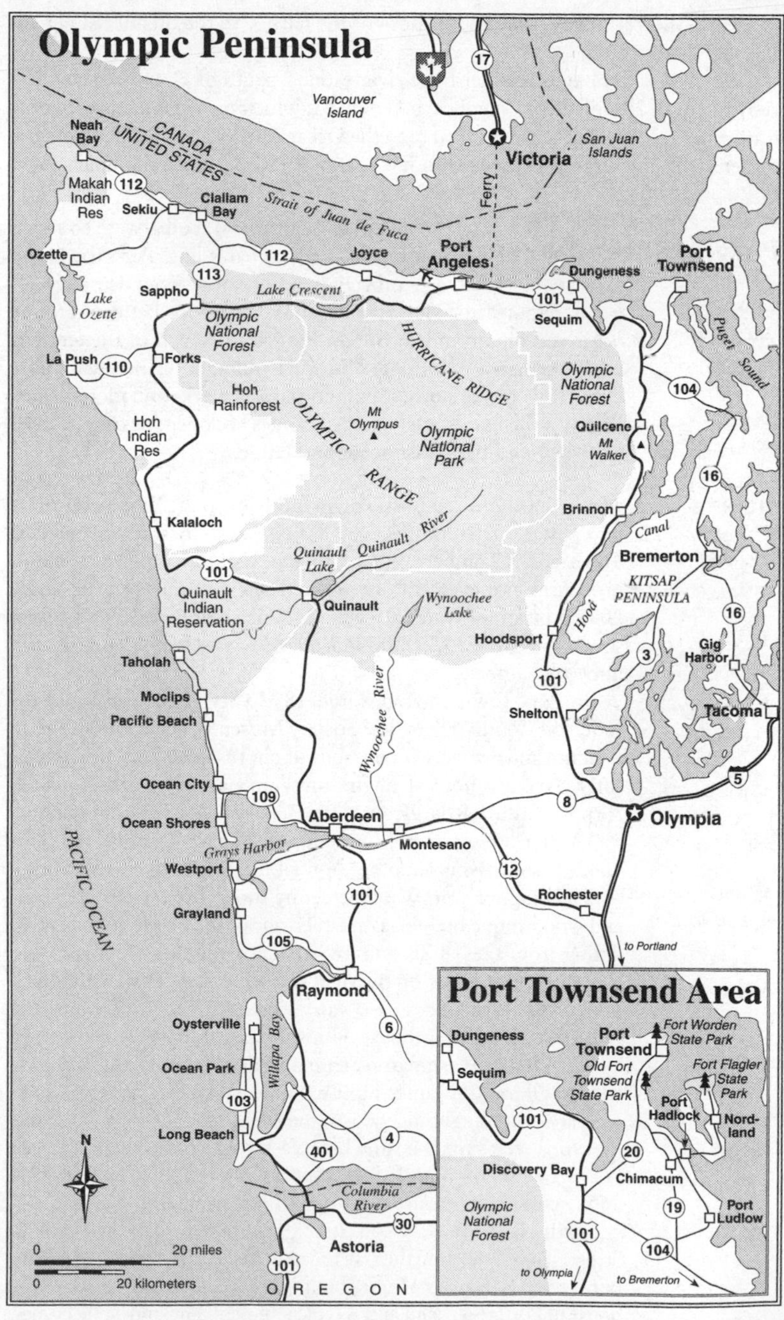
Olympic Peninsula
Vancouver Island
Victoria
San Juan Islands
Ferry
CANADA
UNITED STATES
Neah Bay
Makah Indian Res
Sekiu
Clallam Bay
Strait of Juan de Fuca
Ozette
Lake Ozette
Sappho
Joyce
Port Angeles
Lake Crescent
Dungeness
Port Townsend
Sequim
Puget Sound
Olympic National Forest
HURRICANE RIDGE
La Push
Forks
Hoh Rainforest
OLYMPIC RANGE
Mt Olympus
Olympic National Park
Quilcene
Mt Walker
Hoh Indian Res
Kalaloch
Brinnon
Canal
Hood
Bremerton
KITSAP PENINSULA
Quinault Lake
Quinault River
Quinault
Quinault Indian Reservation
Wynoochee Lake
Wynoochee River
Hoodsport
Gig Harbor
Taholah
Moclips
Pacific Beach
Shelton
Tacoma
Ocean City
Ocean Shores
Aberdeen
Montesano
Olympia
Grays Harbor
Westport
Rochester
Grayland
PACIFIC OCEAN
to Portland
Raymond
Oysterville
Willapa Bay
Ocean Park
Long Beach
Columbia River
Astoria
OREGON
N
0 20 miles
0 20 kilometers
1
17
112
113
110
101
109
105
103
401
4
6
30
12
8
5
3
16
104
Port Townsend Area
Dungeness
Sequim
Port Townsend
Fort Worden State Park
Old Fort Townsend State Park
Fort Flagler State Park
Port Hadlock
Nordland
Discovery Bay
Chimacum
Olympic National Forest
Port Ludlow
101
20
19
104
to Olympia
to Bremerton

of Ocean Shores, or down the south shore of the harbor to the quaint fishing village of Westport.

Serene Willapa Bay is another huge river estuary south of Grays Harbor. The resort strip of 28-mile-long Long Beach Peninsula, which provides a seaward dike for the bay, is older and less contrived than the Ocean Shores area. Wildlife refuges, oyster farms and cranberry bogs lend it a sort of 1950s Cape Cod ambience.

Port Townsend Area

Before either Seattle or Tacoma were so much as a tug on a fisherman's line, Port Townsend was a thriving lumber port. Founded in 1851, it has retained its Victorian seacoast ambience better than any other community north of San Francisco. Much of the city has been designated a National Historic Landmark district, with more than 70 Victorian houses, buildings, forts, parks and monuments. Many of the handsomely gabled homes are open for tours and/or offer bed-and-breakfast accommodations.

SIGHTS

The best way to see **Port Townsend** is on foot. When you drive into town on Route 20, you'll first want to stop at the **Port Townsend Chamber of Commerce** visitors center for maps, brochures and event information. Then continue east on Route 20 as it becomes Water Street. ~ 2437 East Sims Way, Port Townsend; 360-385-2722, 888-365-6978; www.enjoypt.com, e-mail info@ptchamber.org.

In Port Townsend's restored 1892 **City Hall**, you'll find the **Jefferson County Historical Society Museum**, featuring Victorian antiques and artifacts. Thousands of photos from Port Townsend's early days are housed in the museum's archives office (13694 Airport Cutoff Road/Route 19; 360-379-6673). Admission. ~ 540 Water Street, Port Townsend; 360-385-1003, fax 360-385-1042; www.jchsmuseum.org, e-mail marsha@jchsmuseum.org.

Heading west on Water Street by foot, note the elegant stone and wood-frame buildings on either side of the street, most of them dating from the 1880s and 1890s. Turn right on Adams Street; halfway up the block on the right is the **Enoch S. Fowler Building,** built in 1874, the oldest two-story stone structure in Washington. A former county courthouse, it now houses the weekly newspaper.

Turn left at Washington Street and five blocks farther, on your left, you'll see the **James House,** built in 1889. It has five chimneys and a commanding view of the harbor—and in 1973 became the Northwest's first bed and breakfast. ~ 1238 Washington Street, Port Townsend; 360-385-1238, 800-385-1238, fax 360-379-5551; www.jameshouse.com, e-mail info@jameshouse.com.

Turn right up Harrison Street, then right again at Franklin Street. Two blocks farther, at Franklin and Polk streets, the **Captain Enoch S. Fowler Home**, built in 1860, is the oldest surviving house in Port Townsend and is typical of New England–style homes.

Two more blocks ahead, you will encounter the **Rothschild House**, built in 1868 by an early Port Townsend merchant. Notable for its outstanding interior woodwork, it's maintained by the State Parks Commission for public tours. Closed October through April. Admission. ~ Franklin and Taylor streets, Port Townsend; 360-385-1003; www.jchsmuseum.org.

Port Townsend is one of only two Victorian seaports on the U.S. National Historic Register. (Fernandina Beach, Florida, is the other.)

A block north, **Trinity Methodist Church** (1871) is the state's oldest standing Methodist church. Its small museum contains the Bible of the church's first minister. ~ Taylor and Clay streets, Port Townsend; 360-385-0484.

A block east, the 1889 **Ann Starrett Victorian Boutique Hotel Mansion**, now an inn, offers public tours from noon until three during the months of July and August. Admission. ~ 744 Clay Street, Port Townsend; 360-385-3205, 800-321-0644; www.starrettmansion.com, e-mail info@starrettmansion.com.

The **Lucinda Hastings Home** was the most expensive house ever built in Port Townsend when it was erected in 1890 at a cost of $14,000. ~ Clay and Monroe streets, Port Townsend.

Turn right here, and return down Monroe to Water Street and your starting point at City Hall. Get back in your car and drive north on Monroe Street. (The arterial staggers a half-block right at Roosevelt Street onto Jackson Street, then turns right onto Walnut Street.) All roads flow into W Street, the south boundary of **Fort Worden State Park Conference Center**. If the fort looks familiar, it could be because it was used in the filming of the Richard Gere–Debra Winger classic, *An Officer and a Gentleman.* Authorized in 1896, it includes officers' row and a refurbished **Commanding Officer's House** (admission), the **248th Coast Artillery Museum** (admission), gun emplacements, a concert pavilion, marine interpretive center and **Point Wilson Lighthouse**. Fort Worden offers stretches of beach that command impressive views of the Cascades and nearby islands. ~ Port Townsend; 360-344-4400, fax 360-385-7248; www.parks.wa.gov/fortworden.

On the dock at Fort Worden is the **Port Townsend Marine Science Center**. Of special interest are its four large touch tanks, representing different intertidal habitats, where creatures like starfish, anemones and sea cucumbers can be handled by curious visitors. Daily guided walks as well as a birding boat trip around Protection Island National Wildlife Refuge are offered in the summer. Hours vary seasonally; call ahead. Admission. ~ Port Townsend; 360-385-5582, 800-566-3932; www.ptmsc.org, e-mail info@ptmsc.org.

Visitors driving to Port Townsend typically cross the one-and-a-half-mile **Hood Canal Floating Bridge** on Route 104 from the Kitsap Peninsula. Located 30 miles southeast of Port Townsend, it is the world's only floating bridge erected over tidal waters and one of the longest of its kind anywhere. Constructed in 1961, the bridge was washed away during a fierce storm in February 1979, but was rebuilt in 1982.

Traveling south from Port Townsend, Route 20 joins Route 101 at Discovery Bay. Twelve miles south of the junction is the town of **Quilcene** on the Hood Canal, a serpentine finger of Puget Sound. The town is especially noted for its oyster farming and processing and is the location of a state shellfish research laboratory (not open to the public). The **Mount Walker Observation Point**—five miles south on Route 101, then another five miles on a gravel road that starts at Walker Pass—offers a spectacular view of the Hood Canal and surrounding area. On a clear day, you can see Seattle and the Space Needle.

LODGING

The **James House** claims to have been the Pacific Northwest's first bed and breakfast. Just a few steps from shops and restaurants at the foot of the bluff that stands behind lower downtown, it dates from 1889, though it's only been a bed and breakfast since 1973. The house is unmistakable for its five chimneys; inside, the floors are all parquet. All rooms have private baths. There is a fireplace and a library, and a full breakfast is served. Save a few moments to enjoy the English gardens with an impressive view of the water. Two bungalow-style units, adjacent to the James House, are also available. Kids over 12 are welcome. ~ 1238 Washington Street, Port Townsend; 360-385-1238, 800-385-1238, fax 360-379-5551; www.jameshouse.com, e-mail info@jameshouse.com. ULTRA-DELUXE.

For those less than enthralled with bed and breakfasts, the **Palace Hotel** provides historic accommodation in a former seafarers' bordello. Though nicely renovated, this is a bit rustic: After checking in at the main lobby you must climb a long flight of stairs (or two) to your room. There are 15 guest chambers, each with antiques recalling the red-light flavor of the past. Three

LEISURELY LISTENING

Chamber music doesn't come much more idyllic than the annual summer **Olympic Music Festival**, held on a farm near Port Townsend between late June and early September. Founded by members of the Philadelphia String Quartet in 1984, the much-loved weekend Concerts in the Barn now attract 12,000 people a year for a relaxed afternoon of professionally played chamber music, strolls in grassy meadows, and picnics. Concerts are held rain or shine on Saturday and Sunday. ~ 206-527-8839; www.olympicmusicfestival.org, e-mail info@olympicmusicfestival.org.

of the rooms, including the madam's former room, even have kitchenettes. ~ 1004 Water Street, Port Townsend; 360-385-0773, 800-962-0741, fax 360-385-0780; www.palacehotelpt.com, e-mail palace@olympus.net. MODERATE TO DELUXE.

The renowned **Ann Starrett Victorian Boutique Hotel Mansion,** a National Historic Landmark built in 1889, is a classic mansion in Victorian style. High on a bluff overlooking downtown Port Townsend and Puget Sound, it combines diverse architectural elements—frescoed ceilings, a free-hung spiral staircase, an eight-sided dome painted as a solar calendar, the requisite gables and dormer window—into a charming whole. The 11 guest rooms all have private baths and are furnished with antiques, of course. Five-night minimum from November through Christmas. ~ 744 Clay Street, Port Townsend; 360-385-3205, 800-321-0644; www.starrettmansion.com, e-mail info@starrettmansion.com. DELUXE TO ULTRA-DELUXE.

With so many heritage choices, few visitors actually opt for a motel stay. If you do, check out **The Tides Inn,** along the waterfront at the south end of town. Among the 45 rooms are five efficiencies and nine with hot tubs; most units have balconies overlooking the bay. ~ 1807 Water Street, Port Townsend; 360-385-0595, 800-822-8696, fax 360-379-1115; www.tides-inn.com, e-mail tidesinn@cablespeed.com. MODERATE TO ULTRA-DELUXE.

Built in 1936 for use by pilots guiding ships through the Strait of Juan de Fuca, the two-bedroom, weathered-shingle **Pilot's Cottage** exudes oodles of simple rustic charm and atmosphere from its quiet waterfront location overlooking Point Hudson Harbor. Amenities include a kitchen, living room and wood-burning stove. The cottage can be rented by the night, week or longer and sleeps four total; no smoking or pets. It's walking distance to downtown. ~ 327 Jackson Street, Port Townsend; 360-379-0811; www.pilotscottage.com. DELUXE.

For students and backpackers, the **Hostelling International Olympic Hostel** offers some of the least expensive accommodations on the Olympic Peninsula. Housed in a former World War II barracks building, it has 30 beds in men's and women's dorms, along with private rooms for couples and families. ~ 272 Battery Way, Port Townsend; 360-385-0655, 800-909-4776; www.olympichostel.org, e-mail olympichostel@olympus.net. BUDGET.

Another hostel is at **Fort Flagler State Park,** open June through September. ~ Located three miles north of Nordland; 360-385-1259. BUDGET.

South of town about 20 miles, **The Resort at Port Ludlow** is one of the Northwest's premier family resorts. It boasts a championship golf course, tennis courts, swimming pools, a marina, hiking and biking trails and 1500 acres of land. There are 37 guest rooms with fireplaces, six condominiums and one beach house. Other amenities include oversized jetted tubs and decks, and a restaurant with marvelous views of water and mountains. ~ 1 Heron Road, Port Ludlow; 360-437-7000, 877-805-0868, fax 360-437-7410; www.portludlowresort.com, e-mail info@portludlowresort.com. ULTRA-DELUXE.

DINING

For an evening of fine dining, it would be hard to top the **Manresa Castle**. Located in an 1892 hilltop inn that overlooks the town and bay like a German castle on the Rhine River, it combines an elegant restaurant and an Edwardian pub. The menu offers regional and seasonal specialties, everything from curry chicken and bouillabaisse to tiger prawns. Closed Monday; no lunch. Only brunch on Sunday. Closed seasonally; call ahead. ~ 7th and Sheridan streets, Port Townsend; 360-385-5750, fax 360-385-5883; www.manresacastle.com, e-mail info@manresacastle.com. DELUXE TO ULTRA-DELUXE.

The Dungeness crab was the first commercially harvested shellfish on the Olympic coast; it shares its name with the town on Washington's Olympic Peninsula. The town itself was named after a point on the English coast near the Strait of Dover.

Ask locals where to eat, and chances are they'll recommend the **Fountain Café**. You'll probably have to stand in line for a seat, but the wait will be worth it. Occupying the ground floor of a historic building (is there anything else in downtown Port Townsend?), the Fountain serves outstanding seafood and pasta dishes, including oysters as you like 'em. Soups and desserts are homemade. The decor is eclectic and showcases young local artists. ~ 920 Washington Street, Port Townsend; 360-385-1364. MODERATE.

T's showcases excellent service and fresh Northwest cuisine. Start with Dungeness crab pot stickers, or a fresh salad of roasted beets and goat cheese or organic baby greens (entrée-size salads with additional meat options are available). Pan-roasted wild sea scallops and ginger- and scallion-crusted wild salmon top the list of entrées. Other choices include duck, roast chicken, flatiron steak, pastas with homemade sauces and roasted portabello mushrooms. The wine list is extensive. Dinner only. Closed Monday and Tuesday. ~ 2330 Washington Street, Port Townsend; 360-385-0700; www.ts-restaurant.com, e-mail info@ts-restaurant.com. DELUXE.

Breakfasts draw full houses at the **Salal Cafe**. Huge omelettes and various seafood and vegetarian recipes get *oohs* and *ahs*, as do the burgers and meat dishes. Lunch features gourmet home-style cooking, along with crêpes and sandwiches. No dinner. ~ 634 Water Street, Port Townsend; 360-385-6532. BUDGET.

HIDDEN ►

Khu Larb Thai has probably the best Thai food in Washington State. Curries are rich and flavorful; pad thai, usually mundane, is interesting; mussel hot pots are divine. The rich soups, especially the seafood concoctions, are practically enough for a meal by themselves. And the black rice pudding is an unusual treat. Come early for a table on weekend nights. Closed Monday. ~ 225 Adams Street, Port Townsend; 360-385-5023. BUDGET TO MODERATE.

Some say the **Shanghai Restaurant** serves the best Chinese food this side of Vancouver's Chinatown. Forget the view of the RV park across the street, and enjoy the spicy Szechuan and northern Chinese cuisine. ~ Point Hudson, Port Townsend; 360-385-4810, fax 360-385-0660. BUDGET TO MODERATE.

HIDDEN

The **Chimacum Café**, nine miles south of Port Townsend, is a local institution. This is food like grandma should have made—country-fried chicken dinners, baked ham and so forth, followed, of course, by homemade pies brimming with fresh fruit. Breakfast, lunch and dinner are served. ~ 9253 Rhody Drive, Chimacum; 360-732-4631. BUDGET TO MODERATE.

SHOPPING

Port Townsend offers the most interesting shopping on the peninsula with its array of galleries, antique and gift shops, bookstores, gourmet dining and all-purpose emporiums. Proprietors have paid particular attention to historical accuracy in restoring commercial buildings. Many of the shops feature the work of talented local painters, sculptors, weavers, potters, poets and writers.

If you're looking for antiques, try the **Port Townsend Antique Mall** or any of the many other shops along the 600 through 1200 blocks of Water or Washington streets. ~ Antique Mall: 802 Washington Street, Port Townsend; 360-379-8069.

Among the many fine galleries for contemporary arts and crafts are **Ancestral Spirits Gallery**, which features Inuit and Northwest Coast tribal artwork. ~ 701 Water Street, Port Townsend; 360-385-0078. **Artisans on Taylor** specializes in local Northwestern crafts and hand-formed glass beads. ~ 236 Taylor Street, Port Townsend; 360-379-1029.

NIGHTLIFE

Live blues, jazz, opera and folk music accompany dinner at **Lanza's Ristorante** on the weekend. Closed Sunday and Monday. ~ 1020 Lawrence Street, Port Townsend; 360-379-1900.

BEACHES & PARKS

FORT WORDEN STATE PARK A 434-acre estate right in Port Townsend, this turn-of-the-20th-century fort includes restored Victorian officers houses, barracks, theater, parade grounds and artillery bunkers. A beach and a boat launch are on Admiralty Inlet, at the head of Puget Sound. Try the dock or beach for salmon fishing. Restrooms, picnic areas, tennis courts and lodging are found here. ~ The entrance is located on W Street at Cherry Street, at the northern city limits of Port Townsend; 360-344-4431, fax 360-385-7248; www.parks.wa.gov/fortworden, e-mail fwcamping@parks.wa.gov.

▲ There are 80 RV hookup sites ($37 to $38 per night). Primitive sites are also available ($21 per night). Reservations, by mail, by fax or via the internet, are strongly recommended year-round. Reservations: 200 Battery Way, Port Townsend, WA 98368.

KAH TAI LAGOON NATURE PARK This midtown park, which features 21 acres of wetlands and 40 acres of grasslands and woodlands, is a great place for birdwatching: more than 50 species have been identified here. There are two and a half miles of trails, a play area for kids, interpretive displays, restrooms and picnic areas. ~ 12th Street near Sims Way, Port Townsend.

OLD FORT TOWNSEND STATE PARK Decommissioned in 1895 when Indian attacks on Port Townsend (the town) were no longer a threat, the fort site has six and a half miles of trails and a beach on Port Townsend (the inlet). You can fish from the shore. You'll find restrooms and picnic areas. Closed October through April. ~ Old Fort Townsend Road, two miles south of the town of Port Townsend off Route 20; 360-385-3595 or 360-385-3595, fax 360-385-7248.

▲ There are 40 standard sites ($13 per night) and 4 primitive sites ($10 per night). Closed early November to mid-April.

FORT FLAGLER STATE PARK Fort buildings dating from 1898 are a major attraction here. In addition, the saltwater beach on Admiralty Inlet is popular for clamming, beachcombing and fishing for salmon, halibut, sole, crab and shellfish. There are also a boat launch, hiking trails, restrooms, picnic areas and lodging. ~ Off Route 116, on the north tip of Marrowstone Island, eight miles northeast of Hadlock; 360-385-1259, 888-226-7688, fax 360-379-1746.

▲ There are 101 standard sites ($19 to $22 per night) and 12 RV hookup sites ($25 per night). No camping November through February. Reservations: 888-226-7688.

A TASTE OF TOWNSEND

No trip to Port Townsend would be complete without taking back a hunk of the Northwest's freshest catch. The **Key City Fish Co.**, located in one of the harbor marina's warehouses, stocks salmon, halibut, cod, Dungeness crab and everything else in between. It may not be getting it straight off the boat, but then again they'll clean it, pack it and even ship it for you. Closed Sunday in off-season. ~ 307 10th Street, Port Townsend; 360-379-5516, 800-617-3474.

DOSEWALLIPS STATE PARK At the mouth of the Dosewallips River on the Hood Canal, a long, serpentine arm of Puget Sound, this 425-acre park is especially popular among clam diggers and oyster hunters during shellfish season. You'll find a beach of oyster shells and cobble, hiking trails, restrooms, showers and picnic areas. ~ Route 101, in Brinnon, 37 miles south of Port Townsend; 360-796-4415, fax 360-796-3242.

▲ There are 100 standard sites ($17 per night) and 40 RV hookup sites ($24 per night). Reservations: 888-226-7688.

OLYMPIC NATIONAL FOREST Surrounding Olympic National Park on its east, south and northwest sides, this national forest provides ample recreational opportunities, including good fishing for trout and, in some areas, for rock cod and salmon in the forest's many lakes and rivers. It includes five wilderness areas on the fringe of the park. There are restrooms and picnic areas. Dogs and hunting are allowed in the national forest, but not in Olympic National Park. Some areas of the park and some campgrounds close seasonally due to weather. ~ Numerous access roads branch off Route 101, especially south of Sequim, and between Quilcene and Hoodsport, on the east side of the Olympic Peninsula; 360-956-2400, fax 360-956-2330; www.fs.fed.us/r6/olympic.

▲ There are 23 campgrounds throughout the forest. Camping costs range from free to $15 per night. Three cabins, sleeping four to six people, rent for $30 to $40 per night.

Port Angeles Area

The northern gateway to Olympic National Park as well as a major terminal for ferries to British Columbia, the Port Angeles area is one of northwest Washington's main crossroads. Sequim on Route 101, 31 miles west of Port Townsend, and nearby Port Angeles are two of the peninsula's more intriguing towns.

SIGHTS

The town of **Sequim** (pronounced "Squim") is graced with a climate that's unusually dry and mild for the Northwest: it sits in the Olympic rain shadow. A major attraction just north of town is the **Olympic Game Farm**, whose animals—wolves, tigers, bears, buffalo and many others—are trained for film roles. Driving tours of the farm are available year-round; walking tours, including a studio barn, are offered during the summer. Admission. ~ 1423 Ward Road, Sequim; 360-683-4295, fax 360-681-4443; www.olygamefarm.com, e-mail gamefarm@olympus.net.

In the Sequim–Dungeness Valley area, the **Museum and Art Center** preserves the native and pioneer farming heritage of Sequim and showcases the work of local artists. Closed Sunday and Monday. ~ 175 West Cedar Street, Sequim; 360-683-8110; www.sequimmuseum.org.

For visitor information, contact the **Sequim–Dungeness Chamber of Commerce Visitors Center.** ~ 1192 East Washington Street, Sequim; 360-683-6197, 800-737-8462; www.cityofsequim.com, e-mail info@cityofsequim.com.

North off Route 101, the Dungeness Valley is dotted with lavender, strawberry and raspberry fields. Weathered barns left over from the area's dairy farming days are still visible. Pay a visit to the **Cedarbrook Lavender & Herb Farm,** where 300 different varieties of lavender and herbs fill the air with a marvelous (but indefinable!) aroma and inspire many a gourmet chef to go on a culinary buying spree. Limited hours from January through March. ~ 1345 Sequim Avenue South, Sequim; 360-683-7733, 800-470-8423; www.cedarbrookherbfarm.com, e-mail marcella@cedarbrookherbfarm.com.

Opposite the mouth of the Dungeness River is one of the Olympic Peninsula's most remarkable natural features: the **Dungeness Spit,** almost seven miles long and the largest natural sand hook in the United States. A short trail within the adjacent **Dungeness Recreation Area** provides access to this national wildlife refuge. At the end of the spit, the **New Dungeness Lighthouse** rises 63 feet above the sea. Established in 1857, the lighthouse is now on the National Register of Historic Places. Visitors who brave the five-and-a-half-mile walk out along the spit will be rewarded with an in-depth tour of the facilities. ~ 360-683-9166; www.newdungenesslighthouse.com, e-mail lightkeepers@newdungenesslighthouse.com.

Seventeen miles west of Sequim on Route 101 is the fishing and logging port of **Port Angeles,** the Olympic Peninsula's largest town. A major attraction here is the **City Pier.** Adjacent to the ferry terminal, it boasts an observation tower, promenade decks and a picnic area. ~ Port Angeles; 360-452-2363.

The **Arthur D. Feiro Marine Life Center,** where visitors can observe and even touch samples of local marine life, is also found at the City Pier. Call for hours. Admission. ~ Port Angeles; 360-417-6254; www.olypen.com/feirolab.

As the gateway to Olympic National Park, Port Angeles is home to national park headquarters. At the **Olympic National Park Visitor Center,** you'll find an excellent video and exhibits on the natural and human history of the park. Usually open daily in the summer; varying hours the rest of the year. ~ 3002 Mt. Angeles Road, Port Angeles; 360-565-3130; www.nps.gov/olym.

Nestled in the shadow of Olympic National Park, award-winning **Port Angeles Fine Art Center** is located in a leafy five-acre sculpture park and hosts changing mixed-media exhibitions, lectures and concerts, and a stage at the Strait of Juan de Fuca Festival of Fine Arts every Memorial Day weekend. Closed Monday. ~ Take Route 101 westbound to Race Street and the

Olympic National Park Hurricane Ridge turnoff. Turn left (south) and proceed 1 mile towards Hurricane Ridge. Turn left (east) on Lauridsen Boulevard and proceed .25 mile to PAFAC parking adjacent to a domed water silo; 360-417-4590 or 360-457-3532; www.pafac.org, e-mail info@pafac.org.

The **Museum at the Carnegie** has county archival and genealogical records, as well as exhibits like period clothing and old photos. Closed Sunday through Tuesday. ~ 207 South Lincoln Street, Port Angeles; 360-452-2662; www.clallamhistoricalsociety.com, e-mail artifact@olypen.com.

For tourist information, contact the **North Olympic Peninsula Visitor & Convention Bureau.** ~ 338 West 1st Street, Port Angeles; 360-452-8552, 800-942-4042; www.olympicpeninsula.org, e-mail info@olympicpeninsula.org.

LODGING

You'll feel good right down to your cockles—as well as your steamer clams and horse clams—after shellfishing on the saltwater beach outside the **Sequim Bay Resort.** The eight fully equipped housekeeping cottages here are suitable for vacationing families and shoreline lovers. There are no pets allowed in the cottages. There are also guest laundry facilities and hookups for RVs. Two-night minimum stay required. ~ 2634 West Sequim Bay Road, Sequim; 360-681-3853, fax 360-681-3854; www.sequimbayresort.com, e-mail sequimbayresort@yahoo.com. BUDGET TO MODERATE.

Just a spit from the Spit—Dungeness, that is—is the **Groveland Cottage,** by the coast north of Sequim. The early-20th-century building has four carpeted rooms with art, antique decor and private baths; some boast jacuzzis and fireplaces. There is

AUTHOR FAVORITE

Perched on an ocean bluff overlooking the Strait of Juan de Fuca, **BJ's Garden Gate Bed & Breakfast** offers comfortable and luxurious accommodations in a lovely, natural setting. All five guest rooms are individually themed and boast fireplaces, down comforters and an ocean view; three have jacuzzis for two. Both Victoria's Repose and Maria Theresa's suite have a private porch, while the Napoleon Bonaparte has a sitting room. Stroll the three-acre English garden, interlaced with woodland paths and strewn with wild rhododendrons. The area is known for fabulous hiking, and waterfalls, rainforests, beaches and mountains are located a mere 15 minutes away. A full gourmet breakfast is served, and fresh-baked cookies are offered nightly. Reservations are strongly recommended. ~ 397 Monterra Drive, Port Angeles; 360-452-2322, 800-880-1332; www.bjgarden.com, e-mail info@bjgarden.com. ULTRA-DELUXE.

also a private cottage with a queen-size bed and private bath. The rooms may be simple, but service is not: coffee is delivered to your room in anticipation of the gourmet breakfast. Wi-fi is available in all rooms. The accent overall is on comfort. They also rent 32 vacation cottages in the area. ~ 4861 Sequim-Dungeness Way, Dungeness; 360-683-3565, 800-879-8859, fax 360-683-5181; www.sequimvalley.com/groveland.mv, e-mail simone@olypen.com. MODERATE.

Perhaps the nicest motel-style accommodation in these port communities is the **Red Lion Hotel.** A modern building that extends along the Strait of Juan de Fuca opposite the ferry dock, it offers rooms with private balconies overlooking the water. A strand of beach and swimming pool beckon bathers. ~ 221 North Lincoln Street, Port Angeles; 360-452-9215, 877-333-2733, fax 360-452-4734; www.redlionportangeles.com, e-mail pa.frontdesk@redlion.com. ULTRA-DELUXE.

Situated on the water with beautiful gardens and spectacular views of the San Juan Islands, the **Domaine Madeleine Bed and Breakfast** excels in both comfort and hospitality. There are five rooms at this charming inn, including a honeymoon cottage. There's the Renoir Suite, with a 14-foot-high basalt fireplace and impressionist art, and the Ming Room, with antiques, a jacuzzi and a large private balcony. All rooms have wi-fi access, fireplaces, feather beds and French perfumes. Four rooms have jacuzzis for two. Relax in the cozy coffee nook or try your hand at the antique organ. The full gourmet breakfast is elegantly presented—don't miss it. Gay-friendly. ~ 146 Wildflower Lane, Port Angeles; 360-457-4174, 888-811-8376, fax 360-457-3037; www.domainemadeleine.com, e-mail romance@domainemadeleine.com. ULTRA-DELUXE.

The true romance of the Olympic Peninsula is evident throughout **Colette's Bed and Breakfast**, a gorgeous 10-acre waterfront estate in Port Angeles. The five luxurious suites have

AWASH IN PURPLE

In Washington, the town of Sequim is synonymous with lavender—approximately 110,000 plants are grown in the area every year. The three-day **Lavender Festival** in mid-July celebrates this fragrant bit of botany with a street fair bursting with music, food and vendors plying their lavender-themed wares. Enthusiasts can also enjoy a seminar about the plant's many different uses and tour area lavender farms. Contact the Sequim Lavender Growers Association for more information. ~ 360-681-3035, 877-681-3035; www.lavenderfestival.com, e-mail info@lavenderfestival.com.

king-sized beds, fireplaces, large flat-screen TVs, DVD/CD/stereo players, wi-fi access, and private bathrooms with two-person jacuzzi tubs. Private patios adjoining lush gardens have views over the Strait of Juan de Fuca. Breakfast is a multicourse organic feast and might include Northwest eggs Benedict with smoked salmon or minted pancakes with raspberry coulis. ~ 339 Finn Hall Road, Port Angeles; 360-457-9197, 877-457-9777; www.colettes.com, e-mail colettes@colettes.com. DELUXE TO ULTRA-DELUXE.

Victoria, across the strait on Vancouver Island, is said to be "more British than the British"—but the same slogan could almost apply to **The Tudor Inn.** The host serves a gourmet breakfast and afternoon refreshment in the restored Tudor-style home. Most of their antique collection is Old English, and the well-stocked library will steer you to books on a wide variety of subjects. All five bedrooms have private baths; one has a gas fireplace and small balcony. ~ 1108 South Oak Street, Port Angeles; 360-452-3138, 866-286-2224, fax 360-457-9360; www.tudorinn.com, e-mail info@tudorinn.com. DELUXE.

DINING

El Cazador is a casual, family-run restaurant with festive murals. What sets it apart is its use of fresh seafood in traditional Mexican dishes that consistently win local "best of" awards. The burrito à la Veracruz stuffed with baby shrimp is especially good. ~ 531 West Washington Street, Sequim; 360-683-4788; www.el-cazador.com, e-mail info@el-cazador.com. BUDGET.

Dungeness crab doesn't come much fresher than the many variations served up at the **Three Crabs**, an award-winning seafood restaurant right on the beach in Dungeness. A Sequim favorite for 46 years, they also serve fabulous oysters, salmon, halibut and steaks. Reservations recommended. ~ 11 Three Crabs Road, Sequim; 360-683-4264; www.the3crabs.com, e-mail info@the3crabs.com. MODERATE TO DELUXE.

The undisputed winner in the northern Olympic Peninsula fine-dining sweepstakes is **C'est Si Bon**. The decor is modern and dramatic, with handsome oil paintings and full picture windows allowing panoramas of the Olympic Range. The cuisine, on the other hand, is classical French: quails stuffed with mushrooms, veal, pork and chicken, coquilles St. Jacques, filet mignon with dungeness crab. There are French wines and desserts, too. Dinner only. Closed Monday. ~ 23 Cedar Park Road, four miles east of Port Angeles; 360-452-8888; www.cestsibon-frenchcuisine.com. ULTRA-DELUXE.

A New England reader raved about the clam linguine at the charming **Bella Italia** and *Wine Spectator* magazine gave it an award of excellence. Indeed, this restaurant specializing in Olympic Coast cuisine, is a destination in itself for many Puget

Sound–area foodies. In addition to a variety of pasta, this intimate, candlelit eatery whips up Tuscan steak, cioppino and veal Marsala. It also has an extensive wine selection. Dinner only. ~ 118-E East 1st Street, Port Angeles; 360-457-5442, fax 360-457-6112; www.bellaitaliapa.com, e-mail bella@olypen.com. MODERATE TO DELUXE.

Port Angeles Crabhouse, located in the Red Lion Hotel, offers sweeping waterfront views in a casually elegant decor of etched glass and tapestry-covered booth seating. Simple and straightforward seafood dishes such as cracked Dungeness crab and grilled salmon are the specialties. ~ 221 North Lincoln Street, Port Angeles; 360-457-0424, fax 360-452-4734; www.pacrabhouse.com. MODERATE TO ULTRA-DELUXE.

Practically next door is the **First Street Haven**, one of the best places around for quick and tasty breakfasts and lunches. Have a homemade quiche and salad, along with baked goods and the house coffee, and you'll be set for the day. Breakfast and lunch only, but no lunch on Sunday. ~ 107 East 1st Street, Port Angeles; 360-457-0352, fax 360-452-8502. BUDGET.

SHOPPING

Mad Maggi Salon Boutique is a women's clothing shop that doubles as a hair salon. Closed Sunday. ~ 131 East Washington Street, Sequim; 360-683-5733.

NIGHTLIFE

You didn't come to this part of the state for its nightlife, and that's good. What little there is usually exists only on Friday and Saturday nights.

The **Port Angeles Crabhouse Lounge** in the Red Lion Hotel features daily drink specials. ~ 221 North Lincoln Street, Port Angeles; 360-457-0424.

BEACHES & PARKS

SEQUIM BAY STATE PARK Shellfish (clams, oysters and crabs) as well as fishing for salmon and halibut are the main attractions at this park on Sequim Bay, sheltered from rough seas by two spits at its mouth and from heavy rains by the Olympic rain shadow. There's a beach; you'll also find restrooms and picnic areas. ~ Route 101, four miles east of Sequim; 360-683-4235, fax 360-681-5054.

▲ There are 63 standard sites ($16 to $19 per night), 16 RV hookup sites ($22 to $26 per night) and 3 hike- or bike-in primitive sites ($10 to $14 per night). Reservations: 888-226-7688.

DUNGENESS RECREATION AREA The Dungeness Spit is a national wildlife refuge, but a recreation area trail provides access. Marine birds, bald eagles and seals are among the impressive wildlife to be seen; the Dungeness crab is internationally famous as a fine food. There are restrooms, showers and picnic areas. ~ Located at the base of the Dungeness

Spit, five miles west of Sequim on Route 101, then four miles north on Kitchen-Dick Road; phone/fax 360-683-5847.

▲ There are 67 sites (no hookups); $16 per night. Closed October through January.

SALT CREEK RECREATION AREA ◄HIDDEN

One of the finest tidepool sanctuaries on the Olympic Peninsula is this three-mile stretch of rocky beach. Starfish, sea urchins, anemones, mussels, barnacles and other invertebrate life can be observed . . . but not removed. Anglers will find rockfish. Restrooms, picnic areas, playground and hiking trails are all here. ~ Located three miles north from Joyce (or 15 miles west from Port Angeles) on Route 112, then another three miles north on Camp Hayden Road; 360-928-3441, fax 360-417-2395, www.clallam.net/countyparks, e-mail ccps@olypen.com.

▲ There are 51 standard sites ($14 to $16 per night) and 39 RV sites ($20 to $22 per night).

Olympic National Park

The Olympic Peninsula's main attraction—in fact, the reason most tourists come here at all—is Olympic National Park. Rugged, glaciated mountains dominate the 1442-square-mile park, with rushing rivers tumbling from their slopes. The rainier western slopes harbor an extraordinary rainforest, and a separate 57-mile-long coastal strip preserves remarkable tidepools and marvelous ocean scenery. Wildlife in the park includes the rare Roosevelt elk, as well as deer, black bears, cougars, bobcats, a great many smaller mammals and scores of bird species. Besides the main part of the park, which encompasses the entire mountain wilderness in the center of the peninsula and can be entered from the north or west, Olympic National Park includes a separate Coastal Unit spanning 73 miles of Pacific headlands and beaches.

IN MEMORIAM

Much of the Olympic coastline remains undeveloped. Hikers can wander along the high-water mark or on primitive trails, some wood-planked and raised above the forest floor. Offshore reefs have taken many lives over the centuries since European exploration began, and two memorials to shipwreck victims are good destinations for intrepid hikers. Nine miles south of Ozette, the **Norwegian Memorial** remembers seamen who died in an early-20th-century shipwreck. Six miles farther south, and about three miles north of Rialto Beach opposite La Push, the **Chilean Memorial** marks the grave of 20 South American sailors who died in a 1920 wreck.

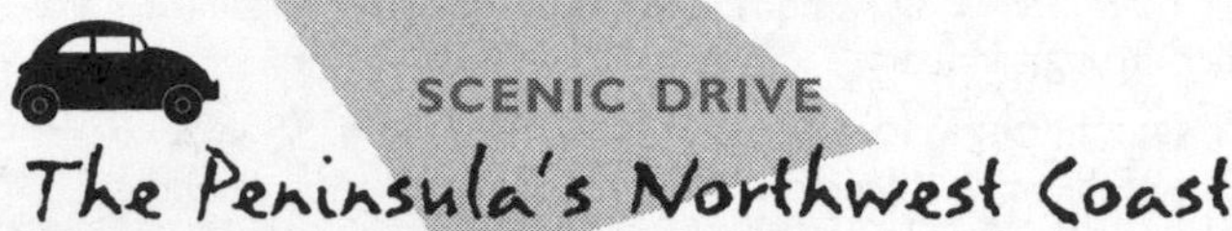

SCENIC DRIVE

The Peninsula's Northwest Coast

Much less traveled than Route 101, Route 112 runs from near Port Angeles to Neah Bay on the northwest tip of the Olympic Peninsula. The drive takes about one and a half hours each way. Allow an additional one and a half to two hours to see the Makah Cultural and Research Center. You may wish to make this an all-day excursion by adding a side trip to Lake Ozette, one of the most hidden spots you can reach by road in Olympic National Park.

THE NORTHWEST COAST From Port Angeles, follow Route 101 west for five miles, then turn off to the right on Route 112. For much of its length, this narrow two-lane highway runs within sight of the Strait of Juan de Fuca and partly traces the water's edge. Travel 46 miles to the sister communities of **Clallam Bay** and **Sekiu** (pronounced "C-Q"). These are prime sportfishing grounds for salmon and huge bottomfish, especially halibut. Check out the wonderful tidepools north of Clallam Bay at **Slip Point**. Just west of Sekiu, at the mouth of the Hoko River, visitors can view the remains of a 2500-year-old Makah Indian fishing village at the **Hoko Archaeological Site**.

NEAH BAY Continue for 18 more miles past Sekiu to the highway's end at Neah Bay, the administrative center of the Makah Indian Reservation. This rather bleak little village has a few motels and a commercial fishing fleet, and visitors can book charter-fishing excursions from the harbor. Beyond the town, roads continue to stormswept beaches on Cape Flattery, strewn with driftwood and shipwrecks. Neah Bay's touristic centerpiece, the **Makah Cultural and Research Center** houses finds from the Ozette Dig at Cape Alava, about 20 miles down the Pacific coast, inter-

SIGHTS

There is no lack of facilities throughout the park: picnic areas, hotels, restaurants and groceries. For general information on the park, call the **Olympic National Park Visitor Center.** ~ 360-565-3130; www.nps.gov/olym.

The most direct route into the park from Port Angeles is the Heart of the Hills/Hurricane Ridge Road. It climbs 5200 feet in just 17 miles to the **Hurricane Ridge Lodge**, where there are breathtaking views to 7965-foot Mt. Olympus, the highest peak in the Olympic Range, and other glacier-shrouded mountains. Summer visitors to Hurricane Ridge can dine in the day lodge, picnic, enjoy nature walks or take longer hikes. In winter, enjoy

preted through the eyes of the Makah themselves. Few relics remain from the ancient culture of the Northwest Coast tribes because their wooden structures and implements rotted away quickly in the damp climate. Ozette, however, was buried 500 years ago by a mudslide that preserved it from the elements until archaeologists discovered it in the 1970s. The artifacts exhibited in an atmospheric longhouse setting at the cultural center include baskets, log canoes, clothing, wood carvings and whaling harpoons. Closed Monday and Tuesday from September through May. Admission. ~ 1880 Bay View Avenue; 360-645-2711, fax 360-645-2656; www.makah.com, e-mail makahmuseum@centurytel.net.

LAKE OZETTE Returning from Neah Bay on Route 112, two miles before you reach Sekiu a paved secondary road turns off to the south (right) and goes 20 miles to Lake Ozette, the northernmost part of Olympic National Park's Coastal Unit. The largest of the park's three lakes, it is separated from the ocean by a strip of land just three miles wide. Several trails lead from here to the sea, including the Indian Village Trail, which leads to the Ozette Dig (no longer open) at Cape Alava, and the Ozette Loop Trail, which weaves past 56 petroglyphs that depict various aspects of historic Makah life. Backcountry permits are required for all overnight trips in the park.

SAPPHO Back on Route 112, six miles east of Clallam Bay Route 113 turns off to the south (right) and goes nine miles through the forest to join Route 101 at Sappho. Here you face a choice: If you turn east (left), you'll return to Port Angeles, a distance of 45 miles through Olympic National Forest and Olympic National Park, passing **Lake Crescent** and **Marymere Falls** (page 171) and the road to **Sol Duc Hot Springs** (page 172). If you turn west (right), Route 101 will take you through Forks to the turnoff for the **Hoh Rainforest** (page 172) and past that to the beaches of the **Olympic National Park Coastal Unit** (page 173), a total distance of 53 miles.

the small downhill ski area here and many cross-country trails. ~ 360-565-3131.

Twenty miles west of Port Angeles on Route 101 is **Lake Crescent**, one of three large lakes within park boundaries. Carved during the last Ice Age 10,000 years ago, it is nestled between steep forested hillsides. A unique subspecies of trout lures many anglers to its deep waters. There are several resorts, restaurants, campgrounds and picnic areas around the lake's shoreline. From National Park Service–administered Lake Crescent Lodge, on the southeast shore, a three-fourth-mile trail leads up Barnes Creek to the beautiful **Marymere Falls**. ~ 416 Lake Cresent Road, Port

Angeles; 360-928-3211, fax 360-928-3253; www.lakecresent lodge.com, e-mail lclodge@olypen.com.

West of Lake Crescent, the Sol Duc River Road turns south to **Sol Duc Hot Springs,** 12 miles off of Route 101. Long known to the Indians, the therapeutic mineral waters were discovered by a pioneer in 1880 and like everything else the white man touched, soon boasted an opulent resort. But the original burned to the ground in 1916 and today's refurbished resort, nestled in a valley of old-growth Douglas fir, is more rustic than elegant. The springs remain an attraction. Sol Duc is a major trailhead for backpacking trips into Olympic National Park; also located here is a ranger station. Closed November through mid-March. ~ 866-476-5382, fax 360-327-3593; www.visitsolduc.com, e-mail info@visitsolduc.com.

The main population center on the Olympic Coast, and the nearest to the Hoh Rainforest, is the lumber town of **Forks.** With over 3000 people, it is the largest town between Port Angeles and Hoquiam. (It's also Washington's rainiest town, with well over 100 inches a year.) Steelhead fishing, river rafting and mushroom gathering are major activities here, but the one most evident to visitors is the timber industry. Some days, in fact, there seem to be more log trucks on the roads than passenger cars.

The **Forks Timber Museum** is filled with exhibits of old-time logging equipment and historical photos, as well as pioneer and Indian artifacts. Interpretive trails, gardens and a logger memorial are next to the visitors center. Open April through October and by appointment in winter. ~ Route 101 South, Forks; 360-374-9663, fax 360-374-9253; www.forkswa.com.

On the coast 14 miles west of Forks is the 800-year-old Indian fishing village of **La Push,** center of the **Quileute Indian Reservation.** Sportfishing, camping and beach walking are popular year-round. An abandoned Coast Guard station and lighthouse here are used as a school for resident children. ~ 360-374-6163, fax 360-374-6311.

A national park road eight miles west of Forks branches off the La Push Road and follows the north shore of the Quileute River five miles to **Rialto Beach,** where spectacular piles of driftwood often accumulate. There are picnic areas and campgrounds here, and a trailhead for hikes north up the beach toward Cape Alava.

On the west side of the national park are three more major points of entry. The **Hoh Rainforest** is 19 miles east of Route 101 via the Hoh River Road, 13 miles south of Forks. For national park information here, call the **Forks Ranger Station** (360-374-5877). There's a less well-known rainforest at the end of the gravel, 19-mile **Queets River Road,** 14 miles off Route 101, 17 miles west of Quinault. Finally, **Lake Quinault,** on Route 101 at the southwestern corner of Olympic National Park, is the site of several resorts and campgrounds, including the venerable Lake Quinault Lodge. Water sports of all kinds are popular at this glacier-fed lake, surrounded by old-growth forest.

The **Hoh Indian Reservation** is 25 miles south of Forks, off Route 101. Of more interest to most visitors is the **Kalaloch Lodge,** 35 miles south of Forks on Route 101. A major national park facility, it affords spectacular ocean views at the southernmost end of the park's coastal strip. ~ Kalaloch Lodge: 157151 Route 101; 360-962-2271, 866-525-2562, fax 360-962-3391; www.visitkalaloch.com, e-mail info@visitkalaloch.com.

The **Olympic National Park Coastal Unit** includes some 3300 square miles of designated marine sanctuary both above and below water level. Although most of the 73-mile seacoast is unreachable by road, trails lead down to six diverse beaches from Route 101 between Kalaloch and Ruby Beach. Here you'll find broad, log-strewn expanses of sand, gravel stretches great for beachcombing, and rocky tidepools teeming with tiny marine life.

LODGING

Set on the south shore of gorgeous Lake Crescent, the 1916 **Lake Crescent Lodge** provides a variety of rooms and cottages with lake or mountain views. Units in the historic main building share bathrooms. Of the 17 cottages, 4 have fireplaces; if you don't opt for one of these, you can relax in front of the lobby's stone fire-

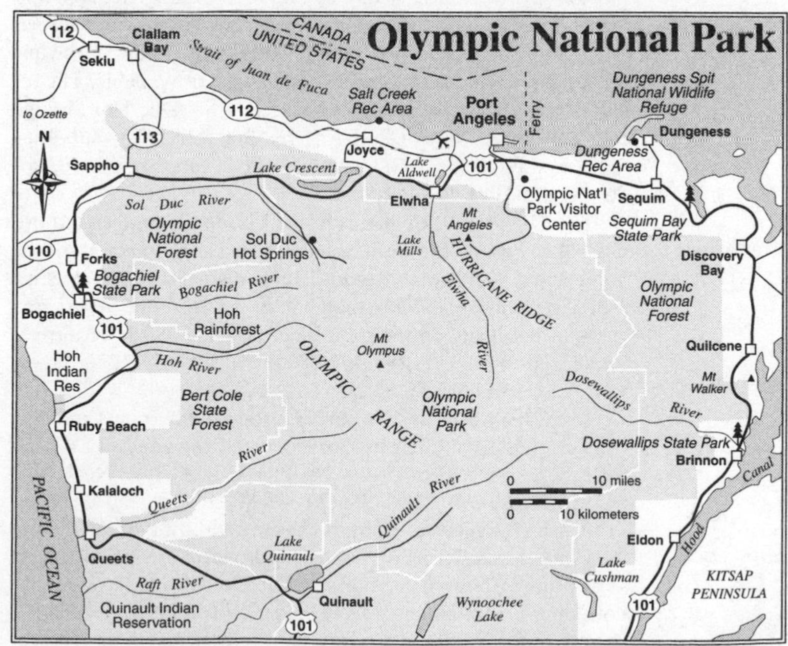

place or in the sunroom. Amenities include an on-site restaurant and lounge, as well as rowboat rentals and wi-fi access. Pets are accepted with a daily charge. The main lodge in closed mid-October through April; the four fireplace cottages are open weekends only during this period. ~ 416 Lake Crescent Road, 20 miles west of Port Angeles; 360-928-3211, fax 360-928-3253; www.lakecrescentlodge.com, e-mail lclodge@olypen.com. MODERATE TO DELUXE.

The rustic **Log Cabin Resort** is a historic landmark also on the shores of Lake Crescent along Route 101. Budget-watchers can stay in the cabins; more upscale are the lakeshore chalets and lodge guestrooms. There is also an RV park with full hookups on Log Cabin Creek. The handsome log lodge has a restaurant and a gift shop; all manner of boats are rented at the marina. Closed October through April. ~ 3183 East Beach Road, 21 miles west of Port Angeles; 360-928-3325, fax 360-928-2088; www.logcabinresort.net, e-mail reservations@logcabinresort.net. MODERATE TO DELUXE.

The **Sol Duc Hot Springs Resort** is another historic property, originally built in 1910 around a series of hot sulphur pools 12 miles south of Route 101. The 32 cabins (six with kitchens) were rebuilt in the mid-1980s and now have indoor plumbing! The River Suite is a three-bedroom cabin that sleeps ten. The best plunge, however, after a day of hiking or fishing, remains the water in three ceramic natural mineral spring pools, kept between 98° and 104°F and cleaned nightly. There is also a full-size swimming pool. Camping sites and RV hookups are available. The resort is closed November to mid-March. ~ Sol Duc Hot Springs Road, 40 miles west of Port Angeles; 360-327-3583, 866-476-5382, fax 360-327-3593; www.visitsolduc.com, e-mail info@solduc.com. DELUXE TO ULTRA-DELUXE.

The hamlet of Sekiu flanks Route 112 on the protected shore of Clallam Bay, on the Strait of Juan de Fuca. The lone waterfront hotel here is **Van Riper's Resort**. Family owned and operated, it's a cozy getaway spot. More than half of the 16 rooms have great views of the boats on the picturesque strait. ~ 280 Front Street, Sekiu; 360-963-2334, 888-462-0803, fax 360-963-2776; www.vanripersresort.com. BUDGET TO DELUXE.

The Cape Motel and RV park has eight motel rooms and two cottages; five have kitchens. Six months of the year, an RV park with restrooms is also open. ~ 1510 Bayview Avenue, Neah Bay; phone/fax 360-645-2250, 866-744-9944. BUDGET.

A peaceful getaway from the hustle and bustle of city living, HIDDEN ► the **Chito Beach Resort** is a virtual nature-lover's paradise and an ideal place to rejuvenate your spirit. Its beachfront accommodations offer breathtaking views of unspoiled beaches and romantic sunsets, and range from a picturesque A-frame cabin to two cot-

The Hoh Rainforest

No matter where you go on this earth, there's only one Hoh Rainforest. It's said to be one of the only coniferous rainforests in the world. Spared the logger's blade after a long-running battle between locals and conservationists, it's been undisturbed since time began. In other words, it's a natural wonder to be cherished.

Reached by traveling 13 miles south from Forks on Route 101, then 19 miles east on Hoh River Road, this is the wettest spot in the contiguous 48 states. In fact, wet isn't the word: even the air drips like a saturated sponge, producing over 30 inches of fog drip in the summer. The average annual precipitation due to rainfall is 145 inches, more than 100 inches of which fall between October and March. But temperatures at this elevation, between 500 and 1000 feet, rarely fall below 40° in winter or rise above 85° in summer. The legacy of this mild climate is dense, layered canopies of foliage.

The forest floor is as soft and thick as a shag carpet, cloaked with mosses, bracken ferns, huge fungi and seedlings. Hovering over the lush rug are vine maple, alder and black cottonwood, some hung with moss, stretching wiry branches to taste any slivers of sunlight that may steal through the canopy. Above them, Douglas fir, Sitka spruce, Western hemlock, Western red cedar and other gigantic conifers rise 200 to 300 feet, putting a lid on the forest. In all, over 300 plant species live here, not counting 70 epiphytes (mosses, lichens and such).

Some compare this environment to a cathedral. Indeed, the soft light is like sun filtered through stained glass, and the arching branches could pass for a vaulted apse. To others, it's simply mystical. The ancient coastal Indians would have agreed.

Though there are similar rainforests in Washington, the rainforest ecology is most conveniently studied at the **Hoh Rainforest Visitor Center** and on the nature trails that surround it. ~ 360-565-3130; www.nps.gov/olym. The **Hoh River Trail** extends for 17.5 miles to the river's source in Blue Glacier, on the flank of Mt. Olympus, but the rainforest can be appreciated by most visitors on one of two loop hikes that are both about a mile long. About three-fourths of a mile in, you'll see enormous old-growth Douglas fir, spruce and hemlock, some over nine feet in girth and at least 500 years old. At about one mile, the trail drops down to Big Flat, the first of several grassy open areas. The winter grazing of Roosevelt elk, whose survival was a major reason for the creation of Olympic National Park, has opened up the forest floor. Keep your eyes open, too, for wildlife. Besides the elk, you may spot river otter or weasel. Black bears and cougars also inhabit these forests. Bald eagles and great blue heron feed on the salmon that spawn seasonally in the Hoh.

tages to a large house that can sleep up to ten people. All have full kitchens stocked with utensils and housewares. Beachcombers are rewarded with regular sightings of sea otters, bald eagles and an occasional whale. ~ 7639 Route 112, Clallam Bay; 360-963-2581; www.chitobeach.com, e-mail chitobch@olympen.com. DELUXE.

Among several low-priced bed and breakfasts in Forks is the **River Inn B&B,** an A-frame chalet on the banks of the Bogachiel River two-and-a-half miles from town. Two bedrooms share a bath and one has a private bathroom, a loft, a sundeck and stairs leading to the hot tub. You can fish from the shore or relax in the hot tub while keeping your eyes open for elk, deer and river otter. Continental breakfast. Closed mid-April to September. ~ 2596 West Bogachiel Way, Forks; 360-374-6526, fax 360-374-6590; www.jeffwoodwardsportfishing.com, e-mail laura.river inn@yahoo.com. MODERATE.

The **Kalaloch Lodge** is perched on a bluff high above the crashing surf. Accommodations here (which may disappoint some) include 10 lodge units, 10 motel units, 20 log cabins with kitchenettes (but no utensils provided) and 18 units atop the bluff, 7 of which are duplexes. The lodge has a dining room overlooking the Pacific Ocean, as well as a general store, gas station and gift shop. ~ 157151 Route 101, 35 miles south of Forks; 360-962-2271, 866-525-2562, fax 360-962-3391; www.visitkalaloch.com, e-mail info@visitkalaloch.com. ULTRA-DELUXE.

Forks also has a youth hostel, complete with the cosmopolitan atmosphere one would expect. The **Rain Forest Hostel**, like other lodgings of its ilk, offers dorm bunks and community bathrooms and kitchen. The common room is a bonus with its fireplace and library. There is also one room for a couple and one room for a family as well as land for camping. ~ 169312 Route 101 North, 23 miles south of Forks; 360-374-2270; www.rainforesthostel.com, e-mail go2hostel@centurytel.net. BUDGET.

If you're planning a stay in the corner of Olympic National Park that includes beauteous Lake Quinault, consider the **Lake**

BRING THE WHOLE FAMILY

Close to shops and restaurants is the **Miller Tree Inn**. A quiet and comfortable farm homestead on one tree-filled acre, it has attractive rooms (eight with private baths) that practice an "open-house" policy not common among bed and breakfasts: children and pets are welcome (with some restrictions)! And visitors love the fresh farmhouse breakfasts. ~ 654 East Division Street, Forks; 360-374-6806, 800-943-6563, fax 360-374-6807; www.millertreeinn.com, e-mail millertreeinn@century tel.net. MODERATE TO ULTRA-DELUXE.

Quinault Lodge—especially if you can get a lakefront room in the historic cedar-shingled lodge itself. The huge building arcs around the shoreline, a totem-pole design on its massive chimney facing the water. Antiques and oversized leather furniture adorn the main lobby, constructed in the 1920s. There is also a sun porch, dining room and bar. There are fireplace and lakeside units available. You can rent boats in the summer, hike year-round or relax in the pool or sauna. ~ 345 South Shore Road, Quinault; 360-288-2900, 800-562-6672, fax 360-288-2901; www.visitlakequinault.com, e-mail info@visitlakequinault.com. DELUXE.

An alternative lodging on the lake is the **Rain Forest Resort Village**, with two suites, 11 deluxe-priced cabins (some with kitchens and whirlpool tubs, all with fireplaces), 16 moderately priced motel rooms and 31 RV spaces (budget). You'll find most of the amenities of the lodge, including restaurant and lounge, boat rentals and general store, but you don't have to pay for the atmosphere. ~ 516 South Shore Road, Quinault; 360-288-2535, 800-255-6936, fax 360-288-2957; www.rainforestresort.com, e-mail mail@rainforestresortvillage.com. BUDGET TO DELUXE.

DINING

The best choice for dining in the park is the **Log Cabin Resort**. Enjoy the view of beautiful Lake Crescent, where anglers dip their lines for the unique crescenti trout, a subspecies of rainbow trout. Dishes range from Cajun chicken quesadillas to clams and mussels sautéed in vermouth. ~ 3183 East Beach Road, 21 miles west of Port Angeles; 360-928-3325, fax 360-928-2088; www.logcabinresort.net, e-mail logcabin@logcabinresort.net. MODERATE.

There's a dining room at the **Sol Duc Hot Springs Resort**, just behind the hot sulphur springs. The food is solid Northwest fare, including some vegetarian dishes. Closed November to mid-March. ~ Sol Duc Hot Springs Road, 40 miles west of Port Angeles; 360-327-3583, 866-476-5382, fax 360-327-3593; www.visitsolduc.com, e-mail info@solduc.com. MODERATE TO DELUXE.

A mile high in the Olympic Range, 17 miles south of Port Angeles, the **Hurricane Ridge Visitors Center** frames glaciers in the picture windows upstairs from its coffee shop. Come for the view, but the standard American snacks served here aren't half-bad, either. Open January through May, weather permitting. ~ Hurricane Ridge Road; 360-565-3131. BUDGET.

Sunsets from the **Kalaloch Lodge**, high on a bluff overlooking the ocean in the national park's coastal strip, can make even the most ordinary food taste good. Fortunately, the fresh salmon and halibut served here don't need the view for their rich flavor. Breakfast, lunch and dinner. ~ 157151 Route 101, 35 miles south of Forks; 360-962-2271, 866-525-2562, fax 360-962-3391; www.visitkalaloch.com. MODERATE TO DELUXE.

The restaurant at the park's **Lake Quinault Lodge** faces another gorgeous lake surrounded by lush cedar forests. As you've come to expect along this coast, the seafood is excellent. Breakfast and dinner year-round. ~ 345 South Shore Road, Quinault; 800-562-6672, fax 360-288-2901; www.visitlakequinault.com, e-mail info@visitlakequinault.com. DELUXE.

Other than the national park lodges, pickings are slim in the restaurant department along this stretch of highway. A mile north of Forks, the **Smoke House Restaurant** serves standard American fare that should stave off hunger pangs if nothing else. ~ 193161 Route 101 North at La Push Road; 360-374-6258. MODERATE.

SHOPPING

For authentic Northwest Indian crafts, you won't do better than the gift shop at the **Makah Cultural and Research Center** on the Makah Indian Reservation near Cape Flattery at the end of Route 112. ~ 1880 Bay View Avenue, Neah Bay; 360-645-2711; e-mail makah@centurytel.net.

BEACHES & PARKS

OLYMPIC NATIONAL PARK This spectacular national park, 922,651 acres in area and ranging in elevation from sea level to nearly 8000 feet, contains everything from permanent alpine glaciers to America's lushest rainforest (the Hoh) to rocky tidepools rich in marine life. Wildlife includes deer in the mountains, elk in the rainforest, steelhead and salmon in the rivers and colorful birds everywhere. Three large lakes—Crescent (near Port Angeles), Ozette (on the coast) and Quinault (on the southwestern edge)—are especially popular visitor destinations. There are restrooms, picnic areas, hotels, restaurants and groceries. A $15 vehicle pass lasts a week. ~ Route 101 circles the park. The numerous access roads are well marked; 360-565-3000, fax 360-565-3015 (Port Angeles); ranger stations in Forks (360-374-5877) and Sol Duc (360-327-3534); www.nps.gov/olym.

▲ There are 16 campgrounds; $10 to $18 per night.

BOGACHIEL STATE PARK Not far from the Hoh Rainforest, this eternally damp park sits on the Bogachiel River, famous for its salmon and steelhead runs. Hiking and hunting in the adjacent forest are popular activities, although this park is more of a campsite than a day-use area. Facilities include restrooms, showers and limited picnic areas. ~ Route 101, six miles south of Forks; 360-374-6356.

▲ There are 36 standard sites ($17 per night), 6 RV hookup sites ($24 per night) and 2 primitive sites ($12 per night).

Ocean Shores–Pacific Beach

A six-mile-long, 6000-acre peninsula, Ocean Shores was a cattle ranch when a group of investors bought it for $1 million in 1960. A decade later, its assessed value had risen to $35 million. Today, it would be hard to put a dollar figure on this strip of condominium-style hotels and second homes, many of them on a series of canals. The main tourist beach destination on the Grays Harbor County coastline, it's located along Route 115, three miles south of its junction with Route 109.

SIGHTS

Folks come to **Ocean Shores** for oceanside rest and recreation, not for sightseeing. One of the few "attractions" is the **Ocean Shores Interpretive Center** four miles south of the town center near the Ocean Shores Marina, which has exhibits describing the peninsula's geological formation and human development. Open daily from April through September; open the rest of the year by appointment only. ~ 1033 Catala Avenue Southeast, Ocean Shores; 360-289-4617, fax 360-289-0189; www.oceanshoresinterpretivecenter.com.

The 22-mile beach that parallels Routes 115 and 109 north to Moclips is an attraction in its own right. Beyond Moclips, however, the coastline gets more rugged. Eight miles past Moclips, the **Quinault Indian National Tribal Headquarters** in the village of Taholah, on the Quinault Indian Reservation, offers guided fishing trips on reservation land and tribal gifts in a small shop and museum. ~ 1214 Aalis Drive, Taholah; 360-276-8215, 888-616-8211, fax 360-276-4191; www.quinaultindiannation.com.

LODGING

The nearest ocean beach area to the Seattle-Tacoma metropolitan area, Ocean Shores' condominiums and motels are frequently booked solid during the summer and on holiday weekends, even though prices can be high. At other times, it can be downright quiet . . . and inexpensive.

sights

AUTHOR FAVORITE

A winding, scenic coastal drive to the end of Route 112 climaxes at **Cape Flattery**, the northwesternmost corner of the contiguous United States. The road at times runs within feet of the water, providing spectacular blufftop views of the Strait of Juan de Fuca and Tatoosh Island—a great location for whale watching between March and May. A short trail leads to the shore. Beach hikers can find some of the last wilderness coast in Washington south of here.

Like almost every other lodging on this stretch of shoreline, **The Polynesian Resort** is as close to the water as you can get—a short quarter-mile trek across the dunes to the high-tide mark. The four-story building has 69 guest rooms ranging from motel units to three-bedroom penthouse suites. It has a restaurant, lively lounge, indoor pool and spa, outdoor games area and indoor game room popular with families. ~ 615 Ocean Shores Boulevard Northwest, Ocean Shores; 360-289-3361, 800-562-4836, fax 360-289-0294; www.thepolynesian.com, e-mail thepoly@techline.com. DELUXE TO ULTRA-DELUXE.

Guesthouse Inn and Suites has 67 units and all the amenities of a larger resort, including a golf course and a heated outdoor pool, as well as oceanside views. Rooms are equipped with microwaves, refrigerators, coffeemakers and TVs. Complimentary breakfast included. ~ 648 Ocean Shores Boulevard, Ocean Shores; 360-289- 3323, 800-214-8378, fax 360-289-3320; www.guesthouseintl.com. MODERATE.

Neighboring units at **The Grey Gull** are fewer in number (37), but they're all studios or suites with fireplaces, wi-fi access, microwaves and private decks or balconies. The Gull has an outdoor pool and jacuzzi guarded by a wind fence. Dogs are welcome in selected rooms. ~ 651 Ocean Shores Boulevard, Ocean Shores; 360-289-3381, 800-562-9712, fax 360-289-3673; www.thegreygull.com, e-mail greygull@thegreygull.com. DELUXE.

The **Caroline Inn** offers four bi-level townhouse suites with great views, just steps from the water. The decor follows a *Gone With the Wind* theme in soft rose colors. The rooms are furnished with sleigh beds and other antiques. Each suite offers all the comforts of home and then some: fireplaces, jacuzzis, complete kitchens and living areas with entertainment centers. ~ 1341 Ocean Shores Boulevard, Ocean Shores; 360-289-0450, 800-303-4297, fax 360-289-5149; www.oceanshoreswashington.com. ULTRA-DELUXE.

One of few accommodations away from "the strip" is the **Discovery Inn**, a condo motel close to the Ocean Shores Marina near the cape's southeast tip, five miles from downtown. Rooms are built around a central courtyard with a seasonal pool. There is an indoor jacuzzi and family game room. A private dock on Ocean Shores' grand canal encourages boating and fishing. ~ 1031 Discovery Avenue Southeast, Ocean Shores; 360-289-3371, 800-882-8821. BUDGET TO MODERATE.

HIDDEN ►

North up the coast from frenetic Ocean Shores are numerous quiet resort communities and accommodations. At Ocean City, four miles north, the **Pacific Sands Motel** is one of the top economy choices on the coast. There are just nine units, but they're well kept; seven have kitchens and three have fireplaces. The extensive grounds include a nice swimming pool, playground, picnic tables and direct beach access across a suspension bridge. ~ 2687 State Route 109, Ocean City; 360-289-3588; www.pacific-sands.net, e-mail info@pacific-sands.net. BUDGET TO MODERATE.

The **Iron Springs Resort** has 28 units in 25 cottages built up a wooded hill and around a handsome cove at the mouth of Boon Creek. The beach here is popular for razor clamming, crabbing and surf fishing; the cottages are equally popular for their spaciousness and panoramic views. All have kitchens and fireplaces. There are an indoor pool and playground. ~ 3707 Route 109, Copalis Beach; 360-276-4230, fax 360-276-4378; www.ironspringsresort.com, e-mail reservations@ironspringsre sort.com. MODERATE TO DELUXE.

Ocean Crest Resort may be the most memorable accommodation on this entire stretch of beach. It's built atop a bluff, so getting to the beach involves a 132-step descent down a staircase through a wooded ravine. But the views from the rooms' private balconies are remarkable, and all but the smallest rooms have fireplaces and refrigerators. There are exercise facilities with a swimming pool, jacuzzi and weight room open to all guests free of charge. ~ Sunset Beach, Route 109, Moclips; 360-276-4465, 800-684-8439, fax 360-276-4149; www.oceancrestresort.com, e-mail info@oceancrestresort.com. DELUXE.

DINING

Mariah's provides a spacious, relaxing cedar dining room with a domed ceiling and skylights. Offerings include fresh seafood, steaks, prime rib and pasta. Dinner only and Sunday breakfast buffet. ~ 615 Ocean Shores Boulevard, Ocean Shores; 360-289-3315, 800-562-4836, fax 360-289-0294; www.thepolynesian.com, e-mail thepoly@techline.com. BUDGET TO DELUXE.

GREEN EGGS AND SPAM?

Part watering hole, part store and part dining "destination," the **Green Lantern Tavern** is quite a roadside stop. Breakfast specials include eggs with spam, giant plate-sized pancakes and a 40-cent cup of joe. Chicken sandwiches and burgers make up lunch, while dinner includes a variety of fried food baskets and steaks. Outside, the beer garden hosts live entertainment on Saturdays; vendors ply handcrafted, Northwest items in the 14-cabin, ramshackle arts and crafts "village" (open Memorial Day through Labor Day). It's quaint, it's quirky and since there's not much else in the area, it's worth stopping off to sample some local flavor. ~ 3119 State Road 109, Copalis Beach; 360-289-2297; www.thegreenlanterntavern.com, e-mail greenlanternpub@hotmail.com. BUDGET TO MODERATE.

The **Home Port Restaurant** is appointed like the private garden of a sea captain home from the waves. Steaks, seafood and pasta dominate the menu. ~ 857 Point Brown Avenue opposite Shoal Street, Ocean Shores; 360-289-2600, fax 360-289-0558. MODERATE TO DELUXE.

Ocean Shores attracts a dedicated breed of beachcomber who rides out winter storms in anticipation of the ultimate reward—driftwood, shells and highly prized, handcrafted glass floats.

No trip to the Washington coast would be complete without having at least one meal that includes seafood. **Mike's Seafood** is a casual eatery that can adequately oblige. Offering a fresh assortment of Pacific Northwest seafood, Mike's is particularly popular with the locals during the winter Dungeness crab season. ~ 830 Point Brown Avenue, Ocean Shores; 360-289-0532. BUDGET TO MODERATE.

The **Sand Castle Drive-in** is the in-spot for hamburgers, with interesting variations such as the oyster burger and the clam burger. ~ 788 Point Brown Avenue, Ocean Shores; 360-289-2777. BUDGET.

A bit of Manzanillo on the Washington coast, **Las Maracas** feels like the tropics with its bright tropical colors and profusion of plants. All the usual Mexican specialties are on the menu, but the best bets are the fajitas, crab and prawn enchiladas and seafood chimichangas. ~ 729 Point Brown Avenue, Ocean Shores; 360-289-2054, fax 360-289-2054. MODERATE.

Authentic Irish pub fare is dished up at **Galway Bay Irish Restaurant and Pub**, where you can ward off the coastal chill with Irish stew, beef sautéed in Guinness, and chicken and mushroom pasties. The pub decor is authentic, with wainscoted walls adorned with Irish prints and memorabilia. Breakfast, lunch and dinner. ~ 880 Point Brown Avenue Northeast, Ocean Shores; 360-289-2300; www.galwaybayirishpub.com, e-mail bgibbons@galwaybayirishpub.com. MODERATE.

For a gourmet Continental dinner in spectacular surroundings, check out the **Ocean Crest Resort**. Attentive service and superb meals (with a focus on seafood and Northwest regional cuisine), amid an atmosphere of Northwest Indian tribal art, only add to the enjoyment of the main reason to dine here: the view from a bluff, through a wooded ravine, to Sunset Beach. Breakfast, lunch and dinner. ~ Sunset Beach, Route 109, Moclips; 360-276-4465, 800-684-8439, fax 360-276-4149; www.oceancrestresort.com, e-mail info@oceancrestresort.com. DELUXE TO ULTRA-DELUXE.

SHOPPING

The most interesting galleries in Grays Harbor County are, not surprisingly, in the beach communities. For oil paintings, watercolors, hand-made jewelry and textile crafts, make sure to seek out **The Cove Gallery**. ~ 3688 Route 109, Iron Springs; phone/fax 360-276-4360; www.covegalleryonline.com. The **Gallery**

Marjuli exhibits recent works by Pacific Northwest artists. ~ 865 Point Brown Avenue Northwest, Ocean Shores; 360-289-2858.

NIGHTLIFE

In Ocean Shores, at the Polynesian Hotel, **Mariah's** is a nice place to enjoy a nightcap. ~ 615 Ocean Shores Boulevard, Ocean Shores; 360-289-3315, 800-562-4836; www.thepolynesian.com.

Along with a convivial atmosphere nightly, **Galway Bay Irish Restaurant** hosts live music on Friday and Saturday nights. ~ 880 Point Brown Avenue Northeast, Ocean Shores; 360-289-2300; www.galwaybayirishpub.com.

BEACHES & PARKS

OCEAN CITY STATE PARK This North Beach park, stretching for several miles along the Pacific coastline, offers a dozen access points. There are clamming and surf fishing (in season), horseback riding on the beach (but not on the dunes or soft sand), surf kayaking in summer, kite flying when the wind blows, birdwatching especially during migratory periods, and beachcombing year-round. Swimming is not recommended because of undertow and riptides. This flat, sandy beach is the same broad expanse that stretches 22 miles north to Pacific Beach. You can drive on some sections of the beach! You'll find restrooms and picnic areas. ~ Off Route 115 and Route 109 north of Ocean Shores; campground is two miles north of Ocean Shores on Route 115; 360-289-3553, fax 360-289-9405.

▲ There are 149 standard sites ($19 per night) and 29 RV hookup sites ($26 per night). Reservations: 888-226-7688.

PACIFIC BEACH STATE PARK Broad, flat and sandy North Beach, extending 22 miles from Moclips (just north of Pacific Beach) to the north jetty of Grays Harbor at Ocean Shores, is the *raison d'être* of the entire park. Beachcombing, kite flying, jogging and (in season) surf-perchfishing and razor-clam digging are popular activities. Swimming is not recommended because of undertow and riptides. Facilities are limited to restrooms and picnic areas. ~ Located along Route 109 in Pacific Beach; 360-276-4297, fax 360-276-4537.

▲ There are 32 standard sites ($19 per night) and 32 RV hookup sites ($26 per night). Reservations: 888-226-7688.

Grays Harbor Area

Industrial towns are not often places of tourist interest. The twin cities of Aberdeen and Hoquiam, on the northeastern shore of the broad Grays Harbor estuary, are an exception. A historic seaport, a rich assortment of bird life and numerous handsome mansions built by old timber money make it worthwhile to pause in this corner of Washington.

Aberdeen has about 16,000 people, Hoquiam around 9000, and the metropolitan area includes some 33,000. Wood-products industries provide the economic base; in fact, more trees are harvested in Grays Harbor County than in any other county in the United States. Boat building and fisheries, both more important in past decades, remain key businesses.

SIGHTS

For information on the region, check with the **Grays Harbor Chamber of Commerce.** ~ 506 Duffy Street at Route 101, Aberdeen; 360-532-1924, 800-321-1924, fax 360-533-7945; www.graysharbor.org.

If you're coming down Route 101 from the north during the summer, it's wise to follow the signs and make your first stop a guided tour of **Hoquiam's Castle.** A stately, 20-room hillside mansion built in 1897 by a millionaire lumber baron, it has been fully restored with elegant antiques like Tiffany lamps, grandfather clocks and a 600-piece, cut-crystal chandelier. With its round turret and bright red color, the house is unmistakable. It is now a bed-and-breakfast inn. Open for tours by appointment. Admission. ~ 515 Chenault Avenue, Hoquiam; 360-533-2005, fax 360-533-9814; www.hoquiamcastle.com, e-mail info@hoquiamcastle.com.

Also in Hoquiam is the **Polson Museum.** Built in the early 1920s by a pioneer timber family and furnished with pieces donated by Hoquiam and Grays Harbor County residents, the 26-room home represents the history of the area. It is surrounded by native trees and the Burton Ross Memorial Rose Gardens. Open Wednesday through Sunday from April through December; open weekends only from January through March. Admission. ~ 1611 Riverside Avenue at Route 101, Hoquiam; phone/fax 360-533-5862; www.polsonmuseum.org, e-mail jbl@polsonmuseum.org.

A couple miles west of Hoquiam on Route 109, at Bowerman Basin on Grays Harbor, next to Bowerman Airfield, is the **Grays Harbor National Wildlife Refuge,** one of four major staging areas for migratory shorebirds in North America. Although this basin represents just two percent of the intertidal habitat of the estuary, fully half of the one million shorebirds that visit each spring make their stop here. April and early May are the best times to visit. An annual shorebird festival occurs the last weekend in April. ~ 360-753-9467, fax 360-534-9302; fws.gov/graysharbor.

A major attraction in neighboring Aberdeen, just four miles east of Hoquiam on Route 101, is the **Grays Harbor Historical Seaport.** Craftspersons at this working 18th-century shipyard have constructed a replica of the *Lady Washington*, the brigantine in which Captain Robert Gray sailed when he discovered Grays Harbor and the Columbia River in 1783. There are also two 18th-century longboat reproductions and a companion tall ship to the *Lady Washington*, the *Tall Chieftain*. Visitors can go for a sail on the *Lady Washington* when the ship isn't touring the West Coast. Call 24 hours ahead for schedules. ~ 712 Hagara Street, Aberdeen; 360-532-8611, 800-200-5239, fax 360-533-9384; www.ladywashington.org.

A few blocks west, the **Aberdeen Museum of History** offers exhibits, dioramas and videos of regional history in a 1922 armory. Displays include several re-created early-20th-century buildings: a one-room school, a general store, a blacksmith's shop and more. Closed Sunday and Monday. ~ 111 East 3rd Street, Aberdeen; 360-533-1976; www.aberdeen-musuem.org, e-mail museum@aberdeen-museum.org.

Route 105 follows the south shore of Grays Harbor west from Aberdeen to the atmospheric fishing village of **Westport**, at the estuary's south head. Perhaps the most interesting of several small museums here is the **Westport Maritime Museum**, housed in a Nantucket-style Coast Guard station commissioned in 1939 but decommissioned in the 1970s. Historic photos, artifacts and memorabilia help tell the story of a sailor's life. The museum also has exhibits of skeletons of marine mammals (including whales), a beachcombing exhibit, a children's discovery room and tours of the Grays Harbor lighthouse. Closed December and January. Admission. ~ 2201 Westhaven Drive, Westport; 360-268-0078, fax 360-268-1288; www.westportwa.com/museum, e-mail westport.maritime@comcast.net.

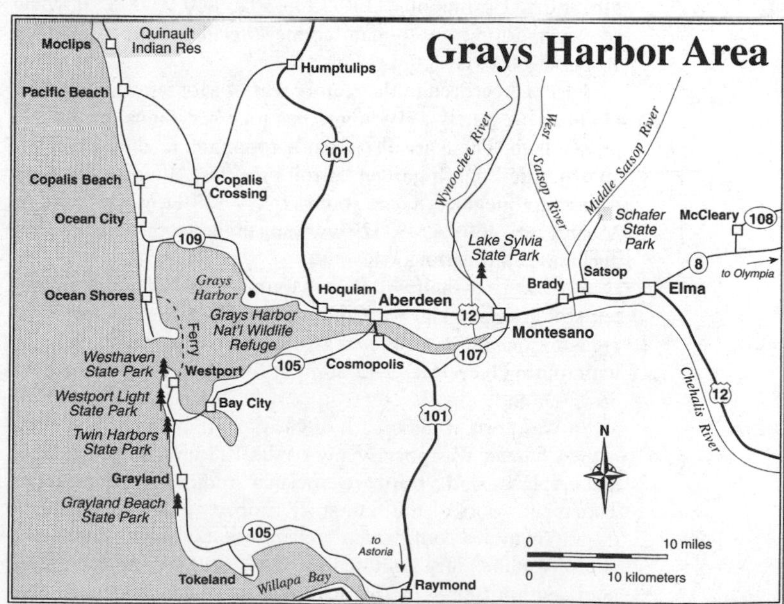

LODGING

There's considerable character at **Hoquiam's Castle Bed & Breakfast**, a three-story Victorian hillside mansion. Each of the four guest rooms, all with private bath, are individually decorated with antiques. A full breakfast is served in the hand-carved oak dining room. Museum-quality period furnishings fill the house, which is open for tours by appointment. ~ 515 Chenault Avenue, Hoquiam; 360-533-2005, fax 306-533-9814; www.hoquiamcastle.com, e-mail info@hoquiamcastle.com. DELUXE TO ULTRA-DELUXE.

The twin cities of Aberdeen and Hoquiam have a strip of look-alike motels along Route 101. Though it's hard to choose one above another, the **Olympic Inn Motel** is notable for its modern, spacious rooms. Decor in the 55 units is simple but pleasant. ~ 616 West Heron Street, Aberdeen; 360-533-4200, 800-562-8618, fax 360-533-6223. MODERATE.

A full-sized replica of another ship commanded by Robert Gray, the 170-ton *Lady Ship* in Aberdeen is a working ship painted in brilliant period colors of red, yellow and blue.

Just southeast of Aberdeen, the **Cooney Mansion** is located in a secluded wooded area on a golf course with an adjoining tennis court and park. A National Historic Landmark built in 1908 by a lumber baron, its interior was designed to show off local woods. Now a B&B, it has nine bedrooms, five with private baths, as well as a jacuzzi, sauna, sundeck and exercise room. Full lumber baron's breakfast included. Call for availability during winter. ~ 1705 5th Street, Cosmopolis; 360-533-0602, 800-977-7823; www.cooneymansion.com, e-mail cooney@techline.com. MODERATE TO ULTRA-DELUXE.

East of Aberdeen in the county seat of Montesano is the **Abel House.** This stately 1908 home has four bedrooms, one with a private bath. There are also a game room and reading room and an exquisite English garden. A full breakfast, afternoon tea and dessert are included in the room rate. ~ 117 Fleet Street South, Montesano; 360-249-6002; www.abelhouse.com, e-mail info@abelhouse.com. MODERATE.

Farther east—halfway from Montesano to Olympia, in fact, but still in Grays Harbor County—**The McCleary Hotel** maintains antique-laden rooms that seem to be especially popular with touring bicyclists. ~ 42 Summit Road, McCleary; 360-495-3678. BUDGET.

In Westport, at the mouth of Grays Harbor, the largest motel is the **Château Westport**. Many of the 108 units have balconies and fireplaces, and a third are efficiency studios with kitchenettes. The upper floors of the four-story property, easily identified by its gray mansard roof, have excellent ocean views to enjoy with your complimentary continental breakfast. Dip into the indoor pool and hot tub. ~ 710 West Hancock Avenue, Westport; 360-

268-9101, 800-255-9101, fax 360-268-1646; www.chateauwestport.com, e-mail chateau@tss.net. MODERATE TO ULTRA-DELUXE.

For value-hunters, **The Islander Resort** offers 32 simple but clean and spacious motel units. Forty-seven RV spaces are also available, some overlooking the harbor. ~ 421 East Neddie Rose Drive, Westport; 360-268-9166, 800-322-1740, fax 360-268-0902; www.westport-islander.com, e-mail info@westport-islander.com. MODERATE.

You can catch a fish, clean it and cook it for dinner all without straying from the **Grayland Motel and Cottages**, located on the beach south of Westport. The grounds offer a fish- and clam-cleaning shed, children's play area, motel units and self-contained cottages with tiled kitchens, pine furnishings and small living/dining areas. ~ 2013 State Route 105, Grayland; 360-267-2395, 800-292-0845; www.westportwa.com/graylandmotel. BUDGET.

DINING

Bridges Restaurant is a handsome, garden-style restaurant with one dining room and a banquet room that's actually a greenhouse. As the size of its parking lot attests, it's very popular locally, for its lounge as well as its cuisine. Local seafood, steaks, chicken and pasta highlight the menu. No lunch on Sunday. ~ 112 North G Street, Aberdeen; 360-532-6563, fax 360-532-5490. MODERATE TO DELUXE.

For historic flavor, you needn't look further than **Billy's Bar and Grill**. Named for an early-20th-century ne'er-do-well notorious for mugging loggers and shanghaiing sailors, Billy's boasts an ornate century-old ceiling and a huge antique bar. This is the place to start the day with a hearty breakfast, or settle back with a burger and a beer and soak up the past. ~ 322 East Heron Street, Aberdeen; 360-533-7144, fax 360-533-7508. BUDGET TO MODERATE.

If you're looking to rub elbows with the locals, **Sidney's Restaurant & Casino** will offer that and a whole lot more. A restaurant, casino and lounge with a motorcycle theme all rolled into one, this noisy and crowded venue is a great place to soak up local flavor. Most of the offerings are typical American fare that includes steak, seafood and pasta. Breakfast, lunch and dinner are served. ~ 512 West Heron Street, Aberdeen; 360-533-0296. MODERATE TO DELUXE.

Elsewhere in the area, the **Hong Kong Restaurant** is surprisingly authentic for a town so far removed from China. It has chop suey and egg foo yung, yes, but it also has egg flower soup, *moo goo gai pan* and other tastes from the old country. Closed Monday. ~ 1212 East 1st Street, Cosmopolis; 360-533-7594. BUDGET.

There aren't many restaurant choices in McCleary, but if you appreciate a good old-fashioned hamburger, head for **Bear's Den**. An authentic 1950s burger stand with drive-up service and a tiny inside dining area, the Den makes burgers to order with heated buns, homemade fries, quality beef and a variety of toppings. Some other specialties are fresh salads and soda fountain treats. ~ 301 Simpson Avenue, McCleary; 360-495-3822. BUDGET.

SHOPPING

Browse vintage nautical baubles such as old ship lanterns and stern wheels at **Olde Mercantile**. Closed Monday and Tuesday. ~ 1820 State Route 105, Grayland; 360-267-0120.

NIGHTLIFE

Folks in the Grays Harbor area show a predilection for **Sidney's Casino**, which features a Harley bar. ~ 512 West Heron Street, Aberdeen; 360-533-6635 or 360-533-0296 (bar).

Also check out the Victorian bar at **Billy's Bar and Grill.** ~ 322 East Heron Street, Aberdeen; 360-533-7144. The posh lounge at **Bridges Restaurant** is also a happenin' spot for drinks. ~ 112 North G Street, Aberdeen; 360-532-6563.

BEACHES & PARKS

LAKE SYLVIA STATE PARK Visitors can circumambulate this narrow, forest-enshrouded lake on a two-mile hiking trail. Also here are trout fishing (from a non-motorized boat or from shore), a swimming beach and boat rentals in season. There are restrooms, picnic areas and groceries. ~ Off Route 12, via North 3rd Street, two miles north of Montesano; 360-249-3621, fax 360-249-5571.

▲ There are 35 standard sites ($19 per night). Closed early October to early April. Reservations: 888-226-7688.

SCHAFER STATE PARK Once a family park for employees of the Schafer Logging Company, this tranquil 119-acre site on the East Fork of the Satsop River is still popular with families. This heavily forested park is ideal for picnics, hikes and fishing. You can fish for rainbow trout, cutthroat trout, salmon and steelhead in the river. Swimmers may find the water too cold. You'll find restrooms and picnic areas. ~ West 1365 Schafer Park Road, 12 miles north of Elma, off Route 12 via Brady; phone/fax 360-482-3852.

▲ There are 43 standard sites ($17 per night), 6 RV hookup sites ($24 per night) and 2 primitive sites ($12 per night). Closed in winter.

WYNOOCHEE LAKE RECREATION AREA Originally an Army Corps of Engineers project, now run by Tacoma Power, this four-and-a-half-mile-long lake was created in 1972 by a water-supply and flood-control dam on the Wynoochee River. A ten-mile trail winds around the lake, past a beach and designated swimming area. Trout fishing, waterskiing, swimming (the water is cold, though), horseback riding and wildlife watching are also popular. Restrooms and picnic areas are the only facilities. ~ Off Route 12, about 35 miles north of Montesano on Wynochee Valley Road. Take a left on Forest Service Road 22 and a right on Forest Service Road 2294; 360-956-2402.

▲ There are 46 developed sites and 10 primitive sites ($10 to $12 per night) in the Coho campground. Closed October through April. Reservations: 888-226-7688.

WESTHAVEN & WESTPORT LIGHT STATE PARKS Westhaven State Park, which occupies the southern headland at the mouth of Grays Harbor, is a great place for watching birds and wildlife, including harbor seals and whales during migratory periods. Surfing is excellent here (try the jetty) and there are yearly competitions. Surfers and swimmers should be very careful of riptides. Westhaven is adjacent to Westport Light State Park, from which you can see a historic lighthouse that's warned coastal ships of the entrance to Grays Harbor since 1897. There's a multi-use paved trail connecting the two parks that's open for hiking, bicycling, inline skating and other nonmotorized forms of transportation. You can fish for salmon, ocean perch, codfish and Dungeness crab from the shores of both parks or the jetty of Westhaven. There are restrooms and picnic areas. ~ Both parks are close to downtown Westport; Westhaven is about one and a half miles from downtown on East Yearout Drive; Westport Light is a half mile from downtown at the end of Ocean Avenue; 360-268-9717, fax 360 268 0372.

Grays Harbor National Wildlife Refuge is the last place to be flooded at high tide and the first to have its mudflats exposed, giving the avians extra feeding time.

TWIN HARBORS STATE PARK The Washington coast's largest campground dominates this 172-acre park. It also includes the Shifting Sands Nature Trail with interpretive signs for dunes explorers. Beachcombing, kite flying and clamming are popular activities on the broad, sandy beach. There's fishing in the surf or from a boat (which you can charter at Westport) for cod, salmon, ocean perch and Dungeness crab, but swimming is not recommended because of riptides. You'll find restrooms and picnic areas. ~ Located along Route 105, four miles south of Westport and four miles north of Grayland; 360-268-9717, fax 360-268-0372.

▲ There are 250 standard sites ($19 per night) and 49 RV hookup sites ($26 per night). Reservations (May 15 to September 15): 888-226-7688.

GRAYLAND BEACH STATE PARK This 400-acre park is broad and flat and ideal for surf fishing, clam digging, beachcombing, kite flying and other seaside diversions. Swimming is discouraged due to riptides. You'll find restrooms, groceries and restaurants in Grayland. ~ 925 Cranberry Road Route 105, one mile south of Grayland; 360-267-4301, fax 360-267-0461.

▲ There are 102 RV hookup sites ($26 to $30 per night) and 14 yurts (call for yurt prices). Reservations: 888-226-7688.

Long Beach–Willapa Bay

This region is the largest "unpopulated" estuary in the continental United States. Its pristine condition makes it one of the world's best places for farming oysters. From Tokeland to Bay Center to Oysterville, tiny villages that derive their sole income from the shelled creatures display mountains of empty shells as evidence of their success. Begin your visit on Route 105 south from Westport, then head east along the northern shore of Willapa Bay.

SIGHTS

Thirty-three miles from Westport, Route 105 rejoins Route 101 at **Raymond**. This town of 3000, and its smaller sister community of **South Bend** four miles south on Route 101, are lumber ports on the lower Willapa River.

You'll find murals—43 of them, to be exact—on walls from Ocean Shores to the Columbia River, Elma to Ilwaco. Chambers of commerce and other visitor information centers have guide pamphlets. But no mural is larger than the 85-foot-wide painting of an early logger on the **Dennis Company Building**. ~ 5th Street, Raymond.

History buffs won't want to miss the **Willapa Seaport Museum**, which houses an eclectic collection of maritime artifacts. Look for displays on local shipwrecks, the slave trade, the Spanish American War and the Spruce Division of World War I. Ahoy, matey. Closed Monday through Wednesday. ~ 310 Alder Street, Raymond; 360-942-4149.

Attractions in South Bend include the **Pacific County Museum**, with pioneer artifacts from the turn of the 20th century. ~ 1008 West Robert Bush Drive, South Bend; 360-875-5224; www.pacificcohistory.org, e-mail museum@willapabay.org.

Also have a look at South Bend's 1910 **Pacific County Courthouse**, noted for its art-glass dome and historic foyer wall paintings. ~ 300 Memorial Drive off Route 101, South Bend; 360-875-9334.

The **Long Beach Peninsula**, reached via Route 101 from South Bend (43 miles), features 28 miles of open sandy beaches, two lighthouses and a boardwalk above grassy dunes. Information is available from the **Long Beach Peninsula Visitor Bureau.** ~ 3914 Pacific Highway at the intersection of Routes 101 and 103, Seaview; 360-642-2400, 800-451-2542; www.funbeach.com, e-mail ask@funbeach.com.

Route 103, which runs north–south up the 28-mile-long, two-mile-wide peninsula, is intersected by Route 101 at **Seaview**. The town of **Long Beach** is just a mile north of the junction.

Long Beach's principal attraction is a 2300-foot-long wooden **boardwalk**, South 10th to Bolstad streets, elevated above the dunes, enabling folks to make an easy trek to the high-tide mark. The beach, incidentally, is open to driving on the hard upper sand, and to surf fishing, clamming (in season), beachcombing, kite flying and picnicking everywhere.

Kite flying is a big thing on the Washington coast, so it's no accident that the **World Kite Museum and Hall of Fame** is in Long Beach. The museum has rotating exhibits of kites from around the world—Japanese, Chinese, Thai and so on—with displays of stunt kites, advertising kites and more. Open daily May through September; closed Tuesday through Thursday from October to April. Admission. ~ 303 Sid Snyder Drive South off Route 103, Long Beach; 360-642-4020; www.worldkitemuseum.com, e-mail info@worldkitemuseum.com.

The **Pacific Coast Cranberry Museum** provides a historic view of the West Coast cranberry industry. Exhibits include hand tools, cranberry boxes, labels, pickers, sorters and separators. Closed mid-December through March. ~ 2907 Pioneer Road, Long Beach; 360-642-5553; www.cranberrymuseum.com, e-mail cranberries@willapabay.org.

During the peak blooming season in May, the **Clarke Rhododendron Nursery** is a dazzling place to view rhododendrons and

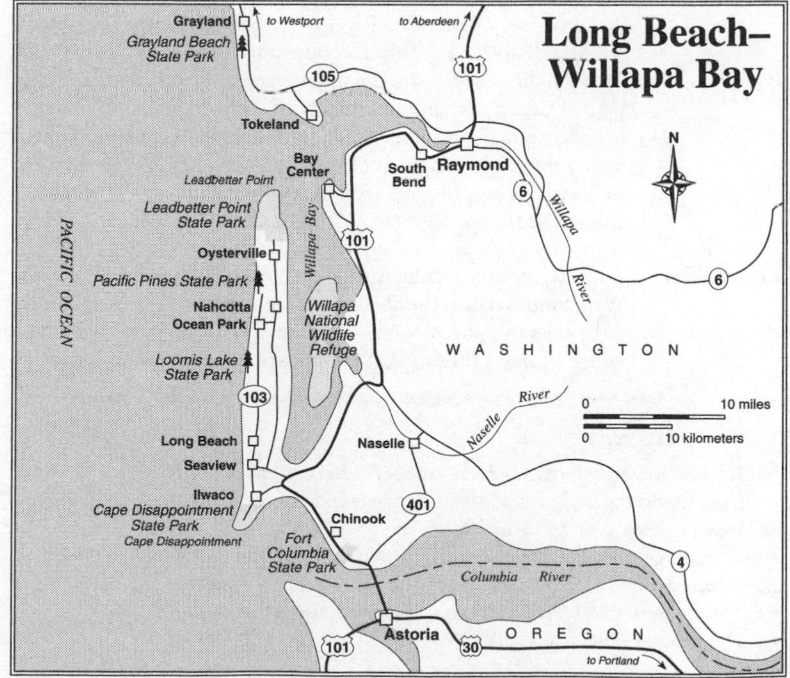

azaleas in all their splendor. ~ 15600 Sandridge Road, Long Beach; 360-642-2241.

North of Long Beach ten miles is **Ocean Park**, the commercial hub of the central and northern Long Beach Peninsula. Developed as a Methodist camp in 1883, it evolved into a small resort town.

Older yet is **Oysterville**, another three miles north via Sandridge Road. Founded in 1854, this National Historic District boasts the oldest continuously operating post office in Washington (since 1858) and 17 other designated historic sites. Get a walking-tour pamphlet from the **Old Church** beside the Village Green. ~ Territory Road, Oysterville.

South of Seaview just two miles on Route 103 is **Ilwaco**, spanning the isthmus between the Columbia River and the Pacific.

Local history is featured at the impressive **Ilwaco Heritage Museum**. A series of galleries depicts the development of southwestern Washington from early Indian culture to European voyages of discovery, from pioneer settlement to the early 20th century. Admission. ~ 115 Southeast Lake Street, Ilwaco; 360-642-3446, fax 360-642-4615; www.ilwacoheritagemuseum.org, e-mail ihm@ilwacoheritagemuseum.org.

About eight miles southeast, a short distance before Route 101 crosses the Columbia River to Astoria, Oregon, **Fort Columbia State Park** is a highly recommended stop for history buffs. Two buildings at the site are museums: the **Fort Columbia Interpretive Center**, exhibiting artifacts of early-20th-century military life in a former coastal artillery post, and the **Columbia House**, which the Daughters of the American Revolution have restored to depict the everyday lifestyle of a military officer of the time. ~ Route 101, Chinook; 360-777-8221.

LODGING

Possibly the most delightful accommodation anywhere on the Washington coast is the **Shelburne Country Inn**. The oldest continually operating hotel in the state, it opened in 1896 and is still going strong. Fifteen guest rooms are furnished with Victorian

CATCH THE WAVE

In October and early November, the cranberry harvest takes precedence over all else on the peninsula. Most fields are owned by local farmers who sell much of their crop to Ocean Spray. The **Pacific Coast Cranberry Research Foundation** offers free self-guided tours of the cranberry bogs year-round. Go in October to see the harvest. ~ 2907 Pioneer Road, Long Beach; 360-642-5553; www.cranberrymuseum.com, e-mail info@cranberrymuseum.com.

antiques and fresh flowers. All have private baths and most have decks. A hearty country breakfast is served in the morning, as well as freshly baked cookies upon arrival. ~ 4415 Pacific Way, Seaview; 360-642-2442, 800-466-1896, fax 360-642-8904; www.theshelburneinn.com, e-mail innkeeper@theshelburneinn.com. DELUXE TO ULTRA-DELUXE.

HIDDEN

Another one-of-a-kinder, but for very different reasons, is **The Historic Sou'wester Lodge, Cabins Tch! Tch! & RV Park.** It's a place much beloved by youth hostelers who, well, grew up. Proprietors Leonard and Miriam Atkins have intentionally kept the accommodation simple and weathered. They advertise it as a B&(MYOD)B—"bed and (make your own damn) breakfast." Common areas include the living room and library. Sleeping options include rooms in the historic lodge, cedar-shingled housekeeping cabins, a dozen-or-so vintage TCH! TCH! RVs and mobile homes ("Trailer Classics Hodgepodge") and an area for RVs and tent campers. Almost every option includes kitchen facilities. The historic lodge draws an artistic clientele and often hosts cultural events such as poetry readings or evenings of chamber music and theater. It also is the closest lodging to the ocean in Seaview, separated from the water only by protected wetlands. ~ Beach Access Road, 38th Place, Seaview; 360-642-2542; www.souwesterlodge.com, e-mail contactus@souwesterlodge.com. BUDGET TO DELUXE.

The Whale's Tale Motel in downtown Long Beach offers amazingly economical one- and two-bedroom suites with living rooms and full kitchens. Though the accommodations are plain and a little frayed around the edges, guests enjoy the use of a recreation hall with a Ping-Pong table, pool table, hot tub, sauna and exercise equipment, as well as free use of a rubber boat, freshwater fishing gear and metal detector during the summer season only. ~ 620 South Pacific Avenue, Long Beach; 360-642-3455, 800-559-4253; www.thewhalestale.com, e-mail whalesta@willapabay.org. BUDGET TO MODERATE.

Numerous beachfront cabin communities speckle the shoreline of the Long Beach Peninsula north from the towns of Ilwaco and Seaview. One of the best is the **Klipsan Beach Cottages.** Each of the ten cottages, in a lovely garden setting, has a kitchen and fireplace or wood-burning stove (with free firewood). There is also a two-bedroom and a three-bedroom unit. Closed in early January. ~ 22617 Pacific Highway, Ocean Park; 360-665-4888, fax 360-665-3580; www.klipsanbeachcottages.com, e-mail cald1947@klipsanbeachcottages.com. MODERATE TO ULTRA-DELUXE.

Shakti Cove is just five minutes from the water. Ten rustic cabins have full kitchens and sleep up to four guests. The units are furnished with queen-size beds, couches and feature eclectic decor. Pets are welcome. Gay-friendly. ~ 25301 Park Avenue,

Ocean Park; 360-665-4000, fax 360-665-6000; www.shakticove.com, e-mail info@shakticove.com. MODERATE.

Caswell's On the Beach overlooking Willapa Bay is an attractive, newly built, Queen Anne–style residence surrounded by acres of tranquil forest and oceanfront. The two-story, 6,700-foot inn has five plush guest rooms with antique beds, sitting areas and TV/VCRs. The full breakfast includes eggs, fresh-baked muffins and fried oysters. There is also a comfortable library, a parlor, a sunroom and relaxing veranda. ~ 25204 Sandridge Road, Ocean Park; 360-665-6535, 888- 553-2319; www.caswellsinn.com, e-mail bcaswell@willapabay.org. DELUXE.

HIDDEN ►

Willapa Bay oyster lovers frequent the beds near the north end of the Long Beach Peninsula, and this is where they'll find the **Moby Dick Hotel**. An eight-room bed-and-breakfast inn that first opened its doors in 1930, it maintains a country nautical atmosphere, with rambling grounds, its own organic vegetable garden and oyster farm. A fireplace, bayside pavilion sauna and piano beckon on rainy days. A new 24-foot yurt with heated bamboo floor, skylight and circular space accommodates up to 30 people for retreats, meditations and workshops. ~ 25814 Sandridge Road, Nahcotta; 360-665-4543, 800-673-6145, fax 360-665-6887; www.mobydickhotel.com, e-mail mobydickhotel@willapabay.org. MODERATE TO DELUXE.

DINING

Housed in the oldest hotel in Washington, the **Tokeland Hotel and Restaurant** pairs delicious local foods with panoramic views of Willapa Bay. Homecooked meals may include dishes ranging from pasta, salmon and crab Louie to steak and a nightly chicken special; breakfast involves blueberry pancakes, and crab and cheddar omelettes. Every Sunday the Tokeland offers a much sought-after cranberry pot roast. ~ 100 Hotel Road, Tokeland; phone/fax 360-267-7006; www.tokelandhotel.com, e-mail scott@tokelandhotel.com. MODERATE TO DELUXE.

HIDDEN ►

For a unique dining experience, visit the **Dock of the Bay**, on an off-the-beaten-track peninsula that juts into Willapa Bay 12 miles south of South Bend just off Route 101. Oysters, of course, are a specialty at this café/tavern; they even serve them for breakfast, along with other seafood omelettes. The fish market here also sells fresh crab and smoked salmon. ~ Bay Center Road at 2nd and Bridge streets, Bay Center; 360-875-5130. MODERATE.

Opposite the Shoalwater Restaurant entrance is **The Heron & Beaver Pub**, with light meals produced by the same kitchen as the Shoalwater Restaurant. ~ Shelburne Country Inn, 4415 Pacific Way, Seaview; 360-642-4142; www.shoalwater.com, e-mail info@shoalwater.com. MODERATE TO DELUXE.

Owned and operated by the former chef and manager of the renowned Shoalwater Restaurant, the **42nd Street Café** is fast making its own reputation. Hand-cut ravioli sautéed in a cider glaze with apples and red onions, iron skillet fried chicken, pot roast with vegetables and other down-home fare are prepared with a gourmet hand. The café is located in a converted army barracks. The dining room is bright and casual with blue and green cloth napery, candles and fresh flowers; in the off season the chef plays her harp for guests on Sunday nights. Breakfast, lunch and dinner. ~ 4201 Pacific Way, Seaview; 360-642-2323, fax 360-642-3439; www.42ndstreetcafe.com, e-mail blaine@42ndstreetcafe.com. MODERATE TO DELUXE.

The **Corral Drive In** claims its Tsunami is the world's largest hamburger—and who's to argue with a five-pounder on a 16-and-a-half-inch bun? Not only is it huge (the drive-in needs 24-hour notice—better have the whole family along), it's actually quite good. The place also has regular burgers, fries, milkshakes and such. ~ North Pacific Highway and 95th Street North, Long Beach; 360-642-2774. BUDGET. ◀HIDDEN

Mountains of oyster shells surround **The Ark Restaurant and Bakery,** located near the north end of the Long Beach Peninsula on oyster-rich Willapa Bay. In fact, the casual, relaxed restaurant has its own oyster beds—as well as an herb and edible-flower garden and a busy bakery. Nearby are cranberry bogs and forests of wild mushrooms. All these go into the preparation of creative dishes like Scotch salmon, sturgeon Szechuan and oysters Italian, and the Ark oyster feed, a decades-old tradition. Dinner Tuesday through Sunday; Sunday brunch. Call for winter hours. ~ 3310 273rd Street and Sandridge Road, Nahcotta; 360-665-4133, fax 360-665-5043; www.arkrestaurant.com, e-mail dine@arkrestaurant.com. MODERATE TO DELUXE.

AUTHOR FAVORITE

I've seen Willapa Bay oysters on the menus at gourmet restaurants throughout the Northwest. The best place to try them is at the source—the highly acclaimed **Shoalwater Restaurant**, located in the historic Shelburne Country Inn, Washington's oldest continuously operated hotel. Expensive, but worth it. Everything is exquisite. From the Dungeness crab and shrimp cakes to the mussel and clam chowder, the roast duck breast to the pan-fried Willapa Bay oysters with a spicy Creole mayonnaise, and the creative preparations of the day's fresh catches, a meal here is one to savor. The turn-of-the-20th-century ambience adds an element of comfort. ~ Shelburne Inn, 4415 Pacific Way, Seaview; 360-642-4142; www.shoalwater.com, e-mail info@shoalwater.com. DELUXE.

SHOPPING

There's wonderful bric-a-brac at **Marsh's Free Museum**, from world-famous Jake the Alligator Man, an authentic shrunken head and freaks-of-nature stuffed animals to antique dishes and saltwater taffy. ~ 409 South Pacific Avenue, Long Beach; 360-642-2188, fax 360-642-8177; www.marshsfreemuseum.com, e-mail jake@marshsfreemuseum.com.

The souvenir most typical of beach recreation here, perhaps, would be a colorful kite. Look for them in Long Beach at **Above It All Kites.** ~ 312 Pacific Boulevard South, Long Beach; 360-642-3541; www.aboveitallkites.com.

Noted watercolorist Eric Wiegardt displays his work at the **Wiegardt Studio Gallery**. Open Monday through Saturday in July and August, Friday and Saturday the rest of the year. ~ 2607 Bay Avenue between Route 103 and Sandridge Road, Ocean Park; 360-665-5976; www.ericwiegardt.com.

NIGHTLIFE

The Lightship Restaurant has the Long Beach Peninsula's only ocean-view restaurant from its third-story loft; come for a sunset drink. ~ Edgewater Inn, 409 Southwest Sid Snyder Drive, Long Beach; 360-642-3252; www.lightshiplb.com. Quiet beers are best quaffed at **The Heron & Beaver Pub** in the Shelburne Inn. ~ 4415 Pacific Way, Seaview; 360-642-4142.

BEACHES & PARKS

LOOMIS LAKE STATE PARK Situated south of Klipsan Beach, this day-use park offers ocean beach access with good fishing from the shore and good clamming on the beach. Swimming is not recommended. Facilities include restrooms and picnic areas. ~ Park Road off Route 103 (Pacific Way), four miles south of Ocean Park; 360-642-3078, fax 360-642-4216.

PACIFIC PINES STATE PARK This day-use park offers beach access for various activities, like beachcombing, kite flying, jogging, surf fishing and razor clam digging in season. The coastal dune environment bristles with foxglove, lupine and a variety of ferns; keep your eye out for hummingbirds, rabbits, deer and raccoons. There are restrooms and picnic areas. ~ At 274th Place off Park Avenue, a mile north of Ocean Park; 360-642-3078, fax 360-642-4216.

LEADBETTER POINT STATE PARK Shifting dunes and mudflats, ponds and marshes, grasslands and forests make this northern tip of the Long Beach Peninsula an ideal place for those who like to observe nature. As many as 100 species of migratory birds stop over here. There are numerous hiking trails. Surf fishing is popular, but riptides discourage swimming. You'll find pit toilets, restrooms and picnic areas. ~ Stackpole Road, via Route 103 and Sandridge Road, three miles north of Oysterville; 360-642-3078, fax 360-642-4216.

CAPE DISAPPOINTMENT STATE PARK

The point where the Columbia River meets the Pacific Ocean has been a crossroads of history for two centuries. The Lewis and Clark expedition arrived at this dramatic headland in 1805 after 18 months on the trail. Two 19th-century lighthouses—at North Head on the Pacific and at Cape Disappointment on a Columbia sandbar—have limited the number of shipwrecks to a mere 200 through 1994. The fort was occupied from the Civil War through World War II. Today, the 1800-acre park contains the Lewis and Clark Interpretive Center, numerous forest, beach and clifftop trails, a boat launch, a swimming beach, fishing (in the surf, from the jetty or from a boat), summer interpretive programs, an interpretive center open year-round, lighthouse tours, restrooms, picnic areas and groceries. ~ Route 101, two and a half miles southwest of Ilwaco; 360-642-3078, fax 360-642-4216.

The Cape Disappointment Lighthouse, built in 1856, is the oldest functioning lighthouse on the West Coast.

▲ There are 152 standard sites ($19 per night), 83 RV hookup sites ($26 per night), and yurts and cabins ($40 per night). Reservations: 888-226-7688.

Southwest Washington

Heading east from the coast via Route 401 and Route 4, you'll want to take the cutoff south to the circa 1905 **Grays River Covered Bridge**. Continue east another 17 miles to Skamokawa, a town that's hard to pronounce and easy to visit. The site of an Indian village that dates back 2000 years, this lumber town is on the Lewis and Clark Trail. Local Skamokawa Vista Park is a good spot to watch traffic on the Columbia River shipping channel. At **Redman Hall**, an 1894 schoolhouse has become a riverlife interpretive center. Step inside the three-story landmark to learn more about this 19th-century riverfront town now on the National Register of Historic Places. Closed Monday through Wednesday. ~ 1394 West Route 4, Skamokawa; 360-795-3007.

To the east, you won't want to miss the **Julia Butler Hansen National Wildlife Refuge.** A sanctuary for the Columbian white-tailed deer, this waterfront refuge is also a place to spot elk and migratory birds. ~ Route 4, Cathlamet; 360-795-3915, fax 360-795-0803.

The refuge is next door to Cathlamet, a historic logging town. Begin your visit at the **Wahkiakum County Museum**. The collection is strong on community artifacts, victrolas, dolls and railway equipment. Closed Monday in summer and Monday through Wednesday in winter. ~ 65 River Street, Cathlamet; 360-795-3954; www.wahkiakumchamber.com/museum.

Outdoor Adventures

SPORT-FISHING

Despite charter operators' complaints that government restrictions hinder their operations, the Strait of Juan de Fuca is still one of the nation's great salmon grounds, with chinook, coho and other species running the waters during the summer months. From April to September, halibut is also big in these waters—literally: one local operator holds the state record, 268 pounds. Bottomfish like ling cod, true cod, red snapper and black bass round out the angling possibilities.

OLYMPIC COAST When **Big Salmon Fishing Resort** isn't breaking state records for halibut (288 pounds), it runs half-day charters for salmon and bottomfish. The store also sells bait and rents tackle. Closed October to March. ~ 1251 Bay View Avenue (or Front Street), Neah Bay; 360-645-2374, 866-787-1900; www.bigsalmonresort.com.

Olson's Resort & Marina runs year-round charters out of Neah Bay and Sekiu for halibut, bottomfish and salmon (in season). ~ Sekiu; 360-963-2311; www.olsonsresort.com.

GRAYS HARBOR AREA **Deep Sea Charters** operates seven boats for one-day bottomfish and overnight tuna charters. Bait and tackle included. ~ Across from Float 6, Westport; 360-268-9300, 800-562-0151; www.deepseacharters.biz.

Angler Charters runs one-day trips for salmon, bottomfish and halibut. Bait and tackle is provided. ~ 2401 Westhaven Drive, Westport, across from Float 18; 360-268-1030, 800-422-0425; www.anglercharters.net.

LONG BEACH–WILLAPA BAY At the mouth of the Columbia River, Ilwaco is another center for deep-sea fishing. Salmon and sturgeon are caught near the river mouth, while tuna, rockfish, cod and sole are in deeper waters. **Seabreeze Charters** arranges day charters, operating seven boats, most of which carry up to 16 people. Large engines cut down run times for deep-bottom trips. ~ 185 Howerton Way Southeast, Ilwaco; 360-642-2300, 800-204-9125; www.seabreezecharters.net.

RIVER FISHING

It's not just the fish—salmon, steelhead, trout—that attract anglers to the mountain streams flowing from the Olympic Mountains. Spectacular scenery and glimpses of eagles, deer, elk and other wildlife sweeten the deal.

PORT ANGELES AREA An hour or two away are several destinations for river fishing: the Sol Duc, Bogachiel, Hoh, Queets and Calawah rivers.

OLYMPIC NATIONAL PARK The lower Quinault River is not "overpacked" with fishermen—yet—partly because nontribal people may not fish rivers on the reservation without a Quinault guide. Contact the **Quinault Indian Nation Department of Natural**

Return of the Monster Slayers

Makah, the tribal name of Neah Bay's native people, means "generous food"—and no wonder! For 2000 years, the main protein in the Makah diet was the meat of the gray whale. Men of the tribe would chase one of the 35-ton leviathans in canoes, harpoon it, and kill it by stabbing it repeatedly with spears as it towed them through the open ocean. So vital was whaling to the Makah culture that in their 1855 treaty the U.S. government guaranteed their right to hunt whales forever—the only treaty ever made by the United States that contains such a guarantee. Thereafter, the tribe also sold whale oil to non-Indian settlers and became the wealthiest Indians in the Northwest. (They are now among the poorest.) They had to stop in the 1920s after the whales nearly disappeared from coastal waters due to industrial whaling.

In recent years, since the California gray whale population has recovered and the whales have been removed from the endangered species list, the Makah intend to hold new whale hunts on a limited scale, still in traditional hand-carved log canoes but using a specially designed rifle—hopefully a single carefully aimed shot at the same instant the harpoon is thrown—as a more humane alternative to spears. Meat from the whales would be divided among the 1800 tribal members, storing any excess in tribal freezers. Under the supervision of the National Marine Fisheries Service, the tribe is allowed to take up to 20 migrating adult whales without calves in a five-year period. After nearly five years of planning the hunt and practicing the use of the harpoon and rifle, and a year of ceremonial purification, tribal hunters killed their first whale in May 1999.

Makah whaling is the subject of one of the biggest animal rights controversies in the Northwest. Opponents interpret the language of the Makah treaty as allowing whaling only as long as non-Indians were also hunting whales, before the present international ban. They also fear that despite federal prohibitions the tribe might find the Japanese importers' $1 million offer for a single whale an irresistible temptation. Tribal leaders say whaling is a matter of cultural preservation, discipline and pride. They claim that many of the tribe's health problems may come from the loss of their traditional whale meat diet and point out that the indigenous Chukotki people of Russia's Pacific coast have been "harvesting" about 165 gray whales a year for the last 40 years, yet the whale population continues to grow. Escalating with each whale hunt, the dispute is unlikely to be resolved soon.

Resources to receive information about available guides for drift boat or walk-in fishing. ~ 1214 Aalis Street, Taholah; 360-276-8211 ext. 374, 888-616-8211; www.quinaultindiannation.com. **Three Rivers Resort & Guide Service** operates four 16-foot drift boats for two anglers on the Sol Duc, Bogachiel and Hoh rivers (another "quiet" spot). The eight-hour trips are for salmon and steelhead. Tackle, continental breakfast, and lunch are provided. ~ 7764 La Push Road, Forks; 360-374-5300; www.forks-web.com/threerivers.

SHELLFISHING

Before you start digging up clams or other shellfish, please remember that just like other forms of fishing, a license is required for this activity. You can pick one up at tackle shops and other locations that sell fishing licenses. Recreational harvesting of shellfish is permitted on public beaches, but you should double-check, because much of the state's tideland is privately owned. Generally, shellfishing is permitted year round; razor clams and oyster harvests are restricted by season and location. Call the **Washington State Department of Fish and Wildlife** for information. ~ 360-902-2700, wdfw.wa.gov, e-mail fishregs@dfw.wa.gov. You can also call the **Shellfish Regulation** hotline. ~ 866-880-5431; wdfw.wa.gov/fish/shellfish/beachreg. You must also check with the Health Department's **Recreational Marine Biotoxin Hotline** to find out which waters are unhealthy for shellfish harvesting. ~ 800-562-5632; www.doh.wa.gov.

RIVER RUNNING

The Elwha River flows from the Olympic Mountains into the Strait of Juan de Fuca. Along the way, there are some Class II whitewater rapids—not quite a thrill ride, but enough excitement for good family fun (it's the only commercially rafted whitewater on the peninsula). Besides that, there's plenty of wildlife to see—elk, osprey, bald eagles, deer, harlequin ducks—as well as a view of a glacier. **Olympic Raft and Kayak** runs multiple trips daily, each lasting about two and a half hours. The trips down the Class II+ Elwha and Class II Hoh rivers are on rafts. Both beginning and

DIGGIN' IN

Folks who like to shellfish will be happy in Washington. There are clams (littleneck, butter, Manila and razor), scallops, oysters (Willapa Bay is famous for its oysters), mussels and crab (Dungeness Spit, north of Sequim, is the home of the renowned Dungeness crab). Then, of course, there's that Northwest oddity, the geoduck (say "gooey-duck"), whose huge foot cannot fit within its shell. See "Shellfishing" for information on this popular activity.

experienced rafters can partake. ~ 123 Lake Aldwell Road, Port Angeles; 360-452-1443, 888-452-1443; www.raftandkayak.com.

KAYAKING

Experienced or novice, kayakers who paddle around a mountain lake, through coastal marshlands or under sea cliffs will be rewarded not only with good exercise but also with the opportunity to observe abundant wildlife in a wilderness setting. Companies offering guided tours generally operate during the warmer months (May through September). But think about this: Many kayakers swear the best time to paddle is in the rain.

PORT TOWNSEND AREA Port Townsend is a sea-kayaking center; call **Sport Townsend**, where you can buy backpacks and kayaks. ~ 1044 Water Street, Port Townsend; 360-379-9711; www.sporttownsend.com. For rentals, lessons and private nature tours guided by well-known kayaker Richard Roshon, contact **Kayak Center at PT Outdoors**. Closed in winter. ~ 1017 Water Street; 360-379-3608, 888-754-8598; www.ptoutdoors.com. **Olympic Outdoor Center** offers private, sunset and overnight kayaking tours in the spring and summer. The center also rents kayaks and offers classes. ~ 18971 Front Street, Poulsbo; 360-697-6095, 800-592-5983; www.olympicoutdoorcenter.com.

PORT ANGELES AREA For kayak rentals and sales in Port Angeles, try **Sound Bikes and Kayaks**. ~ 120 East Front Street, Port Angeles; 360-457-1240; www.soundbikeskayaks.com.

You may have Lake Aldwell all to yourself, aside from the waterfowl nesting along its shores, when you join a two-hour guided tour of this clear blue lake. **Olympic Raft and Kayak** uses the more stable sea kayaks for these lake tours. The service also offers a four-hour trip in the saltwater Freshwater Bay just west of Port Angeles, which teems with bald eagles, otters and endangered marbled murrelets. ~ 123 Lake Aldwell Road, Port Angeles; 360-452-1443, 888-452-1443; www.raftandkayak.com.

KITE FLYING

Several miles of wide, flat beach make the beaches at Ocean Shores and Long Beach ideal kite-flying spots. A nationally sanctioned kite-flying festival in June brings some of the sport's best fliers to Ocean Shores; the same month, competing stunt kites fill the sky over Long Beach. In August, Long Beach hosts the weeklong Washington State International Kite Festival, said to be the biggest kite festival in the country (about 100,000 people attend). You don't have to be up to championship standards, though, to buy a kite and fly it or to visit a museum about kite flying.

OCEAN SHORES–PACIFIC BEACH Pick up a kite and some tips on how to fly it at **Ocean Shores Kites**. Besides dozens of different kites, the store sells windsocks and other wind toys (Frisbees, etc.). ~ Shores Mall, 172 Chance a la Mer, Ocean Shores; 360-289-4103, fax 360-289-0517; www.oceanshoreskites.com.

LONG BEACH–WILLAPA BAY In Long Beach is the **World Kite Museum and Hall of Fame,** which has probably the largest collection of Chinese and Japanese kites outside Asia. Open Friday through Tuesday from October through April, daily the rest of the year. Admission. ~ 303 West Sid Snyder Drive, Long Beach; 360-642-4020; www.worldkitemuseum.com.

WHALE WATCHING

California gray whales and humpbacks head back up to Alaskan waters between March and May. Orcas, or killer whales, are frequently seen in the waters of the Strait of Juan de Fuca, and we land-based mammals can't seem to get enough of the spectacle. Many fishing charter operators convert to whale-watching cruises during these months.

GRAYS HARBOR AREA Two-and-a-half-hour cruises generally head offshore toward the whales' migration path, but occasionally the whales wander into Grays Harbor and the boats never get out to sea. In Westport, contact **Ocean Charters** for whale-watching trips. ~ Across from Float 6; 360-268-9144, 800-562-0105; www.oceanchartersinc.com. In the same harbor, **Deep Sea Charters** offers more of the same from March to mid-October. ~ Across from Float 6; 360-268-9300, 800-562-0151; www.deepseacharters.biz. From Westport, there's a number of specialty whale-cruise operators.

SKIING

The only skiing on the Olympic Peninsula is **Hurricane Ridge Ski Area,** 17 miles south of Port Angeles, in Olympic National Park. Here skiers will find a few downhill runs and several cross-country trails starting from the visitors center. There are two rope tows and a T-bar lift on site. The Hurricane Hill Road cross-country trail (1.5 miles one way) is probably the easiest of the area's six trails; the most challenging is the Hurricane Ridge Trail to Mt. Angeles, a steep three-mile route that's often icy. Rentals of downhill, cross-country and snowshoeing equipment are also available. Open April through October, weekends and weather permitting only. Contact the **Olympic National Park Visitor Center.** ~ 3002 Mt. Angeles Road, Port Angeles; 360-565-3130, for road conditions 360-565-3131.

For ski lift information, call the **Hurricane Ridge Winter Sports Club.** ~ 360-457-2879; www.hurricaneridge.net.

RIDING STABLES

On the Olympic Peninsula, it's possible to saddle up for a guided mountain ride through forests of towering trees or a ride along the beach at sunset.

OCEAN SHORES–PACIFIC BEACH **Nan-Sea Stables** teaches natural horsemanship in Western or English style. A three-hour day camp in summer and Saturdays in winter provides grooming, saddling, riding lessons and a trail ride that is great for kids and beginners, ages seven and up. ~ 255 State Route 115, Ocean Shores; 360-289-0194, fax 360-289-3918; www.horseplanet.com, e-mail nansea@horseplanet.com.

LLAMA TREKKING

Llama lovers will be delighted to accompany an Andean pack animal into the Olympics, thanks to **Kit's Llamas.** ~ P.O. Box 116, Olalla, WA 98359; 253-857-5274; www.northolympic.com/llamas.

Deli Llama Wilderness Adventures leads one- to seven-day trips into the Olympic and North Cascades National Parks. ~ 360-757-4212; www.delillama.com.

GOLF

Bay views, ocean views, mountain views—take your pick. They're part and parcel with the courses in this region, all of which rent power carts, push carts and clubs. Mild Seattle winters easily allow most of the 125-plus public golf courses in the area to operate year-round.

PORT TOWNSEND AREA The public 18-hole **Discovery Bay Golf Club** is set in the woods above Discovery Bay. It is a fairly flat course, although it can get a bit mushy after winter rains. ~ 7401 Cape George Road, Port Townsend; 360-385-0704. The public, double-teed, nine-hole **Port Townsend Golf Club** is located in town. It's considered the driest winter course in the area (it gets only 17 inches of rain), with rolling terrain, small greens and a driving range. ~ 1948 Blaine Street, Port Townsend; 360-385-4547. *Golf Digest* has named the semiprivate 27-hole **Port Ludlow Golf Course** designed by Robert Muir Graves one of the best in the country. Although housing flanks one section, the spectacular views of Ludlow Bay and abundant wildlife prompt comments like "Amazing" and "It's like golfing in a national park" from local duffers. ~ 751 Highland Drive, Port Ludlow; 360-437-0272.

For biking, hiking, canoeing and country life, you can't beat Puget Island, a bucolic retreat just minutes from Cathlamet connecting Washington to Oregon via ferry.

PORT ANGELES AREA Although the 18-hole private **Sunland Golf and Country Club** goes through a housing development, it's well treed and fairly flat. Call for reciprocal play times. ~ 109 Hilltop Drive, Sequim; 360-683-6800. **Dungeness Golf Course** offers a semiprivate, 18-hole course. The number-three hole, called "Old Crabbie," has ten contracts guarding the crab-shaped green. ~ 1965 Woodcock Road, Sequim; 360-683-6344.

OCEAN SHORES–PACIFIC BEACH The front nine of the municipal **Ocean Shores Golf Course** has a links-like layout in the dunes; the back nine wanders into the trees. ~ 500 Canal Drive Northeast at Albatross Street, Ocean Shores; 360-289-3357.

GRAYS HARBOR AREA An old farming tract turned into a public 18-hole golf course in the early 1920s, **Oaksridge Golf Course** is very flat. It's pretty wet in the winter, but drains fast. The front nine is long. ~ 1052 Monte–Elma Road, Elma; 360-482-3511.

BIKING

Except along the southwestern shore areas, bicycling this part of Washington requires strength and stamina. There's spectacular beauty here, but there's also lots of rain and challenging terrain.

PORT TOWNSEND AREA Recreational bicyclists will probably enjoy a ride through **Fort Worden State Park**, which overlooks the Strait of Juan de Fuca, in Port Townsend.

OLYMPIC COAST A recommended road tour is the 85-mile **Upper Peninsula Tour** from Sequim to Neah Bay. The 55-mile trip down Route 101 from **Port Angeles to Forks** is also recommended. A paved six-mile trail loops the Port Angeles waterfront. The trail is flat, mostly following the shoreline, with picnic tables and other stopping spots along the way. On a clear day, you can see across the strait to Victoria.

OCEAN SHORES–PACIFIC BEACH One of the area's gentlest biking opportunities is the 14-mile **Ocean Shores Loop** from North Beach Park. For a map, call the Ocean Shores Chamber of Commerce, 360-289-2451; www.oceanshores.org.

GRAYS HARBOR AREA Worthy of a long ride is the 69-mile **Aberdeen-Raymond-Westport** loop on Routes 101 and 105. A new paved trail has been built in Westport along the beach. It runs for a mile and a half between two small state parks.

LONG BEACH–WILLAPA BAY The 42-mile **Seaview-Naselle** loop in Pacific County is popular.

Bike Rentals In Port Townsend, rent mountain bikes, tandems, running strollers, bike trailers and road bikes at **Port Townsend Cyclery**. ~ 252 Tyler Street, Port Townsend; 360-385-6470; www.ptcyclery.com. **Sound Bikes and Kayaks** rents hybrids and mountain bikes. ~ 120 East Front Street, Port Angeles; 360-457-1240; www.soundbikeskayaks.com.

HIKING

All distances listed for hiking trails are one way unless otherwise noted.

PORT TOWNSEND AREA **Mount Walker Trail** (2 miles) ascends the Olympics' easternmost peak (2804 feet) through a rhododendron forest. The view from the summit, across Hood Canal and the Kitsap Peninsula to Seattle and the Cascades, is unforgettable. The trailhead is one-fifth mile off Route 101 at Walker Pass, five miles south of Quilcene.

PORT ANGELES AREA **Dungeness Spit Trail** (5.5 miles) extends down the outside of the longest natural sandspit in the United

States, and back the inside. The spit is a national wildlife refuge with a lighthouse at its seaward end. The trail begins and ends at the Dungeness Recreation Area.

OLYMPIC NATIONAL PARK Olympic National Park and adjacent areas of Olympic National Forest are rich in backpacking opportunities. Most trails follow rivers into the high country, with its peaks and alpine lakes. **Obstruction Point Trail** (7.4 miles) leads from the Deer Park Campground to Obstruction Point, following a 6500-foot ridgeline.

The easy **Spruce Railroad Trail** (2 miles) begins near North Shore Picnic Area or the west side of Log Cabin Resort on Lake Crescent. It follows the railroad bed of the historic Spruce Railroad and offers spectacular views of glacial Lake Crescent and surrounding mountains. No elevation gain.

Seven Lakes Basin Loop (22.5 miles) has several trail options, starting and ending at Sol Duc Hot Springs.

Coastal areas of the Olympic Peninsula have hiking trails as well. **Cape Alava Loop** (9 miles) crosses from the Ozette Ranger Station to Cape Alava; follows the shoreline south to Sand Point, from which there is beach access to shipwreck memorials farther south; and returns northeast to the ranger station. Prehistoric petroglyphs and an ancient Indian village can be seen en route.

GRAYS HARBOR AREA **Wynoochee Lake Shore Trail** (12 miles) circles this manmade reservoir in Olympic National Forest north of Montesano.

Shifting Sands Nature Trail (.5 mile) teaches visitors to Twin Harbors State Park, south of Westport, about plant and animal life in the seaside dunes.

LONG BEACH–WILLAPA BAY Along the southwestern Washington coast there are few inland trails, but the long stretches of flat beach appeal to many walkers. **Leadbetter Point Loop Trail** (2.5 miles) weaves through the forests and dunes, and past the ponds, mudflats and marshes, of the wildlife sanctuary/state park at the northern tip of the Long Beach Peninsula. Accessible from Oysterville, it's of special interest to birdwatchers.

AUTHOR FAVORITE

One of the most unforgettable hikes I've experienced is the **Hoh River Trail** (17.5 miles), which wanders through lush, primeval rainforest teeming with deer from the Hoh Ranger Station to Glacier Meadows, at the base of the Blue Glacier on 7965-foot Mt. Olympus, the park's highest point. (Afterwards, I felt like a very tired Greek god.)

The Trail of the Ancient Cedars (3.2 miles) goes through an important grove of old-growth red cedar, some as large as 11 feet wide and 150 feet tall, on Long Island, and be sure there is at least a six-foot tide. You must find your own boat access to Long Island. The Willapa Bay National Wildlife Refuge provides interpretive brochures at its headquarters. ~ Milepost 24, Route 101; 360-484-3482.

Transportation

CAR

Route 101 is the main artery of the Olympic Peninsula and Washington coastal region, virtually encircling the entire land mass. Branching off Route 5 in Olympia, at the foot of Puget Sound, it runs north to Discovery Bay, where **Route 20** turns off to Port Townsend; west through Port Angeles to Sappho; then zigzags to Astoria, Oregon, and points south. Remarkably, when you reach Aberdeen, 292 miles after you start traveling on 101, you're just 36 miles from where you started!

Traveling from Seattle, most Olympic Peninsula visitors take either the Seattle–Winslow ferry (to Route 305) or the Edmonds–Kingston ferry (to Route 104), joining 101 just south of Discovery Bay. From Tacoma, the practical route is **Route 16** across the Narrows Bridge. From the north, the Keystone ferry to Port Townsend has its eastern terminus midway down lanky Whidbey Island, off Route 20. Northbound travelers can reach the area either through Astoria, on Route 101, or via several routes that branch off Route 5 north of Portland.

AIR

William R. Fairchild International Airport, near Port Angeles, links the northern Olympic Peninsula with Seattle and western Canada via Kenmore Air and Rite Bros. Aviation charter flights. ~ 360-417-3433.

FERRY

Washington State Ferries serves the Olympic Peninsula directly from Whidbey Island to Port Townsend and indirectly across Puget Sound (via the Kitsap Peninsula) from Seattle and Edmonds. ~ 206-464-6400, 888-808-7977; www.wsdot.wa.gov/ferries. The **Black Ball Transport** offers direct daily service between Port Angeles and Victoria, B.C. ~ 360-457-4491; www.ferrytovictoria.com. **Victoria Express** provides foot-passenger service. ~ 360-452-8088; www.victoriaexpress.com. Some smaller cruise lines may make stops in Port Angeles.

CAR RENTALS

In Port Angeles, **Budget Car and Truck Rental** can be found in town. ~ 800-527-0700.

PUBLIC TRANSIT

For local bus service in the northern Olympic Peninsula, including Port Angeles and Sequim, contact **Clallam Transit System** in Port Angeles. ~ 360-452-4511, 800-858-3747; www.clallamtransit.

com. Port Townsend, Sequim and eastern Jefferson County are served by **Jefferson Transit.** ~ 360-385-4777, 800-371-0497; www.jeffersontransit.com. The **Grays Harbor Transportation Authority** offers bus service to Aberdeen, Ocean Shores and the surrounding region. ~ 360-532-2770, 800-562-9730; www.ghtransit.com.

Bus service between Raymond, Long Beach and Astoria, Oregon, is provided by the **Pacific Transit System.** ~ 360-642-9418; www.pacifictransit.org.

SEVEN

Northern Puget Sound and the San Juan Islands

"Every part of this land is sacred to my people. Every shining pine needle, every sandy shore, every mist in the dark woods, every clearing and humming insect is holy in the memory and experience of my people. . . . We are part of the earth and it is part of us. The perfumed flowers are our sisters; the deer, the horse, the great eagle, these are our brothers. The rocky crests, the juices in the meadows, the body heat of the pony, and man—all belong to the same family." This was part of Chief Seattle's poignant reply when, in 1854, the "Great White Chief" in Washington pressed to purchase some of the land around Puget Sound then occupied by several Northwest Indian tribes. And those sentiments still ring true today as the natural beauty and appeal of Northern Puget Sound and the San Juan Islands remain undiminished.

This awe-inspiring land supported the American Indians, providing for all their needs with verdant woods full of deer and berries and crystal waters full of salmon, letting them live in peaceful coexistence for hundreds of years. Even the weather was kind to them here in this "rain shadow," shielded by the Olympic and Vancouver mountain ranges.

Things slowly began to change for the Northwest Indian tribes and the land with the arrival of Juan de Fuca in 1592, who came to explore the coastline for the Spanish. The floodgates of exploration and exploitation weren't fully opened, however, until Captain George Vancouver came in 1792 to chart the region for the British, naming major landmarks such as Mt. Baker, Mt. Rainier, Whidbey Island and Puget Sound after his compatriots.

Establishment of trade with the American Indians and the seemingly inexhaustible quantity of animals to supply the lucrative fur trade drew many pioneers. Before long, industries such as logging, mining, shipping and fishing began to flourish, supporting the early settlers (and still supporting their descendants today).

Geologists who have studied the record say that a now long-disappeared continent moving eastward out of the Pacific Ocean eons ago collided with, or "docked" against, the Puget Sound mainland, laying the foundation for the multiplicity of land forms—islands, estuaries, mountains, coastlines—that characterize the northern Puget Sound region today.

The geographical layout of the 172 islands of the San Juan Archipelago made for watery back alleys and hidden coves perfect for piracy and smuggling, so the history of the area reflects an almost Barbary Coast–type of intrigue where a man could get a few drinks, a roll in the hay and be shanghaied all in one night. Chinese laborers were regularly brought in under cover of night to build up coastal cities and railroads in the 1800s. This big money "commodity" was replaced by opium and silk, and then booze during Prohibition.

Smuggling has since been curbed, and while things are changing as resources are diminished, logging and fishing are still major industries in the region. However, current booms in real estate and tourism are beginning to tilt the economic scale as more and more people discover the area's beauty.

The area referred to as Northern Puget Sound begins just beyond the far northern outskirts of Seattle, where most visitors first arrive, and extends northward up the coast to the Canadian border. Coastal communities such as Everett, Bellingham and Blaine tend to be more commercial in nature, heavily flavored by the logging and fishing industries, while other small towns such as La Conner and Mt. Vernon are still very pastoral, dependent on an agriculturally based economy. When heading east from Mt. Vernon, for every mile traveled toward the Cascade Mountains, the average annual rainfall increases by one inch. Consequently, springtime along this stretch of land is particularly lovely, especially in the Skagit Valley when the fields are ablaze in daffodils, iris and tulips. The world's biggest single grower of tulip bulbs—Washington Bulb Company—is based in the Skagit Valley.

Of the 172 named islands of the San Juans, we concentrate on the four most popular. These also are very pastoral, with rich soil and salubrious conditions perfectly suited to raising livestock or growing fruit. The major islands are connected to the mainland by bridges or reached by limited ferry service, an inhibiting factor that helps preserve the pristine nature here.

Although it's not considered part of the San Juans, serpentine Whidbey Island, with its thick southern tip reaching toward Seattle, is the largest island in Puget Sound. Situated at Whidbey's northern tip is Fidalgo Island, home of Anacortes and the ferry terminal gateway to the San Juans. Lopez is by far the friendliest and most rural of the islands, followed closely by San Juan, the largest and busiest. Shaw Island is one of the smaller islands, and lovely Orcas Island, named after Spanish explorer Don Juan Vincente de Guemes Pacheco y Padilla Orcasitees y Aguayo Conde de Revilla Gigedo (whew!) rather than orcas, is tallest, capped by 2400-foot Mt. Constitution.

The ferry system is severely overtaxed during the busy summer season when the San Juans are inundated with tourists, making it difficult to reach the islands at times and absolutely impossible to find accommodations if you haven't booked months in advance. The crowds drop off dramatically after Labor Day, a pleasant surprise since the weather in September and October is still lovely and the change of seasonal color against this beautiful backdrop is incredible.

Text continued on page 212.

Three-day Weekend

Island-Hopping to the San Juans

The trip through the San Juan Islands is the longest and most beautiful cruise the Washington State Ferries network has to offer. It's not expensive, but in recent years, as both tourism and population in the Puget Sound area have grown enormously, the San Juan ferries have become so overburdened that even island residents have a hard time getting home during the summer months and on sunny weekends. If visiting during the off-season is out of the question, the best strategy is to arrive in Anacortes the afternoon before, sleep early and get in line for the ferry by dawn. The ferry schedule changes seasonally so obtain a current one at any ferry terminal or toll booth. Study the San Juan Island schedule carefully—it's complicated.

Day 1

- Leaving Seattle, head north on Route 5 to **Edmonds** (Exit 189), where a 30-minute ferry trip will take you to **Kingston** on the Olympic Peninsula (16 to 20 sailings daily from 5:50 a.m. to 11:45 p.m.).
- Drive eight miles north on Route 104 for a look at picturesque, New England–like **Port Gamble** (Chapter Five, page 142). Another 25 miles north via Routes 104, 19 and 20 brings you to **Port Townsend** (Chapter Six, page 156), a quaintly Victorian village on the northwest tip of the peninsula. Along the way, you might stop for lunch at the **Chimacum Café** (page 161), or you can catch a quick bite on the ferry.
- Take the ferry across to Keystone on **Whidbey Island** (page 234), a 30-minute trip (ten sailings daily from 6:30 a.m. to 8:30 p.m.).
- Follow Route 20 for 40 miles up the northern half of Whidbey Island, visiting **Coupeville** (page 236), yet another picture-perfect historic town, along the way.
- Before crossing **Deception Pass** from Whidbey Island to **Fidalgo Island** (page 245), be sure to walk out on the bridge for a magnificent seascape view. You've almost reached today's destination, so if you have time and feel like stretching your legs, the beaches and hiking trails of **Deception Pass State Park** (page 244) are the place to do it.
- Crossing the bridge, drive another six miles to the town of **Anacortes** (page 245); check into your lodging for the evening. Dine out, then go to bed early so you can catch the dawn ferry well rested.

Day 2

- Be at the Anacortes ferry dock no later than (yawn!) 5 a.m. to catch the first ferry of the day to **Orcas Island** (page 257). Otherwise you can expect to wait in line for *at least* three hours to get on another one. The trip to Orcas Island takes about one hour with intermediate stops at Lopez and Shaw islands; there are 10 to 12 sailings daily from 5:35 a.m. to 9:30 p.m. or later; vehicles for Orcas load 20 minutes before sailing.
- Have breakfast on the ferry or upon arrival on Orcas Island.
- Check into your accommodations and buy food for a picnic lunch.
- Head for **Moran State Park** (page 260), the largest and finest park in the Washington State Parks system. Take in the view from the top of Mount Constitution, the highest point in the San Juans. Then take your pick of many hiking possibilities.
- By mid-afternoon you may be ready for a nap.
- For dinner this evening, try a seafood feast at the **Restaurant at the Deer Harbor Inn** (page 259).

Day 3

- It's not quite as critical to catch the first ferry from Orcas to **San Juan Island** (page 251) because any of the ferries, which run from 7:20 a.m. to 9:45 p.m., is likely to unload as many vehicles at Orcas as are waiting to load. The trip to Friday Harbor takes about 30 minutes.
- Visit the **Whale Museum** (page 264).
- Take a driving tour around San Juan Island. On opposite sides of the island you'll find the sites of two historic forts of **San Juan Island National Historical Park** (page 251), where U.S. and British armies faced off in the anticlimactic "Pig War" over control of the San Juans. Several coastal beaches and parks along the way offer opportunities for picnicking and wildlife viewing. You may even see bald eagles or orca whales.
- As evening nears, catch a ferry back to Anacortes. The trip takes one to one and a half hours, depending on whether the ferry makes intermediate stops, and there are 10 or 12 sailings daily from 7:20 a.m. to 9:05 p.m.
- Back in Anacortes, you're less than an hour away from Seattle via Route 5.

Northern Puget Sound

Stretched along the fertile coastline between the Canadian border and the outer reaches of Seattle, communities along Northern Puget Sound are dependent on agriculture, logging and fishing, so the distinct pastoral feel of the area is no surprise. Verdant parks and vista spots taking in the beauty of the many islands not far offshore head the list of sightseeing musts here. But islands and shorelines are just part of the scenic and geographic mix in this region, which also includes rivers and delta wetlands, forests and picturesque farmlands.

SIGHTS

As you drive north from Seattle along Route 5, you'll cross a series of major rivers issuing from the Cascade Mountains. In order, you'll pass the Snohomish River (at Everett), the Stillaguamish (not far from Stanwood), the Skagit (at Mt. Vernon/Burlington) and the Nooksack (Bellingham). The lower reaches of these streams offer wetlands and wildlife to see, fishing villages to poke around in, a vital agricultural heritage in the Skagit and Nooksack valleys, and small towns by the handful.

If you plan to catch the Mukilteo ferry to Clinton on Whidbey Island, be sure to allow enough time to visit the historic **Mukilteo Lighthouse** built in 1906. There are picnic tables above a small rocky beach cluttered with driftwood and a big grassy field for kite-flying adjacent to the lighthouse in little **Mukilteo Lighthouse Park**. A gift shop is located in the former assistant lighthouse-keeper's home. Open April through September, weekend and holiday afternoons only. ~ Mukilteo; 425-513-9602.

In Everett you'll find your best vantage point from the dock behind **Marina Village**, a sparkling complex of upscale shops, microbreweries and restaurants located in the second-largest marina on the West Coast. ~ 1728 West Marine View Drive, Everett.

In summer, a free boat ride will shuttle you from the 10th Street boat launch to picturesque **Jetty Island** for guided nature walks, birdwatching, campfires, a hands-on mudflat safari program to teach children about small marine animals and one of the only warm saltwater beaches on the Sound. For information, call 425-257-8300.

The **Firefighter's Museum** offers a storefront display of antique early-20th-century firefighting equipment. The collection is set up for 24-hour, through-the-window viewing. ~ 13th Street Dock, Everett.

The **Everett Area Chamber of Commerce** can provide you with more information. Closed Saturday and Sunday. ~ 2000 Hewitt Avenue, Suite 205, Everett; 425-257-3222, fax 425-257-2074; www.everettchamber.com, e-mail info@everettchamber.com.

On the hillside above the marina, ornate **mansions** of the lumber barons that once ruled the economy here line Grand and

Rucker streets from 16th Street north. None are open to tour, but a slow drive up and down these avenues will give you a feel for the history of the city.

Everett is the home of the **Boeing Company's** largest aircraft assembly plant—in fact, the largest building in the world by volume at 472 million cubic feet. As the largest aerospace business in the U.S., Boeing employs nearly 80,000 people in the Puget Sound area alone. Begin a visit at the **Future of Flight Aviation Center,** located at the western edge of Paine Field 30 miles north of Seattle. Hourly tours of the assembly plant are available (reservations recommended). The factory visit begins with a video of how airplanes are built, then leads past assembly lines for the 747, 767 and 777—and soon the 787—in various stages of assembly, manufacture and flight testing. Children must be four feet tall to take factory tours. Closed Thanksgiving, Christ-

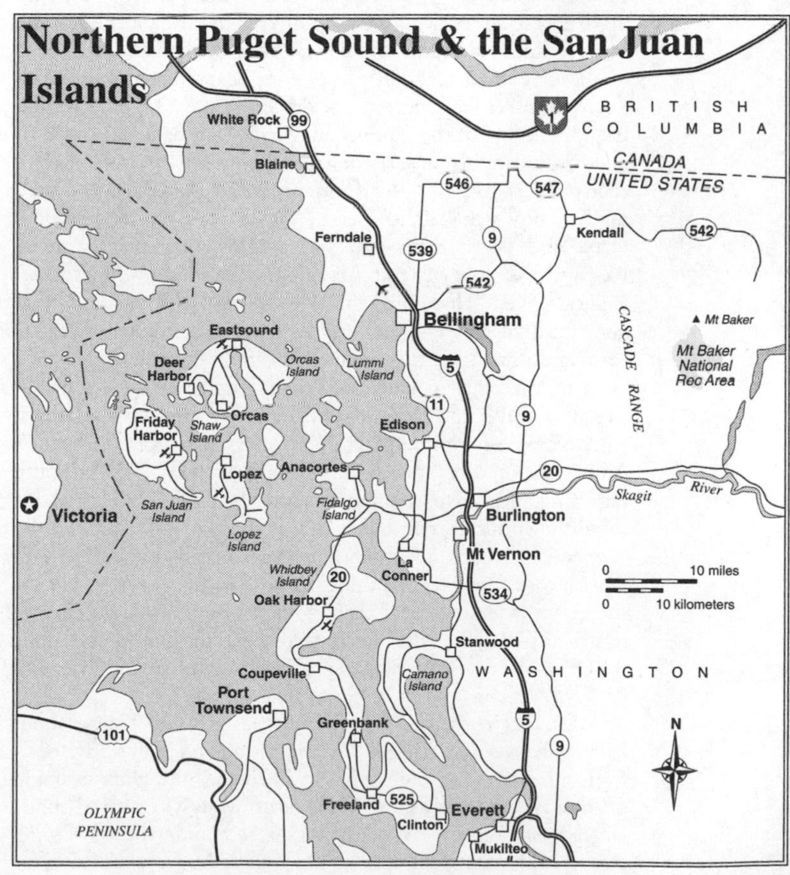

mas and New Year's Day. Admission. ~ 8415 Paine Field Boulevard, Mukilteo; 425-438-8100, 888-467-4777, fax 425-265-9808; 360-756-0086 (reservations), 800-464-1476; www.futureofflight.org.

HIDDEN ►

Visitors to **Biringer Farm** can not only pick fresh strawberries and raspberries (in summer) and pumpkins (in fall), they can also participate in fun farm harvest celebrations. Seasonal events include wandering a giant corn maze and visiting the "Not So Scary Boo Barn." Kids of all ages can ride the barrel-train and the whole family can take a tractor-drawn trolley to the fields. But the prime reason to visit remains the incomparable fresh berries. Watch carefully for direction signs off Route 529 north of downtown Everett. ~ 4625 40th Place, Everett; 425-259-0255; www.biringerfarm.com, e-mail farm-info@biringerfarm.com.

Just west of Route 5, in the delta of the Stillaguamish River, the small farming town of **Stanwood** hides its main street away, signing it 271st Street. Many tourists never discover its shops and pubs, ethnic restaurants and bakery specializing in "lefse," popular among the descendants of pioneer Scandinavian farmers.

A few miles west, across a bridge on Route 532, lies **Camano Island**, not one of the famous San Juans, but boasting five bed-and-breakfast inns (at last count) and blessed with one magnificent public park, 134-acre **Camano Island State Park**. Located midway down the island's west shore, the park offers splendid forest and beach trails and sweeping views across Saratoga Passage to Whidbey Island. Also on the island is a wonderful art gallery. Called **"History of the World—Part IV,"** the name suggests the owners' whimsical way with art. Jack Gunter is quickly earning a reputation as a painter and folk artist, but prefers to describe himself as a creator of "pseudo naive surrealistic narrative art." You'll find plenty to chuckle over here—wry paintings, entertaining sculpture, playful art glass and Karla Matzke's American pop art. Open Friday through Sunday. ~ 3311 South East Camano Drive, Camano Island; 360-387-5225; www.historyoftheworldfineart.com.

Someday, the Skagit Valley may become as famous as the well-known tourist attractions that surround it. But for now, out-of-state visitors tend to speed through this 25-mile-wide floodplain, missing its beauty as they hurry to or from the San Juan Islands, the Olympic Peninsula, Whidbey Island, North Cascades National Park, or Vancouver and Victoria, B.C.

Alas, they're missing something special. **Skagit Valley**, about halfway between Seattle and Vancouver (and an hour's drive or so from either city via Route 5) is very likely the most glorious union of countryside and seashore in the Northwest. It's centered on the largest, most pristine river delta on Puget Sound, whose sweeping estuary—an important stop on the Pacific Flyway—nurtures an extraordinary diversity of marine life and waterfowl. With topsoil up to several feet deep, the Skagit is the world's third-most fertile river delta, according to Skagitonians to Preserve Farmland. These farmlands, estuaries and tide flats attract several species of hawks, making the area one of the best places in all of North America to go "hawkwatching."

Nowadays, big-city folk from both sides of the border flock to the Skagit to explore the valley's country roads and small towns, especially historic La Conner (see "Walking Tour"). They come to pedal a bike or stroll a beguiling stretch of coast, to boat and fish for salmon in season. To watch in winter for the delta's

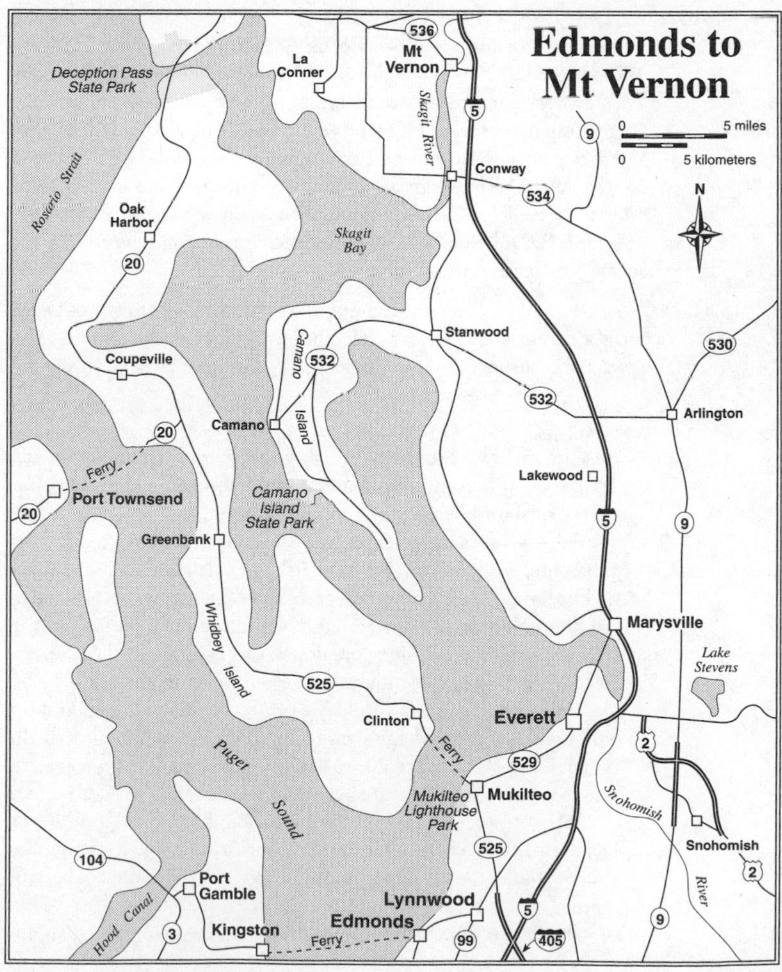

WALKING TOUR
La Conner

Built on pilings above the bank of Swinomish Channel, La Conner got its start in the 1880s as a market center for farmers in the Skagit Flats. Now a historic district, this small village of fewer than 800 people is easy to explore on foot and, with its many well-preserved homes and buildings, offers a glimpse of turn-of-the-20th-century life.

SKAGIT COUNTY HISTORICAL MUSEUM Park your car at the **La Conner Chamber of Commerce**. ~ 606 Morris Street; 360-466-4778, 888-642-9284, fax 360-466-0204; www.laconnerchamber.com. Walk a short distance up 4th Street to the top of the hill to visit the Skagit County Historical Museum, where you'll find a collection of farm and fishing equipment, vintage clothing, household furnishings, dolls and photographs. The museum also has a video theater and a section for temporary exhibits. Closed Monday. Admission. ~ 501 4th Street; 360-466-3365, fax 360-466-1611; www.skagitcounty.net/museum, e-mail museum@co.skagit.wa.us.

GACHES MANSION From the museum, head south along 4th Street, which turns a corner and becomes Calhoun Street. Follow Calhoun downhill toward the channel for two blocks to the Gaches Mansion. This grand

treasure of hawks and eagles, snow geese and trumpeter swans. To marvel at blooming tulips that paint the valley in vivid colors every April and herald the return of spring.

Other visitors from Seattle and Vancouver, seeking respite from urban life, come to unwind in the Skagit's delightful country inns and bed-and-breakfast homes. Here, you can sprawl before a roaring fire with a good book in hand. Or idle away a Sunday morning over a splendid country breakfast. Or just stare in silent reverie from a farmhouse veranda across open fields to the sea.

Today, the Skagit is gateway both to Whidbey Island and the San Juans (westward on Route 20 from Route 5), and to the North Cascades (Route 20, eastbound). The valley is a travelers' crossroads, with adventures enough for a month of sightseeing.

Mt. Vernon, situated on the broad banks of the Skagit River, has done little to capitalize on its superior riverside location. But it does claim the liveliest "main street" in the valley. The true main street is signed as 1st Street here; it is lined with a variety of vintage architecture in both brick and wood dating to the

Victorian home was built in 1891 by a local merchant who wanted the finest house in town. The mansion houses the **La Conner Quilt Museum**, the Pacific Northwest's only quilt museum. Closed Monday and Tuesday, and the first two weeks of January. Open weekends only in December. Admission. ~ 703 South 2nd Street; phone/fax 360-466-4288; www.laconnerquilts.com, e-mail lacquiltm@aol.com.

MAGNUS ANDERSON CABIN Stroll a block south of the Gaches Mansion to see the Magnus Anderson Cabin next to city hall. The oldest structure in Skagit County, the 1869 cabin was moved here from a solitary location on the north fork of the Skagit River to save it from decay. ~ 2nd and Douglas streets.

MUSEUM OF NORTHWEST ART Walk one more block west to 1st Street, then proceed north. This time-capsule waterfront street has been gentrified with boutiques, galleries and restaurants yet still retains a palpable air of history. Two longish blocks up the street you'll find the Museum of Northwest Art, which exhibits the works of regional artists, presenting a cohesive look at the distinctive school of visual arts that has developed in the Pacific Northwest—an often surrealistic blend of Northwest Coast Indian and Asian motifs. Admission. ~ 121 South 1st Street; 360-466-4446, fax 360-466-7431; www.museumofnwart.org. Walking three blocks up Washington Street and five blocks south on 3rd Street will bring you back to the chamber of commerce and your car.

turn of the century. Preservation or recycling of old buildings is in full swing.

Don't miss **Calico Cupboard Restaurant** (360-466-4451). Nearby is the valley's land trust, **Skagitonians to Preserve Farmland** (360-336-3974), where you can learn how concerned citizens are working to save farmlands and the valley's agricultural heritage. ~ 414-A Snoqualmie Street, Mt. Vernon.

Across railroad tracks just to the west is the old **Condensary Building**, now remodeled into offices.

South of Division Street, but still on 1st Street, is the Uptowne Centre. The **Deli Next Door** (360-336-5087) serves appetizing organic vegetarian fare.

Stroll south on 1st and you'll find more old buildings housing vintage books and records, handcrafts from around the valley, jewelry, art and outdoor gear, and the 1926 **Lincoln Theatre** (360-336-2858; www.lincolntheatre.org), now an art-film house. Several more eateries and coffee bars also compete for your patronage.

Each spring, the fields of the Skagit Valley are alive with color as the tulips and daffodils begin to appear. **The Skagit Valley Tulip Festival Office** provides a guide to the festival that runs the entire month of April; the guide lists events and includes a tour map of the fields, children's activities and display gardens. ~ 100 East Montgomery Street, Suite 250, Mt. Vernon; 360-428-5959, fax 360-428-6753; www.tulipfestival.org, e-mail info@tulipfestival.org.

There are interesting gardens to view year-round. The prettiest is **RoozenGaarde** with display gardens and a great little gift shop. ~ 15867 Beaver Marsh Road, Mt. Vernon; 360-424-8531, 866-488-5477, fax 360-424-4920; www.tulips.com, e-mail info@tulips.com.

West of Mount Vernon, across the channel from the Swinomish Indian Reservation, **La Conner** (see "Walking Tour" on pages 216–17) is in the running for the title of quaintest little seaside town in the Puget Sound area.

Burlington, the next city north of Mt. Vernon, is famous for a different sort of shopping. Bargain-hunters from Seattle and Vancouver come to seek out the discount designer merchandise at Pacific Edge Outlet Center. Neighboring Cascade Mall offers a more classic array of mall shops.

For the perfect counterpoint to the sort of creeping suburbanism encountered in Burlington, drop in on **Bay View, Edison** and the town of **Bow**. These three country hamlets (located in the northern valley across Route 20) are treasures of the old way of life and are rarely discovered by the average tourist. Here, you'll see century-old farmhouses rising behind white picket fences, boatworks (some still active) that once turned out fishing boats, country taverns alive with the rustic merriment of farmers, loggers, truck drivers and dairymen. Here, too, are a smattering of art galleries, antique shops, country cafés and upscale eateries.

Located just north of Bay View, **Padilla Bay National Estuarine Research Reserve** is the place to find bald eagles, great blue

SCENIC SKAGIT VALLEY

The Skagit Valley has become a year-round retreat for city visitors, as nourishing to the soul in winter as it is inspiring to the adventurous spirit in summer. Indeed, artists and writers have been gathering in the Skagit for decades, including members of the famed "Northwest School" beginning in the 1930s—Mark Tobey, Morris Graves, Kenneth Callahan, Clayton James, Guy Anderson and many others. They were drawn by the Skagit's enchanting blend of meandering river levees and farm fields, bayous and bays, nearby islands and distant misty mountains, along with the extraordinary quality of the valley's ever-changing light.

herons and dozens of other species of waterfowl and raptors. The interpretive center offers exhibits on the region's natural and maritime history. The center is closed Monday and Tuesday. ~ 10441 Bay View–Edison Road, Mt. Vernon; 360-428-1558, fax 360-428-1491; www.padillabay.gov, e-mail alex@padillabay.gov.

For a view-rich and slow-paced alternate to Route 5 that will take you north to Bellingham, opt for **Chuckanut Drive** (Route 11), a signed exit from the freeway just north of Burlington. The "drive" takes you north through gorgeous farmlands, in and out of the village of Bow in a twinkling, and then along the rocky and precipitous shoulder of the Chuckanut Mountains overlooking the San Juan Islands (you can stop and savor the scene from numerous pullouts). The drive continues all the way to the funky 1880s brick district of **Fairhaven.** This slightly counterculture community is a treasure of refurbished brick Victorians housing shops, galleries, artists' studios and bohemian eateries. Most are concentrated around 11th Street and Harris Avenue.

But Fairhaven also boasts the **Bellingham Cruise Terminal**, southern terminus for ferries of the Alaska Marine Highway (foot of Harris Avenue). The terminal presents dynamite views over the harbor, a deli and a variety of shops. Here, too, the sightseeing vessel *Victoria Star* 2 (360-738-8099, 800-443-4552; www.whales.com) is moored for daily departures in summer through the San Juan Islands to Victoria, B.C. After hours of sightseeing in Victoria, enjoy a dinner of fresh salmon and baked chicken served on the return trip to the San Juans.

Early growth in **Bellingham** centered around the industries of mining and logging. To this day, the city retains an industrial nature with thriving ports that are home to a large fishing fleet and, more recently, the Alaska Marine Highway Ferry System terminal, tempered by a firm agricultural base. Perhaps it is because of this outward appearance that visitors are often amazed at the array of cultural arts and international dining experiences to be enjoyed here.

Bellingham has two noteworthy museums. The first is the **Whatcom Children's Museum**, which has several hands-on exhibitions to delight the kids (ages 2–10). Closed Monday. Admission. ~ 227 Prospect Street, Bellingham; 360-733-8769, fax 360-738-7409; www.whatcommuseum.org, e-mail museum info@cob.org.

Just down the street, the red-brick Victorian architecture of the **Whatcom Museum** is as interesting as the fine collections of contemporary American art, Northwest art and regional history featured inside. It's also a good point to start a walking tour of the many outdoor sculptures scattered around downtown. Closed

Monday. Admission for special shows. ~ 121 Prospect Street, Bellingham; 360-676-6981, fax 360-738-7409; www.whatcommuseum.org, e-mail museuminfo@cob.org.

A Sculpture Walk route guide is available at the museum or from **Bellingham/Whatcom County Tourism.** ~ 904 Potter Street, Bellingham; 360-671-3990, 800-487-2032, fax 360-647-7873; www.bellingham.org, e-mail tourism@bellingham.org.

At the **Maritime Heritage Park** you can observe outdoor hatchery tanks, watch fish make their way up the ladder (recommended in October and November), learn about the life cycle of salmon, or just toss a line (with the proper license and only in October) into the abutting creek for steelhead or chinook salmon. ~ 1600 C Street, Bellingham; 360-676-6985.

HIDDEN ►

No visit to Bellingham is complete without a trip to the **Big Rock Garden**, a serene Japanese garden with plantings, a patio and deck areas overlooking Lake Whatcom where visitors can sit and take it all in. ~ 2900 Sylvan Street, Bellingham; 360-676-6985, fax 360-647-6367; www.cob.org.

The **T.G. Richards & Co. building** is the oldest brick building still standing in the state, dating from 1858. Its bricks came around Cape Horn from Philadelphia. ~ 1308 E Street, Bellingham.

Don't miss the opportunity to stroll through the grounds of **Western Washington University** on the Western Sculpture Tour to enjoy the many fountains, sculptures and rich variety of architecture on this green campus. Brochures are available at the visitors information center on campus or at the Western Gallery. ~ McDonald Parkway, Bellingham; 360-650-3900; westerngallery.wwu.edu/sculpture.

Immediately adjacent to the campus is **Sehome Hill Arboretum,** 180 acres laced with six miles of hiking trails and fern-lined footpaths under a cool green canopy of moss covered trees; only the hum of traffic and the view from the observation tower remind you that you are in the city rather than some forest primeval. ~ 25th Street at Bill McDonald Parkway, Bellingham; 360-676-6985, fax 360-647-6367.

The **Nooksack River Valley** located east of Bellingham is a treasure of rolling green dairy pastures, berry fields, Christmas tree farms and charming small towns, like **Lynden.** The Darigold plant here produces some 340,000 pounds of non-fat dry milk a day and is the largest powdered milk factory in the U.S. Settled by Dutch dairymen more than a century ago, Lynden and its main street (Front Street) offer a colorful collection of storefronts looking as if they were plucked right out of Amsterdam, including a windmill hotel. A beguiling array of import shops proffers wooden shoes, Delft tiles, kitchenware and other goods from Holland. Several eateries also specialize in Dutch fare. Festivals such as Sinterklaas (Santa Claus) in December and Holland Days in May also reflect the rich Dutch heritage.

The **Lynden Pioneer Museum** tells the story of early Dutch and Northern European settlers. The five galleries that comprise the museum are filled with life-size replicas of street scenes of Lynden from days gone by. Don't miss the Fred K. Polinder buggy collection. Admission. ~ 217 Front Street, Lynden; 360-354-3675; www.lyndenpioneermuseum.com, e-mail info@lyndenpioneermuseum.com.

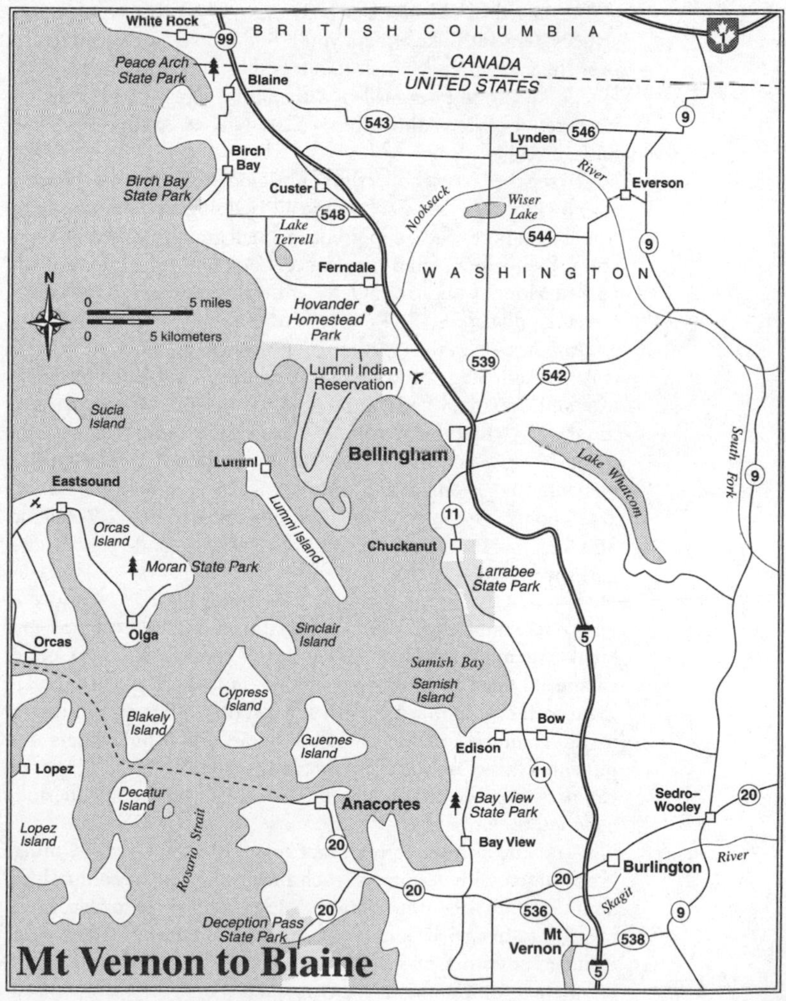

Mt Vernon to Blaine

Just outside of town begin several superb bike routes that follow winding and picturesque country roads, one of which brings you to a first-rate winery, **Mt. Baker Vineyards,** famous for its excellent German-style white wines. ~ 4298 Mt. Baker Highway, Everson; 360-592-2300, fax 360-592-2526.

When in Lynden, take a tour of Holmquist Hazelnut Orchards and stay for a sampling of the rich-tasting nuts. Call ahead. ~ 800-720-0895.

North of Bellingham in Ferndale, **Hovander Homestead Park** features a handsome Victorian residence and a cheery red farmhouse alive with cows, goats and even peacocks (closed October to April). Laced by the Nooksack River, the 720-acre park also includes **Tennant Lake,** where you'll find a boardwalk leading out over the swamp and marsh habitats that border the edge of the lake, and a fragrance garden with braille signs. There's also an interpretive center. Admission. ~ 5299 Nielsen Avenue, Ferndale; 360-384-3444.

To see the largest collection of original log homes in the state, stop by **Pioneer Park.** Each of the 12 buildings is a minimuseum. You'll see a post office, a stagecoach inn, a granary, a veteran's museum, a schoolhouse and a residence. Look for the little log church. Closed Monday and from October through April. ~ 2004 Cherry Street, Ferndale; 360-384-6461.

Another site in the Northern Puget Sound area worth taking in is **Peace Arch State Park.** The large white arch, flanked by American and Canadian flags, is surrounded by bountiful formal gardens with sculptures throughout and symbolizes the ongoing friendship between the two neighboring countries. The park is meticulously groomed, and spills across the international boundary. ~ Follow the signs to the park off Route 5, Exit 276, Blaine; 360-332-8221; www.peacearchpark.org, e-mail peacearch@parks.wa.gov.

LODGING

La Conner and the Skagit Valley now boast several bed and breakfasts and first-class inns. One of them is the **La Conner Channel Lodge,** a handsome luxury inn, the only hostelry in town on the Swinomish Channel. Most of its 40 rooms looks out to the channel and the ceaseless parade of fishing boats and pleasure craft. Continental breakfast. ~ 205 North 1st Street, La Conner; 360-466-1500, fax 360-466-1525; www.laconnerlodging.com. ULTRA-DELUXE.

A private in-town retreat, **La Conner Maison Garden Cottage** is decorated with country French furnishings discovered in local antique shops. Resting behind a 19th-century Victorian home mere steps from La Conner's shops and restaurants, the cottage includes a two-person jacuzzi tub and a kitchen stocked with coffee and tea. Complimentary breakfast is served on the first morning of your stay. ~ 205 East Morris Street, La Conner; 360-391-

0506, 866-552-5526; www.laconnermaison.com, e-mail info@laconnermaison.com. DELUXE.

Tucked amid fir trees and overlooking Skagit Bay, the **Skagit Bay Hideaway Bed and Breakfast** offers two guest suites located in a separate guesthouse. Both feature fireplaces, private rooftop decks with hot tubs and magnificent views of Puget Sound. A gourmet breakfast is included in the price of your stay. It's an ideal place in which to relax and pamper yourself. Minimum two-night stay is required during the Tulip Festival (the month of April), and from June through September. ~ 17430 Goldenview Avenue, La Conner; 360-466-2262, 888-466-2262; www.skagitbay.com, e-mail hideaway@skagitbay.com. ULTRA-DELUXE. ◄ HIDDEN

The **Wild Iris** is on the edge of town overlooking farm fields and mountains. Each of its 18 rooms is decorated individually in bold and fearless strokes. Many rooms feature a jacuzzi spa, a fireplace and a deck. Breakfast fare is generous and varied, a hallmark of this inn's overall attention to quality. ~ 121 Maple Avenue, La Conner; 360-466-1400, 800-477-1400, fax 360-466-1222; www.wildiris.com, e-mail info@wildiris.com. DELUXE TO ULTRA-DELUXE.

Next door to the Wild Iris, **The Heron & Watergrass Day Spa** offers the same views in smaller, cozier style, with 12 rooms. Highlights here include a jacuzzi in the garden, a variety of spa treatments (fee), a wine bar and a complimentary full breakfast. ~ 117 Maple Avenue, La Conner; 360-466-4626, 877-883-8899, fax 419-844-2190; www.theheron.com, e-mail info@theheron.com. MODERATE TO DELUXE.

The Hotel Planter, originally built in 1907, is right in the thick of things when it comes to shopping and dining in downtown La Conner. The 12 rooms have skylights, light paint and carpeting, floral chintz comforters and pine furnishings. There's also a jacuzzi under the gazebo on the garden terrace out back. ~ 715 1st Street, La Conner; 360-466-4710, 800-488-5409, fax 360-466-1320; www.hotelplanter.com, e-mail hotelplanter@aol.com. MODERATE TO DELUXE.

Opened in 1977, **La Conner Country Inn** was the first inn in these parts. It's still a favorite with long-time visitors, partly because several of its 28 rooms are so comfortable. It's also close to shops and restaurants. Continental breakfast. ~ 107 South 2nd Street, La Conner; 360-466-3101, fax 360-466-0199; www.laconnerlodging.com. MODERATE TO DELUXE.

In a home loaded with a lifetime's collection of art, **Art's Place Bed & Breakfast** offers a one-room guesthouse with balcony bedroom, jacuzzi bath. ~ 511 Talbot Street, La Conner; 360-466-3033. MODERATE.

About half a mile east of historic La Conner, the **Queen of the Valley Inn** is surrounded by farm fields. This classic Craftsman built in 1908 offers four guest rooms, two suites and oodles of luxury with a British colonial flair. Full breakfast. ~ 12757 Chilberg Road, La Conner; 360-466-4578, 888-999-1404; www.queenofthevalleyinn.com, e-mail innkeeper@queenofthe valleyinn.com. DELUXE.

White Swan Guest House offers accommodations in a country setting. The rooms are country casual and there's a superb collection of samplers spread across the house. The English country garden features a big orchard where you're welcome to pick your own apples and plums as well as pears. A separate cottage offers kitchen facilities. Vegetarian country continental breakfast and homemade chocolate chip cookies are included. ~ 15872 Moore Road, Mt. Vernon; 360-445-6805; www.thewhiteswan.com. MODERATE TO DELUXE.

Boeing means big. The largest aerospace, electronic and computer business in the U.S. employs over 52,000 people in the Puget Sound area alone.

South Fork Marina is one of those true hideaways (dare we say, "unique") that travelers yearn to discover. The "moorage" is comprised of a houseboat floating in the usually placid waters of the South Fork of the Skagit River adjacent to a wildlife reserve. Bring your canoe, kayak or raft, and the owner will shuttle you up to Burlington for a lazy float back to the moorage. Or paddle across the river to an island full of wildlife. Or just sprawl like Huck Finn on the docks for a picnic as you watch the peaceful river unspool before you. No river shack this—the Tea House is decorated in Japanese style. It features a fully equipped kitchen and is outfitted as a housekeeping cabin accommodating up to three people. And yet the price is only moderate! Small pets are allowed for a fee. Continental breakfast. Closed Tuesday through Thursday. ~ 21357 Mann Road, Mt. Vernon; 360-445-4803; e-mail ree cered@earthlink.net. MODERATE.

Built in 1914, the **Benson Farmstead Bed and Breakfast** is a four-room charmer in the heart of "the Skagit Valley" farms. Some guests come for the big farm breakfasts and cozy rooms full of country antiques, each with a private bath and queen bed. Others come for the chance to stay on a working crop farm that's been in operation for more than eight decades. Still others stay for the proximity to some of the state's best country bicycling. Or perhaps they seek the English garden and the garden of flowers filled with antique machinery. There is also the barn cottage, which can sleep up to ten people. Closed in the winter except to groups. ~ 10113 Avon Allen Road, Bow; 360-757-0578, 800-441-9814; www.bbhost.com/bensonbnb. MODERATE.

Anderson Creek Lodge, a soaring Northwest-style, glass-and-wood inn on 35 wooded acres near Bellingham, offers the privacy of a hotel with the intimacy of a bed and breakfast. Each of the five lodge rooms has a king or queen-sized bed, a tiled shower, wi-fi access, hair dryers and large view windows. The sitting area in the great room has comfy couches around a massive stone fireplace. Amenities also include a hot tub and full breakfast. Trails follow Anderson Creek and lead to the inn's own llama herd. ~ 5602 Mission Road, Bellingham; 360- 966-0598; www.andersoncreek.com, e-mail andersoncreek@msn.com. MODERATE TO DELUXE.

Nestled in Bellingham Cove, the luxurious, European-style **Hotel Bellwether** offers 50 standard rooms and 15 suites with views of the San Juan Islands. Italian-style furniture and down comforters are a cozy complement to the bathroom's chic granite and marble countertops and two-person jacuzzi. If you're looking for an impressive retreat, reserve the three-story lighthouse condo with a 360-degree observation deck. A private dock, bistro and piano bar round out the amenities. ~ 1 Bellwether Way, Bellingham; 360-392-3100, 877-411-1200, fax 360-392-3101; www.hotelbellwether.com, e-mail reservations@bellwether.com. ULTRA-DELUXE.

Dutch Village Inn Hotel is a local landmark. Besides several conventional motel-style rooms, it also has two rooms in the colorful windmill tower (ask for the "windmill rooms"). All rooms boast Dutch decor and artifacts, and some present views across the Nooksack River Valley. Breakfast is included in the rates. ~ 655 Front Street, Lynden; 360-354-4440, fax 360-354-3390. MODERATE.

About six miles south of Blaine is the small village of Birch Bay, where you'll find the largest tidal flats in Washington. Here, the two restored 1930s **Cottages by the Beach** are great for an old-fashioned self-catering holiday. Lora's Cottage has two bedrooms with a bathroom and soaking tub. Seashell Cottage has three bedrooms, one-and-three-quarter baths with a vintage tub. It has a large, open-plan kitchen/dining room and a brick fireplace. Both cottages have a washer and a dryer, cooking utensils, bedding, DVD/CD players, yards and barbecues. Two-night minimum. Call ahead for directions. ~ 425-339-8081; www.ilovecottages.com, e-mail www.ilovecottages.com. ULTRA-DELUXE.

Housed in the old Blaine Air Force Base a few miles from the Canadian border and Birch Bay State Park, the **Birch Bay Hostel & Guesthouse** offers family- and dormitory-style rooms with three or four beds. The common room is equipped with a television and a DVD/VCR player. From November to April the hostel is open for groups only. ~ 7467 Gemini Street, Blaine; 360-371-2180; www.birchbayhostel.org. BUDGET.

There is something for everyone at the sumptuous **Semiahmoo Resort-Golf-Spa**, located on the tip of the sandy spit stretched between Semiahmoo Bay and Drayton Harbor. History buffs will enjoy browsing through the resort's collection of early photography, romantics will delight in a walk on the beach or a leisurely sunset meal in one of the restaurants or lounges, and sports fanatics will flip over the array of activities, including tennis, golf at two of the top-rated courses, and biking and hiking throughout an 1100-acre wildlife preserve. Treat yourself to a massage at the full-service European spa. The guest rooms are spacious and nicely appointed; some rooms have decks or patios, and others have woodburning fireplaces. ~ 9565 Semiahmoo Parkway, Blaine; 360-318-2000, 800-770-7992, fax 360-318-2087; www.semiahmoo.com, e-mail info@semiahmoo.com. ULTRA-DELUXE.

The **Willows Inn** was built in 1910 as a "farm resort." Today, it offers a cottage amid flower gardens, a two-bedroom guesthouse and five rooms in the main house. The cottage has a private deck with a fantastic view, and the guesthouse offers a fireplace and walk-in steam shower. Both have full kitchens. Views here are outstanding—west and northwest across other San Juan Islands to Vancouver, British Columbia. Full breakfast is included in the rate; you'll also find a coffeehouse here (it turns into a pub at night) and a restaurant serving lunch and dinner Wednesday through Sunday. ~ 2579 West Shore Drive, Lummi Island; 360-758-2620; www.willows-inn.com, e-mail innkeeper@willows-inn.com. DELUXE TO ULTRA-DELUXE.

DINING

Anthony's Home Port is the spot for seafood when it comes to waterfront dining in Everett. Prime picks on the seasonal menu include Whidbey Island mussels, ginger-sesame steak, Dungeness crab cakes, roasted garlic prawns sprinkled with gremolatta and a variety of fresh oysters. Their four-course Sunset Dinner (served Monday through Friday from 4:30 to 6 p.m.) is a bargain and includes everything from appetizer to dessert. You can dine alfresco on the deck or pick a spot in the considerably less breezy dining room or lounge. ~ 1726 West Marine View Drive, Everett; 425-252-3333, fax 425-252-7847. MODERATE TO ULTRA-DELUXE.

Best bet for breakfast or lunch in La Conner is the **Calico Cupboard** at the south end of the main drag, where they serve hearty and wholesome baked goods, soups, salads, sandwiches and vegetarian fare as good for the heart as for the taste buds. Don't be surprised if there is a line to get into this modest café. No dinner. ~ 720 South 1st Street, La Conner; 360-466-4451, fax 360-466-2181; www.calicocupboardcafe.com. BUDGET TO MODERATE.

Whisker's Café is a lunch house featuring hearty sandwiches, soups and chowders, salads, fish and chips, and burgers. Try one of the flavored floats from its old-fashioned soda fountain. ~128 South 1st Street, La Conner; 360-466-1008; www.ksmenterprises.com. BUDGET TO MODERATE.

Palmer's Restaurant on the Waterfront may just be the best restaurant in town. All dishes on the wide-ranging French Continental menu (seafood, pasta, chicken, beef) are served with distinctive Northwest and European flair. All ingredients are fresh and, when possible, local. ~ 512 South 1st Street, La Conner; 360-466-3147, fax 360-466-3270; www.nwcuisine.com, e-mail chef@nwcuisine.com. MODERATE TO ULTRA-DELUXE.

Fish, free-range meat and organically grown Skagit Valley produce shine in the family-run **Nell Thorn Restaurant,** adjoining La Conner Inn. To start, try herb-dusted oysters, followed by the Beach Bowl, a fresh-catch melange of fin fish and shellfish in a tomato-herb broth. Vegetarians will find homemade soups and pastas, fresh salads and the Buddha Bowl, a black olive-chevre risotto with grilled zucchini. Closed Monday; dinner only from Tuesday to Thursday. Soups, salads, ploughman's lunches and sandwiches are served in the cozy pub downstairs until 11 p.m. on weekends. ~ 214 Washington Street, La Conner; 360-466-4261; www.nellthorn.com, e-mail info@nellthorn.com. MODERATE TO DELUXE.

The **Farmhouse Restaurant**, a large eatery with country decor dominated by heavy oak tables and chairs, believes in serving solid, old-country-style portions of meat and potato classics—pot roast, turkey potpie, New York steak and baked potatoes—along with a hearty selection of daily baked goods like their famous pies thrown in for good measure. The lunch buffet and kids' menu are great bargains. Breakfast, lunch and dinner. ~ 13724 La Conner–Whitney Road, outside of Mt. Vernon; 360-466-4411, fax 360-466-4413; www.thefarmhouserestaurant.net. MODERATE.

The drive to **Chuckanut Manor Bed & Breakfast** near Bow is one of the most scenic in Washington. Chuckanut Drive winds along the coast between Bellingham and Mt. Vernon, overlook-

AUTHOR FAVORITE

Speak E-Z's was born when barbecue master Dennis Rayborn was told "You should start your own restaurant" one too many times. Good thing, too—his Memphis-style joint is pure heaven for meatlovers. Drawing from old family recipes, Rayborn dishes out Southern soul food classics such as pulled pork and beef brisket sandwiches, ribs and chicken; he smokes his meat for so long that it melts the moment it touches your tongue. Platters come with the requisite sides of slaw, baked beans, collard greens and hush puppies. Other offerings include grilled prawns, seafood gumbo and (gasp!) a vegan garden burger. Closed Sunday. ~ 2400 Meridian Street, Bellingham; 360-714-0606, fax 360-714-0607; www.speakezs.com, e-mail rosie@speakezs.com. BUDGET TO MODERATE.

ing Samish Bay. Not surprisingly, the restaurant's fare centers on expertly prepared seafood—oysters, salmon and halibut. Closed Monday in winter and spring. ~ 3056 Chuckanut Drive, Bow; 360-766-6191, fax 360-766-8515; www.chuckanutmanor.com. DELUXE TO ULTRA-DELUXE.

The **Archer Ale House**, tucked in the basement of one of Fairhaven's historic Victorians, is a smoke-free English-style pub that's considered one of the country's best Belgian beer bars by *All About Beer* magazine. The main fare is upscale pub grub (check out the pizza) and an array of microbrewery and imported beers. ~ 1212 10th Street, Bellingham; 360-647-7002. BUDGET.

There are cows everywhere—from the pictures on the walls to the salt and pepper shakers—at the **Colophon Cafe**, which shares a historic brick building with Village Books. Don't look for beef on the menu, though. Instead, you'll find café fare by a master chef. Soups are the specialty; try the African peanut soup. There are also appetizer platters, salads, big sandwiches, quiche and such desserts as chocolate chunk cake. ~ 1208 11th Street, Bellingham; 360-647-0092, fax 360-676-1742. BUDGET.

Locals rave about the excellent dining at the light-filled **Pacific Cafe** in Bellingham, next to the Mt. Baker Theater. This attractive bistro has been serving up Asian- and European-inspired Northwest dishes since 1985, and has fans from as far away as Seattle. Among the most popular appetizers are seasonal fried oysters and Dungeness crab cakes with ginger apricot sauce, and fried calamari with garlic aioli sauce. The wild-caught salmon here is justly famous, even in salmon-savvy Washington, as are the Gulf prawns in lemon passionfruit sauce. No dinner Sunday or Monday. ~ 100 North Commercial Street, Bellingham; 360-647-0800; www.thepacificcafe.com, e-mail info@thepacificcafe.com. DELUXE.

In addition to coffees and teas, **Harris Avenue Cafe**, serves up fresh daily soups, salads, sandwiches and pastries to an eclectic crowd of regulars. It's almost too bohemian, but the cocoa mocha makes it worth the trip. Breakfast and lunch only. ~ 1101 Harris Avenue, Bellingham; 360-738-0802. BUDGET.

Giuseppe's Italian Restaurant dishes out good, albeit typical, Italian fare. The menu relies heavily on fresh seafood (many of its requisite pasta dishes feature shellfish) but it also offers a wide variety of chicken, veal, lamb and steak entrées served in classic Italian sauces such as marsala and lemon caper. Of course, you'll also find *pollo alla parmigiana*, sure to please the little ones. A large variety of desserts are available. No lunch on the weekends. ~ 1414 Cornwall Avenue, Bellingham; 360-714-8412; www.giuseppesitalian.com, e-mail info@giuseppesitalian.com. MODERATE TO DELUXE.

At the **Boundary Bay Brewery**, bare woodplank floors and simple wooden tables and chairs create an unpretentious setting for "Northwest pub fusion food." What's that, you ask? In this case, it means eclectic offerings such as olive tapenade and yam ale *chiladas*. Wash it all down with a sampler of small glasses of all seven beers and ales they make in plain sight on the premises. Watch a movie in the beer garden while enjoying your meal. ~ 1107 Railroad Avenue, Bellingham; 360-647-5593, fax 360-671-5897; www.bbaybrewery.com, e-mail info@bbaybrewery.com. MODERATE.

The tables at **Café Toulouse** are always full, a testament to the quality breakfast, lunch and dessert selections served here. Favorites include fresh fruit pancakes, curried chicken salad, roast pork with mint jelly or smoked turkey with cranberry-apple cream-cheese sandwiches. You will also find pizzas and calzones from their wood-fire stove, and many selections from the fresh daily dessert board accompanied by piping espresso or latte to finish the meal. ~ 114 West Magnolia Street, Crown Plaza Building, #102, Bellingham; 360-733-8996. BUDGET.

Dutch Mother's Restaurant is *the* place in Lynden for traditional (that's to say, hearty) Dutch cuisine such as pot roast, meatloaf, beef cutlet, sausage and pirogies. Waitresses sport Dutch dress and often can be overheard speaking Dutch with locals. Closed Sunday. ~ 405 Front Street, Lynden; 360-354-2174, fax 360-354-8440. MODERATE.

For Mexican dining, try **Chihuahua**. Decorated with Mexican murals, paintings and parrot sculptures, the dining room offers booth and table seating. There's also dining in an enclosed patio. Popular specialties are fajitas, *carne asada* and a wide variety of combination plates. ~ 5694 3rd Avenue, Ferndale; 360-384-5820, fax 360-384-0644. BUDGET TO MODERATE.

Just north of the ferry dock and across the street from The Beach Store Café is the only public access beach on Lummi Island.

For romantic waterfront dining, it's hard to beat the Semiahmoo Resort's elegant dining room, **Stars**. Soft piano music fills the room as diners feast on grilled king salmon, rainbow trout, seared sea scallops, roasted longline cod and other rich entrées. For lighter fare, try the livelier, moderately-priced **Packers Lounge** just down the corridor for French onion soup, a salmon sandwich, crab caesar salad or homestyle burgers. No lunch at Stars; closed Sunday and Monday in off-season. ~ 9565 Semiahmoo Parkway, Blaine; 360-318-2000, 800-770-7992, fax 360-318-2087; www.semiahmoo.com, e-mail f&b@semiahmoo.com. DELUXE TO ULTRA-DELUXE.

Near the ferry landing and offering gorgeous water views, **The Beach Store Café** is the only place on Lummi Island where visitors can find deli quality picnic supplies and lunches to go. But it's also a terrific little restaurant where everything is homemade, where herbs, lettuce and other produce is grown in its own garden or elsewhere on the island. Seafood, a specialty, is also local—crab, salmon, halibut. The café serves lunch and dinner, along with weekend breakfast during the busy tourist season. Closed Monday and Tuesday in winter. ~ 2200 South Nugent Road, Lummi Island; 360-758-2233, fax 360-758-2266. BUDGET TO MODERATE.

SHOPPING

Antique hounds will want to make the quick 15-minute trip east of Everett to Snohomish, home to **Star Center Antique Mall**, a five-level mall with over 200 dealers and dozens of other antique shops to browse through. ~ 829 2nd Street, Snohomish; 360-568-2131; www.myantiquemall.com, e-mail starmall@myantiquemall.com.

In Everett, the **Everett Public Market** is the prime browsing spot for antiques as well as Northwest arts and crafts. The market also houses a natural foods co-op that offers organically grown fruits and vegetables. ~ 2804 Grand Avenue, Everett; 425-304-1000.

Shopping is a major drawing card of little La Conner, with most of the boutiques and galleries concentrated along 1st and Morris streets. Focus on **Earthenworks** for fine art. ~ 713 1st Street, La Conner; 360-466-4422; www.earthenworksgallery.com. **The Scott Collection** also has a selection of fine art. ~ Pier 7 Building on 1st Street, La Conner; 360-466-3691; www.scottcollection.com. Stop by **Bunnies by the Bay** for collectibles and unique gifts. ~ 623-A Morris Street, La Conner; 360-293-8037; www.bunniesbythebay.com.

If it's raining, pull up a chair by the fire, order an espresso or cup of tea, and read to your heart's content at **The Next Chapter Bookstore & Coffeehouse**. Housed in the former "Nevada Bar," built in 1890, this small, independent bookstore has a great selection of titles. ~ 721 South First Street, La Conner; 360-466-2665; www.nextchapter.com.

The historic **Tillinghast Flowers and Gifts** has been in business for over 100 years. You'll find a flower shop, foods of the Northwest and gift baskets. ~ 623 Morris Street, La Conner; 360-466-3329. At **Go Outside**, the owners' remarkable taste is reflected in an appealing collection of garden tools, clothing and art selected with great care. ~ 111 Morris Street, La Conner; 360-466-4836.

Don't miss **Cascade Candy**—it produces first-class truffles and other chocolate concoctions at about half the price of similar candy-makers in Seattle or Vancouver, B.C. ~ 605 South 1st Street, La Conner; 360-466-2971.

Rosabella's Garden Bakery is the perfect place to pick up unique vintage gifts as well as supplies for a picnic. The shop, located on a working farm and 50 acres of fruit orchards, sells apples, baked goods, wine and lunches. Their five-pound apple pies and homemade hard cider are not to be missed. Closed in winter. ~ 8933 Farm to Market Road, Bow; 360-766-6360, fax 360-766-6365; e-mail rmerritt@wavecable.com.

The greatest concentration of wintering bald eagles can be found at the Skagit River Bald Eagle Natural Area, 7800 acres located between Marblemount and Rockport.

The best shops and galleries in Bellingham are generally located in the Fairhaven District.

Artwood is a co-op gallery of fine woodworking by Northwest artists. ~ 1000 Harris Avenue, Bellingham; 360-647-1628; www.artwoodgallery.com. Try **Inside Passage** for gifts made in Pacific Northwest. ~ 355 Harris Street, inside the Bellingham cruise terminal, Bellingham; 360-734-1790.

Dutch Village Mall is a collection of 12 shops specializing in imported Dutch lace, foodstuffs, wooden shoes and the like. The "mall" is built around a 150-foot-long canal to re-create a typical Dutch street scene. ~ 655 Front Street, Lynden; 360-354-4440.

NIGHTLIFE

Everett's **Club Broadway Big Apple** has both a large sports bar and a danceclub. Cover. ~ 1611 Everett Avenue, Everett; 425-259-3551; www.clubbroadway.com. Things are jumping at **Anthony's Home Port**, with great happy-hour prices and a nice sheltered deck overlooking the marina. Outdoor seating is only available during the warm months. ~ 1726 West Marine View Drive, Everett; 425-252-3333; www.anthonys.com.

The **La Conner Pub and Eatery**, housed in a waterfront structure that was at one time Brewster's Cigar Store, is the primary watering hole in La Conner and does a booming business through the wee hours of the morning. There are always at least six microbrews on tap. ~ 702 1st Street, La Conner; 360-466-9932.

There are a half-dozen other country taverns scattered across the Skagit Valley, well known to locals but nearly unknown to tourists, which also serve up terrific burgers, microbrewery ales and bitters and weekend jazz and dancing. The **Conway Pub and Eatery** is best for burgers. ~ 18611 Main Street, Conway; 360-445-4733. The **Old Edison Inn** is also very popular. ~ 5829 Cains Court, Bow; 360-766-6266.

HIDDEN

You'll find great happy-hour specials and the best sunset views in the little bar of **The Black Cat.** ~ 1200 Harris Avenue, Sycamore Square, Suite 310, Fairhaven; 360-733-6136.

BEACHES & PARKS

MUKILTEO LIGHTHOUSE PARK A swath of beach adjacent to the Whidbey Island–Mukilteo Ferry facilities on Puget Sound, Mukilteo Lighthouse Park is a day-use-only facility known primarily as a prime salmon-fishing spot with seasonal public boat launch (fee). Noble little Elliott Point Lighthouse, also known as Mukilteo Lighthouse, on the tip will keep shutterbugs happy; it's also a fine spot for beachcombing or picnicking while waiting for the ferry to Whidbey Island. There are restrooms, picnic grounds and seasonal floats. Boat launch parking fee. ~ Take the Mukilteo exit off Route 5 and follow the signs to the ferry; 425-355-4141, fax 425-347-4544.

CAMANO ISLAND STATE PARK There are a handful of tiny beachfront pocket parks and boat ramps scattered around Camano Island. For instance, Cama Beach State Park nearby is an old 1930s fishing resort. But there's just one true park, Camano Island State Park, and it's a real stunner, boasting the finest stretch of shoreline in this part of Puget Sound. Here is well over a mile of enchanting beach to wander, in view of the Olympic Mountains rising to the west. Anglers fish for clams, salmon, perch, bottomfish, flounder, sole and rock cod. You can find camping facilities and places to picnic; forest and beach hiking and nature trails; and plenty of opportunities for swimming, but cold water. Day-use fee, $5. ~ From Stanwood, drive west on Route 532 for five miles, then follow signs to West Camano Drive and the park; phone/fax 360-387-3031.

▲ There are 86 sites (no hookups); $17 to $22 per night.

BAY VIEW STATE PARK This tiny park on the north side of the town of Bay View overlooks the **Padilla Bay National Estuarine Research Reserve**, an ecological pocket with over 11,000 acres of marsh and tidelands tucked between the north Skagit Valley at Bay View and March Point. The Breazeale Padilla Bay Interpretive Center, half a mile north on Bay View–Edison Road, is a good place to get better acquainted with the many forms of wildlife that inhabit the area. A nature trail winds through parts of the wildlife habitat area just beyond the center. Restrooms, showers (fee), fireplaces, picnic tables and shelter, and a kitchen are some of the facilities here. Day-use fee, $5. ~ Exit 230 off Route 5 in Burlington, follow Route 20 west to Bayview–Edison Road. Turn right, then follow the signs to the park; 360-757-0227, fax 360-757-1967.

Padilla Bay's nearly 8000 acres of ellgrass serve as a nursery for salmon, perch, crab and herring.

▲ There are 4 cabins ($45 per night), 46 standard sites ($19 per night), 30 RV hookup sites ($25 to $30 per night) and 3 primitive sites ($14 per night). Reservations: 888-226-7688.

LARRABEE STATE PARK This 2683-acre park on Samish Bay offers 14 miles of hiking trails, including two steep trails to small mountain lakes (Fragrance and Lost lakes), and a one-and-a-half-mile stretch of beach with numerous tidepools for views of the local marine life. There's good freshwater fishing for trout in either of the mountain lakes and crabbing (with a license), clamming and saltwater fishing in Chuckanut and Samish bays and newly acquired Clayton Beach. You'll find restrooms, showers, picnic tables and shelters, a playground, barbecue grills and kitchens. ~ On scenic Chuckanut Drive (Route 11), seven miles south of Bellingham; 360-676-2093, fax 360-676-2061.

▲ There are 51 standard sites ($19 per night), and 26 RV hookup sites ($26 per night) and 8 primitive sites ($10 per night). Reservations: 888-226-7688.

TEDDY BEAR COVE This secluded, narrow stretch of white sand bordered by thick trees just south of the Bellingham city limits is a public beach that lacks facilities—and the water is very cold in case you're thinking of swimming. The beach area curves out around the shallow cove, like a thumb jutting out toward Chuckanut Bay. ~ There's a well-signed parking lot along Chuckanut Drive, Route 11, at the intersection of California Street. The trail to the beach is marked with signs at the parking lot and meanders down a steep bank for 100 yards or so from the road; 360-733-2900, fax 360-676-1180.

◄ HIDDEN

WHATCOM FALLS PARK This popular park sprawls across 209 acres along the tumbling waters of Whatcom Creek. It's just the place to discover cooling breezes on a hot summer day as you stroll next to the woodland-bordered stream. There are hiking trails, waterfalls, fishing ponds and a hatchery, picnic shelters and barbecue stands. ~ 1401 Electric Avenue, five miles east of the Maritime Heritage Center; 360-676-6985, fax 360-647-6367.

BIRCH BAY STATE PARK The highlight of this 192-acre park with 6000 feet of shoreline is the warm, shallow bay, which is suitable for wading up to half a mile out in some spots. The bay is bordered by a mile-long stretch of driftwood and shell-strewn beach edged by grassland. Swimming, clamming and crabbing are popular here. The camping area is inland in a stand of cedar and Douglas fir; nestled in the lush greenery it's hard to tell that the park sits in the shadow of BP's Cherry Point Refinery. Birdwatchers frequent the park to visit the marshy estuary at the south border that attracts more than 100 varieties of birds. Facilities include restrooms, fireplaces, picnic tables, shelters and trails; some facilities for the disabled. ~ Located eight miles south of Blaine off Birch Bay; 360-371-2800, fax 360-371-0455.

▲ There are 147 standard sites ($19 per night), and 20 RV hookup sites ($25 per night) and 2 primitive hike- or bike-in sites ($10 per night). Reservations: 888-226-7688.

SEMIAHMOO PARK This long, slender spit dividing Semiahmoo Bay and Drayton Harbor is a favorite among beach lovers, who can stroll sandy, narrow beaches on both sides of the spit, and of birdwatchers who come here to observe bald eagles, loons, herons and others supported by this protected, nutrient-rich habitat. Kite flying is also ideal here. The spit has been an important site for native peoples of the United States and Canada. It was also the site of a fish cannery, the history of which is reviewed in the park's museum. Restrooms, picnic tables, and a bike path are found here. ~ Located near Blaine. Take the Birch Bay–Lynden Road exit west off Route 5, turn north onto Harbor View Road then west onto Lincoln Road, which becomes Semiahmoo Parkway and leads into the park; 360-733-2900, fax 360-676-1180.

Whidbey Island

Whidbey Island, stretching north to south along the mainland, is the longest island in the continental United States aside from Long Island. This slender, serpentine bit of land is covered in a rolling patchwork of loganberry farms, pasturelands, sprawling state parks, hidden heritage sites and historic small towns. The artistic hamlet of Langley near Whidbey's southern tip is a current hotspot for weekend escapes from Seattle.

SIGHTS

Most of the sights in **Langley** are concentrated along 1st and 2nd streets, where falsefront shops house small galleries, boutiques and restaurants. There's a lovely stretch of public beach flanked by a concrete wall adorned in Northwest Indian motifs just below **Seawall Park** (look for the totem pole on 1st Street), and a wonderful bronze statue by local artist Georgia Gerber above a second stairwell leading down to the beach.

In the spring months, you'll find a colorful tulip display at **Holland Gardens.** During the balance of the year come to see the beautiful floral displays that make this small garden a local favorite. ~ Corner of Southeast 6th and Ely streets, Oak Harbor.

Beautiful greenery typifies Whidbey Island, and one Greenbank area establishment offers visitors a close look at cultivating the landscape. The famous **Meerkerk Rhododendron Gardens** feature hundreds of varieties of these showy bushes—with 2000 types spread across 53 acres—which find Whidbey's climate one of the best on earth. Magnolia, maple and cherry trees and exotic conifers add to the beauty of this spot, creating an arboretum. April and May are the peak months for blooms, with daffodils providing additional color. The nursery has rhodies for sale from the end of March through May. Admission. ~ Just off Route 525 south of Greenbank; 360-678-1912; www.meerkerkgardens.org, e-mail meerkerk@whidbey.net.

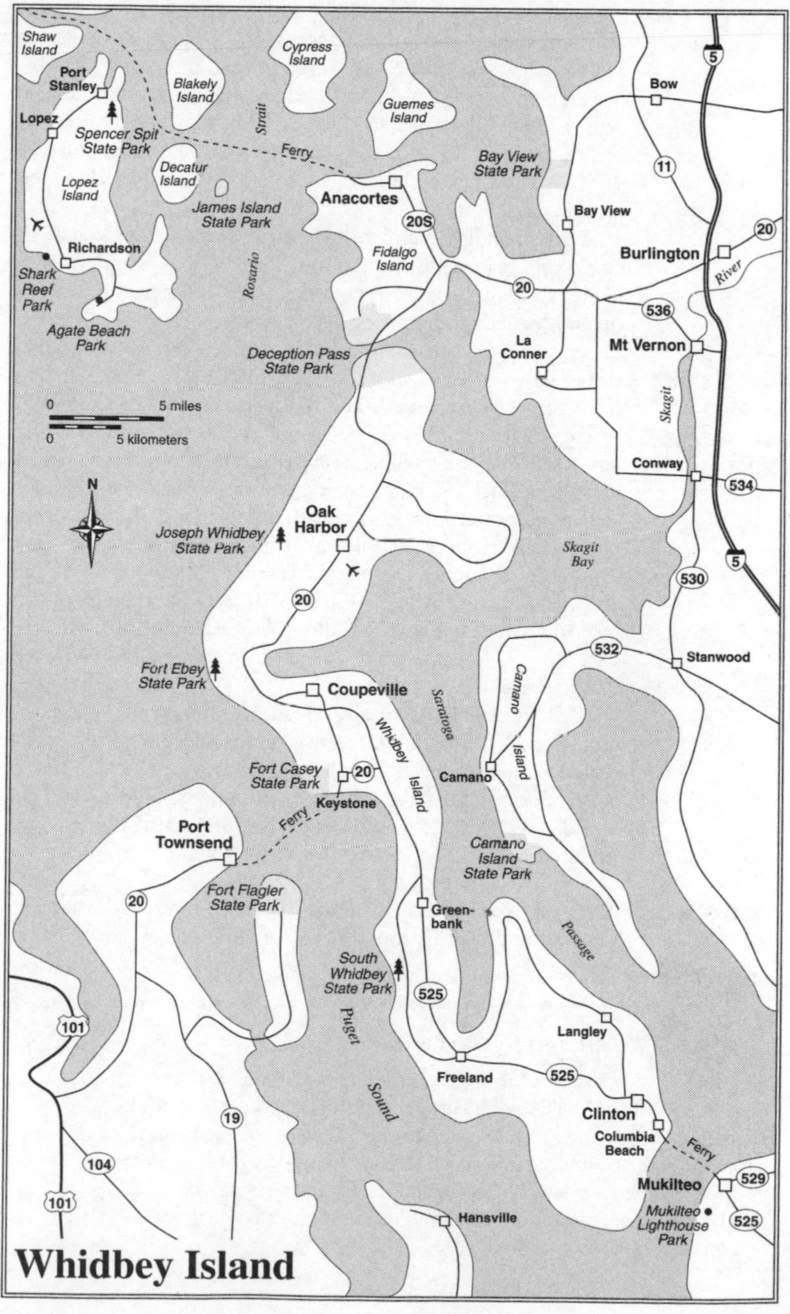
Shaw Island
Port Stanley
Lopez
Spencer Spit State Park
Lopez Island
Richardson
Shark Reef Park
Agate Beach Park
Blakely Island
Decatur Island
James Island State Park
Cypress Island
Guemes Island
Strait
Ferry
Rosario
Anacortes
Fidalgo Island
Bay View State Park
Bay View
Bow
Burlington
River
La Conner
Mt Vernon
Skagit
Conway
Deception Pass State Park
0
5 miles
0
5 kilometers
N
Oak Harbor
Joseph Whidbey State Park
Skagit Bay
Stanwood
Fort Ebey State Park
Coupeville
Saratoga
Camano Island
Whidbey Island
Camano
Fort Casey State Park
Keystone
Ferry
Port Townsend
Camano Island State Park
Fort Flagler State Park
Green-bank
Passage
South Whidbey State Park
Puget
Sound
Langley
Freeland
Clinton
Columbia Beach
Ferry
Mukilteo
Mukilteo Lighthouse Park
Hansville
5
11
20S
20
536
534
530
532
525
529
19
104
101
Whidbey Island

Only a few wine grapes ripen in Puget Sound's cool climate; **Whidbey Island Vineyard & Winery** specializes in clean, crisp vintages, such as Madeleine Angevine and Siegerrebe, that are rarely grown elsewhere, in addition to other whites and a full range of reds. Closed Tuesday in summer, and Monday and Tuesday the rest of the year. ~ 5237 South Langley Road, Langley; 360-221-2040; www.whidbeyislandwinery.com, e-mail winery@whidbeyislandwinery.com.

Ebey's Landing National Historical Reserve, set aside as the first such reserve in the country in 1978, lies midway up Whidbey Island. The reserve protects 17,400 acres of beaches, uplands, woods and prairies; historic pioneer farms homesteaded under the Donation Land Law of 1850; Fort Ebey and Fort Casey state parks; Penn Cove, long used by the Skagit Indians from across Puget Sound; and the historic town of **Coupeville**, where falsefront buildings line Front Street above the wharf. Here you'll find Alexander Blockhouse (Alexander and Front streets) and Davis Blockhouse (Sunnyside Cemetery Road), built by early settlers for protection against possible Indian attacks, and a good collection of pioneer agricultural artifacts and historical displays in the **Island County Historical Museum** (908 Northwest Alexander Street, Coupeville; 360-678-3310). Reduced hours in winter. Admission. ~ Ebey's Landing National Historical Reserve, P.O. Box 774, Coupeville, WA 98239; 360-678-6084; www.nps.gov/ebla.

Built in 1903, **Admiralty Head Lighthouse** at Fort Casey State Park features an interpretive center offering history on the region's military past. You'll also enjoy excellent views of Admiralty Inlet and the Olympic Mountains. Hours vary; call ahead. ~ 1280 Engle Road, Coupeville; 360-240-5584; www.admiraltyhead.wsu.edu, e-mail gloriaw@wsu.edu.

LODGING

There are some 11 hotels on the island, all motel-style and clustered around Oak Harbor. But the big draw on Whidbey has al-

sights

AUTHOR FAVORITE

Spanning the "Grand Canyon of Puget Sound," **Deception Pass Bridge** links Whidbey with Fidalgo Island. Most visitors just drive slowly by, taking in the sights. But if you want a little more excitement, stroll out onto the bridge for vertigo-inducing views—straight down into the swift, churning currents of Deception Pass. You can also walk down to the shore on the footpaths of Pass Island to watch the streaming waters up close and personal.

ways been bed-and-breakfast inns, over 80 of them at last count. Your choices run the gamut from log cabins in the forest to beach cabins and posh retreats. For a comprehensive list, contact the **Langley Chamber of Commerce**. Closed Sunday in winter. ~ P.O. Box 403, 208 Anthes Avenue, Langley, WA 98260; 360-221-6765, 888-232-2080; www.visitlangley.com, e-mail langley@whidbey.com.

Overlooking the Maxwelton Valley near Clinton in west Whidbey Island, **Lapis Lane Guesthouse & Cabin** offers two earth-friendly guest quarters in a wooded artist compound featuring hand-blown glass. The one-bedroom cabin has a queen-sized bed, a gas fireplace, hardwood floors and throw rugs. The guesthouse sleeps six and has two bedrooms, a foldout sofa, steam bath and jacuzzi. Both accommodations have handcrafted furniture, a washer and dryer, barbecue, DVD/CD player and a kitchen stocked with breakfast items and fruits and veggies from the onsite organic garden. Two-night minimum. Note: The entire property is fragrance-free and nonsmoking. ~ 3645 Lapis Lane, Clinton; 360-579 2009; www.lapislane.com, e-mail dimitri@whidbey.com. MODERATE TO DELUXE.

The view over Useless Bay is the selling point for the charming, cedar-shingled **Heron Beach Cottage** in west Whidbey. The cottage sleeps six in two bedrooms (one has a queen-sized bed, the other has twin beds) and a foldout sofa. Two bathrooms, a kitchen, separate dining and sitting areas, a woodstove and a washer and dryer round out the amenities. There is also a deck with a gas barbecue as well as extensive cottage gardens. Three-night minimum in summer; two-night minimum rest of year. ~ 7495 Maxwelton Road, Clinton; 360-319-5111; www.heronbeachcottage.com, e-mail ruth@heronbeachcottage.com. DELUXE.

The beautiful **Inn at Langley** has perfected the fine art of hospitality at a polished property worthy of its magnificent waterfront setting. With a decorator's color palette taken directly from the beach, guest rooms in zen-like shades of gray, cream, tan and brown accented by lots of natural wood are elegant, presenting a delicate balance of modern art and furnishings, and are decked out with every possible amenity (fireplace, jacuzzi, Krups coffee set, wi-fi and large deck to take advantage of the 180° view). A serene oriental garden set in front of the grand dining room is an added touch. If you can afford the tariff, this is the most luxurious selection available on the island. Buffet breakfast. ~ 400 1st Street, Langley; 360-221-3033, fax 360-221-3033; www.innatlangley.com, e-mail info@innatlangley.com. ULTRA-DELUXE. ◄ HIDDEN

Garden Path Suites, one of the older establishments in town, presents two luxurious and private suites decorated by the designer-owner with original art from the Northwest and around the world. ~ 111 1st Street, Langley; 360-221-5121, fax 360-221-

6050; www.thegardenpathsuites.com, e-mail lll@whidbey.com. DELUXE TO ULTRA-DELUXE.

Ashingdon Manor Bed and Breakfast is a typical country house built by the owner on ten acres of woods and pasture. The large inn includes six guest rooms, all decorated with European pine furnishings and each with an open fireplace. A spacious guest cottage is also available. Guests can relax in the large living room, appointed in elegant country-manor style. Dinner offered on Saturday. ~ 5023 Langley Road, Langley; 360-221-2334, 800-456-5006; www.ashingdonmanor.com, e-mail stay@ashingdonmanor.com. MODERATE TO ULTRA-DELUXE.

The majestic orca, with its distinctive black and white markings, is Washington's official marine mammal.

Country Cottage of Langley sits on two acres of handsomely landscaped garden with an English country feel and oodles of lawn for endless games of croquet. Despite the country feel, this bed and breakfast is still within easy walking distance of downtown Langley. Choose from six cottages, each with water views. All have private decks or patios, and three feature jacuzzis and fireplaces. Antiques from various periods and materials decorate all the rooms. Full breakfast is delivered to your door. ~ 215 6th Street, Langley; 360-221-8709, 800-713-3860; www.acountrycottage.com, e-mail stay@acountrycottage.com. DELUXE TO ULTRA-DELUXE.

From the deck of **Eagles Nest Inn**, you can gaze east across Saratoga Passage and Camano Island to Mt. Baker and the Cascades. Guests come to enjoy the very rural setting, soak up the pampering country hospitality, and take long strolls on a nearby cobbled beach. Four traditional rooms and a honeymoon cottage offsite. Full breakfast. ~ 4680 Saratoga Road, Langley; phone/fax 360-221-5331, 800-243-5536; www.eaglesnestinn.com, e-mail eaglesnest@whidbey.net. DELUXE TO ULTRA-DELUXE.

Home By The Sea Guest Cottages gives guest a choice of locales. The Sandpiper Suite is a quintessential sandy beach property next to a bird sanctuary. It features a king-sized feather bed, a fully equipped kitchen and a private entrance through the perennial garden. Though the address is Clinton, Home By The Sea is actually closer to Langley. ~ 2388 East Sunlight Beach Road, Clinton; 360-321-2964; www.homebytheseacottages.com, e-mail info@homebytheseacottages.com. ULTRA-DELUXE.

Cliff House is an architecturally stunning two-story structure of wood and sweeping panes of glass set on a wooded bluff overlooking Puget Sound. Guests have the run of the two-bedroom house, with its open central atrium, wonderful gourmet kitchen, sunken sitting area with fireplace and wraparound cedar deck with large jacuzzi. A stairway leads down to miles of empty beach. There is also a separate small cottage with one bedroom. ~ 727

Windmill Drive, Freeland; 360-331-1566, 800-297-4118; www.cliffhouse.net, e-mail wink@whidbey.com. ULTRA-DELUXE.

Bush Point Wharf Bed and Breakfast has it all: spectacular views of shipping lanes, the Olympic Mountain ranges and romantic sunsets. Located at the tip of Bush Point Wharf on some 175 feet of beachfront, its main draw is the huge 50-by-70 foot private docks that skirt its two rooms and penthouse suite. Each room is comfortably furnished and includes a coffee maker and refrigerator. The penthouse suite features comfortable leather sofas and can accommodate up to six people. Closed mid-October to mid-April. ~ 229 Spyglass Drive, Freeland; 360-331-0405, 800-460-7219; www.whidbeyisland.com/bushpoint. DELUXE TO ULTRA-DELUXE.

Built as officer's housing just prior to World War I, the **Fort Casey Inn** has been converted into inviting cottages overlooking Puget Sound. Its access to Fort Casey State Park and Crockett Lake makes this inn a prime location for outdoor recreation. Each of its ten units features a plethora of patriotic military memorabilia, including walls decked out with nostalgic post-cards sent by soldiers overseas to their sweethearts at home. All have a bathroom, and most have a living room and a large kitchen with a breakfast nook as well as cast-iron gas fireplaces. A favorite with children, Fort Casey Inn is a historical treasure and a delightful retreat rolled into one. ~ 1124 South Engle Road, Coupeville; 360-678-5050, 866-661-6604; www.fortcaseyinn.com, e-mail stay@fortcaseyinn.com. DELUXE.

The **Captain Whidbey Inn**, a well-preserved and maintained log inn on Penn Cove, is a fine example of the type of Northwest retreat all the rage years ago and now coming back into fashion. This walk into the past offers several cozy, antique furnished rooms that share two baths and waterfront views; two rows of spacious, pine-paneled rooms with baths and a few private cottages with fireplaces. This is one of only a handful of waterside accommodations in the region. ~ 2072 West Captain Whidbey Inn Road, Coupeville; 360-678-4097, 800-366-4097, fax 360-678-4110; www.captainwhidbey.com, e-mail info@captainwhidbey.com. MODERATE TO ULTRA-DELUXE.

The **Blue Goose Inn** dates to 1889, and its two rooms are furnished with early American antiques and plush comforters. A full breakfast is included. ~ 602 North Main Street, Coupeville; 360-678-4284; www.whidbeyvictorianbandb.com. MODERATE TO DELUXE.

Within walking distance of shops and restaurants, the **Inn at Penn Cove** is actually a pair of elegant century-old Victorian homes converted into bed and breakfasts. Together, they offer six spacious rooms, some fitted with gas fireplaces, one suite with double jacuzzi; all but one have views over Penn Cove. Each house boasts plenty of antiques. Full breakfast and afternoon tea. ~ 702 North Main Street, Coupeville; 360-678-8000, 800-688-2683; www.whidbey.net/penncove, e-mail penncove@whidbey.net. MODERATE TO DELUXE.

The **Coupeville Inn** has a French mansard–style roof that adds a touch of class to this otherwise straightforward two-story inn with two large apartment-like units that sleep up to four. Breakfast featuring homemade muffins is included in the room rates. Of the two dozen rooms, most have balconies, about half have water views. Possibly the best motel value on the island, given the free continental breakfast and excellent location. ~ 200 Northwest Coveland Street, Coupeville; 360-678-6668, 800-247-6162, fax 360-678-3059; www.thecoupevilleinn.com, e-mail onisland@whidbey.net. MODERATE TO DELUXE.

The **Auld Holland Inn** is a reasonably priced roadside motel with flair, from the flowering window boxes on the European exterior to the immaculately clean, antique-filled rooms. Some rooms have fireplaces and princess canopied beds. For those seeking budget prices, there are 34 mobile home units with two or three bedrooms tucked behind the full-sized windmill housing the motel's office. If you're looking for more luxury, there are six deluxe-priced units furnished with jacuzzis and fireplaces. Continental breakfast. ~ 33575 Route 20, Oak Harbor; 360-675-2288, 800-228-0148, fax 360-675-2817; www.auldhollandinn.com, e-mail dutchvillage@oakharbor.net. MODERATE TO DELUXE.

DINING

Since 1989, **Cafe Langley** has served Mediterranean favorites such as spanikopita, moussaka, dolmas and lamb shish kabobs along with fresh seafood (Penn Cove mussels, grilled salmon and Dungeness crab cakes), pastas and steaks. The atmosphere here is airy Mediterranean, with stucco-like walls, exposed beams and an assortment of exotic fish etched on a glass partition. There are often people waiting in the park across the street for a table in this popular café. Closed Tuesday during winter. ~ 113 1st Street,

AUTHOR FAVORITE

An unassuming little eatery tucked away downtown, the **Oystercatcher** offers a small, carefully prepared menu. Mussels and oysters are a mainstay, but entrées may include New Zealand lamb medallions with lemon-caper sauce as well as salmon *en papillote*. Since there's only a smattering of tables, reservations are highly recommended. Dinner only. Closed Sunday through Tuesday. ~ 901 Grace Street, Northwest Coupeville; 360-678-0683. DELUXE.

Langley; 360-221-3090, fax 360-221-8542; www.langley-wa.com/cl, e-mail garibyan@whidbey.net. MODERATE TO DELUXE.

Prima Bistro is a laid-back European-style eatery on the waterfront in Langley. The main attractions are the reliably good fresh seasonal foods and dining outside on the deck. Choose from a range of interesting appetizers, such as housemade paté, organic beet salad and Penn Cove mussels mariniere, then follow with a bistro classic like steak frites, roast free-range chicken, quiche, croque monsieur or cassoulet. ~ 201½ 1st Street, Langley; 360-221-4060; www.primabistro.com. MODERATE.

The **Doghouse Tavern** is the place to go for burgers, fish-and-chips and chowder. A totem on the side of this waterfront building points the way to their separate family dining room in case you've got the kids along. ~ 230 1st Street, Langley; 360-221-4595. BUDGET TO MODERATE.

The chef provides a floor show as well as fine cuisine at the **Chef's Kitchen** inside the Inn at Langley. The dining area is a huge gourmet kitchen where gleaming pots and pans hang from the ceiling and most tables have a view of the culinary action. Served Friday to Sunday and Thursday night during the summer only, the dinners consist of six courses emphasizing regional flavors such as duck breast with loganberries, baked salmon with apples, leeks and chanterelles, or fresh Penn Cove mussels harvested on Whidbey Island. Make reservations well in advance. Note: If canceling, do so a week ahead or pay 50 percent of the dinner cost. ~ 400 1st Street, Langley; phone/fax 360-221-3033; www.innatlangley.com, e-mail info@innatlangley.com. ULTRA-DELUXE.

The **Braeburn Restaurant** provides a homey atmosphere and friendly, country-style fare. Look for downhome specialties like pot roast, meatloaf and liver and onions. Fresh omelettes, apple french toast, homemade granola and giant mimosas grace the breakfast menu. ~ 197 2nd Street, Langley; 360-221-3211, fax 360-221-8182; www.appledumpling.com. MODERATE TO ULTRA-DELUXE.

The tranquil **Edgecliff Restaurant** is well named: it sits atop the cliffs in Langley and has the best views in town. The Mediterranean and Northwest cuisine is quite tasty, too. Try a new twist on the ubiquitous Whidbey oysters, cooked Thai style with a sesame-seed crust and served with a Thai peanut dipping sauce. If it's on the menu, don't miss the butternut ravioli with black butter- brandy sauce, caramelized walnuts, roasted garlic and sage. ~ 510 Cascade Avenue, Langley; 360-221-8899. MODERATE TO DELUXE.

Original pine walls, bright pink tablecloths and large entrées make **Tyee's Restaurant** just the place for a put-up-your-feet-and-feel-at-home meal. A long lunch counter adds to the down-home comfort as do the round-backed chairs and family-friendly menu items such as the hot turkey sandwich, sirloin steak, taco salad, and fish and chips. A full salad bar and dessert menu are also available. ~ 405 South Main Street, Coupeville; 360-678-6616, fax 360-678-3774; www.tyeehotel.com, e-mail cheyenne@coupeville.net. BUDGET TO MODERATE.

Toby's Tavern serves up a cheeseburger that was rated tops by actress Kathleen Turner, who starred in the film *War of the Roses*, which was filmed partly in and around Coupeville in 1989. Good fish-and-chips, Penn Cove steamed mussels and an upscale atmosphere add a touch of class to this waterfront watering hole. ~ 8 Northwest Front Street, Coupeville; 360-678-4222; www.tobysuds.com, e-mail info@tobysuds.com. MODERATE.

Christopher's Front Street Cafe specializes in "creative contemporary cuisine" with a menu that changes seasonally. The emphasis is on fresh, local fare, especially seafood, and runs the gamut from superb Penn Cove mussels, to beef and chicken, vegetarian dishes, and pasta; regional wines and microbrews are also available. Closed Sunday from Labor Day to Memorial Day. ~ 103 Northwest Coveland Street, Coupeville; 360-678-5480; www.christophersonwhidbey.com, e-mail info@christophersonwhidbey.com. BUDGET TO DELUXE.

Splendid views across Penn Cove from the rooftop patio are the chief attraction at **Mad Crab**. Live music is featured on some Friday and Saturday nights along with the hearty fare. ~ 10 Front Street, Coupeville; 360-678-0241. MODERATE TO DELUXE.

SHOPPING

There's plenty to keep shoppers and browsers busy on Whidbey Island, especially in artsy Langley and historic Coupeville. The best art galleries are concentrated in Langley. **Museo** specializes in art glass made by local Whidbey Island artists. ~ 215 1st Street, Langley; 360-221-7737; www.museo.cc. The **Gaskill/Olson Gallery** showcases bronzes, paintings, sculpture and pottery. ~ 302 1st Street, Langley; 360-221-2978; www.gaskillolson.com. **Soleil** carries double-sided aluminum-alloy pieces by Arthur Court, silver, bone, pewter and glass jewelry, candles, stationery, photo albums and soaps. ~ 308 1st Street, Langley; 360-221-0383. The **Hellebore Glass Gallery** has fine handblown glass created on the premises. ~ 308 1st Street, Langley; 360-221-2067.

Another noteworthy shop in town is **The Star Store**, a modern mercantile selling fun clothing and housewares. ~ 201 1st Street, Langley; 360-221-5222; www.starstorewhidbey.com. You can also browse the two shops of **Whidbey Island Antiques**. ~ 2nd Street and Anthes Avenue, Langley; 360-221-2393; www.whidbeyislandantiques.com.

There's an array of charming shops in the revitalized waterfront district of Coupeville. You'll find wonderful antiques and collectibles at **Elk Horn Trading Company**. ~ 15 Front Street,

Coupeville; 360-678-2250. Nautical gifts, artifacts and sportswear can be found at **Nautical 'N' Nice.** ~ 22 Front Street, Northwest Coupeville; 360-678-3565.

If it's sunny out and a picnic is in order, stock up at **Bayleaf** for imported cheeses, cold cuts, olives, wines and rustic, fresh-baked bread. Closed Monday and Tuesday. ~ 101 Northwest Coveland Street, Coupeville; 360-678-6603; www.bayleaf.us.

Just three miles south of Coupeville is **Salmagundi Farms,** which specializes in estate liquidations, tag sales and auctions. It's listed on the National Historic Register and filled with antiques and old farm equipment. Open weekends only. ~ 19162 South Route 20; 360-678-5888.

NIGHTLIFE

Hong Kong Gardens has a pool table and karaoke every Friday and Saturday night. The occasional band plays on Saturday nights. ~ 9324 State Route 525, Clinton; 360-341-2828.

Or drop by **Toby's Tavern,** where they filmed the bar scene from the movie *War of the Roses.* ~ 8 Northwest Front Street, Coupeville; 360-678-4222; www.tobysuds.com.

BEACHES & PARKS

SOUTH WHIDBEY STATE PARK There are 347 acres with 4500 feet of rocky shoreline to explore in this lovely state park. Hikers here will enjoy the one-and-a-quarter-mile loop trail through an old-growth stand of fir and cedar. Anglers seek silver salmon, and climbing is popular. Black-tailed deer, herons and osprey are among the many creatures here. Only the hardy will venture into the cold waters of Admiralty Inlet for a dip. There are restrooms, showers, picnic tables, shelter and firepits. ~ Take Route 525 nine miles north of Clinton to Bush Point Road, which after six miles becomes Smuggler's Cove Road; 360-902-8844, fax 360-331-5202.

▲ There are 46 standard sites ($19 per night) and 8 RV hookup sites ($26 per night). Closed December and January. Reservations: 888-226-7688.

Fort Casey was used as a military training center during both World Wars I and II.

FORT CASEY STATE PARK History buffs and children will enjoy exploring the military fortification of this 467-acre park. While most of the big guns are gone, you'll still find panoramic views of the Olympic Mountains across the Strait of Juan de Fuca from the top of the concrete bunkers built into the escarpment. Wild roses and other flowers line the paths to the museum housed in pretty Admiralty Head Lighthouse and the beachside campground that overlooks the Keystone Harbor ferry terminal. Scuba enthusiasts swarm to the underwater trail through the park's marine wildlife sanctuary off Keystone Harbor, and anglers try for salmon and steelhead. Facilities include restrooms, showers, picnic tables, fireplaces and an underwater marine park. ~ At Coupeville turn south off Route 20 onto Engle Road and follow the Keystone Ferry signs to the park; 360-678-4519, fax 360-428-1094.

There are 35 standard sites ($19 per night) and 3 primitive sites ($14 per night).

FORT EBEY STATE PARK The massive guns are long gone from this coastal World War II fortification, but there are still bunker tunnels and pillboxes to be explored. The picturesque beach at Partridge Point is the hands-down favorite of the islanders; at low tide it's possible to walk the five-mile beach stretch to Fort Casey. Anglers cast a rod for bass on Lake Pondilla. There are restrooms, showers, picnic tables, fireplaces and nature trails. ~ From Route 20 turn west onto Libbey Road, then south onto Hill Valley Drive and follow the signs; 360-678-4636, fax 360-678-5136.

There are 38 standard sites ($19 to $22 per night), 12 RV hookup sites ($25 to $30 per night) and 3 primitive sites ($14 per night). The secluded campsites under a canopy of Douglas fir are much nicer than the crowded sites at nearby Fort Casey. Reservations accepted May through September: 888-226-7688.

OAK HARBOR WINDJAMMER PARK A full-scale windmill and an A-6 Prowler, first used in Vietnam and donated by the Navy, are just two of the features of this day-use park on Oak Harbor Bay next to the sewage processing plant (not a deterrent, believe it or not). A sandy beach slopes down from the lighted walking path bordering expansive green fields suitable for flying kites or playing frisbee. Anglers will find salmon, bottomfish and bass. There are two wading pools in summer and a protected swimming area. There are bathhouses, picnic tables, ball fields, tennis and volleyball courts and a playground. ~ Located in downtown Oak Harbor off Pioneer Parkway, east of Route 20; watch for the windmill; 360-679-5551, fax 360-679-3902, e-mail info@oakharbor.org.

An RV park with 56 full hookups and hot showers can be accessed at Beeksma Drive or City Beach Street ($20 per night). An overflow area has campsites with no hookups.

DECEPTION PASS STATE PARK The most popular state park in Washington, it encompasses over 4100 acres laced with 35 miles of hiking trails through forested hills and wetland areas and along rocky headlands. There are several delightful sandy stretches for picnics or beachcombing. Breathtaking views from the 976-foot steel bridge spanning the pass attract photographers from around the world. There's swimming in Cranberry Lake in the summer and flyfishing for trout on Pass Lake. Facilities include restrooms, showers, bathhouses, picnic tables, kitchens, shelters, fireplaces, a concession stand, a retreat center and an underwater park. ~ Take the Mukilteo ferry to Whidbey Island and follow Route 525 and Route 20, or take Route 5 to Exit 230 and follow Route 20 West to the park on the northern tip of the island; 360-675-2417, fax 360-675-8991; www.deceptionpassfoundation.org, e-mail deception.pass@parks.wa.gov.

▲ There are 167 standard sites ($19 per night), 13 RV hookup sites ($26 per night) and 5 primitive sites ($14 per night). Reservations: 888-226-7688.

Fidalgo Island

A two-hour drive northwest of Seattle, Anacortes on Fidalgo Island is a good place to enjoy folk art, ride a charming excursion train and see impressive murals. Quiet inns and waterfront restaurants make this town a pleasant retreat.

But Anacortes is only the beginning of adventures on this charming island. Often called the first of the San Juans, Fidalgo is actually linked to the mainland by the Route 20 bridge over Swinomish Channel in the Skagit Valley, and to Whidbey Island by another bridge. Access is easy. Nevertheless, you can still find quiet beaches and parks to explore. Lonely trails wind through an enormous forest reserve to superb viewpoints. A mini "Lake District" clusters more than half a dozen splendid lakes. And a marvelous resort complex—Scimitar Ridge Ranch—combines a working Northwest horse ranch and a deluxe campground that includes covered wagons outfitted for camping.

SIGHTS

In the late 1800s, the bustling city of **Anacortes** was also referred to as the "Magic City," "Liverpool of the West" and "New York of the West." Because of its ferry terminal, Anacortes is known as "the gateway to the San Juans," but don't just zip on through because there's plenty to see and do here. One of the best ways to get acquainted with the city and its history is to take a walking tour of downtown to view over 100 life-size murals attached to many of the historical buildings. As part of the **Anacortes Mural Project**, these murals are reproductions of early-20th-century photographs depicting everyday scenes and early pioneers of the town. A tour map of the murals is available from the **Anacortes Chamber of Commerce**. ~ 819 Commercial Avenue, Suite F, Anacortes; 360-293-7911, fax 360-293-1595; www.anacortes.org, e-mail info@anacortes.org.

In 1877, postmaster Amos Bowman changed the town of Ship Harbor's name to Anacortes in honor of his wife, Anna Curtis.

Another reminder of earlier days is the **W. T. Preston**, a drydocked sternwheeler that once plied the waters of the sound and rivers breaking up log jams. Closed weekdays in April, May, September and October, and from November through March.

Admission. ~ 7th Street and R Avenue, Anacortes; 360-293-1916; http://museum.cityofanacortes.org, e-mail coa.museum@cityofanacortes.org.

At the **Anacortes Museum**, you'll find an entertaining collection of memorabilia from Anacortes, Fidalgo and Guemes islands, as well as exhibits detailing the history of the islands. In front of the museum there's a highly amusing (but non-functional) drinking fountain with varying levels suited for dogs, cats, horses and humans, which was donated to the city by the Women's Temperance Union. Closed Tuesday and Wednesday. ~ 1305 8th Street, Anacortes; 360-293-1915, fax 360-293-1929; http://museum.cityofanacortes.org, e-mail coa.museum@cityofanacortes.org.

The **Anacortes Community Forest Lands** is a 2200-acre treasure of fishing and swimming lakes, wildlife wetlands, and tall conifers climbing the slopes of 1270-foot **Mt. Erie**, about five miles south of downtown Anacortes. Some 20 miles of foot trails offer days of wandering. For maps and information, stop at the Anacortes Chamber of Commerce. ~ 819 Commercial Avenue, Anacortes; 360-293-3832; www.anacortes.org, e-mail info@anacortes.org.

You can also simply drive to the top of Mt. Erie and enjoy a series of vista points carved into its rocky summit that look out in all directions of the compass from the Cascades to the Olympics, across the San Juans, over Skagit Bay to Whidbey and all the way to Mt. Rainier.

Within the park and all around it are a handful of lakes—Heart, Erie, Campbell, Whistle, Cranberry, Pass. You can swing past Campbell Lake and Pass Lake (good fishing) on Route 20 between Anacortes and Deception Pass. And you can visit Heart and Erie (picnicking, fishing) from Mt. Erie Road leading into the park. Whistle and Cranberry (good fishing) are reached by foot trail.

LODGING

At the **Holiday Motel**, one of the only motels that keeps its prices low even during high season, you get what you pay for. Aging rooms are very basic but tidy, with nicked furnishings in both the

HANDCRAFTED HOUSE

The **Ship House Inn** is an attractive high-waterfront property facing the San Juan Islands. Handcrafted by the owner in knotty cedar, accommodations are in three pleasant cabins, with nautical bunk-style beds, fridges, microwaves, TVs and private decks. Continental breakfast included. Closed November to mid-April. ~ 12876 Marine Drive, Anacortes; 360-293-1093; www.shiphouseinn.com, e-mail info@shiphouseinn.com. MODERATE TO DELUXE.

cramped bedroom and separate sitting room. ~ 2903 Commercial Avenue, Anacortes; 360-293-6511. BUDGET.

The **Anaco Bay Inn** is a step up, with 18 spacious, well-appointed rooms, all featuring a cozy fireplace. Some rooms have kitchens while others offer jetted tubs. Rooms without kitchens have microwaves and mini-fridges. Four two-bedroom suites are also available. A public jacuzzi, a library and laundry facilities round out the amenities. An expanded continental breakfast is included. ~ 916 33rd Street, Anacortes; 360-299-3320, 877-299-3320; www.anacobayinn.com, e-mail anacobay@fidalgo.net. MODERATE TO DELUXE.

DINING

The **Deception Cafe & Grill** serves traditional hand-breaded oysters and prawns, grilled burgers and mouth-watering, homemade desserts. Look for this unpretentious roadside establishment on the hill four miles north of Deception Pass. Breakfast, lunch and dinner. ~ 5596 Route 20, Anacortes; 360-293-9250. MODERATE.

Treat your eyes and your stomach with a meal at **Adrift**, located in a century-old building in rustic Old Town Anacortes. Its limpid water-blue floors, midnight blue ceiling and blue-gray walls (reminiscent of a foggy Anacortes morning) reflect the moody Northwest environs, while the eclectic menu makes good of the sea's bounty. Among the specialties are the Samish burger with pan-fried Blau oysters, the fish tacos with cinnamon black beans, the grilled polenta with basil and artichokes, and the grilled flank steak topped with spicy ginger garlic sauce. Breakfast served all day. Closed Sunday. ~ 510 Commercial Way, Anacortes; 360-588-0653; www.adriftrestaurant.com. MODERATE TO DELUXE.

Potted plants, taped light jazz and tablecloths soften the rough edges of **Charlie's**, a hash house overlooking the ferry terminal and water. Captive diners, here during the long wait for the ferry, choose from soups, salads, sandwiches and seafood at lunch and pasta, steak and seafood for dinner. ~ 5407 Ferry Terminal Road, Anacortes; 360-293-7377; www.charliesrestaurant.com. MODERATE TO DELUXE.

SHOPPING

Most of the great shops on Fidalgo Island are scattered along Anacortes' Commercial Avenue. **Left Bank Antiques**, housed in two floors of a renovated barn, absolutely bulges with American and European antiques and architectural items. ~ 1904 Commercial Avenue, Anacortes; 360-293-3022, fax 360-299-8888; www.leftbankantiques.com.

◄ HIDDEN

The historic **Marine Supply and Hardware** is packed to the rafters with nautical antiques and memorabilia. Closed Sunday. ~ 202 Commercial Avenue, Anacortes; 360-293-3014; www.marinesupplyandhardware.com.

Resist the temptation to buy smoked salmon to take home until you visit **SeaBear Smokehouse**, which has been producing authentic smoked salmons since 1957. Not only does the smokehouse sell smoked salmon, smokehouse chili and smoked salmon chowder, it also offers tours Monday through Friday. Pose with a salmon, learn to fillet, or just taste the goods. ~ 605 30th Street, Anacortes. Take 22nd Street east toward the Anacortes Marina, turn right onto T Avenue and you'll find the warehouse in an industrial complex a block down on the right; 360-293-4661, 800-645-3474; www.seabear.com, e-mail smokehouse@seabear.com.

Lopez Island

Life on pastoral Lopez Island is slow and amiable; residents wave to everyone and are truly disappointed if you don't wave back. Lopez didn't earn its nickname as the "Friendly Island" for nothing. Even better, it remains much less developed than San Juan and Orcas islands.

SIGHTS

The history of the island is well mapped out at the **Lopez Island Historical Museum** with its exhibit of pioneer farming and fishing implements, stone, bone and antler artifacts and fairly large maritime collection. While you're here, pick up a historical landmark tour guide to the many fine examples of Early American architecture scattered around the island. Closed Monday and Tuesday, and October through April. ~ 28 Washburn Place, Lopez Village; 360-468-2049; www.rockisland.com/~lopezmuseum, e-mail lopezmuseum@rockisland.com.

Stroll out to **Agate Beach Park** on MacKaye Harbor Road to watch the sunset. Another good sunset view spot is **Shark Reef Park** on Shark Reef Road, where you might see some harbor seals, heron and, if you're lucky, a whale or two.

Shaw Island is one of only four of the San Juan Islands that can be reached by ferry, but most visitors to the San Juans miss it. You need to stay on the ferry from Anacortes and get off at Shaw, one stop beyond Lopez Island. Those who do make the trip are in for a treat. Stop by the general store near the ferry landing for picnic supplies before heading out to **South Beach County Park** on Squaw Bay Road, two miles to the south.

Afterward, continue east along Squaw Bay Road, turn north on Hoffman Cove Road and make your way to the picturesque little red schoolhouse. Park by the school and cross the street to see the **Shaw Island Library and Historical Society**, a tiny log cabin housing a hodgepodge of pioneer memorabilia. Open limited hours on Tuesday, Thursday and Saturday. ~ Blind Bay Road and Ben Nevis; 360-468-4068.

LODGING

The **Lopez Islander Bay Resort**, once a dog-eared motel, has turned upscale. All of the 26 rooms and two suites have been refurbished. All rooms have decks overlooking Fisherman's Bay, perfect for a view of the sunset. Rental houses on the bay are also available. The marina has been upgraded (new floats and piers, a seaplane dock). An ambitious outings program for guests includes opportunities to bike, kayak and fish. Laundry and fitness facilities are included. ~ 2864 Fisherman Bay Road, Lopez Village; 360-468-2233, 800-736-2864, fax 360-468-3382; www.lopezislander.com, e-mail desk@lopezislander.com. MODERATE TO ULTRA-DELUXE.

Edenwild, a welcome addition to the scant list of lodgings on the island, is a two-story Victorian. The eight guest rooms are pretty, with carpeted floors and clawfoot tubs; three rooms have romantic fireplaces, one is handicapped accessible and four have views of Fisherman's Bay or San Juan Channel. Included in the room rates is breakfast, served in the sunny dining nook or on the delightful garden terrace. Apéritifs and truffles are served in the rooms. ~ Lopez Village; phone/fax 360-468-3238, 800-606-0662; www.edenwildinn.com, e-mail edenwild@rockisland.com. ULTRA-DELUXE.

You might feel a bit like Little Red Riding Hood as you bound up a footpath to your cabin at **Lopez Farm Cottages and Tent Camping**, nestled in an ancient cedar grove teeming with wildlife. Thankfully, only an inviting queen-size bed—not a wolf—awaits. These light and airy efficiencies feature a contemporary design with fireplaces, kitchens, decks and plenty of windows; an outdoor spa is an additional amenity. In the morning, continental breakfast arrives at your doorstep in a basket. For a more rustic experience, there are 13 campsites available. ~ Fisherman Bay Road, Lopez Island; 360-468-3555, 800-440-3556, fax 360-468-3966; www.lopezfarmcottages.com. MODERATE TO ULTRA-DELUXE.

◄HIDDEN

The best bet on Lopez Island is the **Inn at Swifts Bay**, a delightful bed and breakfast in an elegant Tudor home. Posh best describes the interior, with a comfortable mix of modern, Williams Sonoma–style furnishings and antique reproductions adorned in crocheted antimacassars and needlepoint pillows. There are two rooms sharing one bath, as well as three suites

AUTHOR FAVORITE

Set off to one side within the **Lopez Island Pharmacy** is an old-fashioned, red, white and black soda fountain, the best spot for lunch on Lopez. Grab a booth or a stool at the bar and order a sandwich, bowl of soup or slice of pie to go with your phosphate, malt, float or other fountain treat. No dinner. Closed Sunday. ~ 157 Lopez Village Road; 360-468-4511, fax 360-468-3825; www.lopezislandpharmacy.com, e-mail biz@lopezislandpharmacy.com. BUDGET.

with private entrances and baths; each has a gas-lit fireplace. A hot tub, an exercise studio, a sauna and a private beach are on the premises. The leisurely gourmet breakfast is without a doubt the most delicious morning repast available in the islands. ~ Port Stanley Road; 360-468-3636, 800-903-9536; www.swiftsbay.com, e-mail inn@swiftsbay.com. MODERATE TO ULTRA-DELUXE.

The **Lopez Lodge** in the village has two no-frills, motel-like rooms that share a bath. One studio has a private bath and full kitchen. ~ 35 Weeks Point Road, Lopez Village; 360-468-2816; www.lopezlodge.com, e-mail needle@rockisland.com. BUDGET TO DELUXE.

DINING

The **Bay Cafe** has an imaginative menu featuring fresh Northwest products. There are always daily specials to choose from, and regular entrées may include duck confit, handmade vegetable ravioli and filet of beef tenderloin. Check out the surprising garlic cheesecake. Reservations are essential, especially during summer. Closed Monday and Tuesday in the winter. ~ Lopez Village Road, Lopez Village; 360-468-3700, fax 360-468-4000; www.bay-cafe.com, e-mail thebaycafe@aol.com. DELUXE TO ULTRA-DELUXE.

Located next to the Lopez Village Market in a handsome Cape Cod–style building with weathered shingles and a terrace overlooking the water, the **Love Dog Cafe** uses fresh ingredients to create an eclectic blend of world cuisine. The seasonal menu changes regularly, offering anything from simple, juicy burgers to pesto cappelini to Alaskan halibut. The casual, warm atmosphere draws a real local crowd—hang out with a book or borrow a boardgame and enjoy the easy rhythm of island life. Dinner only. Reservations recommended. ~ 1 Village Center, Lopez Village; 360-468-2150. BUDGET TO ULTRA-DELUXE.

The **Lopez Islander Restaurant** is a true waterfront restaurant, looking west across Fisherman Bay to spectacular evening sunsets. In summer, ask for a table on the outdoor dining patio. Specialties of the house include an award-winning clam chowder and a daily fresh sheet of local seafood—salmon and halibut, for example. The resort's tiki bar stays open later with a limited menu. ~ Fisherman Bay Road, Lopez Village; 360-468-2233, fax 360-468-3382; www.lopezislander.com. MODERATE TO DELUXE.

SHOPPING

For the most part, shopping here is limited to establishments in Lopez Village. **Archipelago** sells cotton T-shirts and women's casual apparel. Limited hours during the off-season. ~ Lopez Village Road; 360-468-3222. **Islehaven Books and Borzoi** stocks an admirable selection of new books and regional music. ~ 210 Lopez Village Road; 360-468-2132. For fine art, visit **Chimera Gallery**, the cooperative showcase for prints, paintings, weaving, pottery, handblown glass and jewelry produced by local artists. Closed Tuesday in June; closed Tuesday and Wednesday the rest of the year. ~ Lopez Village Road; 360-468-3265.

Sometimes there's nothing quite like a picnic to cap off a pleasant daytrip. **Blossom Organic Grocery** stocks organic and natural treats, beverages and lunch fixings. If you'd rather have someone else do the work for you, there's also pre-packaged sandwiches as well as a small deli counter. ~ 135B Lopez Road, Lopez Island; 360-468-2204.

BEACHES & PARKS

SPENCER SPIT STATE PARK This long stretch of silky sand on Lopez Island encloses an intriguing salt-water lagoon. The mile-long beach invites clamming, crabbing, shrimping, bottom fishing, wading and swimming during warm summer months. Facilities include restrooms, beach firepits and picnic shelters. Day use fee, $5. ~ Take the ferry from Anacortes to Lopez Island, then follow the five-mile route to the park on the eastern shore of the island; 360-468-2251.

▲ There are 37 standard sites ($19 per night) and 7 primitive sites ($14 per night). Closed November through February. Reservations: 888-226-7688.

San Juan Island

San Juan Island, the namesake of the archipelago, is a popular resort destination centered around the town of Friday Harbor. This 20-mile-long island has a colorful past stemming from a boundary dispute between the United States and Great Britain. The tension over who was entitled to the islands was embodied in American and British farmers whose warring over, get this, a pig, nearly sent the two countries to the battlefield. When an American farmer shot a British homesteader's pig caught rooting in his garden, ill feelings quickly escalated. Fortunately, cooler heads prevailed so that what is now referred to as the "Pig War" of 1859 only resulted in one casualty: the pig.

SIGHTS

The history of this little-known incident is chronicled through interpretive centers in the **San Juan Island National Historical Park**, which is composed of English Camp and American Camp.

A WHALE OF A TIME

If you're in town in mid-May, you likely can't miss the annual **Orca Festival of the San Juan Islands.** The three-day event includes a whale symposium, a Taste of Friday Harbor event complete with art and music, and whale and wildlife tours on land and sea. ~ www.orcafestival.com.

Located on West Valley Road at the north end of the island is **English Camp**, which features barracks, a formal garden, cemetery, guardhouse, hospital and commissary. **American Camp**, on Cattle Point Road at the south end of the island, is where the officers and laundress' quarters, and the Hudson Bay Company's Bellevue Sheep Farm remain. ~ 360-378-2240, fax 360-378-2615; www.nps.gov/sajh.

San Juan Historical Museum is located on the 1891 James King farmstead. The museum complex consists of the original farmhouse, milk house and carriage house, as well as the original county jail. A variety of memorabilia is displayed throughout, including American Indian baskets and stone implements, an antique diving suit, period furniture and clothing. A great place to learn about the region's maritime history, the museum also features an excellent collection highlighting the region's proud past. Hours vary seasonally, so call ahead. ~ 405 Price Street, Friday Harbor; phone/fax 360-378-3949; www.sjmuseum.org, e-mail curator@sjmuseum.org.

HIDDEN ►

Oyster lovers and birdwatchers should make the trip down the dusty road to **Westcott Bay Sea Farms**, where they'll find saltwater bins of live oysters, mussels and clams (available in spring and summer only) and an array of birds attracted to the oyster beds that stretch out into the bay. Closed Sunday in winter. ~ 904 Westcott Drive, Friday Harbor; 360-378-2489, fax 360-378-6388; www.westcottbay.com, e-mail kathleen@westcottbay.com.

The lavender fields at **Pelindaba Lavender Farm** are awash with color in the summertime, the best time to visit this working organic farm. An old farmhouse serves as the general store here, offering all things lavender, from soaps and essential oils to honey, pepper and even vinegar. Self-guided tours and signage explain the farming and distilling operations. Closed Monday through Thursday in October. Closed Monday and Tuesday from October to December; closed January to April. ~ 33 Hawthorne Lane, Friday Harbor; 360-378-4248, 866-819-1911, fax 360-378-8946; www.pelindaba.com, e-mail admin@pelindaba.com.

The fir-paneled tasting room at **San Juan Vineyards** was once a one-room schoolhouse. And they still hand out lessons here—but they're a lot more fun than arithmetic. Instead, you'll learn all about the unusual varietals, like Madeleine Angevine and Siegerrebe, grown on this pretty semi-wooded patch of excellent grape-growing land. This is an up-and-coming island outpost of Washington's burgeoning wine industry. Closed in January and on the weekends in February. ~ 3136 Roche Harbor Road, Friday Harbor; 360-378-9463, fax 360-378-2668; www.sanjuanvineyards.com, e-mail sjvineyards@rockisland.com.

Afterglow Vista is the mausoleum of one of the region's wealthy families. The structure itself is fascinating; an open, Grecian-style columned complex surrounds six inscribed chairs, each containing the ashes of a family member, set before a round table of limestone. A seventh chair and column have obviously been removed, some say as part of Masonic ritual, others believe because a member of the family was disinherited or because the seventh member considered life unending. ~ Roche Harbor Resort, 4950 Reuben Tarte Memorial Drive, Roche Harbor.

LODGING

Conveniently located one and a half blocks from the ferry terminal, **Harrison House Suites** provides home-away-from-home comfort in five spacious suites. The suites, set in a turn-of-the-20th-century Craftsman and a 1930s cottage, sleep from two to ten guests and include private baths and kitchens. Most have sundecks and two have private outdoor hot tubs while one features a wood stove and upright piano. In addition, laundry facilities, bikes and kayaks are available. For those without the luxury of an in-room whirlpool, relax in the outdoor hot tub. Transportation from the ferry can be provided by request. Full gourmet breakfast and afternoon tea are included. ~ 235 C Street,

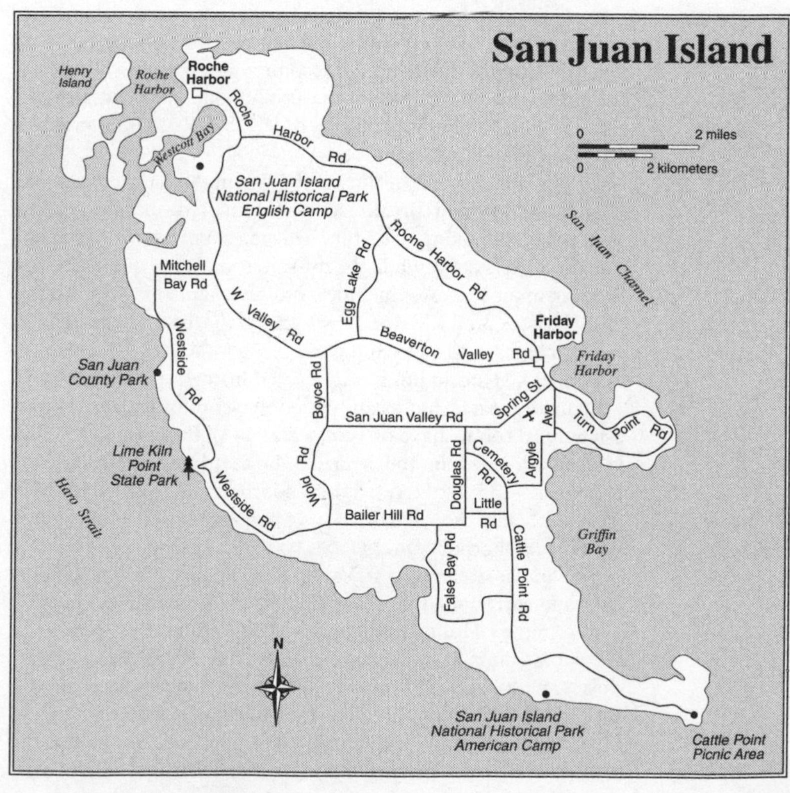

Friday Harbor; 360-378-3587, 800-407-7933, fax 360-378-2270; www.harrisonhousesuites.com, e-mail innkeeper@harrisonhouse suites.com. DELUXE TO ULTRA-DELUXE.

Named for its view, **Olympic Lights** is a remodeled 1895 farmhouse set on five grassy, breeze-tossed acres overlooking the Olympic Peninsula across the Strait of Juan de Fuca. Guests kick off their shoes before heading up to the cream-carpeted second floor with three comfortably appointed, pastel-shaded rooms; a fourth room on the ground floor is also available. You'll find no frilly, Victoriana clutter here, just a peaceful night snuggled under down comforters topped off by a farm-fresh breakfast. ~ 146 Starlight Way, Friday Harbor; 360-378-3186, 888-211-6195, fax 360-378-2097; www.olympiclights.com, e-mail olympiclights@ rockisland.com. DELUXE.

The **Tower House Bed & Breakfast** is a romantic Queen Anne–style B&B located on ten acres overlooking the San Juan Valley. It features two large suites with private baths and sitting rooms. Its crown jewel is the tower room with a tufted window seat and stained-glass window. Popular with honeymooners, the Tower House strives to cater to its guests every need. A large vegetarian breakfast is served on fine china and antique linens. If given notice, the owners will accommodate vegans. Of course, no inn would be complete without a couple of friendly cats. ~ 392 Little Road, Friday Harbor; 360-378-5464, 800-858-4276; www.san-juan-island.com. ULTRA-DELUXE.

If you've dreamed of life on the water, you'll appreciate the **Wharfside Bed and Breakfast**, a 60-foot, two-masted sailboat with two guest rooms. The forward stateroom with a queen and bunkbeds feels cozy, while the aft stateroom with queen bed is a little roomier. The rates include a cruise in summer. ~ Port of Friday Harbor; 360-378-5661; www.fridayharborlodging.com, e-mail slowseason@rockisland.com. DELUXE TO ULTRA-DELUXE.

Friday's Historic Inn is a renovated historic inn with 15 individually decorated rooms, all with down comforters and wildlife art. Several rooms have private jacuzzis. All this romance is conveniently located in the heart of Friday Harbor. Continental breakfast. ~ 35 1st Street, Friday Harbor; 360-378-5848, 800-352-2632, fax 360-378-2881; www.friday-harbor.com, e-mail stay@friday-harbor.com. DELUXE TO ULTRA-DELUXE.

Set in the rolling West Valley near English Camp National Park and surrounded by a working ranch, **States Inn & Ranch** is a bit of Sleepy Hollow in San Juan. Each of the ten rooms has a decor that hints at its namesake state—tiny Rhode Island comes closest, with shells and brass dolphins on the fireplace mantle, various renditions of ships on the walls and copies of the New England publication *Yankee* to peruse. The friendly and informative innkeepers and the multicourse country breakfasts with prize-winning dishes make up for the slight sulphur odor of the tap water. The inn is also disabled-accessible (hard to find in the islands), and menus can be arranged for special diets. Full breakfast. ~ 2687 West Valley Road, Friday Harbor; 360-378-6240, 866-602-2737; www.statesinn.com, e-mail ranch@statesinn.com. MODERATE TO ULTRA-DELUXE.

Roche Harbor has something for everyone. You can check in to the 1886 **Hotel de Haro**, where gingerbread trim, parlor beds, antiques and a roaring fireplace bring back memories of the good old days. In addition to this three-story, 20-room establishment, nine former workers' cottages have been converted into two-bedroom units, ideal for families. The cottages are convenient to the swimming pool. Also available are the **McMillin Suites**, newly constructed carriage houses for families or larger groups, and four luxury guest suites in the recently remodeled **McMillin Family Home**. Each suite has a king-size bed, two TVs, a fireplace in the sitting room, a clawfoot iron bathtub, and lovely views of the harbor. For contemporary lodging, choose one- to three-room harbor-view condominiums. ~ 248 Reuben Memorial Drive, Roche Harbor; 360-378-2155, 800-451-8910, fax 360-378-6809; www.rocheharbor.com, e-mail roche@rocheharbor.com. MODERATE TO ULTRA-DELUXE.

DINING

The Blue Dolphin is an unpretentious diner serving hearty portions of home-cooked breakfast favorites like biscuits and gravy, eggs Benedict, blueberry pancakes and chicken-fried steak. No dinner. ~ 185 1st Street, Friday Harbor; 360-378-6116. BUDGET.

Among the best restaurants on the island, the rustic look and rural setting of the **Duck Soup Inn** hardly hints at the creative bill of fare. Several seafood and beef options are available, but why not try the inn's namesake—duck stew seasoned with chipotle chiles, lime and cilantro or perhaps with African spices and lemon-zest dumplings? For starters, there are appetizers such as Westcott Bay home-smoked oysters or sea scallop ceviche; as well as fine Northwestern and European wines. Dinner only.

MUSIC WITH A VIEW

If you're around Orcas at the end of August, don't miss the annual **Orcas Island Chamber Music Festival**. Created by a group of Seattle-based professional musicians, this event features both classical and experimental pieces performed by internationally renowned musicians. This very brief concert series always sells out, so call ahead for tickets. ~ P.O. Box 646, Eastsound, WA 98245; 360-376-6636, 866-492-0003; www.oicmf.org.

Closed November through March. Call for hours. ~ 50 Duck Soup Lane, Friday Harbor; 360-378-4878; www.ducksoupinn.com. ULTRA-DELUXE.

SHOPPING

Most of the shops are located within blocks of Friday Harbor, giving you plenty to do while waiting for the ferry. Near Sunshine Alley, **Cotton Cotton Cotton** (360-378-3531) sells original screenprint art on cotton sportswear, natural fiber clothing, dance shoes and custom jewelry. ~ 165 1st Street, Friday Harbor.

If you've never donned an alpaca sweater or coat, you're in for a treat. An animal closely related to the llama, alpacas are renowned for their long, silky wool. At **Krystal Acres Alpaca Ranch & Country Store**, you buy all manner of alpaca wear and stuffed toys. ~ 152 Blazing Tree Road, Friday Harbor; 360-378-6125, fax 360-370-5330; www.krystalacres.com.

At Krystal Acres Alpaca Ranch & Country Store, you can tour the ranch and come face to face with a herd of these South American mammals. Be sure to call ahead.

Art lovers visiting Friday Harbor will want to stop by several galleries. **Waterworks Gallery** features a collection of contemporary eclectic Northwest art in media such as glass, sculpture, oil and watercolor. Limited hours in winter. ~ 315 Spring Street, Friday Harbor; 360-378-3060; www.waterworksgallery.com, e-mail info@waterworksgallery.com. **The Garuda & I** carries an amazing selection of ethnic arts, beads, crafts, musical instruments as well as jewelry from local artisans. ~ 60 1st Street, Friday Harbor; 866-488-5294; www.thegarudaandi.com.

NIGHTLIFE

On San Juan Island, **Herb's Tavern** is the local sidle-up-to-the-bar joint with pool tables. ~ 80 1st Street, Friday Harbor; 360-378-7076. To watch the game on several TVs visit **Haley's Bait Shop**, a sports bar and grill. ~ 175 Spring Street, Friday Harbor; 360-378-4434. The **Roche Harbor Resort Lounge** has weekend dancing to live music in the summer. ~ 248 Reuben Memorial Drive, Roche Harbor; 360-378-2155.

BEACHES & PARKS

SAN JUAN COUNTY PARK Orca whales frequently pass by the rocky shoreline of this 12-acre park on the western edge of San Juan Island. Swimming is good in the shallow, protected bay; fishing is fair for bottomfish, rockfish, salmon and crab. There are restrooms, picnic tables and fire pits. ~ On Westside Road just north of Lime Kiln Point State Park; 360-378-8420, fax 360-378-2075; www.co.san-juan.wa.us/parks, e-mail parks@co.san-juan.wa.us.

▲ There are 20 standard sites ($25 per night), two mooring buoys ($8 per night) and one premium site ($50 per night). Group camping sites for up to 30 people are available. Reservations: 360-378-1842.

LIME KILN POINT STATE PARK Situated on a rocky bluff overlooking Haro Strait, the park is named for an early lime kiln operation, with remnants of old structures still visible to the north of the lighthouse. The bluff is the prime whale-watching spot on San Juan Island. A footpath takes you to picturesque Lime Kiln Lighthouse, listed on the National Register of Historic Places. Restrooms, picnic tables and interpretive displays are found here. ~ Off Westside Road on the western shore of San Juan Island; 360-378-2044.

CATTLE POINT NATURAL AREA Though it takes a precarious scramble down a rocky ledge to reach it and picnic tables on the bluff above lend little privacy, this gravelly half-moon is arguably the prettiest public beach on San Juan Island. Anglers will find bottomfish and salmon. Facilities include picnic tables, shelter, restrooms, interpretive signs and a nature trail. ~ Follow Cattle Point Road through American Camp and on to the southern tip of the island. ~ 360-856-3500, fax 360-856-2150.

FOURTH OF JULY BEACH This secluded, gravelly crescent is where the locals head when they're looking for privacy. There are often bald eagles nesting in the nearby trees, a poignant sign of this aptly named stretch. The shallow, little bay area extends out a long way and is suitable for wading on hot days. Anglers can try for bottomfish and salmon. There are pit toilets, picnic tables and a fenced grassy area off the parking lot suitable for frisbee. Large groups should call for a permit. ~ Located on the northeastern edge of American Camp; 360-378-2240, fax 360-378-2996.

Orcas Island

Trendy, artsy-craftsy and lovely to look at, Orcas Island is a resort that caters to everyone from backpackers to the well-to-do. A nature sanctuary pocketed with charming towns, the island also boasts more sun than some of its neighbors.

SIGHTS

HIDDEN

One of Orcas Island's leading landmarks is **Rosario Resort & Spa.** Even if you're not planning to stay here during your trip, make sure to visit the original mansion here for a fantastic evening show that includes music performed on a 1910 Steinway grand piano and an amazing pipe organ along with entertaining narration and slides of life on the island in the early 1900s. Call ahead for show schedule. ~ 1400 Rosario Road, Eastsound; 360-376-2222, fax 360-376-2289; www.rosarioresort.com.

Of the many small historical museums in the San Juans, the **Orcas Island Historical Museum** is our favorite. Six interconnected log cabins of prominent early settlers house a fine assemblage of artifacts representing the culture of the Coast Salish and area homesteaders. Island industry, home and social life, farming and oral histories comprise some of the featured exhibits. Closed Monday and from October through May. Admission. Note: The museum will be closed for renovations until 2009. ~ 184 North Beach Road, Eastsound; 360-376-4849; www.orcasmuseum.org, e-mail orcasmuseum@rockisland.com.

HIDDEN ► **Madrona Point**, a pretty madrone tree–dotted waterside park saved from condo development by the Lummi Indians and local residents, is a fine spot for a picnic. It's at the end of the unmarked road just past Christina's Restaurant in Eastsound. No dogs are allowed.

LODGING

Overlooking the water and shrouded by giant trees is **Wescott Woods,** one of Orcas Island's best-kept secrets. The rustic two-bedroom cabin was built from reclaimed materials found at historic sites on San Juan Island and includes a full kitchen with a wood stove, a laundry area and an herb garden available for guest use. Both bedrooms feature a platform full-sized bed, a deck and a skylight that provides a natural glow throughout the day. Privately owned, this tranquil getaway is perfect for rest and relaxation. Closed November through March. Three-night minimum. ~ Call for specific directions; 206-320-9127; www.westcottwoods.com, e-mail sungrebe@mac.com. DELUXE.

A stay at **Turtleback Farm Inn** is like stepping into the much-loved story *The Wind in the Willows*, surrounded as it is by acres of forest and farm tracts full of animals as far as the eye can see. Rooms in this lovely, late-19th-century farmhouse vary in size and setup, but all 11 rooms have a charming mix of contemporary and antique furniture, cozy quilts and antique fixtures in private baths. The newer Orchard House offers four spacious rooms with king-sized beds, a sofa sitting area, a gas fireplace, a dining corner, refrigerators and large decks overlooking the valley. Full breakfast. ~ 1981 Crow Valley Road, Eastsound; 360-376-4914,

AUTHOR FAVORITE

When you want to really get away from it all, a stay at the **Laughing Moon Farm** fits the bill. Set on 21 acres of farm and woodlands on Eastsound Bay, there's not much to do but relax, explore nature and visit the resident sheep and llama. Accommodations consist of three cabins that may appear rustic on the outside but are fully equipped and can sleep up to eight people; one offers a fireplace and a view of the bay. It's a great place to catch up on some reading or soak up that legendary Puget Sound beauty. ~ Call ahead or visit the website for specific directions; 360-376-7879; www.laughingmoonfarm.com, e-mail laughingmoonfarm@yahoo.com. ULTRA-DELUXE.

800-376-4914, fax 360-376-5329; www.turtlebackinn.com, e-mail info@turtlebackinn.com. DELUXE TO ULTRA-DELUXE.

The **Outlook Inn** is right in Eastsound, overlooking the bay and close to the town's many shops and restaurants. A classic turn-of-the-20th-century maritime inn, it's been restored with light pine and fir floors and wood furnishings helping bring in the light off the harbor. In addition to the original inn, there are 16 contemporary suites. The inn's restaurant focuses on organic and seasonal ingredients, and serves breakfasts seasonally. ~ Main Street, Eastsound; 360-376-2200, 888-688-5665, fax 360-376-2256; www.outlookinn.com, e-mail info@outlookinn.com. MODERATE TO ULTRA-DELUXE.

It's not unusual to find semi-tame deer roaming around the ample grounds of **Rosario Resort & Spa**, tucked away on Cascade Bay on the east side of the horseshoe of Orcas Island. The motel-style rooms scattered along the waterfront or perched on the hillside overlooking the bay are spacious and comfortable; some feature fireplaces and private balconies. Three pools, a fitness room, a jacuzzi and sauna round out the amenities. A marina is available for guests arriving by boat. ~ 1400 Rosario Road, Eastsound; 360-376-2222, 800-562-8820, fax 360-376-2289; www.rosarioresort.com, e-mail info@rosarioresort.com. ULTRA-DELUXE.

Expect a wide variety of accommodations at the funky **Doe Bay Resort & Retreat**, including hostel beds, camping, yurts and cabins, some of which are fully equipped. There are shared central bathrooms, a community kitchen and a small seasonal café on the grounds of this large retreat along with a splendid three-tiered sauna and three mineral baths perched on a covered deck. Clothing optional. Be aware of the strict 14-day, advance-notice cancellation policy. ~ 107 Doe Bay Road, Olga; 360-376-2291, fax 360-376-5809; www.doebay.com, e-mail contact@doebay.com. BUDGET TO ULTRA-DELUXE.

DINING

Bilbo's Festivo specializes in Southwestern fare. A margarita or *cerveza* on the tiled garden patio surrounded by adobe walls is a great way to relax. Bilbo's serves dinner only, but opens **La Taqueria,** a lunch outlet in the courtyard, during the summer. ~ North Beach Road, Eastsound; 360-376-4728. BUDGET TO MODERATE.

The Restaurant at the Deer Harbor Inn, is tucked away in an expanse of orchard grove peering out over Deer Harbor and the Olympic Range and is where locals come for that special night out. The daily menu is chalked on the board; rock cod, coho salmon and choice steaks are prime picks. For diners on the deck, this is a great spot to watch the sunset. Dinner only; reservations recommended. ~ 33 Inn Lane, Deer Harbor; 360-376-1040, 877-377-4110, fax 360-376-2237; www.deerharborinn.com, e-mail stay@deerharborinn.com. DELUXE TO ULTRA-DELUXE.

SHOPPING

An 1866 cabin houses the original **Crow Valley Pottery & Gallery**, a long-established studio that got its start making ceramic wind bells inspired by Northwest tribal arts. It has expanded to represent numerous island artists and craftspeople working in art glass, metal sculpture, watercolors, jewelry, pastels and more. ~ 2274 Orcas Road, Eastsound; 360-376-4260, fax 360-376-6495; www.crowvalleypottery.com, e-mail pottery@crowvalley.com.

HIDDEN ►

Don't spend all your time and money in Eastsound proper because you won't want to miss **Orcas Island Pottery**, the oldest existing craft studio on Orcas. You can watch potters at work through the windows of the studio while your kids enjoy the onsite treehouse. ~ 338 Old Pottery Road, off West Beach Road, Eastsound; 360-376-2813; www.orcasislandpottery.com, e-mail orcaspots@rockisland.com.

The Right Place has pottery strewn about the garden and in the showroom. In the summertime you can try using the wheel yourself. ~ 2915 Enchanted Forest Road, Eastsound; 360-376-4023; www.rightplacepottery.com.

HIDDEN ►

At a bend in Horseshoe Highway as you reach Olga is **Orcas Island Artworks**, the cooperative art gallery showcasing fine arts, handicrafts and furniture all produced locally. Closed January to mid-February. ~ 360-376-4408; www.orcasartworks.com.

Sallie Bell Designs carries a curious selection of boutique items—jewelry and clothing, both elegant and casual. ~ 140 Sedum Hill Road, Orcas; 360-376-2275; www.monkeypuzzle.com.

NIGHTLIFE

Moran Lounge is the place to go for live entertainment throughout the year. ~ Rosario Resort, 1400 Rosario Road, Eastsound; 360-376-2222.

For convivial pub action, step into the **Lower Tavern** and amuse yourself with darts and pool. Beer and wine only. ~ 1 Prune Alley and Main Street, Eastsound; 360-376-4848.

HIDDEN ►

Or hang out in **The Living Room**, a yoga studio/community arts center that hosts concerts, poetry readings, storytelling and stand-up comedy. ~ 474 North Beach Road, Eastsound.

BEACHES & PARKS

MORAN STATE PARK Washington's fifth-largest park consists of 5252 verdant acres dotted with five freshwater lakes and crowned by sweeping Mt. Constitution. There are 38 miles of forest trails connecting the four mountain lakes, numerous waterfalls and five campgrounds. There is fishing for rainbow, cutthroat and kokanee trout on several lakes, with boat rentals available seasonally. Facilities include restrooms, showers, kitchen shelters and picnic tables. ~ Located near Eastsound, accessible by state ferry from Anacortes; 360-376-2326, fax 360-376-2360.

▲ There are 136 standard sites ($19 to $22 per night) and 15 primitive sites ($14 per night). Reservations: 888-226-7688.

OBSTRUCTION PASS STATE PARK This primitive, heavily forested locale located on the southeastern tip of Orcas Island is tricky to get to, so the crowds are kept to a minimum, a reward for those who care to search it out. The area has a hiking trail, campsites and a beach with cold water for brave swimmers. Anglers will find bottomfish and rockfish. There are vault toilets, picnic tables and trails. ~ From the town of Olga follow Point Lawrence Road east, turn right on Obstruction Pass Road and keep right on Trailhead Road until you hit the parking area. From there it's a half-mile hike to the campground; 360-376-2326, fax 360-376-2360.

◄HIDDEN

▲ There are ten, hike-in, primitive sites ($14 per night); no potable water.

OTHER PARKS Many of the smaller islands are preserved as state parks including **Doe, Jones, Clark, Sucia, Stuart, Posey, Blind, James, Matia, Patos** and **Turn**. They are accessible by boat only and in most cases have a few primitive campsites, nature trails, a dock or mooring buoys off secluded beaches, but no water (except Jones, Stuart and Sucia, in season) or facilities except for composting toilets. Costs are $10 for mooring buoys, $12 for camping, $10 plus $.50 per foot for boats to dock overnight. Washington watertrail sites cost $12 per night and must be reached by a beachable human-powered watercraft. For more information, contact Washington State Parks: 360-902-8844, e-mail infocent@parks.wa.gov.

Outdoor Adventures

BOATING

Spending time on the water is a part of daily life here, and certainly something that visitors should not miss. In fact, many of the 100-plus islands of the San Juans are accessible only by boat. Rental options are numerous; on the mainland, contact **Fairhaven Boatworks** for kayaks, rowboats and sailboats. Closed Monday and weekdays in winter. ~ 501 Harris Avenue, Bellingham; 360-714-8891; www.whatcomboatworks.org.

In the islands, try **North Isle Sailing**, which offers sea cruises around Whidbey, the San Juans and Canada. Trips last from a half day to a week. ~ 1856 North Swantown Road, Oak Harbor; 360-675-8360, 800-580-8360; www.northislesailing.com.

Captain Bob Plank of **Viking Cruises** has been leading tours since 1979 aboard his wooden-hulled custom-built boat, which holds 49 people. Choose from a wide variety of trips including a three-hour Skagit Bay float and crabfeast. In winter, consider taking a birdwatching tour to see the more than 200 species that flock to the islands. ~ 109 North 1st Street, La Conner; 360-466-2639; www.vikingcruises.com.

Fortunate divers may encounter the giant Pacific octopus on their deep-sea adventure. The largest of its species in the world, it's relatively docile unless provoked.

Skipper Ward Fay of **Classic Daysailing** offers sunset and day sails in a classic 1940s Blanchard Sloop "Aura" from Deer Harbor in Orcas Island. Excursions range from three to eight hours. Personalized as well as dinner trips to Friday Harbor are available. ~ 360-376-5581 (May 1 through September 30); www.classicdaysails.com, e-mail wardfay@rockisland.com.

SPORT-FISHING

Catching some salmon is the hoped-for reward when you head out on a fishing charter through Northern Puget Sound and the San Juan Islands. As a bonus, you're also likely to encounter seals, eagles and whales as you sail past islands wooded with red-bark madrone trees.

In winter, of course, the temperature on the water can get chilly and the water a bit choppy. All the charter fishing services listed here provide boats with heated, enclosed cabins to keep you comfortable. Charter fees include bait and tackle, but do not include a fishing license or food and drink.

NORTHERN PUGET SOUND **Jim's Salmon Charter** specializes in arranging full-day trips to fisheries in the San Juan and Canadian islands for groups of no more than six people. Jim has more than three decades of experience. Bait, tackle and license are included. ~ Marine Drive, Blaine Marina; 360-332-6724; www.jimssalmoncharter.com.

In Everett, Gary Krein is president of the Charter Boat Association of Puget Sound and owner of **All Star Fishing Charters.** He operates a 28-foot fiberglass-bottom boat that can carry up to six people each, and encourages "angler participation" on his full-day trips (two daily in summer, one in winter). The boat comes fully equipped with electronic fishfinding equipment that seeks out the salmon and bottomfish. Bait and tackle are in-

SOUND BITE

With thousands of miles of tidal coastline, Puget Sound and the San Juan Islands once boasted some of the best sportfishing opportunities in North America. These days, the fish—especially salmon—are in great peril from various abuses. For the present, there are still five varieties of Pacific salmon (chinook, coho, chum, pink and sockeye), and anglers can also try for cod, flounder, halibut, ling, rockfish, sea perch, squid and sturgeon. Scuba divers often concentrate their efforts on harvesting abalone, crab, octopus, shrimp and squid, while shellfishers are rewarded with butter and razor clams. Clamming and fishing licenses are required and are available in sporting goods stores. For more information, contact Washington's Department of Fish and Wildlife. ~ 360-902-2700; www.wdfw.wa.gov/fishcorn.htm, e-mail fishregs@dfw.wa.gov.

cluded. ~ Port of Everett; 425-252-4188, 800-214-1595; www.allstarfishing.com, e-mail gary@allstarfishing.com.

Mike Dunnigan is the skipper of **Sea Hawk Salmon Charters**. He runs year-round, exclusive eight-hour charters for up to four people to fish for salmon, bottomfish and halibut. Bait and tackle are included. ~ Skyland Marina, Anacortes; 360-424-1350; www.seahawksalmoncharters.com.

SAN JUAN ISLANDS **A Trophy Fishing Charters** will pick anglers up from the other islands before heading out on a four- to six-hour fishing trip seeking salmon and bottomfish in a 29-foot sportfisher that holds six. Captain Monty runs a fast boat (up to 30 mph), so travel time is reduced. ~ Friday Harbor; 360-378-2110; www.fishthesanjuans.com.

RIVER FISHING

Several rivers in the area—the Snohomish, Skykomish, Skagit and Sauk, for example—provide year-round catches, notably steelhead and all species of salmon except sockeye (it's not permitted to take this fish from rivers). **All Rivers Guide Service** offers customized, seven- to nine-hour fly-fishing trips in a 16-foot heated drift boat. All bait and tackle are included, and the knowledgeable professional guides also offer instruction in fishing. ~ 425-736-8920; www.allriversguideservice.com, e-mail mark@allriversguideservice.com.

KAYAKING

For nonadventurers who want an outdoor experience that's a lot of fun but not extremely challenging, a guided water excursion in a sea kayak may be just the thing. No previous kayaking experience is necessary to join one of these groups for a paddling tour on the gentle waters of Chuckanut Bay, with its sandstone formations near Bellingham; of sea caves around Deception Pass State Park on Whidbey Island; or off San Juan Island, where you are likely to see whales, seals and other marine wildlife. Unless noted, the operators listed here generally offer a regular schedule of excursions from April–May to September–October. Cost for a sea kayak excursion ranges from $30 to $60. Most operators can also arrange overnight or longer trips.

NORTHERN PUGET SOUND **Moondance Sea Kayaking Adventures** leads half-day to five-day trips to nearby locations such as Chuckanut Bay, Cypress Island and Clark's Point (where you'll see a fossil of the entire trunk of a palm tree). A slightly longer trip to sea caves occasionally heads down to Deception Pass State Park, where the wave action is rougher. ~ Bellingham; 360-738-7664; www.moondancekayak.com, e-mail sharmon@moondancekayak.com.

LOPEZ ISLAND **Lopez Kayaks** offers morning and afternoon sea-kayaking tours in double kayaks for eight people to

Text continued on page 266.

Whale Watching in the San Juan Islands

Here in the waters of the San Juan archipelago there are three resident pods, or extended families, of *Orcinus Orca*, otherwise known as "killer" whales. Because they are so frequently and easily spotted in the protected waters, these gentle black and white giants have been carefully studied by scientists since 1976.

Their research is documented at the **Whale Museum**, where you can learn more about whales. A photo collection with names and pod numbers will help you identify some of the 90 resident orcas, distinguished by their grayish saddle patches and nicks, scars or tears in the dorsal fins. There are displays of full-sized skeletons, videos and models of local marine mammals. Call ahead for winter hours. Admission. ~ 62 1st Street North, Friday Harbor; 360-378-4710, 800-946-7227, fax 360-378-5790; www.whalemuseum.org.

The Whale Museum also has an orca adoption program set up to help fund the ongoing research and all sorts of whale-related educational material, art and souvenirs available in their gift shop. They operate a 24-hour hotline (Washington only, 800-562-8832) for whale sightings and marine mammal strandings as well.

From May to September you can often see the whales from shore when they range closest to the islands to feed on migrating salmon. The best shoreline viewing spots are **Lime Kiln Point** on San Juan Island or **Shark Reef Park** on Lopez Island. Sightings drop dramatically in the winter as the pods disperse from the core area in search of prey.

If you want to get a closer look, put on your parka and sunglasses, grab your binoculars and camera and climb aboard one of the **wildlife cruises** that ply the waters between the islands. Even if you don't see any orca during the trip, you will almost certainly spot other interesting forms of wildlife such as sleek, gray minke whales, Dall's porpoises (which look like miniature orca), splotchy brown harbor seals, bald eagles, great blue heron, cormorants or tufted puffin.

Deer Harbor Charters offers four-hour whale-watching tours from April to October on a 36-foot boat that carries 20 people from Rosario Resort or on a 47-foot boat that carries 30 people from Deer Harbor Marina. Both boats have a naturalist guide. ~ P.O. Box 303, Deer Harbor, WA 98243; 360-376-5989, 800-544-5758; www.deerharborcharters.com.

Island Mariner Cruises boasts a high success rate for spotting whales. It's no wonder: the naturalist has worked there for years. Enjoy day-long nature and whale-watching expeditions with commentary on the history, flora and fauna of the San Juans as you cruise through the islands on a boat designed for whale watching that holds over 100 people. ~ 5 Harbor Loop, Bellingham; 360-734-8866, 877-734-8866; www.orcawatch.com, e-mail mariner@orcawatch.com.

Western Prince Cruises has similar naturalist-accompanied wildlife tours on a half-day basis. Boats normally carry fewer than 30 people and the environmentally friendly *Western Prince II* is powered by biodiesel. ~ Friday Harbor; 360-378-5315, 800-757-6722; www.orcawhalewatch.com. **Viking Cruises** offer three-hour nature tours to Deception Pass from La Conner. Their three-day excursion to Rosario Resort in Eastsound combines a crabfeast and pipe-organ concert with whale-watching trips. The captain claims an 80 percent success rate for spotting whales. ~ 109 North 1st Street, La Conner; 360-466-2639, 888-207-2333; www.vikingcruises.com. You can also try **San Juan Boat Tours Inc.** for a three-and-a-half-hour whale-sighting excursion aboard a 100-foot tour vessel. ~ Friday Harbor; 360-378-3499, 800-232-6722; www.whales.com.

Happy spotting!

MacKaye Harbor, which is also popular with seals. If you have experience, you can also rent a kayak for your own use without joining a tour or buy your own vessel, accessories or related books. Closed November through April. ~ 2845 Fisherman Bay Road; 360-468-2847; www.lopezkayaks.com.

SAN JUAN ISLAND Since the waters just off the west side of San Juan Island are in the main whale-migration corridor, your chances of seeing whales are good. If not, there's plenty of other wildlife to view, notably seals and bald eagles. (The highest density of bald-eagle nestings in the lower 48 states is in the San Juan Islands.) There are also kelp forests, jutting cliffs, sea caves and rocky outcroppings. A biologist or scientist accompanies the day excursions led by **Sea Quest Kayak Expeditions** for groups of four to twelve. There are also camping trips lasting from two to five days that go through primary orca viewing areas. ~ Friday Harbor; 360-378-5767, 888-589-4253; www.sea-quest-kayak.com. **Crystal Seas Kayaking** escorts up to ten people on morning or afternoon sunset excursions. You can also arrange custom camping trips from two to six days. Paddlers will see eagles, seals and whales. ~ Friday Harbor; 360-378-4223, 877-732-7787; www.crystalseas.com.

San Juan Islands' 172 named islands make up over 375 miles of shoreline. That's nearly as much saltwater shoreline as Washington and Oregon combined.

ORCAS ISLAND **Osprey Tours** brings a different, historical twist to half-day, full-day and overnight sea-kayaking tours. Following the Alaskan Aleut tradition, owner Randy Monge makes these woodframe kayaks with bifurcated (T-shaped) bows, which, he says, split the water and provide lift going through waves. Monge also gives each kayaker an Aleutian whale-hunter's hat, shaped like a conical visor that resembles a bird's beak. The hats helped disguise Aleutian hunters and, acting like a hearing aid, collect sound. ~ P.O. Box 580, Eastsound, WA 98245; 360-376-3677; www.ospreytours.com. For lessons or tours contact **Shearwater Sea Kayak Tours,** which offers half- and full-day tours. Custom overnight trips can also be arranged. Shearwater has also sold accessories and clothing since 1982, making it the oldest outfitter on the islands. ~ P.O. Box 787, Eastsound, WA 98245; 360-376-4699; www.shearwaterkayaks.com.

SCUBA DIVING

The protected waters of Puget Sound hold untold treasures for the diver: Craggy rock walls, ledges and caves of this sunken mountain range and enormous forests of bull kelp provide homes for a multitude of marine life. Giant Pacific octopus thrive in these waters, as do sea anemones and hundreds of species of fish.

"Within 15 minutes of Friday Harbor on San Juan Island, there are hundreds of great dive spots," says one local diver who grew up in the area. The west side of San Juan Island and the south side of Lopez Island are particular favorites, largely because the absence of silt means the water is cleaner and therefore clearer. There are also lots of ledges along these rocky coasts, which abound with exceptional wall-dive spots. Acres of bull kelp forests, with their teeming marine life, are also popular dive spots. But just as these waters hold great beauty, they can also be treacherous with tremendous tidal changes and strong currents.

NORTHERN PUGET SOUND **Washington Divers, Inc.** offers complete rental and diving services, including a full schedule of diving activities year-round, from one-day trips to two-week-long international excursions. A one-day dive charter to the San Juan Islands is the most popular trip. In the summer, extended daylight hours make it possible to make up to two dives during the six- to seven-hour trip. The shop also runs night dives and a free "come along" beach dive at least two weekend days a month. Scuba certification classes (open water) are also available. ~ 903 North State Street, Bellingham; 360-676-8029, fax 360-647-5028; www.washingtondivers.com, e-mail hurricanejones@comcast.net.

WHIDBEY ISLAND Besides air fills, diving lessons and rental of wetsuits and other equipment, **Whidbey Island Dive Center** offers half- to full-day dive charters using two tanks per dive. One popular spot for experienced divers is under the bridge at Deception Pass State Park, where currents reach seven knots—"a diving rush." For the less experienced, the charter to the diving sanctuary off Keystone Jetty is an excellent spot to view marine life. The Dive Center also teaches all types of certification. ~ 1020 Northeast 7th Avenue #1, Oak Harbor; 360-675-1112, 360-679-2247; www.whidbeydive.com, e-mail info@whidbeydive.com.

SAN JUAN ISLAND **Island Dive & Water Sports** is a full-service dive shop, retail and rental. It specializes in daily half-day charters, guaranteeing you at least two dives using one tank per dive, in different locations during the trip. One might be a vertical wall dive, another may be in a grotto filled with marine life. Its vessels can accommodate up to 18 divers. Open-water certification classes are also available. Closed Wednesday and Thursday. ~ 2-A Spring Street Landing, Friday Harbor; 360-378-2772, 800-303-8386; www.divesanjuan.com, e-mail info@divesanjuan.com. **Underwater Sports Inc.** offers full-day chartered trips to the islands, night dives, rentals, open-water certification, classes and air fills. ~ 205 East Casino Road, Everett; 425-355-3338; www.underwatersports.com, e-mail everett@underwatersports.com.

SHELLFISHING

Many of the public parks and tidelands in north Puget Sound offer clamming opportunities in season. Licenses are necessary, and it's imperative to check first with the **Red Tide Hotline**. Shellfish poisoning can be deadly. ~ 800-562-5632.

Beaches in the immediate Seattle area are often polluted as well; most outlying beaches are safe until late summer. For information on seasons, licenses and limits, call the **Washington Department of Fish & Wildlife.** ~ 1111 Washington Street, 360-902-2200. Most sporting goods and fishing supply stores sell licenses.

One of the best beaches is on Whidbey Island. **Double Bluff State Tidelands** is a long beach stretch looking south across Useless Bay. This is a fine place for a walk; the beach stretches two miles to the headland, and the southern exposure means it's warm on almost any sunny day.

It's also a top-notch spot during low tides to dig for steamer clams and for the native Washington butter clam, which is excellent for steaming or chowder. Clams and mussels are available year-round, but there are no oysters. ~ At the end of Double Bluff Road, turn west off State Route 525 about ten miles west of Clinton, a mile north of the Langley turnoff.

RIDING STABLES

Saddle up for a gentle, leisurely ride around an 85-acre ranch or take in the scenic beauty of the San Juan Islands.

NORTHERN PUGET SOUND A year-round operation, **Lang's Pony and Horse Farm** takes up to 14 riders on a leisurely guided trail ride (half-hour to two hours) around the hilly and wooded ranch, which is about 30 miles south of Bellingham. The farm also offers a Mom's Camp so mothers can ride in tranquility, as well as summer camps and riding lessons. Call for reservations. ~ 21463 Little Mountain Road, Mt. Vernon; 360-424-7630; www.comeride.com.

WHIDBEY ISLAND Put on jeans and a pair of sturdy leather shoes (leave your Birkenstocks and sneakers at home) for a guided trail ride through the hilly, wooded **Madrona Ridge Ranch**. Please call ahead (evenings are best) to arrange a one-and-a-half-hour ride; groups are limited to up to two people at a time. Riding lessons are available for all ages, but the trail rides are for teens and adults only. Nonriders can enjoy nature walks and the nearby beach. ~ Madrona Way, Coupeville; 360-678-4124.

GOLF

Award-winning design, lush scenery and the Northwest's only par-5 to an island green are among the distinctions of golf courses in this part of the state.

NORTHERN PUGET SOUND **Dakota Creek** was named one of the most challenging 18-hole courses by the Pacific Northwest Golf Association. This public course, carved out of a mountain, is quiet, well maintained and hilly. ~ 3258 Haynie Road, Custer; 360-366-3131, 888-465-3515; www.dakotacreekgolf.com.

The 18th hole at **Homestead Farms Golf Course** is the Northwest's only par-5 on an island green. The public course is flat, but has lots of water. ~ 115 East Homestead Boulevard, Lynden; 360-354-1196, 800-354-1196; www.homesteadfarmsgolf.com.

A good choice is the **Walter E. Hall Memorial Golf Course,** an 18-hole public facility with well-kept grounds, a restaurant and cart rentals. ~ 1226 West Casino Road, Everett; 425-353-4653; www.walterhallgolf.com. The 18-hole **Kayak Point Golf Course** has an 18-hole putting course, a driving range, a full-service restaurant and lounge, and cart, shoe and club rentals. ~ 15711 Marine Drive, Stanwood; 360-652-9676. **Overlook Golf Course**, a nine-hole public course with a view of Big Lake, offers club and cart rentals. ~ 17523 State Route 9, Mt. Vernon; 360-422-6444.

It's easy to tell when the chinook salmon are running—bald eagles line up along the river banks, eagerly awaiting their shimmering prey.

There's a hilly front nine at **Lake Padden Municipal Golf Course**, located in Lake Padden Park. It's a tight, densely treed public course. ~ 4882 Samish Way, Bellingham; 360-738-7400; www.lakepaddengolf.com. **Sudden Valley Golf and Country Club** is an 18-hole semiprivate course that sits on a lake. There are cart rentals, a driving range and a snack shop. ~ 4 Club House Circle, Bellingham; 360-734-6435; www.suddenvalleygolfclub.com.

The most expensive course (up to $65 greens fees) in the area is the semiprivate **Semiahmoo Golf and Country Club.** It's ranked as one of nation's best resort courses and was designated as a sectional qualifying course for the 1997 U.S. Open. The 18-hole, par-72 course was designed by Arnold Palmer; hole number 4 has a scenic view of Mt. Baker and the valley beyond. ~ 9565 Semiahmoo Parkway, Blaine; 360-371-7015.

The **Avalon Golf Club** has the hottest new links around the Sound. The 27-hole public course will keep you busy for a while. You can rent pull-carts, too. ~ 19345 Kelleher Road, Burlington; 360-757-1900; www.avalonlinks.com.

FIDALGO ISLAND **Similk Beach Golf Course** is a public 18-hole facility that rents carts. ~ 12518 Christiansen Road, Anacortes; 360-293-3444.

LOPEZ ISLAND The nine-hole **Lopez Island Golf Course** is a private, flat course. ~ 589 Airport Road, Lopez Island; 360-468-2679; www.lopezislandgolfclub.com.

SAN JUAN ISLAND It's only nine holes, but the **San Juan Golf and Country Club** "plays like 18." Private, but open to the public, the course is set on a wooded, rolling tract next to Griffin Bay. Cart rentals are available. ~ 806 Golf Course Road, Friday Harbor; 360-378-2254; www.sanjuangolf.com.

ORCAS ISLAND For a distinctive, lesser-known golf experience, try the **Orcas Island Golf Club**, a quaint, challenging 9-hole public course that plays like an 18-hole course. The regular nine alternates tees on the back nine to make play a little more interesting. The pro shop and clubhouse are like a touch of Scotland, and wildlife abounds. ~ 2171 Orcas Road, Eastsound; 360-376-4400; www.orcagolf.com.

TENNIS

No need to leave your racquet at home with so many public courts to take advantage of. In Everett, you'll find six first-come, first-served lighted courts at **Clark Park.** ~ 2400 Lombard Street. Or try the courts at **Fairhaven Park** in Bellingham. ~ 107 Chuckanut Drive; 360-676-6985.

On Whidbey Island, you can use the four lighted courts at **Coupeville High School** at South Main Street or the four clay courts at **Oak Harbor City Park** at 1501 City Beach Street. On Fidalgo Island, try the six courts at **Anacortes High School facility.** ~ 20th Street and J Avenue. On San Juan, try the four courts at the **Friday Harbor High School** at Guard Street or head out to the **Roche Harbor Resort** at Roche Harbor Road.

BIKING

For bicycling in the Bellingham area, the best map is "Bicycling in Bellingham and Whatcom County," which outlines trails according to traffic volume, surface status (gravel, paved, etc.) and hill difficulty; it also categorizes trails as City Ride, City Trail or Country Ride. The map is available in many bicycle stores and during the summer from the **Bellingham/Whatcom County Convention and Visitors Bureau.** ~ 904 Potter Street, Bellingham; 360-671-3990, 800-487-2032; www.bellingham.org.

The hardy cyclist might prefer a 20-mile hilly and winding route around San Juan Island or 16 miles of steep, twisting roads beginning at the ferry landing on Orcas Island.

For bike trails here and in other parts of the state, contact the **Washington Department of Transportation** to request a route map and informative brochure, or call 360-705-7277 for the Bicycle Hotline. ~ P.O. Box 47300, Olympia, WA 98504.

NORTHERN PUGET SOUND Some of the best country bike routes in the state can be found in the **Skagit and Nooksack val-**

CYCLE SAFELY

If you plan to bike on the San Juan Islands, it's important to remember that the islands' narrow roads don't have special lanes or other provisions for cyclists. Lopez Island is probably the best bet for the occasional bicyclist: you'll be able to bike long, flat country roads, rather than the steeper, twisting roads of some of the other islands. You can rent a bike on the island or in Anacortes before ferrying over for the day.

leys. Use the backroads east, northeast and southeast of La Conner to fashion loop tours from a few miles to over 20. Or, head for the north Skagit Valley and create a route using backroads starting in Bow on Chuckanut Drive, and heading west to Edison, south to Bay View, west over Bay View Ridge to Chuckanut Drive, then north back to Bow.

Do the same in the slightly hillier Nooksack Valley, beginning in Lynden and circuiting Sumas, Everson and Nooksack, before returning to Lynden.

There are no designated bike lanes along the dusty rural roads of Mt. Vernon, but you'll see rich fields and quiet lanes for miles.

Bellingham offers several bike routes, some arduous, some easy, all highlighting the scenery and history of the area. One is the moderate **Interurban Trail** (also known as the Chuckanut Trail). The seven-mile trail, which follows an old trolley route, begins at the Fairhaven Parkway and ends at Larrabee State Park. The best of the bunch is the fairly easy, 45-minute **Lake Padden Loop** in Lake Padden Park. It connects to a series of trails on **Mt. Galbraith**, a local hot spot for mountain biking.

WHIDBEY ISLAND Those looking for a long-distance ride will enjoy the 50-mile Island County Tour, which begins at Columbia Beach on Whidbey Island and continues on to Deception Pass at the northern tip of the island. This trip is moderately strenuous, with high traffic on a good portion of the ride, but the spectacular views of the Strait of Juan de Fuca and the Saratoga Passage are reward enough.

SAN JUAN ISLAND The slightly difficult, 30-mile **San Juan Island Loop** leads along hilly, winding roads through Friday Harbor, Roche Harbor, San Juan Island National Historical Park and along the San Juan Channel.

ORCAS ISLAND The **Horseshoe Route** is by far the most difficult island bike route, with 16 miles of steep, twisting roads beginning at the ferry landing in Orcas, continuing through Eastsound, then on to Olga. An alternative route for the very hardy starts in Olga, passes through Moran State Park and ends in Doe Bay, with a possible challenging 3.5-mile sidetrip up and back down Mt. Constitution.

Bike Rentals For mountain-bike sales and repairs in the Northern Puget Sound region, contact **The Bicycle Center.** ~ 4707 Evergreen Way, Everett; 425-252-1441. For year-round mountain-bike rentals, sales and repairs in the Bellingham area, try **Fairhaven Bike & Mountain Sports.** ~ 1108 11th Street, Bellingham; 360-733-4433.

Located off Route 20, the main drag into Anacortes, the **Skagit Cycle Center** rents bikes (and helmets) by the week. The center's location is ideal for cyclists heading to the San Juans ferry or just pedaling around nearby Skagit Valley. ~ 1620 Commercial Avenue, Anacortes; 360-588-8776; www.skagitcyclecenter.com.

Lopez Bicycle Works rents, repairs and sells mountain bikes, touring bikes and hybrids and will let you drop off the bike at the ferry landing when you leave for the day. Closed October through April. ~ 2847 Fisherman's Bay Road, Lopez Island; 360-468-2847; www.lopezbicycleworks.com.

For bike rentals on San Juan Island, contact **Island Bicycles**, which offers hybrids and road bikes, as well as bike sales, repairs and friendly advice. Limited winter hours. ~ 380 Argyle Avenue, Friday Harbor; 360-378-4941; www.islandbicycles.com.

Rent, buy or repair mountain bikes and hybrids on Orcas Island at **Dolphin Bay**, which also offers custom tours for 10 to 30 people. ~ Ferry Landing; 360-376-4157. Mountain bikes, road bikes, tandems, bike trailers and trail-a-bikes can be found for sale or rent at **Wildlife Cycles**, which also does repairs and offers off-road tours. ~ 350 North Beach Road, Eastsound; 360-376-4708; www.wildlifecycles.com.

HIKING

All distances listed for hiking trails are one way unless otherwise noted.

NORTHERN PUGET SOUND On the **Langus Riverfront Park Nature Trail** (2.5 miles) in Everett, hikers are likely to spot red-tailed hawk or gray heron as they make their way through towering spruce, red cedar and dogwood trees along the banks of the Snohomish River, past Union Slough and on toward Spencer Island, a protected haven for nesting ducks.

The Padilla Bay National Estuarine Reserve (360-428-1558) in the tiny community of Bay View (about six miles west of Burlington) offers the best hikes in the area. The **Padilla Bay Shore Trail** (2.3 miles) is a bicycle/pedestrian path with views of the estuary, mudflat, sloughs and tidal marsh. The Breazeale Interpretive Center is one mile north of the Shore Trail. Binoculars and trail guides can be checked out at the center to aid your exploration of the forest and meadow along the **Upland Trail** (.8 mile).

There are several good choices for hikes in Bellingham. The **Interurban Trail** (6 miles) begins near the entrance to Larrabee State Park and hugs the crest above Chuckanut Drive overlooking the bay and the San Juan Islands. Chuckanut Drive passes the rose gardens of Fairhaven Park on its way into the revitalized Fairhaven District of the city.

There are 5.9 miles of rolling trails through the lush **Sehome Hill Arboretum**, crowned by views of Mt. Baker and the San Juans from the observation tower at the summit. Since no motorized boats are allowed on **Lake Padden**, the path (3 miles) around the glistening lake and through some of the park's 1008 acres is both peaceful and rejuvenating.

In Birch Bay State Park in Blaine, the gently sloping **Terrell Marsh Trail** (.5 mile) winds through a thickly wooded area of birch, maple, red cedar, hemlock and fir, home to pileated woodpeckers, bald eagle, ruffed grouse, blue heron, muskrats and squirrels, and on to Terrell Marsh, the halfway point on the loop, before passing back through the forest to the trailhead.

WHIDBEY ISLAND The most picturesque hikes on Whidbey Island are found in and around Fort Ebey State Park. The **Ebey's Landing Loop Trail** (3.5 miles) has some steep sections on the bluff above the beach, but carry your camera anyway to capture the views of pastoral Ebey's Prairie in one direction and Mt. Rainier and the Olympic Mountains framed by wind-sculpted pines and fir in the other. Trimmed in wild roses, the trail swings around Perego's Lagoon and back along the driftwood-strewn beach. Be aware that the trail passes over some private property.

The **Partridge Point Trail** (3.5 miles) in Fort Ebey State Park climbs through a mix of coastal wildflowers on a windswept bluff rising 150 feet above the water with wide views of Port Townsend, Admiralty Inlet, Protection Island and Discovery Bay. A fenced path at the southern end drops down the headland to the cobbly beach below.

There are numerous trails to choose from in Deception Pass State Park. Locals prefer **Rosario Head Trail** (.3 mile) on the Fidalgo Island side, stretching over the very steep promontory between Rosario Bay and Bowman Bay with sweeping views of San Juans, Rosario Strait and the Strait of Juan de Fuca; the **Lighthouse Point Trail** (1.5 miles), near Bowman Bay. On the Whidbey Island side of the bridge, climb the steep switchback on **Goose Rock Perimeter Trail** (3.5 miles) and you might see great blue heron on Cornet Bay, then follow the path down under the bridge next to the swirling waters of the pass and on to quiet North Beach. Heartier hikers might want to tackle the **Goose Rock Summit Trail** (.5 mile), with an altitude gain of some 450 feet for an unparalleled view of Deception Pass and the Cascades.

FIDALGO ISLAND In Anacortes, your best bet is to head for the **Washington Park Loop Road** (3 miles), located on Fidalgo Head

AUTHOR FAVORITE

On Lopez Island, the easiest and most popular bike route here is the **Lopez Island Perimeter Loop**, 32 miles of gently rolling hills and narrow, paved roads passing by Fisherman's Bay, Shark Reef Park, MacKaye Harbor and Agate Beach on the west side of the island and Mud Bay, Lopez Sound and Shoal Bay on the east side.

at the end of Sunset Avenue four miles west of downtown. Rewarding views on this easy, paved path with a few moderate slopes include incredible glimpses of the San Juan Islands, Burrows Pass and Burrows Island. You'll also find quiet, cool stretches through dense woods and access to beaches and romantic, hidden outcroppings suitable for a glass of champagne to toast the breathtaking sunsets.

LOPEZ ISLAND On Lopez, ideal hiking choices include the **Shark Reef Park Trail** (.5 mile), a mossy path that meanders through a fragrant forest area and along a rock promontory looking out over tidal pools, a large kelp bed, a jutting haul out spot for seals and across the channel to San Juan Island. Spencer Spit State Park's **Beach Trail** (2 miles) travels down the spit and around the salt marsh lagoon alive with migratory birds; at the end of the spit is a reproduction of a historic log cabin built by early settlers, a fine spot for a picnic or brief rest stop with a nice view of the tiny islands offshore.

The best place to spy whales from land is at Whale Watch Park on the western side of San Juan Island. There's no entrance fee, and the area provides an unobstructed view of the orca's favorites feeding haunts.

SAN JUAN ISLAND Two of the best hiking alternatives on San Juan are the established hiking trails of the San Juan Island National Historical Park. The **Lagoon Trail** (.5 mile) in American Camp is actually two trails intertwined, starting from a parking area above Old Town (referred to on maps as First) Lagoon and passing through a dense stand of Douglas fir connecting the lovely, protected cove beaches of Jakle's Lagoon and Third Lagoon. The highlight of the short but steep **Mt. Young Trail** (.75 mile) in English Camp are the plates identifying the many islands dotting the waters as far as the eye can see. If you want a closer view of the water, you can take the flat, easy **Bell Point Trail** (2 miles), also in English Camp, which runs along the edge of the coast.

ORCAS ISLAND Unless you plan to spend an extended period of time here, there's little chance of covering the many hiking trails that twist through Moran State Park on Orcas Island connecting view spots, mountain lakes, waterfalls and campgrounds. The **Mountain Loop** (3.9 miles) is fairly easy and takes in sights such as log cabins and a dam and footbridge at the south end of Mountain Lake. For a little more challenge, try a section of the two-part **Twin Lakes Trail:** one part (2.2 miles) heads up the valley at the north end of Mountain Lake; the other (3.7 miles) takes you from the summit of Mt. Constitution along a rocky ledge to Twin Lakes and the Mountain Lake Campground, with occasional views through the thick trees. If you're a waterfall lover, take the **Cascade Creek Trail** (4.3 miles) from the south end of Mountain Lake past Cascade and Rustic falls and on to Cascade Lake.

Transportation

CAR

Route 5, also known as the Pacific Highway, parallels the Northern Puget Sound coastline all the way up to the Canadian border. **Route 20** from Burlington takes you into Anacortes, the main jump-off point for ferry service to the San Juan Islands. **Route 16** leads from Tacoma across The Narrows and onto the Kitsap Peninsula where it connects to **Route 3** skirting the Sinclair Inlet and continuing north to Port Gamble.

AIR

Visitors flying into the Northern Puget Sound area usually arrive at either **Bellingham International Airport** (360-671-5674) or the much larger and busier **Seattle-Tacoma International Airport** (see Chapter Two for further information). Carriers serving the Bellingham airport include Casino Express, EliteAir, Horizon Airlines and San Juan Airline.

Charter and regularly scheduled commuter flights are available into the tiny **Friday Harbor Airport** through Kenmore Air Express, Island Air and San Juan Airline. ~ 360-378-4724. Small commuter airports with limited scheduled service include **Anacortes Airport**, **Eastsound Airport** and **Lopez Airport**; all are served by San Juan Airline.

FERRY

Washington State Ferries, which are part of the state highway system, provide transportation to the main islands of the San Juans —Lopez, Orcas, Shaw and Friday Harbor on San Juan—departing from the Anacortes Ferry Terminal (Ferry Terminal Road; 888-808-7977 in Washington). Schedules change several times per year, with added service in the summer to take care of the heavy influx of tourists. The system is burdened during peak summer months, so arrive at the terminal early and be prepared to wait patiently (sometimes three hours or more) in very long lines if you plan to take your car along; walk-on passengers seldom wait long. ~ 206-464-6400; www.wsdot.wa.gov/ferries.

BUS

Greyhound Bus Lines (800-231-2222; www.greyhound.com) provides regular service into Bellingham, Everett and Mt. Vernon. Stations are in Bellingham at 401 Harris Avenue in Fairhaven Station, 360-733-5251; in Everett at 3201 Smith Avenue, 425-252-2143; and in Mt. Vernon at 105 Kincaid Street, Suite 100, 360-336-5111.

The **Bellingham/Sea-Tac Airporter** provides express shuttle service between Bellingham, Mt. Vernon, Stanwood, Anacortes, Marysville, Oak Harbor and the Sea-Tac airport. ~ 360-380-8800, 866-235-5247.

TRAIN

Amtrak offers service into Everett on the Puget Sound shoreline via the "Empire Builder," which originates in Chicago and makes its final stop in Seattle before retracing its route. West Coast connections through Seattle on the "Coast Starlight" are also available. ~ 3201 Smith Avenue, Everett; 800-872-7245; www.amtrak.com.

CAR RENTALS

At the Bellingham International Airport, you'll find **Avis Rent A Car** (800-331-1212), **Budget Rent A Car** (800-527-0700) and **Hertz Rent A Car** (800-654-3131).

A less expensive local rental agency is **U-Save Auto Rental** (360-293-8686) in Anacortes.

PUBLIC TRANSIT

Whatcom Transportation Authority provides public transit in Lynden, Bellingham, Blaine, Birch Bay, Ferndale and Gooseberry Point. ~ 360-676-7433; www.ridewta.com. **Skagit Transit** services the Mt. Vernon, Sedro Woolley, Anacortes and Burlington areas. ~ 360-757-4433; www.skagittransit.org. In Everett you can get just about anywhere for 50 cents via **Everett Transit.** ~ 425-257-7777. **Island Transit** covers Whidbey Island, with scheduled stops at Deception Pass, Oak Harbor, Coupeville, the Keystone Ferry, Greenbank, Freeland, Langley and the Clinton Ferry. ~ 360-678-7771, 800-240-8747; www.islandtransit.org. In smaller towns like La Conner and Mt. Vernon and on most of the islands there are no public transportation systems set up; check the Yellow Pages for taxi service.

TAXIS

A cab company serving the Bellingham International Airport is **City Cab, Inc./Yellow Cab** (360-733-8294). For service from the Friday Harbor Airport contact **Bob's Taxi Service** (360-378-3550). **Triangle Taxi** (360-293-3979) serves the Anacortes Airport.

EIGHT

The Cascades and Central Washington

Perhaps without even realizing it, many Americans have a burning image of this region. For it was here, in the Cascade Range, that Mt. St. Helens blew its top in 1980. But the area has a lot more going for it than one hyperactive mountaintop. Indeed, think of the Cascades and Central Washington as one wild place for anyone who loves the outdoors.

The Cascade Range contains some of the most beautiful mountain scenery in the United States, much of it preserved by two major national parks, several national recreation areas and numerous wilderness areas that make this a major sports haven. There are also glaciers galore; 316 are in the North Cascades National Park Service Complex alone. Thousands of miles of trails and logging roads lace the Cascades, leading to mountaintop lookout towers, old gold mines, lakes, streams and gorgeous sights.

The hand of man has done little to alter the Cascades. When the North Cascades Highway (Route 20) was finally completed in 1972, it was with the understanding that it would be closed during the heavy snows, usually from November until April. Thus, most of the Cascades are still wild and remote, seen and experienced by humans but not transformed by them.

The range, about 700 miles long, begins at the Fraser River in southern British Columbia and extends southward through Washington and Oregon and into California just beyond Lassen Peak. The most dominant features of the Cascades are its 15 volcanoes. Washington lays claim to five, with Mt. Rainier the granddaddy at 14,411 feet. Most peaks are under 10,000 feet, and Harts Pass, the highest pass in the state, is only 6197 feet.

Although the range is not a comparatively high one, it served as an effective barrier to exploration and development until well into the 20th century. The pioneers who came over the Oregon Trail avoided it, choosing instead to go down the Columbia River to the Cowlitz River, travel up to present-day Toledo, then move overland to Puget Sound at Tumwater and Olympia.

Mining has always been part of the Cascades story. Although no major gold strikes have been found, several smaller ones have kept the interest alive, and there's probably never been a day since the mid-1870s when someone wasn't panning or sluicing in the mountains.

The range supports a wide variety of plants and wildlife because it has so many climatic zones. Naturalists have given names to eight distinct ones: Coastal Forest Zone, Silver Fir Zone, Sierran Mixed-Conifer Zone, Red Fir Zone, Subalpine Zone, Alpine Zone, Interior Fir Zone and Ponderosa Pine Zone. Each zone has its own community of plants, animals and birds.

Although most of the range is under the stewardship of the Forest Service, which by law has to practice multiple-use policies, most people think of the Cascades as their very own. It is used by mushroom hunters, hikers, runners, birdwatchers, anglers, hunters, photographers, painters, skiers, horse riders, loggers and miners. Whichever of these apply to you, enjoy.

North Cascades

Extending from the Canadian border south into the Mt. Baker–Snoqualmie National Forest, the North Cascades region has over 300 glaciers, valleys famous for their spring tulip fields and some of the best skiing in the Pacific Northwest. Backroads wind through old logging towns past mountain lakes to unspoiled wilderness areas. The North Cascades National Park Service Complex forms the core of this realm that includes Rainy and Washington passes, two of the Cascades' grandest viewpoints.

SIGHTS

Beginning at the northernmost approach, **Route 542** enters the Cascades from Bellingham, a pleasant, two-lane, blacktop highway that is shared by loggers, skiers, anglers and hikers. Much of the route runs through dense forest beside fast streams and with only rare glimpses of the surrounding mountains. The road deadends a few miles beyond the Mt. Baker day-use lodge for skiers, at a lookout called Artist Point. In clear weather you will see 9127-foot **Mt. Shuksan**, one of the most beautiful peaks in the Cascades. It can't be seen from any other part of the range, but it probably appears on more calendars and postcards than its neighbor Mt. Baker or even Mt. Rainier.

The **Mt. Baker** ski slopes usually open in November and run all the way into April, making for the longest ski season of any area in Washington. During summer the mountain is popular with day hikers and backpackers. Several hiking trails wind through high alpine meadows dotted with wildflowers in the Heather Meadows area. ~ Mt. Baker Ranger District; 360-856-5700, fax 360-856-1934.

Mt. Baker was named by George Vancouver in May 1792, in honor of Joseph Baker, a lieutenant on his ship. It was first climbed on August 17, 1868, by a party of four led by an experienced alpinist named Edmund T. Coleman. Although it is listed as an active volcano and occasionally steam is seen rising from it, Mt. Baker hasn't erupted since 1880.

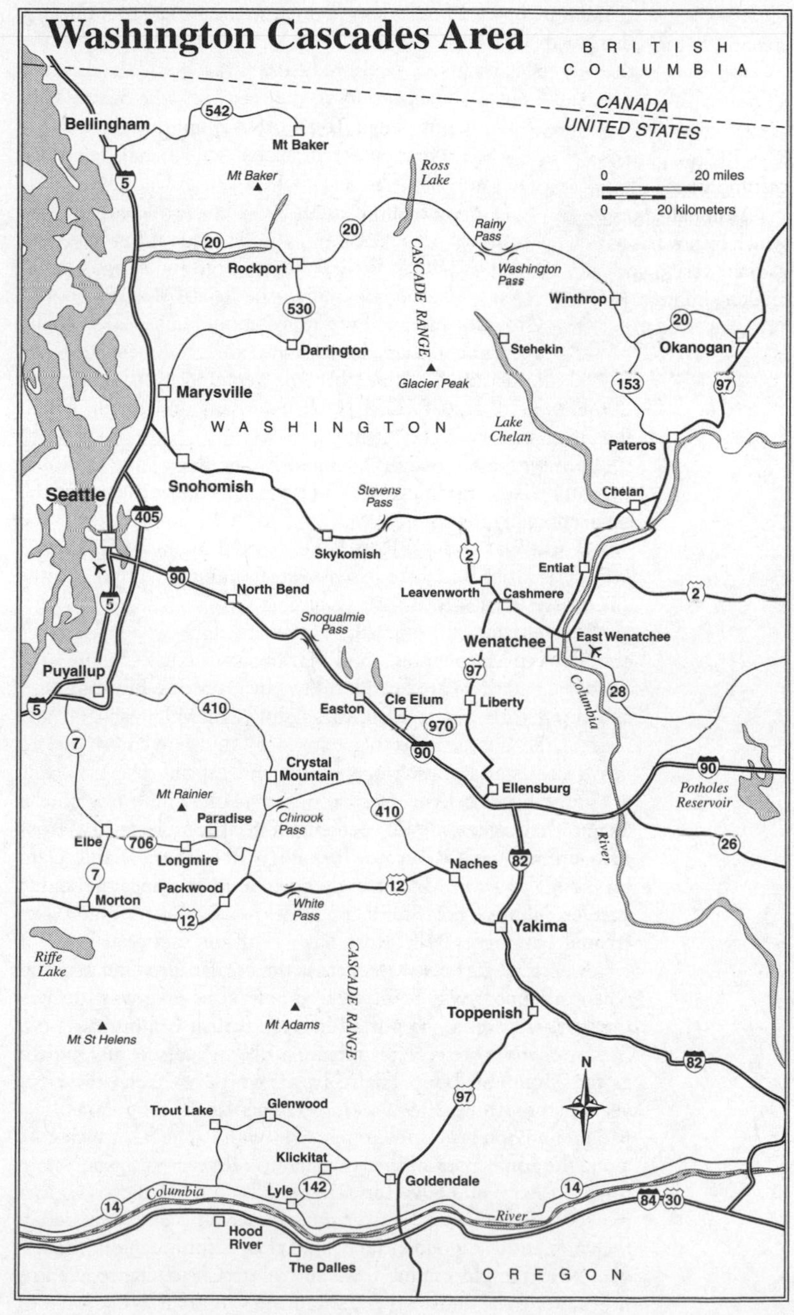
Washington Cascades Area
BRITISH COLUMBIA
CANADA
UNITED STATES
0 20 miles
0 20 kilometers
Bellingham
542
Mt Baker
Mt Baker
5
Ross Lake
20
20
Rockport
Rainy Pass
Washington Pass
CASCADE RANGE
530
Winthrop
20
Okanogan
Darrington
Stehekin
153
97
Glacier Peak
Marysville
WASHINGTON
Lake Chelan
Pateros
Snohomish
Seattle
405
Stevens Pass
Chelan
Skykomish
2
Entiat
90
North Bend
Leavenworth
Cashmere
2
5
Snoqualmie Pass
Wenatchee
East Wenatchee
97
Columbia
28
Puyallup
Easton
Cle Elum
Liberty
5
410
970
7
90
Crystal Mountain
90
Potholes Reservoir
Mt Rainier
Ellensburg
Paradise
Chinook Pass
410
River
26
Elbe
706
Longmire
Naches
82
7
Packwood
12
Morton
White Pass
12
Yakima
Riffe Lake
CASCADE RANGE
Toppenish
Mt Adams
Mt St Helens
N
82
97
Trout Lake
Glenwood
Klickitat
Goldendale
Lyle
142
14
Columbia
River
14
84
30
Hood River
The Dalles
OREGON

Built between 1916 and 1918, the Henry Thompson Bridge was the longest single-span cement bridge of its time, and is now listed on the National Historic Register.

Route 20, one of America's premier scenic routes, goes through the North Cascades National Park Service Complex and along the way provides hiking trails, roadside parks, boat launches and one of the more unusual tours in the Cascades, the **Seattle City Light Skagit Tours** offers a unique opportunity to experience the rugged wilderness. The two-and-a-half-hour Diablo Lake Adventure travels across Diablo Dam. It includes a scenic cruise (with dinner on Monday and Thursday in July and August) deep into the Skagit Gorge and across Diablo Lake. Often compared to the Swiss Alps, the North Cascades offer snow-capped mountains peaks, alpine valleys and glaciers. Reservations are recommended. Tours run seasonally June through September. Admission. ~ 206-684-3030, fax 206-233-1642; www.skagittours.com, e-mail skagittours.reservations@seattle.gov.

Because the highway is enclosed by the Ross Lake National Recreation Area, new development is virtually nonexistent, and the small company towns of Newhalem and Diablo look frozen in the pre–World War II days. **Ross Lake**, created by the hydroelectric project, is a fjordlike lake between steep mountains that eventually crosses over into British Columbia.

When driving on Route 20, be forewarned: No gasoline is available between Marblemount and Mazama, a distance of more than 70 miles, and there are few places to buy groceries. Fill your tank and bring your lunch. Also, the highway at Milepost 134, just west of the Cascade Crest, is closed by mid-November due to heavy snows and doesn't open again until April.

Three historic hydroelectric power plants and dams on the Skagit River generate 25 percent of Seattle's electricity. Ross Lake on the Skagit River was formed by Ross Dam. Diablo Dam was built a short distance downstream, creating the much smaller Diablo Lake. Stairstepped below Diablo is Gorge Lake, created by Gorge Dam. Ross Lake is an international body of water because its backwaters cross the border into Canada, and when the timber was being cleared before the lake was formed, the work was done via a road in from British Columbia.

Another way to reach Route 20 is over what is locally known as the **Mountain Loop Highway**, a favorite weekend drive for years before Route 20 was completed across the mountains. The Mountain Loop begins in Granite Falls with Route 92, which goes along the South Fork of the Stillaguamish River past the one-store towns of Robe and Silverton. The road is crooked and slow driving because it follows the river route closely. It is always closed in the winter and sometimes landslides close it for much of the summer. Near the old mining town of Monte Cristo, the road turns north along the Sauk River and emerges in the logging town of

Darrington. Here you can drive north to catch Route 20 at Rockport or turn west on Route 530 and return to Route 5.

Route 20 plunges into the Cascades and goes over two passes—**Rainy Pass**, 4860 feet, and **Washington Pass**, 5477 feet—before descending into the Methow Valley. Stop at each viewpoint and turnout for stunning views of the region. One viewpoint above Ross Lake shows miles of the lake, and another just beyond Washington Pass gives a view of the mountains behind the pass.

The only way to visit the resort town of **Stehekin**, at the tip of Lake Chelan, is by boat, plane or hiking. Most visitors take the trip up the lake on the **Lady of the Lake**, the tour-mail-supply boat for Stehekin and points between. The schedule allows you up to three hours in Stehekin, and you can buy lunch at the Stehekin landing. Bike and bus tours coordinated with the ferry schedule are available. Reservations suggested. Admission. ~ 509-682-4584, fax 509-682-8206; www.ladyofthelake.com.

If you'd like to fly into Stehekin, contact **Chelan Airways.** ~ 1328 West Woodin Avenue (one mile west of Chelan on Route 97A); 509-682-5555, fax 509-682-5065 (call first); www.chelanairways.com, e-mail info@chelanairways.com.

LODGING

The closest B&B to the Mt. Baker Ski Area is the **Mt. Baker Bed and Breakfast**, a mountain chalet with three rooms. While the rooms themselves are clean and comfortable but nothing to write

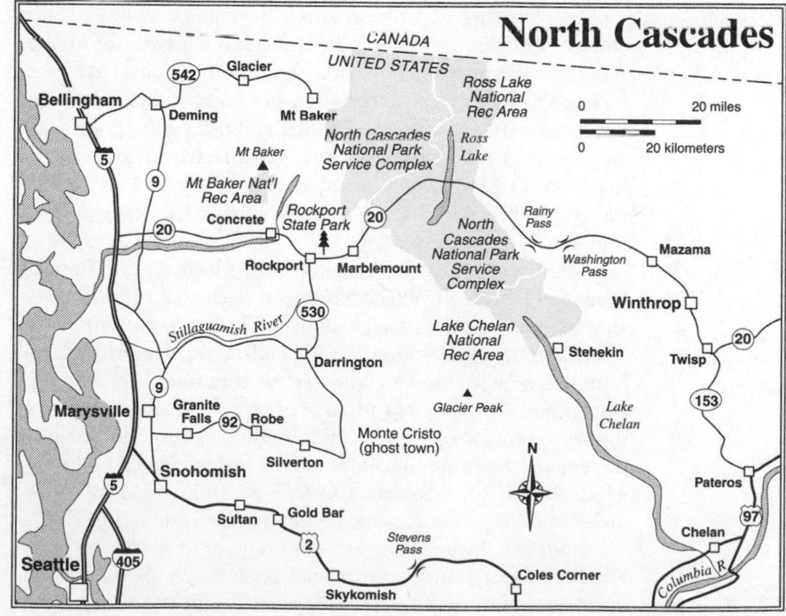

home about, guests appreciate the gorgeous mountain views and idyllic forest locale. Still, all accommodations have queen-sized beds and private bathrooms and entrances; two offer private decks. A secluded hot tub with mountain views soothes away hiking and skiing pains. A continental breakfast is served. ~ 9447 Mt. Baker Highway, Glacier; 360-599-2299, fax 360-599-1193; www.mtbakerbedandbreakfast.com, e-mail mtbakerbnb@msn.com. MODERATE

The **Glacier Creek Lodge** is a rustic motel with nine units and thirteen blue-and-white cabins. The cabins are one or two bedrooms, with bath, double bed, bedside table and tired furniture. The motel units are so small there's no room for a table. In addition to a hot tub, there is a large lobby where continental breakfast is served. ~ 10036 Mt. Baker Highway, Glacier; 360-599-2991, 800-719-1414, fax 360-599-1048; www.glaciercreeklodge.com. BUDGET TO ULTRA-DELUXE.

In 1889 the **Buffalo Run Inn** was built as a meeting place for the gold miners and pack mule train drivers heading up the Skagit River. The two-story inn now boasts 15 Northwest-themed suites with kitchenettes, private bathrooms and queen-sized beds. There is a jacuzzi on the premises, and a self-serve continental breakfast is provided. Register across the street in the restaurant. No smoking or pets. ~ Route 20, Marblemount; 360-873-2103, 877-828-6652, fax 360-873-4078; www.buffalorunrestaurant.com, e-mail buffalo_run@hotmail.com. BUDGET TO MODERATE.

One of the larger lakeside resorts is **Baker Lake Resort,** 20 miles north of Concrete on Baker Lake Road. It is a mixture of RV sites and nine rustic cabins on the lake. Four of the cabins have bathrooms, showers and a refrigerator, but guests must bring their own cookware and utensils. Boating and fishing are popular on the lake; boat rentals are available. Closed early October to late May. ~ 46110 East Main Street, Concrete; 360-853-8341, 888-711-3033, fax 425-462-3118; e-mail bakerlakerecpse@puget.com. BUDGET TO MODERATE.

A lodge with bed-and-breakfast ambience, the **Cascade Mountain Lodge** is a vintage Northwest cedar-shake hostelry with an adjoining restaurant and lounge. There are 13 refurbished rooms, some with antique and hand-carved furnishings. All rooms come with modern comforts such as microwaves, refrigerators and TVs. Guests can have breakfast, lunch or dinner in the restaurant or on an adjoining outdoor patio adorned by a three-tiered fountain and dozens of hanging flower baskets. ~ 44628 Route 20, Concrete; 360-853-8870, 800-251-3054, fax 360-853-7123; www.cascademountainlodge.com. MODERATE.

Rustic reigns in remote Stehekin. The most outdoorsy is the **Stehekin Valley Ranch**, owned and operated by the Courtneys, the major family in the valley. The ranch is nine miles from town, up the Stehekin River Valley. Guests are housed in tent cabins with wooden walls and canvas-covered roofs. Showers and toilets are in the main building. Five newer cabins have private baths. All meals are included and served in the dining room, which has split logs for tables and seats. Horseback rides, river rafting and kayaking trips are offered. Closed October to mid-June. ~ P.O. Box 36, Stehekin, WA 98852; 800-536-0745, fax 509-682-4677; www.stehekin.biz, e-mail ranch@courtneycountry.com. MODERATE.

The fanciest Stehekin lodging is **Silver Bay Inn**, at the head of the Stehekin River a short distance from the village. In the owners' home there is a room with a kitchenette and private bath. Also on the property are three spacious, well-appointed cabins that will sleep six and are complete with kitchens, dishwashers and decks. Bikes, kayaks and canoes are available for guests, as is the riverside hot tub. ~ 10 Silver Bay Road, Stehekin; 800-555-7781, fax 509-687-3142; www.silverbayinn.com, e-mail stehekin@silverbayinn.com. ULTRA-DELUXE.

DINING

A popular place along the Mt. Baker Highway is **Milano's Market and Deli,** a combination small restaurant and deli offering a hearty supply of soups, salads, fresh pasta dishes and homemade bread and desserts. This is a good place to have a picnic lunch made up. If the weather is right, the deck is open for outside dining. ~ 9990 Mt. Baker Highway, Glacier; 360-599-2863. BUDGET.

A big, airy place decorated with family memorabilia dating back to the 1800s, **The Eatery Restaurant** at the Skagit River Resort specializes in downhome fare. Breakfast features biscuits and gravy, while lunch touts bistro sandwiches and dinner means steaks, chops and fish. Don't miss the housemade pies and milkshakes. ~ Route 20, Marblemount; 360-873-2250, fax 360-873-4077; www.northcascades.com. BUDGET TO MODERATE.

AUTHOR FAVORITE

If you're traveling the scenic North Cascades Highway between May and October, plan on stopping for delicious homemade organic ice cream, berries and shortcake, shakes and espresso at the 27-acre **Cascadian Farm,** near Rockport. The farm marks the birthplace, 35 years ago, of the Cascadian Farm Organic brand. Seasonal blueberries, raspberries and strawberries infuse the creamiest ice cream imaginable. Picnic tables are available, and you can pick your own berries or buy produce. ~ 55749 State Route 20, Rockport; 360-853-8173; www.cascadianfarm.org.

After a long day hiking or bicycling, stop in for one of the popular buffalo burgers at **Buffalo Run Restaurant**, a unique roadhouse diner specializing in exotic game meat. The buffalo is raised on the restaurant's own nearby ranch. You can also try venison, elk and ostrich, or play it safe with chicken, beef, fish, pasta or vegetarian fare. A lovely garden patio is open for summer dining. Closed Sunday. ~ 60084 Route 20, Marblemount; 360-873-2461; www.buffalorunrestaurant.com, e-mail buffalo_run@hotmail.com. BUDGET TO DELUXE.

On the western edge of Concrete, **Cascade Mountain Lodge** has established a local reputation for good, plain American food (steaks, chops, burgers) and delicious pie (made by a local woman especially for the restaurant). The interior is decorated with antique furnishings and decorations. ~ 44628 Route 20, Concrete; 360-853-8771, 800-251-3054; www.cascademountainlodge.com. BUDGET.

SHOPPING

If you're in Concrete on Saturday from mid-May through August, hit the **Saturday Market** in the **Concrete Senior Center** for arts and crafts and baked goods. ~ 45821 Railway Avenue.

Potter Stephen Murray is known for his wood-fired ceramic dinnerware that comes in a variety of lustrous glazes. He also works with stoneware and porcelain. Individual pieces are sold at his **Sauk Mountain Pottery** store east of Concrete. ~ 50303 Route 20, Concrete; 360-853-8689.

NIGHTLIFE

The Cascades isn't the place to go for stellar nightlife. After a day traipsing around in the mountains, most people return to town tired and only want to eat and go to bed. Consequently, only the busiest areas even have live music.

PARKS

MT. BAKER–SNOQUALMIE NATIONAL FOREST This 1.7-million-acre forest begins at the Canadian border and goes south along the western slopes

sights

Over 300 feet high and spanning 35 feet, **Rainbow Falls** in the Lake Chelan National Recreation Area are perhaps my favorite cascades in Washington State. They're only accessible by foot or by going through the tiny hamlet of Stehekin via a 3.5-mile bus ride up the valley. Purported to be one of the country's most impressive, Rainbow Falls were created by an ancient glacier that scraped out the walls of the Stehekin River Valley. The falls' tiers result in multiple plunges and a cascade at the bottom. For tour information, contact the Lady of the Lake (page 281).

of the Cascades to Mt. Rainier National Park. It is dominated on the north by the inactive volcano, 10,778-foot Mt. Baker. Another inactive volcano, 10,568-foot Glacier Peak, lies in the middle of the forest. The Forest Service controls the land for the ski areas at Crystal Mountain, Mt. Baker, Stevens Pass and Snoqualmie Pass. Its best-known wilderness area is Alpine Lakes Wilderness, but it also includes the Glacier Peak, Noisy Diobsud, Boulder River, Henry M. Jackson, Clearwater, Norse Peak and Mt. Baker Wilderness areas. Within the forest is excellent fishing for rainbow trout, salmon and steelhead in Baker Lake and many other streams and lakes. There are picnic areas, restrooms and showers. Parking permit, $5 per day or $30 for an annual pass. ~ Four east–west highways cross the national forest: Routes 90, 20, 2 and 410; 425-775-9702, 800-627-0062, fax 425-744-3255; www.fs.fed.us/r6/mbs.

▲ Camping is permitted (unless otherwise posted) along the highways, trails and the Pacific Crest Trail, as well as at established campsites. Most of the 40-plus campgrounds are primitive with vault toilets and vary from walk-in to drive-in sites (RV sites are available); $10 to $16 per night. Roughly 60 percent of sites are available for reservation: 877-444-6777.

ROCKPORT STATE PARK There are picnic areas, restrooms, showers, good steelhead fishing spots and five miles of hiking trails in this 670-acre park along the Skagit River. The David Douglas Historical Marker, named for the noted horticulturalist who discovered the Douglas fir, is located in the park. This is a great place to view bald eagles in winter (open weekends only in winter). ~ Route 20, one mile west of Rockport; phone/fax 360-853-8461.

▲ Heavy rains in the winter of 2006–2007 destabilized the old-growth forest of Douglas fir that has long been a popular place for camping. Unfortunately, the campground is closed indefinitely.

RASAR STATE PARK This 169-acre park is located approximately 15 miles west of Rockport along the Skagit River and offers 4,000 feet of shoreline for boating, fishing, birdwatching and wildlife viewing. There are nearly four miles of hiking trails a mile- long accessible trail. ~ Off Route 20, about 12 miles northwest of Rockport; 360-826-3942.

▲ There are 18 standard campsites ($17 per night), 20 campsites with hookups ($24 per night), 2 ADA-accessible campsites, 8 walk-in sites, 3 primitive hiker/biker sites ($12 per night) and 3 three-sided Adirondack sleeping shelters ($23 per night). Reservations: 888-226-7688.

HOWARD MILLER STEELHEAD COUNTY PARK One of the most popular parks on the Skagit River for steelheaders and travelers alike, this county park covers 97 acres and has exhibits of a historic cabin, an old river ferry and dugout canoe. Anglers will find salmon and trout, and birders will enjoy bald-eagle watching from December to February. Facilities include picnic areas, a playground, a clubhouse, restrooms, showers and a trailer dump. ~ Located in the middle of Rockport at the junction of Routes 20 and 530; 360-853-8808, fax 360-853-7315.

▲ There are both tent and RV sites available ($18 to $20 per night). Call the park for more information and reservations.

NORTH CASCADES NATIONAL PARK SERVICE COMPLEX Covering 684,313 acres in the north central part of the state, this park is divided into two units. The northern unit runs from the Canadian border to **Ross Lake National Recreation Area.** The southern unit continues on to the **Lake Chelan National Recreation Area.** Much of its eastern boundary is the summit of the Cascade Range, and the western boundary is the Mt. Baker–Snoqualmie National Forest. It is the most rugged and remote of the national parks in Washington and has the fewest roads. All visitor facilities and most roads in the northern portion are inside the Ross Lake National Recreation Area. On the southern end, the Lake Chelan National Recreation Area covers the heavy-use area on the north end of the lake, including the village of Stehekin. Try for rainbow trout in Ross Lake, steelhead in the Skagit River downstream from Newhalem and rainbow and eastern brook trout in high lakes. There are visitors centers in Newhalem and Stehekin, and rangers sometimes lead nature walks. Picnic areas, restrooms and nature walks are located here. ~ Only Route 20 goes through Ross Lake National Recreation Area, and in winter the road closes after the visitors center. 360-854-7200, fax 360-856-1934; www.nps.gov/noca, e-mail noca_information@nps.gov.

▲ There are over 350 campsites at four campgrounds. You can camp year-round at Goodell Creek, which has potable water in summer and vault toilets; $10 per night. Colonial Creek and Newhalem Creek campgrounds have potable water, flush toilets and dump stations; $12 per night. Gorge Lake sites are free, but you'll have to bring in your own drinking water. The adjacent Okanogan Forest has more sites, including the popular Lone Fir and Early Winters campgrounds. Backcountry camping is free, but requires a permit. Reservations: 877-444-6777.

Methow Valley

The scenery changes quickly and dramatically once you have crossed Washington Pass into the Methow Valley. Located along Route 20 between Mazama and Pateros, this region includes the tourist center of Chelan, gateway to one of the state's most popular lake-resort areas.

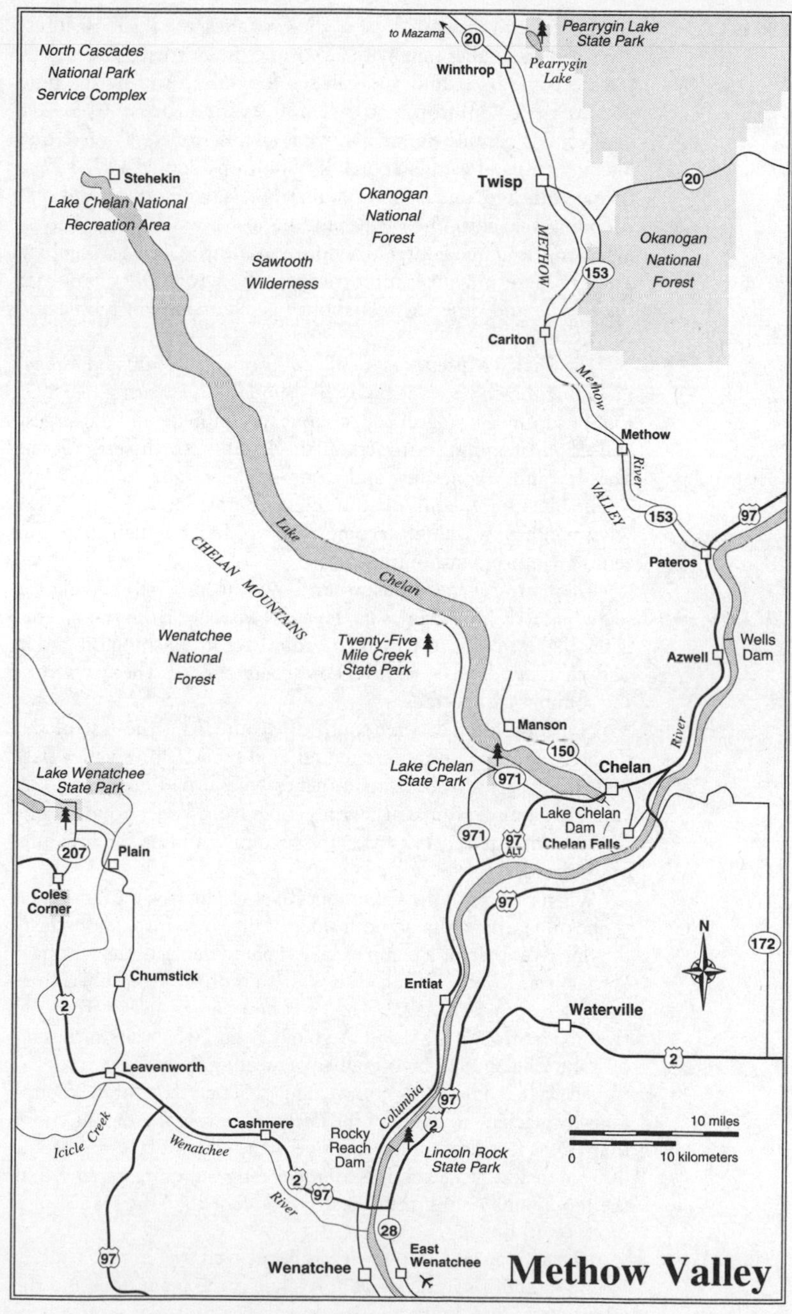
to Mazama
20
Pearrygin Lake State Park
North Cascades National Park Service Complex
Winthrop
Pearrygin Lake
Twisp
20
Stehekin
Lake Chelan National Recreation Area
Okanogan National Forest
METHOW
Okanogan National Forest
Sawtooth Wilderness
153
Carlton
Methow
Methow
River
VALLEY
153
97
Pateros
Lake
Chelan
CHELAN MOUNTAINS
Wenatchee National Forest
Twenty-Five Mile Creek State Park
Wells Dam
Azwell
Manson
River
150
Lake Wenatchee State Park
Lake Chelan State Park
971
Chelan
Lake Chelan Dam
Chelan Falls
971
97 ALT
207
Plain
Coles Corner
97
N
172
Chumstick
Entiat
2
Waterville
2
Leavenworth
Columbia
97
2
0
10 miles
0
10 kilometers
Icicle Creek
Wenatchee
Cashmere
Rocky Reach Dam
Lincoln Rock State Park
2
97
River
28
97
Wenatchee
East Wenatchee
Methow Valley

SIGHTS

As you descend the east slope of the Cascades, the thick, fir forest gives way to smaller pine with almost no underbrush. The mountains become bare, and you can see for miles. And by the time you arrive in **Winthrop**, you will wonder if you are in Colorado or Wyoming because the small town is all falsefronts, saloon doors, hitching rails and wooden porches. Winthrop adopted a Wild West theme years ago, and it has revitalized the sawmill town and surrounding area into one of the state's most popular destinations. Winthrop is named after Theodore Winthrop, a 19th-century Yale graduate and adventurer/traveler who wrote *The Canoe and the Saddle* and other novels about his excursions in the Pacific Northwest.

The **Shafer Museum** is a collection of early-1900s buildings, including the cabin built by town founder Guy Waring in 1897. Exhibits include a stagecoach, antique automobiles and the largest collection of mining artifacts in the Pacific Northwest. Closed Tuesday and Wednesday, and from late September to late May. ~ One block up the hill off Route 20, Winthrop; 509-996-2712; www.winthropwashington.com/winthrop/shafer, e-mail shafermu seum@winthropwashington.com.

HIDDEN ►

There are several areas around Winthrop worth driving to, including 6197-foot **Harts Pass** a short distance from town. This is the highest point to which you can drive in Washington and is only an hour's drive on a gravel Forest Service road. The views from the summit are spectacular.

Not long after driving south on Route 153, the last of the timbered mountains are left behind, and the Methow Valley flattens into a series of irrigated ranches with broad hayfields. The valley is gaining popularity with people from Puget Sound looking for more space, so houses are beginning to line the low hills on both sides.

When you reach the **Columbia River** at Pateros, the landscape is one of basaltic cliffs on both sides of the river. Instead of a fast-flowing river there is a chain of lakes behind dams all the way past Wenatchee. Route 97 hugs the west side of the Columbia, then splits off onto 97A at Chelan Falls and swings away from the river to go through the resort town of Chelan, which sits at the end of **Lake Chelan**. The two highways meet again at Wenatchee.

The lake is a remnant of the Ice Ages. Scoured out of the mountains by glaciers, it is one of the deepest lakes in the region, more than 1500 feet deep in at least one area, which places its bed at 400 feet below sea level. It is 50 miles long but quite narrow, and the mountains rising from its shores give it the appearance of a Norwegian fjord.

Chelan is a small town that has been given over almost entirely to apples and tourism. Woodin Avenue is the main drag and the lakefront is lined with resorts, but the small-town atmosphere remains intact, so a farmer can come to town and still buy a two-by-four or a cotter pin.

The best way to get to Stehekin is also an incomparably scenic way to see Lake Chelan and its surroundings. **Chelan Airways** has been flying the lake for more than a half-century, and its experienced floatplane pilots not only give passengers the best views, they know every nook and cranny of the lake and all the stories that accompany them. Round-trip passage is not too expensive, but it's worth a flight just to see the sights even if you don't stay "uplake." Closed November through March. ~ 1328 West Woodin Avenue (one mile west of Chelan on Route 97A); 509-682-5555, fax 509-682-5065 (call first); www.chelanairways.com, e-mail info@chelanairways.com.

Lake Chelan, nestled in North America's deepest gorge, extends for 55 miles into the Cascades and is flanked by towering peaks over 9000 feet tall.

The **Lake Chelan Historical Society Museum** displays American Indian artifacts and early farming equipment. One room depicts a miner's cabin, and another shows a typical country kitchen. Limited hours October through May. Closed Sunday from June through September. ~ Woodin Avenue and Emerson Street, Chelan; 509-682-5644; www.chelanvalley.com/history, e-mail historical@chelanvalley.com.

LODGING

If you want to get up close and personal with the North Cascades, head for the **Freestone Inn and Cabins**. The 15 cabins sit across the highway from the Forest Service/National Park Service information center at the foot of the mountains. Varying in size and widely spaced, each cabin is heated with a propane fireplace; the bathrooms are heated. All cooking utensils are provided. In the inn, all 21 rooms have fireplaces. The inn has one hot tub, the cabins have another. The Recreation Center offers cross-country ski rentals in the winter and mountain-bike rentals in the summer for adventurers who want to explore the Methow Valley Nordic Ski Trails—a 175-kilometer network of trails that intersect the property. ~ 31 Early Winters Drive, Mazama; 509-996-3906, 800-639-3809, fax 509-996-3907; www.freestoneinn.com, e-mail info@freestoneinn.com. DELUXE TO ULTRA-DELUXE.

The most elaborate place in the Methow Valley, and one of the best resorts in the Pacific Northwest, is **Sun Mountain Lodge**. Built at the 3000-foot level atop a small mountain, this low-rise, stone-and-timber resort gives a 360-degree view of the Cascades, Pasayten Wilderness, Okanogan Highlands and Methow Valley. The 112 units are spread over three buildings atop the mountain and down the road in 16 rustic, cozy cabins. The resort has just about everything: several miles of hiking trails that become cross-country ski trails in the winter, two pools, two hot tubs, an exercise room, a full-service spa, saddle-and-pack horses, mountain-bike rentals, canoe and sailing on the lake, heli-skiing and tennis. It also has a great restaurant. Rooms feature bentwood furniture, a fireplace (only the suites have real-wood fireplaces), coffee, the thickest and softest towels and robes you can hope for and no television. ~ 604 Patterson Lake Road, Winthrop; 509-996-2211, 800-572-0493, fax 509-996-3133; www.sunmountain lodge.com, e-mail sunmtn@methow.com. ULTRA-DELUXE.

Hotel Rio Vista has a facade that looks like it was made out of matchsticks. The 29 bright and airy rooms all overlook the Methow River and have mini-fridges and private decks. A hot tub and quaint riverside picnic area round out the amenities. Located on the south side of town, this lodging is within walking distance of downtown's eateries. It also runs a fully equipped Aspen loft cabin, ten miles west of town, which has a fireplace and sleeps six. ~ 285 Riverside Avenue, Winthrop; 509-996-3535, 800-398-0911; www.hotelriovista.com, e-mail info@hotelriovista.com. MODERATE TO DELUXE.

On the south edge of Winthrop is the **Virginian Resort**. Located on the high bank of the Methow River, the riverfront rooms in this 32-unit motel have balconies. There are also seven cabins, which are a bit more expensive, but several have wood stoves and room enough for four. Kitchens are equipped with microwaves. Also available is a three-bedroom cottage that has five beds and a full kitchen. ~ 808 North Cascades Highway, Winthrop; 509-996-2535, 800-854-2834, fax 509-999-2468; www.virginian-resort.com, e-mail info@virginian-resort.com. BUDGET TO MODERATE.

The oldest and most reliable resort in Chelan is **Campbell's Resort**, which has been in business since 1901. With 170 rooms, it is still growing along the lakeshore in the heart of town. It has two heated pools, two outdoor jacuzzis, a day spa, a good beach and boat moorage. The larger rooms have kitchenettes and one king or two queen beds, and are decorated in soft pastels or earth tones. ~ 104 West Woodin Avenue, Chelan; 509-682-2561, 800-553-8225, fax 509-682-2177; www.campbellsresort.com, e-mail info@campbellsresort.com. ULTRA-DELUXE.

One of the most complete resorts inside the Chelan city limits is **Darnell's Lake Resort**, a few blocks southwest of the city

ORCHARDS, ORCHARDS EVERYWHERE

Chelan has some of the best orchards along the eastern slopes of the Cascades. If you take a drive northwest of town on Route 150 to Manson, you will see thousands of acres of apple orchards climbing up the sun-baked hills from the lake.

center on Route 150. It has a heated pool and hot tub, putting greens, lighted tennis courts, swimming beach, waterskiing, volleyball, badminton and game rooms. The resort is divided into two three-story buildings. All rooms have balconies with views of the lake. All units are suites; some have two bedrooms. The penthouse suites have two fireplaces and private jacuzzi. Closed mid-October through March. ~ 901 Spader Bay Road, Chelan; 509-682-2015, 800-967-8149, fax 509-682-8736; www.darnellsresort.com, e-mail info@darnellsresort.com. ULTRA-DELUXE.

On the eastern edge of Chelan is the clean and comfortable **Apple Inn Motel** with white stucco walls and black wood trim. The 41 rooms are small and clean; some have kitchenettes, all have microwaves; coffeemakers and TVs. The heated outdoor pool is open in the summer, and a hot tub is open year-round. ~ 1002 East Woodin Avenue, Chelan; 509-682-4044, 800-276-3229, fax 509-682-3330; www.appleinnmotel.com, e-mail info@appleinnmotel.com. MODERATE.

DINING

The dramatic **Sun Mountain Lodge Dining Room** garners statewide attention. The room is cantilevered with views down into the Methow Valley and Winthrop 1000 feet below. All seats here have a view. The food is wonderful. The menu features seafood and creatively prepared grilled or roasted meats. ~ Sun Mountain Lodge, Patterson Lake Road, Winthrop; 509-996-2211, 800-572-0493, fax 509-996-3133; www.sunmountainlodge.com, e-mail sunmtn@methow.com. ULTRA-DELUXE.

One of Winthrop's most trendy restaurants is the oddly named **Duck Brand Cantina** in the hotel of the same name. The menu reflects an effort to please several palates, including Mexican, Continental and American. The restaurant is divided into two areas: a dining room filled with antiques and old photographs, and a deck overlooking Winthrop's sole street. Breakfast, lunch and dinner. ~ 248 Riverside Avenue, Winthrop; 509-996-2192, 800-996-2192, fax 509-996-2001; www.methownet.com/duck, e-mail duckbrand@methow.com. DELUXE.

Decorated in rustic Western style with wooden tables, hardwood floors, and elk heads mounted on the walls, **Three Fingered Jack's Saloon and Restaurant** offers fresh meats and vegetables, homemade soups, salads and desserts. The New York steaks are cut in-house in this family-run establishment. Vegetarians might try the pasta primavera. ~ 176 Riverside Avenue, Winthrop; phone/fax 509-996-2411; www.3fingeredjacks.com. MODERATE.

Although Campbell's Resort is so large it overwhelms some people, it is hard to find a better place in the area for a good meal than the resort's **Campbell's House Cafe**. The large room seats about 130 and is pleasantly decorated in early American furnishings with walls covered with an eclectic collection of prints, documents and paintings. The menu is large: prime rib, medallions of pork, Asian-style jumbo prawns, the catch of the day and a variety of pasta. In summer, open daily for all three meals; no breakfast on weekdays in winter. ~ 104 West Woodin Avenue, Chelan; 509-682-2561, 800-553-8225, fax 509-682-2177; www.campbellsresort.com, e-mail info@campbellsresort.com. MODERATE.

Winthrop's town hall was originally the Duck Brand Saloon, built in 1891.

A few doors down from Campbell's on the lakefront is **J.R.'s Bar and Grill**. It has two floors—with open-air seating on the top level—and specializes in lunches of sandwiches (some are purely vegetarian), soups and salads. Dinner offers a series of specials throughout the week, seafood, steak and several pastas. ~ 116 East Woodin Avenue, Chelan; 509-682-1031. BUDGET TO MODERATE.

SHOPPING

Art is popular, and quite often very good, in Winthrop, especially at **Hildabob's Gallery**, where you will find paintings, sculpture and handknit apparel. Closed January to mid-April. ~ 231 Riverside Avenue, Winthrop; 509-996-2094. Art by local artists is available in the gift shop. **Sun Mountain Lodge**. ~ Patterson Lake Road, Winthrop; 509-996-4716.

Art is also a growth industry in the Chelan area. **Main Street Gallery** features watercolors, oils, pottery, glass and sculpture by local artists, as well as clothing and accessories. ~ 208 East Woodin Avenue, Chelan; 509-682-9262; www.mainstreetgallerychelan.com.

However, the apple is king in Chelan, and **Culinary Apple** is a mail-order store with more than 1500 apple gift items, packaged apples and other Northwest-produced foods. ~ 109 East Woodin Avenue, Chelan; 509-682-3618, 800-568-6062; www.culinaryapple.com.

NIGHTLIFE

In Winthrop the **Winthrop Palace** offers live rock and rhythm-and-blues music most nights during summer. Cover on occasion. ~ 149 Riverside Avenue, Winthrop; 509-996-2245.

Not much happens in Chelan after dark, which may be fine if you're planning to wake up in time to catch the *Lady of the Lake* cruise in the morning. If you simply must go out, your best bet may be the **Ruby Theatre**, a small but historic pink theater that presents double-feature movies and weekend matinees. ~ 135 East Woodin Avenue, Chelan; 509-682-5016; www.rubytheatre.com.

Seven miles west of Chelan, the Colville Indian Reservation operates the **Mill Bay Casino**, with blackjack, roulette, craps and slot machines. ~ 455 Wapato Lake Road, Manson; 509-687-2102, 800-648-2946; www.colvillecasinos.com.

PARKS

PEARRYGIN LAKE STATE PARK This 696-acre park is popular for travelers in RVs because it is close to Winthrop and has a sandy beach on a small lake surrounded by mountains. Anglers will find rainbow trout off the fishing dock. Facilities include picnic areas, barbecue pits, restrooms and showers. Closed November through March. ~ Bear Creek Road, four miles northeast of Winthrop; 509-996-2370.

▲ There are 92 standard sites ($19 per night), two primitive sites ($14 per night) and 71 RV hookup sites ($26 per night). Reservations: 888-226-7688.

LAKE CHELAN STATE PARK This is a favorite park for youths yearning for sunshine, and in July and August the shoreline looks more like California than Washington with its broad, sandy beach (great swimming) and play area. Because it has docks and launching areas for skiers, it is equally popular with powerboaters and waterskiers. Anglers fish for rainbow trout, kokanee salmon, burbot, lake trout and bass as far away from the powerboats as possible. There are picnic tables, restrooms, a concession stand and showers. ~ Route 971, nine miles west of Chelan; 509-687-3710.

▲ There are 109 standard sites ($19 per night) and 35 RV hookup sites ($26 per night). Reservations highly recommended for summer: 888-226-7688.

TWENTY-FIVE MILE CREEK STATE PARK More remote than Lake Chelan State Park but popular with those more interested in mountain scenery than body scenery, this park is quiet, with the Chelan Mountains behind and the jagged peaks of the Sawtooth Wilderness across the lake. The small beach is mostly for wading, though boaters fish in the lake. There are picnic areas, restrooms, showers and moorage at the marina; a concession stand offers snacks, groceries and fishing supplies. Closed October through March. ~ Route 971, 20 miles up-lake from Chelan; 509-687-3610.

▲ There are 46 standard sites ($19 per night) and 21 RV hookup sites ($26 per night). Closed in winter. Reservations: 888-226-7688.

LINCOLN ROCK STATE PARK Named for a rock outcropping that resembles Abraham Lincoln's profile, this state park in the Columbia River canyon is a short distance north of Wenatchee. There is swimming, fishing for trout and salmon, and boating. Several species of wildlife reside in the park, including marmots, rabbits, deer, beaver, nighthawks and swallows. Facilities include picnic shelters, restrooms, showers, volleyball courts, a playfield and play equipment for children. Closed mid-October to early March. ~ Route 97/2, six miles north of East Wenatchee; 509-884-8702, fax 509-886-1704.

▲ There are 27 standard sites ($19 per night) and 67 RV hookup sites ($26 per night). Reservations: 888-226-7688.

Wenatchee Area

Famous for its apple orchards, the sunny Wenatchee Area is located in the heart of Washington. Popular with rafters and gold panners, this region is also home to one of the state's most picturesque gardens.

SIGHTS

You have a choice of two highways when leaving Chelan: You can continue along Route 97A, which cuts through the Cascade foothills back to the Columbia River and south to Wenatchee, or cross the Columbia at Chelan Falls, hardly more than a junction, and follow Route 97 south through the orchard town of Orando to East Wenatchee. Stop at **Rocky Reach Dam** to visit the Fish Viewing Room where healthy numbers of migratory salmon and steelhead swim past the windows. The dam also has a museum showing the natural and human history of the Columbia River, along with a Nez Perce Indian portrait collection and other rotating exhibits. Closed November to March. ~ Located 28 miles south of Chelan; 509-663-7522, fax 509-661-8149; www.chelanpud.org.

Wenatchee is the largest town in this region and directed more toward orchards than tourists, although you will certainly feel welcome. On the northern edge of town, overlooking the Columbia River, Wenatchee and Rocky Reach Dam, is **Ohme Gardens**. You will find nine acres of alpine gardens developed by the Ohme family on the steep, rocky outcroppings at the edge of their property overlooking the Columbia River. Closed mid-October to mid-April. Admission. ~ 3327 Ohme Road, Wenatchee; 509-662-5785, fax 509-662-6805; www.ohmegardens.com.

Downtown, the **Wenatchee Valley Museum & Cultural Center** has several permanent exhibits including a 1919 Wurlitzer theater pipe organ and an apple-packing shed featuring an apple wiper, sizing machine and a 1924 orchard truck. In the gift shop area is an original WPA mural by Peggy Strong depicting the change of the postal service from its pioneer days to a modern, organized unit. Closed Sunday and Monday. Admission. ~ 127 South Mission Street, Wenatchee; 509-664-3340, fax 509-664-3356; www.wenatcheevalleymuseum.com, e-mail info@wenatcheevalleymuseum.com.

Ten miles west via Routes 2 and 97, **Cashmere**, so-named because it reminded a pioneer of Kashmir, India, has an early American theme to its downtown buildings. The **Cashmere Pioneer Village and Museum** has almost two dozen original structures from Chelan and Douglas counties assembled to recreate a pioneer village, including a blacksmith shop, school, gold mine and hotel. Closed weekdays from November to late December; closed completely from late December through February. ~ 600 Cotlets Way, Cashmere; 509-782-3230, fax 509-782-3219.

From Cashmere, Routes 2 and 97 follow the swift Wenatchee River into the Cascades. Shortly before reaching Leavenworth, Route 97 turns south toward the Route 90 Corridor towns of Cle Elum and Ellensburg by going over 4101-foot **Blewett Pass.** An alternative route, in the summer only, is to follow the **Old Blewett Pass Highway**, which has been preserved by the Wenatchee National Forest. The old highway is a series of switchbacks with sweeping views of the Cascades. No services are available until you reach Cle Elum and Ellensburg, other than a small grocery store at **Liberty**, a gold-mining town just off the highway that is making a comeback as people move into its modest cabins along the main street.

LODGING

Most hotels in Wenatchee are along North Wenatchee Avenue. The largest hotel in this part of the state is the **Coast Wenatchee Center Hotel**, at nine stories one of the tallest buildings along the eastern edge of the Cascades. The 147 rooms are newly remodeled and larger than those at most other hotels in town, and suites have desks, armoires and potted plants. A large lobby has a baby grand piano. There's a restaurant, an indoor-outdoor pool and jacuzzi and a fitness center. ~ 201 North Wenatchee Avenue, Wenatchee; 509-662-1234, 800-716-6199, fax 509-662-0782; www.coasthotels.com. DELUXE.

For a low-priced place, try the **Super 8**. It has 103 rooms on three floors decorated with subtly flowered bedspreads, unobtrusive furniture and wallhangings. There is a heated pool and hot

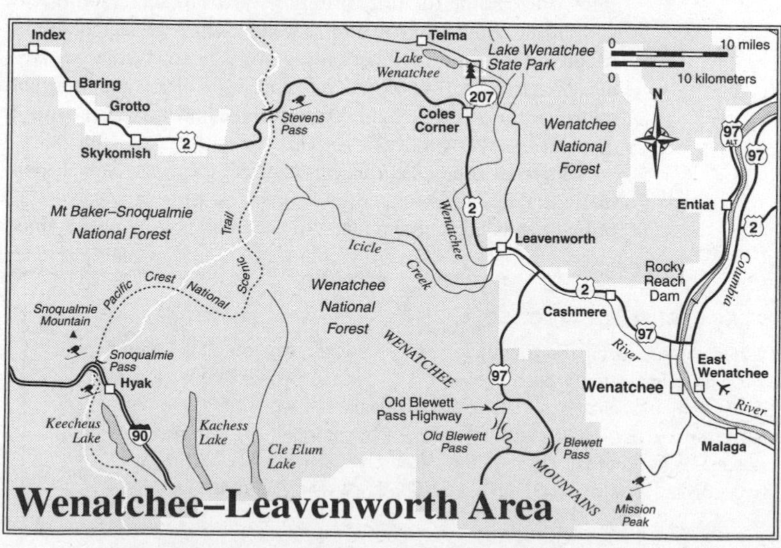

Wenatchee–Leavenworth Area

tub. Continental breakfast included. ~ 1401 North Miller Street, Wenatchee; 509-662-3443, 800-800-8000, fax 509-665-0715; www.super8wenatchee.com. MODERATE TO DELUXE.

The **Cedars Inn** offers 94 rooms with king- and queen-sized beds, fridges and microwaves; some king suites have whirlpool tubs. While comfortably adequate, the decor is standard motel. The large, 24-hour indoor pool, spa and fitness room helps set the Cedars Inn apart from others. Pets are welcome. A continental breakfast is served. ~ 80 9th Street Northeast, East Wenatchee; 509-886-8000, 800-358-2074, fax 509-886-0711; www.cedars-inn.net. MODERATE TO DELUXE.

The **Village Inn Motel** is in the heart of town. The white-and-green motel has 21 units, six with refrigerators. A bit impersonal, but it's clean, quiet and reasonably priced. ~ 229 Cottage Avenue, Cashmere; 509-782-3522, 800-793-3522, fax 509-782-8190; www.cashmerevillageinn.com. BUDGET.

DINING

Want Italian? Try **Visconti's Italian Restaurant.** Both Southern and Northern Italian dishes are offered in a family-friendly atmosphere. Their wood-fired oven is used to "broil-roast" seafood and prime cuts of meat. ~ 1737 North Wenatchee Avenue, Wenatchee; 509-662-5013, fax 509-667-9543; www.viscontis.com, e-mail wenatchee@viscontis.com. MODERATE TO DELUXE.

A top-notch steakhouse is **The Windmill.** It's a down-to-earth place, with waitresses who have been there for years. A blackboard keeps a running total of the number of steaks sold there since 1962. Prime rib and lobster are now offered in addition to a wide selection of meat and seafood dishes. Fresh-baked pies round out the meals. Dinner only. ~ 1501 North Wenatchee Avenue, Wenatchee; 509-665-9529, fax 509-662-5030; www.thewindmillrestaurant.com, e-mail greatsteaks@thewindmillrestaurant.com. MODERATE TO ULTRA-DELUXE.

As a reflection of Central Washington's growing Hispanic population, **Tequila's** is owned by former residents of Mexico. The refried beans are homemade, and the salsa is as tangy as you'd

STREETSIDE SHOWCASE

While you're touring the town, keep an eye out for **Art on the Avenues**, a town beautification project composed of over 65 bronze statues located in and around Wenatchee's public places. Mainly the work of Pacific Northwest artists, the pieces vary in size from as small as eight inches to as large as five feet tall. Contact the Wenatchee Downtown Association for information and a map. ~ 509-662-0059; www.artontheavenues.org.

get in Guadalajara. ~ 800 North Wenatchee Avenue, Wenatchee; 509-662-7239. MODERATE.

Wenatchee's top restaurant, **Shakti's**, has a sophisticated supper-club ambience and creative Northwest cuisine inspired by European traditions. To start, try homemade french onion soup or a salad of baby greens paired with locally smoked Columbia steelhead and capers. Entrées include handcut dry-aged steak, and Washington-grown chicken breast with artichoke hearts, kalamata olives, roma tomatoes, lemon and demiglace. Closed Sunday; no lunch on Saturday. Garden dining in spring and summer. ~ 218 North Mission Avenue, Wenatchee; 509-662-3321; www.shaktisfinedining.com, e-mail shaktis@charter.net. MODERATE TO DELUXE.

SHOPPING

A wide range of Washington souvenirs and products, everything from jam to smoked salmon, can be found at **Pak It Rite**. ~ 126 North Wenatchee Avenue, Wenatchee; 509-663-1072, 800-666-2730; www.pakitrite.com.

If you need a fix for an urban-size mall, the **Wenatchee Valley Mall** has 50 stores, making it the largest shopping center you'll encounter in the shadow of the Cascades. ~ 511 Valley Mall Parkway, East Wenatchee; 509-884-6645; www.wenatcheevalley mall.com.

Victorian Village is a small mall constructed in the best of the Victorian Carpenter Gothic style—round towers, falsefronts and steeples. You will find a hair salon, an equestrian shop and, interestingly for a Victorian theme, a Mexican restaurant. ~ 611 South Mission Street, Wenatchee.

For cider or wine tastings and gifts with an apple theme, check out the **Washington Apple Country Gift Shop**, located at the Cashmere Cider Mill. Open Monday through Friday from May through October; limited hours through February. ~ 5420 Woodring Canyon Road, Cashmere; 866-459-9614; www.washington applecountry.com.

Cashmere is the place to shop for a wide range of apple-based food products and gifts. Especially tempting is **Liberty Orchards**, which has been making fruit confections since 1920. Known for their Aplets and Cotlets, fruit-and-nut concoctions sprinkled with powdered sugar, Liberty Orchards also sells a wide variety of apple-themed gifts. Tours of the candy factory are offered on weekdays, and the company store is open weekends during the summer. ~ 117 Mission Street, Cashmere; 509-782-2191; www.libertyorchards.com, e-mail service@libertyorchards.com.

NIGHTLIFE

Although Wenatchee is the largest town in the Cascades, the nightlife choice is slim. Your best bet may be the lounges in some of the chain motor inns, but don't expect much. For a quick game of pool or a crack at a jukebox, try **Igloo.** ~ 1308 North Miller Street, Wenatchee; 509-663-4791.

PARKS

OKANOGAN-WENATCHEE NATIONAL FORESTS At 4 million acres, this is one of the largest national forests in the United States. It encompasses eight wilderness areas, hundreds of lakes, downhill-ski areas and more than 4000 miles of trails for hiking, riding and biking (including the Pacific Crest National Scenic Trail). Salmon, steelhead, searun cutthroat trout, bull trout, bass, crappie, walleye and sturgeon are among the fish found in streams and lakes. There are picnic areas and restrooms. ~ The forest is crossed by Routes 12, 97/2 and 90; 509-664-9200, fax 509-644-9280.

▲ There are more than 120 campgrounds; RVs accommodated in some campgrounds (no hookups); prices range from free to $18. Most campgrounds do not take reservations; the five that do can be reached at 877-444-6777.

Leavenworth Area

Think Bavarian! If you like cuckoo clocks, fancy woodwork, beer steins and alpenhorns, you'll love making a stop in Leavenworth.

SIGHTS

One of the major tourist spots in the Cascades, **Leavenworth** welcomes visitors with oompah bands, specialty stores and impressive alpine scenery. Almost everything here—architecture, hotels, restaurants, annual events—is centered around the Bavarian theme. Mountains are on three sides, and a river rushes through town. During most of the summer, free concerts and dancing exhibitions are given in the City Park, and outdoor art exhibits are held on weekends.

The only museum in the country devoted exclusively to nutcrackers, the **Leavenworth Nutcracker Museum** displays artifacts from as early as the 14th century up to modern times. The collection consists of more than 5000 nutcrackers from around the world, including Italy, Germany, Turkey, the U.S. and India. You'll see the popular soldier nutcracker, as well as nutcrackers in the shape of dragons, dogs and rams. Moses, Abraham Lincoln, Bugs Bunny, Thomas Edison and Shakespeare have all been immortalized as, you guessed it, nutcrackers in the museum's gift shop. Open daily 2 p.m. to 5 p.m. from May through October; open weekends only November through April. Admission. ~ 735 Front Street, Leavenworth; 509-548-4573, 509-548-4708, fax 509-548-4760; www.nutcrackermuseum.com, e-mail curator@nutcrackermuseum.com.

Just west of Leavenworth, Route 2 enters **Tumwater Canyon**, which follows the Wenatchee River some 20 miles. It is marked by sheer canyon walls, plunging river rapids and deciduous trees along the riverbank that turn into brilliant colors in autumn.

Route 2 continues over **Stevens Pass**, a popular ski area and where the **Pacific Crest National Scenic Trail** (see "Hiking" at the end of this chapter) crosses the highway. Soon after crossing the summit and passing Skykomish, the **Skykomish River** parallels the highway. This is one of Western Washington's most popular white-water rivers. Most trips originate in the small alpine village of **Index**, a short distance off the highway. The sheer-faced, 5979-foot **Mt. Index** looms behind the town. From there, the river rumbles down past the small towns of Gold Bar and Sultan, then flattens out onto the Puget Sound lowlands.

LODGING

One of the most pleasant spots in Leavenworth is the **Hotel Pension Anna.** It has 16 rooms with furniture and decor imported from Austria and Germany. Heavy wooden bed frames and cupboards are used throughout, along with feather beds and down comforters. Three suites come with fireplace and jacuzzi, and all rooms have private baths. Breakfast is included. ~ 926 Commercial Street, Leavenworth; 509-548-6273, 800-509-2662, fax 509-548-4656; www.pensionanna.com, e-mail info@pensionanna.com. MODERATE TO ULTRA-DELUXE.

A Bavarian wood carver was imported to fashion the rails and ceiling beams of the **Enzian Inn**, and the entire 105-room motel with its turret and chalet-styled roofs shows similar touches. The eight suites have king-size beds, spas and fireplaces. It has indoor and outdoor pools and hot tubs. During the win-

sights

AUTHOR FAVORITE

Salmon is everywhere around these parts, and there's no better place to learn about the mighty chinook than at the **Leavenworth National Fish Hatchery Complex**, devoted to the famous Northwest salmon's life cycle. In spring, millions of juvenile salmon and steelhead are released into the Icicle, Entiat and Methow rivers for migration to the Pacific Ocean. During summer, adult chinook salmon return to spawn. The newly spawned eggs develop in fall, and winter offers an opportunity to spy growing fish in indoor and outdoor holding pens. All tours are self-guided—the visitors center has comprehensive exhibits and artwork about salmon. ~ 12790 Fish Hatchery Road, Leavenworth. From Route 2, turn south on Icicle Road for about two miles then turn left on Fish Hatchery Road; 509-548-7641; www.fws.gov/leavenworth, e-mail leavenworth@fws.gov.

ter, cross-country ski equipment is available to guests; in summer, guests get a free round of putting at Enzian Falls Championship Putting Course. The complimentary buffet breakfast is served in the big solarium on the fourth floor. ~ 590 Route 2, Leavenworth; 509-548-5269, 800-223-8511, fax 509-548-9319; www.enzianinn.com, e-mail info@enzianinn.com. DELUXE.

For a change of pace, try renting one of the townhouses at the **Linderhof Inn**, next door to the Enzian Inn. The 11 townhouses are divided into one- and two-bedroom units that sleep six and eight respectively. They have cathedral ceilings with balcony bedrooms and full kitchens with all appliances. There are 22 additional units, some with fireplaces and spas, all with handcrafted furniture. There is an outdoor pool and hot tub. Continental breakfast is included, and there's wireless internet throughout the property. ~ 690 Route 2, Leavenworth; 509-548-5283, 800-828-5680, fax 509-548-6705; www.linderhof.com, e-mail info@linderhof.com. MODERATE.

More and more bed and breakfasts and inns are opening outside town. One is **Run of the River Inn & Refuge**, a mile east of Icicle River from Route 2. The building is made of logs and has cathedral ceilings with pine walls and handmade log furniture. The six rooms come with private baths and cable television, as well as jacuzzis, river-rock fireplaces and private decks. A private lodge sleeps two. Stay here, kick back and just contemplate the beautiful setting. There are complimentary mountain bikes for exploring the many surrounding trails and backroads and complimentary snowshoes in winter. Breakfasts are country-style. The inn accepts nonsmoking adults only. ~ 9308 East Leavenworth Road, Leavenworth; 509-548-7171, 800-288-6491, fax 509-548-7547; www.runoftheriver.com, e-mail info@runoftheriver.com. ULTRA-DELUXE.

Located in a wooded setting on the banks of the Wenatchee River, the **All Seasons River Inn** offers spacious rooms and suites overlooking the river, all with jacuzzis and most with fireplaces and private decks. The inn provides full breakfasts and bicycles for touring the nearby Icicle Loop. Nonsmoking; no children or pets. ~ 8751 Icicle Road, Leavenworth; 509-548-1425, 800-254-0555; www.allseasonsriverinn.com, e-mail info@allseasonsriverinn.com. ULTRA-DELUXE.

Farther down the mountain you'll find the **Dutch Cup Motel**, which is popular with skiers. The two-story motel has 20 environmentally friendly units with refrigerators, microwaves, wi-fi access and cable television. Small, quiet, supervised pets are welcome. ~ 918 Main Street, Sultan; 360-793-2215, 800-844-0488, fax 360-793-2216; www.dutchcup.com, e-mail dutchcup@mac.com. BUDGET TO MODERATE.

DINING

Café Mozart Restaurant's wall sconces, gold chandeliers, floral carpeted floors and candlelit tables create an intimate baroque-style atmosphere in each of the four dining rooms. The German-born chef prepares Central European favorites such as *kaesespaetzle* and smoked half duck glazed with orange-raspberry confiture. You might also find almond-crusted halibut with champagne-orange hollandaise sauce. If you have room for dessert or if you stop by between meals, treat yourself to Mozart's chocolate torte (seven layers of rich marzipan wine crème covered with dark chocolate). Reservations recommended. Open daily for lunch and dinner from June through October; no lunch Monday through Thursday from November through May. ~ 829 Front Street, Leavenworth; 509-548-0600; www.cafemozartrestaurant.com, e-mail mozart@crcwnet.com. MODERATE TO DELUXE.

Customers can watch the staff pull taffy on Saturday at the Taffy Shop. ~ 725 Front Street, Leavenworth; 509-548-4857.

What would a visit to the "Bavarian village" be without a meal of authentic German fare? At **King Ludwig's Restaurant**, the host's *leiderhosen* and the waitstaff's costumes add to the experience. Diners feast family-style on weinerschnitzel, *schweine schitzel* (ham cutlets) and a host of other *schnitzels* in this family-owned and -operated restaurant. Wash down the *schweinshax'n* (Bavarian-style pork hocks) with a large stein of German brew. On weekends, when the oompah or polka band takes the stage, diners enthusiastically cut up the well-worn dancefloor. ~ 921 Front Street, Leavenworth; 509-548-6625, fax 509-548-4101; www.kingludwigs.com, e-mail info@kingludwigs.com. MODERATE TO DELUXE.

The Gingerbread Factory is a delight for children and parents alike, with decorated cookies and gingerbread houses. The café sells pastries, bagels, quiches, sandwiches, soups, salads, espresso and all sorts of gifts related to gingerbread. Lunch only; although coffee and pastries are available for breakfast. Closed Wednesday and another weekday in winter; call for hours. ~ 828 Commercial Street, Leavenworth; 509-548-6592, 800-296-7079; www.gingerbreadfactory.com, e-mail sales@gingerbreadfactory.com. BUDGET.

The Dutch Cup Restaurant is one of the most popular restaurants on the Stevens Pass route. It opens at 7 a.m. to catch the ski crowd as they head up the highway and stays open until 8 p.m. to get them on the way home. The home-cooking menu includes country breakfasts, burgers, soups and sandwiches for lunch, and offers steaks, prime rib and chicken for dinner. ~ 927 Route 2, Sultan; 360-793-1864, fax 360-793-3447. MODERATE.

The **Index Café** offers breakfast and lunch to travelers heading up and down Route 2. Stop in for fish and chips, pot roast sandwiches and chicken with artichokes. ~ 49315 Route 2, Index; 360-799-1133. BUDGET.

SHOPPING

A Book for All Seasons offers a wide variety of books, cards and author readings. ~ 703 Route 2, Leavenworth; 509-548-1451.

The Feathered Nest carries a variety of American crafts, including ceramics, jewelry, metalwork and a complete line of Black Forest cuckoo clocks. ~ 715 Front Street, Leavenworth; 509-548-2064.

Nussknacker Haus specializes in all kinds of themed nutcracker dolls and "smokers," or figurines that puff incense smoke instead of cracking nuts. ~ 735 Front Street, Leavenworth; 509-548-4708, 800-892-3989; www.nussknackerhaus.com.

Die Musik Box imports elaborate music boxes from all over the world, including boxes shaped like instruments (pianos, guitars) and eggs. ~ 933 Front Street, Leavenworth; 800-288-5883; www.musicboxshop.com.

At **Bavarian Clothing Company**, you can try on feather-bedecked hats and boiled-wool jackets, and order custom-made lederhosen. ~ 933 Front Street, Leavenworth; 509-548-2442, fax 509-548-0479.

NIGHTLIFE

In a family-themed fun park, the **Icicle Junction Cinema** shows first-run films daily. ~ 565 Route 2, Leavenworth; 509-548-2400; www.iciclejunction.com.

True to its Germanic roots, Leavenworth offers plenty of live accordion music, including the annual summertime Leavenworth International accordion Celebration.

Andreas Keller German Restaurant offers live accordian music on weekends in winter and spring, nightly in summer and fall. ~ 829 Front Street, Leavenworth; 509-548-6000; www.andreaskellerrestaurant.com. For live rock and blues in the summer, try **Uncle Uli's Pub** on weekends. ~ 901 Front Street, Leavenworth; 509-548-7262.

Leavenworth's major sports bar is the **Old Post Office Tavern,** with TVs, pool tables and karaoke on Friday and Saturday nights. ~ 213 9th Street, Leavenworth; 509-548-7488.

PARKS

LAKE WENATCHEE STATE PARK The lake is tucked away near Stevens Pass and is popular in summer for canoeing, kayaking, sailing, swimming and fishing (kokanee and whitefish) and in the winter for cross-country skiing. The secluded, wooded campsites are great. Picnic areas, restrooms and showers are found here, and in July and August there are interpretive programs on Saturdays. ~ Route 207, 18 miles northwest of Leavenworth and four miles off Route 2; 509-763-3101.

▲ There are 155 standard sites ($19 per night) and about 42 RV hookup sites ($26 per night). Reservations: 888-226-7688.

Route 90 Corridor

This pristine area remains one of America's scenic icons. From snow-capped peaks to dramatic waterfalls, the corridor is one of the Northwest's hidden treasures. It extends from Snoqualmie across the Cascades to Ellensburg and the Kittitas Valley. Fasten your seat belts for a breathtaking ride past volcanic peaks, fir forests and rivers where you're likely to land tonight's dinner.

SIGHTS

The Cascades begin rising only a half-hour's drive east of Seattle. The town of **Snoqualmie** has an ornate, 1890 railroad depot that is the oldest continually operating train station in the country. It's also home to the **Snoqualmie Valley Railroad**, which makes a five-mile trip through the Snoqualmie Valley on weekends (April through October) and runs a special Christmas train. Admission. ~ 38625 Southeast King Street, Snoqualmie; 425-888-3030, fax 425-888-9311; www.trainmuseum.org; e-mail info@trainmuseum.org.

Inside the depot, the **Northwest Railway Museum** displays old railroad equipment and sleeper and dining car paraphernalia. ~ 425-888-3030.

Nearby is **Snoqualmie Falls**, a thundering cataract with a small park, observation platform and trails leading to the river below the 270-foot falls.

The town of **North Bend** has adopted an alpine theme for its downtown buildings, but it hasn't caught on with the vigor of Winthrop and Leavenworth. Not to be confused with the Oregon coastal town of the same name, this hamlet sits snugly in the shadow of the looming Mt. Si. The **North Bend Ranger District Forest Service Station** offers maps, books and other outdoor-recreation information. Closed Sunday; also closed Saturday in

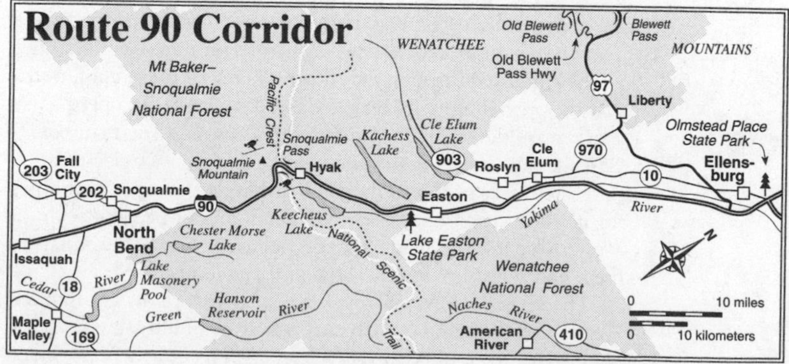

off-season. ~ 42404 Southeast North Bend Way, North Bend; 425-888-1421.

The Summit at Snoqualmie Pass has four major ski areas, for downhill and snowboarding, and one cross-country ski area with more than 35 miles of groomed trails. ~ 1001 State Route 906, Snoqualmie Pass; 425-434-7669; www.summitatsnoqualmie.com. **Snoqualmie Pass Visitor Center** offers maps and books. Closed Monday through Thursday and Labor Day to Memorial Day. ~ Exit 52 off Route 90 on State Route 906; on Snoqualmie Pass; 425-434-6111.

In **Cle Elum**, an American Indian name meaning "swift water," you will find the unusual **Cle Elum Historical Telephone Museum**, which commemorates and explains (through exhibits of ethnic costumes, old switchboards and railroad, logging and mining items) why Cle Elum was the last U.S. town to switch over from a manual long-distance switchboard. (Twenty-seven dialects were commonly heard during the town's early days as a mining center.) Closed weekdays and from Memorial Day to Labor Day. ~ 221 East 1st Street, Cle Elum; 509-674-5939; www.nkcmuseums.org, e-mail nkchs@yahoo.com.

The **Carpenter Museum** is actually a 1914 house that belonged to the first successful banker in Cle Elum. It's one of the few historic houses in the state that still has original furnishings. An art gallery features work by local artists. Closed Monday through Thursday. ~ 302 West 1st Street, Cle Elum; 509-674-9766.

At the foot of 4th Street is the access point for the 113-mile-long **Iron Horse State Park**, a section of the former railroad right of way with the rails and ties removed and the roadbed smoothed over for walking, jogging, cross-country skiing and biking. It is part of the **John Wayne Pioneer Trail** that will eventually run the width of the state.

Three miles away from Cle Elum is the tiny town of **Roslyn**, used as the set for TV's quirky "Northern Exposure." It was formerly a coal-mining town with a large population of Italian, Croatian and Austrian immigrants who worked in the mines. There are separate cemeteries—23 in fact—for these nationalities.

As you drive through the Kittitas Valley to Ellensburg, notice that the prevailing wind off the Cascades gives trees a permanent lean toward the east. When you reach Ellensburg, you're out of the Cascades and entering the arid climate that characterizes most of the eastern side of Washington. **Ellensburg** is perhaps best known for its rodeo each Labor Day weekend, and in keeping with the Western legacy, the Western Art Association has its headquarters there and holds an annual show and auction each May.

The **Clymer Museum of Art** displays work by the famous Western artist, John Ford Clymer, who lived in Ellensburg. Closed Sunday from January through April. ~ 416 North Pearl Street,

Ellensburg; 509-962-6416, fax 509-962-6424; www.clymermuseum.com, e-mail clymermuseum@charter.net.

The **Kittitas County Historical Museum** displays American Indian and pioneer artifacts and has extensive rock and doll collections. Closed Sunday. ~ 114 East 3rd Avenue, Ellensburg; 509-925-3778; www.kchm.org, e-mail kchm@kchm.org.

Four miles east of town is the **Olmstead Place State Park**, a working farm that uses pioneer equipment. The 217-acre farm and all its buildings were deeded to the state. Restrooms and picnic tables are available, and weekend tours are offered from Memorial Day to Labor Day. ~ 921 North Ferguson Road, Ellensburg; 509-925-1943.

LODGING

The Edgewick Inn, located two miles east of town, is a straightforward motel with 42 clean and quiet units and two suites with jacuzzis. ~ 14600 468th Avenue Southeast, North Bend; 425-888-9000, fax 425-888-9400; www.edgewickinn.com. MODERATE.

About the only place to stay at Snoqualmie Summit is the **Summit Lodge at Snoqualmie Pass.** Outfitted for skiers, its 81 rooms come with king-size or two queen-size beds, and it has a complimentary ski-storage area and coin-operated laundry. Tired guests also enjoy the indoor sauna, jacuzzi and heated outdoor pool. The large lobby is stocked with comfortable leather sofas set around the native-stone fireplace. ~ P.O. Box 163, Snoqualmie Pass, WA 98068; 425-434-6300, 800-557-7829, fax 425-434-6396. DELUXE.

A former Milwaukee Railroad crew house and recognized in the National Historic Register, **Iron Horse Inn** has been converted into one of the state's best inns. The 11 rooms, three with

AUTHOR FAVORITE

When I want to spend a pricey night in the lap of luxury, I can't think of a more dramatic setting to do it in than the clifftop **Salish Lodge and Spa at Snoqualmie Falls**, perched on the cliff overlooking the spectacular falls. Visitors might recognize it as the backdrop for the eerie David Lynch TV drama *Twin Peaks*. The 89 rooms and suites are decorated in an upscale-country motif with down comforters, wicker furniture, woodburning fireplaces and jacuzzis. Only a few rooms have views of the falls, but the interiors are so well done that most visitors console themselves by watching the falls from the lounge or observation deck. There is also a full-service spa. ~ 6501 Railroad Avenue Southeast, Snoqualmie; 425-888-2556, 800-272-5474, fax 425-888-2420; www.salishlodge.com, e-mail reservations@salishlodge.com. ULTRA-DELUXE.

shared baths, are named for former occupants. All are decorated in turn-of-the-20th-century antiques—with an emphasis, not surprisingly, on railroad trinkets and tools. Four remodeled cabooses sport queen-size beds, refrigerators and sundecks with hot tub. A third caboose and the deluxe honeymoon suite has a jacuzzi; an outdoor hot tub serves everyone else. The Iron Horse is adjacent to the Iron Horse State Park Trail, where cross-country skiing, bicycling, horseback riding and walking are popular. Full breakfast is included in the rate. ~ 526 Marie Avenue, South Cle Elum; 509-674-5939, 800-228-9246; www.ironhorseinnbb.com, e-mail maryp@ironhorseinnbb.com. MODERATE TO DELUXE.

In summer, when the water is really low, you can cross the river and explore behind Snoqualmie Falls.

For more impersonal lodgings, the **TimberLodge Inn**, on the western edge of town, has 35 bright, clean rooms and one deluxe suite with fridge, microwave and wi-fi, far enough off the street to deaden the noise of the busy main drag. Amenities include a hot tub. There is a daily breakfast bar. ~ 301 West 1st Street, Cle Elum; 509-674-5966, 800-584-1133, fax 509-674-2737. MODERATE.

A restored Victorian home located near the Central Washington University campus in downtown Ellensburg, the **Ellensburg Guest House** has two guest suites furnished with antiques and private baths. ~ 606 North Main Street, Ellensburg; 509-962-3706. DELUXE.

A restored Victorian home located near the Central Washington University campus in downtown Ellensburg, the **Meadowlark Guest House** has two guest suites furnished with antiques and private baths. A fruit-and-pastry breakfast is provided. ~ 606 North Main Street, Ellensburg; 509-962-3706, 888-699-0123. DELUXE.

DINING

The **Salish Lodge & Spa at Snoqualmie Falls** offers spectacular views over the falls and canyon below, and the food is first rate. The menu leans toward what has become known as Northwest cuisine: lots of seafood, fresh fruits and vegetables, and game. The restaurant boasts the largest wine list in the state and a dessert list almost as long. ~ 6501 Railroad Avenue, Snoqualmie; 425-888-2556, 800-272-5474; www.salishlodge.com, e-mail reservations@salishlodge.com. ULTRA-DELUXE.

Twede's Café, which served as the model for the diner in television's *Twin Peaks*, has faux gas lamps, wood paneling and neon across the ceiling. Stay for a cup of "damn good coffee" and their infamous cherry pie. ~ 137 West North Bend Way, North Bend; 425-831-5511. BUDGET.

Cle Elum is better known for its inns and small hotels, but it has at least one good restaurant, **Mama Vallone's Steak House**, where you never have to wait for someone to replenish your water or bring more bread. A specialty is *bagna cauda*, a fondue-style mixture of olive oil, anchovy and garlic served with dipping strips of steak or seafood. Lunch served only in summer on weekends. ~ 302 West 1st Street, Cle Elum; 509-674-5174. MODERATE TO DELUXE.

The **Starlight Lounge** offers updates on comfort food such as pan-fried chicken, cinnamon-crusted pork chops and the classic martini. Weekend brunch, too. ~ 402 North Pearl Street, Ellensburg; 509-962-6100. MODERATE TO DELUXE.

A short walk away is **The Valley Café**. Food is American with a Northwest flair. Fish (frequently salmon) and chicken dominate the dinner menu. There are also lamb, steak, pasta and vegetarian options on the menu. ~ 105 West 3rd Avenue, Ellensburg; 509-925-3050. MODERATE.

SHOPPING

In North Bend, 31 miles east of Seattle, the **Factory Stores at North Bend** is a mall with 50 stores selling well-known brands—Nike, the Gap, Van Heusen, Big Dog, Bass—at discount prices. ~ 461 South Fork Avenue Southwest, North Bend; 425-888-4505; www.factorystoresatnorthbend.com.

Antique hunters will enjoy Ellensburg, which has at least half a dozen antique stores in a three-block area, including a mall. The **Showplace Antique Mall** is a restored art deco theater with up to 40 antique dealers displaying at a time. ~ 103 East 3rd Avenue, Ellensburg; 509-962-9331.

NIGHTLIFE

Cle Elum has almost nothing in nightlife other than taverns with jukeboxes, although occasionally **Iron Horse Inn** guests will bring their own instruments to the piano in the lobby area for a sing-along. ~ 526 Marie Avenue, South Cle Elum; 509-674-5939; www.ironhorseinbb.com.

In Ellensburg between the rodeos there is little entertainment, but **The Tav** keeps 'em at the bar with brews and jukebox music. Occasional live music and cover. ~ West 4th Avenue, Ellensburg; 509-925-3939.

PARKS

LAKE EASTON STATE PARK

On Route 90, near the summit at Snoqualmie Pass, this lakeside park with forested trails is used as a base for skiers and snowmobilers in winter, as a lunch stop for travelers in spring and fall, and for hiking, swimming and trout fishing in the summer. Facilities include picnic areas, a swimming beach and restrooms. ~ Route 90, a mile west of Easton; 509-656-2230.

▲ There are 95 standard sites ($19 per night) near the Yakima River and 45 RV hookup sites ($26 per night) near the lake. Reservations: 888-226-7688.

Mt. Rainier Area

It is always a dramatic moment when Mt. Rainier suddenly appears ahead of you (in the Northwest it is often just called The Mountain). You could spend weeks in this area and only sample a small portion of its recreational possibilities. Whether you approach from the east or the west, the forest gets thicker and thicker and the roadside rivers get swifter and swifter. The national park is almost surrounded with national forest wilderness areas as buffer zones against clear-cut logging. Located southeast of Seattle, this peak is the site of the aptly named town of Paradise. *Note: Mount Ranier experienced massive flooding in November 2006 and severe damage to visitors services and trails closed the park for nearly six months. Some areas have already reopened, including the Stevens Canyon Entrance, the National Park Inn and the Road to Paradise, but the superintendent states it may take two years for the park to fully recover.*

SIGHTS

Coming from Route 5 down Route 7 toward Mt. Rainier, right before the town of Elbe is a turnoff that will take you north on Route 161 to **Northwest Trek Wildlife Park.** A free-roaming animal park owned by the Tacoma Metro Parks Department, it provides a rare opportunity to see native wildlife of the Pacific Northwest up close. The highlight is a 55-minute tram ride around a 435-acre expanse of forest and meadows inhabited by hundreds of large grazing animals, including bison, caribou, bighorn sheep, mountain goats, Roosevelt elk and a few elusive moose. Migratory sandhill cranes and geese also live in the park. There is often a wait of an hour or more for the tram ride. In the meantime, you can walk around the more conventionally zoolike area near the tour station and see predators such as wolves, bears, cougars, owls and eagles as well as smaller animals like beavers, raccoons and badgers that would be hard to spot in a free-roaming setting. There's also a network of paved and unpaved nature trails that can take an hour or more to explore fully, plus a hands-on discovery center for kids. The gift shop features animal-motif gift items made by regional artisans, and the café has a full lunch menu as well as an outdoor picnic area. If you're planning to visit Mt. Rainier, Northwest Trek is right on the way. Closed Monday through Thursday from November to mid-February. Admission. ~ 11610 Trek Drive East (off Route 161), Eatonville; 360-832-6117, fax 360-832-6118; www.nwtrek.org.

If you arrive via Route 706 you will have to go through Elbe on Route 7 which has the **Mt. Rainier Scenic Railroad**, a steam-powered train that makes a 14-mile trip through the lush forest and across high bridges to Mineral Lake. It runs daily from July through September and on Saturday and Sunday in June and

December. ~ P.O. Box 250, Mineral, WA 98355; 360-492-5588, 888-783-2611; www.mrsr.com.

Once inside the park you may be almost overwhelmed by the scenery. **Mt. Rainier** is so monstrous (14,410 feet) that it makes everything around it seem trivial. In fact, Mt. Rainier is the tallest mountain in the Northwest and has more glaciers—25—than any other mountain in the contiguous 48 states. **Mt. Rainier National Park** has numerous visitor centers and interpretive exhibits along winding roads. For park information, contact the National Park Service in the Longmire Museum at 360-569-2211 ext. 3314; www.nps.gov/mora.

In **Paradise**, head to the **Henry M. Jackson Visitor Center,** which has several exhibits and audiovisual shows. Paradise is one of the most beautiful places in the park, and the visitors center is one of the busiest. It has a snack bar and gift shop. Closed weekdays (except holidays) between October and April. *Note: The visitors center also contains the Guide Center for those wishing to arrange a climb to the summit. This visitors center will close permanently in fall 2008 and be replaced by the smaller but more energy-efficient new Paradise Visitor Center, which is under construction nearby.* ~ Paradise, WA; 360-569-2211 ext. 2328.

The **Longmire Museum** emphasizes the natural history of the park with rock, flora and fauna exhibits as well as with exhibits on the human history of the area. Its old historic buildings have stood since the 1880s when the Longmire family lived there. The museum also has information for hikers, and next door at the National Park Inn you can rent cross-country skis or snowshoes. ~ Longmire, WA; 360-569-2211 ext. 3314; www.nps.gov/mora.

The **Ohanapecosh Visitor Center**, located down in the southeast corner near a grove of giant, ancient cedar trees, has history and nature exhibits. Closed mid-October through May. ~ 360-569-6046.

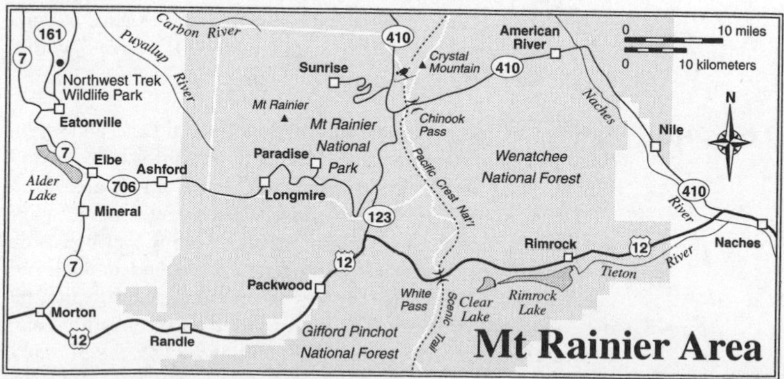

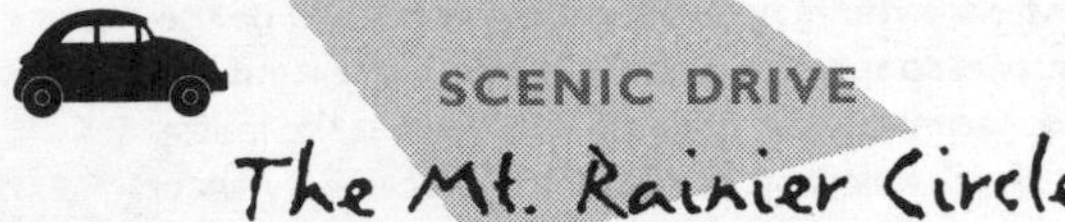

SCENIC DRIVE

The Mt. Rainier Circle

Mt. Rainier, the huge landmark mountain visible (on clear days) from everywhere in the Puget Sound area, makes for a spectacularly scenic all-day trip from Seattle. Heading south from the city on Route 5, take Exit 149, drive two miles to Kent, and turn south on Route 167, another wide, fast, divided highway. Go seven miles to Puyallup, turn off on Route 161, and suddenly you're off the freeway and on your way through the forests and farmlands of Pierce County.

NORTHWEST TREK WILDLIFE PARK Located about 17 miles south of Puyallup is Northwest Trek Wildlife Park (page 308), Washington's premier animal park, where you can take an hour-long tram tour for an up-close look at large animals native to the Pacific Northwest roaming in a 435-acre natural habitat. There's usually a wait, so expect to spend two to three hours here.

PARADISE Ten miles south of Northwest Trek, Route 161 meets Route 7. Turn south (left) and go nine miles to Elbe, where Route 706, the well-marked road to **Mt. Rainier National Park** (page 314), turns off to the east (left). Passing Alder Lake, it's about 15 miles to the park's Nisqually Entrance, where on sunny weekends you may have to wait in a long line to pay the $10-per-vehicle entrance fee. As you drive through

The **Sunrise Visitor Center** has geological displays and at 6400 feet is the closest you can drive to the peak. Numerous trails fan out from the center for day hikes, but be aware that even into July, there is often snow on the trails. ~ 360-663-2425.

Nearby, at the intersection of Routes 410 and 12 east of the mountain, you can watch elk and bighorn sheep being fed by game officials during the middle of winter at the **Oak Creek Wildlife Recreation Area**, which is accessible only from Route 12.

LODGING Two inns are located inside Mt. Rainier National Park, and several other places to stay are around the park in Ashford, Packwood, Elbe, Crystal Mountain, Morton and the White Pass area.

The most popular is **Paradise Inn**. Nineteen miles into the park, this nonsmoking inn has 126 rooms and a lobby that boasts exposed beams, peeled-log posts, wooden furniture, Indian-made rugs and two huge fireplaces. The views from outside are grand, but the rooms are ordinary. The inn is closed for renovations until May 2008. ~ Paradise, WA 98398; 360-569-2275, fax 360-569-

lofty primeval forest at the base of the mountain, you'll see signs of a vast mudslide that occurred when the sleeping volcanic giant stirred and melted part of the glacier that caps its summit. About 15 miles into the park, a turnoff on the left takes you up to timberline at Paradise, where the busy visitors center has a cafeteria, trails that wend through alpine meadows, and exhibits about climbing the mountain.

SUNRISE Beyond the Paradise turnoff, Route 706 is closed in the winter but stunning in the summer as it traverses Backbone Ridge, offering panoramic views of the jagged Catamount Range to the southeast. In about 15 miles you'll join Route 123 northbound. Another ten miles brings you to the summit of 4675-foot Cayuse Pass. Four miles farther on is the turnoff on the left that winds by switchbacks up the east slope of the mountain to **Sunrise Visitor Center**, a 16-mile climb to the highest point in the park that you can reach by car. Another network of alpine hiking trails starts here, and it's usually much less crowded than Paradise.

HOMEWARD When you descend from Sunrise, turn north (left) on Route 123 and you're on your way out of the park. The highway takes you 38 miles through **Mt. Baker–Snoqualmie National Forest** (page 284) to Enumclaw. Angle to the right on Route 164, drive 15 miles to Auburn, and hop onto divided four-lane Route 18 westbound. Three quick miles and you're back on Route 5, just 20 miles south of downtown Seattle. Allow one and a half hours for the return trip from Mt. Rainier to Seattle.

2770; http://ranier.guestservices.com, e-mail mtranierreservations@guestservices.com. MODERATE.

The other in-park hotel is the **National Park Inn**, six miles from the Nisqually entrance. Built in 1916, the inn offers much of the rustic charm of the Paradise Inn, yet is much smaller with only 25 rooms, 18 with private baths. Some rooms have views of the mountain. In keeping with the rustic theme, there are no telephones or televisions. The lobby has an enormous stone fireplace. ~ Longmire, WA 98397; 360-569-2275, fax 360-569-2770; ranier.guestservices.com, e-mail mtranierreservations@guestservices.com. MODERATE TO DELUXE.

Equally popular with lovers of old inns is **Alexander's Country Inn & Restaurant**. This inn was built in 1912 as a small hotel designed to look like a manor with turret rooms and grand entrance hall. It retains the Old World look while adding modern conveniences such as a hot tub in a backyard gazebo, a media room and a day spa. A full-course country breakfast is included, as is wine in the evening. ~ 37515 Route 706 East, Ashford; 360-

569-2300, 800-654-7615, fax 360-569-2323; www.alexanderscountryinn.com, e-mail info@alexanderscountryinn.com. MODERATE TO DELUXE.

In Packwood on the southern flank of the national park is the **Cowlitz River Lodge.** It is notable for clean, brightly decorated rooms and views of the mountains, although not "The Mountain." It is set back from the busy Route 12 far enough for the logging trucks to be a distant hum rather than an immediate roar. ~ 13069 Route 12, Packwood; 360-494-4444, 888-305-2185, fax 360-494-2075; www.escapetothemountains.com, e-mail cowlitz000@centurytel.com. MODERATE.

On the northeast boundary of the park is **Crystal Mountain Resort,** a year-round resort that is best known for its skiing. Visitors can choose from a number of places to stay, ranging from condominiums to inexpensive hotels, all of which are nonsmoking. Don't expect much charm because skiing, not hotel amenities, is the focus. Typical is **Silver Skis Lodge and Crystal Chalets,** which has a cluster of one- and two-bedroom units, some with fireplaces and views. All have kitchens and televisions and can sleep from four to eight people. They are decorated in the traditional rental-condo manner of wood furniture and durable fabrics. ~ Crystal Mountain Lodging, 33000 Crystal Mountain Boulevard, Crystal Mountain; 360-663-2558, 888-668-4368, fax 360-663-0145; www.crystalmtlodging-wa.com. MODERATE TO ULTRA-DELUXE.

A bit farther east toward Yakima is the White Pass ski area with **The White Pass Village Inn.** The complex has 50 rental units designed for large groups, up to eight in many units, and they have a bit of variation in decor since all are privately owned. Some have fireplaces and sleeping lofts, while all have full kitchen facilities. ~ P.O. Box 3035, White Pass, WA 98937; 509-672-3131, fax 509-672-3133; www.whitepassvillageinn.com, e-mail info@whitepassvillageinn.com. MODERATE TO DELUXE.

DINING

Good restaurants are hard to find around Mt. Rainier but there are a few worth mentioning.

A funky little roadside burger stand, **Scale Shack Burgers** delights the Mt. Rainier visitors who make yearly pilgrimages to the mountain. The Overload Burger (a quarter-pounder with two slices of bacon and cheese) and the frothy milkshakes will tide over any roadtrip hunger pangs. Closed weekdays in the off-season. ~ Route 706, Elbe; 360-569-2247. BUDGET.

The traditional **Alexander's Country Inn & Restaurant** boasts a dining room with windows that look out over the forest. Trout from the glacier-fed trout pond is a favorite, along with seafood; all the breads and desserts are homemade. They also prepare box lunches. Breakfast, lunch and dinner served. Open weekends only in winter. ~ 37515 Route 706 East, Ashford; 360-569-2300, 800-654-7615, fax 360-569-2323; www.alexanderscountry inn.com. MODERATE TO DELUXE.

Set on three wooded acres, which also include log cabins and an RV park, the **Gateway Inn** offers a wood-paneled coffee shop–style restaurant serving breakfast, lunch and dinner. The standard road fare of burgers, steaks and omelettes is enhanced by local trout and freshly baked breads and fruit pies. ~ 38820 Route 706 East, Ashford; 360-569-2506. BUDGET TO MODERATE.

Mt. Rainier last erupted around 1845, and the mountain has been quiet since. However, steam vents on the summit are still active, and geologists warn another eruption is inevitable—someday.

One of the most popular restaurants between Mt. Rainier and Mt. St. Helens is **Peters Inn**, a large, old-fashioned place where they serve burgers, steaks and some seafood. In busy seasons, they have a large salad bar. Pies and cinnamon rolls are made locally. ~ 13051 Route 12, Packwood; 360-494-4000. MODERATE.

The **Whistlin' Jack Lodge** is a rustic lodge 20 miles east of Mt. Rainier National Park that offers a sophisticated level of dining unusual in these parts. Pan-fried rainbow trout boned tableside and a signature appetizer of crab-stuffed artichoke hearts served with garlic toast points are among the specialties. Prime rib, lobster and "bubbleberry" pie (a blend of apples, cherries, raspberries and huckleberries) round out the menu. Breakfasts are also exceptional, with items such as huckleberry coffee cake. The spacious dining area is set with white linen napery and the lounge features a huge fireplace built from local river rock. Picture windows overlook the Naches River. ~ 20800 State Route 410, Naches; 509-658-2433, 800-827-2299; www.whistlinjacklodge.com. MODERATE TO ULTRA-DELUXE.

PARKS

NORTHWEST TREK WILDLIFE PARK Located 35 miles south of Tacoma this 635-acre nature preserve is operated by the Metropolitan Park District of Tacoma, which provides close but safe encounters with grizzly bears and other wildlife. Walking along the five miles of trails at Northwest Trek, visitors are also likely to see bobcats, martens, wolverines, eagles and owls. In the park's Bear Exhibit, one of the largest in North America, grizzlies and black bears live in outdoor enclosures designed to mimic their natural habitats. A tram tour takes visitors through 435 acres, where they will see bison, deer, elk, mountain goats, caribou, big horn sheep and moose. There is also the Cheney Discovery Center where children can handle reptiles and observe bee and ant societies at work. Closed Monday through Thursday from November to mid-February. Day-use fee, $13.50. ~ 11610 Trek Drive East, Eatonville; 360-832-6117, fax 360-832-6118; www.nwtrek.org.

MT. RAINIER NATIONAL PARK One of the most heavily used national parks in Washington, Mt. Rainier is everybody's favorite because the mountain can be approached from so many directions and the area around it is glorious no matter the time of year. The mountain is open for climbing for individuals or groups, and may be done under the leadership of Rainier Mountaineering Inc. (360-569-2227; www.rmiguides.com, e-mail info@rmiguides.com), or by direct registration with the climbing rangers, for experienced mountaineers. The park charges a climbing fee per person, per climb above 10,000 feet. Otherwise, you can hike the lower stretches of the mountain. The lower elevations are notable for the great views of vast meadows covered with wildflowers from July until August, and for dramatic fall colors in September and October. Numerous trails lead day hikers to viewpoints, and backpackers can register on a permit system for backcountry campsites. A backcountry fee may be charged for a reservation for overnight trips during the summer months. The park is open year-round with special areas set aside for winter sports at Paradise. Fishing is permitted in designated waters without a state license. Check with a ranger for regulations. You will find picnic areas, restrooms, four information centers, museums and self-guided nature trails. Day-use fee, $15 per vehicle (good for seven days). ~ Entrances to the park are located on Route 410 on the northeast, Route 706 on the southwest and Route 123 on the southeast; 360-569-2211 ext. 3314, 888-892-5462.

▲ There are four car campgrounds, one walk-in campground, and one campground accessible only to high-clearance vehicles. Overnight hike-in backcountry areas are first-come, first-served, though you can reserve a spot ($20 reservation fee). RVs are allowed (no hookups). Fees range from free to $15 per night. Information about making reservations for two campgrounds during the summer months can be found at www.nps.gov/mora.

Mt. St. Helens Area

There are few certitudes in travel writing, but here's one: Don't miss Mt. St. Helens. At the southern end of the Washington Cascades an hour north of Portland, this peak might best be described as a cross between a geology lesson and a bombing range. East of this landmark is Gifford Pinchot National Forest and Mt. Adams Wilderness, the heart of a popular recreation area ideal for rafting and fishing.

On May 18, 1980, Mt. St. Helens, dormant for 123 years, blew some 1300 feet off its top and killed 57 persons, causing one of the largest natural disasters in recorded North American history.

Today, access to the volcano remains limited because the blast and resulting mudslides and floods erased the roads that formerly entered the area.

SIGHTS

A major sightseeing destination, **Mt. St. Helens Visitor Center** is on Route 504 at Silver Lake, five miles east of Route 5. The center is elaborate and includes a walk-in model of the inside of the volcano and other volcanoes in the Cascades. Two short films about the eruption play almost continuously. ~ 3029 Spirit Lake Highway, Silver Lake; 360-274-0962, fax 360-274-9285.

Windy Ridge is the closest you can get to the volcano, and it is reached by driving south from Randle on a series of Forest Service roads. Hourly talks are given by rangers in the amphitheater there in summer. **Meta Lake Walk** is on the way to Windy Ridge, and rangers tell how wildlife survived the blast. A 30-minute talk is given in **Ape Cave** on the southern end of the monument. It includes a walk into the 1900-year-old lava tube that got its name from the first group of people who mapped and explored the cave, a boy scout group called St. Helens Apes.

East of Mt. St. Helens, continue south through **Gifford Pinchot National Forest** on paved national forest roads. First, buy a copy of the national forest map at the forest headquarters visitors centers, or from a ranger station. You can drive to the edge of **Indian Heaven Wilderness Area** and hike through peaceful meadows and acres of huckleberry bushes, or continue east to the edge of the **Mt. Adams Wilderness Area** with views of that mountain reflected in lakes. Day and overnight permits are required to enter

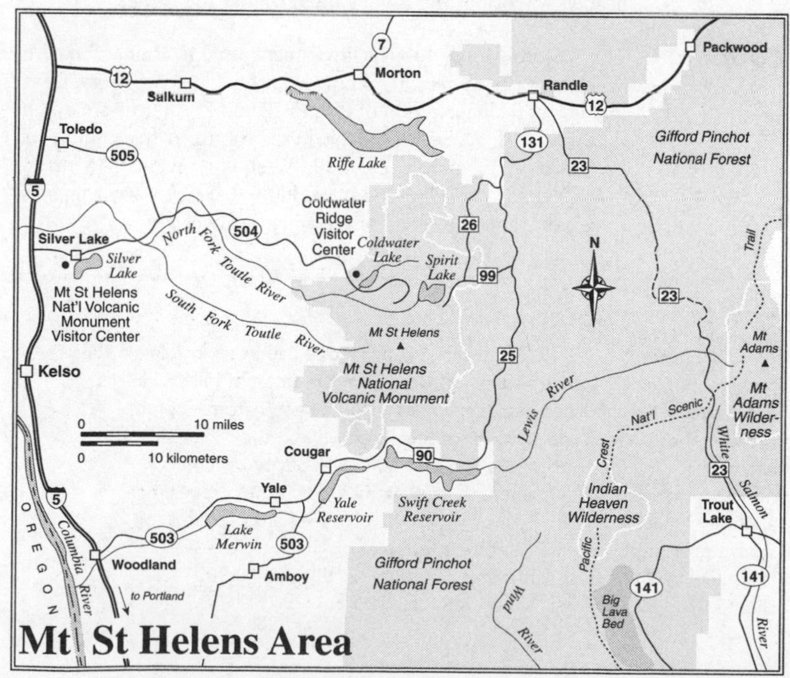

wilderness areas in the Gifford Pinchot National Forest. This whole area is known for wild huckleberries, and there are two seasons for them; in the lower elevations, they ripen in July and into August, then a week or two later the higher-elevation berries ripen. For more information, call the Gifford Pinchot National Forest Headquarters. ~ 360-891-5001, fax 360-891-5045; www.fs.fed.us/gpnf.

The roads will eventually take you to **Trout Lake,** a small town close to a wetland area of the same name near Mt. Adams. Here you'll find all services and a Forest Service Ranger Station. Just west of town is a vast lava flow called the **Big Lava Beds** and a lava tube called **Ice Cave**, which is chilly all through the summer. Both are reached on Forest Service roads.

HIDDEN ► From Trout Lake, drive east 16 miles to the small cowboy town of **Glenwood.** There's not much more than a country tavern and post office to the town, but in the Shade Tree Inn tavern you can get directions to some of the more unusual sights in the area, such as 300-foot-high basalt columns and what is locally called "volcano pits," a series of small craters left behind by cinder cones.

From Glenwood, take the Glenwood-Goldendale Road to the junction with Route 142 and drive back southwest to Klickitat and the Columbia Gorge at Lyle. This takes you through the deep, winding Klickitat River Canyon with views of the river, a steelheaders' favorite. Mt. Adams often frames the scene.

LODGING

The **Seasons Motel**, about halfway between Mt. Rainier and Mt. St. Helens, has 49 recently renovated rooms in a two-story, frame building at the intersection of Routes 12 and 7. All beds are queen-sized and wi-fi access is available in the rooms. A free continental breakfast is available. ~ 200 Westlake Avenue, Morton; 360-496-6835, 877-496-6835, fax 360-496-5127; www.whitepasstravel.com, e-mail reservations@whitepasstravel.com. MODERATE.

THE DAY THE MOUNTAIN BLEW

At 8:32 a.m. on May 18, 1980, the growing bulge that had been forming in the past weeks pushed a small section of rock down the slope of Mt. St. Helens, and suddenly the mountain exploded with the force of 500 atomic bombs the size of the one dropped on Hiroshima. It powdered the mountainside and blew it into the atmosphere at about 500 miles per hour. Simultaneously, practically the whole north flank lurched down the mountain at about 200 miles per hour. By evening, ash had covered a quarter-million square miles in three states and the silhouette of Mt. St. Helens was left standing with a huge bite taken out of its north slope—1300 feet shorter than its 9677-foot stature the day before.

Located 17 miles west of Morton in the tiny town of Salkum, **The Shepherd's Inn** is about 45 minutes away from Mt. Rainier and one hour away from Mt. St. Helens. The inn's five rooms offer country Victorian furnishings and brass beds. If you have the urge to tickle the ivories, you may do so on the grand piano. There's also a double jacuzzi. Full breakfast includes wild huckleberry crêpes. ~ 168 Autumn Heights Drive, Salkum; 360-985-2434, 800-985-2434; www.theshepherdsinn.com, e-mail shepherd@theshepherdsinn.com. MODERATE.

◄ HIDDEN

The Farm Bed and Breakfast is on six acres in Trout Lake, close to Mt. Adams. Two rooms decorated in antiques with cozy quilts are available in this three-story 1890 farmhouse. Surrounding the B&B are perennial gardens, a barn and a vegetable garden. Hosts Rosie and Dean Hostetter serve a full breakfast with fresh raspberries and strawberries in season. ~ 490 Sunnyside Road, Trout Lake; 509-395-2488; www.thefarmbnb.com, e-mail innkeeper@thefarmbnb.com. MODERATE.

Also on the southeastern edge of Mt. Adams is the outdoor-oriented **Flying L Ranch**. Originally a working ranch, since 1960 the Flying L has been a guest ranch but now without horses. Hiking and photography are popular here. Bikes are available free of charge to get around the mostly flat roads in the area. In the winter, cross-country skiing and snowshoeing access is nearby. The main lodge has six rooms, five with private baths; a two-story guesthouse has five rooms with private baths, and three separate cabins sleep four to six. The main lodge has a large common kitchen where guests can prepare their own lunches and dinners. ~ 25 Flying L Lane, Glenwood; 509-364-3488, 888-682-3267; www.mt-adams.com, e-mail flyingl@mt-adams.com. MODERATE TO DELUXE.

◄ HIDDEN

DINING

The **Wheel Café** has long been a local fixture in downtown Morton, with its all-pine paneling. Breakfast specialties include blueberry or strawberry pancakes, while dinner choices are a large salad bar, steaks, prime rib, burgers, fish and chips and housemade pies. There is also an adjoining bar area with dart boards, pool table and pull tabs. ~ 185 Main Street, Morton; 360-496-3240. BUDGET TO MODERATE.

Plaza Jalisco offers classic Mexican fare, with daily specials such as *pollo loco*. ~ 200 Westlake Avenue, Morton; 360-496-6660. MODERATE.

PARKS

MT. ST. HELENS NATIONAL VOLCANIC MONUMENT The monument covers 110,000 acres and was created to preserve and interpret the area that was devastated by the 1980 eruption. Interpretive centers and overlooks along Route 504 show vast mud flows and the forests that were flattened by the blast. Access to the east side of the monument is limited to a few Forest Service roads, most of which are closed in the winter. Fishing is excellent for bass and trout in nearby Silver Lake and good for trout in lakes behind dams on the Lewis River, south of the monument. Facilities include interpretive centers, picnic areas, scenic overlooks and self-guided nature walks; viewpoints on the east side are closed during the winter. ~ From the west, Route 504 (Exit 49 from Route 5) leads to the Mt. St. Helens Visitor Center on the shores of Silver Lake, as well as the Coldwater Ridge Observatory (Milepost 43) and the Johnson Ridge Observatory (Milepost 52); Southside attractions are along Route 503 (Exit 21 from Route 5). The eastside blast area, including Windy Ridge, is located on Route 99, accessible from the north via Route 12 to Forest Road 25 and from the south via Route 503 to Forest Road 25; 360-449-7800, fax 360-449-7801.

GIFFORD PINCHOT NATIONAL FOREST This 1.37-million-acre forest covers most of the southern Cascades to the Columbia River, marked by the Mt. St. Helens Volcanic National Monument on the west and Mt. Adams on the east. Enclosing seven wilderness areas, the forest is well-accessed by a network of roads and trails used for a variety of recreational uses. Of particular interest are the **Big Lava Beds**, 14 miles west of Trout Lake, where unusual formations of basalt are found, and the **Ice Cave**, six miles southwest of Trout Lake, a lava tube where ice remains until late summer. Rivers and frequently stocked lakes offer excellent fishing. In late summer, huckleberry picking is very popular. You'll find picnic areas and restrooms. Parking fee, $5. ~ The easiest way to reach the forest is by Route 12 from the north. There is also access on smaller roads such as State Route 14, State Route 141, State Route 503 off Route 5 at Woodland, and Route 504 off Route 5 at Castle Rock; 360-891-5000, fax 360-891-5010.

A WINDOW TO THE PAST

American Indian culture is alive and well throughout Klickitat County, the north shore site of over 10,000 years of coastal Chinook and interior Sahaptin tribes habitation. Collectively known today as the Yakama Nation, these traditional fishermen can be seen fishing using specialized long-handled nets while precariously perched on platforms that extend out over falls and turbulent rapids. The Fisher Hill Bridge near Klickitat is one of the best places to witness their catch during spring and fall salmon and smelt runs.

▲ There are 24 campgrounds ($10 to $91 per night), 21 primitive campgrounds and 10 horse camps. Reservations: 877-444-6777; www.fs.fed.us/gpnf.

Outdoor Adventures

FISHING

Winter steelhead, Dolly Varden, rainbow trout, eastern brook trout, walleye, sturgeon, catfish, bass, perch and crappie all can be caught in the interior and along the flanks of the Cascade Range. Fishing is typically done from the banks or on private boats, but most resorts on lakes and rivers have boats and fishing tackle for rent.

The other Cascade rivers, such as the Methow, Wenatchee, Yakima, Snake and Klickitat, drain into the Columbia River. All have good trout, walleye and steelhead fishing. The Klickitat River has an excellent summer steelhead run as does the Columbia. As their numbers continue to dwindle, fewer and fewer salmon can be caught upstream from the Bonneville Lock and Dam, the first of 14 dams on the river.

You'll need a Washington State Fishing License to fish in most places, although not in all national parks. You can buy one at most bait shops.

NORTH CASCADES Several rivers in the area—Skykomish, Snohomish, Sauk and Skagit for example—provide year-round catches, notably steelhead and all species of salmon except sockeye (it's not permitted to take this fish from rivers). **John's Guide Service** offers fishing trips for small groups throughout the North Cascades region. ▸ Concrete; 360-853-9801; www.johnsguideservice.com, e-mail johnsguidesvc@hotmail.com.

RIVER RUNNING

"Mild to wild"—that's how one outfitter describes the range of whitewater-rafting experiences in the Cascades. From the easy Class I and II rapids on the Skagit, to the steady Class II and III staircase rapids on the Suiattle, to the Tieton's Class IV and the Skykomish's Class IV-plus rapids, whitewater-rafting trips are fun and popular throughout the Cascades. In the Wenatchee–Leavenworth area, the Wenatchee River, which has a relatively easy Class III rapid, makes a great trip for families with children. Depending on the river, outfitters generally operate April through October. From mid-December through January, the Skagit is the place for float trips to observe bald eagles, who migrate to the area to feed on salmon from the river. A caveat, though: One guide warns that classifications can be misleading, and inexperienced rafters may think they can handle rapids beyond their skill.

NORTH CASCADES **Downstream River Runners** rafts the Skagit, Sauk and Suiattle rivers in the North Cascades region, as well as several others elsewhere in the state. They do trips at all levels of difficulty (rivers range from Class I to Class V). Eagle-viewing trips are offered in December and January. Downstream doesn't rent boats, but it offers many years of experience. ~ Monroe; 206-906-9227; www.riverpeople.com, e-mail rafting@riverpeople.com.

WENATCHEE AREA Besides whitewater trips, **All Adventures Rafting** offers eagle-viewing and scenic floats (accompanied by a naturalist) on rafts or inflatable kayaks on three rivers in Washington and one in Oregon. They can arrange rafting trips of all levels of experience, and for individuals using wheelchairs or with other special needs. ~ BZ Corner; 509-493-3926, 800-743-5628; www.alladventuresrafting.com, e-mail driver@gorge.net.

LEAVENWORTH AREA **Alpine Adventures' Wild and Scenic River Tours** concentrates its operation on eleven rivers found within the Cascade Loop (the Route 2–Route 20 driving loop), including the Skykomish, Sauk, Nooksack, Wenatchee, Methow and Skagit. They also run trips on the Tieton River in September. Alpine's trips range from scenic floats to all classes of whitewater rafting, last from one hour to several days, and can accommodate from six to 200 people. ~ Seattle; 206-323-1220, 800-723-8386; www.alpineadventures.com, e-mail info@alpineadventures.com. Experienced guides at **Leavenworth Outfitters** lead rafting trips on the Wenatchee River. They also arrange trips or provide gear for snow-shoeing, kayaking and cross-country skiing. ~ 21312 Route 207, Leavenworth; 509-548-0368; www.leavenworthoutfitters.com. Located on the farthest reaches of Lake Chelan, accessible only by boat or floatplane, **Stehekin Valley Ranch** offers rafting on the Stehekin River (Class II) in summer. Children should be at least six. The trips are half-day and the rivers are tame. ~ P.O. Box 36, Stehekin, WA 98852; 509-682-4677, 800-536-0745. **Orion Expeditions** offers one- to seven-day raft trips on most of the Washington rivers ranging from Class I to IV. Lunch and lodging (camping) included. Closed October through March. ~ 1746 North 128th Street, Seattle; 206-547-6715, 800-553-7466; www.orionexp.com.

SKIING

In the winter, the Cascades turn into a wonderland for all types of skiing—cross-country, downhill and snowboarding. See the "Snow Bound" feature for more information. For skiing conditions call the Forest Service's Avalanche Center at 206-526-6677.

GOLF

It seems that nearly every community in the foothills has a golf course. And the courses are as varied as the individual communities that host them.

METHOW VALLEY Along the eastern slopes of the North Cascades, in the Methow Valley, the public **Lake Chelan Golf Course** is fairly challenging, with small elevated greens and a tenth-hole canyon to hit over. This 18-hole course is open March through November, weather permitting, and has golf lessons, a driving range and full-service restaurant and bar. ~ 1501 Golf Course Road, Chelan; 509-682-8026, 800-246-5361. The privately owned, public **Bear Creek Golf Course** has 9 holes and two sets of tees. Designed by Herman Court, the course is scenic with valleys, hills and mountains. Closed in winter. ~ 19 Bear Creek Golf Course Road, Winthrop; 509-996-2284.

Leavenworth's Lake Minotaur, one of the most breathtaking bodies of water in the area, can be reached in one day via the Lake Minotaur Trail. It may be only six miles long, but it's all uphill. Scenic views and a refreshing dip in the lake will be your reward.

WENATCHEE AREA **Three Lakes Golf Course** is a pretty tough par-69, 18-hole public course, set on rolling terrain with a few water hazards. It includes a driving range, snack shop and restaurant. Weather permitting, it's open year-round. ~ 2695 Golf Drive, Malaga; 509-663-5448; www.threelakesgolf.com.

LEAVENWORTH AREA The Wenatchee River runs around the **Leavenworth Golf Club**, a semiprivate golf course that is closed to the public for a few hours each week. The spectacular mountain valley setting makes it worth the effort to get a tee time at this short, tight 18-hole course. The club, designed by members, is open April through October. ~ 9101 Icicle Road, Leavenworth; 509-548-7267.

ROUTE 90 CORRIDOR The 18-hole public **Mt. Si Golf Course** has breathtaking views of its namesake. ~ 9010 Boalch Avenue Southeast, Snoqualmie; 425-888-1541. **Tall Chief Public Golf Course** has 12 easy holes. ~ 1313 West Snoqualmie River Road South East, Fall City; 425-222-5911. Although it's relatively flat, **Cascade Golf Course**, with good drainage, is probably the best winter course in the area. The public nine-hole course, designed by Emmett Jackson, has three sets of tees and easy access from Route 90. ~ 14303 436th Avenue Southeast, North Bend; 425-888-0227; www.cascadegolfcourse.com. **Sun Country Golf Course**, a public nine-hole course, is equipped with RV spots for golfers who want to stay. Closed in winter. ~ 841 St. Andrews Drive, Cle Elum; 509-674-2226. The semiprivate **Ellensburg Golf Club**, designed by the Elks Club in the 1930s, has a nine-hole course available to the public. The Yakima River runs alongside the course. ~ 3231 Thorp Highway South, Ellensburg; 509-962-2984.

RIDING STABLES

Seen from atop a horse, the Cascades wilderness areas—deep mountain valleys, alpine meadows ablaze with wildflowers, heavily forested slopes and high peaks—take on new beauty. Winter weather limits horseback riding to the warmer months, from mid-April through October.

Text continued on page 324.

Snow Bound

It's all downhill from here: Yes, friends, we are going to take you skiing. Whether you are into slopes or cross-country, the best ski areas in Washington are stretched along the Cascades from Mt. Baker to Mt. Rainier.

Beginning at the northernmost ski area and working south toward the Columbia River, **Mt. Baker** is 56 miles east of Bellingham and has an elevation range of 3500 to 5090 feet. Receiving the highest amount of average snowfall of any ski area in North America, Mt. Baker's ski park has two options, one all natural, including their half pipe, and a six-acre manmade area. Seven lifts and two rope tows take you up to over 38 trails. ~ Route 542; 360-734-6771, snowline 360-671-0211; www.mtbaker.us, e-mail snow@mtbaker.us. The state's only helicopter skiing is **North Cascade Heli-Skiing**, which operates out of the Freestone Inn in Mazama. ~ 509-996-3272; 800-494-4354; www.heli-ski.com, e-mail info@heli-ski.com.

Some skiers prefer **Stevens Pass**, located on Route 2 about 65 miles east of Everett, because it has an annual average of 450 inches of snowfall. Closed late November to mid-April. ~ 206-812-4510; www.stevenspass.com, e-mail info@stevenspass.com. One of the area's smaller mountains is **Leavenworth Winter Sports Club**, a mile north of Leavenworth with a 400-foot vertical drop and a network of cross-country trails. ~ 509-548-5477; www.skileavenworth.com, info@skileavenworth.com.

Probably the best powder snow at a large ski area is at **Mission Ridge**, 13 miles southwest of Wenatchee. Its base elevation is 4570 feet (the highest base area in the state of Washington), with a 2200-foot vertical rise and views of Mt. Rainier and the Columbia River. Closed Tuesday and Wednesday during non-holiday weeks. ~ On Mission Ridge Road, up Squilchuck Canyon; 509-663-6543, snowline 509-663-3200; www.missionridge.com, e-mail info@missionridge.com. But the largest operation of all is **The Summit at Snoqualmie Pass**, 47 miles east of Seattle. Four major ski areas are to be found in a space of two miles: **Alpental, Summit East, Summit West** and **Summit Central**. The average summit elevation is 4100 feet and the average base is 2900 feet. The Summit at Snoqualmie offers the largest night-skiing operation in the country, as well as a tubing center, a lodge and a Nordic center where you can cross-country ski, telemark and snowshoe. ~ 425-434-7669, snow conditions 206-236-1600, road conditions 800-695-7623, information 206-236-7277; www.summitatsnoqualmie.com.

Way up in the sky is **Crystal Mountain**. Forty miles east of Enumclaw just off Route 410 and in the shadow of Mt. Rainier, the summit has an elevation of 7012 feet. Crystal has 2300 acres including 1000 acres of backcountry terrain. The vertical drop is 3100 feet, and there are 50 trails, 13 percent of which are beginner, 57 percent of which are intermediate and 30 percent of which are advanced. ~ 360-663-2265, 888-754-6199; www.skicrystal.com, e-mail comments@skicrystal.com. In the same general area, **White Pass** is 20 miles east of Packwood on Route 12 southeast of Mt. Rainier. A family-oriented ski area, this place is rarely crowded. Six lifts serve 32 runs. Their 18-kilometer cross-country trail system is double tracked with a skating lane. Closed May through October. ~ 509-672-3101, snowline 509-672-3100; www.skiwhitepass.com.

Cross-country skiing is particularly popular on the eastern slopes of the mountains. Some of the best is in the Methow Valley, where 90 miles of trails are marked, the majority of which are groomed. The **Methow Valley Sport Trails Association** has a hotline for ski-touring information (509-996-3860) and a brochure showing the major trails. ~ P.O. Box 147, Winthrop, WA 98862; 509-996-3287; www.mvsta.com, info@mvsta.com.

Echo Valley offers downhill and cross-country skiing as well as rope tows, one lift, 14 miles of trails and a six-foot-wide skating lane for freestyle cross-country skating. A full-service rental shop stocks ski gear, and a school offers both downhill and cross-country lessons. In summer, there's a mountain-biking/hiking center. Echo Valley is seven miles northwest of Chelan on a dirt road off Route 150 and has elevations of 3000 feet. ~ 509-687-3167. The Leavenworth area maintains several ski trails, including the **Icicle River Trail** (7.5 kilometers), kid-friendly **Ski Hill** (5 kilometers) and **Leavenworth Golf Course** (8 kilometers). You can actually ski from your hotel in downtown Leavenworth to the golf course trails (2 kilometers). ~ 509-548-7267; www.echovalley.org, e-mail info@echovalley.com.

Leavenworth Outfitters, located a half mile from five snow parks in the Lake Wenatchee area, offers cross-country ski lessons, and the store rents 120 pairs of cross-country skis and snowshoes. ~ 325 Division, Leavenworth; 509-548-0368; www.leavenworthoutfitters.com.

Besides guided rides, some outfitters also schedule pack trips that last overnight or longer. Always call ahead to make arrangements.

NORTH CASCADES For a two-and-one-half-hour "nose-to-tail" guided ride—six riders maximum—through a pine forest to Coon Lake, which is in the North Cascades Wilderness Park, contact **Stehekin Valley Ranch**. ~ Stehekin; 509-682-4677, 800-536-0745; www.courtneycountry.com.

METHOW VALLEY Guided rides at **Sun Mountain Lodge** are open to the public. The lodge's stable of 35 horses is one of the largest in the Cascades. The 90-minute ride is perfect for beginners; a four-hour trip through the aspen, pine and fir trees of the valley up to a lookout ridge is popular with more experienced riders. Private rides are also available, as are winter sleigh rides. ~ Patterson Lake Road, Winthrop; 509-996-4735, 800-572-0493; www.sunmountainlodge.com.

LEAVENWORTH AREA At **Eagle Creek Ranch**, a guided ride into Wenatchee National Forest follows a trail through alpine meadows blooming with dozens of varieties of wildflowers before reaching a lookout peak for a spectacular view of the Cascades. The ranch also offers horse-drawn sleigh rides in the winter. ~ 7951 Eagle Creek Road, Leavenworth; 509-548-7798, 800-221-7433; www.eaglecreek.ws, e-mail ranch@eaglecreek.ws. Located in Lake Wenatchee State Park, **Icicle Outfitters and Guides** has seasonal hourly guided rides, sleigh rides, day trips and summer pack trips that take two to ten people through timber past Nason Creek. Closed late September through May. ~ P.O. Box 322, Leavenworth, WA 98826; 509-763-3647, 800-497-3912; www.icicleoutfitters.com.

BIKING

For the most part, bicycling in the Cascades is not for the faint of heart or inexperienced. Besides that, unless you bring your own bike, it's hard to find bikes to rent. One exception is the Leavenworth area, where a relatively easy seven-mile loop will take you along the river and through town. You can pick up a free map at the **Leavenworth Chamber of Commerce**. ~ 940 Route 2, Leavenworth; 509-548-5807; www.leavenworth.org.

Several loop routes have been established along the eastern slopes of the Cascades. The **Leavenworth–Lake Wenatchee loop** is 50 miles long and goes from Leavenworth along Route 209 north to Route 207 at Lake Wenatchee State Park and south to Route 2 and back to Leavenworth.

The **Wenatchee–Chelan loop** is 90 miles along the Columbia River and Lake Entiat. It goes north on Route 2 from East Wenatchee, then north on Route 151 to Chelan Station, across the Columbia River, then south on Route 97 to Wenatchee again.

HIKING

The Cascades are a backpacker's paradise laced with thousands of miles of maintained trails. All distances listed are one way unless otherwise noted.

NORTH CASCADES The **Pacific Crest National Scenic Trail** (480 miles) has its northern terminus just north of Washington at the Canadian border. It is a hard hike in many places but can be broken into easier chunks, such as from Stevens Pass to Snoqualmie Pass. Contact the **Outdoor Recreation Information Center** for further details. Closed Monday in winter. ~ REI building, 222 Yale Avenue North, Seattle; 206-470-4060.

Beat writer Jack Kerouac spent a summer at the lookout tower atop Desolation Peak.

The **Heliotrope Ridge Trail** (2.7 miles) leads to a precipice where you can look down on Coleman Glacier. This popular hike has three hazardous stream crossings and can be accessed from Road 39 at Heliotrope Ridge, just east of the town of Glacier. Purchase a one-day trail parking pass ($5) before parking at the trailhead. Contact the visitors center for more information (360-856-5700, 360-599-2714; www.fs.fed.us/r6/mbs).

In Ross Lake Recreation Area, try the hike up Desolation Peak on the **East Bank Trail** (19.3 miles from the highway). The views of the surrounding mountains and Ross Lake are spectacular.

Perhaps the most historic route in the North Cascades is **Cascade Pass Trail** (3.5 miles), the American Indians' route across the mountains for centuries. It is also a route from Marblemount to Stehekin (9 miles), if you want to really make a trip of it.

All along **Route 20** are signs for trailheads—all are worth exploring.The signs show the destination and distance of each trail.

For a long trip—allow three or four days—**Image Lake** (16 miles) is considered one of the most beautiful in the Central Cascades. The lake mirrors Glacier Peak, the most remote and inaccessible of the Washington volcanoes.

METHOW VALLEY **Goat Peak Trail** (2.5 miles) leads to a 7001-foot summit that has a staffed lookout tower. The fairly steep trail starts from a Forest Service road near Mazama; it is hikeable only from July through September. Contact Methow Ranger Station (509-996-4000; www.fs.fed.us/r6/oka).

LEAVENWORTH AREA **Icicle Gorge Trail** (3.5 miles roundtrip) is an interpretive loop trail a short distance west of Leavenworth.

Enchantment Lakes (15 miles) is Washington's most beloved backpacking trip because the lakes are so otherworldly. They are approached from Icicle Creek near Leavenworth. The hike is a hard one, and permits ($5) must be obtained through the Leavenworth Ranger Station (509-548-6977; www.fs.fed.us/r6/wenatchee).

ROUTE 90 CORRIDOR **Iron Horse Trail State Park** (113 miles) is a former railroad right-of-way that is used by hikers, horse riders, cross-country skiers and bicyclists. No motorized vehicles are allowed on the trail, which goes from North Bend over Snoqualmie Pass to Vantage.

MT. RAINIER AREA **Wonderland Trail** (93 miles) goes entirely around Mt. Rainier and can be made in stages ranging from the 6.5-mile section between Longmire and Paradise to the 39-mile section from Carbon River to Longmire.

Northern Loop Trail (34 miles roundtrip) runs through the wilderness with frequent views of the mountain between Carbon River and Sunrise.

MT. ST. HELENS AREA **Klickitat Trail** (17 miles) takes you through a remote part of the Gifford Pinchot National Forest and is part of an old American Indian trail network. Closed November through May. For more information contact Randle Ranger Station (one mile east of Randle on Route 12; 360-497-1100), or the Klickitat Trail Conservancy (www.klickitat-trail.org).

Willard Springs Trail (3 miles roundtrip) winds through the **Conboy Lake National Wildlife Refuge** just south of Glenwood. It skirts the lake, which is dry in summer, and passes back through Ponderosa pines.

Indian Heaven (13 miles) is a beautiful section of the **Pacific Crest National Scenic Trail** that people return to again and again. It is near Trout Lake and goes past numerous lakes reflecting the surrounding mountains.

Transportation

CAR

Route 542 travels east from Bellingham through Glacier to dead-end at Mt. Baker Lodge. **Route 20**, also known as the North Cascades Highway, is one of the state's most popular highways and goes east from Route 5 at Burlington to the Methow Valley. **Route 2**, one of the last intercontinental, two-lane, blacktop highways, runs from Everett to Maine and is called the Stevens Pass Highway in Washington. From Seattle, **Route 90** goes over Snoqualmie Pass to Cle Elum and Ellensburg.

AIR

Only one airport, **Pangborn Memorial Airport** in Wenatchee, serves this large area, and only one carrier, Alaskan Airlines/Horizon Air, offers scheduled service. ~ 509-884-2494; www.pangbornairport.com. The roadless Lake Chelan area is served by **Chelan Airways**, which makes charter flights between Chelan and Stehekin. ~ 509-682-5555; www.chelanairways.com.

FERRY

The Lady of the Lake provides daily transportation between Chelan, Manson, Fields Point, Prince Creek, Lucerne, Moore, Moore Point and Stehekin. You can also catch the smaller **Lady Express**, which has fewer stops but faster service and runs in the winter (except on Tuesday, Thursday and Saturday). ~ 1418 West Woodin Avenue, Chelan; 509-682-4584; www.ladyofthelake.com, e-mail info@ladyofthelake.com.

BUS

Greyhound Bus Lines (800-231-2222; www.greyhound.com) offers service to Leavenworth and Wenatchee and a stop in Cashmere. The Wenatchee station is at 300 South Columbia Street, 509-662-2183; while the Centralia/Chehalis Station is at 1232 Mellen Street, Centralia, 360-736-9811.

Link Transit serves Ardenvoir, Cashmere, Chelan Falls, Dryden, East Wenatchee, Entiat, Lake Wenatchee, Leavenworth, Malaga, Manson, Monitor, Orondo, Peshastin, Plain, Rock Island, Waterville and Wenatchee. ~ 509-662-1155; www.linktransit.com.

TRAIN

Amtrak travels from Seattle, Portland and Spokane to Wenatchee via the "Empire Builder." ~ 800-872-7245; www.amtrak.com.

CAR RENTALS

At the Wenatchee airport are **Budget Rent A Car** (800-527-0700) and **Hertz Rent A Car** (800-654-3131). In Wenatchee is **John Clark Motors** (509-663-0587, 800-972-2298). Ellensburg has **Budget Rent A Car** (800-527-0700).

NINE

East of the Cascades

If state boundaries were determined by similar geography, customs and attitude, Washington and Oregon as we know them would simply not exist. Instead, they'd be split into two more states using the crest of the Cascades as the dividing line or would run vertically from California on the south to Canada on the north with one state taking either side of the mountain range. Well, who ever said life was perfect? So what we have are two states whose eastern and western halves bear almost no resemblance to each other. From the Cascades west, the land is damp, the forests thick and the climate temperate. The eastern side of the range is almost exactly the opposite: Very little rain falls and most crops are irrigated by water from the Columbia Basin Project created by Grand Coulee Dam, or by water from deep wells. Here, the winters are cold and the summers are hot.

Only bits and pieces of eastern Oregon are irrigated because it has not been blessed with any large rivers other than the Snake. It remains mostly arid, the northern reaches of the Great American Desert that runs north from Mexico through Arizona, California and Nevada. It is land more suitable for cattle grazing than growing crops, although in some valleys ranchers have drilled wells or dammed small streams to enable them to irrigate meadows. This kind of open and sparsely populated countryside doesn't appeal to all travelers, so you tend to see more recreational vehicles and truck stops than hotels and restaurants.

If urban amenities such as hotels, finer restaurants, theater and shopping centers are what you're after, head to Washington's larger cities—Spokane, Walla Walla, the Tri-Cities and Yakima. Elsewhere you'll find RV parks and inexpensive but clean motels. On the lakes and streams are rustic resorts, some with log cabins.

Away from the cities, hunting and fishing abound. Many streams and lakes are stocked regularly with trout, and a few sturgeon are still caught in the Snake and Columbia rivers. Deer, elk and an occasional black bear are popular quarry, as are waterfowl, pheasant, grouse and quail. Don't be startled while driving along a mountain road during hunting season if you spot someone in camouflage clothing carrying a rifle emerge from the forest.

Some of the most interesting geology in North America can be found in this region due to its tortured creation by volcanoes, lava flows through vast fissures and floods gigantic beyond imagining. Throughout the two states' eastern sides you will find vivid reminders of this creation process. In Oregon it is shown by hundreds if not thousands of dead volcanoes and cinder cones, the lava flows that have not yet been covered by windblown soil, the brilliantly colored volcanic ash deposits, and sheer canyons whose basalt walls were created by these lava flows. In Washington it is the dramatic Coulee Country along the Columbia River and the beautiful Palouse Country with its steep, rolling hills.

The forests are mainly pine with very little underbrush. Along some parts of the eastern slope of the Cascades you will find larch, the only species of coniferous trees that are deciduous. They are brilliantly colored in the fall and stand out as vividly as sumac and maples in the dark green forest.

East of the mountains is another treasure: peace and quiet. There are lonesome roads undulating off into the distance, small rivers stocked with trout, open pine forests, vast lakes made by man, working cowboys and mornings so tranquil you can hear a door slam.

As is true elsewhere in America, the general rule is the smaller the town the friendlier the people, so don't be surprised if folks stop to talk about anything or nothing in particular. Also, nearly everything is less expensive than along the coast.

Traveling these remote areas you will have a continual sense of discovery as you visit places barely large enough to get themselves onto state maps. And you will find small towns that don't bother opening tourist bureaus but have a clean motel, a good café, friendly people to talk to and a small city park for your picnic.

A few remnants of the pioneer years still remain standing in eastern Oregon and Washington. Here and there you'll see the remains of a cabin with the tall tripod of a windmill where a homesteader tried but failed to "prove up" the land given him by the Homestead Act. You'll also see remains of ghost towns (although some have been rediscovered and are peopled again). Most of these towns were built at or near mines and abandoned when the mines began coughing up only rocks and sand.

To help you explore this fascinating eastern strip of Washington, which extends from the Canadian border on the north to the Columbia Gorge that separates Washington from Oregon on the south, we've divided this chapter into the following sections:

The Okanogan Highlands, often called the Okanogan Country or simply the Okanogan, has boundaries that are fairly easy to determine: Route 97 to the west, the Canadian border to the north, the Columbia River on the east and the Colville Indian Reservation on the south.

Grand Coulee Area includes all the Columbia River system from where it swings west at the southern end of the Colville Indian Reservation and follows past Grand Coulee Dam south to the Vantage–Wanapum Dam area, where the Columbia enters the Hanford Nuclear Reservation.

The Spokane Area covers the only true metropolitan center east of the Cascades.

Southeastern Washington encompasses the famed Palouse Hills between Spokane and Pullman; the Snake River town of Clarkston; Walla Walla; the Tri-Cities of Pasco, Kennewick and Richland; and Yakima and the agricultural and wine-producing valley of the same name.

Okanogan Highlands

One of the pleasures of touring the Okanogan Country is simply driving down country roads to see where they lead. A number of ghost towns, some no more than a decaying log cabin today, dot the map.

Most visitors enter the Okanogan Country from Route 97, the north–south corridor that runs up the Columbia River Valley to Bridgeport, then follows the Okanogan River Valley north toward Canada. This is desertlike country with irrigated orchards on either side of the highway and open range climbing back up the mountains.

SIGHTS

First, contact the **Omak Visitor Information Center** for brochures and maps. Closed weekends in winter. ~ 401 Omak Avenue, Omak; 509-826-4218, 800-225-6625, fax 509-826-6201; www.omakchronicle.com/omakvic, e-mail omakvic@northcascades.net.

The **Okanogan County Historical Museum**, also headquarters for the county historical society, has a collection of pioneer farm and ranch implements and historical photos. This is also a good place to start your travels because members of the volunteer staff have lived in the region for many years and know where everything is, including skeletons in the county's closets. Open from Memorial Day to Labor Day. Admission. ~ 1410 2nd Avenue North, Okanogan; 509-422-4272; e-mail ochs@ncidata.com.

Northwest of Omak is a region that was a silver mining area in the 1880s. Here, adventurers will find the remote town site for the short-lived **Ruby**. Named for either the type of silver prospectors hoped to find there or for a prospector's girlfriend or prostitute, the site has no structures left, only foundations and wagon roads. ~ Salmon Creek Road, 10 to 15 miles northwest of Omak.

HIDDEN ►

West of Oroville, is **Nighthawk**, which was a ghost town until recently. The paved county road, which heads west from Route 97 near the Canadian border, curves along the Similkameen River Valley, then swings south into a valley between the mountains of the Pasayten Wilderness of the North Cascades National Park and a series of steep ridges to the east. This area is dotted with old mines, some still worked from time to time, but most of the land along the valley floor and stretching up the hillsides a few hundred feet has been turned into orchards or expanses of alfalfa with grazing cattle. Nighthawk now has two permanent residences, but mostly consists of a historic old store, post office, hotel and pink house from the few-year boom when prospectors found precious metals there in the 1890s. **Loomis**, the other mining town farther south on this loop drive, is no longer a ghost town. The highway passes Palmer Lake and Spectacle Lake, both of which have public beaches, before rejoining Route 97.

HIDDEN ►

One of the most interesting drives is to **Molson**, a ghost town 15 miles east of Oroville off Route 97 near the Canadian border.

Molson was founded when a nearby mine was attracting hundreds of prospectors and workers. Owing to a land-claim mix-up, a farmer took over the whole town, so a new one had to be built and it was named New Molson. The two towns, less than a mile apart, fought over everything except education for their children. They built a school halfway between the towns, and it became Center Molson. Today **Old Molson** is an outdoor museum with one historic building, two homesteads, sheds, early 1900s machinery, a steam engine and more. The **Center Molson school**

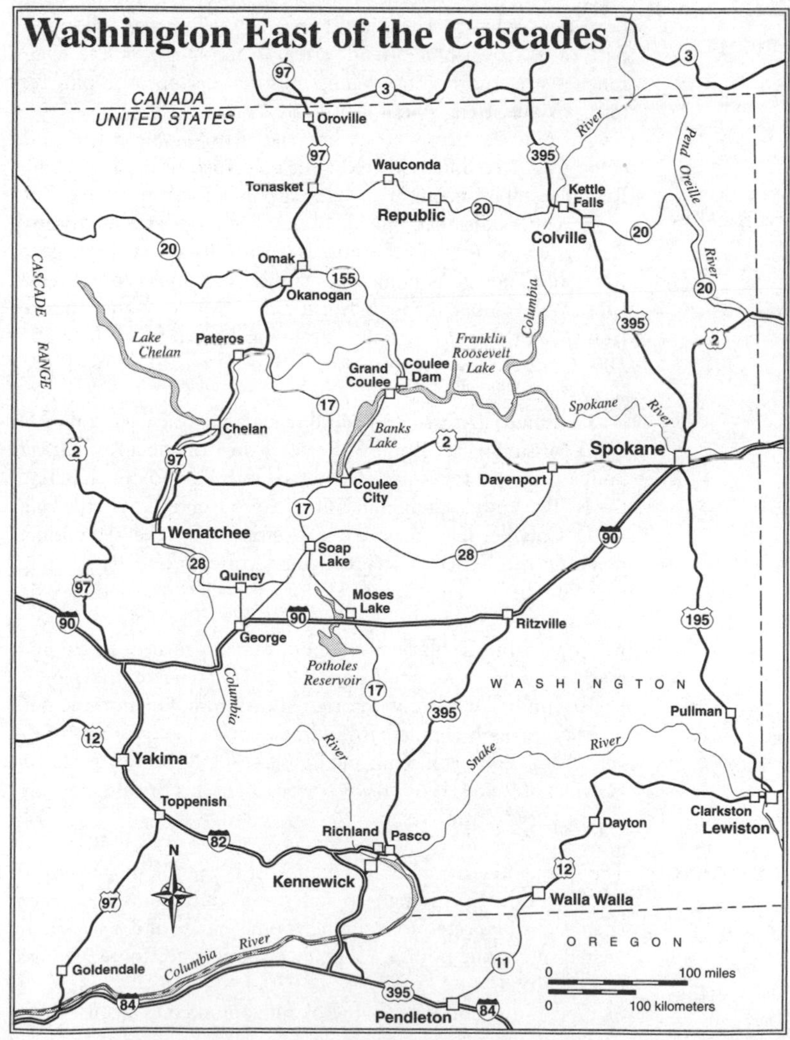

building has three stories of artifacts and a tea room. Open Memorial Day weekend to Labor Day weekend. ~ Information, 509-485-3292 (ask for Mary Louise Lowe).

Route 20 is one of Washington's best highways for leisurely rural driving, especially as it traverses the Okanogan Country on its way to the Idaho border. It comes in from the Cascades to Omak-Okanogan, joins Route 97 north to Tonasket, swings east across the heart of the highlands through Wauconda and Republic, crosses the Columbia River at Kettle Falls and continues on to Tiger, where it follows the Pend Oreille River south to the Idaho border at Newport. There it disappears. The highway follows the path of least resistance beside streams and along valleys where ranches stretch off across rolling hills that disappear in pine forests. ~ Main Street, Okanogan.

Heading east from Tonasket, the first notable town you'll come to is **Republic**. Created by a gold rush in the late 1890s, Republic still hosts one last operative gold mine, the Kinross Gold mine, a short distance outside town. The **Stonerose Interpretive Center** lets visitors dig for fossils on a hillside on the edge of Republic. The site is named for family rose fossils found there. Closed November through April; closed Monday and Tuesday from May through October. Admission to the fossil dig site. ~ 509-775-2295; www.stonerosefossil.org, e-mail srfossils@rcabletv.com.

HIDDEN ►

Continue eastward and you'll reach a historical site called **St. Paul's Mission** where Route 395 crosses the Columbia River. It was built as a chapel for American Indians in 1845 and operated until the 1870s. A modest museum is also here. ~ Route 395, Kettle Falls.

In **Colville**, ten miles east of Kettle Falls, several buildings make up the **Keller Heritage Center Museum and Park**. Sponsored by the Stevens County Historical Society, the complex has a museum, a fire lookout tower, Colville's first schoolhouse, a trapper's cabin, a blacksmith shop, mine, a farmstead cabin, a machine shop, a sawmill and the 1910 home of the pioneer Keller family complete with original furniture. Open to the public May through September and by appointment the rest of the year. Admission to museum and house. ~ 700 North Wynne Street, Colville; 509-684-5968; www.stevenscountyhistoricalsociety.org, e-mail schs@ultraplix.com.

LODGING

The most modern motel in Okanogan is the **Okanogan Inn**. It has 77 rooms (including two suites and four rooms with kitchenettes), an unpretentious dining room, lounge and a seasonally heated swimming pool. ~ 1 Appleway Street and Route 97, Okanogan; 509-422-6431, 877-422-7070, fax 509-422-4214; www.okanoganinn.com, e-mail inn@okanoganinn.com. MODERATE.

A cheaper Okanogan motel is the 25-room **Ponderosa Motor Lodge** downtown, a clean one-story motel of basic design with a pool. Two-bedroom suites with kitchens are available. ~ 1034 South 2nd Avenue, Okanogan; 509-422-0400, 800-732-6702, fax 509-422-4206; www.ponderosamotorlodge.com, e-mail pond@communitynet.org. BUDGET.

The **U and I Motel** has nine small "cabinettes" with rustic paneling; each unit has a microwave and refrigerator. They come with deck chairs, so you can sit and look across a lawn and flower garden to the Okanogan River. You can also fish from one of the benches along the river. ~ 838 2nd Avenue, Okanogan; 509-422-2920. BUDGET.

In Omak are several small, inexpensive motels including the **Rodeway Inn & Suites**, which has rooms with refrigerators and microwaves. ~ 122 North Main Street, Omak; 509-826-0400, 888-700-6625, fax 509-826-5635. BUDGET.

The **Royal Motel** offers clean and simple accommodations. ~ 514 East Riverside Drive, Omak; 509-826-5715. BUDGET.

Several small resorts are scattered along lakes in the area. Among them is the **Bonaparte Lake Resort.** This resort, 26 miles from both Republic and Tonasket, has ten airy and clean log cabins along the lake shore. Three have bathrooms and kitchens; the "Penthouse" also comes with linens. There are public showers and a bathroom. RV and tent sites are also available. A general store and lakeside café round out the amenities. Closed in winter. ~ 615 Bonaparte Lake Road, Tonasket; 509-486-2828, fax 509-486-1987; www.bonapartelakeresort.com. BUDGET.

For a trip back to the Old West, head to the **Hidden Hills Country Inn**, a rustic-style bed and breakfast surrounded by

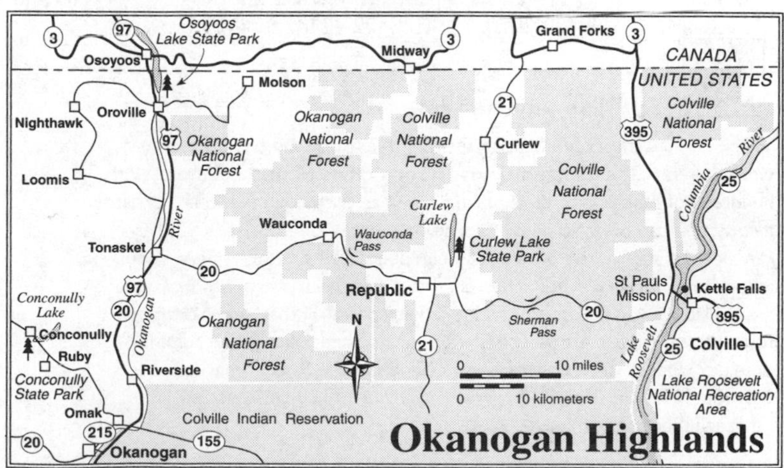

fields of wildflowers and pine trees. The eight guest rooms, most of which offer mountain views, have a turn-of-the-20th-century feel with floral wallpaper, pedestal sinks, brass beds and gleaming woodwork. Full breakfast. ~ 104 Hidden Hills Lane, Tonasket; 509-486-1895, 800-468-1890, fax 509-486-8264; www.hiddenhillsresort.com, e-mail information@hiddenhillsresort.com. MODERATE.

Farther east, near Republic, the **K Diamond K Ranch** offers total immersion in ranch living: sleeping in a group lodge, riding lessons, eating with the ranch owners, relaxing with campfire sing-alongs and hayrides. Guests can also hike, bike, fish, explore old mines and pan for gold. A working ranch, the K Diamond K is open year-round. ~ 15661 Route 21 South, Republic; 509-775-3536, 888-345-5355, fax 509-775-3520; www.kdiamondk.com, e-mail kdiamond@kdiamondk.com. DELUXE.

Farther east is **Dominion Mountain Retreat**, a Craftsman-style bungalow in the foothills of Old Dominion Mountain, six and a half miles from Colville. The loft cabin can sleep up to four people (a fifth on the window seat) and has a fully equipped kitchen stocked with breakfast foods, a propane heating stove, private tiled bath, two decks (one of them rooftop) and a covered porch. Hot tub shared with owner. Access by four-wheel drive only in winter. Fresh cookies on arrival. No credit cards. ~ 694 Mosby Road, Colville; 509-684-6878; www.dominionmountainretreat.com, e-mail lwaters@plix.com. MODERATE.

DINING

Basic, standard fare is pretty much the order of the day here. For starters, there is the **Sun Valley Restaurant and Lounge**, which serves adequate, straightforward lunches and dinners and farmer-sized breakfasts. ~ Appleway Street and Route 97, Okanogan; 509-422-2070, fax 509-422-4214. BUDGET TO DELUXE.

AUTHOR FAVORITE

To experience the excitement of the Old West, nothing beats a stay at a working ranch. The **Canaan Guest Ranch** offers all that and more. With hundreds of ranch acres to explore as well as Okanogan National Forest nearby, you can bring your own horse or borrow one of theirs. Guests can elect to stay in one of two fully equipped cabins with Western decor, a bunkhouse or an RV spot. There's a bathhouse with sauna, and massages are available if you find yourself a bit saddle sore. If all that weren't enough to make you fell like a true cowpoke, you can participate in the summertime hay rides or barn dances. ~ 474 Cape LaBelle Road, Tonasket; 509-486-1191, 866-295-4217; www.canaanguestranch.com, e-mail canranch@bossig.net. BUDGET TO DELUXE.

The choices are few in Omak, but one café and bakery that rates high is the antique-decorated **Breadline Cafe**, where lunch features big sandwiches on fresh-baked, whole-grain breads and dinner includes shrimp Creole, jambalaya, pepper steak, portobello and eggplant marinara over pasta, and beef burgundy crepe. Closed Sunday and Monday. ~ 102 South Ash Street, Omak; 509-826-5836; www.breadlinecafe.com; e-mail info@breadlinecafe.com. MODERATE.

Omak's **North Country Pub** serves nothing fancy—burgers, steaks, tacos and barbecue—but it's solid, filling food. The lunch specials are usually pretty good, and if you're there on a Thursday night, the steak special is a bargain. ~ 15 South Main, Omak; 509-826-4271. BUDGET TO MODERATE.

One of the few deluxe dining choices in the region is provided by **Hidden Hills Country Inn**. This contemporary hotel has created a dining room built to resemble an 1890s mansion. The large room overlooks a pond and is handsomely decorated with cherry and maple furnishings, China cabinets and fringed lamps. The menu offers just one multicourse dinner selection that changes every night. Steaks and chicken breast are among the possibilities. ~ 104 Hidden Hills Lane, Tonasket; 509-486-1895, 800-486-1895, fax 509-486-8264; www.hiddenhillsresort.com, e-mail information@hiddenhillsresort.com. ULTRA-DELUXE.

One of the more interesting places to stop for a snack or down-home American meal is **Wauconda**, the one-store town on Route 20 east of Tonasket. A breakfast and lunch counter to the left of the door is between the cash register and a large dining room overlooking a valley and low mountains beyond. The food is uncomplicated and hearty, and the portions are generous. No dinner Thursday through Sunday. ~ 2360 Route 20, Wauconda; 509-486-4010. MODERATE.

Downtown Oroville sports a few restaurants, including **Fat Boys Diner**, a classic joint specializing in burgers, steaks and barbecued ribs, with a few pasta dishes on the side. Breakfast is served daily. ~ 1518 Main Street, Oroville; 509-476-4100. BUDGET.

SHOPPING

Omak's Main Street provides a few good browsing spots such as **Mustard Seed Gallery & Gifts**, which features handmade Polish pottery, plus crafts, jewelry and collectibles. Closed Saturday through Monday. ~ 21 North Main Street, Omak; 509-826-2463.

Western wear of all kinds plus handcrafted silver jewelry, Pendleton blankets and saddles are stock and trade at the **Detros Western Store**, a few miles north of Omak in Riverside. Closed Saturday. ~ 107 Main Street, Riverside; 509-826-2200.

You don't have many retail options in the small town of Oroville. However, **Prince's Center** may be all you need (or find). Half of Prince's is devoted to groceries; the other side carries general merchandise—everything from footwear and apparel to toys and garden tools. ~ 1000 23rd Avenue, Oroville; 509-476-3651.

NIGHTLIFE

Most nightlife in this cowboy and fruit-picking area is limited to taverns, a few of which have live bands on weekends.

Big-screen TV, pool, darts, karaoke on weekends and beer on tap are provided by **Shorthorn Tavern** in downtown Omak. ~ 3 North Main Street, Omak; 509-826-0338.

PARKS

CONCONULLY STATE PARK Strung along the edge of the town of the same name, this site is popular with boaters, swimmers, families and anglers seeking kokonee, large- and smallmouth bass, rainbow trout, German brown trout and Eastern brook trout. For hikers, there is a nature trail. Other facilities here include picnic areas, restrooms, a children's play area and a wading pool. Day use fee, $5. ~ Located 22 miles north of Omak on Conconully-Okanogan Highway; 509-826-7408.

▲ There are 82 standard sites ($17 per night) and 2 primitive sites ($12 per night). Closed weekdays in winter except holidays or by appointment.

OSOYOOS LAKE STATE PARK This lakeshore park is one quarter mile north of Oroville and stretches along the southern end of Osoyoos Lake. It has some of the few trees in the area for shade while picnicking and camping and is the most popular state park in the area. It is heavily used by Canadians and Americans alike since it is almost on the Canadian border. For nature lovers, the lake is a prime nesting area for Canadian geese; for anglers, this is a year-round spot for bass and salmon. Facilities are limited to picnic areas and restrooms. Closed weekdays (except holidays) in winter. ~ Route 97, on the northern end of Oroville; 509-476-3321.

▲ There are 86 standard sites ($19 per night) that accommodate RVs (no hookups). Reservations: 888-226-7688.

CURLEW LAKE STATE PARK This 128-acre setting is on the southeastern shore of a lake in a pine forest with several islands. Remnants of homesteaders' cabins can be seen near the park, and a large variety of animals, including chipmunks, squirrels and deer, lives in the area. Several species of birds also can be seen. The park is bordered on the south by Colville National Forest. Picnic area and restrooms are the facilities here. Closed November to April. ~ Route 21, ten miles north of Republic; 509-775-3592.

▲ There are 57 standard sites ($17 per night), 25 RV hookup sites ($24 per night), and 2 primitive sites ($12 per night). First-come, first-served.

Grand Coulee Area

This area is frequently baffling to visitors because of the similarity of place names. The towns of Coulee Dam and Grand Coulee are at the site of Grand Coulee Dam itself, while Coulee City is 30 miles away at the southern end of Banks Lake. In the same area are still two more small towns with names that often get confused: Elmer City and Electric City.

The centerpiece of the Grand Coulee Area, not surprisingly, is Grand Coulee Dam with its spectacular laser light shows during the summer months. The sheer mass of the dam is almost overwhelming and for decades was the largest concrete structure in the world.

Electric City's North Dam Park harbors an intriguing collection of whimsical windmills built out of household scraps. Look for the folk art display on Route 155 about a half mile southwest of Grand Coulee.

Also of interest are the many lakes created by the dam that have become some of the Northwest's most popular recreation areas. The backwaters of the dam itself, named in honor of President Franklin D. Roosevelt, reach far north nearly to the Canadian border and east into the Spokane River system. A chain of lakes and some smaller dams were built to hold irrigation water for distribution south and east of the dam. These include Banks Lake and the Potholes Reservoir, known as the Winchester Wasteway. These lakes continue south to the Crab Creek Valley before re-entering the Columbia River below Vantage.

SIGHTS

Grand Coulee Dam was built in the 1930s and memorialized by the songs of Woody Guthrie. The area that became known as the Columbia Basin was so barren before the dam that locals liked to say you had to prime yourself to spit and that jackrabbits crossing the basin had to carry canteens. The dam was the largest concrete pour in the world for many decades after its completion at the beginning of World War II. It stands 550 feet above bedrock, as tall as a 46-story building, and at 5223 feet is nearly a mile long. While its 12 million cubic yards of concrete may be difficult to imagine, the Bureau of Reclamation points out that this is enough to build a standard six-foot-wide sidewalk around the world at the equator.

In addition to powering the hydroelectric system with the 151-mile-long Lake Roosevelt, the dam serves the additional purpose of irrigating more than 500,000 acres. Water is pumped 280 feet up the canyon wall to fill Banks Lake's reservoir, from which the water is moved through canals and pipes to the area's farmland.

Visitors are welcome at the dam and can go on guided tours. One of the most popular events is the nightly **laser show**, a free,

40-minute demonstration that uses the spillway of the dam for its screen. It is shown nightly from Memorial Day through September. ~ 509-633-9265; www.grandcouleedam.org, e-mail chamber@grandcouleedam.org.

The **Colville Tribal Museum, Gallery and Gift Shop** displays authentic village and fishing scenes, coins and metals dating from the 1800s and many ancient artifacts. The gift shop sells local beadwork and other artwork by tribal members. ~ 512 Mead Way, Coulee Dam; 509-633-0751.

The best way to appreciate the stark beauty of the Grand Coulee Area is to drive south from the dam on Route 155 along **Banks Lake**. The artificial lake is used for all water sports, and its color and character change dramatically with the time of day and weather.

At Coulee City you come to the **Dry Falls Dam**, which holds Banks Lake water and sends it on south into a system of canals. Pinto Ridge Road heads due south from Coulee City and passes **Summer Lake**, a favorite picnic spot. The falls are created by the irrigation water from Banks Lake.

The main route out of Coulee City is across Dry Falls Dam, then south on Route 17 past Dry Falls and Sun Lakes State Park, along a series of smaller lakes in the coulees—Park Lake, Blue Lake, Lake Lenore (where you can see the form of a small rhinoceros that was trapped in a prehistoric lava flow) and finally to Soap Lake.

Soap Lake was so named because the water used to foam before the ground water rose. The water is rich in minerals—sodium, chloride, carbonate, sulfate, bicarbonate and plenty of others—and matches the contents of water in the Baden Baden Spa in Germany. It has attracted a number of motels that pump water for use in the rooms or into spas where people go to soak themselves seeking comfort for a variety of skin, muscle and bone afflictions.

South of Soap Lake the coulees flatten out, and the landscape away from the Columbia River becomes the gently rolling wheat-growing region. **Moses Lake** in the center of the Columbia Basin, is better known as a hub for farmers of the basin than as a tourist destination. The lake for which the town is named joins the Potholes Reservoir to the south.

LODGING

If you want a room with a view, there are two good places near the dam. The **Columbia River Inn** is right across the street from Grand Coulee Dam. Most rooms have a view of the spillway, and nightly laser light shows are across the street in the summer. The motel has 35 rooms, a sauna, an exercise facility, an outdoor pool and a hot tub. Two rooms have jacuzzis. ~ 10 Lincoln Avenue, Coulee Dam; 509-633-2100, 800-633-6421, fax 509-

633-2633; www.columbiariverinn.com, e-mail info@columbiariverinn.com. MODERATE.

The other is **Coulee House Motel**, which is up a hill and provides a top-notch view. It has clean, unremarkable rooms and a swimming pool and hot tub. Free internet is available. ~ 110 Roosevelt Way, Coulee Dam; 509-633-1101, 800-715-7767, fax 509-633-1416; www.couleehouse.com, e-mail info@couleehouse.com. MODERATE.

Several budget-priced motels and resorts are located near Banks Lake and Lake Roosevelt. **Ala Cozy**, a mile and a half from the marina at the end of Banks Lake, offers 14 motel-style

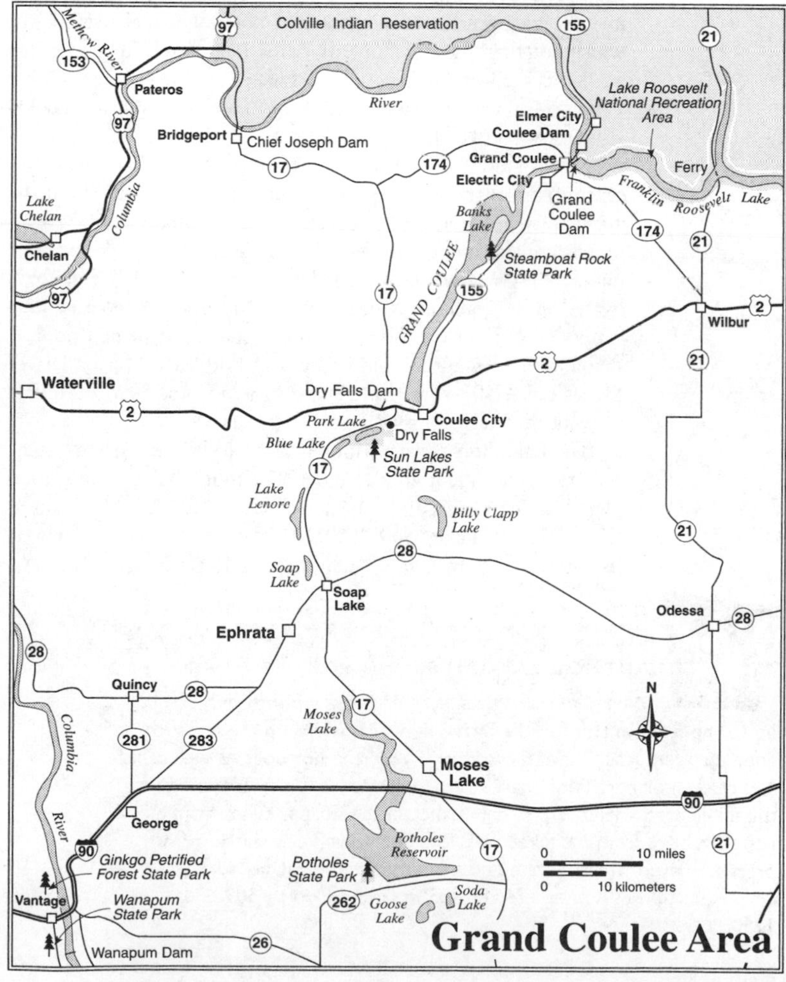

units with private bathrooms and refrigerators. There's a pool on the premises. ~ 9988 Route 2 East, Coulee City; 509-632-5703, 877-678-2918, fax 509-632-5383; alacozymotel.com, e-mail ala cozy@hotmail.com. BUDGET TO MODERATE.

In Soap Lake, **Notaras Lodge** is the best-known and one of the most modern motels in town. The four-building complex plus restaurant has 15 rooms, 7 of which have jacuzzis. The rooms boast unusual decor, with names like the "Old Mexico" room—with a red roof, stucco walls and wrought-iron balcony—and the "Bunkhouse," complete with a wooden pack horse saddle and a 1900 cistern pump that turns the water on for the copper kettle sink. The accommodations are spacious and equipped with microwave ovens, refrigerators and coffee makers. Massages, whirlpool therapy and mineral baths in Soap Lake water are available. ~ 236 Main Street, Soap Lake; 509-246-0462, fax 509-246-1054; www.notaraslodge.com, e-mail notaras@televar.com. MODERATE TO DELUXE.

Moses Lake is one of the most popular RV destinations in the central part of the state because several lakes are in the immediate vicinity, and hot, sunny weather is almost guaranteed. Several motels are also along the Route 90 corridor and the lake, including the **Best Western Lakefront Hotel**, which has 159 fully renovated units, some on Moses Lake. In addition to boating and waterskiing, right off the dock, the motel has a heated pool, a sauna, and a restaurant and lounge. ~ 3000 West Marina Drive, Moses Lake; 509-765-9211, 800-235-4255, fax 509-766-0493; www.bestwestern.com. MODERATE TO DELUXE.

The **Lakeshore Resort Motel** is also on the lake, where a marina and waterskiing are available. The motel has 24 units, nine housekeeping cabins and a heated pool. ~ 3206 West Lakeshore Court, Moses Lake; 509-765-9201, fax 509-765-1800; www.lakeshoreresortmotel.com, e-mail hapnravi@yahoo.com. BUDGET.

AUTHOR FAVORITE

When I'm craving a side of nostalgia with my burger, I pull up to the **Rock'n Robin 50's Drive-in**, which whips up classics such as cheeseburgers (called the "Big Bopper"), BLTs and hot dogs, as well as fish and chicken dinners. Sure, there's carhop service, but it's hard to resist the full-fledged "Happy Days" experience inside. Snappy tunes from a bygone era blare from the jukebox; Elvis and Marilyn keep watch from practically everywhere. Limited hours in the winter; call ahead. ~ At the junction of Routes 174 and 155 in Grand Coulee; 509-633-1290. BUDGET.

DINING

A well-known eatery in this region is the **Melody Restaurant & Lounge.** With views of the Grand Coulee Dam and its summer laser light show, the Melody offers standard American fare, seafood and pasta. Breakfast, lunch and dinner. ~ 512 River Drive, Coulee Dam; 509-633-1151, fax 509-633-2925. BUDGET TO MODERATE.

If you want Asian food, **Siam Palace** will have it. Thai, Chinese and American dishes are served. No lunch on Saturday. Closed Sunday and Monday. ~ 213 Main Street, Grand Coulee; 509-633-2921. BUDGET.

A light-filled, contemporary restaurant built of native stone, **Michael's on the Lake** offers both indoor and outdoor dining. A spacious deck overlooks Moses Lake. Prime rib, hamburgers, oriental chicken salad and home-style desserts like cobblers are especially popular here. ~ 910 West Broadway, Moses Lake; 509-765-1611, fax 509-766-2804; www.michaelsonthelake.com, e-mail michaels@michaelsonthelake.com. MODERATE TO DELUXE.

SHOPPING

The **Colville Tribal Museum, Gallery and Gift Shop** sells local beadwork and other items crafted by the tribal members. Closed Sunday. ~ 512 Mead Way, Coulee Dam; 509-633-0751.

NIGHTLIFE

Moses Lake has a series of free concerts, all beginning at 8 p.m., on most Saturdays from July to September, in its 5000-capacity outdoor amphitheater on the lakeshore. Nationally known musicians perform here. ~ Located 49 miles south of Coulee City; 509-765-7888, 800-992-6234.

PARKS

LAKE ROOSEVELT NATIONAL RECREATION AREA This area stretches 151 miles along the entire length of Lake Roosevelt, including parts of the Spokane and Kettle rivers. Owing to the arid climate, the lake has miles and miles of sandy beaches and outcroppings of dramatic rocks. Only when you get close to the Spokane River do trees begin appearing along the shoreline. It is a particular favorite for waterskiers. Sailing and windsurfing are also popular activities. More than 30 species of fish are found here, including walleye, rainbow trout, sturgeon, yellow perch and kokanee, the land-locked salmon. There are only picnic areas. ~ The lake can be accessed from Grand Coulee and Davenport in the South and Kettle Falls to the north; 509-633-9441, 800-824-4916 for lake levels, fax 509-633-9332; www.nps.gov/laro.

▲ There are 27 campgrounds with over 600 sites; $10 per night from May through September, $5 per night from October to April.

STEAMBOAT ROCK STATE PARK This is one of Washington's most popular state parks and thus is one of the many parks where camping-space reservations are a necessity. The park is on the shores of Banks Lake at the foot of the butte by the same name. The ship-shaped butte rises 800 feet above the lake and has a good trail to the 640-acre flat top. Fishing for bass, walleye, trout, crappie, kokanee and perch is good year-round, and it's a popular place to ice fish. You'll find picnic tables, playground equipment, a bathhouse and a seasonal snack bar. ~ Route 155, 12 miles south of Grand Coulee; 509-633-1304, fax 509-633-1294.

▲ There are 26 standard sites ($19 per night), 100 RV hookup sites ($26 per night) and 19 primitive sites ($14 per night). Reservations: 888-226-7688.

SUN LAKES STATE PARK This park is located on the floor of the coulee that was scoured out when the Columbia River's normal course was blocked by ice and debris at the end of the Ice Age. The river, three and a half miles wide, flowed over nearby 400-foot-high Dry Falls, which was the original name of the state park but was changed because of the lakes and recreation. It is now home to boating, riding, jetskiing, hiking and golfing. Picnic areas and restrooms are here. Included in the park is 76-person Camp Delaney, an environmental learning center. ~ Route 17, seven miles southwest of Coulee City.

▲ There are 152 sites and 39 with RV hookups; $19 to $26 per night. Note: A private concessionaire (Sun Lakes Park Resort, 34228 Park Lake Road Northeast, Coulee City, WA 99115; 509-632-5291; www.sunlakesparkresort.com) operates a portion of the park and offers 50 cabins ($65 to $93 per night for three to four people, $119 to $149 for lake views), 10 mobile homes ($99 to $129 per night for up to six people) and 112 full hookups ($20 to $33 per night). There's a general store, a snack bar, a heated swimming pool, boat rentals and marina, laundry, an 18-hole mini-golf course and a nine-hole golf course.

POTHOLES STATE PARK The potholes were created by floods following large lava flows during the Pleistocene

WASHINGTON GEM

Centuries ago, Washington's swampy and mild interior boasted a variety of trees such as gingko, elm and cypress. And then came the lava that oozed from volcanic fissures. With each new lava flow, logs became waterlogged in deep marsh and were preserved as the layers deepened. Over time, water and silica permeated the wood through the lava. Eventually, silica replaced the original wood fiber, essentially petrifying the log into a perfect representation of itself. The best place to see examples of petrified wood is at Gingko Petrified Forest State Park (page 343) in Vantage.

era. Now the dunes stand above the water level and are used for campsites, bird blinds and picnic areas. The area supports a large population of waterfowl and other birds, including blue herons, white pelicans, sand-hill cranes, hawks and eagles. A lawn and shade trees, tables and stoves are beside the lake. Rainbow trout, bass, perch, crappie, bluegill and walleye are found in the park. There are restrooms and showers. ~ Route 262, 17 miles southwest of Moses Lake; 509-346-2759, fax 360-664-8112.

▲ There are 60 RV hookup sites ($22 per night) and 61 primitive sites ($10 per night). Reservations: 888-226-7688.

GINKGO PETRIFIED FOREST STATE PARK More than 30 species of fossilized trees have been identified in this area of barren hillsides and lava flows, making it one of the largest fossil forests in the world. The park has an interpretive center overlooking the Columbia River with a wide selection of petrified wood and also has a ten-mile interpretive hiking trail. No camping, fishing or swimming are permitted at Ginkgo, but you can head four and a half miles south on the Columbia River to **Wanapum State Park** for camping and swimming. Fishing is popular and boat ramps are available. There are picnic areas and restrooms. ~ Located on the edge of Vantage, a tiny town on Route 90 where it crosses the Columbia River; 509-856-2700, fax 509-856-2294.

▲ Wanapum has 50 RV hookup sites ($22 per night). Open weekends only in winter. Reservations: 888-226-7688.

Spokane

The northeastern corner of Washington is an area of pine forests, sparkling lakes, sprawling wheat farms and urban pleasures in a rural setting. Spokane is where the Midas-rich miners from Idaho came to live in the late 19th century, so the city has an abundance of historic homes, museums, bed and breakfasts and inns, and one of the most beautiful city park systems in the West.

SIGHTS

The best way to become acquainted with Spokane is to take the self-guided "City Drive Tour" outlined in a brochure from the city that is available at the **Spokane Convention and Visitors Bureau.** ~ 201 West Main Avenue; 509-747-3230, 888-776-5263; www.visitspokane.com.

Another useful brochure is the self-guided tour of historic architecture in downtown Spokane. The "City Drive Tour" takes you along Cliff Drive where many of the finest old homes stand and through **Manito Park**, one of the city's largest parks. Manito Park includes the Japanese Garden built by Spokane's sister city in Japan and the **Duncan Formal Gardens**, whose lush scenery looks like something out of a movie set in 18th-century Europe. ~ Grand Avenue between 17th and 25th avenues.

The tour continues past **Coeur d'Alene Park**, off 2nd Avenue, and the stately **Patsy Clark Mansion** at 2nd Avenue and Hemlock Street. It goes on to the **Northwest Museum of Arts & Culture** with its major collection of regional history and fine art. Closed Monday. Admission. ~ 2316 West 1st Avenue; 509-456-3931, fax 509-363-5303; www.northwestmuseum.org.

Next is **John A. Finch Arboretum**, which features an extensive collection of deciduous and evergreen trees from all over the world. From there the tour leads you back to the downtown area. ~ 3404 West Woodland Boulevard, off Sunset Boulevard; 509-363-5455, fax 509-363-5454.

The city is most proud of its **Riverfront Park**, located in the heart of downtown and known for the natural beauty of its waterfall and island. A glorious addition to Spokane built for the 1974 World's Fair, the park has the restored 1909 Looff Carrousel and various other rides and food concessions, plus an IMAX Theater (admission). The Spokane Falls Skyride offers aerial views of the waterfall. It also has footpaths, natural amphitheaters, lawns and hills, and always the roar of the waterfall for a backdrop. ~ 507 North Howard Street; 509-625-6600, 800-336-7275, fax 509-625-6630; www.spokane riverfrontpark.com.

Commemorating Spokane's most famous native son, Gonzaga University's **Bing Crosby Memorabilia Room** is home to the crooner's Oscar, gold records, photographs and other items. ~ 502 East Boone Avenue; 509-328-4220.

Another must see is the château-style **Spokane County Courthouse** across the river from downtown. Oddly enough, it was designed in the 1890s by a young man whose only formal training in architecture came from a correspondence course. It is a magnificent conglomeration of towers and turrets, sculpture, iron and brickwork in the French Renaissance manner. ~ Broadway just off Monroe Avenue.

Spokane has several wineries with sales and tasting rooms. On a bluff overlooking the Spokane River, **Arbor Crest Wine Cellars** is in a building designated as a National Historic Site. ~ 4705 North Fruit Hill Road; 509-927-9463, fax 509-927-0574; www.arborcrest.com, e-mail info@arborcrest.com.

Latah Creek Wine Cellars has a Spanish-style building with a large courtyard and a tasting room decorated with oak. ~ 13030 East Indiana Avenue; 509-926-0164, fax 509-926-0710; www.latahcreek.com, e-mail info@latahcreek.com.

Knipprath Cellars is in the old Parkwater Schoolhouse and offers Northwest wines in a lovely tasting room with a European flair. Tasting room closed Monday and Tuesday except by appointment. ~ 5634 East Commerce Avenue; 509-534-5121, fax

509-534-5141; www.knipprath-cellars.com, e-mail winemaker@knipprath-cellars.com.

LODGING

Spokane has some pleasant hotels that don't carry big-city rates like those found in Seattle and Portland. You won't find deluxe or luxury accommodations here, but the down-home hospitality of the hotel staffs more than makes up for it.

Two of the largest offer perhaps the best rooms and service. The **Ridpath Hotel** is a renovated establishment downtown divided into two buildings across the street from each other with a second-story skywalk connecting them. The second building has the larger rooms, which all look inside to the courtyard and large swimming pool. The lobby is small, but the staff is cheerful. There are two restaurants and a weight room. ~ 515 West Sprague Avenue; 509-838-2711, fax 509-747-6970; www.theridpathhotel.com. MODERATE.

The **Doubletree Hotel Spokane City Center** was built for Spokane's 1974 World's Fair and has the best location, right along the Spokane River and on Riverfront Park. The lobby is impressive, and most rooms have good views of the river, park or downtown. It also has two restaurants. ~ 322 North Spokane Falls Court; 509-455-9600, 800-222-8733, fax 509-455-6285; www.doubletree.com. MODERATE TO DELUXE.

The **Spokane House Travelodge** is a favorite of many who visit Spokane frequently. Built on a hill west of town, it is roughly

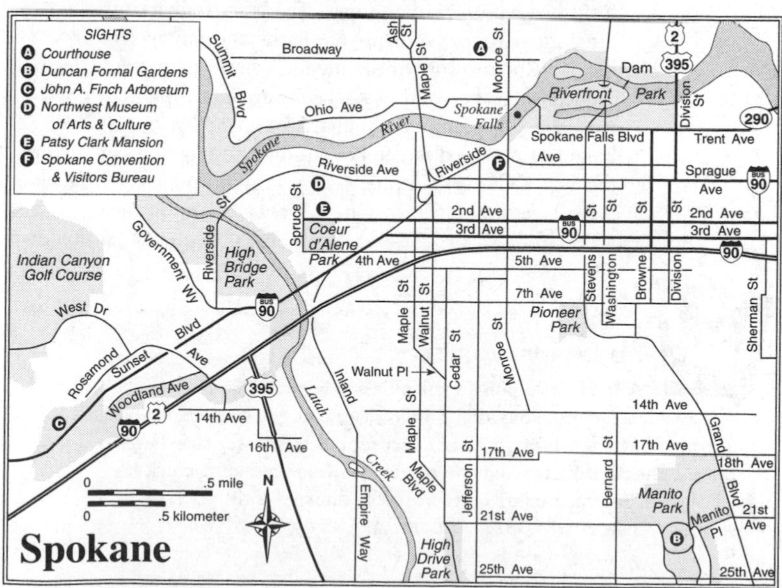

halfway between the airport and downtown, is quiet and affords good views of the city's growing skyline. ~ 4301 West Sunset Highway; 509-838-1471, 800-550-7635, fax 509-838-1705. BUDGET TO MODERATE.

The **Davenport Hotel**, housed in a restored building in downtown Spokane, is the region's classiest place to stay. The 1914 building has 283 rooms outfitted with hand-carved mahogany furniture and suites with whirlpool tubs. Be sure to check out the Hall of the Doges, a ballroom decorated in Venetian palatial style, and the stained-glass ceiling of the Peacock Room. Amenities include a spa and health club, as well as a restaurant, café and lounge. The Davenport Tower is a new extension of the hotel just across the street with an additional 328 rooms. ~ 10 South Post Street; 509-455-8888, 800-899-1482, fax 509-624-4455; www.thedavenporthotel.com, e-mail info@thedavenporthotel.com. ULTRA-DELUXE.

The **Red Lion Hotel at the Park** has 400 rooms and 25 suites and is directly across the river from Riverfront Park. Unfortunately, it is just far enough away from the river to lose some of the waterfront charm. The inn is walking distance from downtown, and some of the rooms have private decks. ~ 303 North River Drive; 509-326-8000, 800-733-5466, fax 509-325-7329; www.redlion.com. MODERATE TO DELUXE.

Built in 1889 as a personal residence for the Roberts family, the 23-room **E. J. Roberts Mansion** is now a bed and breakfast furnished with period antiques. There are four beautifully decorated guest rooms with private baths and vintage fixtures. The Marian Room is softly decorated in velvet and brocade, includes a queen-sized bed and is washed with sunset light. A library, a parlor, a sunroom and a billiard room are also available. Full breakfast is served in the large dining room. You can also rent the Secret Garden Cottage complete with full kitchen facilities, just 30 feet from the mansion. ~ West 1923 1st Avenue, Spokane; 509-456-8839 or 866-456-8839; www.ejrobertsmansion.com. MODERATE.

AUTHOR FAVORITE

A local institution, **Frank's Diner** is one of Spokane's most revered breakfast joints. Housed in a 1906 railcar, it's got everything you'd want from a bustling, all-American comfort food eatery: tasty fare, huge portions, a cheeky waitstaff, and line cooks that aren't afraid to crack a joke or two. Be prepared to wait for a table on weekends. ~ 1516 West 2nd Avenue; 509-747-8798. BUDGET.

DINING

Spokane's most popular Asian cuisine comes from one of several **Mustard Seed Asian Cafés.** The menu offers specialties from several provinces in China, as well as Japanese dishes. Sample traditional fare such as sweet-and-sour shrimp, or check out fusion dishes like Asian tacos with curry chicken. ~ Northtown Mall, 4750 North Division Street; 509-483-1500, fax 509-483-1599; and 9806 East Sprague Avenue, 509-924-3194, fax 509-924-7288; www.mustardseedweb.com. MODERATE.

A favorite lunch and dinner spot is **The Onion**. Occupying a vintage downtown building, The Onion has a 1904 mahogany bar, 1890s prints and brass accents. A wide menu of appetizers and entrées includes onion rings, deep-fried mozzarella, burgers, caesar and taco salads, vegetable stir-fries and baby back ribs. ~ 302 West Riverside Street; 509-747-3852, fax 509-624-9965. MODERATE.

Located in the opulent Davenport Hotel, the **Palm Court Grill** serves up a winning mixture of big-city elegance and small-town informality. Lunches and dinners are unabashedly gourmet, featuring artfully arranged plates. Dishes include crabcakes with yellow cherry tomato vinaigrette, salmon with huckleberry sauce and papaya salad, and fresh papardelle pasta. Breakfasts and the celebrated champagne Sunday brunch are more traditional, but with a twist: omelettes made with crab and avocado, french toast made with baguettes, and fresh pastries. Reservations recommended. ~ 10 South Post Street; 509-789-6848; www.thedavenporthotel.com, e-mail info@thedavenporthotel.com. MODERATE TO ULTRA-DELUXE.

SHOPPING

The Skywalk in the downtown core, a series of weatherproof bridges that connects 15 blocks on the second level, makes downtown shopping pleasant year-round. It leads to the major downtown department stores such as **Nordstrom** at Lincoln Street and Main Avenue (509-455-6111) and **Macy's** at Wall Street and Main Avenue (509-626-6015), several specialty shops, restaurants and art galleries.

With more and more Canadians driving just over a hundred miles to Spokane, where nearly all goods are less expensive, the city has had a surge of discount stores, from national chain stores to the West Coast warehouse stores. Shopping centers have sprung up on the north and northeast edges of town. Covered shopping areas include **Northtown Mall** at Division Street and Wellesley Avenue, **Franklin Park Mall** at Division Street and Rowan Avenue and **University City** at Sprague Avenue and University Street.

If you're using Spokane as an urban stopover in-between more rugged adventures, drop by **N.W. Map & Travel Book Center** for their extensive selection of maps (including USGS topographic, Forest Service, public land and fishing maps) and guidebooks to the Northwest region. Closed Saturday and Sunday. ~ 525 West Sprague Avenue; 509-455-6981; www.nwmaps.com.

The **Flour Mill** is one of the more charming places to shop. It was built as a flour mill but was turned into a specialty shopping center in 1974 with more than a dozen shops, including gift stores, cafés and restaurants. ~ 621 West Mallon Avenue; 509-755-7551, fax 509-458-4014; www.spokaneflourmill.com.

NIGHTLIFE A lively bar that attracts a young, vibrant crowd, **Mootsy's** has a cozy atmosphere that features red walls, funky fixtures, and a pool table. Live music on the weekend. ~ 406 West Sprague Avenue, Spokane; 509-838-1570; www.mootsys.com.

Dempsey's Brass Rail is a popular gay and lesbian nightspot with a dancefloor and drag shows. Cover on Friday and Saturday. ~ West 909 1st Street; 509-747-5362.

The **Spokane Jazz Orchestra**, the oldest continually performing professional community jazz orchestra in the country, performs big band–style concerts as well as Latin, jazz, blues and more throughout the year at various venues around town. ~ P.O. Box 174, Spokane, WA 99210; 509-838-2671, fax 509-747-3739; www.spokanejazz.com, e-mail sales@spokanejazz.com.

The **Spokane Symphony Orchestra** performs more than 60 orchestral concerts per year, including 10 concert classic performances, six superpops shows and three pairs of chamber orchestra concerts. ~ Ticket office, 818 West Riverside Avenue, Suite 100; 509-624-1200, fax 509-326-3921; www.spokanesymphony.org.

The **Spokane Civic Theatre** presents musicals, comedies and dramas from late September through June. ~ 1020 North Howard Street; 509-325-1413; www.spokanecivictheatre.com.

sights

AUTHOR FAVORITE

A life-size diorama that fires my imagination is the **Yakama Nation Cultural Heritage Center**'s depiction of the Yakama catching salmon by hand at Celilo Falls. Imagining is all one can do since the falls vanished when The Dalles Dam was constructed and the Yakama turned to growing asparagus and hops. The history of the tribe is told in dioramas and writings by and about the tribe preserved in a large library. The center also has a theater for films and concerts and a restaurant that serves traditional dishes. Admission (to museum). ~ Route 97, 100 Spilyay Loop, Toppenish; 509-865-2800, fax 509-865-5749; www.yakamamuseum.com, e-mail inquiries@yakama.com.

PARKS

RIVERSIDE STATE PARK On the edge of Spokane, this 10,000-acre park includes nearly eight miles of Spokane River shoreline (perfect for rainbow trout fishing), odd basaltic formations in the river and Indian paintings on rocks. It houses the Spokane House interpretive center (open weekends), which tells the history of the oldest trading post in Washington. Canoes and kayaks area available for rent and interpretive hikes and tours are available for an additional fee. Facilities include a 600-acre off-road vehicle park, picnic areas with shelters, restrooms, hot showers and horse trails; wheelchair accessible. ~ Located six miles northwest of Spokane at 9711 West Charles Road, Nine Mile Falls; 509-465-5064, fax 509-465-5571; www.riversidestatepark.org, e-mail riverside@parks.wa.gov.

▲ There are two campgrounds with tent and TV sites rang ing from $19 to $30. Reservations: 888-226-7688.

MT. SPOKANE STATE PARK This 5881-foot mountain is used as much or more in the winter as it is in summer, but warm-weather visitors find its views spectacular. It is especially pretty during the spring when its slopes are blanketed with flowers and in the fall when the fields are brown and the leaves have turned. For those into winter sports, there are skiing (downhill and cross-country) and snowmobiling. During warm weather, the park has some of the best mountain biking in Washington. There are picnic areas and restrooms. ~ Located at the end of Route 206, 30 miles northeast of Spokane; 509-238-4258, fax 509-238-4078.

▲ There are 12 standard sites ($17 per night). All sites are first-come, first-serve. Closed in winter.

TURNBULL NATIONAL WILDLIFE REFUGE One of the most popular natural places for day trips in the Spokane area, the refuge was established in 1937 primarily for waterfowl. It has several lakes and wooded areas and a marked, self-guided auto-tour route. You will also find hiking trails, cross-country skiing areas and restrooms. Day-use fee March through October. ~ Cheney Plaza Highway, five miles south of Cheney; 509-235-4723, fax 509-235-4703.

Southeastern Washington

The drive from Spokane south into Oregon is one of unusual beauty, especially early or late in the day, or in the spring and fall. The entire region between the wooded hills around Spokane to the Blue Mountains is known as the Palouse Country. Here the barren hills are low but steep, and wheat is grown on nearly every acre. In fact, it is acknowledged as the best wheat-growing land in the world.

SIGHTS

Proceeding south from Spokane along Route 195, you'll find that the two best places to view the Palouse Hills are **Steptoe Butte State**

Park (see "Parks" below) and **Kamiak Butte County Park.** Kamiak Butte stands 3360 feet high and offers bird's-eye views of the Palouse Hills. The park has picnic areas, a hiking trail and, unlike Steptoe Butte, a fringe of trees on its crest and over 100 kinds of vegetation, including the Douglas fir more common to the damp, coastal climate. Kamiak Butte is 18 miles east of Colfax and 15 miles north of Pullman just off Route 27.

The town of **Pullman** is almost entirely a product of Washington State University, although a few agricultural businesses operate on the edge of town. Continuing south from this campus town, Route 195 gains elevation through the small farming communities of Colton and Uniontown, then crosses over into the edge of Idaho just in time to disappear into Route 95 and then take a dizzying plunge down the steep Lewiston Hill, where you drop 2000 feet in a very short time over a twisting highway. The old highway with its hairpin turns is still passable and is exciting driving if your brakes and nerves are in good condition.

Clarkston, Washington, and Lewiston, Idaho, are separated by the Snake River, which flows almost due north through Hells Canyon before taking a sudden westward turn where Idaho's Clearwater River enters in Lewiston. Boat operators will take you up to the Snake River—you can't drive there. Most of the Snake River boat operators are headquartered in these two towns. For more information, contact the **Clarkston Chamber of Commerce.** ~ 502 Bridge Street, Clarkston; 509-758-7712, 800-933-2128, fax 509-751-8767; www.clarkstonchamber.org, e-mail info@clarkstonchamber.org.

The population has followed the Snake on its way west to join with the Columbia, but it is a tamed river now, a series of slackwater pools in deep canyons behind a series of dams: Lower Granite, Little Goose, Lower Monumental and Ice Harbor. The main highway doesn't follow the Snake River because of the deep canyon it carved, so from Clarkston you follow Route 12 west through the farming communities of Pomeroy and Dayton to Walla Walla, then on to the Tri-Cities area around Richland, where the Snake enters the Columbia River. Along the way is Dayton, an agricultural town with over 117 buildings listed on the National Register of Historic Places. Most impressive is the beautiful 1881 **Dayton Historic Depot,** a classic Victorian building that had an upper floor for the stationmaster's quarters. Closed Sunday and Monday. ~ 222 East Commercial Street, Dayton; 509-382-2026; dayton.bmi.net.

Walla Walla looks much like a New England town that was packed up and moved to the rolling hills of Eastern Washington, weeping willows, oak and maple trees included. Best known for its colleges, Whitman and Walla Walla College, the town with a double name has many ivy-covered buildings, quiet streets lined with

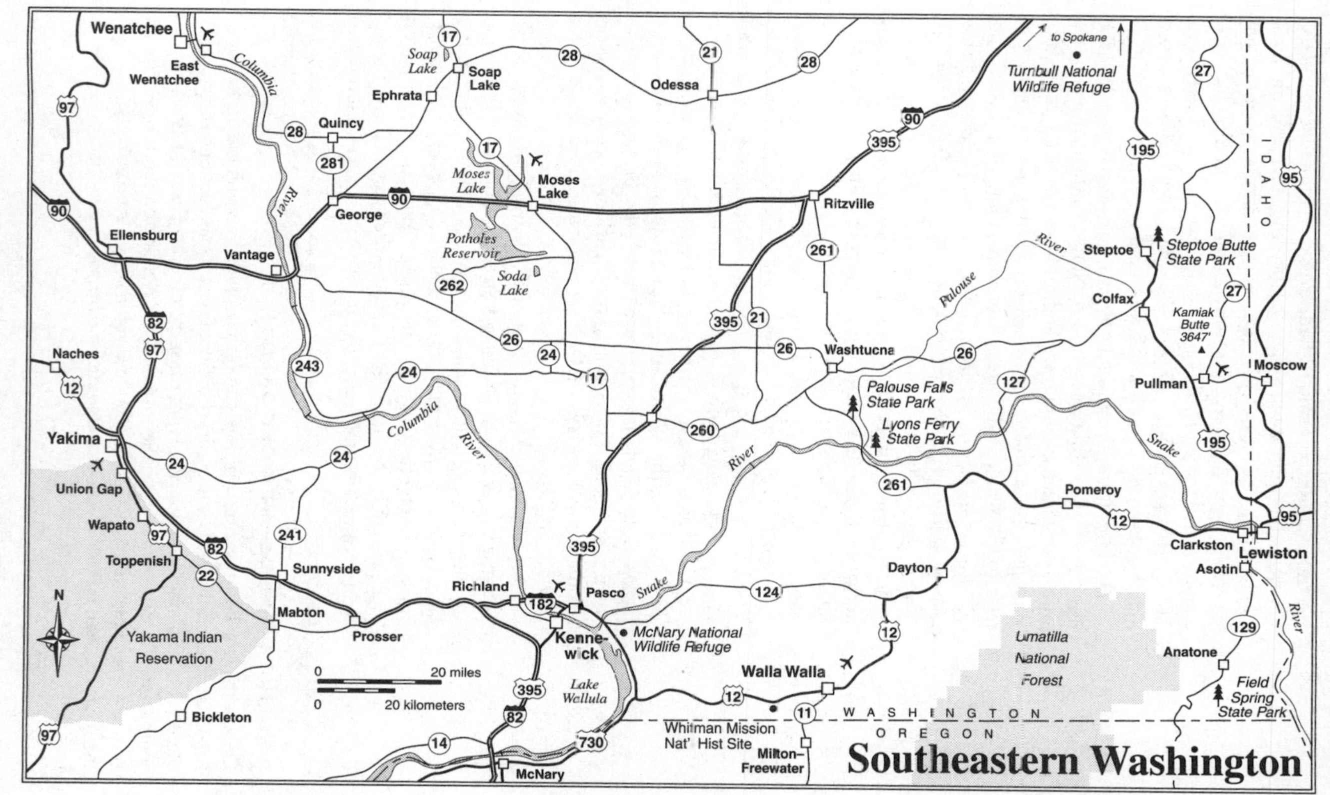
Southeastern Washington
IDAHO
WASHINGTON
OREGON
to Spokane
Turnbull National Wildlife Refuge
Steptoe Butte State Park
Kamiak Butte 3647'
Moscow
Lewiston
Clarkston
Asotin
Anatone
Field Spring State Park
Pullman
Colfax
Steptoe
Pomeroy
Umatilla National Forest
Palouse Falls State Park
Lyons Ferry State Park
Palouse River
Snake River
Dayton
Washtucna
Ritzville
Odessa
Walla Walla
Whitman Mission Nat' Hist Site
Milton-Freewater
McNary National Wildlife Refuge
Pasco
Kenne-wick
Lake Wallula
Richland
McNary
Moses Lake
Soap Lake
Ephrata
Potholes Reservoir
Soda Lake
Columbia River
George
Quincy
Vantage
Wenatchee
East Wenatchee
Ellensburg
Sunnyside
Mabton
Prosser
Bickleton
Yakama Indian Reservation
Toppenish
Wapato
Union Gap
Yakima
Naches
0 20 miles
0 20 kilometers
N

old frame houses, enormous shade trees and, rather incongruously amid this Norman Rockwellian beauty, the state penitentiary.

To see more of the city by foot, stop by the **Chamber of Commerce** for four different historic walking trail guides, including the *Historic Homes Trail Guide*. ~ 29 East Sumach Street, Walla Walla; 509-525-0850, 877-998-4748, fax 509-522-2038; www.wwchamber.com, e-mail info@wwchamber.com.

You can learn about the heritage of southeast Washington at the **Fort Walla Walla Museum**. A pioneer settlement composed of 17 early frontier buildings and replicas and five large exhibit buildings make this museum an excellent place to begin your visit to the Walla Walla area. A pioneer cabin built in 1877 and furnished with period artifacts, an old country rail depot, a completely outfitted one-room school and a doctor's office are among the highlights. Above the pioneer settlement, you'll find wide-ranging displays featuring American Indian, military, and agricultural displays including a combine with a 33 mule team hitch. The museum presents living-history re-enactments every Sunday and on Saturday from June through August. Closed November through March. Admission. ~ 755 Myra Road, Walla Walla; 509-525-7703, fax 509-525-7798; www.fortwallawallamuseum.org, e-mail info@fortwallawallamuseum.org.

You'll enjoy seeing the stately old trees centered around Pioneer Park and the Whitman College campus. With 360 acres of parks, Walla Walla is a pleasure to explore. Be sure to visit the town's splendid late-19th-century **Kirkman House**. Closed Monday and Tuesday. ~ 214 North Colville Street, Walla Walla; 509-529-4373.

At **Whitman Mission National Historic Site**, one of the Northwest's worst tragedies occurred because of a basic misunderstanding of American Indian values by an American missionary, Marcus Whitman. He and his wife, Narcissa, founded a mission among the Cayuse Indians in 1836 to convert the Cayuse to Christianity. As traffic increased on the Oregon Trail, the mission became an important stop for weary travelers. Eleven years

A SCENIC DRIVE DOWN A CROOKED HIGHWAY

Only in the late 1980s was the highway completely paved between the Snake River Canyon and the Wallowas in Oregon. But now you can take one of the prettiest mountain drives in the Northwest by following **Route 129** south from Clarkston in the southeastern corner of Washington through Anatone, then down into the Grande Ronde River valley over probably the most crooked highway in the Northwest. Be sure your brakes (and fortitude) are in good condition.

later the Cayuse felt betrayed by Whitman because his religion hadn't protected them from a measles epidemic that killed half the tribe. On November 29, 1847, the Cayuse killed both Whitmans and 11 others and ransomed 50 to the Hudson's Bay Company. The site is run by the National Park Service. There's a visitors center, a memorial monument, a millpond and walking paths to sites where various buildings once stood. None of the original buildings remain. Admission. ~ Route 12, seven miles west of Walla Walla; 509-529-2761, fax 509-522-6355; www.nps.gov/whmi.

The **Columbia River** runs free for about 60 miles through the Hanford Reservation, but when it swings through the Tri-Cities (Richland, Pasco and Kennewick) it becomes Lake Wallula, thanks to McNary Dam. Several city parks with picnic and boating facilities are along the river, such as **Columbia Park.** ~ Off Route 240, between Edison and Columbia Center Boulevard, Kennewick.

The Tri-Cities are best known for the nuclear-power plant and research center in nearby Hanford. It was here that the components for the first atomic bombs were assembled. A nuclear-related visitors center tells the nuclear story. The **Columbia River Exhibition of History, Science and Technology** features exhibits and historical displays that focus on people's interaction with the environment, such as hydroelectric power, nuclear energy and environmental restoration. Admission. ~ 95 Lee Boulevard, Richland; 509-943-9000, fax 509-943-1770; www.crehst.org, e-mail gwen@crehst.org.

From the Tri-Cities, the population follows the Yakima River, which flows into the Columbia at the Tri-Cities. The **Yakima Valley** is the state's richest in terms of agriculture: Yakima County ranks first nationally in the number of fruit trees, first in the production of apples, mint and hops and fifth in the value of all fruits grown. It is also the wine center of the state: Some 40 wineries have been built between Walla Walla and Yakima, and they have helped create a visitor industry that has encouraged the growth of country inns and bed and breakfasts. Brochures listing the wineries and locations are available in visitors centers and many convenience stores, and once you're off Route 82, signs mark routes to the wineries.

Fort Simcoe State Park is probably the best-preserved frontier army post in the West and was one of the few forts where no shots were fired in anger. It was used in the late 1850s during the conflict with the local American Indian people. There's a museum/interpretive center (closed Monday and Tuesday from April to September; closed October through March). Five of the original buildings are still standing, including the commanding officer's home. Closed weekdays from October through March. ~ Located at the end of Fort Simcoe Road, about 35 miles south of Yakima; 509-874-2372, fax 509-874-2351.

Washington Wine

For a long time, Washington's liquor laws were so restrictive that it was illegal to bring wine into the state; you had to buy it from the state-run stores. The best Washington wine in those days was made by an Italian immigrant, Angelo Pelligrini, who taught Shakespeare at the University of Washington and made wine in his basement—illegally.

That has changed completely. Over 500 wineries are spread across the state, most in Eastern Washington, and many of those in the Puget Sound region own vineyards in Eastern Washington or buy their grapes there. The soil and climate are excellent for wine grapes, and the **Washington Wine Commission** likes to remind us that Eastern Washington is on the same latitude as some of France's great winegrowing regions. ~ 1000 2nd Avenue, Suite 1700, Seattle; 206-667-9463, fax 206-583-0573; www.washingtonwine.org.

Washington has four viticultural regions: Columbia Valley, which extends southward from the Okanogan Country into Oregon and east to Idaho; Yakima Valley, which runs from the foothills of the Cascades east to the Kiona Hills near Richland and is bisected by Interstate 82, making it the most convenient for visits; the Walla Walla Valley region, which straddles the Oregon–Washington border, taking in some vineyards in the Milton-Freewater area; and the Puget Sound region, which covers areas from Olympia in the south to Bellingham in the north, and includes various Puget Sound and San Juan Islands in between.

In keeping with the French adage that the best grape vines "like to be in sight of the water but don't want to get their feet wet," some of the best vineyards in Eastern Washington are on south-facing slopes above the Columbia, Yakima and Snake rivers, where they get as much as 16 hours of sunlight a day and fresh irrigation water on well-drained soil. As with all wine-producing areas, many wineries have been built in palatial settings.

One of the most dramatic is the **Columbia Crest Winery**. Built on a hillside overlooking the Columbia River, it produces more than a million gallons of wine annually and has a reflecting pool, fountain and courtyard, a luxurious lobby and tasting-and-sales room. ~ Route 221, Paterson; 509-875-2061, 800-309-9463, fax 425-415-3657; www.columbia-crest.com.

Running a close second is **Château Ste. Michelle**. This is the state's oldest continuously operating winery. ~ 14111 145th Street Northeast, Woodinville; 425-488-1133, fax 425-415-3657; www.chateau-ste-michelle.com.

Featuring syrah and bordeaux varieties, **White Heron Cellars** emphasizes a natural winemaking process, leaving as much of the ecosystem undisturbed as possible. It also features a concert venue showcasing jazz and blues with a spectacular view. Closed Tuesday and Wednesday. ~ 10035

Stuhlmiller Road, Quincy; 509-797-9463; www.whiteheronwine.com, e-mail info@whiteheronwine.com.

A wine that keeps gaining new fans is the **Silver Lake** label. The tasting room stands on a hill overlooking the winery's acres of grapes. They have three tasting rooms in the area. ~ 1500 Vintage Road, Zillah, 509-829-6235; 715 Front Street, Suite A1, Leavenworth, 509-548-5788; 15029 Woodinville-Redmond Road, Woodinville, 425-485-2437; www.silverlakewinery.com.

The Puryear family, Gail and Shirley, call **Bonair Winery** a "hobby that got out of hand." The winery not only offers a versatile range of wines, including fine chardonnays and cabernets. The setting, on a curve of land inside one of the valley's main irrigation canals, is inviting. ~ 500 South Bonair Road South, Zillah; 509-829-6027, fax 509-829-6410; www.bonairwine.com, e-mail shirley@bonairwine.com.

The quirky **L'Ecole N° 41** got its name from the retired schoolhouse near Walla Walla in which it was built. ~ 41 Lowden School Road, Lowden; 509-525-0940, fax 509-525-2775; www.lecole.com; e-mail info@lecole.com.

Joel Tefft focuses on very limited bottlings of fine handcrafted wines at **Tefft Cellars** outside Sunnyside. Aside from cabernet sauvignon and lush, velvety merlot, the Teffts make unique, light, dry sparkling wines and ports, a rarity in Washington. ~ 1320 Independence Road, Outlook; 509-837-7651, 888-549-7244, fax 509-839-7337; www.tefftcellars.com.

The most homey of the wineries is probably **Kiona Vineyards**. It is a family operation, with a tasting room, winery and the Kiona Vineyard at the home of John and Ann Williams. The winery was one of the originals to produce lemberger. ~ 44612 North Sunset Road, Benton City; 509-588-6716, fax 509-588-3219; www.kionawine.com, e-mail kiona1wine@aol.com.

Sagelands Vineyards is located in a French-country building set on a rolling hillside above the Yakima River. The tasting room features a stone fireplace and cathedral ceilings. ~ 71 Gangl Road, Wapato; 509-877-2112, 800-967-8115, fax 509-877-3377; www.sagelandsvineyard.com, e-mail sagelands.info@sagelandsvineyard.com.

Pontin del Roza came into being because the Pontin family's Italian heritage included a love of wine. They decided to add wine grapes to the crops they had been growing on their Prosser farm for two decades and produce both reds and whites. ~ 35502 North Hinzerling Road, Prosser; 509-786-4449; e-mail pontindelroza@msn.com.

Founded in 1982 with a planting of riesling grapes, **Hogue Cellars**, located in the Columbia Valley, is known for grapes with intense fruit flavor and natural acidity. ~ 2800 Lee Road, Prosser; 509-786-4557 ext. 208, 800-565-9779, fax 509-786-4580; www.hoguecellars.com, e-mail info@hoguecellars.com.

Cheers!

The **Central Washington Agricultural Museum** has a large collection of early farm machinery including a working windmill, a blacksmith shop, a furnished log cabin and a tool and artifact collection. Closed Monday and Tuesday in summer, Monday through Wednesday in winter. ~ 4508 Main Street, Union Gap; 509-457-8735.

The **Yakima Valley Museum** has a comprehensive collection of horse-drawn vehicles, a re-creation of the office of the late Supreme Court Justice William O. Douglas and a unique collection of neon signs. There is also an interactive children's museum and an operating ice cream soda fountain. Closed Monday from November to March. Admission. ~ 2105 Tieton Drive, Yakima; 509-248-0747, fax 509-453-4890; www.yakimavalleymuseum.org, e-mail info@yakimavalleymuseum.org.

Another museum that recalls the early days of the region is the **Sunnyside Historical Museum**. The elegant white building houses statues of early pioneers, a library of historical texts and a pioneer kitchen and dining room. Across the street is the Ben Snipes Cabin, dating from 1859. Closed Monday through Wednesday. ~ 704 South 4th Street, Sunnyside; 509-837-6010.

The main road leading from the Yakima Valley to the beautiful Columbia River Gorge (see Chapter Ten) is Route 97, which runs south from Toppenish, crosses Satus Pass (3107 feet) and reaches the Gorge just past Goldendale. An alternate route from HIDDEN ► the Yakima Valley down to the Columbia River is the **Mabton-Bickleton Road**, which heads south from the small town of Mabton through the even smaller Bickleton. An unincorporated town

THE OLDEST MAN IN WASHINGTON

The Tri-Cities area was the site of the 1996 discovery of the controversial Kennewick Man, one of the oldest human skeletons ever found in North America, radiocarbon-dated to between 8400 and 9200 years old. Because the skull was much different from those of modern American Indians, the find was first thought to suggest the presence of Caucasians in archaic America but is now believed to be "proto-Mongolian," with possible genetic links both Russian Europeans and to native peoples' Asian ancestors. The Colville, Yakima, Umatilla and Nez Perce tribes each claim Kennewick Man as an ancestor, demanding reburial rights under the Native American Graves Protection Act. The ancient bones were locked up at the University of Washington's Burke Museum until 2005, when a court cleared the way for scientists to study the skeleton. Preliminary findings suggest that he was indeed American Indian, about 45 years old, 5 feet 9 inches, and may have been a hunter when the climate was cooler and wetter.

with a scattering of Victorian houses and falsefront store buildings, Bickleton's claim to fame is hundreds of houses for (are you ready for this?) bluebirds. Maintained by residents, the houses are on fence posts along the highway and country lanes and literally all over town. The one in front of the community church is a miniature copy of the church itself.

Opened in 2007, the **Alder Creek Pioneer Association Carousel Museum** celebrates East Klickitat County's past. Displays include an exhibit about the area's wheat farming, collections of barbed wire and bit and spurs, a turn-of-the-century medical office, and American Indian artifacts accompanied by old photographs and petroglyphs. The focal point is the rare 1905, 24-horse Herschel Spillman Carousel, which has been used since 1929 in Bickleton's Pioneer Picnic and Rodeo—the state's oldest rodeo. Closed Monday through Wednesday. Admission. ~ Market Street, Bickleton; www.bickleton.org.

LODGING

It's difficult to find anything other than your basic, cookie-cutter motel in southeastern Washington, although Yakima shows some imagination.

Pullman has about half a dozen motels, none particularly distinguished. The best view is at the **Hawthorn Inn & Suites**. ~ 928 Northwest Olson Street at Davis Way, Pullman; 509-332-0928, 800-527-1133, fax 509-334-5275; www.hawthorn.com, e-mail hawthorn@pullman.com. The **Quality Inn** is near both the campus and the airport. ~ 1400 Southeast Bishop Boulevard, Pullman; 509-332-0500, 800-669-3212, fax 509-334-4271. MODERATE TO DELUXE.

Dayton seems to be out in the middle of nowhere—gateway to the Blue Mountains and an agricultural center. The **Purple House B&B** is thus an unexpected pleasure. This elegant inn, on the National Register of Historic Places, is housed in an 1882 Queen Anne mansion that was built by a pioneer physician. Two upstairs bedrooms share a bath; the master suite downstairs has a private bath. All rooms are furnished in period antiques; there's a library and heated outdoor pool. A separate carriage house has full amenities and a private bath. The full breakfast is cooked to order. Small pets are welcome. ~ 415 East Clay Street, Dayton; phone/fax 509-382-3159, 800-486-2574. MODERATE TO DELUXE.

Walla Walla has about ten motels, most of them in the budget to moderate range. The **Budget Inn** offers a continental breakfast. ~ 305 North 2nd Avenue, Walla Walla; 509-529-4410, 888-529-4161, fax 509-525-5777. BUDGET.

The Tri-Cities area has several fair-size motels, many with meeting rooms since the Hanford Nuclear Center is nearby. One of the largest is the **Clover Island Inn**, built on an island in the Columbia River. Half of the rooms have views of the river. The complex has a pool, hot tub, restaurant and lounge. ~ 435 Clover Island, Kennewick; 509-586-0541, 866-586-0542, fax 509-586-6956; www.cloverislandinn.com, e-mail cloverisland.inn@verizon.net. MODERATE.

Quiet is the overwhelming virtue of the **Apple Country B&B**, located between Naches and Yakima. With five antique-furnished bedrooms in a 1911 house on a working farm, hard-working hostess Shirley Robert wants her guests to feel as serene as the setting suggests. Sit outside your room overlooking the back yard and orchards beyond, sipping lemonade, and peace prevails. ~ 4561 Old Naches Highway; 509-965-0344, 877-788-9963, fax 509-965-1591; www.applecountryinnbb.com, e-mail apple@applecountryinnbb.com. MODERATE.

Yakima does a lively convention business, and one of the best places to stay is next door to the convention center. **Red Lion Yakima Center Hotel** has 153 large, comfortable rooms with colorful furnishings and spacious bathrooms, two heated pools, a dining room and a lounge. ~ 607 Yakima Avenue East, Yakima; 509-248-5900, 800-733-5466, fax 509-575-8975. MODERATE.

DINING

The **Hilltop Restaurant** shares the steep hill with the Hawthorn Inn & Suites, looking down on the city of Pullman. It caters to the local trade with thick steaks, fresh seafood and a full-service lounge. No lunch Saturday and Sunday. ~ 920 Olson Street at Davis Way, Pullman; 509-334-2555, fax 509-332-3120; www.hilltoprestaurant.com, e-mail hilltop@pullman.com. MODERATE.

If you're good at what you do, so goes the saying, the world will beat a path to your door. This could be the slogan for **Patit Creek Restaurant**. It has been in business since 1978 and has built a national reputation for excellent dishes in what is most accurately described as French country cuisine. Meat is the specialty—beef and lamb. Most of the food is grown locally, some by the staff, and since some of the luxurious plants inside and around the outside are herbs, they may one day season your food. No lunch Saturday through Tuesday. Closed Sunday through Tuesday. ~ 725 East Dayton Avenue, Dayton; 509-382-2625. ULTRA-DELUXE.

If you're feeling nostalgic for New York delis, **Merchants Ltd.** will help. It has a wide choice of foods and a sidewalk café ideal for Walla Walla's mostly sunny weather. ~ 21 Main Street East, Walla Walla; 509-525-0900, fax 509-522-3065; www.merchantsdeli.com. BUDGET TO MODERATE.

The Cedars is one of the Tri-Cities' most striking restaurants. It is cantilevered over the Columbia River with boat-docking facilities. The specialties are steaks, seafood and prime rib. Favorites include the *biergarten* steak and the daily fresh fish specials. Dinner only. ~ 355 Clover Island, Kennewick; 509-582-2143, fax 509-582-2144; www.cedarsrest.com. MODERATE TO DELUXE.

Emerald of Siam serves authentic Thai food in a former drugstore. A buffet lunch is served on weekdays, or you may order from the menu. Closed Sunday. ~ 1314 Jadwin Avenue, Richland; 509-946-9328. BUDGET.

Prosser is a farm town, pure and simple. But what better place for fine, gourmet country cuisine? At **The Blue Goose**, local wine and produce form the basis for a Tuscan/Northwest menu that ranges from veal marsala to chicken-fried steak (well, it is a country restaurant). The wine list features more than 50 local wines, some of them superb vintages, at prices you'll never see in any urban restaurant. ~ 306 7th Street, Prosser; 509-786-1774, fax 509-786-7557. MODERATE TO DELUXE.

Washington's wine-making history dates back to 1824, when grape seeds from England were planted in Vancouver.

Over the years, **Birchfield Manor** has won more magazine awards than any other Washington restaurant outside the Puget Sound region. The owners restored an old farmhouse and filled it with antiques, then opened the restaurant with a menu of seven entrées including fresh salmon in puff pastry, filet mignon, rack of lamb and lobster linguini. Local fruit and vegetables are used, and the fixed menu includes an appetizer, a salad and a homemade chocolate treat. Closed Sunday through Wednesday except for large groups. ~ 2018 Birchfield Road, Yakima; 509-452-1960, 800-375-3420, fax 509-452-2334; www.birchfieldmanor.com, e-mail reservations@birchfiled manor.com. ULTRA-DELUXE.

SHOPPING

Yakima offers several intriguing shopping areas. One is the **North Front Street Historical District**, where the city's oldest buildings, some of them made of rough-hewn local rock, now house an assortment of boutiques, restaurants and brew pubs.

Yesterday's Village is a collection of shops in the former Fruit Exchange Building. The remodeled building houses some 75 shops that sell antiques, glassware, collectibles, furniture and jewelry. ~ 15 West Yakima Avenue, Yakima; 509-457-4981.

At **Inklings Bookshop**, you'll find cards, candles, and new and used titles on a wealth of subjects. Settle in with your new read on one of the plush couches and sip your beverage from the espresso bar. ~ 5629 Summitview Avenue, Yakima; 509-965-5830; www.inklingsbookshop.com.

NIGHTLIFE

Yakima has frequent concerts put on by the **Yakima Symphony Orchestra**. Season runs October through April. ~ 32 North 3rd Street #333, Yakima; 509-248-1414; www.yakimasymphony.org.

Square dancing is very popular in the Yakima Valley, and numerous clubs welcome travelers to their dances. Dances are held Thursday and Saturday nights at the Yakima Square and Round Dance Center. ~ 207 East Charron Road, Moxee; 509-452-6438.

PARKS

STEPTOE BUTTE STATE PARK This park consists of the butte, a picnic area and primitive toilets at the base and summit. The reason for the park's existence is the butte itself, which rises to an elevation of 3567 feet out of the rolling Palouse Hills with panoramic views that are popular with photographers. The butte is actually the top of a granite mountain that stands above the lava flows that covered all the other peaks. The word "steptoe" has entered the international geological vocabulary to represent any similar remnant of an earlier geological feature standing out from the newer feature. There are seven picnic sites at the foot of the butte; no water. ~ Off Route 195, roughly 50 miles south of Spokane; 509-646-9218, fax 509-646-9288; e-mail cpt.central@parks.wa.gov.

FIELD SPRING STATE PARK This 792-acre park is in forested land on the eastern slope of the Blue Mountains. It is just below Puffer Butte, a 4500-foot mountain that overlooks the Grand Ronde River Canyon. For hikers, there are a one-mile trail to the summit of Puffer Butte and ten miles of hiking paths. Winter brings cross-country skiing, snowshoeing and tubing. There are restrooms and showers. ~ Route 129, four miles south of Anatone; 509-256-3332.

▲ There are 20 standard sites ($16 per night) and 2 primitive sites ($10 per night). A teepee for eight people is $20 per night.

FORT WALLA WALLA PARK AND MUSEUM This collection of pioneer buildings is located on a 208-acre former Army fort and cemetery containing victims from both sides of the first conflicts with the Indians. It also has 20 buildings, some authentic and others replicas, of pioneer homes, schools and public buildings. One of the largest collections of horse-drawn farm equipment in the Northwest is also owned by the museum (admission; closed November through March; 755 Myra Road, Walla Walla; 509-525-7703; www.fortwallawallamuseum.org, e-mail info@fortwallawallamuseum.org). There are also nature and bicycle trails in the park. Other facilities include picnic areas, a skate park and BMX track, restrooms, play equipment and volleyball courts. ~ Located on the southeast side of Walla Walla on Dalles Military Road at Myra; 509-527-4527.

PALOUSE FALLS/LYONS FERRY PARK This two-part, remote park is out in the rugged Channeled Scablands. The Lyons Ferry section consists of a pleasant, grassy area with boat ramps at the confluence of the Snake and Palouse rivers. About seven to eight miles up the Palouse River is the Palouse Falls section, with a dramatic picnic area and viewpoint overlooking the thundering 200-foot-tall Palouse Falls. There are picnic areas and restrooms; a wheelchair-accessible hiking trail there and at Lyons Ferry, as well as a boat launch ramp, concessionaire, hiking areas and a restaurant, are nearby. ~ Route 261, 23 miles southeast of Washtucna; Lyon's Ferry 509-751-0240; Palouse 509-646-9218.

▲ Palouse Falls has 10 tent sites ($17 per night); Lyons Ferry has 52 standard sites ($17 per night). Both close in winter.

McNARY NATIONAL WILDLIFE REFUGE This is one of the major resting areas in the Pacific Flyway for migratory waterfowl, especially Canada geese, American widgeon, mallards, pintails and white pelicans. The population peaks in November, and the few summer migratory birds, such as the pelicans and long-billed curlews, arrive in the spring and summer. The refuge covers over 15,000 acres that stretch along the confluence of the Snake River downstream into the mouth of the Walla Walla River. Hunters look for waterfowl and upland birds, while anglers cast a rod for largemouth black bass, catfish and crappie. Self-guided wildlife trail through the marsh and croplands. ~ 500 East Maple Street, southeast of Pasco just off Route 395 on the Snake River; 509-547-4942, fax 509-544-9047.

Outdoor Adventures

FISHING

Although eastern Washington is not, as one local guide puts it, "blue ribbon" fishing territory for most of the year, the region has its moments: come August, some big salmon show up in the Klickitat River; September starts the steelhead run in the Snake River; and trout in June and July make the Yakima River the most popular flyfishing stream in the Northwest. Some outfitters can also arrange hunting trips for game like elk, deer and bighorn sheep.

GRAND COULEE AREA For information on fishing in Banks and Roosevelt lakes, contact **Coulee Playland.** ~ P.O. Box 457,

IT'S ALL RECENT HISTORY

Compared with the rest of the country, the Northwest's history is both recent and benign. The Northwest is so new that East Coast visitors look askance when they find that the major cities weren't founded until the latter part of the last century. Very little recorded history goes back before 1800; the Lewis and Clark Expedition of 1804–1806 was the first overland crossing between the original 13 states and the Pacific Coast, and they were the first to describe the lower Snake River.

Electric City, WA 99123; 509-633-2671; www.couleeplayland.com. In winter, Banks Lake, near Grand Coulee, is a popular place to ice fish.

SPOKANE AREA G. L. Britton of **Double Spey Outfitters** has been flyfishing since he was a boy; he now guides visiting anglers for half-day walk-and-wade flyfishing trips for trout on the Spokane during August and September, and full-day steelhead trips on a driftboat on the Snake and Grande Rhonde rivers in October and November. The rest of the year, Britton will take you out to one of the local lakes for a full day of fishing that's more "teach-you" than "trophy." Flies, rods and leaders are provided. ~ West 11254 Meadowview Lane, Nine Mile Falls; 509-466-4635.

Check with the Washington Department of Fish and Wildlife for updates on fish counts and restrictions before setting off with rod and reel *sans* guide. ~ www.wdfw.wa.gov.

Fishing excursions on the Snake River between the Idaho/Washington border are offered by **Beamer's Hells Canyon Tours.** Spring and summer half-day to four-days trips on a fishing sled seek bass, trout and sturgeon; in fall, it's steelhead. Bait and tackle provided. ~ 1451 Bridge Street, Clarkston; 509-758-4800, 800-522-6966, fax 509-758-3643; www.hellscanyontours.com, e-mail beamerstours@bhct.net. **Snake River Adventures** provides day tours as well as single or multiday guided trips for steelhead, sturgeon, bass and trout on the Snake, Salmon and Clearwater rivers. ~ 4832 Hells Gate Road, Lewiston, ID; 208-746-6276, 800-262-8874, fax 208-746-9906; www.snakeriveradventures.com, e-mail sra@lewistondsl.com.

RIVER RUNNING

In September on the Tieton River, in southeastern Washington, water is released from the dam that controls the flow, creating Class III and some Class IV rapids and drawing ever-increasing crowds of rafters. It may not be a "hidden" spot, but it's still a thrill. Whitewater thrills come on the Snake River in Northeastern Oregon, where it cuts through walls of black basalt, forming Hells Canyon, the deepest gorge in the country. Spring is the best time to hit good whitewater, but be forewarned: classifications are arbitrary and the hard classes aren't necessarily the best. Watch water levels more closely than class.

SOUTHEASTERN WASHINGTON **Chinook Expeditions** has been leading guided trips and wildlife-watching tours since 1974. Rivers rafted include the Skagit, Snohomish, Skykomish, Toutle and Queets. Guide Shane Turnbull says all trips are very interpretive. All river and camping gear is included. ~ P.O. Box 256, Index, WA 98256; 360-793-3451, 800-241-3451; www.chinookexpeditions.com. **Rivers, Inc.** offers full-day guided trips on paddle rafts down the Wenatchee, Methow, Suiattle and Tieton rivers in the summer. ~ P.O. Box 2092, Kirkland, WA 98083; 425-822-5296; www.raftriverinc.com. **Idaho Afloat** leads one- to six-day rafting trips down Class II to Class IV rivers. ~ P.O. Box 542, Grangeville, ID 83530; 208-983-2414, 800-700-2414; www.idahoafloat.com.

Snake Dancer Excursions provides full- and half-day jet boat tours down the Snake River and through Hells Canyon, with a stop at Kirkwood Ranch. Trips cover 85 sets of rapids that rate as high as Class IV. Lunch provided. ~ 1550 Port Drive, Suite B, Clarkston; 509-758-8927, 800-234-1941, fax 509-758-8925; www.snakedancerexcursions.com, e-mail sdexcursions@qwest.net.

Another popular location for rafting is the Snake River between the Washington and Idaho border. Contact **O.A.R.S. Dories** for guided tours on rafts, dories and inflatable kayaks on Class III and Class IV rivers. Trips on the Snake River last three to five days; Salmon River expeditions are four to seventeen days. ~ P.O. Box 67, 2687 South Route 49, Angels Camp, CA 95222; 209-736-4677, 800-346-6277, fax 209-736-2902; www.oars.com, e-mail info@oars.com.

GOLF

Mountain valleys and high desert vistas give golfers satisfying course options, and greens fees that are lower than in urban areas sweeten the deal. Winter weather closes many courses for two to five months.

OKANOGAN HIGHLANDS Hilly terrain makes a cart rental highly recommended at the nine-hole **Oroville Golf Club**. The scenic semiprivate course runs beside a river. Closed Thursday afternoon. ~ 3468-A Nighthawk Road, two miles west of Oroville; 509-476-2390, fax 509-476-2408. Between Omak and Okanogan is the **Okanogan Valley Golf Club**. This public course is surrounded by hills on one side and orchards on the other. Closed in winter. ~ 105 Danker Cutoff, off the Okanogan–Conconully Route; 509-826-6937; www.okanoganvalleygolf.com.

GRAND COULEE AREA **Banks Lake Golf and Country Club** offers 18 holes for golf enthusiasts. The public course is next to Banks Lake, and offers a few canyons and wide fairways. Closed in winter. ~ 19849 Lundolph Road Northeast, one mile south of Electric City; 509-633-0163.

SPOKANE AREA If you've seen San Francisco's Lincoln Park Municipal Golf Course with its view across the city skyline, Spokane's **Indian Canyon Golf Course** will seem familiar. Set on a hillside that undulates downward toward Spokane, the public 18-hole course is well known throughout the region. Closed in winter. ~ West 4304 West Drive; 509-747-5353, fax 509-747-0622.

SOUTHEASTERN WASHINGTON In Yakima the public, 18-hole **Suntides Golf Course** is fairly flat, so it's very walkable, making it popular with seniors and junior golfers. There's water on 13 of the holes. You'll find a restaurant on the premises. ~ 231 Pence

Road, Yakima; 509-966-9065, fax 509-966-2742; www.sun tidesgolf.com. The 17th hole at public **Apple Tree Golf Course** is called Apple Island, and is shaped like an apple and surrounded by water (this is apple country, after all). ~ 8804 Occidental Road, Yakima; 509-966-5877.

Sun Willows Golf Course is a public, 18-hole course that's very playable for all handicaps. It's fairly flat, but has several lakes. Carts are available for rent. ~ 2535 North 20th Avenue, Pasco; 509-545-3440; www.sunwillowsgolfcourse.com. A canyon runs through **Canyon Lakes Golf Course**, which makes for plenty of interesting shots on this 18-hole public course. Rated one of the top ten courses in the Northwest, Canyon Lakes also has a champion putting course and full practice facilities. ~ 3700 West Canyon Lakes Drive, Kennewick; 509-582-3736; www.canyon lakesgolfcourse.com.

SKIING

Ski areas in this part of the state, particularly the southeast part, are little farther away from the hustle and bustle of the larger, more popular spots elsewhere. The full-service resorts all offer equipment rentals for downhill skiing, cross-country skiing and snowboarding. In addition, lessons are available for all levels.

OKANOGAN HIGHLANDS Downhill and cross-country skiing are both popular in this region, particularly the latter because there is so much open country and powdery snow. Cross-country trails are maintained at most downhill areas, but any country road, most golf courses and parks may be used by skiers. **Loup Loup Ski Area** has a 1240-foot vertical drop for downhill skiing and snowboarding. Its four lifts serve over a dozen runs. There is a small half-pipe for snowboarders, and 25 kilometers of groomed trails for cross-country skiers. Closed Monday, Tuesday and Thursday, and April to mid-December. ~ Route 20, between Twisp and Okanogan; 509-826-2720, fax 509-826-5469; www.skitheloup.com, e-mail info@skitheloup.com.

Sitzmark Ski Lodge has a base elevation of 4950 feet and a modest 650-foot drop. There is a chair lift, a rope tow and runs for snowboarders. The majority of runs are intermediate (60 percent). Closed mid-March to mid-December. ~ Located 20 miles northeast of Tonasket on Havillan Road; 509-485-3323; www. skisitzmark.com. **49° North** has six chairlifts on 1900 feet as well as a snowboard park and 380 miles of groomed trails. Closed mid-April to mid-November. ~ Located ten miles east of Chewelah; 509-935-6649, 866-376-4949; www.ski49n.com.

SOUTHEASTERN WASHINGTON **Ski Bluewood**, 22 miles southeast of Dayton at the end of a Forest Service road, has 1125 vertical feet of downhill skiing. There are two triple-chair lifts and one surface lift, as well as a snowboard terrain park. Closed

North America's Deepest Gorge

The Snake River's colorful Hells Canyon, deeper by 2000 feet than Arizona's Grand Canyon, is the center piece of a 652,488-acre parcel, much of it wilderness. The gorge defines the border between Idaho on one side and the Oregon–Washington boundary on the other, although the largest section of wilderness surrounding the gorge lies in Oregon. America's deepest gorge (with an average depth of 6000 feet), this 72-mile stretch of the Snake River (31.5 miles designated as wild; 36 miles designated as scenic and 4.2 miles unspecified) is accessible from Clarkston, Washington, and neighboring Lewistown, Idaho. It was saved from flooding after conservationists blocked a frightening proposal to dam this scenic region popular with anglers, rafters and jet boat operators. Visitors from all over the world make the pilgrimage to eastern Washington just to see **Hells Canyon National Recreation Area**, which encompasses three mountain ranges in Washington, Idaho and Oregon. ~ 88401 Route 82, Enterprise, OR; 509-758-0616; www.fs.fed.us/hellscanyon.

The incredible scope of the gorge is apparent even to those who only see it from the surrounding hills. Visitors who continue farther into the canyon, either by water or by land, discover more than stark and spectacular scenery. Hells Canyon was well known to prehistoric American Indians and early white settlers alike, as evidenced by petroglyphs and 8000-year-old artifacts from Chief Joseph's Nez Perce, remnants of turn-of-the-20th-century gold mines and homesteads.

On your trip you're likely to spot bighorn sheep, elk, deer and bald eagles, as well as American Indian petroglyphs and Nez Perce tribal landmarks. You'll also see old mining townsites and the site of one of the regions great tragedies, the Deep Creek Massacre of 1887, which took the lives of 32 Chinese gold miners.

Whitewater rafters, kayakers and drift boaters put in at the mouth of Hells Canyon Creek, just below Hells Canyon Dam, for trips downriver on the "national wild and scenic" portion of the Snake that extends north 79 miles to the mouth of the Grande Rhonde River in Heller Bar. In the fall, steelhead fishing trips are extremely popular on the Snake. The **Clarkston Chamber of Commerce** can provide the names of jet-boat and rafting operators. Overnight fishing trips can also be arranged with convenient stays at rustic Hells Canyon lodges. ~ 502 Bridge Street, Clarkston, WA; 509-758-7712, 800-933-2128; www.clarkstonchamber.org, e-mail info@clarkstonchamber.org. For private float boat reservations, call 509-758-1957. For private power boat reservations, call 509-758-0270.

Monday and Tuesday, and from mid-April to mid-November. ~ 262 East Main Street; 509-382-4725, fax 590-382-4726; www.bluewood.com, e-mail info@bluewood.com.

BIKING

For the most part, automobile traffic is sparse in these regions, so bicyclists have little trouble finding long stretches of road that are practically deserted, and scenically beautiful. But they're also challenging and attract avid cross-country bicyclists, especially along Routes 3 and 86 in the Wallowa National Forest near Hells Canyon. Recreational bicyclists, however, have a couple of options. Along the bank of the Spokane River, the paved **Centennial Trail** extends from Riverside State Park to the Washington–Idaho state line (37 miles) and continues on to Coeur d'Alene, Idaho, 25 miles farther. The trail is a relatively flat, easy ride with a few hills in the park (and nobody says you have to go the full distance; you might just want to go as far as Plante's Ferry Park, where you'll find some interesting basalt rock formations in the water). Just west of Spokane is the forested Riverside State Park, which has several gravel trails for mountain biking. Mt. Spokane, which rises some 5800 feet, is another recommended destination.

In the Yakima area, besides an easy five-mile multi-use route along the **Yakima Greenway**, which meanders along the river, there are several possible routes through the local wine country. The **Yakima Valley Visitors and Convention Bureau** has information and maps. ~ 10 North 8th Street; 509-575-6062, 800-221-0751; www.yakimacenter.com.

The **Snake River Bikeway** runs six miles between Clarkston and Asotin along both the Clearwater and Snake rivers. Access it from Beachview Park at the corner of Beachview and Chestnut in Clarkston. Also, a 24-mile tour from **Palouse** leads south on Route 27 to Clear Creek Road to Route 272 back to Palouse.

In some cities, you'll find some bicycle routes that double as hiking trails (see "Hiking," below).

Bike Rentals & Tours There are three bike shops along Spokane's main street. Rent or repair a mountain bike or buy equipment at **North Division Bicycle Shop.** ~ 10503 North Division Street, Spokane; 509-467-2453, 888-222-2453; www.northdivision.com. **Spoke 'N Sport** rents and sells mountain bikes, racks and trailers. There's also a full-service bike shop. ~ 212 North Division Street, Spokane; 509-838-8842.

In the Yakima area, contact the **Yakima Valley and Convention Bureau** for a map of bike routes through the local wine country. ~ 101 North Fair Avenue; 509-575-6062, 800-221-0751. Mountain-bike sales and repairs are available through **Valley Cycling and Fitness.** ~ 1802 West Nob Hill Boulevard, Yakima; 509-453-6699; www.valleycyclingandfitness.com.

For a variety of scheduled rides in the Yakima area, check out **Mount Adams Cycling.** ~ P.O. Box 745, Yakima, WA 98907; www.mountadamscycling.org.

HIKING

All distances listed for hiking trails are one way unless otherwise noted.

OKANOGAN HIGHLANDS Backpackers and day hikers alike enjoy this area because the weather is often clear and dry. A number of established hiking trails are shown on Forest Service maps and in free brochures given out at the ranger station in Okanogan. ~ 1240 South 2nd Avenue; 509-826-3275, fax 509-826-3789.

A good walk for a family with small children is the one-mile trail leading from Bonaparte Campground just north of the one-store town of Wauconda to the viewpoint overlooking the lake. Another easy one is the **Big Tree Trail** (1 mile) loop from Lost Lake Campground, which is only a short distance north of Bonaparte. This one goes through a signed botanical area.

Forest areas in the Okanogan Highlands are more open than in the Cascades and Olympics, making it a favorite among hikers.

One of the most ambitious highlands trails is the southern segment of the **Kettle Crest Trail** (15 miles). The trek begins at the summit of Sherman Pass on Route 20 and winds southward past Sherman Peak and four other major mountains, the highest peak measuring 7135 feet. The trail is through mostly open terrain, and you'll have great views of the mountains and Columbia River Valley. ~ 509-684-7000.

GRAND COULEE AREA A system of paths and trails connects the four towns clustered around Grand Coulee Dam. The Bureau of Reclamation built a paved route about two miles long called the **Community Trail**, which connects Coulee Dam and Grand Coulee. An informal system of unpaved paths connects these two towns to Elmer City and Electric City.

The newest is the walking/biking trail called the **Down River Trail** (6.5 miles). It runs north along the Columbia River from Grand Coulee, beginning in the Coulee Dam Shopping Center. Some access points are accessible for wheelchairs. ~ 509-633-9503.

Bunchgrass Prairie Nature Trail (.5-mile roundtrip) begins in the Spring Canyon Campground, which is three miles up Lake Roosevelt by water and two miles from Grand Coulee. This loop trail starts in the campground and goes through one of the few remaining bunchgrass environments here. ~ 509-633-9441.

SOUTHEASTERN WASHINGTON **Cowiche Canyon** (3 miles) starts five miles from Yakima. The trail is actually an old railroad bed that ran through the steep canyon. The canyon has unusual rock formations, and you can expect to see some wildlife.

Noel Pathway (4.6 miles) is a trail inside the city limits of Yakima that follows the Yakima River. The pathway is used by bicyclists, as well.

Transportation

CAR

Eastern Washington and Oregon is served by a network of roads that range from interstates to logging roads that have been paved by the Forest Service. **Route 97** serves as the north–south dividing line between the Cascade Mountains and the arid, rolling hills that undulate to the eastern boundaries of the states.

Route 90 runs through the center of the Washington, from Spokane southwest through Moses Lake, George and across the Columbia River at Vantage, where the highway turns almost due west for its final run to Puget Sound.

Route 5 bisects Portland, Oregon, and provides access from the north via Vancouver, Washington. This highway is also the main line from points south like the Willamette Valley and California.

Route 82 begins near Hermiston, Oregon, crosses the Columbia River to the Tri-Cities (Richland, Kennewick and Pasco) and runs on up the Yakima Valley to join Route 90 at Ellensburg. **Route 84** runs almost the entire length of the Columbia River Gorge in Oregon before swinging southeast at Hermiston and connecting Pendleton, La Grande and Baker City with Ontario on the Idaho border.

Other major highways are **Route 395**, starting south of Lakeview, Oregon, and continuing into Washington at the Tri-Cities to Ritzville. It joins with Route 90 at Ritzville only to emerge again at Spokane, where it continues north into British Columbia. Smaller but important highways include **Route 12** between Clarkston and Walla Walla, and **Route 195** running between Spokane and the Clarkston–Lewiston area.

Perhaps the most beautiful of all the highways in Washington is **Route 20**, which starts at Whidbey Island and continues to the North Cascades, through the Methow Valley, then straight through the Okanogan Highlands to Kettle Falls, where it merges with Route 395. It becomes Route 20 again at Colville, and continues southeast to Newport on the Idaho border.

AIR

Spokane International Airport is by far the busiest in Eastern Washington with ten airlines serving the area: Alaska Airlines, America West, Delta Airlines, Frontier, Horizon Air, Northwest Airlines, Skywest, Southwest Airlines, United Airlines and United Express ~ www.spokaneairports.net.

Other airports with scheduled service in Washington are **Moses Lake, Pullman, Wenatchee, Yakima,** the **Tri-Cities** and **Walla Walla.** All of these smaller cities are served by either Horizon Air or United

Express, or both. In addition, Delta Airlines serves the Tri-Cities. Empire Airlines serves the Tri-Cities and Yakima.

BUS

Three bus lines operate in the region. From the Spokane terminal at 221 West 1st Avenue are **Greyhound Bus Lines** (509-624-5251, 800-231-2222; www.greyhound.com) and **Northwestern Trailways** (509-838-5262). Greyhound also serves Yakima at the depot at 602 East Yakima Avenue (509-457-5131).

Operating from Medical Lake (just southwest of Spokane) is **Alpha Omega Tours and Charters.** ~ 419 North Jefferson Street; 509-299-5545, 800-351-1060; www.alphaomegatoursandcharters.com.

TRAIN

Washington is one of the few states to have two **Amtrak** routes. Both start in Spokane. The first route runs from Spokane due west with stops in Ephrata, Wenatchee, Everett and Edmonds before arriving in Seattle. The other route runs southwest from Spokane to the Columbia River Gorge with stops in Pasco, Bingen and Vancouver, and ultimately goes to Portland, Oregon. ~ 800-872-7245; www.amtrak.com.

CAR RENTALS

Car-rental agencies in Spokane include the following: **Budget Car and Truck Rental** (800-527-0700) and **Thrifty Car Rental** (800-367-2277).

Agencies in the Tri-Cities include **Avis Rent A Car** (800-331-1212), **Budget Rent A Car** (800-527-0700) and **Hertz Rent A Car** (800-654-3131). Walla Walla is served by **Budget Rent A Car** (800-527-0700).

PUBLIC TRANSIT

The Tri-Cities area has **Ben Franklin Transit.** ~ 509-735-5100; www.bft.org. **Valley Transit** serves Walla Walla and College Place. ~ 509-525-9140; www.valleytransit.com. Pullman has **Pullman Transit.** ~ 509-332-6535; www.pullmantransit.com. Yakima has **Yakima Transit.** ~ 509-575-6175.

TAXIS

Major taxi companies in the area are **Valley Cab** (509-535-7007) and **Spokane Cab** (509-568-8000).

TEN

The Columbia River Gorge

The Columbia River cuts an 80-mile swath through the Cascade Mountains on its way to the Pacific, leaving in its wake a magnificent landscape of towering basalt cliffs, waterfalls and forested bluffs known as the Columbia River Gorge. Because it forms a natural border between Oregon and Washington, exploring the Gorge is a two-state proposition, with a lot to see and do on both sides of the river.

Since long before the two states existed, the Gorge has both fascinated and terrified travelers. For centuries this part of the river was a major trading ground for American Indians who came from as far away as Northern California and British Columbia to meet, talk and barter. Lewis and Clark marveled at the Gorge as they journeyed down the Columbia on the last stretch of their westward trek. Less captivated were the Oregon Trail immigrants of the 1840s who had to detour south around Mt. Hood or else mount their wagons on homemade rafts for a treacherous ride through the rocks and rapids west of The Dalles.

Today, visitors have it a lot easier. On the Oregon side, Route 84 parallels the Columbia River from Portland through such prime Gorge sightseeing areas as Cascade Locks and The Dalles. On the Washington side, Route 14 follows a mostly water-level route through the Gorge on the north bank, providing good views of the Oregon shore and such river traffic as tugboats pushing grain-laden barges downstream. Frequently sighted at the eastern edge of the Gorge, particularly near Hood River, are the bright sails of windsurfers attracted to some of the best conditions for their sport in North America. Although it's possible to tour the Gorge in a loop drive, taking Route 14 one way and Route 84 the other, we recommend crisscrossing it at various points in between. Declared a national scenic area by Congress in 1986, the Columbia Gorge, less than an hour east of Portland, has been a busy area for tourism development during the past several years. Although most hotels and restaurants are still concentrated on the Oregon side, it is the Washington side around Stevenson, with its interpretive center and deluxe resort, where the most recent activity has taken place. Fortunately, the Gorge is still largely unspoiled and provides much to keep waterfall lovers, windsurfers, kayakers, hikers and history buffs enthralled for days.

SIGHTS

Although it's only half an hour from downtown Portland and the logical starting point for touring the Columbia Gorge region, many visitors to the region miss **Fort Vancouver**. What a pity. Located across the Columbia River from Portland, on the Washington side, this National Historic Site is a cornerstone of Pacific Northwest history. Organized by the Hudson Bay Company in 1825, the fort was originally a British fur-trading post and focal point for the commercial development of an area extending from British Columbia to Oregon and from Montana west to the Hawaiian Islands.

Ten structures have been reconstructed on their original fort locations. Collectively known as Fort Vancouver National Historic Reserve, they give a feel for life during the arrival of the first white settlers. One of the best ways to start your tour is at the visitors center with the introductory video. On your tour you'll see the re-created Chief Factor's House, once home to Dr. John McLoughlin, the British agent who befriended American settlers and is remembered as the "Father of Oregon." The phenomenal ability of the British to instantly gentrify the wilderness is reflected in the fine china, copper kettles and elegant furniture of this white clapboard home wrapped with a spacious veranda. You may be surprised to learn that the male officers dined without their wives.

The **Fur Warehouse** interprets how furs were collected and prepared for shipment to England. Also worth a visit are the **Blacksmith Shop, Bake House, Kitchen, Wash House, Palisade, Bastion, Jail** and a **Carpenter Workshop**. At the **Indian Trade Shop and Dispensary**, you'll learn how American Indians skillfully bartered their collected furs for British-made goods. Because most of the items were imported, there was a two-year hiatus between ordering goods and receiving them. Fort Vancouver: Admission May 1 to September 30. ~ 612 East Reserve Street, Vancouver, WA; 360-816-6230, fax 360-816-6363; www.nps.gov/fova.

On nearby **Officer's Row**, you'll see 21 grand homes built for American Army leaders who served here during the latter half of the 19th and the early 20th centuries. These charming Victorians are the focus of a rehabilitation program combining interpretive and commercial use. Among the residences you can tour is the **Grant House**, which currently houses a restaurant serving classic Northwestern food. ~ 360-906-1101. The **George C. Marshall House**, an imposing Queen Anne structure, also offers tours every day. Call for weekend hours; tours are available Saturday and Sunday except during weddings or other event rentals. ~ 360-693-3103.

HIDDEN ►

Next to Fort Vancouver is **Pearson Air Museum.** The field, opened in 1905, is the oldest operating airfield in the United States. Exhibits feature a display on the world's first nonstop transpolar flight (Moscow to Vancouver) in 1937—the Soviet aviators were greeted by General George Marshall, who hosted them at his residence—as well as the last remaining artifact from the *Hindenburg*. The airpark exhibit features flyable vintage aircraft, an aviation theater, a hands-on activity room, the nation's oldest wooden hangar and the world's first bomber. Closed Monday. Admission. ~ 1115 East 5th Street, Vancouver, WA; 360-694-7026, fax 360-694-0824; www.pearsonairmuseum.org, e-mail director@pearson airmuseum.org.

Originally constructed in 1909 as a Carnegie Library, **Clark County Historical Museum** has a better than good regional collection—from the American Indian artifacts and handicrafts to the historical doctor's office and general store. Not to be missed is the downstairs train room with a Pullman unit, railway telegram office, dining car china, a model train layout and photos of noteworthy local derailments. Closed Sunday and Monday. ~ 1511 Main Street, Vancouver, WA; 360-993-5679, fax 360-993-5683; www.cchmuseum.org, e-mail cchm@pacifier.com.

To see more of Vancouver stop by the **Greater Vancouver Chamber of Commerce** and pick up the handy downtown walking tour brochure. ~ 1101 Broadway, Suite 100, Vancouver, WA; 360-694-2588, fax 360-693-8279; www.vancouverusa.com, e-mail yourchamber@vancouverusa.com.

Returning to the Oregon side of the river take Route 84 east up the Gorge to the **Historic Columbia River Highway** (see "Scenic Drive").

The taming of the Columbia River to provide low-cost power is one of the most controversial issues associated with the river. You'll get the pro side of the picture at **Bonneville Lock and Dam,** including the **Bradford Island Visitors Center**. You can also witness salmon swimming up underwater fish ladders. Extensive interpretive displays and an informational film provide an overview of the dam's operation and history. ~ Route 84, Exit 40, three miles west of Cascade Locks, OR; 541-374-8820, fax 541-374-4516.

On the Washington side of the Gorge, you can also learn how the dam operates, enjoy underwater views of fish ladders and visit the **Fort Cascades National Historic Site**. To get there, cross the Columbia River at Cascade Locks, Oregon, using the **Bridge of the Gods** (named after an Indian legend) and head west two miles on Route 14. The 59-acre historic site includes a one-mile self-guided trail featuring the sites of the old Portage Railroad, a one-time Chinook Indian village, a pre–Civil War military fort and a nature preserve ~ 503-230-1221, fax 541-374-4516.

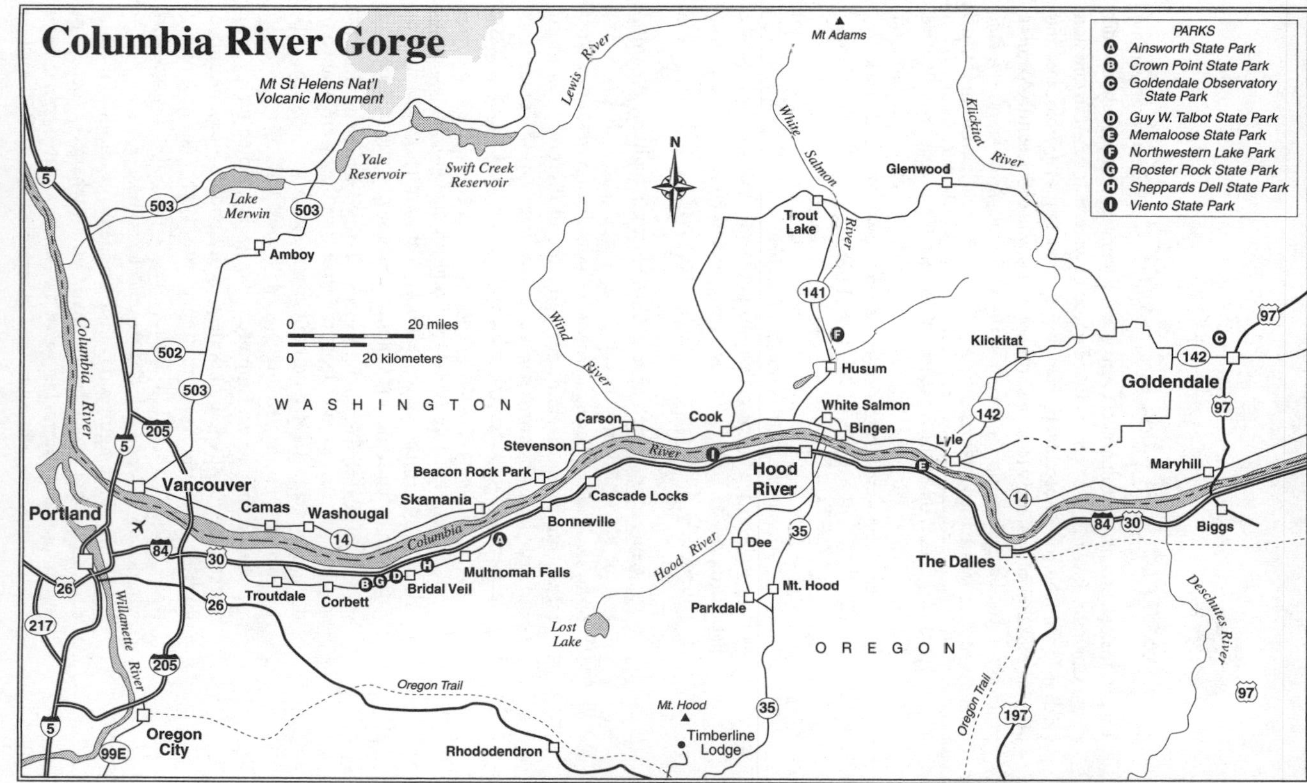
Columbia River Gorge
Mt St Helens Nat'l Volcanic Monument
PARKS
A Ainsworth State Park
B Crown Point State Park
C Goldendale Observatory State Park
D Guy W. Talbot State Park
E Memaloose State Park
F Northwestern Lake Park
G Rooster Rock State Park
H Sheppards Dell State Park
I Viento State Park
Mt Adams
Lewis River
Yale Reservoir
Swift Creek Reservoir
Lake Merwin
White Salmon River
Klickitat River
Wind River
Columbia River
Willamette River
Hood River
Deschutes River
Oregon Trail
Lost Lake
Mt. Hood
N
0 20 miles
0 20 kilometers
WASHINGTON
OREGON
Amboy
Trout Lake
Glenwood
Husum
Klickitat
Goldendale
Carson
Cook
White Salmon
Bingen
Lyle
Maryhill
Biggs
Stevenson
Beacon Rock Park
Skamania
Cascade Locks
Bonneville
Hood River
The Dalles
Vancouver
Portland
Camas
Washougal
Multnomah Falls
Bridal Veil
Troutdale
Corbett
Dee
Mt. Hood
Parkdale
Timberline Lodge
Rhododendron
Oregon City
5
503
502
205
84
30
26
217
99E
14
141
142
97
35
197

SCENIC DRIVE

Historic Columbia River Highway

This magnificent scenic route parallels Route 84, skirting the foot of sheer cliffs of the Columbia River Gorge with its wonderland of waterfalls, side canyons and verdant forest. The road was built by concrete tycoon Sam Hill, creator of the Maryhill Museum of Art, in 1916 as an attempt to convince Oregon legislatures to let him extend a highway up the length of the Columbia River. It was the first rural paved road in the Pacific Northwest.

VISTA HOUSE Turn off Route 84 at Troutdale (Exit 17) to reach the Historic Columbia River Highway. At the mouth of the gorge, a road turns off to the right and winds up to Vista House in Crown Point State Park. This octagonal structure, perched 733 feet above the river, has an information desk, a gift shop, an espresso bar and an awesome view.

WATERFALLS Among the major waterfalls that plunge into the gorge alongside the highway are **Latourelle Falls** (249 feet) in Guy W. Talbot State Park, **Sheppards Dell Falls** (two tiers, 50 and 60 feet) in Sheppards

A quiet nine-mile segment of the historic highway continues east of Hood River, between Mosier and The Dalles, winding onto the Rowena Plateau. Views include channeled scabland terraces, fruit orchards, and the **Tom McCall Preserve**, a beautiful and little-known nature reserve run by The Nature Conservancy that protects many of the hundreds of unique Columbia River Gorge wildflower species.

Retrace your route across the Bridge of the Gods to the Oregon side and stop at the **Cascade Locks Museum** to see exhibits on American Indians, the first Columbia River locks, the portage road, logging and fishwheels. Water-powered, these rotating devices scooped so many salmon from the river that they were banned by the state in 1926. Closed November through April. ~ Marine Park, 1 Northwest Portage Road, Cascade Locks, OR; 541-374-8535.

The sternwheeler **Columbia Gorge** is docked in Cascade Locks year-round. The multidecked old paddlewheel steamboat leads daytime and weekend dinner cruises through the Gorge. ~ 503-224-3900, 800-224-3901, fax 503-231-9089; www.sternwheeler.com, e-mail sales@sternwheeler.com.

On the Washington side of the bridge in Stevenson is the spacious **Columbia Gorge Interpretive Center**, where the focus is on the cultural and natural history of the Gorge. Located on a ten-acre site overlooking the river, the center includes a 37-foot-high

Dell State Park, **Bridal Veil Falls** (two tiers, 100 and 60 feet) and **Wahkeena Falls** (242 feet), where a mile-long trail leads to **Fairy Falls**, a magical 30-foot fan-shaped fall.

MULTNOMAH FALLS The most popular tourist attraction in Oregon, this cascade plunges 620 feet, making it the second-tallest waterfall in the United States. Walk up the paved trail to the observation bridge between the upper and lower falls, where you'll get a misty view of the entire falls. In 1995, a 400-ton rock the size of a Greyhound bus fell from the top of the falls to the upper pool as a result of the ongoing erosion that originally formed the gorge. It caused about 20 minor injuries from flying debris, reminding us that the amazing geology here is still transforming on a grand scale.

STILL MORE FALLS Two and a half miles beyond Multnomah Falls is **Horsetail Falls** (176 feet). Nearby, a trail leads almost two miles through the lush greenery of Oneonta Gorge to **Triple Falls**, a 135-foot segmented fall. The historic highway rejoins the interstate at Ainsworth State Park—unbelievably a mere 18 miles from where it began.

replica of a 19th-century fishwheel, a restored Corliss Steam Engine, a theater with a nine-projector slide show re-creating the cataclysmic formation of the Gorge and several exhibits drawn from the oral histories of local American Indians and pioneer settlers. The world's largest rosary collection is also housed here. Admission. ~ 990 Southwest Rock Creek Drive, Stevenson, WA; 509-427-8211, 800-991-2338, fax 509-427-7429; www.columbiagorge.org, e-mail info@columbiagorge.org.

Farther east on Route 14 is **Carson Mineral Hot Springs Resort**. On the Wind River, this resort is well-known by weary travelers for its mineral baths and massages, and can provide a restful stop for those who have been hiking all day on its beautiful hiking trails; there's also an 18-hole golf course. From here you can drive east along Route 14 to Route 141, which leads north along the White Salmon River Valley to Trout Lake, then return to Route 14 and the town of White Salmon. ~ 372 St. Martin's Spring Road, Carson, WA; 509-427-8292, 800-607-3678, fax 509-427-7242; www.carsonhotspringsresort.com, e-mail carsonhotspring@earthlink.net.

If Carson Hot Mineral Springs starts to feel too hectic, head to the secluded **Wind River Hot Springs** nearby for a calmer alternative. Well off the beaten path, you can relax and float in these steamy hidden pools reached by a rough half-mile trail that

HIDDEN

runs alongside the river. Parking fee, $10 per car with two passengers, $2 per additional passenger. ~ Continue east on Route 14, past Carson, and cross the Wind River bridge. Turn left on Berge Road, continue for a mile, then left on Indian Cabin Road to the registration stand and parking lot; www.nwhotsprings.net/wind_river.

Just east of White Salmon in the small town of Bingen, Washington, is the **Gorge Heritage Museum**, where you can view historic photographs and American Indian artifacts, including tools, arrow points and beadwork. Closed Monday through Wednesday, and October through May. ~ 202 East Humboldt Street, Bingen, WA; 509-493-3228; e-mail ghm@gorge.net.

Your next stop should be on the Oregon side at **Hood River,** which has become a windsurfing capital thanks to the strong breezes here. Stop at the **Hood River County Visitors Center** for information on this scenic hub. Closed weekends from mid-October to mid-April. ~ 405 Portway Avenue, Hood River, OR; 541-386-2000, 800-336-3530, fax 541-386-2057; www.hoodriver.org, e-mail hrccc@hoodriver.org.

If you're in town from mid-May to mid-October, visit the **Hood River Saturday Market**, which features local foods, crafts and artwork. ~ 5th Street and Cascade Avenue, across from the Full Sail Brewing Company; 541-387-8349.

The **Hood River County Historical Museum** features exhibits on American Indian culture, the westward migration, pioneer farming, logging and the Columbia River. Also found here is a collection of period furniture and early-20th-century artifacts. Closed November through March. ~ 300 East Port Marina Park, Hood River, OR; phone/fax 541-386-6772.

HIDDEN ►

One of the prettiest drives in Oregon is the 20-mile trip from Hood River to **Lost Lake** (elevation 3140 feet). At the lake you'll have a stunning angle on Mt. Hood—have your camera ready—and can rent a canoe or paddleboat (motorized boats are banned

sights

AUTHOR FAVORITE

You'll enjoy panoramic views of the Cascades from the restored coaches of the scenic **Mt. Hood Railroad**. Two- and four-hour journeys link the Gorge with Mt. Hood along a route pioneered in 1906. The trains climb up the Hood River Valley through steep canyons, orchards and forests. Special events are offered throughout the high season. The railroad runs April through October, with selected holiday trips between Thanksgiving and Christmas. ~ 110 Railroad Avenue, Hood River, OR; 541-386-3556, 800-872-4661; www.mthoodrr.com, e-mail mthoodrr@gorge.net.

on the lake). In addition to fishing for rainbow trout, visitors like to walk the three-mile Lakeshore Trail that circles the lake. To reach the idyllic retreat, take Route 281 south to Dee and then follow the signs west to the lake. Do keep an eye out for logging trucks en route.

Although many visitors miss it, we strongly recommend a visit to **The Dalles,** on the Oregon side of the Gorge. The end of the Oregon Trail, where immigrants boarded vessels to float down the Columbia (the Barlow Trail later made it possible to complete the overland journey), this city has a superb old-town walking tour. Pick up a copy of the route map at **The Dalles Area Chamber of Commerce.** Closed weekends from Labor Day to Memorial Day. ~ 404 West 2nd Street, The Dalles, OR; 541-296-2231, 800-255-3385, fax 541-296 1688; www.thedalleschamber.com, e-mail td acc@gorge.net.

Highlights on this walk include the state's oldest bookstore, **Klindt's** (315 East 2nd Street), and the circa-1863 **Waldron Brothers Drugstore** nearby.

Don't miss the attractive 26,100-square-foot **Columbia Gorge Discovery Center and Wasco County Historical Museum** in The Dalles. This is the official Columbia River Gorge National Scenic Area interpretive center and has exhibits on the natural and cultural history of the gorge, as well as artifacts from local collectors in its airy, barnlike structure. ~ 5000 Discovery Drive, The Dalles; 541-296-8600, fax 541-298-8660; www.gorgedis covery.org.

The **Fort Dalles Museum** is a favorite stop. Only two fort buildings, the Surgeon's Quarters and the Garden Cottage, remain today. But the museum does preserve an excellent collection of pioneer artifacts, rifles, quilts and historic photographs. Closed December through February. Call for hours otherwise. Admission. ~ 500 15th at Garrison Street, The Dalles, OR; phone/fax 541-296-4547; e-mail fortdallesmuseum@netcnct.net.

From here, take Route 30 east to Route 197 north. Cross the freeway to Bret Clodfelter Way and follow signs to **The Dalles Dam.** Perhaps the saddest part of this story focuses on the demise of the Gorge's best-known Indian fishing grounds. Wherever you go along this part of the Columbia River, in coffee shops and hotel lobbies, phone company offices and visitors centers, you're likely to see classic photographs of Indians dipping their nets into the river at heavenly Celilo Falls. To get the full picture, leaf through the scrapbook of Celilo Falls fishing pictures at the Fort Dalles Museum. One hopeful sign, though. If you look carefully below The Dalles Dam, you may see contemporary Indian dipnet subsistence fishermen fishing from platforms. Treaties have upheld the right of Indian fishers to half the annual take of fish along the river for subsistence and cultural use only.

If you continue on Route 84 east of The Dalles for 12 miles you'll come to a small **Celilo Falls Marker**, which indicates where these bounteous fishing waters prospered before being destroyed by the dam in the late 1950s.

HIDDEN ►

A few miles farther east, on the Washington side, is one of the most isolated museums in America. **Maryhill Museum of Art** was designed in 1914 as the mansion residence of eccentric millionaire Sam Hill, and was supposed to oversee a Quaker agricultural town. But the plan for a new town flopped and the house on the hill eventually became a museum. This eclectic assemblage was dedicated in 1926 by Queen Marie of Rumania, which helps explain the presence of treasures from that nation's royal collection. Also here are Russian icons, a large collection of Rodin sculptures, Charles M. Russell's *Indian Buffalo Hunt*, French decorative arts, a good display of American Indian handicrafts and artifacts, and contemporary Pacific Northwest art, as well as one of the world's great chess collections. The museum also includes the world's only collection of post–World War II fashion mannequins. Views of the Columbia Gorge are spectacular, as are the sunsets. Closed mid-November to mid-March. Admission. ~ 35 Maryhill Museum Drive, Goldendale, WA; 509-773-3733, fax 509-773-6138; www.maryhillmuseum.org, e-mail maryhill@maryhillmuseum.org.

Three miles east of Maryhill Museum of Art is **Stonehenge**, Sam Hill's memorial to local soldiers who died in World War I.

Although most are built with public funds, astronomical observatories are seldom accessible to the general public. One exception is the **Goldendale Observatory State Park Interpretive Center**. Just 11 miles north of the Maryhill Museum and Columbia River, this gem was created by four amateur astronomers and later taken over by the state. Afternoon instructional tours feature an opportunity to gaze at occasional sunspots and the bright planet Venus. Depending on night sky conditions, interpretive specialist Stephen R. Stout may allow visitors to view moon craters, planets, binary stars, star clusters, nebulas and galaxies through a 24-inch telescope. Be sure to call first for the observation schedule. ~ 1602 Observatory Drive, Goldendale, WA; 509-773-3141,

MUSEUMS GALORE

There are many different visitors centers and museums in Columbia River Gorge National Recreation Area because it is managed cooperatively by a board made up of representatives from the states of Washington and Oregon and each of the counties in which it falls, as well as the U.S. Forest Service.

fax 509-773-6929; www.perr.com/gosp.html, e-mail goldendale.observatory@parks.wa.gov.

LODGING

The **Cedarplace Inn Bed and Breakfast**, a yellow two-story home built in 1907, offers three large guest rooms and a two-bedroom suite, decorated with antique furnishings including canopy beds and soft featherbeds with down pillows and comforters. All these attributes may sound fairly typical of Victorian-style luxury B&Bs everywhere, but the location of this one, at the gateway to the Columbia River Gorge Scenic Area, makes it an extra special spot for a romantic getaway. ~ 2611 South Troutdale Road, Troutdale, OR; 503-491-1900, 877-491-1907, fax 503-465-1046; cedarplcinn.com, e-mail cedarplace@comcast.net. MODERATE TO DELUXE.

Located just above the Columbia Gorge Interpretive Center in Stevenson, Washington, is the **Skamania Lodge**, a modern resort built in the tradition of the grand mountain lodges of the late-18th century. Guests can congregate in the wood-paneled Gorge Room with its deep sofas and three-story river-rock fireplace. Public areas and the 254 guest rooms are handsomely decorated with mission-style furniture, Pendleton fabrics, petroglyph rubbings and American Indian–inspired rugs. The grounds include an 18-hole golf course, fitness center, whirlpools, swimming pool, and more. ~ 1131 Skamania Lodge Way, Stevenson, WA; 509-427-7700, 800-221-7117, fax 509-427-2547; www.skamania.com. ULTRA-DELUXE.

One of the frustrating facts of life on the road is the Sunday brunch. If you crave broccoli quiche, Italian sausages, artichoke frittatas, baklava, date tarts, fresh fruit and a dozen other treats, Monday to Saturday just won't do. Fortunately, the **Inn of the White Salmon** has solved this problem in an imaginative way. This lovely bed and breakfast offers brunch seven days a week. All you need do is check in to one of the inn's 16 countrified rooms featuring brass beds and antiques, and this splendid feast is yours. Across the Columbia from Hood River, this inn also features a comfortable parlor. ~ 172 West Jewett Boulevard, White Salmon, WA; 509-493-2335, 800-972-5226; www.innofthewhitesalmon.com, e-mail innkeeper@innofthewhitesalmon.com. MODERATE TO DELUXE.

With rooms often in short supply during the summer windsurfing season, visitors who arrive in the Hood River area without reservations may want to call the **Hood River Bed and Breakfast Association** room-finder hotline for information on what is available at local inns. ~ 541-386-6767; www.gorgelodging.com.

In Cascade Locks, 20 miles west of Hood River, **Bridge of the Gods Motel** provides affordable rustic rooms. All 17 units have queen-size beds; 11 of them offer kitchens. ~ 630 WaNaPa Street,

Cascade Locks, OR; 541-374-8628; e-mail bridgeofgodsmotel@msn.com. BUDGET TO MODERATE.

The **Columbia Gorge Hotel** is a 40-room landmark where strains of Bach waft through the halls, sculptured carpets highlight the public areas and the fireplace is always roaring. This Mediterranean-style hotel tucks guests into wicker, brass, canopy or hand-carved antique beds. The dining room, home of a popular five-course farm breakfast, offers splendid riverfront dining. Relax in the Valentino Lounge, take a walk through the manicured gardens or enjoy a mineral wrap at the in-house spa. ~ 4000 Westcliff Drive, Hood River, OR; 541-386-5566, 800-345-1921, fax 541-386-9141; www.columbiagorgehotel.com, e-mail cghotel@gorge.net. ULTRA-DELUXE.

The chandeliered **Hood River Hotel** is a restored brick landmark with 41 rooms and suites. Brightly painted rooms are appointed with oak furniture, four-poster beds, casablanca fans, wing chairs and antiques. Some offer views of the Columbia River. Comfortable sitting areas and a cheery restaurant add to the charm. Kitchenette suites are available. ~ 102 Oak Street, Hood River, OR; 541-386-1900, 800-386-1859, fax 541-386-6090; www.hoodriverhotel.com, e-mail hrhotel@gorge.net. BUDGET TO DELUXE.

Situated in a restored 1909 historic downtown home, the charming **Oak Street Hotel** offers nine guest rooms (one of which is a suite). Queen-sized beds with intricate iron frames and handcrafted furnishings enliven the rooms, all of which have a private bath. There's a comfortable lounge downstairs with a fireplace. ~ 610 Oak Street, Hood River; 866-386-3845, fax 541-387-8696; www.oakstreethotel.com, e-mail reservations@oakstreethotel.com. MODERATE.

AUTHOR FAVORITE

As its name suggests, **Panorama Lodge Bed and Breakfast** offers sweeping views of Mt. Hood and Mt. Hood Valley. Most of the five bedrooms in this charming log home face the mountain, while two boast garden and forest views. Accommodations are spacious and comfortable, with cedar-paneled walls, early American decor and king- and queen-sized antique beds. A big country-style breakfast is served, with fluffy pancakes, home-baked bread, home fries seasoned with fresh herbs from the garden, and up to 15 different kinds of omelettes. Many of the repeat guests enjoy gathering around a campfire with the hosts before turning in. Reservations recommended. No credit cards. ~ 2290 Old Dalles Drive, Hood River; 541-387-2687, 888-403-2687; www.panoramalodge.com, e-mail info@panoramalodge.com. MODERATE TO ULTRA-DELUXE.

Beautifully located overlooking the Columbia, **Vagabond Lodge** offers 42 spacious, carpeted rooms—some opening right onto the riverfront. All feature contemporary furniture, doubles or queens, microwaves, refrigerators, wi-fi access and a secluded garden setting. Some suites have fireplaces, whirlpools and full kitchens. For the price, it's hard to beat this motel west of town. ~ 4070 Westcliff Drive, Hood River, OR; 541-386-2992, 877-386-2992, fax 541-386-3317; www.vagabondlodge.com, e-mail info@vagabondlodge.com. BUDGET TO MODERATE.

Located just five blocks from downtown Hood River is the 1908 Victorian **Inn at the Gorge Bed & Breakfast**. Three suites and two bedrooms have antique furnishings and private baths. Enjoy the surrounding gardens, nap in the hammock beneath the cedar tree or just laze the day away on the wraparound porch. Full breakfast included. ~ 1113 Eugene Street, Hood River, OR; phone/fax 541-386-4429; www.innatthegorge.com, e-mail stay@innatthegorge.com. MODERATE TO DELUXE.

The family-run **Riverview Lodge** provides simple and reasonably priced motel accommodations as well as some two-room suites with kitchens and fireplaces year-round. You'll also find a heated indoor pool and hot tub. This place is great for families. ~ 1505 Oak Street, Hood River, OR; 541-386-8719, 800-789-9568; www.riverviewforyou.com. BUDGET TO ULTRA-DELUXE.

The **Columbia Windrider Inn** is operated by an avid Columbia Gorge sailor and windsurfer who likes to play host to other sailboard afficionados. Situated on a quiet residential street, this historic 1921 home has maple wood floors and four large guest rooms, each with private bath, air conditioning, complimentary wi-fi internet and a queen- or king-size bed. Facilities include a swimming pool, a hot tub and a recreation room. ~ 200 West 4th Street, The Dalles, OR; 541-296-2607; www.windriderinn.com, e-mail chuck@windriderinn.com. BUDGET.

For contemporary motel accommodations try the **Cousins Country Inn**. The 93 fully carpeted rooms have oak tables and queen-size beds. Some have kitchenettes. Guests receive free use of the nearby health club. There's a pool on the premises, as well as Cousins, the only restaurant we know that has a John Deere tractor in the middle of the dining room. ~ 2114 West 6th Street, The Dalles, OR; 541-298-5161, 800-848-9378, fax 541-298-6411; www.cousinscountryinn.com, e-mail info@cousinscountry inn.com. BUDGET TO MODERATE.

DINING

Vancouver now boasts its own **Pizzicato Gourmet Pizza**, part of a popular Oregon chain known for sophisticated toppings and unique combinations. Try the *melanza*, with sweet red and yellow peppers, roasted eggplant, and fontina and goat cheese. Meat-eaters will love the *patate e prosciutto*, with rosemary red potatoes, prosciutto ham, smoked mozzarella and mushrooms. ~ 1900 Northeast 162nd Avenue, Vancouver, WA; 360-891-2081, fax 360-891-2057; www.pizzicatogourmetpizza.com. MODERATE TO DELUXE.

In Stevenson, Washington, the **Cascade Room** at Skamania Lodge has a grand dining room with massive wooden ceiling beams and superb views of the Gorge. The specialties are Northwest-inspired dishes prepared in a wood-burning oven, including wild salmon, meats and seafood, not to mention a Sunday champagne brunch. ~ 1131 Skamania Lodge Way, Stevenson, WA; 509-427-7700, 800-221-7117, fax 509-427-2547; www.skamania.com. DELUXE TO ULTRA-DELUXE.

The **Big River Grill** in downtown Stevenson is a convivial place with wooden booths and old photographs on the walls. Both locals and visitors come here to enjoy salmon chowder in bread bowls (Fridays only), daily specials, salads topped with grilled meats and such vegetarian entrées as portobello ravioli and nutty garden burgers. ~ 192 Southwest 2nd Avenue, Stevenson, WA; 509-427-4888. MODERATE.

HIDDEN ►

About 20 minutes north of the Gorge, and well worth the trip, is one of the Gorge's most intriguing restaurants, **The Logs**. You'll be impressed by the roasted chicken, hickory-smoked ribs, giant fries and huckleberry pie served in this log-cabin setting. The battered and deep-fried chicken gizzards and cheese sticks are a big hit with the regular clientele, who include locals, rafters, skiers and devotees of the rich mud pie. In business for six decades, this is the place where city slickers will come face to face with their first jackalope, safely mounted on the wall. ~ 1258 Route 141, White Salmon, WA; 509-493-1402; e-mail thelogs@earthlink.net. BUDGET TO MODERATE.

You can tour (and taste) delicious and unique brews from the employee-owned **Full Sail Brewing Company** and then grab a pint and something to eat in the onsite English pub. Fare includes light bites such as an Oregon ploughman's lunch featuring Crater Lake blue cheese. More substantial entrées showcase amber-ale barbecue pork loin, halibut and fries and Malaysian-style tofu curry. Try one of the seasonal brews such as Wassail Winter Ale or Old Boarhead Barleywine Ale. ~ 506 Columbia Street, Hood River; 541-386-2281; www.fullsailbrewing.com, e-mail fullsail@fullsailbrewingcompany.com. MODERATE TO DELUXE.

HIDDEN ►

Tucked away in the woods on the Oregon side is **Stonehedge Gardens**, an antique-filled home preparing Continental and Northwest dining at its finest. Set in a beautiful garden, this paneled restaurant has a tiny mahogany bar and a roaring fireplace. Among the dishes are scallop sauté, jumbo prawns and filet of salmon. Light entrées, such as a seafood platter, are also recommended. Dinner only. Closed Monday in winter. ~ 3405 Cascade Avenue,

Hood River, OR; 541-386-3940; www.hoodriverrestaurants.com, e-mail stonehedge@gorge.net. MODERATE TO DELUXE.

Locals enjoy **Sixth Street Bistro & Loft** for its casual dining and tasty cuisine. Pastas, salads and hamburgers are joined by more international items like *pad thai*, chicken satay or "Mexican stir-fry." The dinner menu includes steak, seafood and daily specials with a focus on local, organic ingredients. After dinner you can shoot pool or relax with a drink in the upstairs loft. ~ 509 Cascade Avenue, Hood River, OR; 541-386-5737; www.sixthstreetbistro.com. BUDGET TO MODERATE.

It's hard to beat the breakfasts at **Bette's Place**, a small, mauve-toned café. Bette's bakes 13 kinds of muffins daily, including cinnamon and Oregon blackberry, and also serves eggs Benedict, omelettes, strawberry waffles and pancakes topped with fresh fruit. ~ 416 Oak Street, in the Oak Mall, Hood River, OR; 541-386-1880; e-mail bettesr@gorge.net. BUDGET.

Cornerstone Cuisine has breezy indoor and sidewalk seating in the center of this resort town. The heart of the dining room is a handcrafted bar with an etched-glass mirror. Entrées include almond-crusted salmon, paella and braised lamb shank with gnocchi, dates and cinnamon butter. ~ In the Hood River Hotel, 102 Oak Street, Hood River, OR; 541-386-1900, 800-386-1859, fax 541-386-6090; www.hoodriverhotel.com, e-mail hrhotel@gorge.net. MODERATE TO DELUXE.

As its name suggests, **The Mesquitery Restaurant & Bar** is best known for its meat and seafood dishes cooked on a mesquite grill. Barbecue-glazed baby-back ribs and and garlic-and-parmesan-crusted salmon are among the highlights, as are heaping main-dish cobb and caesar salads. The inside dining area is filled with high-backed booths and rich wood paneling, while outside you'll find a two-level enclosed deck area with colorful planters. No lunch Saturday through Tuesday. ~ 1219 12th Street, Hood River, OR; 541-386-2002, fax 541-387-4002. MODERATE.

AUTHOR FAVORITE

A hip little café serving *pommes frites* rather than french fries, **Congusto** caters to a 30-something crowd. The slate-tiled floor and cool, modern decor provide a sleek setting for the satisfying and expansive bistro-style menu—crisp salads, thick sandwiches and a variety of seafood and meat dishes. Try a cocktail from the lengthy liquor menu. Sunday brunch is served. ~ 704 Oak Avenue, The Dalles; 541-387-3087, fax 541-387-3089; www.congustocafe.com, e-mail info@congustocafe.com. BUDGET TO DELUXE.

An elegant dining room overlooking the Gorge, **Simon's Restaurant** at the Colombia Gorge Hotel is a romantic place to dine on roast pork tenderloin, fresh Oregon salmon, rack of lamb or Dungeness crab with lobster sauce and risotto. Done in an Early American design with oak furniture and candlelit tables, this establishment is well known for its lavish farm breakfast. ~ 4000 Westcliff Drive, Hood River, OR; 541-387-5428, 800-345-1921, fax 541-387-5414; www.columbiagorgehotel.com, e-mail cghotel@gorge.net. DELUXE TO ULTRA-DELUXE.

Located in one of the most historic buildings in The Dalles, the **Baldwin Saloon** was built in 1876 and has an 18-foot-long mahogany back bar and turn-of-the-20th-century oil paintings on the brick walls. The restaurant is known for its seafood and oyster dishes (baked and on the half shell) and also serves thick sandwiches, burgers, soups and desserts. Breads and desserts are baked on the premises. Closed Sunday. ~ 205 Court Street, The Dalles, OR; 541-296-5666; www.baldwinsaloon.com. MODERATE TO DELUXE.

For heaping platters of chicken, steak or shrimp fajitas, the place to go is **Casa El Mirador**, a cozy family-run restaurant with embroidered sombreros and decorative items from Mexico adorning the walls. Crabmeat burritos, chimichangas, tacos and other south-of-the-border staples also make good choices. ~ 1424 West 2nd Street, The Dalles, OR; 541-298-7388. MODERATE.

After a visit to Multnomah Falls it makes sense to dine at **Multnomah Falls Lodge.** The smoked-salmon-and-cheese platter and generous salads are recommended. The European-style lodge building with a big stone fireplace, scenic paintings of the surroundings and lovely views will add to your enjoyment of the Gorge. Buffet champagne brunch on Sunday. ~ Off Route 84, Bridal Veil, WA; 503-695-2376, fax 503-695-2338; www.multnomahfallslodge.com, e-mail info@multnomahfallslodge.com. MODERATE TO DELUXE.

SHOPPING

Fort Vancouver Gift Shop is the place to go for books, maps and pamphlets on Pacific Northwest history. We recommend picking up a copy of *Outpost* by Dorothy Morris. ~ 1501 East Evergreen Boulevard, Vancouver, WA; 360-816-6230.

Aviation buffs will want to stop by the gift shop at **Pearson Air Museum.** The shop has an ace collection of memorabilia and souvenirs for adults and juniors alike. Closed Sunday through Tuesday. ~ 1115 East 5th Street, Vancouver, WA; 360-694-7026, fax 360-694-0824; www.pearsonairmuseum.org.

Pendleton Woolen Mills and Outlet Store offers big savings on irregulars. Tours of the mill, in operation since 1912, are available, but call first for schedule information. ~ #2 17th Street, Washougal, WA; 360-835-1118, fax 360-835-5451.

Locally made jams, jellies, wine and other food products make terrific presents for the folks back home. **The Gift House** carries a variety of home-grown products, including wine and jams. ~ 204 Oak Street, Hood River, OR; 541-386-9234; www.hoodrivergifthouse.com. Pick up a fine Oregon white or red at **The Wine Sellers.** ~ 514 State Street, Hood River, OR; 541-386-4647; www.wine-sellers.com. **Rasmussen Farms** sells strawberries, Hood River apples, Comice pears and cherries. Apples, cherries and pears can be shipped as gift packs. ~ 3020 Thomsen Road off Route 35 south of Hood River, OR; 541-386-4622, 800-548-2243, fax 541-386-4702; www.rasmussenfarms.com, e-mail info@rasmussenfarms.com.

The first Friday of each month in downtown Hood River unites patrons of the arts with local artists in friendly meet-and-greets. Participating businesses showcase artworks in all mediums and extend their hours. Live entertainment adds to the festive atmosphere.

A good place to find books on the region is **Waucoma Bookstore,** which is also well stocked with fiction, children's books, cards, magazines, children's toys and handcrafted pottery. Closed Sunday in winter. ~ 212 Oak Street, Hood River, OR; 541-386-5353.

Columbia Art Gallery represents over 150 artists, primarily from the Columbia Gorge region. Featured are the works of photographers, printmakers, potters, glassblowers, jewelers, weavers, sculptors and painters. ~ 215 Cascade Avenue, Hood River, OR; 541-387-8877; www.columbiaartgallery.org.

On the Washington side of the Gorge, Stevenson's small, walkable downtown has some distinctive art galleries and gift shops.

The Dalles is home to Oregon's oldest bookstore, **Klindt's,** which dates from 1870 and still has an old-time ambience with high ceilings and glass-topped counters. Books on the Pacific Northwest, both new and used, are a specialty, as are rare and out-of-print books. ~ 315 East 2nd Street, The Dalles, OR; 541-296-3355.

The Dalles Art Center, located in the historic Carnegie Library, exhibits work by local and regional artists. Most of this fine art is available for purchase. The gallery showcases paintings, pottery, jewelry, glasswork, photography and baskets. Closed Sunday and Monday. ~ 220 East 4th Street, The Dalles, OR; 541-296-4759; www.thedallesartcenter.org.

NIGHTLIFE

A popular gay and lesbian nightspot in Vancouver, Washington, is **North Bank Bar & Grill,** which has a dancefloor and outdoor patio. Cover for cabaret shows. ~ 106 West 6th Street, Vancouver, WA; 360-695-3862.

The **Power Station Pub and Theater** is located in the former Multnomah County poor farm. The theater presents second-run movies in the farm's former power plant. The pub serves a full menu in the converted laundry building. Also on the premises is the **Edgefield Brewery** and a working winery and distillery. ~ 2126 Southwest Halsey Street, Troutdale, OR; 503-492-4686, 800-669-8610; www.mcmenamins.com, e-mail power@mcmenamins.com.

The **Skamania Lodge** has occasional live music or speakers before a woodburning fireplace in summer. ~ 1131 Skamania Lodge Way, Stevenson, WA; 509-427-2527, fax 509-427-2547.

Bungalow Bar & Grill has televised sports, two pool tables and dart boards. ~ 812 Wind River Highway, Carson, WA; 509-427-4523.

Full Sail Brewing Company offers tastings of their very popular hand-crafted beers, as well as a pub-style menu and deck seating with fine views of the Columbia. ~ 506 Columbia Avenue, Hood River, OR; 541-386-2247, 888-244-2337; www.fullsailbrewing.com.

PARKS

ROOSTER ROCK STATE PARK Offering more than three miles of sandy Columbia River frontage, this 872-acre park is near the Gorge's west end. The rock, named for a towering promontory, is near a camping site chosen by Lewis and Clark in 1805. Well-known for swimming and beginner windsurfing, Rooster Rock also has excellent hiking trails, a small lake and a forested bluff. Anglers can fish for salmon. There are picnic tables and restrooms. Day-use fee, $3, or $25 for an annual pass. ~ Located in Oregon 22 miles east of Portland on Route 84 at Exit 25; 503-695-2261, 800-551-6949, fax 503-695-2226.

"Memaloose," in case you were wondering, is a Chinook word linked to the sacred burial ritual.

VIENTO STATE PARK Originally a rest stop on the old Columbia River Highway, this 247-acre park includes a riverfront and Viento Creek forest section. Dramatic views of the Columbia River make this a popular camping and picnicking facility. It can get very windy, and be aware that trains pass through the gorge at night. Facilities include picnic tables, barbecue pits, showers and restrooms. Closed October through April. Day-use fee, $3. ~ Route 84 Exit 56, eight miles west of Hood River in Oregon; 541-374-8811, 800-551-6949.

▲ There are 18 tent sites ($10 to $14 per night) and 56 RV hookup sites ($12 to $16 per night).

AINSWORTH STATE PARK Ranking high among the treasures of the Columbia River Scenic Highway is this 156-acre park. Near the bottom of St. Peter's Dome, the forested park has a gorgeous hiking trail that connects with a network extending throughout the region. A serene getaway, the only sound of civilization you're likely to hear is that of passing trains. There are picnic tables, showers and restrooms. Closed November through March. ~ Route 30, the Columbia River Scenic Highway, 37 miles east of Portland on the Oregon side; 503-695-2301, 800-551-6949, fax 503-695-2226.

▲ There are 45 RV hookup sites; $12 to $16 per night. There are also six walk-in sites; $10 to $14 per night.

MEMALOOSE STATE PARK The park is named for an offshore Columbia River island that was an American Indian burial ground. This 336-acre site spreads out along a two-mile stretch of riverfront and is forested with pine, oak and fir. Much of the park is steep and rocky. It can also be very windy. There are horseshoes, a playground, interpretive programs in summer, showers and restrooms. Closed November through March. ~ Off Route 84, 11 miles west of The Dalles in Oregon. Take the Memaloose Rest Stop exit, then make a right into the park. Westbound access only; 541-478-3008, fax 541-478-2369.

▲ There are 66 tent sites ($12 to $16 per night) and 44 RV hookup sites ($16 to $20 per night). Reservations: 800-452-5687.

Outdoor Adventures

FISHING

This is a prime fishing spot: Salmon, steelhead, walleye and sturgeon are all found in the Columbia River area. For guides or charters in the Portland area, contact **Page's Northwest Guide Service**. They will set up a one-day Tillamook Bay fishing trip, or arrange an outing on the Willamette, Clackamas, Columbia or Sandy rivers. ~ 14321 Southeast Bush Street, Portland, OR; 503-760-3373, 866-760-3370; www.fishingoregon.net. In The Dalles, **River's Bend Outfitters** offers fishing information. ~ P.O. Box 436, The Dalles, OR 97058; 541-296-5949; www.riversbandoutfitters.com. For both fishing and flyfishing information on steelhead, salmon and walleye in the Columbia and John Day rivers, contact **Fly by Nyte Guide Service.** ~ 2624 Old Dufur Road, The Dalles, OR 97058; 541-298-2770; www.flybynyteguideservice.com. Also offering guided fishing trips in the Gorge area is **Northwest Guide Service.** ~ Woodard Creek Road, Skamania, WA; 509-427-4625.

The art of flyfishing abounds on rivers in the Gorge region. **The Gorge Fly Shop** arranges flyfishing excursions to such popular destinations as Deschutes. All levels of lessons are available. ~ 201 Oak Street, Hood River, OR; 541-386-6977; www.gorgeflyshop.com.

WINDSURFING

Between the high cliff walls of the Columbia Gorge, east of Portland, winds on the river can hit 60 knots, so it's no wonder this is one of the world's best windsurfing areas, with Hood River its capital. According to a local expert, "Once you learn the tricks and let the wind do the work for you, it's not as hard as it looks." And if you don't mind cool temperatures (50°F and lower) in winter, you can windsurf year-round.

Text continued on page 390.

South of the Gorge

Since you've already dipped your toe into Oregon while visiting the Columbia River Gorge, you may now want to visit the place named the "Most Livable U.S. City" by the U.S. Conference of Mayors—Portland. Near the entrance to the Gorge, Portland boasts a rich cultural life and is blessed with some of the prettiest urban streets in the Northwest. A good place to orient yourself is the **Portland Oregon Information Center**. Here you can pick up helpful maps and brochures. Closed Sunday. ~ Pioneer Courthouse Square; 503-275-8355, 877-678-5263; www.travelportland.com.

Pioneer Courthouse Square is a popular gathering point. A waterfall and 64,000 red bricks inscribed with the names of residents who donated money for the square's construction are all here. Named for adjacent **Pioneer Courthouse**, the oldest public building in Oregon (completed in 1873), the square offers a variety of special events including concerts.

Head west on Yamhill Street for one block then south on Park Avenue to the **Oregon Historical Society**, the place to learn the story of the region's American Indians, the arrival of the Europeans and the westward migration. Admission. ~ 1200 Southwest Park Avenue; 503-222-1741, fax 503-221-2035;. www.ohs.org, e-mail orhist@ohs.org.

Adjacent to the Oregon Historical Society is the **First Congregational Church**, dating from 1895. This Venetian gothic–style basalt structure is modeled on Boston's Old South Church and crowned by a 175-foot tower. ~ 1126 Southwest Park Avenue; 503-228-7219.

Across the street is the **Portland Art Museum**, known for its collection of Asian and European art as well as 20th-century American sculpture. The collection of American Indian art and artifacts showcases excellent tribal masks and wood sculptures. The pre-Columbian pieces are notable, and the Cameroon collection is nationally known. Don't miss the skylit sculpture courtyard. The Silver gallery has more than 100 rare objects on display. Closed Monday. ~ 1219 Southwest Park Avenue; 503-226-2811, fax 503-226-4842; www.portlandartmuseum.org, e-mail info@pam.org.

Head east to 11th Avenue and then turn south to **The Old Church**. Built in 1883, this gothic classic is one of the city's oldest and best-loved buildings. Closed Sunday. ~ 1422 Southwest 11th Avenue; 503-222-2031, fax 503-222-2981; www.oldchurch.org, e-mail staff@oldchurch.org.

Head east on Columbia Street to Southwest 5th Avenue. Take 5th north to the **Portland Building**, a postmodern office landmark. This whimsical skyscraper represents the Northwest with an American Indian motif, making extensive use of turquoise and earth tones. Above the entrance to the Portland Building is *Portlandia*, the world's second-largest hammered-bronze sculpture. ~ 1120 Southwest 5th Avenue; 503-823-4000, fax 503-823-6924.

On the Portland Building's second floor is the **Metropolitan Center for Public Art**. Here you'll find a portion of the *Portlandia* mold and renderings of the building, as well as pieces from the *Visual Chronicle of Portland*, a continually evolving series of works on paper. ~ 1120 Southwest 5th Avenue; 503-823-5111, fax 503-823-5432; www.racc.org, e-mail info@racc.org.

Walk east on Main Street to Southwest 3rd Avenue; head south to the **Ira Keller Memorial Fountain**, across from the Civic Auditorium. Situated in a pretty park, this is a lovely spot to rest your weary feet. ~ Clay Street between 3rd and 4th avenues. Farther south, past the Hawthorne Bridge on Harbor Way, you'll come to the sloped-roof buildings of **RiverPlace**, a popular shopping, hotel, restaurant and nightclub complex on the water. A promenade overlooks the Willamette River and the marina's many plush yachts.

Then return north to **Mill Ends Park**, located in the median at Southwest Front Avenue and Taylor Street. Just two feet wide, this is one of the smallest parks in the world. Proceed northward to **Tom McCall Waterfront Park**, which is notable for being the green river frontage that in the 1970s replaced a busy, ugly stretch of freeway blocking the Willamette. ~ Front Avenue.

Walk west on Yamhill to the shops, food stands and outdoor produce stalls of **Yamhill Marketplace**. ~ 110 Southwest Yamhill Street; 503-224-3450. Then stroll back to the waterfront and walk north on Front to the **Oregon Maritime Center and Museum**. Here's your chance to learn Northwestern maritime history, all aboard the steam sternwheeler *Portland*. Closed Monday through Thursday. Admission. ~ River Wall, between Morrison and Burnside bridges at the foot of Pine Street; 503-224-7724, fax 503-224-7767; www.oregonmaritimemuseum.org, e-mail info@oregonmaritimemuseum.org.

The **Skidmore/Old Town** area illustrates Portland's commitment to adaptive reuse. This area between Front and 3rd streets both north and south of Burnside Street boomed in the later 19th century when the harbor was bustling. Eventually this became the rowdy part of town where sailors caroused, and polite society began to keep away as the buildings fell into disrepair. But interest has grown in the waterfront over the past 30 years, and historic commercial buildings and warehouses have been reborn as trendy shops, galleries, restaurants and nightclubs.

Next, head north through **Chinatown** on 4th Avenue. Not as large as it was at the turn of the 20th century, it is still packed with Chinese restaurants and markets. The ornate entry gate to Chinatown at the corner of Burnside Street and 4th Avenue looks a bit out of place among the neighboring adult bookstores. Continue north on 4th to Northwest Everett Street and turn right. In one block you'll arrive at the **Portland Classical Chinese Garden**, a walled oasis of plants, ponds, stone sculptures and pavilions linked by winding pathways. Admission. ~ Corner of Northwest 3rd Avenue and Northwest Everett Street; 503-228-8131; www.portlandchinesegarden.org, e-mail rdecker@portlandchinesegarden.org.

For more information, consult *Hidden Oregon* (Ulysses Press).

Big Winds offers rentals and instruction for children and adults, and a full-service retail shop. Kitesurfing equipment is also available. ~ 207 Front Street, Hood River, OR; 541-386-6086, 888-509-4210; www.bigwinds.com.

Swiss Swell also offers lessons in the Hood River area. Closed in winter. ~ 13 Oak Street, Hood River, OR; 541-490-7570; www.swiss-swell.com.

If you're experienced and want to rent equipment, contact **Doug's Sports.** ~ 101 Oak Street, Hood River, OR; 541-386-5787, 800-211-8207; www.dougsports.com. **Hood River WaterPlay** offers lessons and equipment, and has a beginner beach area in front of the Hood River Inn. ~ Port Marina Park, Hood River, OR; 541-386-9463, 800-963-7873; www.hoodriverwaterplay.com.

RIVER RUNNING

The White Salmon River north of the Columbia is a popular whitewater rafting spot.

There are some 30 Class II, III and IV rapids along the short course of the White Salmon River, a pool-and-drop mountain stream that is fed by rainfall and snowmelt from Mt. Adams, 30 miles distant. For half-, full- or multiple-day guided whitewater adventures on the White Salmon Klickitat rivers, call **Zoller's Outdoor Odyssey.** ~ 1248 Route 141, White Salmon, WA; 509-493-2641, 800-366-2004; www.zooraft.com. Also try **North Cascades River Expeditions.** ~ P.O. Box 116, Arlington, WA 98223; 360-435-9548, 800-634-8433; riverexpeditions.com.

River Drifters Whitewater Tours in Bend will outfit trips on the White Salmon, Deschutes and Owyhee rivers. ~ P.O. Box 7962, Bend, OR 97708; 800-972-0430; www.riverdrifters.net.

Another often-rafted river in the Gorge is the Klickitat. An outfitter to contact is **River Recreation.** ~ P.O. Box 2124, Bothell, WA 98041; 800-464-5899; www.riverrecreation.com.

In Washington, there's also **All Adventures Rafting,** which offers day trips to the Klickitat as well as three-day trips elsewhere. ~ P.O. Box 544, White Salmon, WA 98672; 509-493-3926, 800-743-5628; www.alladventures.net.

SKIING

With Hood River and the Columbia River Gorge practically at the foot of snowcapped Mt. Hood, it's possible to ski in the morning and windsurf in the afternoon. **Mt. Hood Meadows** spreads across 2150 acres and offers 87 trails, most of which are intermediate and expert level. In addition to alpine skiing, there are terrain parks and half pipes. Night skiing and 15 kilometers of cross-country trails are also available. ~ Take Route 84 Exit 64 in Hood River then follow Route 35 south to the Meadows entrance; 800-754-4663, 503-227-7669 (snowline), fax 503-337-2217; www.skihood.com, e-mail info@skihood.com.

GOLF

Hood River Golf and Country Club has 18 holes, full mountain views, pear orchards and a driving range. ~ 1850 Country Club Road, Hood River, OR; 541-386-3009; www.hoodrivergolf.com. Indian Creek Golf Course, with its gentle rolling hills, is a dry, year-round 18-hole course. ~ 3605 Brookside Drive, Hood River, OR; 541-386-7770, 866-386-7770; www.indiancreekgolf.com. In Stevenson, Washington, there's the 18-hole **Skamania Lodge Golf Course**, with views of the Columbia River and Bridge of the Gods. ~ 1131 Skamania Lodge Way; 509-427-2541, 800-293-0418. In Carson, Washington, the **Hot Springs Golf Course** has 18 holes and is great for beginners. ~ Hot Springs Avenue and St. Martins Road; 509-427-5150. Located on Route 14 in Washington between Beacon Rock and North Bonneville is **Beacon Rock Public Golf Course.** There's nine holes near the Columbia with sand traps and water hazards. ~ 509-427-5730.

RIDING STABLES

For equestrians, the Gorge area has limited options. **Northwest Lake Riding Stables** provides one- to four-hour guided trips that take in views of Mt. Adams and Mt. Hood, and also offers rides for children. ~ 126 Little Buck Road, White Salmon; 509-493-4965; www.nwstables.com.

BIKING

The Columbia River Gorge along Route 84 is prime cycling territory, particularly along any portion of the 62-mile route from Portland to Hood River. The old Columbia River Highway, which parallels Route 84, is less trafficked, calmer, scenic and a wonderful way to experience the Gorge. The Dalles Riverfront Trail, a paved bike trail, extends from the west part of The Dalles to Dalles Dam.

The Oregon Department of Transportation (ODOT) publishes the **Columbia River Gorge Bike Map,** a free 15-page brochure of this scenic area's cycling opportunities. Look for the publication at Welcome Centers and bike shops, or contact the ODOT. ~ 123 Northwest Flanders Street, Portland; 503-731-8200; www.oregon.gov/ODOT.

AUTHOR FAVORITE

A little Washington gem on the White Salmon River north of the Columbia, **Northwestern Lake** is an ideal destination for a day trip where you can swim, fish, hike or just loaf. There are also summer cabins nearby for those who want to stay longer. ~ Head west from White Salmon on Route 14 to Route 141. Continue north five miles to the park.

Bike Rentals For rentals of mountain bikes, road bikes and trail maps, try one of **The Bike Gallery**'s six locations in and around Portland and Beaverton. ~ In Portland at 1001 Southwest Salmon Avenue, 503-222-3821, and 5329 Northeast Sandy Boulevard, 503-281-9800; in Beaverton at 12345 Southwest Canyon Road, 503-641-2580. **Discover Bicycles** rents and sells mountain and road bikes and can provide information about guided bike tours. ~ 116 Oak Street, Hood River, OR; 541-386-4820; www.discoverbicycles.com.

HIKING

All distances listed for hiking trails are one way unless otherwise noted.

Latourell Falls Trail (2.2 miles), on the Columbia River Highway three miles east of Crown Point, is a moderately difficult walk leading along a streambed to the base of the upper falls. To extend this walk another mile, take a loop trail beginning at the top of lower Latourell Falls and returning to the highway at Talbot Park.

Near the Bridal Veil exit off Route 84 is **#415 Angels Rest Trail** (4.5 miles), an easy hike leading to an overlook. This route can be extended another 15 miles to Bonneville Dam by taking the **#400 Gorge Trail**, an amazing path that passes many of the Gorge's stunning cascades, including Multnomah Falls, Triple Falls and Horsetail Falls.

Eagle Creek Campground at Exit 41 on Route 84 is the jump-off point for the easy **#440 Eagle Creek Trail** to Punch Bowl Falls (2 miles) or Tunnel Falls (6 miles). You can continue to follow the wildflower-riddled path (part of the Pacific Crest Trail) through the Columbia Wilderness, up to Wahtum Lake (13 miles). Four campsites provide rest between Eagle Creek and the lake.

On the Washington side of the river west of Bonneville Dam is the one-mile trail leading to the top of **Beacon Rock**, an 800-foot monolith noted by Lewis and Clark. Ascended by a series of switchbacks guarded by railings, this trail offers numerous views of the Gorge.

East of Home Valley, Oregon, on Route 14 is the **Dog Mountain Trail** (6 miles), a difficult climb up 2900 feet for impressive views of Mt. Hood, Mt. St. Helens and Mt. Adams. During May and June, the surrounding hills are covered with wildflowers, making this an extraordinary time to hike the trail.

AUTHOR FAVORITE

An excellent cycling getaway in the area is **Sauvie Island**, located ten miles northwest of Portland. Light traffic makes it a pleasure to pedal through this wildlife sanctuary. You can drive or take a Tri-Met bus to the island.

Transportation

CAR

Route 84 along the Columbia River is the preferred way to enter Portland. From the west, **Route 26** is a major highway into town. Secondary routes include **Route 30** from the west and **Route 99** from the south. For road conditions, call 503-222-6721.

AIR

If you plan on flying to the Columbia River Gorge Area, **Portland International Airport** is the closest airport. It is served by Air Canada Jazz, Alaska Airlines, American Airlines, Big Sky Airlines, Continental Airlines, Delta Air Lines, Frontier Airlines, Hawaiian Airlines, Horizon Air, JetBlue Airlines, Lufthansa, Mexicana, Northwest Airlines, Southwest Airlines, United Airlines and US Airways. ~ www.flypdx.com.

Limousines, vans and buses take visitors to downtown locations, including **Limousines Dot Com** (866-546-6726; www.limos.com).

BUS

Greyhound Bus Lines offers bus service to Portland from across the nation. The main downtown terminal is at 550 Northwest 6th Avenue. ~ 503-243-2361, 800-231-2222; www.greyhound.com.

Also consider the **Green Tortoise**, a New Age company with a fleet of funky buses. Each is equipped with sleeping platforms allowing travelers to rest as they cross the country. The buses stop at interesting sightseeing points en route. The Green Tortoise, an endangered species from the '60s, travels to and from the East Coast, Portland, Seattle, Los Angeles and elsewhere. It provides a mode of transportation as well as an experience in group living. ~ 494 Broadway, San Francisco, CA 94133; 415-956-7500, 800-867-8647; www.greentortoise.com.

TRAIN

Amtrak provides service from Washington and California via the "Coast Starlight." There is also a northerly connection to Spokane on the "Empire Builder." ~ 800 Northwest 6th Avenue; 800-872-7245; www.amtrak.com.

CAR RENTALS

In The Dalles, contact **Enterprise Rent A Car.** ~ 100 East 2nd Street; 541-506-5007. Car rentals in Hood River are provided by **Reliable Rental Cars.** ~ 2755 Cascade Avenue, Hood River; 877-287-9913.

PUBLIC TRANSIT

Hood River is served by the **Columbia Area Transit.** Buses run to Parkdale, Odell and Cascade Locks. ~ 541-386-4202.

TAXIS

In Hood River, call **Hood River Taxi and Transportation.** ~ 541-386-2255.

Index

Lodging Index

HOSTELS

LODGING SERVICES

Dining Index

HIDDEN GUIDES

Adventure travel or a relaxing vacation?—"Hidden" guidebooks are the only travel books in the business to provide detailed information on both. Aimed at environmentally aware travelers, our motto is "Where Vacations Meet Adventures." These books combine details on unique hotels, restaurants and sightseeing with information on camping, sports and hiking for the outdoor enthusiast.

THE NEW KEY GUIDES

Based on the concept of ecotourism, The New Key Guides are dedicated to the preservation of Central America's rare and endangered species, architecture and archaeology. Filled with helpful tips, they give travelers everything they need to know about these exotic destinations.

PARADISE FAMILY GUIDES

Ideal for families traveling with kids of any age—toddlers to teenagers—Paradise Family Guides offer a blend of travel information unlike any other guides to the Hawaiian islands. With vacation ideas and tropical adventures that are sure to satisfy both action-hungry youngsters and relaxation-seeking parents, these guides meet the specific needs of each and every family member.

Ulysses Press books are available at bookstores everywhere. If any of the following titles are unavailable at your local bookstore, ask the bookseller to order them.

You can also order books directly from Ulysses Press
P.O. Box 3440, Berkeley, CA 94703
800-377-2542 or 510-601-8301
fax: 510-601-8307
www.ulyssespress.com
e-mail: ulysses@ulyssespress.com

HIDDEN GUIDEBOOKS

____ Hidden Arizona, $16.95
____ Hidden Baja, $14.95
____ Hidden Belize, $15.95
____ Hidden Big Island of Hawaii, $13.95
____ Hidden Boston & Cape Cod, $14.95
____ Hidden British Columbia, $18.95
____ Hidden Cancún & the Yucatán, $16.95
____ Hidden Carolinas, $17.95
____ Hidden Coast of California, $18.95
____ Hidden Colorado, $15.95
____ Hidden Disneyland, $13.95
____ Hidden Florida, $19.95
____ Hidden Florida Keys & Everglades, $13.95
____ Hidden Georgia, $16.95
____ Hidden Hawaii, $19.95
____ Hidden Idaho, $14.95
____ Hidden Kauai, $13.95
____ Hidden Los Angeles, $14.95
____ Hidden Maine, $15.95
____ Hidden Maui, $14.95
____ Hidden Miami, $14.95
____ Hidden Montana, $15.95
____ Hidden New England, $19.95
____ Hidden New Mexico, $15.95
____ Hidden Oahu, $14.95
____ Hidden Oregon, $15.95
____ Hidden Pacific Northwest, $19.95
____ Hidden Philadelphia, $14.95
____ Hidden Puerto Vallarta, $14.95
____ Hidden Salt Lake City, $14.95
____ Hidden San Diego, $14.95
____ Hidden San Francisco & Northern California, $19.95
____ Hidden Seattle, $14.95
____ Hidden Southern California, $19.95
____ Hidden Southwest, $19.95
____ Hidden Tahiti, $18.95
____ Hidden Tennessee, $16.95
____ Hidden Utah, $16.95
____ Hidden Walt Disney World, $13.95
____ Hidden Washington, $15.95
____ Hidden Wine Country, $14.95
____ Hidden Wyoming, $15.95

PARADISE FAMILY GUIDES

____ Paradise Family Guides: Kaua'i, $17.95
____ Paradise Family Guides: Maui, $17.95
____ Paradise Family Guides: Big Island of Hawai'i, $17.95

Mark the book(s) you're ordering and enter the total cost here ⇨ ☐

California residents add 8.75% sales tax here ⇨ ☐

Shipping, check box for your preferred method and enter cost here ⇨ ☐

☐ Book Rate — **FREE! FREE! FREE!**

☐ Priority Mail/UPS Ground — cost of postage

☐ UPS Overnight or 2-Day Air — cost of postage

Billing, enter total amount due here and check method of payment ⇨ ☐

☐ Check ☐ Money Order

☐ VISA/MasterCard ______________________ Exp. Date __________

Name ______________________ Phone __________

Address ______________________________

City ______________ State ______ Zip ________

Money-back guarantee on direct orders placed through Ulysses Press.

ABOUT THE AUTHORS

ERIC LUCAS, a writer and editor, is also author of Ulysses Press' *Hidden British Columbia.* He has been a newspaper editorial columnist, travel writer, magazine editor and business journalist. An avid gardener, fisherman, backpacker and runner, he lives in Seattle.

NICKY LEACH, the update author for this edition, is a Santa Fe–based author specializing in writing books on the natural and cultural history of the American West. She has written over 40 guidebooks, including several award-winning visitor guides to national parks. Nicky lives in a historic artist's home off the Santa Fe Trail with her tabby cat Molly.

ABOUT THE ILLUSTRATOR

GLENN KIM is a freelance illustrator residing in the San Francisco Bay Area. His work appears in numerous Ulysses Press titles including *Hidden Southwest* and *Hidden Belize*. He has also illustrated for the National Forest Service, several Bay Area magazines, book covers and greeting cards, as well as for advertising agencies.